STANDARD LESSON COMMENTARY
1989-90

International Sunday School Lessons

published by

STANDARD PUBLISHING

Eugene H. Wigginton, *Publisher*

Richard C. McKinley, *Director of Curriculum Development*

James I. Fehl, *Editor*   Hela M. Campbell, *Office Editor*

Thirty-seventh Annual Volume

Minister F. Lewis

© 1989

The STANDARD PUBLISHING Company
division of STANDEX INTERNATIONAL Corporation
8121 Hamilton Avenue, Cincinnati, Ohio 45231

Printed in U.S.A.

In This Volume

Cover photo by Comstock

Index of Printed Texts, 1989-90

The printed texts for 1989-90 are arranged here in the order in which they appear in the Bible. Opposite each reference is the number of the page on which it appears in this volume.

Cumulative Index

A cumulative index for the Scripture passages used in the *Standard Lesson Commentaries* for the years September, 1986—August, 1990, is set forth below.

How Adults Learn

by Gary Bussman

IN CONSIDERING THE QUESTION, "How do adults learn?" we may be inclined to think in terms of the methods by which teaching is accomplished. Adults learn as they are exposed to or participate in visuals, discussions, dramas, etc. But the issue is broader than finding the most efficient teaching techniques. Instead of looking for the answer in the science of teaching methodology, I want to shift the focus to the life situation of the learner.

From my teaching experience, I find that those adults who are more than twenty-three years of age are generally more highly motivated learners than their younger counterparts. Basically, they learn the same way high school and college students do: by reading, listening, experience, and trial and error. The difference is that most adults find their life situations surrounding them with challenges that require and instill a desire for learning.

This increased motivation on the part of adults may be traced to their having resolved, or made progress in, such life identity issues as career choices, value choices, and mate selection. Hence, energy that previously was spent in these areas is now available for the pursuit of life and career advancement.

Example

Not long ago a young adult, who was in his late twenties or early thirties, returned to my college classes to complete a degree. Originally, he had entered Bible college right out of high school. At that time, he had been unmotivated and had not selected a career in which to invest his life energies. Consequently, he had done poorly in his college work.

He finally had left school and had taken up a local church ministry. Soon he was deeply involved in ministering to teens who were struggling with severe life issues. He found his own type of ministry limited in its ability to deal with these problems, so he decided to focus his ministry in such a way as to speak more directly to the problems of youth.

The pursuit of this more specialized ministry brought him face-to-face with the need for more formal education and the earning of a degree. When he returned to my classes, he was animated and enthusiastic. He read everything I assigned and requested additional reading. He was one of my finest students.

Did this man have new learning abilities? No. But it is very evident that he was a better learner. He now had a life goal and mission to meet the needs of these unfortunate teens. He was learning information and acquiring skills and attitudes that related to his life needs, goals and identity.

Application

What does all this mean to the teacher of adults in Sunday school? Simply this: Relate insights to your pupils' life situations. This task requires at least two steps. The first step is to clarify the truths of the passage you are considering. Developing a theme and an outline of the passage will help you zero in on, and convey, its teachings. To help isolate a theme, begin with the following questions:

1. Who wrote the passage?
2. To whom was it written?
3. What special issues or cultural situations were involved?

To develop an outline, ask these questions:" "What does this passage say about the theme?" or "How does it illustrate the theme?"

For example, the Biblical story of Ruth can be expressed by means of the theme of "Selfless Love." It is illustrated in this outline:

I. Naomi's Selfless Love
II. Ruth's Selfless Love
III. Boaz's Selfless Love

Although the author is unknown, the custom of levirate marriage is keenly illustrated. It is a beautiful story of devotion and selflessness, which can be clarified and clearly articulated by focusing on the above theme and describing the involvement of Naomi, Ruth, and Boaz.

The second step needed to key your Bible lesson to the life situations of your pupils is to become familiar with your students' lives. This is not to suggest that you become a busybody, but rather that you develop a genuine concern for your students. This can be done by visiting in their homes, by being present and supportive in times of crisis, and by listening carefully to them in class discussions, in casual conversation during fellowship gatherings, and during chit-chat before and after church services.

These two steps suggested above will enable you to make your Bible teaching more meaningful to your adult students and will motivate them to increased learning.

1

Sep
3

Sep
10

Sep
17

Sep
24

Oct
1

Oct
8

Oct
15

Oct
22

Oct
29

Nov
5

Nov
12

Nov
19

Nov
26

Autumn Quarter, 1989

Theme: Vision of God's Rule

Special Features

Lessons

Unit 1: Ezekiel: God's Care for Judah

Unit 2: Daniel: Through Oppression to Victory

Unit 3: 1 and 2 Thessalonians: The Coming of the Lord

Unit 4: Revelation: A Message of Hope

Related Resources

The following publications are offered to give more detailed help on the subjects of study presented in the Autumn Quarter. They may be purchased from your supplier. Prices are subject to change.

Revelation, by Alger Fitch. Order #R40113, $5.95. This non-speculative study is an overview that looks at the message of Revelation from five perspectives.

Revelations Workbook, by Terry Hicks. Order #40213, $1.95.

This workbook is designed to complement the study of Revelation.

The King Is Coming, by David McCord. Order #R41026, $2.95. This book will help you understand Revelation, live as a happy and loyal subject to the King, and look forward eagerly to His coming again.

Who's in Control?

WHO'S IN CONTROL HERE? Perhaps that question has crossed your mind in recent years. You watch TV or read the newspaper and you are reminded of evil that seemingly goes unchecked. Terrorists victimize the innocent with impurity. Drug dealers have an ever-tightening stronghold on our youth. The strong take advantage of the weak.

God's people in every age have asked that question. To some, reminders were given through prophets and apostles that there is One who is in control of all things. God is the eternal ruler, and ultimately His cause and His people will be vindicated. These messages will be studied in the Autumn quarter.

If God is the ruler, how do we submit to His rule? How do we demonstrate in our daily lives that we are His subjects? The answers are found in the studies of the Winter and Spring quarters. John's Gospel and his three epistles reveal that God is enthroned in our hearts as we make Jesus, His Son, the Lord of our lives. And as we abide in love, we show that that enthronement is real.

The Summer quarter focuses on wisdom literature in the Bible in two ways: the way of man's devising and the way revealed by God. The wise align themselves with God now; they know that one day He will reveal that He is the ruler, and then the ungodly shall perish.

International Sunday School Lesson Topics
September, 1986 — August, 1992

	AUTUMN QUARTER (Sept., Oct., Nov.)	WINTER QUARTER (Dec., Jan., Feb.)	SPRING QUARTER (Mar., Apr., May)	SUMMER QUARTER (June, July, Aug.)
1986-1987	Beginning of the Covenant People (Old Testament Survey)	The Arrival of a New Age (New Testament Survey)	God's Constant Love (Luke and Hosea)	The Righteousness of God (Romans)
1987-1988	Genesis: Book of Beginnings	The Call to Discipleship (The Gospel of Matthew)	Facing the Future With Confidence (Matthew, Hebrews)	Moses and His Mission (Exodus, Numbers, Deuteronomy)
1988-1989	Through Suffering to Hope (Job, Isaiah, Jeremiah)	Scenes of Love and Compassion (Luke)	Letters From Prison (Philemon, Colossians, Philippians, Ephesians)	Conquest and Challenge (Joshua, Judges, Ruth)
1989-1990	Visions of God's Rule (Ezekiel, Daniel, 1 and 2 Thessalonians, Revelation)	John: The Gospel of Life and Light	The Gospel of John (cont'd) Abiding in Love (1, 2, 3 John)	Wisdom As a Way of Life (Ecclesiastes, Proverbs, Psalms, James)
1990-1991	Prophets, Priests, and Kings (Conflicts and Concerns)	Stories Jesus Told (Parables)	Counsel for a Church in Crisis (1 and 2 Corinthians)	After the Exile (Ezra, Nehemiah, and Prophets)
1991-1992	From the Damascus Road to Rome (Life of Paul—Acts)	Songs and Prayers of the Bible (Song of Solomon, Psalms, others)	The Strong Son of God (Mark) God's People in the World (1 and 2 Peter)	God's Judgment and Mercy (Minor Prophets) Organizing for Ministry (Pastoral Epistles)

Who Is in Charge?

by Orrin Root

WHO'S IN CHARGE HERE? God is, that's who. This has been demonstrated so many times that no one ought to doubt it.

Even Eve should have known better, but we can see how she made a mistake. She had no history to guide her, and not much experience. A snake in the garden convinced her that she could take charge, and she tried it. As a result, she and her compliant husband lost not only the garden, but their lives as well.

After such a demonstration, wouldn't you think all of Eve's children for a million years would be content to let God be in charge? That would seem reasonable, but human reasoning ran in another direction. Many of Eve's children followed her example instead of learning from her mistake. They took charge of their own living, and the results were disastrous. Mankind sank to such a level that "Every imagination of the thoughts of his heart was only evil continually" (Genesis 6:5).

Then again God showed who was in charge. With forty days of rain and some flooding from the fountains of the great deep, He covered the earth with water and drowned all the people who thought they were in charge. The human race survived because one family still was content to let God be the general manager.

Wouldn't you think all of Noah's children for a million years would obey God as carefully as Noah did? Unreasonable as it seems, they did not. More and more of them tried to take charge and manage things for their own profit and pleasure, regardless of God and right.

This time God did not drown all the people who wanted to run things. Instead, He picked one man, Abraham, who was willing to believe Him and obey Him. He gave that man such power and prosperity that all the world could see that it was good to obey God. He made Abraham the father of a nation designed to show the benefits of letting God be in charge.

Then did all the children of Abraham worship God and obey Him as Abraham had done? No. As centuries went by, more and more of them gave their worship to Baal and their obedience to their own selfish desires. After seventy years of captivity in Babylon they gave up Baal, but not their selfishness. They wanted to be in charge. When God's Son called them to repent because the kingdom of Heaven was at hand, they crucified Him. Only forty years later their nation was demolished and they were scattered to the four winds.

Then wouldn't you think everybody in the world could see that it was best to let God be in charge? As a matter of fact, atheistic communists have taken charge of much of the world and are reaching for more. As a matter of fact, some people in your own town are managing things for their own profit and pleasure, ignoring both God and the welfare of their neighbors—and in many cases they seem to be getting away with it. It is no wonder that skeptics ask who is in charge. If God is in control, they say, why is there so much ungodliness?

Through September, October, and November, our Bible lessons will be drawn from two periods when many people might ask who was in charge. God's people were oppressed and distressed. How could anyone think their God was almighty? But He was, and He still is.

Captivity in Babylon

Nebuchadnezzar of Babylon took charge of the Jewish nation about 606 B.C. Twenty years later he destroyed Jerusalem and deported most of the surviving Jews to Babylon. When God's people were ruled by heathen foreigners, who would say God was in charge?

One who said so was Ezekiel. He was one of the captives in Babylon, and he gave his fellow Jews a message direct from God. Three great thoughts stand out in that message.

1. The heathen Babylonians were God's servants, though they did not know it. He was using them to punish His chosen people who had rebelled against Him. Refusing to obey Him, they had meant to do as they pleased, and now they had to do as the Babylonians ordered.

2. When the Jews were transported to Babylon, God was not left behind in the ruins of Jerusalem. He was with His people wherever they were, and ready to help and bless them when they were ready to acknowledge that He was in charge.

3. Captivity was not forever. God was going to set His people free and lead them back to their homeland. That would be convincing proof that He was indeed in charge.

Four lessons are from the book of Ezekiel.

Daniel was another captive prophet who said God was in charge. Boldly he said it even to haughty Nebuchadnezzar: "The God of heaven hath given thee a kingdom, power, and strength, and glory" (Daniel 2:37). Nebuchadnezzar thought he himself was in charge, but he learned to say, "Now I Nebuchadnezzar praise and extol and honor the King of heaven" (Daniel 4:37).

In those days God revealed that He was in charge of future centuries. In visions, He pictured the empires that would rule after the fall of Babylon: The Medo-Persian Empire, the Greek Empire of Alexander the Great, the Roman Empire. Beyond all these was to be the greatest empire of all: "In the days of these kings shall the God of heaven set up a kingdom, which shall never be destroyed: and the kingdom shall not be left to other people, but it shall break in pieces and consume all these kingdoms, and it shall stand for ever" (Daniel 2:44).

Lessons 5, 6, and 7 are from the book of Daniel.

When the Church Was Young

The first Christian century was another time when an observer might doubt that God was in charge. Christians were His chosen people then, but, like Christ himself, they were despised and rejected.

The church began at Jerusalem, and the first Christians were Jews; but their own rulers persecuted them so furiously that they were driven from their homes (Acts 8:1). As they moved out into the heathen world, they took the good news of Jesus, and everywhere they won followers for Him. But everywhere they were in trouble with unconverted Jews because they preached the gospel, and with unconverted heathen because they would not worship imaginary gods. Neither would they worship the emperor, who was supposed to be a god, too. For that reason, they were often in trouble with the government.

In such a time, Christian teachers insisted that God was still in charge. To the Thessalonian Christians Paul wrote that Jesus would come back in triumph and take His people to be with Him forever. In the meantime, His people must be true to Him in spite of persecution.

Lessons 8 and 9 are from Paul's letters to the Thessalonians.

It was near the end of the first century when earthly rulers imprisoned John the apostle on a little island, but God invited him to Heaven to see "things which must be hereafter" (Revelation 1:9; 4:1). In majestic visions he saw mighty conflict, but he saw victory. He saw death and the devil cast into the lake of fire. He saw all mankind stand before the throne of God for judgment. He saw God's people triumphant, purified, glorified. He saw the new Jerusalem gleaming with jewels and gold, bright with God's own presence. He saw the water of life like a river from the throne of God. He heard the invitation: "Whosoever will, let him take the water of life freely" (Revelation 22:17). But with all the joy and glory of that vision, he knew that some would not have a share of the water of life. "Whosoever was not found written in the book of life was cast into the lake of fire" (Revelation 20:15).

Lessons 10-13 are from the book of Revelation.

The Twentieth Century

Jails are overcrowded almost everywhere.

We spend millions trying to control the flow of illegal drugs.

In some areas, elderly people are afraid to leave their homes at night.

Child abuse is becoming more frequent.

In spite of sex education, schoolgirls are becoming pregnant in increasing numbers.

Homosexuals are "coming out of the closet" to say their practice is not perverted.

The divorce rate is horrendous.

Newspapers headline the adulteries of preachers and politicians.

Increasing numbers of financiers are being caught in illegal tricks.

We face these problems and more because people are not content to have God in charge. They try to manage things for their own advantage.

"Thou shalt love the Lord thy God with all thine heart, and with all thy soul, and with all thy might" (Deuteronomy 6:5).

"Thou shalt love thy neighbor as thyself" (Leviticus 19:18).

"Honor thy father and thy mother" (Exodus 20:12).

"Thou shalt not commit adultery" (Exodus 20:14).

"Thou shalt not steal" (Exodus 20:15).

"Thou shalt not covet . . . any thing that is thy neighbor's" (Exodus 20:17).

These are not arbitrary rules devised by Moses. They are not theories dreamed up by philosophers. They are not bits of wisdom distilled from centuries of experience.

These are the Creator's explanation of how His creation is designed to work. The moral laws are built into the nature of man and society as surely as the law of gravity is built into the nature of material things. We can try to ignore God's laws, but the results will be bad.

The thirteen lessons ahead of us will show that God has always been in charge, and always will be.

Don't Give Up

by Knofel Staton

DO YOU EVER GET DOWN IN THE DUMPS? Do you ever feel that everything you have planned for, worked for, invested in, dreamed about, waited for, planned for, sacrificed for, and lived for is coming apart at the seams? You wonder—when will the storm end? When will the clouds break and the sky become blue again? Then it dawns on you that life may never be free from the storms, and you just want to throw up your hands and quit.

Just recently it happened to our eleven-year-old daughter as she faced tragedy—the unraveling of life for a girl her age. The tire on her bike was flat. Not only that—but the right pedal came off. She looked up at me with deep agony in her eyes and said, "Dad, my whole bike is falling apart." From the viewpoint of an eleven-year-old, it was. She did not know how to fix the tire, and she did not know that one screw would fix the pedal. It was "all over" as far as she was concerned. It was "junkville." Her life—not just her bike—was ready to be taken to the landfill.

If each of us could only remember the times we have thought like that! But we forget. You see, they passed by.

It Happens to Us All

Not only does it happen to little girls with their bikes. It can happen to the owners of a business, to parents of teenagers, to a couple in a marriage, to employers and employees, to members in a church, to singles in a couples world, to an entire area that depends on oil when the oil prices go down. It can happen when the doctor says, "It is cancer," or when the banker says, "We will be starting foreclosure proceedings."

It happened to God's people when they were captives in Babylon. They were discouraged. They were downhearted. They wondered if there was any future for them, or if they should just quit. At that point, God carried the prophet Ezekiel out "in the Spirit of the Lord" to give him a message to relay to the people. We read about it in Ezekiel 37.

God took Ezekiel to a valley. How was it in the valley? It was full, but full of what? It was full of bones—dry, bleached bones. Now that seems like quite an empty valley to me. The graveyard in the valley had the appearance of a hopeless situation.

This Too Shall Pass

In the midst of our troubles, the question is, "Can new life spring up—not the same life as before—but a new beginning, a freshness with laughter, gaiety, activity, celebrations, and holiday fun times?" Can a new heart follow a code blue? How many say, "No possible way," when they see the piles of dry bones before them?

As Ezekiel viewed the valley of dry bones, God asked him a penetrating question: "Can these bones live?" Ezekiel knew better than to say no to God, so he replied, "O Lord God, thou knowest." That was Ezekiel's way of saying that if it was possible, God was the one who knew it, and God was the one who knew how to bring them to life.

Help It Pass

1. *Hear the Word of the Lord* (Ezekiel 37:4).

Quit looking at the mess. Quit looking down—feeling down, talking down, and putting self down. Quit comparing life now to what it used to be and to what you think it will never be again. Hear the positive word of God who says hundreds of times in the Bible, "I am with you."

Not only hear it, but also breath in.

2. *Breath in God's Holy Spirit* (Ezekiel 37:5).

To breathe in God's Spirit is to be filled with His Spirit. It is to act and speak the way God would have us act and speak. It is to give up our ways, our littleness, our complaints, our bitterness. Breathe in God's Spirit and then breath out God's disposition. That is, as we face the tough times in life, we are to breathe out love instead of animosity, joy instead of sadness, patience instead of giving up, peace instead of factions, kindness instead of ugliness, goodness instead of power plays, faithfulness instead of fickleness, gentleness instead of the "get-even" philosophy, and self-control instead of falling apart.

What really determines our true condition is not what happens outside of us, but what happens inside of us. We may not be able to control the actions outside of us, but we can control our reactions.

Hear, breathe, and then *wait*, because things change when God touches us on the inside. Things start to change in the "hopeless" situation.

So it was in the valley before Ezekiel. Upon hearing the word of the Lord spoken by the prophet, the dry bones came together, muscles and ligaments came upon them, and skin covered them. Receiving the breath of life they then stood up upon their feet—an exceeding great army. New life and strength and hope for the future was theirs because of the power of God.

3. *Run From Negative Reactions.*

Even in the midst of positive changes, negative attitudes try to control. God was working in the midst of the captives through His prophets, yet the people compared their lot to dry bones. They said, "Our bones are dried, and our hope is lost" (v. 11). Isn't it easy for the negative attitudes to block our view of the positive realities in life?

It is often our perspective of life around us, not the reality, that makes the difference. For instance, two different people can look at a snowstorm in opposite ways. One may say, "Oh, no, this storm is terrible. I will have to shovel snow, and it will be so cold." But another may say, "Great. Life can slow down. I won't have to get out for awhile. I can sit by the fire and read."

One person may look at retirement and say, "Oh, no. My life will count for nothing now." Another may say, "Great. Now I can do some things I have always wanted to do."

One person may look at a promotion at work and say, "Oh, no. More responsibility." Another may say, "Great. More responsibility."

4. *Run With Positive Reactions.*

Don't let the negative control you. Whatever it is you are facing, apply Philippians 4:8,9. Look for what is true about a situation, not for just hearsay. Then if what is true is negative reality, look for the positive in it. Look for what is honorable, look for what is right, look for what is pure, look for whatever is lovely, look for any excellence in the situation. Look for anything that is worthy of praise. When you find those things, let your mind dwell on these things. When you do, the peace of God that surpasses all understanding will be with you.

God Over Circumstances

While Israel was letting the negative attitudes blur their sight from the positive realities, God spoke up and said, "I will open your graves. I will cause you to come up out of that situation. I will bring you to the promised land." That's God's way of saying your tomorrows will be better than your yesterdays. Your next twenty years can be better than your last twenty years.

There is enough in life to cause anyone to say, "I quit." But there is also enough in life to cause

us to say, "God is bigger than any circumstances I face."

Is your bicycle falling apart? Is the tire flat? Does the trip seem bumpy? Is the pedal off? Is there not much motivation?

I know Someone who knows all about it. What is death to us is life for Him. What is hopeless to us is easy with Him. We are out of hope when we are out of rope. He is not out of hope. He can bring freshness to dryness. He can bring sweetness to spoilage. That is, if we don't give up, give in, or give out.

Have you noticed that in spite of the cost of living, living is still popular today? Be assured of this—in spite of the crisis in your life, God is still powerful today. He is *for you.*

God is the same yesterday, today, and forever. His power does not change. When God created the universe, He brought something out of nothing; (when He brings the world to an end, He will turn something into nothing; He can make a lot out of a little. He can take our sin-scarred lives and make us fit to be the sons of God.

As God's power does not change, neither does His presence. God did not create this world and then take off on a celestial coffee break to do something else, while we struggle and try to make it without Him. He is the God who is both there and here. We do not serve an impotent God, and neither do we serve an absentee God. There is no need to quit when we know that God is on board.

As God's power and presence do not change, neither does His providence. He has enough provisions to meet every need we face. Trust Him and don't give up!

You Might Ask . . .

by Ronald G. Davis

JESUS ASKED QUESTIONS AS A primary teaching strategy. He asked various types of questions for a variety of purposes. Some of His questions called for a simple, matter-of fact response. For example, "Whose image and inscription is this (on this Roman coin)?" Using the answer that was given, He then taught a basic life lesson.

But Jesus asked more difficult questions also. Near Caesarea Philippi, He checked His own disciples' knowledge of the general public's opinion of Him: "Who do men say that I am?" He asked. After they had accurately reported what the people were saying of Him, He challenged their own understanding of what they had seen and heard: "But who do you say that I am?" When Peter answered boldly, "You are the Christ," perhaps Jesus felt as any teacher does when a student answers a question correctly.

Jesus might ask His learners to project a future decision on the basis of information given, as He did following the parable of the wicked vinedressers. "When the owner of the vineyard comes, what will he do to those vinedressers?" Calling for a learner to identify a logical consequence was common to Jesus' teaching. Jesus knew the value of questions.

The Adult Teacher and Questioning

Questions may arise in the contemporary Sunday-school class in three basic ways. One, the teacher may ask questions of individuals or of the class as a whole. Two, the learners may ask questions of the teacher. Three, the class members may direct questions to one another. Though questions of all three sorts will come up spontaneously in most adult classes, specific ideas for the various strategies follow.

As a teacher, you can introduce questions to your learners orally or in print. Either way, there are three types of questions you will want to use: (1) "revelation" questions, which ask, "What does the Bible say?" (2) "interpretation" questions, which ask, "What does the Bible mean?" And (3) "speculation" questions, which ask, "Why did. . . ?" and "What do you think?" to stretch thinking. Occasionally writing out a series of lesson questions will allow you to see if you are maintaining a balance among the three.

Handing written questions to learners as they arrive will direct their attention to the study of the day and will allow them to consider their response in advance. (Some learners appreciate not being put on the spot by an oral question that demands immediate response!) To get class members to examine the Bible text and to consider its meaning and application, you may, on occasion, give a "quiz" orally or in print and ask students to respond in writing. Then, as the session proceeds, they may contribute orally.

For variety you may choose to have either an individual or a small group of learners stand/sit before the group and answer your questions, letting the members of the "audience" agree-disagree with the respondent's answers.

Turning the Tables

Class interest and learning is likely to increase if the learners ask the teacher questions too. But some learners may be hesitant to do this. One way to get such questioning stimulated is to have volunteers from the class construct some questions in advance. These could be distributed to learners randomly to be asked of the teacher. Also, a learner can become comfortable asking questions of his teacher by being assigned in advance a verse of the study text, for which he is to word and ask his own question.

Finally, the successful teacher of adults will want the class members to question one another (there *is* a great deal of insight and understanding sitting in those classroom chairs!) Initially, to limit the threat a bit, prepare question-and-answer match cards. Distribute *question* cards to one group and *answer* cards to another, and have the group simply identify matches. (Some will enjoy this more in a "Jeopardy" format—have the answers read and then find questions to match.) A "Circle of Questions" is one step closer to spontaneous interrogative interaction. With the class members seated in a circle, each is assigned a verse and writes a question based on it. Then the group goes around the circle, each asking his question to the person next to him. When one answers his neighbor's question, he is "free" to ask his. (Some will be happy if these questions are limited to the "revelation" type.) By the time the circle is completed, an overview of the text will be gained, and no doubt some discussion ideas will have been introduced.

Jesus asked questions. And any teacher of adults who would model the Master Teacher will also use questions as a teaching strategy.

Quarterly Quiz

The questions below may be used as a pretest at the beginning of the quarter, as a review at the end of the quarter, or as a review after each lesson. The questions are based on the Scripture text of each lesson (King James Version). **The answers are on page 6.**

Lesson 1

1. In Ezekiel's vision of a whirlwind and a fiery cloud, the four living creatures that he saw had the likeness of what? *Ezekiel 1:5*
2. In the vision, high above the living creatures and wheels was what appeared to be a throne on which a man sat. (T/F) *Ezekiel 1:26*

Lesson 2

1. God affirmed that all souls—all people—belong to Him. (T/F) *Ezekiel 18:4*
2. Neither the wicked nor the righteous can change from his ways. (T/F) *Ezekiel 18:21-24*
3. Each person is accountable to God for his behavior. (T/F) *Ezekiel 18:30*

Lesson 3

1. Ezekiel described the rich and powerful in Judah as _____ cattle, and the poor and weak as _____ cattle. *Ezekiel 34:20, 21*
2. God said He would set up one _____ over His flock, who would feed them and be a prince among them. *Ezekiel 34:23, 24*

Lesson 4

1. In one of Ezekiel's visions, he saw a valley full of what? *Ezekiel 37:4*
2. The vision was meant to comfort Israel with God's assurance that one day they would return to their homeland. (T/F) *Ezekiel 37:12*

Lesson 5

1. Who was the king whose dream Daniel both revealed and interpreted? *Daniel 2:1, 31*
2. The huge image that the king had seen in his dream was made up of what five substances? *Daniel 2:32, 33*

Lesson 6

1. In Daniel's night visions, one like whom came with the clouds of heaven and was brought before the Ancient of days? *Daniel 7:13*
2. According to Daniel's visions, the saints will suffer persecution but ultimately will rule in God's kingdom. (T/F) *Daniel 7:25-27*

Lesson 7

1. Daniel records that the dead will be raised to everlasting life, or to everlasting shame and contempt. (T/F) *Daniel 12:2*

2. Although we may not understand all of the revelation given to Daniel, Daniel himself understood it perfectly. (T/F) *Daniel 12:8*

Lesson 8

1. Christians are not to sorrow over the death of loved ones as do others who have no (faith, hope, love). *1 Thessalonians 4:13)*
2. Paul indicates that "the day of the Lord" will come as a "_____ in the night." *1 Thessalonians 5:2*

Lesson 9

1. Paul warns us not to let anyone _____ us by any means regarding the time of the Lord's return. *2 Thessalonians 2:3*
2. What two events does Paul say must occur before the day of the Lord comes? *2 Thessalonians 2:3*

Lesson 10

1. In John's vision of the throne of God, what (and how many) beings did he see round about the throne? *Revelation 5:6, 8*
2. Why was the Lamb worthy to take God's book and open its seals? *Revelation 5:9*

Lesson 11

1. John saw a vast multitude of people standing before God's throne. What were they doing? *Revelation 7:9, 10*
2. These persons had come out of great _____ and had washed their robes in the _____ of the Lamb. *Revelation 7:14*

Lesson 12

1. The one called Faithful and True sat on a white horse, and the _____ in heaven followed him on white horses. *Revelation 19:14*
2. John saw that the dead were judged out of those things that were written in the books, according to what? *Revelation 20:12*

Lesson 13

1. In John's vision of the new Jerusalem, what did the voice out of Heaven say about "the former things"? *Revelation 21:4*
2. The One who sat upon the throne said, "I make all things _____ ." *Revelation 21:5*

God's Presence With Judah

LESSON SCRIPTURE: Ezekiel 1.

PRINTED TEXT: Ezekiel 1:4-6, 15-20, 26-28b.

Ezekiel 1:4-6, 15-20, 26-28b

4 And I looked, and, behold, a whirlwind came out of the north, a great cloud, and a fire infolding itself, and a brightness was about it, and out of the midst thereof as the color of amber, out of the midst of the fire.

5 Also out of the midst thereof came the likeness of four living creatures. And this was their appearance; they had the likeness of a man.

6 And every one had four faces, and every one had four wings.

. . . .

15 Now as I beheld the living creatures, behold one wheel upon the earth by the living creatures, with his four faces.

16 The appearance of the wheels and their work was like unto the color of a beryl: and they four had one likeness: and their appearance and their work was as it were a wheel in the middle of a wheel.

17 When they went, they went upon their four sides: and they turned not when they went.

18 As for their rings, they were so high that they were dreadful; and their rings were full of eyes round about them four.

19 And when the living creatures went, the wheels went by them: and when the living creatures were lifted up from the earth, the wheels were lifted up.

20 Whithersoever the spirit was to go, they went, thither was their spirit to go; and the wheels were lifted up over against them: for the spirit of the living creature was in the wheels.

. . . .

26 And above the firmament that was over their heads was the likeness of a throne, as the appearance of a sapphire stone: and upon the likeness of the throne was the likeness as the appearance of a man above upon it.

27 And I saw as the color of amber, as the appearance of fire round about within it, from the appearance of his loins even upward, and from the appearance of his loins even downward, I saw as it were the appearance of fire, and it had brightness round about.

28 As the appearance of the bow that is in the cloud in the day of rain, so was the appearance of the brightness round about. This was the appearance of the likeness of the glory of the Lord.

GOLDEN TEXT: As the appearance of the bow that is in the cloud in the day of rain ... This was the appearance of the likeness of the glory of the Lord.
—Ezekiel 1:28.

Lesson Aims

After this lesson a student should be able to:
1. Tell the main features of Ezekiel's vision.
2. Realize that God is everywhere and has work everywhere for His people to do.
3. Specify one thing he will do in the Lord's work this week.

Lesson Outline

INTRODUCTION
    A. Away From Home
    B. Lesson Background
I. VISION OF LIVING CREATURES (Ezekiel 1:4-6)
    A. Wind, Cloud, and Fire (v. 4)
    B. Living Creatures (vv. 5, 6)
II. VISION OF HUGE WHEELS (Ezekiel 1:15-20)
    A. Description of the Wheels (vv. 15-18)
    B. Motion of the Wheels (vv. 19, 20)
      Close Encounters
III. VISION OF GOD'S THRONE (Ezekiel 1:26-28b)
    A. The Sapphire Throne (v. 26a)
    B. The One on the Throne (vv. 26b-28b)
      The Glory of the Lord
CONCLUSION
    A. God Is Glorious
    B. God Is Everywhere
    C. God Has Work for His People
    D. Prayer
    E. Thought to Remember

Display visual 1 from the visuals packet. Refer to it in connection with the "Introduction" section and whenever else you deem appropriate. The visual is shown on page 13.

Introduction

A. Away From Home

"Vacation time is testing time," a wise old man said. "What you do when you feel free reveals what you really are. When you're away from home, are you as sober and responsible, as honest and generous, as kind and considerate as you are at home? Some people forget that being away from home is not being away from God."

B. Lesson Background

Ezekiel was about sixteen years old when Nebuchadnezzar of Babylon first subdued Judah

and forced it to pay tribute. He was less than twenty when his king rebelled and refused to pay tribute, and about twenty-five when Nebuchadnezzar came back to subdue Judah again. This time Nebuchadnezzar took the king to Babylon. He took also the statesmen and the military men, along with the blacksmiths skilled in making swords and spears. He hoped to prevent another rebellion by leaving Judah with neither leaders nor weapons for a war against mighty Babylon. As a promising young man of a priestly family, Ezekiel was one of the captives. Weakened Judah was left in the charge of a puppet king, who swore allegiance to Nebuchadnezzar (2 Kings 23:36—24:17). We come now to a summer day in Babylonia in the fifth year of Ezekiel's captivity. He was a long way from home, but he was reminded that he had not left God back in Jerusalem (Ezekiel 1:1-3).

I. Vision of Living Creatures (Ezekiel 1:4-6)

That summer day was momentous because "the word of the Lord came expressly unto Ezekiel the priest" (v. 3). But before Ezekiel heard a word, he saw a dramatic vision.

A. Wind, Cloud, and Fire (v. 4)

4. And I looked, and, behold, a whirlwind came out of the north, a great cloud, and a fire infolding itself, and a brightness was about it, and out of the midst thereof as the color of amber, out of the midst of the fire.

The meaning of some Hebrew terms is uncertain, and many students think what Ezekiel saw was not necessarily *a whirlwind.* Other versions call it "a windstorm," "a tempestuous wind," and "a great storm." Impressively it swept down from the north, carrying *a great cloud.* Perhaps the cloud was big enough to blot out the whole northern sky, but it was not a black storm cloud. It was bright with *a fire infolding itself.* It was not a fire running wild, but a fire self-contained, a fire self-controlled. Of course *a brightness was about it,* illuminating the vast cloud. *And out of the midst thereof* shone something like *the color of amber.* Here is another Hebrew word of uncertain meaning. Instead of *the color of amber,* other versions have "glowing metal" or "gleaming bronze." Perhaps it looked as if some metal in the fire was white hot, so hot that it was incandescent.

B. Living Creatures (vv. 5, 6)

5. Also out of the midst thereof came the likeness of four living creatures. And this was their appearance; they had the likeness of a man.

Notice how often the words *likeness* and *appearance* are seen in this chapter. It seems that Ezekiel realized he was not seeing actual material things, but a vision that had the appearance of material things. *Out of the midst* of the cloud and fire came what looked like *four living creatures.* In general, each had *the likeness of a man.* Each figure was standing upright on two feet, not on four like an ox or a lion.

6. And every one had four faces, and every one had four wings.

In these respects each creature was different from a man. He had the face of a man, but also the faces of an ox, a lion, and an eagle. These looked in four directions. Other details are given in the rest of the chapter. The creature did not need to turn when he wanted to go another way, for one of his faces was already turned that way. The meaning of the faces is not explained, but it is easy to imagine a suggestion that all living things are as one in subjection to the rule of God: not only human beings, but also domestic animals like the ox, wild animals like the lion, and birds like the eagle. The Lord Jehovah made them all, and all of them ought to do His will and accomplish His purposes.

Each creature had also *four wings.* One pair was used to cover his body, and the other pair was stretched out. Apparently it was used for flying, for when the creature stood still, he let down his wings, and when he went, the sound of wings was heard. The creatures were brilliant with light, and they went back and forth like a flash of lightning. "Straight feet" (v. 7) probably means the creatures' legs were straight as in standing upright, not bent as in sitting or kneeling. The feet themselves were like the hooves of calves. Each creature had human hands, however, perhaps four pairs of them. Wings suggest the ability to go where God commands; hands suggest the ability to do His work.

II. Vision of Huge Wheels (Ezekiel 1:15-20)

Even more puzzling than the living creatures are the wheels that appeared with them in Ezekiel's vision. Their meaning is not explained, nor is it so easily guessed as is the meaning of the creatures with four faces. But we can consider what Ezekiel saw and recorded.

A. Description of the Wheels (vv. 15-18)

15. Now as I beheld the living creatures, behold one wheel upon the earth by the living creatures, with his four faces.

Ezekiel saw *one wheel upon the earth by* each of *the living creatures*, four wheels in all.

16. The appearance of the wheels and their work was like unto the color of a beryl: and they four had one likeness: and their appearance and their work was as it were a wheel in the middle of a wheel.

Their work means the way they were made. Some versions have "chrysolite" instead of *beryl.* From either translation we understand that the wheels sparkled like gemstones. *They four* indicates that there were four wheels, one beside each of the four living creatures; but *they four had one likeness:* they all looked alike. In our translation *a wheel in the middle of a wheel* sounds as if each wheel had a smaller wheel within it in the same plane, but the next verse suggests a different meaning. Instead of *a wheel in the middle of a wheel* the New International Version has "a wheel intersecting a wheel." *The Living Bible* has "each wheel was constructed with a second wheel crosswise inside."

17. When they went, they went upon their four sides: and they turned not when they went.

The *New International Version* makes this clearer: "As they moved, they would go in any one of the four directions the creatures faced." Each living creature could go north, south, east, or west without turning, because he had four faces, one looking in each direction. The wheel likewise could roll either north and south or east and west, because it was made with a second wheel of the same size intersecting it crosswise at its diameter. The second wheel pointed east and west when the first one pointed north and south. A wheel revolved as it rolled along, but it *turned not* from a north or south direction to an east or west direction because its intersecting wheel was already in that direction.

18. As for their rings, they were so high that they were dreadful; and their rings were full of eyes round about them four.

Their rings were the rims at the circumference of the wheels, and *eyes* were all around the rims. In today's English we would say *awesome* instead of *dreadful*, but it is clear that the height of the wheels was impressive. We have no estimate of how high they were or how tall the living creatures were, but we remember that creatures and wheels came out of a great cloud.

VISUALS FOR THESE LESSONS

The *Adult Visuals/Learning Resources* packet contains classroom-size visuals designed for use with the lessons in the Autumn Quarter. The packet is available from your supplier. Order no. ST 192.

How to Say It

EZEKIEL. E-*zeek*-yul or E-*zeek*-ee-ul.
NEBUCHADNEZZAR. *Neb*-you-kad-*nezz*-er
(strong accent on *nezz).

B. Motion of the Wheels (vv. 19, 20)

19. And when the living creatures went, the wheels went by them: and when the living creatures were lifted up from the earth, the wheels were lifted up.

The *living creatures* were darting to and fro like lightning (v. 14). Swift and mobile as they were, the wheels *went by them:* that is, each wheel moved beside its living creature wherever the creature went. We recall also that the living creatures were not earthbound. They had wings (v. 6). The wheels had no wings, but *when the living creatures were lifted up from the earth, the wheels were lifted up* with them.

20. Whithersoever the spirit was to go, they went, thither was their spirit to go; and the wheels were lifted up over against them: for the spirit of the living creature was in the wheels.

The four living creatures were directed by a spirit: they went wherever the spirit wanted to go (v. 12). The same spirit directed the wheels. That explains why they were able to match every move of the living creatures. The living creatures moved on the ground or were lifted up as the spirit wished; and *the wheels were lifted up over against them*, or alongside them, *for the spirit of the living creature was in the wheels* as well. Some guess that this was the Spirit of God, but our text does not say so. God's angels are spirits (Hebrews 1:13, 14), and He could have assigned one of them to direct the figures in Ezekiel's vision.

If we suppose the four living creatures were symbols of all the living creatures in the world, we need to remember that this is our supposition, not God's word. And if we suppose these creatures were symbols of all earthly creatures, shall we suppose the wheels were symbols of all the mechanical things that help mankind and other creatures—all the wheels and tools and machines? That too is only supposition, and it may be doubted because it seems that the wheels themselves were living things rather than lifeless tools or machines. They had eyes around their rims and a spirit within them.

We are about to consider Ezekiel's vision of God's throne (vv. 26-28). Some suggest that the wheels in the vision were the wheels of a huge chariot or other vehicle that transported the throne. That also is more than is written. Ezekiel

does not mention any other parts of a vehicle. On the contrary, above the creatures and wheels, between them and the throne, was a firmament (vv. 22-25). A firmament is an expanse, an open space like the sky (Genesis 1:6-8, 17, 20).

No doubt those great wheels had some profound meaning, some symbolism related to the glory of God. But until God reveals their meaning to us, let's not be too sure about our guesses.

CLOSE ENCOUNTERS

The human race has long been fascinated by the idea of visitors from outer space. In the twentieth century, perhaps the most bizarre result of this fascination occurred in 1938, when Orson Welles' radio show pretended to report an invasion from Mars. Thinking they were hearing an actual news broadcast of an interplanetary invasion, thousands of people panicked.

More recently, several movies have portrayed extraterrestrial visitors in more benign terms. In *E.T.* and *Close Encounters of the Third Kind*, we saw both the visitors and the vehicles that brought them to earth.

Ezekiel's cultural framework did not cause him to think he was seeing extraterrestrials. On the contrary, when the vision of the living beings and wheels came to him, he recognized it as a message from God.

We live in a secular age that offers a naturalistic explanation for everything. We must resist the temptation to exclude God from the events of our lives. When unusual events occur, a Christian should ask, "Is there a spiritual lesson that I can learn from these things?" Be inquisitive; use the Bible to put it in perspective; let God speak to you.
—C. R. B.

III. Vision of God's Throne (Ezekiel 1:26-28b)

Above the wheels and living creatures was a firmament, an open space, clear and bright as awesome crystal (v. 22). Under that space were loud sounds of huge wings (v. 24); but when the creatures stood still and folded their wings, Ezekiel heard a voice from the firmament above (v. 25). He now directs our attention higher still, to the glory above the crystal sky.

A. The Sapphire Throne (v. 26a)

26a. And above the firmament that was over their heads was the likeness of a throne, as the appearance of a sapphire stone.

Can you imagine a royal throne carved from one huge sapphire? Ezekiel might have described the beauty of its deep, rich color and exquisite workmanship, but he did not. In-

visual 1

Don't forget,
being away
from home
is not
being away
from
God!

stead he passed over it briefly to go on to the greater glory of the one who sat on the sapphire throne.

B. The One on the Throne (vv. 26b-28b)

26b. And upon the likeness of the throne was the likeness as the appearance of a man above upon it.

Upon what looked like a throne of sapphire was someone who seemed to have the form of a man. Nothing is said about the size of this human form. Remembering that the vision was introduced by a great cloud and included wheels of awesome size, we may well imagine a huge throne and a man-like form many times larger than a man.

27. And I saw as the color of amber, as the appearance of fire round about within it, from the appearance of his loins even upward, and from the appearance of his loins even downward, I saw as it were the appearance of fire, and it had brightness round about.

It may be better to translate *look* instead of *color*. Literally, the primary meaning of the Hebrew word is *eye*, but sometimes it means the look or appearance of something seen. The look may include color and form and brightness. The man-like form had the brightness of fire, but not the instability of fire. It seemed to be solid as *amber*. Here, as in verse 4, some versions translate "glowing metal" instead of *amber*. The humanlike figure was all aglow, both above and below the waist: *and it had brightness round about*, perhaps like a halo around the whole body.

28a. As the appearance of the bow that is in the cloud in the day of rain, so was the appearance of the brightness round about.

All the colors of the rainbow were in the halo about the figure on the throne. If the form appeared to be superhuman in size, we may well imagine that the brightness filled the sky.

28b. This was the appearance of the likeness of the glory of the Lord.

Ezekiel was a priest (v. 3). Probably he read the Scriptures and knew that the full glory of God's face is more than a human being can endure (Exodus 33:17-23). But in his vision he saw some resemblance of that glory, some *appearance of the likeness* of it. Even that appearance was so impressive that Ezekiel fell on his face, overwhelmed with awe and reverence (v. 28c). But the reality is far more glorious than the prophet's vision. With what humility and awe we ought to fall on our faces, ready to hear and follow the word of the Lord!

THE GLORY OF THE LORD

In the thinking of some people, southern California is almost synonymous with all that is new, bizarre and cultish in American culture. They may be right, whether we speak of cultural fads and fancies, philosophy, or religion!

Some of the strangest aberrations of Christian teaching come from a minister in the area, who claims that all prayers must ascend to God from the million-dollar golden altar in his church building. The altar and the near-life-size statue of Christ standing nearby are a gaudy arrangement of baubles, tinsel, and gold. The minister asserts without embarrassment that Christ will return at the site of the golden altar.

The radiance of the Lord God is not a garish gleam of light reflected from a tawdry statue. It is the glow of His holiness, untarnished by the sins of pride, deceit, or self-aggrandizement. It was this vision of God's glorious holiness that Ezekiel saw and proclaimed to Israel. It is this same glory of God that people should see in our lives and teaching.   —C. R. B.

Conclusion

We may not understand all the symbols that appeared in Ezekiel's vision; but as we try to imagine the grandeur of it, some great thoughts cannot be avoided.

A. God Is Glorious

No one on earth can see the full glory of God's face (Exodus 33:17-23). Not everyone can see a brilliant vision of the Lord on His throne. But in the Scriptures, everyone can see the Son of God, who took a human form and lived awhile among men. "We beheld his glory, the glory as of the only begotten of the Father" (John 1:14). John, who wrote those words, once saw Jesus' divine glory shining as visible light through His human form (Matthew 17:1, 2). But almost everyone in Galilee and Judea saw His glory in His miracles as He went about "Healing all that were oppressed of the devil" (Acts 10:38).

We do not need to see a towering vision of the Lord on His throne (Isaiah 6:1). We have the record of the visions of Moses, Isaiah, and Ezekiel. Better still, we have the record of Jesus. He is God's Son, "the brightness of his glory, and the express image of his person" (Hebrews 1:3). As Paul put it, "In him dwelleth all the fulness of the Godhead bodily" (Colossians 2:9). Or as Jesus put it, "He that hath seen me hath seen the Father" (John 14:9). So come to Jesus, and fall down in reverence and awe.

B. God Is Everywhere

Captive in Babylon, miles from home, Ezekiel could understand his people's cry, "How shall we sing the Lord's song in a strange land?" (Psalm 137:4). They may have felt that God was in Jerusalem and not in Babylon.

But God was in Babylon. Ezekiel was reminded of His presence when a huge, bright cloud swept in from the north with an awesome vision. The climax of the vision was the Lord sitting on His throne and speaking to Ezekiel—in Babylon.

Every day people are moving miles from home. In their homesickness, many get the feeling that they have left God behind with all their friends. They took Him for granted in the old home; but now they are in a new home, and it is hard to feel His presence there.

But God is there. He does not lose track of us, even if we lose track of Him. We need to know Him so well that we will feel His presence wherever we are. Even in utterly strange surroundings, we can see Him in our personal quiet hour, in family worship, and in the meeting of the church. And meeting Him in worship, we can see Him also in sunshine and cloud and rain, in tree and bird and flower. If we keep in touch with Him, soon we shall see Him also in the lives of new friends who are His people, and the new home will be as dear as the old.

C. God Has Work for His People

Our lesson text describes the majestic vision that Ezekiel saw, but we must look to the next chapter of Ezekiel to see the purpose of it. God had work for Ezekiel to do. He showed himself in lofty vision to assign a task. Ezekiel was to give God's word to his countrymen who were exiled with him in Babylon. It would seem to be a thankless task, for the people were rebellious. Even though their rebellion was punished by exile, they were still rebellious. Ezekiel must speak God's word, whether they would listen or not (Ezekiel 2:1-7). Back home in Jerusalem, Jeremiah was giving the Lord's message; but God wanted a spokesman in Babylon, too.

Home Daily Bible Readings

Monday, Aug. 28—God and Israel at Sinai (Exodus 19:1-9)

Tuesday, Aug. 29—The Tent of Meeting (Exodus 40:1-10, 16)

Wednesday, Aug. 30—Led by Cloud and Fire (Exodus 40:34-38)

Thursday, Aug. 31—Crossing the Jordan (Joshua 3:1-6)

Friday, Sept. 1—The Temple in Jerusalem (1 Kings 8:1-11)

Saturday, Sept. 2—Dwelling in Mount Zion (Micah 4:1-7)

Sunday, Sept. 3—The Spirit Comes at Pentecost (Acts 2:1-11)

God has work for His people everywhere. He does not come in radiant vision to assign our tasks, but work is there to be done.

Are you a stranger in a strange land, feeling homesick and forsaken and lonely? There is no better way to recover than to find your place in God's work. Not everyone is called to be a prophet. Not often does a newcomer find a prominent place to serve. But look for the lowliest place, the most unwanted task. Other ways to serve will appear soon enough.

Perhaps you have lived in one place for years or for your whole life, and yet you do not feel very close to the Lord. Perhaps it seems that He and His church are not doing much for you. The way to remedy that is to do more for them. Perhaps no one bothers to inquire about you when you are absent, no one gives you a lift when you are discouraged. Then make it your duty and pleasure to visit the sick, check up on the absent, encourage the downhearted. If you do such things often and with good will, you will find that you are very near to the Lord and His people. In service, you become a partner of one who came not to be ministered unto, but to minister (Matthew 20:28).

D. Prayer

There's a place, oh, may I find it,
  Where my mission I can fill,
Be it humble or exalted,
  May I hold it with a will;
Help to serve my generation
  With a heart of love and grace,
Help me, Lord, from this time onward,
  Find and occupy my place.

E. Thought to Remember

God has something for *me* to do *now*.

Learning by Doing

This page contains an alternate lesson plan emphasizing learning activities. Classes desiring such student involvement will find these suggestions helpful.

Learning Goals

This lesson should lead a student to:

1. List the main features of Ezekiel's vision.
2. Acknowledge that God is everywhere and has work everywhere for His people to do.
3. Specify one thing he will do in the Lord's work this week.

Into the Lesson

As the pupils arrive, divide them into groups of three or four. Give them the following problem situation and ask them to solve it.

"Barry and Theresa James are newcomers to your community and congregation. They were deeply involved in the life of the congregation they recently left. But your congregation is different from that one. The worship service is different. Your congregation is less bound by tradition than their previous one. The main points that the two congregations have in common are the emphasis upon the Word of God and the names of the churches. Barry and Theresa are having difficulty adapting to this new situation, and often remark longingly about the way it was back home. What advice would you give to them about adapting to this situation? How can they begin to feel at home here?"

Allow the groups five minutes to discuss the situation and to develop some helpful guidelines. Then call for a sharing of this work.

Make the transition into the Bible study section of the lesson by stating that Ezekiel and the people of God experienced feelings that were similar. They had been removed from their homeland and from their familiar patterns and place of worship. Today's lesson deals with the matter of becoming involved in God's work wherever we are.

Into the Word

Briefly present the lesson material in the "Lesson Background" section. Have someone read aloud the printed text for this lesson. Then use a question-and-answer approach to examine the text. Use the questions below to work through the text. After the answer to each question is given, you may need to add some detail on the basis of your study of the lesson, especially to provide some interpretation to each of the visions. But be sure to accept as much of a student's answer as you can.

1. Describe the setting for this message from God to Ezekiel (Ezekiel 1:4-6).
2. Describe what Ezekiel saw (vv. 4-6).
3. What is the significance of this vision?
4. Describe Ezekiel's vision that is recorded in verses 15-20.
5. What is the significance of this vision?
6. Describe Ezekiel's vision that is recorded in verses 26-28.
7. What is the significance of this vision?

Briefly summarize the material covered in the text. Make a transition to the application of this text stating that the text may be important for us today also.

Into Life

Ask the students this question: Given the facts of Ezekiel 1, as we have examined them, what is the importance of this section of Scripture for us? The pupils may have several responses, but be sure that they mention the three stated in the conclusion of the lesson: (1) God is glorious; (2) God is everywhere; and (3) God has work for His people wherever they are.

Ask, How does this vision speak to Barry and Theresa James's situation? Let the pupils share their thoughts. You may have to restate the original question occasionally to keep the discussion on target. Be sure that the students see the analogy—Ezekiel was displaced, he could not worship in the manner he had in the past, and he was lonely for the sights and sounds of home. Yet God assured him that He was present and that His work could be done anywhere.

Continue the discussion by asking the following question: How does this Scripture relate to those of us who have been displaced for the first time and must learn to worship and work in a new setting? Be sure that your students see the difference between their customs and traditions and what is essential to the worship of God.

Ask, What truth from this lesson can you apply to your life this week? Be sure that the pupils acknowledge that God's work is for everyone, and that they can carry it out in the midst of their daily circumstance.

In closing, give each person a small index card. Have the class members complete this sentence: I will acknowledge the presence of God and the need to do His work this week by—

Let's Talk It Over

The questions on this page are designed to encourage review of the lesson Scriptures and to promote discussion of the lesson by the class. The answers provided are only discussion starters. Let your class talk it over from there.

1. What does the *apocalypse* mean?

An apocalypse is a disclosure or prediction of the future, usually expressed in symbolic imagery. It is intended to be understood by the faithful, but to be clouded and puzzling to "outsiders." The books of Ezekiel, Daniel, and Revelation are examples of apocalyptic literature in the Old and New Testaments. *The* Apocalypse is always a reference to the book of Revelation, in which symbolic images are used to describe events that will take place when God finally destroys the forces of evil and raises the righteous to a place in His eternal kingdom. Many of the Biblical texts for this quarter are examples of apocalyptic literature.

2. Many families in our society move fairly often. What are the effects of such mobility on contemporary life?

There are both negative and positive effects. Some negative effects are these: (1) The family loses its support system and social network; family and friends are usually left behind. (2) Patterns of life are disrupted; stability and security seem threatened with the demand for change and adjustment. (3) Financial loss—moving tends to be costly.

Some positive effects are the following: (1) Family members are given opportunity for new experiences, relationships, and friendships. (2) The family is forced to draw on its own relational resources; often neglected family ties experience new vitality out of mutual need and new focus. (3) Family members are challenged to grow in response to the crises of change, of newness; stagnation frequently accompanies "sameness."

Psychologists and sociologists tend to feel that the negative factors outweigh the positive in the mobility of American families.

3. How do people respond most frequently to significant change?

With resistance. People feel more secure with the familiar, the usual, the traditional. Change disturbs their comfort zone. It often forces adjustment and adaptation, which require flexibility and work. Most people would rather not bother. And they often experience anxiety in the face of the unknown and the uncertain.

4. What is the healthiest perspective for crisis?

The wisdom of the Chinese offers crucial insight. The word for *crisis* in Chinese consists of two characters. The first represents danger; the second represents opportunity. Usually, crisis is viewed solely in terms of danger. But the eye of faith views crisis as the context for opportunity—to see God at work, to experience His power, to stretch and grow in Him.

5. What factors tend to be present when a person feels distant, or estranged, from God?

(1) Guilt. Unforgiven sin erects barriers between God and His children. The distance increases the longer the guilt remains. (2) Emotional dynamics. Emotional inflation and deflation foster feelings of distance from God. When one experiences emotional inflation, grandiose feelings often set in, causing one to think, Who needs God? With deflation—for example, depression, feelings of despondency, worthlessness, and helplessness feed the feeling, Where is God? (It should be noted that depressed emotions are not trustworthy indicators of reality. When someone is in the deep, dark pit, everything gets distorted—including the presence of God.) (3) Shifts in values and/or priorities. When a person who has valued the eternal gives priority to the temporal, distance from God occurs. Neglect of private devotions, public worship, and "the fellowship of the saints," fosters increased distance from God. A popular poster has this succinct message: "Do you feel God is far away? Guess who moved!"

6. What positive effects may a strong awareness of the presence of God have on an individual?

(1) Security. A person who is aware of God's presence can experience the feelings that he is not alone, and that God will provide for his needs. (2) Stability. Such a person can have the assurance that no matter what vicissitudes and changes life may bring his way, the unchanging God is with him. This provides strength for the soul. (3) Serenity. The awareness of God's presence enables one to say, "Despite the chaos and crisis that flow around me, at the center of my life He brings calm and peace.

Personal Accountability Before God

LESSON SCRIPTURE: Ezekiel 18.

PRINTED TEXT: Ezekiel 18:2-4, 19-24, 30, 31.

Ezekiel 18:2-4, 19-24, 30, 31

2 What mean ye, that ye use this proverb concerning the land of Israel, saying, The fathers have eaten sour grapes, and the children's teeth are set on edge?

3 As I live, saith the Lord God, ye shall not have occasion any more to use this proverb in Israel.

4 Behold, all souls are mine; as the soul of the father, so also the soul of the son is mine: the soul that sinneth, it shall die.

. . . .

19 Yet say ye, Why? doth not the son bear the iniquity of the father? When the son hath done that which is lawful and right, and hath kept all my statutes, and hath done them, he shall surely live.

20 The soul that sinneth, it shall die. The son shall not bear the iniquity of the father, neither shall the father bear the iniquity of the son: the righteousness of the righteous shall be upon him, and the wickedness of the wicked shall be upon him.

21 But if the wicked will turn from all his sins that he hath committed, and keep all my statutes, and do that which is lawful and right, he shall surely live, he shall not die.

22 All his transgressions that he hath committed, they shall not be mentioned unto him: in his righteousness that he hath done he shall live.

23 Have I any pleasure at all that the wicked should die? saith the Lord God: and not that he should return from his ways, and live?

24 But when the righteous turneth away from his righteousness, and committeth iniquity, and doeth according to all the abominations that the wicked man doeth, shall he live? All his righteousness that he hath done shall not be mentioned: in his trespass that he hath trespassed, and in his sin that he hath sinned, in them shall he die.

. . . .

30 Therefore I will judge you, O house of Israel, every one according to his ways, saith the Lord God. Repent, and turn yourselves from all your transgressions; so iniquity shall not be your ruin.

31 Cast away from you all your transgressions, whereby ye have transgressed; and make you a new heart and a new spirit: for why will ye die, O house of Israel?

GOLDEN TEXT: I will judge . . . every one according to his ways, saith the Lord God.—Ezekiel 18:30.

Lesson Aims

After studying this lesson a student should be able to:

1. Recall the proverb of sour grapes and tell why it was mistaken.

2. Briefly summarize what Ezekiel taught about personal accountability.

3. Shape his life this week so that he will be glad to give account of it before God.

Lesson Outline

INTRODUCTION
    A. Not My Fault
    B. Lesson Background
 I. LIFE AND DEATH (Ezekiel 18:2-4, 19, 20)
    A. Mistaken Proverb (vv. 2, 3)
       An Evil Family
    B. Personal Justice (vv. 4, 19, 20)
 II. A CHANCE TO CHANGE (Ezekiel 18:21-24)
    A. From Bad to Good (vv. 21-23)
    B. From Good to Bad (v. 24)
III. A PLEA TO LIVE (Ezekiel 18:30, 31)
    A. God's Justice (v. 30a)
    B. Plea to Choose Life (vv. 30b, 31)
       God Sees What No One Else Can
CONCLUSION
    A. No Way Out
    B. I Do Choose
    C. Choose Life
    D. Prayer
    E. Thought to Remember

Display visual 2 from the visuals/learning resources packet and refer to it when you consider verse 20. The visual is shown on page 21.

Introduction

In powerful drama, the book of Job declares that one's misfortune is not necessarily due to any fault of his own. No less powerfully the book of Ezekiel declares that one's misfortune may be the result of his own sin. But no one likes to say, "It's my fault."

A. Not My Fault

If two cars collide, each driver claims that he had the right of way. If a marriage breaks up, each party says the other is at fault. If there is a strike, the management and the union blame each other. If there is a split in a church, each side says the other side caused it.

This game of pinning the blame has been going on for a long time. Guilty Adam blamed guilty Eve, and she blamed the serpent. But there was blame enough to go around, and punishment for all the guilty (Genesis 3).

B. Lesson Background

The overpowering army of Babylon swept down on Judah, and tiny Judah had no strength to resist. In return for freedom and safety, the king of Judah agreed to pay tribute to Babylon. But after three years he rebelled. A few years later the king of Babylon came back with his mighty army, and again Judah had to submit. This time the king of Babylon weakened Judah by taking away its king, along with ten thousand of its statesmen and military men and blacksmiths.

We can well imagine that the king blamed his advisers for this disaster, and his advisers blamed the king or each other. Common people hated to pay taxes to far-off Babylon, so the officials may have claimed that popular demand forced the rebellion. Or perhaps they blamed Egypt for failing to send troops to defend Judah. The Bible does not record these efforts to pin the blame on someone else, but our text does reveal another effort that was popular among the ten thousand captives in the land of Babylon.

I. Life and Death
(Ezekiel 18:2-4, 19, 20)

Ezekiel was God's prophet in Babylon. As we saw in last week's lesson, he was called to deliver the word of the Lord to the ten thousand captives, whether they would welcome it or not. Directed by the Lord, he took note of a popular effort to shift the blame.

A. Mistaken Proverb (vv. 2, 3)

2. What mean ye, that ye use this proverb concerning the land of Israel, saying, The fathers have eaten sour grapes, and the children's teeth are set on edge?

Biting sour grapes and having your teeth set on edge is an unpleasant feeling, to say the least. Likewise unpleasant was the feeling of being captive in Babylon, but the captives used this proverb to say their captivity was not their fault. Their fathers—their ancestors in former generations—had done wrong, and now the present generation was suffering the consequences—or so they said. There was reason enough to say their ancestors had done wrong.

God's prophets had made that plain a century earlier (Isaiah 1:2-4; Micah 2:1, 2). Isaiah said the people of Israel would be captives in Babylon (Isaiah 39:5-7). Now ten thousand of them were captives, and they said it was because their fathers had sinned. But in truth, they themselves had continued the sins of their fathers. Ezekiel made that plain among the captives (Ezekiel 20:30, 31), and Jeremiah proclaimed it among the people who were still living in Judah (Jeremiah 5:20-31). The fathers had sinned, yes; but God sent the present generation into captivity because of its own sin.

3. As I live, saith the Lord God, ye shall not have occasion any more to use this proverb in Israel.

The captives would no longer have any *occasion*, any reason or excuse, to use that proverb, for the Lord was going to make it plain that the meaning they gave it was false. They could not truthfully blame their fathers and not themselves for their captivity.

AN EVIL FAMILY

In 1875, a report was published on research into the lives of seven hundred members of one family's seventy-three-year history. Describing them as prostitutes, lechers, paupers, drunkards, fornicators, murderers, rapists, and thieves, the researcher concluded that more than five hundred of them were morally corrupt as a result of inherited "bad seed."

Other studies have purported to prove that there is a "bad seed" inherited by some people that makes it difficult or impossible for them to make anything positive of their lives. It's all a part of the old "heredity versus environment" argument.

While most of us don't go that far, we all enjoy the diminished responsibility implied when we can blame someone else for what we have done. But the Bible will have none of it.

The ancient Israelites were forbidden to find any peace in their proverb. God does not make the child pay for the sins of his father. Neither should the child try to blame his father for predisposing him to be a sinner. Each of us stands responsible before God.   —C. R. B.

B. Personal Justice (vv. 4, 19, 20)

4. Behold, all souls are mine; as the soul of the father, so also the soul of the son is mine: the soul that sinneth, it shall die.

In one sense, it is correct to say that God's people are those who accept Him and try to do His will, while those who rebel against His rule are not His people. But in another sense, *all souls*, all lives, all people, belong to Him because He made them. In this sense, even the most rebellious are His. All people ought to do His will; all are in His power; all must face His judgment. His rule is the same for all: *The soul that sinneth, it shall die.* This was made plain to the very first man on earth (Genesis 2:16, 17). It is reaffirmed in Christian teaching, but Christian teaching adds that a sinner can accept the gift of life instead of the wages of sin (Romans 6:23).

Verses 5-9 emphasize this rule, specifying some of the sins that were common in Judah. If a person avoids these sins and does right, "he shall surely live, saith the Lord God."

Verses 10-18 deny the captives' theory that children are punished for their father's sins. If a man who does right has a son who does wrong, the son will not be saved by the father's goodness. The wicked son "shall surely die; his blood shall be upon him." But if that wicked son has a son who does right, that righteous son "shall not die for the iniquity of his father, he shall surely live."

19. Yet say ye, Why? doth not the son bear the iniquity of the father? When the son hath done that which is lawful and right, and hath kept all my statutes, and hath done them, he shall surely live.

The captives were not ready to give up the belief that their fathers' sins had brought them to captivity. Their sharp question may be put in modern English thus: "What? Do you mean to tell us that a son does not have to bear his father's sins?" There was some basis for their mistaken belief, because in many cases a son does suffer because of his father's wrongdoing. For example, a drunken driver with his son in the car may veer across the center line and collide head-on with a truck. So the son may die as a result of his father's sin. Or a father may abuse his children physically. He may be put in jail, or he may run away, leaving his children and their mother with no means of support. The Lord took note of such cases when He said He visits the iniquity of the fathers upon the children (Exodus 20:5). Some of the captives may have accused Ezekiel of contradicting that Scripture. But there is no real contradiction. A son may indeed bear some of the *results* of his father's sin, but he does not bear any of the *guilt* of it. No matter how evil the father may be, if the son himself does right, *he shall surely live.*

20. The soul that sinneth, it shall die. The son shall not bear the iniquity of the father, neither shall the father bear the iniquity of the son: the righteousness of the righteous shall be upon him, and the wickedness of the wicked shall be upon him.

The principle of divine justice is stated again. Each person is responsible for his own sins and no others. Sins of others may bring him suffering and even physical death, but only his own sins can keep him from eternal life. Of course, that principle alone does not give us hope, for all of us have sinned (Romans 3:23; 1 John 1:10). Therefore, all of us deserve to die (Romans 6:23). The gift of eternal life is possible because Christ bore our sins and died in our place (1 Peter 2:24). In that one case, it was possible for one person to take the punishment for another's sins. Jesus took the sins of the whole world (1 John 2:2), and anyone in the world can be free from sin if he puts his trust in Jesus and obeys Him.

II. A Chance to Change (Ezekiel 18:21-24)

"The soul that sinneth, it shall die." That is a principle of divine justice, but it is not the whole story. The soul that sins has a chance to change. He can stop sinning. If his way of life is changed, so is his destiny. Every sinner needs to be transformed.

Sad as it seems, the upright person also has a chance to change. He can become a sinner, and so he can forfeit his life. Every upright person needs to be on guard.

A. From Bad to Good (vv. 21-23)

21. But if the wicked will turn from all his sins that he hath committed, and keep all my statutes, and do that which is lawful and right, he shall surely live, he shall not die.

The sinner can change his way of life. He can do right instead of wrong. If he becomes a righteous man, he will be treated as a righteous man, not a sinner. *He shall surely live, he shall not die.*

22. All his transgressions that he hath committed, they shall not be mentioned unto him: in his righteousness that he hath done he shall live.

In God's court of justice, a man is judged by what he is, not by what he used to be. If a sinner has become righteous, his sins of the past are not even mentioned. Ezekiel was not permitted to announce that Jesus would atone for those past sins, but he was permitted to say of the reformed sinner, *in his righteousness that he hath done he shall live.*

23. Have I any pleasure at all that the wicked should die? saith the Lord God: and not that he should return from his ways, and live?

God wants every sinning soul to *return from his ways, and live.* If any soul dies in sin, it is by his own choice, not God's. "The wages of sin is death," but sin does not pay off at sunset every day. If it did, the world would have been depopulated when there were only two people in it. And if every sin would bring instant death today, would there be a living person in the world tomorrow? Death is the sinner's due, but death is delayed to give the sinner a chance to change. Adam and Eve had a long time to learn about life after Eden and to return to obedience. God waited long in the time of Noah while the ark was being built (1 Peter 3:20). Noah was "a preacher of righteousness" (2 Peter 2:5). Most of the people ignored his preaching and died, but that was their choice, not God's. The people of Judah were deep in sin for centuries, while prophets shouted that defeat and captivity were sure unless they would stop their sinning; but the people chose to keep on sinning, and defeat and captivity came. In later times came Jesus to be the world's Savior, and He promised to come again to be its judge (Matthew 25:31-46). But nineteen centuries have passed, and still He has not come again. Peter tells us why He is waiting. "The Lord is . . . not willing that any should perish, but that all should come to repentance" (2 Peter 3:9). But He will come and He will judge, and some people will go into everlasting punishment (Matthew 25:41-46). That is their choice, not His. Every sinner has a chance to change, to become righteous. If the righteousness he can attain by his own effort is not enough (and it is not), he can have "the righteousness which is of God by faith" (Philippians 3:8-11). By coming to Jesus, the sinner can find forgiveness of sins and the gift of the Holy Spirit (Acts 2:38).

B. From Good to Bad (v. 24)

24. But when the righteous turneth away from his righteousness, and committeth iniquity, and doeth according to all the abominations that the wicked man doeth, shall he live? All his righteousness that he hath done shall not be mentioned: in his trespass that he hath trespassed, and in his sin that he hath sinned, in them shall he die.

A bad person can become good, and a good person can become bad; and destiny changes along with character and action. If a good person becomes bad, his past goodness will not even be mentioned in God's court of justice. We need to be good and stay good.

Even when we have been redeemed and cleansed by the blood of Christ, even when we have "the righteousness which is of God by faith," we must not be smug, complacent, and self-satisfied. We need to be on guard against

visual 2

"the sin which doth so easily beset us." We need to press on steadfastly to victory in "the race that is set before us" (Hebrews 12:1, 2). We need to exert ourselves to keep ourselves in line with God's will (1 Corinthians 9:24-27). Remember the Pharisee who reveled in his own goodness? It was not he who was justified, but a confessed sinner who cried for mercy (Luke 18:9-14). "If we say that we have no sin, we deceive ourselves, and the truth is not in us. If we confess our sins, he is faithful and just to forgive us our sins, and to cleanse us from all unrighteousness" (1 John 1:8, 9).

III. A Plea to Live (Ezekiel 18:30, 31)

"It's not fair!" As the *King James Version* has it, "The way of the Lord is not equal." That was the complaint of the captives when they said God had sent them into captivity because of their fathers' sins.

God rejected that complaint. Those captives were not being punished for their fathers' sins; they were being punished for their own sins, and that was fair. It was unfair for them to complain. God gave the charge of unfairness right back to them: "Are not your ways unequal?" (vv. 25-29)

A. God's Justice (v. 30a)

30a. Therefore I will judge you, O house of Israel, every one according to his ways, saith the Lord God.

God will judge each person individually, according to what that person himself does. What could be fairer than that?

B. Plea to Choose Life (vv. 30b, 31)

30b. Repent, and turn yourselves from all your transgressions; so iniquity shall not be your ruin.

God's way is never less than fair; sometimes it is much better than fair. "The soul that sinneth,

it shall die," and that is fair. Fair warning has been given ever since creation, and the way to do right has been made plain. But if that fair rule were rigidly enforced, every soul on earth would die, for "all have sinned" (Romans 3:23). In divine mercy and grace, God makes a way for sinners to escape death, and that is much better than fair.

31. Cast away from you all your transgressions, whereby ye have transgressed; and make you a new heart and a new spirit: for why will ye die, O house of Israel?

Would you rather live than die? The choice is up to you. If you choose life, there are two things for you to do. First, *cast away from you all your transgressions.* Stop your wrongdoing, all of it. Clean up your way of living and acting. Do right. Second, *make you a new heart and a new spirit.* Clean up your way of thinking and feeling. Cultivate a love for the right. Banish unclean thoughts, selfish desires, unworthy motives. Be pure in heart as well as pure in life.

Why will ye die? Why would any person choose to die rather than to live? Is it because death is far away, and the pleasures of sin are now? Today I can make a thousand dollars by a big deal that is crooked, or maybe two or three dollars by a small but crooked deal. Today I can profit by another's loss without being dishonest—just unkind and selfish. Today I can prove how clever I am by hiding some income from the IRS. Today I can build up my vanity by humiliating a neighbor or insulting a friend. Today I can flaunt my independence by committing adultery or shoplifting a steak or ignoring the speed limit.

The time comes when death is today. Happy is the person who has chosen life long before that time.

GOD SEES WHAT NO ONE ELSE CAN

Jermaine Gardiner is blind. At his birth, his parents were told he would also be deaf and mentally retarded. But they would not accept that verdict. They determined to treat him just as they would a child they believed to be normal. When he was eight months old, his mother was holding him on her lap as she helped his older brother with his piano lessons. A few minutes later, Jermaine played the same song his brother had been practicing!

At thirteen months of age, Jermaine played his first sonata. At two years, he was playing Beethoven with skill; and by the time he was three years old, he had composed his first song. He eats his breakfast at the piano. Sometimes his parents will awaken in the night to the sound of his playing.

There may be times when even Christians decide that a person is "too far gone" for a life to be redeemed. Sin has destroyed a life; only a hollow shell of a person remains. But the verdict may be given too early.

When that life is turned over to God, He takes what no one else can see and begins to create something remarkable out of it. God sets that person "on His knee" and, with His help, a beautiful life results. Where sin and despair had been, God puts in their place a new heart and a new spirit.   —C. R. B.

Conclusion

"Personal Accountability Before God." Our lesson on that theme is drawn from an Old Testament prophet, but it is confirmed in Christian teaching. "Every one of us shall give account of himself to God" (Romans 14:12). Every careless word we say enters into the account (Matthew 12:36). There is no escape: living and dead alike will face judgment (1 Peter 4:5).

A. No Way Out

In recent years some thinkers have made a fad of excusing almost anyone who commits a crime. They say, "He never had a chance. He grew up in abject poverty. His parents neglected him. He never had the things other kids had. Naturally he was angry; naturally he struck back at the system that oppressed him." Or they say, "He never had a chance. He grew up in luxury. Doting parents gave him anything he asked, let him do anything he wanted to do. Naturally he thought he could go on doing as he pleased. We can't hold him accountable." But the Bible says, "Every one of us shall give account of himself to God."

Home Daily Bible Readings

Monday, Sept. 4—A Watchman for Israel (Ezekiel 3:16-21)
Tuesday, Sept. 5—Promise of Restoration (Ezekiel 11:14-21)
Wednesday, Sept. 6—You Can't Save Anyone Else (Ezekiel 14:12-20)
Thursday, Sept. 7—Matters of Life and Death (Ezekiel 18:5-18)
Friday, Sept. 8—Who Can Question God's Way? (Ezekiel 18:25-29)
Saturday, Sept. 9—God Doesn't Want People to Die (Ezekiel 33:7-16)
Sunday, Sept. 10—"Cleanse Me From My Sin" (Psalm 51:1-12)

Some philosophers have a theory that everything I do is determined by what I am and the circumstances I face. In any set of circumstances, they say, such a person as I am will inevitably respond in a certain way. I really have no choice, they say. Some theologians have a similar theory. They say every act of mine is predestined by the Almighty, so that I really have no choice.

I knew a philosopher who scoffed at such theories. He said they are destroyed by a simple fact. The fact is that *I do choose*.

I do choose. That is a fact. My choices have consequences in this world and in eternity, and I have to face those consequences. That too is a fact. There is no way out.

B. I Do Choose

Mom tells me to come straight home after school; the kids want me to stop at the playground with them. I choose, and I face the consequences. If I choose to obey Mom, the kids ridicule me as "mama's boy." If I choose to please the kids, I face Mom's displeasure and maybe her switch.

I choose a college, a life work, a wife or husband, a house to live in, a car to drive. Each choice has consequences, good or bad. Most choices have consequences of both kinds, and I have to balance the good against the bad. But I do choose, and I do face the consequences.

I choose to worship God and do as He directs because that is right, or I choose to ignore God and take my own way because it is more pleasant or more profitable. That is a choice of life or death.

C. Choose Life

Long ago, centuries before Ezekiel spoke, before Israel entered the land of promise, Moses put a challenge before his people: "I have set before you life and death, blessing and cursing: therefore choose life, that both thou and thy seed may live: that thou mayest love the Lord thy God, and that thou mayest obey his voice, and that thou mayest cleave unto him: for he is thy life" (Deuteronomy 30:19, 20). The challenge still stands. "Therefore choose life."

D. Prayer

O Lord our God, thank You for setting before us the way of life. As we make our choices day by day, may we have wisdom and courage to choose that way and to walk in it. In Jesus' name, amen.

E. Thought to Remember

Choose life.

Learning by Doing

This page contains an alternate lesson plan emphasizing learning activities. Classes desiring such student involvement will find these suggestions helpful.

Learning Goals

At the conclusion of this lesson from Ezekiel 18:2-4, 19-24, 30, 31, a student will be able to:

1. Explain the law of personal accountability before God.

2. Identify an area of his life in which he needs to be more aware of his accountability to God.

3. Choose a way to shape his life so that he will be glad to give account of it before God.

Into the Lesson

Before the class members arrive, place the sentence below on the chalkboard or a sheet of newsprint.

"The sins of the fathers will be visited on the children."

As the class members arrive, ask them to read the statement and decide whether they agree or disagree with it. Have them record their responses on the chalkboard or newsprint. Then ask them to work with one other person to see if they can find Scripture to support their views.

When most of the students have arrived, summarize the responses. Ask those who responded each way to provide a brief rationale for their response.

Make the transition into the Bible study section by stating that this question will be answered in today's Bible text.

Into the Word

Provide a brief background for the lesson by using the material in the "Introduction" section. Read the text aloud for the class.

Have your students continue to work in the same pairs as in the activity suggested in the "Into the Lesson" section. Each pair is to write a paraphrase of the text in words that even a child can understand. Allow seven to ten minutes for the pairs to do this. Then have them share their paraphrases with the entire class.

Use the following questions to pursue the meaning of the text.

1. What do you think is the major lesson of this text?

2. What does this text say to those who believe that sin is a social evil?

3. What does this text say to those who believe that a person from a bad environment cannot be expected to do better?

4. What is the only way to avoid penalty for sin?

5. What does Ezekiel mean by a "new heart" and a "new spirit"? Why is this desirable?

Into Life

Continue your discussion by asking the following questions:

1. What does this text have to say to a person who lives in twentieth-century America?

2. How can this text be helpful in promoting evangelism?

3. How can this text be helpful to those who would promote social programs?

4. How accountable do you think people in this day and age feel for their sins?

5. What can the church do to make those who come under its influence more aware of their personal accountability to God?

6. How can the church keep the fine balance between preaching accountability for sin on the one hand and being judgmental on the other? Should that even be a concern?

7. What is the most positive thing you gain from this passage?

Give each student a copy of the following self-evaluation form. Continue your application by asking them to fill it out.

My Life Before God

1. I have to say that in the area of accountability for sin, I am _____

_____ .

2. I have to acknowledge that in the following area of my life I need to have a greater awareness of my accountability to God: _____

_____ .

This week, I will make myself more ready to give an account of my life to God by _____

_____ .

After the students have had enough time to complete the self-evaluation, have them form groups of three. They need not share what they wrote, although they may if they choose. But the groups of three should conclude the session by praying for each other, asking God to work in their lives to help them be more aware of their accountability before Him.

Let's Talk It Over

The questions on this page are designed to encourage review of the lesson Scriptures and to promote discussion of the lesson by the class. The answers provided are only discussion starters. Let your class talk it over from there.

1. Cite some Old Testament examples of those who attempted to refuse responsibility for their actions.

We naturally think of the original pair. When God confronted Adam with his responsibility for eating of the forbidden fruit, Adam adroitly passed the buck to Eve and to God (imagine that!). He said, "The woman *You* gave me, *she* gave me the fruit of the tree, and I ate it" (see Genesis 3:12). And Eve wasn't to be outdone: her response was "The *serpent* beguiled me, and I ate it" (see Genesis 3:13). Another example is Aaron. When Moses called him to account for building an idol—the golden calf—he responded, "You know how *the people* are—*they* are set on mischief. *They* asked for the idol; *they* gave me their gold. I just threw it into the fire— and out came this calf!" (see Exodus 32:22-24). Today's lesson brings us the example of those people of Judah who were captives in Babylon in the time of Ezekiel. They complained, "We're suffering because of the sins of *our fathers.* It's all *their* fault" (see Ezekiel 18:2). God's response to such rationalizing has always been the same "Each person is responsible for his choices and his own conduct."

2. Are parents ultimately responsible for how their children turn out? Give reasons for your response.

No—even though most of them feel they are. Family, friends, and even some in the church often state or imply to parents, "You are responsible for how your adult children turn out—especially if they fail." And too many Christian parents whip themselves with the litany of guilt—"Where did we fail? Where did we go wrong?"—if their adult children reject the Christian life-style. All of this overlooks one profound Biblical and psychological principle: Parents are responsible for faithful parenting, *not for results.* Paul declares, "It is required in stewards, that a man be found faithful" (1 Corinthians 4:2). Parenting is a stewardship of life and responsibility, and God requires *faithfulness.* Parents are to set before their children the ways in which God would have them live. Parents are to do this, both by their instruction and by their consistent example. And all of this is to be done in an atmosphere of love. But the time comes when the child must choose his own way. The principle is emphasized in both Old and New Testaments: responsibility is *personal —* each must give account of himself or herself before God! Ezekiel affirmed that children are not responsible for the deeds of their parents nor are parents responsible for the deeds of their children.

3. Compare the Old Testament and New Testament concepts of righteousness.

In the Old Testament, a person was considered righteous if he kept God's law. Righteousness was seen as a matter of personal action and achievement. This concept was expressed in statements such as these in Ezekiel 18: "If the wicked will . . . keep all my statutes, and do that which is lawful and right, he shall surely live" (v. 21), and "In his righteousness that he has done he shall live" (v. 22). In the New Testament, being *declared* righteous, on the basis of what Christ has done, establishes a new and superior concept. The New Testament makes it plain that a person cannot attain righteousness in the sight of God by keeping the law. In Romans 3, Paul declares, "There is none righteous, no, not one" (v. 10); and again, "All have sinned, and come short of the glory of God" (v. 23). Verses 20-22 of the same chapter differentiate between the two concepts of righteousness. The old righteousness was based in human effort, in the need to obey the law perfectly. The new based in what God has done for us. This righteousness of God can be ours only through faith in Jesus Christ (vv. 24-28).

4. Today's text makes it plain that it is possible for a person to change his behavior, How should we respond to those who say, "People will have to accept me the way I am"?

We find such individuals within and outside the church, wherever we must deal with people. They will either claim they are unable to change the way they are, or they will admit they are unwilling to try to change. And so they go on offending, irritating, embarrassing, and trying the patience of others. Perhaps we can impress them by pointing out how impossible life would be if everyone else lived according to their philosophy.

God Promises to Bless

LESSON SCRIPTURE: Ezekiel 34:11-31.

PRINTED TEXT: Ezekiel 34:17, 20-31.

Ezekiel 34:17, 20-31

17 And as for you, O my flock, thus saith the Lord God; Behold, I judge between cattle and cattle, between the rams and the he goats.

. . . .

20 Therefore thus saith the Lord God unto them; Behold, I, even I, will judge between the fat cattle and between the lean cattle.

21 Because ye have thrust with side and with shoulder, and pushed all the diseased with your horns, till ye have scattered them abroad;

22 Therefore will I save my flock, and they shall no more be a prey; and I will judge between cattle and cattle.

23 And I will set up one shepherd over them, and he shall feed them, even my servant David; he shall feed them, and he shall be their shepherd.

24 And I the Lord will be their God, and my servant David a prince among them; I the Lord have spoken it.

25 And I will make with them a covenant of peace, and will cause the evil beasts to cease out of the land: and they shall dwell safely in the wilderness, and sleep in the woods.

26 And I will make them and the places round about my hill a blessing; and I will cause the shower to come down in his season; there shall be showers of blessing.

27 And the tree of the field shall yield her fruit, and the earth shall yield her increase,

and they shall be safe in their land, and shall know that I am the Lord, when I have broken the bands of their yoke, and delivered them out of the hand of those that served themselves of them.

28 And they shall no more be a prey to the heathen, neither shall the beast of the land devour them; but they shall dwell safely, and none shall make them afraid

29 And I will raise up for them a plant of renown, and they shall be no more consumed with hunger in the land, neither bear the shame of the heathen any more.

30 Thus shall they know that I the Lord their God am with them, and that they, even the house of Israel, are my people, saith the Lord God.

31 And ye my flock, the flock of my pasture, are men, and I am your God, saith the Lord God.

GOLDEN TEXT: Ye my flock, the flock of my pasture, are men, and I am your God, saith the Lord God.—Ezekiel 34:31.

Lesson Aims

After this lesson a student should be able to:

1. Summarize God's promise to rescue His people from their bad leaders (vv. 17, 20-24).

2. Summarize God's promise to rescue His people from Babylon (vv. 25-31).

3. Point out indications that our text refers also to God's promise of rescue from sin through Christ (vv. 23, 24).

Lesson Outline

INTRODUCTION

    A. No Help, No Hope

    B. Lesson Background

 I. BAD SHEPHERDS (Ezekiel 34:17, 20, 21)

    A. Judgment (vv. 17, 20)

    B. Mistreatment (v. 21)

       Poor and Powerless

 II. GOOD SHEPHERD (Ezekiel 34:22-24)

    A. The Rescue (v. 22)

    B. The Shepherd (v. 23)

    C. The Lord (v. 24)

       The Promised Deliverer

III. BLESSED FLOCK (Ezekiel 34:25-31)

    A. Safety and Plenty (vv. 25-29)

    B. A Nation Under God (vv. 30, 31)

CONCLUSION

    A. The Knowledge of God

    B. The Power of God

    C. The Choice Is Ours

    D. Prayer

    E. Thought to Remember

Display visual 3 from the visuals/learning resources packet as you consider verses 25-31. The visual is shown on page 29.

Introduction

This is the third of four lessons from Ezekiel. The whole group of four is titled "God's Care for Judah," but in the first two lessons we have seen care offered rather than care received. God was ready to help His people, but they were not ready to be helped.

A. No Help, No Hope

In the first lesson, we saw that God was with the people of Judah, even when they were cap-tives in Babylon. But they were too rebellious to welcome His message, so there was little hope that it would help them.

In the second lesson, we saw a plain message to straighten out the people's thinking. But still they grumbled that God's way was not fair, so still there was little hope that they would profit by the care that was offered.

Now, in a third lesson, we see the dawn of hope. As the lesson title puts it, "God Promises to Bless." He was going to rescue His people from Babylon, but first He was going to rescue them from the evil oppressors that were among themselves.

B. Lesson Background

In the first two lessons, we saw that ten thousand people of Judah were captives in Babylon, while the rest were still living in the homeland. But in the twelfth year of their captivity, Jerusalem was destroyed (Ezekiel 33:21). Most of the remaining people were then transported to Babylon. That catastrophe was not due to the Babylonians only. God used it to punish His people because they persisted in doing wrong. Their land would be desolate until they would learn that God was the Lord (Ezekiel 33:23-29).

Chapter 34 describes Israel as the flock of God, but a flock scattered and distressed. Their beloved fold, Jerusalem, had just been destroyed. Three thoughts are seen in the first part of the chapter.

1. Verses 1-6 denounce the shepherds of Israel, the officials of government and the leaders of industry and commerce. As shepherds, they should have cared for the welfare of the whole nation, but they had been mistreating the people in order to enrich themselves.

2. Verses 7-10 say those shameless shepherds must be removed. No longer would they be able to enrich themselves by mistreating others.

3. Verses 11-16 promise that God himself would gather the scattered flock and bless it with peace and prosperity.

These thoughts are continued in our text.

I. Bad Shepherds (Ezekiel 34:17, 20, 21)

Attention is given first to the bad shepherds, the greedy men of power and influence who exploited the rest of the people, mistreating others for their own gain.

A. Judgment (vv. 17, 20)

17. And as for you, O my flock, thus saith the Lord God; Behold, I judge between cattle and cattle, between the rams and the he goats.

God's judgment here was not against Babylon. If the captives had a case against their captors, it is not mentioned at this point. They had a case against some of their own people, their greedy and conscienceless leaders. God's judgment was between people of His own flock, *between cattle and cattle*. In the *King James Version*, the word *cattle* means livestock of any kind. The bovine kind we now call cattle does not appear in this chapter. All the people of Israel are sheep and goats. The oppressors—the rulers, the rich and powerful members of the flock—are pictured as utterly heartless and ruthless. They not only seized the best pasture, but also trampled the rest to impoverish the poor and helpless yet more (vv. 18, 19).

20. Therefore thus saith the Lord God unto them; Behold, I, even I, will judge between the fat cattle and between the lean cattle.

In our modern slang, rich and powerful and arrogant people are called fat cats. Ezekiel called them *fat cattle*. The *lean cattle* were the poor and powerless, hungry because the fat cattle robbed them in legal or illegal ways. But God knew what was going on, and He would give His judgment against the wrongdoers.

B. Mistreatment (v. 21)

21. Because ye have thrust with side and with shoulder, and pushed all the diseased with your horns, till ye have scattered them abroad.

The rich and powerful people were pushy. Heartlessly they shouldered the poor and weak out of their way. Not only that, they attacked them violently with their horns. *Diseased* here does not mean anything evil, but only weakness. The lean cattle had no strength to resist the onslaught of the fat cattle. So they were driven and scattered. Many were in Babylon, but the word *abroad* does not necessarily mean a foreign land. It means the poor people were driven out of their proper places. Perhaps they were evicted from homes and farms when mortgages were foreclosed without mercy.

POOR AND POWERLESS

A major social problem of the twentieth century is found in Latin America, Africa, India, and Asia. Throughout the Third World, masses of people live in the squalor of unremitting poverty. Their homes are tin or cardboard shanties. At an early age, children are pressed into labor or learn to beg and steal to help the family eke out a meager existence.

But their basic problem is not poverty. It is powerlessness. The rich and politically powerful control the institutions of society that ought to protect the weak and downtrodden. Little wonder that Marxism and revolution hold such attraction for many of the oppressed.

In Ezekiel's time, the number of the poor and powerless was not as great, but their suffering was no less real. The oppressors were "religious" people, but their religion gave them no conscience on the matter. God was forced to act as Israel's judge, the last refuge of the powerless.

What is the Christian response to the great injustices in our world? Do our riches insulate us from God's call for justice? How can we bring about change? Can we be truly Christian and still not care?   —C. R. B.

II. Good Shepherd (Ezekiel 34:22-24)

Not forever would the Lord's flock be left to the mistreatment of bad shepherds. The Lord had other plans.

A. The Rescue (v. 22)

22. Therefore will I save my flock, and they shall no more be a prey; and I will judge between cattle and cattle.

God's flock had been mistreated, driven, and scattered by bad shepherds; but He himself would rescue His sheep. This verse does not speak of rescue from the Babylonian invaders. It speaks of rescue from the bad shepherds, the corrupt rulers and masters of commerce among the people of Judah. God's judgment was *between cattle and cattle*, between members of His flock and other members of it. The captivity was God's instrument to destroy the power of the powerful and crooked men who had been dominating Judah.

B. The Shepherd (v. 23)

23. And I will set up one shepherd over them, and he shall feed them, even my servant David; he shall feed them, and he shall be their shepherd.

After breaking the power of all the bad shepherds, God would appoint one good shepherd for his flock, *even my servant David*. King David had led Israel from weakness to power and glory, but now he had been dead for centuries. This Scripture does not mean God was promising to bring him back from the dead to rule again in Jerusalem. But one of David's descendants would be a shepherd-king who would rule forever over a kingdom not of this world, but a kingdom far more glorious than David's kingdom was. This points to Jesus Christ, though His coming was more than five hundred years in the future, and the perfection of His kingdom is in the future still. *He shall feed them.* The bad shepherds had sacrificed the sheep to feed themselves (Ezekiel 34:2-4), but the good shepherd would sacrifice himself to give life to His sheep (John 10:11).

C. The Lord (v. 24)

24. And I the Lord will be their God, and my servant David a prince among them; I the Lord have spoken it.

God said, "All souls are mine" (Ezekiel 18:4). In a sense, He is God even of the bad shepherds. He created them, and finally He will judge them. But now He speaks of those who follow the good shepherd, Jesus. He is *their God* in a different sense. They accept Him as their God; they worship Him reverently and obey Him gladly, and He gives them His special blessing both here and hereafter. Among them is *a prince*, one lifted up, exalted. He is David: that is, the son of David who rules forever—Jesus. Twenty-five centuries ago the Lord promised this, and the promise is sure forever.

The Promised Deliverer

Fidel Castro and his band of ragtag followers hid for years in the mountains of Cuba. In the villages and towns, they pled their cause, gradually gaining support. Stealthily, they awaited their chance to overthrow Fulgencio Batista, the dictator of their land. Finally, in 1959, Castro struck and Batista fell.

Then came the surprises: Castro turned out to be a Communist, and the common man in Communist Cuba was no freer than he had been before the revolution. The "savior" did not deliver on many of the promises that had gained supporters for his cause.

However, we should not be surprised. Throughout history, reformers and revolutionaries, rescuers and redeemers have consistently failed to fulfill their promises. The problem occurs even in democracies, with their elected officials, doesn't it? Often it seems that campaign platforms are to run on, not to enact into law.

But it was different with Jesus, who would come as the "David" of Ezekiel's prophecy. He would be a prince with authority, of course. But He would also be a shepherd who knew His sheep and cared for them, feeding them as He led them. He will still do the same for us. *All* of God's promises are fulfilled in Jesus! —C. R. B.

III. Blessed Flock (Ezekiel 34:25-31)

When Jehovah is our God and Jesus is our prince and shepherd, the flow of blessings is ceaseless and eternal.

A. Safety and Plenty (vv. 25-29)

25. And I will make with them a covenant of peace, and will cause the evil beasts to cease out of the land: and they shall dwell safely in the wilderness, and sleep in the woods.

Jeremiah was God's prophet in Jerusalem while Ezekiel was His prophet in Babylon, and through Jeremiah also Jehovah gave His promise of a new covenant. It was to be *a covenant of peace* written on the hearts of His people, and it was to provide forgiveness for their sins (Jeremiah 31:31-34). When we devote ourselves to Jesus, the covenant in our hearts leads us to do right, and the blood of Christ atones for our wrongs. So "we have peace with God through our Lord Jesus Christ" (Romans 5:1).

However, it seems plain that verses 25-29 point also to a time nearer to Ezekiel's own time. A prophetic word from God may have more than one meaning. For example, see Hosea 11:1: "When Israel was a child, then I loved him, and called my son out of Egypt." This was a statement of history. God loved the infant nation of Israel, regarded it as His son, and called it out of slavery in Egypt to a new life of freedom in the promised land. But the verse pointed also to the future, to the time when God was going to call His infant Son, Jesus, out of Egypt to live in that same promised land (Matthew 2:13-15). In a similar way, our text speaks plainly of a time when God would free His people from Babylon and restore them to peace and prosperity in their own land. But with the clue given in verses 23 and 24, we can see that it speaks also of the peace and safety we have in Jesus.

In the time of north Israel's punishment, *evil beasts* had been a danger to the inhabitants of Israel (2 Kings 17:24, 25). There would be no such danger when God's people would return to their own land. They would be able to sleep safely, even in the most lonely desert or forest. In the days of the New Covenant, people who would behave as beasts would be doomed (2 Peter 2:12).

26. And I will make them and the places round about my hill a blessing; and I will cause the shower to come down in his season; there shall be showers of blessing.

God's *hill* was Zion, the temple hill in Jerusalem. There His people had worshiped Him through many centuries. The Babylonians had destroyed the temple, but God's people would go back to rebuild it and to make their homes in *the places round about* it. There, God would *shower* them with His *blessing*, not only literal rainfall in the time it was needed, but uncounted blessings besides.

visual 3

Zion is a symbol of the church, whose people enjoy blessings innumerable through this life and look for perfect happiness in the new Jerusalem pictured in Revelation 21 and 22.

27. And the tree of the field shall yield her fruit, and the earth shall yield her increase, and they shall be safe in their land, and shall know that I am the Lord, when I have broken the bands of their yoke, and delivered them out of the hand of those that served themselves of them.

The first part of our text has told us that rich and powerful men of Israel had *served themselves* by mistreating the poor and powerless. God had broken the power of these oppressors and delivered the people from them by letting the whole nation be taken captive. Now rich and poor alike were in the hand of Babylon and used for the purposes of the conquerors. But in time, God would break the power of Babylon and set His people free. They would go back to their own land, God would give them good crops from fruit trees and grainfields, and they would be *safe in their land.* All of this would be convincing evidence of the power of God. Set free by His power, His people would know that He was the Lord, the eternal ruler, the controller of all the nations of earth.

All of us have sinned (Romans 3:23). Thus we have become captives, slaves of sin (John 8:34). But Christ's sacrifice has broken the power of sin and set us free. Free to worship God and blessed abundantly by the fruit of the Spirit (Galatians 5:22), how can we ever doubt the presence and power and love of Jehovah?

28. And they shall no more be a prey to the heathen, neither shall the beast of the land devour them; but they shall dwell safely, and none shall make them afraid.

The captives in Babylon, or some of them, would realize that their sinning had brought them there. They would give up their sinning. They would worship God sincerely and obey Him. In time they would be free to go back to their homeland. Then they would not be troubled either by *heathen* invaders like the Babylonians or by wild *beasts* like lions.

History records that this prophecy was fulfilled. Fifty years after Jerusalem was destroyed, about fifty thousand of its people went back to start rebuilding it. The process was slow, and there were setbacks, as we see in the books of Ezra and Nehemiah; but the people did live safely in their land. Of course, their safety depended on their faithfulness to God. When that failed in later years, they became again *a prey to the heathen:* to Alexander the Great and his successors, and then to the Romans.

So it is when Jesus rescues us from captivity to sin. Our spirits are safe even in the midst of persecution and every kind of trouble (Romans 8:35-39). But our safety depends on our faithfulness as well as on the Savior's power (Revelation 2:10; 1 Corinthians 9:24-27).

29. And I will raise up for them a plant of renown, and they shall be no more consumed with hunger in the land, neither bear the shame of the heathen any more.

Instead of a *a plant* we can translate *a plantation*, a large area planted and renowned for producing abundant crops. Back in the homeland, God's people would not be *consumed with hunger.* The fruitful fields would keep them safe from famine. They would not have to *bear the shame of the heathen,* either the shame of acting like heathen as their forefathers had done, or the shame of being defeated by heathen, or the shame of being ridiculed and scorned by heathen because of their poverty and weakness.

Likewise when Christ sets us free from sin and we serve Him faithfully, we find that He supplies all our needs (Matthew 6:33; Philippians 4:19).

B. A Nation Under God (vv. 30, 31)

30. Thus shall they know that I the Lord their God am with them, and that they, even the house of Israel, are my people, saith the Lord God.

Liberated from Babylon and living lives of faith and obedience, the people of Israel would know that the Lord was with them. They would know it, because He would give them safety, peace, and prosperity.

So it is with us who are liberated by Christ. The more thoroughly we are devoted to Him, the more certainly we know that He is with us. We are "the Israel of God" (Galatians 6:16).

31. And ye my flock, the flock of my pasture, are men, and I am your God, saith the Lord God.

Men here means human beings, both men and women. This verse applies equally to ancient Israelites and modern Christians. We are people made in God's image (Genesis 1:27). We are not mere animals. We must not act like "brute beasts," though some people do (2 Peter 2:12-22). On the other hand, we are only *men*, not God. We must not ignore God's Word and set our own standards of right and wrong. We must not imagine that our own wisdom and power are all we need, "for in him we live, and move, and have our being" (Acts 17:28).

Conclusion

"O come, let us worship and bow down:
let us kneel before the Lord our maker.
For he is our God;
and we are the people of his pasture,
and the sheep of his hand" (Psalm 95:6, 7).

A. The Knowledge of God

"O the depth of the riches both of the wisdom and knowledge of God! how unsearchable are his judgments, and his ways past finding out! For who hath known the mind of the Lord? or who hath been his counselor?" (Romans 11:33, 34).

When Assyria was the mightiest nation in the world, Babylon was only a little country down the river. But God said Babylon and not Assyria would make prisoners of the people of Judah (Isaiah 39:5-7). It was a hundred years before that happened, but it happened.

When Babylon took away ten thousand captives, optimists in Jerusalem blithely promised that the captives would be back in a couple of years. God did indeed promise that the captives would go back, but He said it would be in seventy years instead of two (Jeremiah 29:10). That was what happened.

In those days God said He would make a New Covenant with His people, putting His law in their hearts and forgiving their sins (Jeremiah 31:31-34). About five hundred years later, Jesus came to establish the New Covenant and seal it with His blood.

Jesus said He will come again to reign in glory. He said He will welcome some to the kingdom prepared for them from the foundation of the world, and consign some to everlasting fire prepared for the devil and his angels (Matthew 25:31-46). That will happen. Count on it.

B. The Power of God

Not by any power of their own would the people of Israel escape from Babylon and go back to live happily in their own land, Observers who did not know God might think it was the power of the Medes and Persians that crushed Babylon and set God's people free. But students of Scripture know the power of God was working through the Medes and Persians.

Not by any power of our own are we rescued from bondage to sin and made free as children of God. The power and grace of God save us (Ephesians 2:8). Jesus gives us the right to become God's children (John 1:12, 13). Dead bodies have no power, but Jesus has power to call them from their graves to life or to judgment (John 5:26-29).

C. The Choice Is Ours

"Death is so permanent!" Sometimes we hear that old saying quoted, but it is not true. Death is only a passing phase.

"The Lord himself shall descend from heaven with a shout, with the voice of the archangel, and with the trump of God: and the dead in Christ shall rise first" (1 Thessalonians 4:16). But the dead in Christ are not the only ones who will rise at His call. The dead outside of Christ will rise too. "All that are in the graves shall hear his voice, and shall come forth; they that have done good, unto the resurrection of life; and they that have done evil, unto the resurrection of damnation" (John 5:28, 29).

We cannot choose whether we shall rise from the dead or not, but we can choose whether we shall rise to everlasting life or to shame and everlasting contempt (Daniel 12:2).

D. Prayer

Almighty God, we know Your wisdom and Your power. Thankfully we put ourselves in Your hand. If we commit ourselves fully, we know You will keep that which we have committed unto You until the day of resurrection.

E. Thought to Remember

Death is *not* permanent.

Home Daily Bible Readings

Monday, Sept. 11—False Shepherds, Beware! (Ezekiel 34:1-10)

Tuesday, Sept. 12—God is the Good Shepherd (Ezekiel 34:11-16)

Wednesday, Sept. 13—Vindicated Among the Nations (Ezekiel 36:6-15)

Thursday, Sept. 14—From Ruin to Renewal. (Ezekiel 36:33-38)

Friday, Sept. 15—A Righteous Branch Will Grow (Jeremiah 33:10-16)

Saturday, Sept. 16—Sing Praise to God! (Jeremiah 31:1-9)

Sunday, Sept. 17—Joy and Gladness Will Come (Jeremiah 31:10-14)

Learning by Doing

This page contains an alternate lesson plan emphasizing learning activities. Classes desiring such student involvement will find these suggestions helpful.

Learning Goals

After studying Ezekiel 34:17, 20-31, a student will be able to:

1. List ways God served as a shepherd to Israel.

2. List ways God serves as a shepherd to His children today.

3. Identify the responsibility of those to whom God serves as a shepherd.

4. Thank God for His shepherding in our lives.

Into the Lesson

As the class members arrive, give each person a sheet with the word *shepherd* printed on it vertically. Ask each to write words or phrases beginning with the letters of the word *shepherd* A sample acrostic is completed below.

Shepherd Acrostic

S—seeks
H—helps
E—exhorts
P—protects
H—herds
E—endures hardship
R—rescues
D—directs

Allow five to seven minutes for this activity; then have the class members share their responses. As they do so, write the words on a master acrostic on the chalkboard or a chart. Your class members will suggest words that aren't included here. If you aren't sure of what the words mean, have the students explain them.

Make the transition into the Bible study by stating that today's lesson will deal with shepherding, particularly the way in which God serves as a shepherd for His people.

Into the Word

Have someone previously appointed to read aloud the text for today. Use the material in the "Lesson Background" section to clarify the setting for the lesson.

Ask someone earlier in the week to prepare a report on the work of shepherds. Have the report presented at this time. Your own research on this subject during the week will enable you to add any facts the reporter may omit.

Divide the class into groups of four to six. Ask them to read the text and find the ways God indicated that He would shepherd His people. Each group may also add ideas of how God served as a shepherd as recorded in other portions of Scripture. Possible responses from this text are:

1. God promised to save His people (v. 22).

2. He would provide a leader for them (v. 23).

3. He would make a covenant of peace (v. 25).

4. He would protect His people (vv. 25, 28).

5. He would bless them (v. 26).

6. He would provide what they needed (v. 27).

7. He would feed them (v. 29).

8. They would know that He was their God (v. 30).

Allow the groups six to eight minutes to do their work. Then lead a time of sharing. As the groups share their ideas, add insights from your study that may be helpful to the development of the lesson.

Make the transition into the application section by having someone read Psalm 95:6, 7, followed by another person reading Psalm 23.

Into Life

Ask, How does God serve as a shepherd for His people now? Let the class members suggest ways that He cares for His people. You may want to organize this around the eight points listed in the Bible study section. Be sure that your students mention that God has rescued us from the power and penalty of sin.

Now have the class work in the same groups of four to six as they did earlier. Have each group read the following Scriptures and note what they indicate that God does for His people: Jeremiah 31:31-34; Ephesians 2:8; John 1:12-13; and 1 Thessalonians 4:16. Then ask each group to write a song, a prayer, or a poem expressing God's care for us as described in these verses and as mentioned in the previous discussion. You may want to make your way from group to group as they work, so you will know what each group is preparing.

Call on the groups in an order that will bring the lesson to a fitting climax. When the groups are finished, briefly summarize the main points emphasized.

Let's Talk It Over

The questions on this page are designed to encourage review of the lesson Scriptures and to promote discussion of the lesson by the class. The answers provided are only discussion starters. Let your class talk it over from there.

1. Why do people seek political office? Why do politicians seek to remain in office?

At least four reasons exist for seeking political office: (1) to be of service to one's community, state, and/or nation; (2) to wield power; (3) to become wealthy; (4) to make a name for oneself. Undoubtedly, a significant number of persons seek office for the first reason given above. Yet just as surely, others are motivated by one or more of the other reasons listed. Once a person is in office, the temptation to enhance his or her power, wealth, and status increases. It takes a person of uncommon strength and integrity to resist these corrupting influences. In Ezekiel's day, the leaders of Israel (particularly the politicians) were corrupt.

2. Speaking through Ezekiel, the Lord described some of the people in that day as "fat cattle." As our lesson writer indicates, we moderns use the term "fat cats" to describe these people in our society. What are some common characteristics or traits of "fat cats"?

These people in ancient Judah have their counterparts in every modern society. *Often* (but not always) fat cats behave in ways that are pushy, arrogant, ruthless, self-centered and self-serving, coercive or manipulative, greedy (of money and power), and unethical. The potential corrupting impact of wealth can be seen in the deterioration of character.

3. How may we describe *the measure* of God's blessing upon His people?

The Twenty-third Psalm depicts the measure of blessing best in these words: "my cup runneth over" (Psalm 23:5). Whenever God blesses, it is always to overflowing measure, to super saturation. He is the giver of "every good gift and every perfect gift" (James 1:17). When Ezekiel promised Jehovah's blessings upon His people, He described the outpouring in terms of abundance and plenty, of bounteous provision for every need—and more! And what the new Israel experiences in Jesus Christ far surpasses anything known by Israel under the Old Covenant. "God is great, God is good!"

4. Does God always bless His people with material prosperity? Amplify your answer.

No. The blessings that God promised ancient Israel for faithful obedience to His law were couched in material terms. But it is not so in the New Covenant. In the New Testament, the prosperity of the righteous is spiritual. Although God had promised to meet *all* our material *needs*, He has never promised that His blessing will always be expressed in material prosperity. The prime example was Jesus himself. Come to earth to do only the will of His Heavenly Father (John 5:30), Jesus described himself as one who didn't even have a place where He could count on spending the night (Luke 9:58). And in death, His body had to be placed in a borrowed tomb. Materially prosperous? Hardly!

The current, enticing message assuring "health and wealth" to Christ's followers is opposed to the revelation of the New Testament. The Christian faith, as a way of life, emphasized instead sacrifice and service. That doesn't appeal to the multitudes lusting for "health and wealth."

5. We know that Jesus is our advocate with our Heavenly Father (1 John 2:1). In light of this lesson, how may Christians function as advocates in our society?

Advocates plead the cause of others; they work for the well-being of other persons. In our time, advocacy implies all of this in behalf of the powerless and the helpless—those who do not possess the power or resources to champion their cause or call attention to their desperate need. The poor, the handicapped, the uneducated, the aging, the deprived, the disadvantaged usually need *advocacy*. Christian responsibility calls for the followers of the Servant-Lord to function in this way. In a very real sense, Ezekiel functioned in an advocacy role for the poor sheep of Israel against the unfaithful and corrupt shepherds of his time.

6. Cite some of the most crucial marks of a "servant-leader," after the example of Jesus.

Such a leader possesses these traits: (1) refusal to abuse power (Matthew 20:25, 26); (2) self-sacrifice, expressed in giving (laying down) one's own life (John 10:11, 15); and (3) humble service (John 13:3-16). How winsome and meaningful are these characteristics!

God Gives New Life

LESSON SCRIPTURE: Ezekiel 37:1-14.

PRINTED TEXT: Ezekiel 37:3-14.

Ezekiel 37:3-14

3 And he said unto me, Son of man, can these bones live? And I answered, O Lord God, thou knowest.

4 Again he said unto me, Prophesy upon these bones, and say unto them, O ye dry bones, hear the word of the Lord.

5 Thus saith the Lord God unto these bones; Behold, I will cause breath to enter into you, and ye shall live:

6 And I will lay sinews upon you, and will bring up flesh upon you, and cover you with skin, and put breath in you, and ye shall live; and ye shall know that I am the Lord.

7 So I prophesied as I was commanded: and as I prophesied, there was a noise, and behold a shaking, and the bones came together, bone to his bone.

8 And when I beheld, lo, the sinews and the flesh came up upon them, and the skin covered them above: but there was no breath in them.

9 Then said he unto me, Prophesy unto the wind, prophesy, son of man, and say to the wind, Thus saith the Lord God; Come from the four winds, O breath, and breathe upon these slain, that they may live.

10 So I prophesied as he commanded me, and the breath came into them, and they lived, and stood up upon their feet, an exceeding great army.

11 Then he said unto me, Son of man, these bones are the whole house of Israel: behold, they say, Our bones are dried, and our hope is lost: we are cut off for our parts.

12 Therefore prophesy and say unto them, Thus saith the Lord God; Behold, O my people, I will open your graves, and cause you to come up out of your graves, and bring you into the land of Israel.

13 And ye shall know that I am the Lord, when I have opened your graves, O my people, and brought you up out of your graves,

14 And shall put my Spirit in you, and ye shall live, and I shall place you in your own land: then shall ye know that I the Lord have spoken it, and performed it, saith the Lord.

GOLDEN TEXT: [I] shall put my Spirit in you, and ye shall live, and I shall place you in your own land.—Ezekiel 37:14.

Lesson Aims

After this lesson a student should be able to:
1. Describe Ezekiel's vision of dry bones and explain its meaning.
2. Mention two or three events of history that show that God is the Lord.
3. Believe that Jesus will come and judge the world.
4. Find one way to do God's will better this week than he did last week.

Lesson Outline

INTRODUCTION
    A. Hope and Despair
    B. Lesson Background
  I. THE VOICE OF THE LORD (Ezekiel 37:3-6)
    A. Amazing Question (v. 3)
    B. Amazing Order (v. 4)
    C. Amazing Promise (vv. 5, 6)
 II. PROPHECY AND RESPONSE (Ezekiel 37:7-10)
    A. Building Bodies (vv. 7, 8)
    B. Breathing Life (vv. 9, 10)
      Dry Bones
III. EXPLANATION (Ezekiel 37:11-14)
    A. Hopeless Israel (v. 11)
    B. Message of Hope (vv. 12-14)
      Hope for New Life
CONCLUSION
    A. "Ye Shall Know"
    B. Promise and Performance
    C. Double Demonstration
    D. Prayer
    E. Thought to Remember

Display visual 4 from the visuals/learning resources packet. Refer to it at appropriate times throughout the lesson. It is shown on page 36.

Introduction

"Hope springs eternal in the human breast." So wrote Alexander Pope, a famous English author who was born 301 years ago. Indeed, hope is hard to extinguish. If a home is destroyed by fire or earthquake, we hope to rebuild. If we ourselves are laid low by injury or sickness, we hope to recover. In the presence of death, we hope for life eternal. But to some there comes such a time of despair that there is no hope.

A. Hope and Despair

The people of Judah clung to hope when ten thousand of them were deported to Babylon. Gladly they heard the false promise that the captives would be free within two years (Jeremiah 28:1-4). They resented the true promise that there was worse to come, that Jerusalem would be taken and destroyed (Jeremiah 34:1-3). Deluded by false hope, they ignored the call to stop the sinning that was bringing ruin (Ezekiel 18:30, 31).

Then came the time when the troops of Babylon besieged Jerusalem till the starving people had no will to resist. Taking the city, the Babylonians burned everything they could and battered down the stone walls they could not burn. The people who survived were driven over weary miles to Babylon.

That was when the captives were submerged in despair. How could they hope to go back home when home was no longer there? But then hope lived on in the promises of God. Read Ezekiel 36 with its prophecies of new life in a land restored and fruitful. Chapter 37 brings the same promise in an unforgettable way.

B. Lesson Background

We who are not prophets can only dimly imagine what it was like to be "in the Spirit," to have the word of God sound clear and unmistakable, or to be enlightened by vast visions. The opening verses of Ezekiel 37 tell us that Ezekiel was taken by the hand of the Lord to a valley full of bones. We need not wonder whether it was a real valley or only a vision. In either case its message is clear. It looked as if a terrible battle had been fought there in bygone years. Countless people had been killed. With none to bury them, the dead bodies were left on the ground till they were devoured by jackals and vultures and decay. Only bare bones remained. Bleached by the sun, "they were very dry" (vv. 1, 2).

I. The Voice of the Lord
(Ezekiel 37:3-6)

Wandering and wondering among the dry bones that littered the floor of the valley, Ezekiel heard the voice of the Lord.

A. Amazing Question (v. 3)

3. And he said unto me, Son of man, can these bones live? And I answered, O Lord God, thou knowest.

Can these bones live? What a question! An ordinary wanderer in that valley would never have thought of it; and if he had heard it, he would have answered with a scornful no. But Ezekiel was God's prophet. He knew God's power was unlimited, and he knew he was in that valley for a purpose. With mind wide open to whatever God had to say, Ezekiel answered, *O Lord God, thou knowest.*

B. Amazing Order (v. 4)

4. Again he said unto me, Prophesy upon these bones, and say unto them, O ye dry bones, hear the word of the Lord.

What an order! Those bones had no ears, no minds, no life. How could they hear anything? But the deaf, the mindless, and the lifeless can respond to the word of God. There was no ear to hear Him say, "Let there be light"; but "there was light" (Genesis 1:3). In another beginning "the dead shall hear the voice of the Son of God: and they that hear shall live" (John 5:25).

C. Amazing Promise (vv. 5, 6)

5. Thus saith the Lord God unto these bones; Behold, I will cause breath to enter into you, and ye shall live.

What a promise! Those brittle bones had no lungs. How could they breathe? But if God gives breath, He gives what is needed to receive it as the next verse shows.

6. And I will lay sinews upon you, and will bring up flesh upon you, and cover you with skin, and put breath in you, and ye shall live; and ye shall know that I am the Lord.

In short, God promised to build human bodies on those dry bones. *Sinews* are bands or thongs. Such are the ligaments that tie bone to bone and the tendons that tie bone to muscle. *Flesh* is often a general term for the whole body, including internal organs, glands, brain, blood vessels, nerves as well as the muscles that give a body its shape. Covered with *skin*, the completed body would be ready to receive *breath* and life, and God would supply these. This reminds us of the way man was made in the beginning. Shaped from the dust of earth, he received from God the breath of life (Genesis 2:7). Any person so made and endowed with life ought to know that the Creator is the Lord. There is no other way to account for the marvelous construction of a human being.

II. Prophecy and Response (Ezekiel 37:7-10)

Speak to bones that have no ears? Promise breath to bones without lungs, life to bones long dead, dried by years of sunshine? It seemed preposterous. But Ezekiel was God's prophet. He spoke as God told him to speak.

A. Building Bodies (vv. 7, 8)

7. So I prophesied as I was commanded: and as I prophesied, there was a noise, and behold a shaking, and the bones came together, bone to his bone.

Some suggest that the *shaking* was an earthquake accompanied by a thunderous *noise*. Others think perhaps the *noise* was just the rattling of countless thousands of dry bones as they were shaken from their resting places and assembled into skeletons. In either case, the point is that God's word gets results. Genesis 1 records that God spoke, and what He ordered was done. In Ezekiel's vision, the word of God was likewise creative, even when spoken by a prophet. *The bones came together*, each one coming to the one that belonged next to it in a skeleton.

8. And when I beheld, lo, the sinews and the flesh came up upon them, and the skin covered them above: but there was no breath in them.

Ezekiel watched, and before his very eyes the *sinews* tied the bones together in skeletons, the *flesh* of human bodies came upon them, and *skin* covered the bodies to make them complete. But they were lifeless bodies.

B. Breathing Life (vv. 9, 10)

9. Then said he unto me, Prophesy unto the wind, prophesy, son of man, and say to the wind, Thus saith the Lord God; Come from the four winds, O breath, and breathe upon these slain, that they may live.

This is a very interesting verse because the Hebrew word used here can mean either *wind* or *breath* or *spirit*. Translators of the *King James Version* chose to translate it first as *wind* and then as *breath*. That too seems reasonable; but the *New International Version* translates it "breath" throughout the verse except in the phrase "the four winds." That too seems reasonable. Notice the various possibilities: "Then said he unto me, Prophesy unto the wind [or breath or spirit], Thus saith the Lord God; Come from the four winds [or breaths or spirits], O breath [or wind or spirit], and breathe [or blow] upon these slain, that they may live." However we translate it, Ezekiel was to summon wind or breath or spirit to enter those lifeless bodies and make them alive.

10. So I prophesied as he commanded me, and the breath came into them, and they lived, and stood up upon their feet, an exceeding great army.

Again God's word was given by God's prophet, and again it was obeyed. The lifeless bodies became alive and *stood up*. Ezekiel did not try to estimate the number of them, but called them *an exceeding great army*. Were rusted swords revived to arm that army? Did the men have armor, or any clothes at all? We are not told. The point is that God can restore life to those long dead. Some students see here a prediction of the final resurrection of all the dead (John 5:28, 29). Others see a suggestion of new life for those dead in sin (Ephesians 2:1, 2). But neither of these is the meaning given to the vision in the explanation that follows.

DRY BONES

The word *desert* is almost synonymous with *dead* to most people: vast wastes of sand stretching to the horizon; mirages taunting the thirsty wanderer with the promise of water that is not there; an occasional rattlesnake scurrying from the shade of one prickly, cactus to another. "Death Valley" says it all, verbally and emotionally.

Not necessarily. The Hoover Dam, completed in 1936, was constructed at a cost of $120 million dollars. But that dam brought life for the desert of the American southwest. The water and the electric power that it made available turned the small cities of southern California, Nevada, and Arizona into booming metropolises.

When Ezekiel surveyed the valley full of dry bones, he must have had little concept of what they could become. But he prophesied as he was told, and the bones came together as God had said they would. The word of the Lord was the power that brought them back to life.

The word of the Lord can be a reconstituting power in our lives as well. In the dusty desert of the sinful heart, it will begin its work of turning death into life.   —C. R. B.

III. Explanation
(Ezekiel 37:11-14)

The Lord gave the vision, and without the Lord's explanation it must have been as mystifying to Ezekiel as it is to us. But the Lord promptly explained it. Whether it carried an additional meaning or not, we can be sure it meant what the Lord said it meant.

A. Hopeless Israel (v. 11)

11. Then he said unto me, Son of man, these bones are the whole house of Israel: behold, they say, Our bones are dried, and our hope is lost: we are cut off for our parts.
Many people of Israel were living in Babylon, but their national life was ended. As a nation they were dead, dead as those bleached bones in the visionary valley. That was their own opin-

visual 4

ion; it was what they were saying. Their nation was no more, and they had no hope that it would ever live again. *We are cut off for our parts* is literally *We are cut off for us*. The Keil-Delitzsch commentary aptly expresses what the Israelites were saying: "It is all over with us." They were cut off from their homeland; they were cut off from the temple and ceremonial worship; it must have seemed to them that they were cut off from God. By the streams of Babylon they sat down and cried (Psalm 137:1).

B. Message of Hope (vv. 12-14)

12. Therefore prophesy and say unto them, Thus saith the Lord God; Behold, O my people, I will open your graves, and cause you to come up out of your graves, and bring you into the land of Israel.
As the captives saw themselves, they were not only dead but buried. The places where they lived in Babylon were like graves. Escape was no more possible for them than it was for dead men buried in the ground. But with God nothing is impossible. Plainly He promised, *I will open your graves*. He would free them from their captivity. He would take them back into the land of Israel. Like the long-dead army in the vision, they would live again as a nation.

13. And ye shall know that I am the Lord, when I have opened your graves, O my people, and brought you up out of your graves.
God was going to do the impossible. He was going to rescue the people of Israel from their living death in Babylon. He was going to take them back to their land and give them freedom, peace, security, prosperity. He was going to make dead Israel live and stand upon its feet. He was going to do this before their very eyes. Yes, with their own feet He was going to take them back to their homeland; with their own hands He was going to fill that land with fruitful fields and vineyards and orchards. Then they would know, surely they would know, that He was the Lord.

14. And shall put my Spirit in you, and ye shall live, and I shall place you in your own land: then shall ye know that I the Lord have spoken it, and performed it, saith the Lord.

Again we see the Hebrew word that means *wind* or *breath* or *spirit.* Like those lifeless bodies in the vision, dead Israel was going to receive a breath or spirit that would make it alive. This time God specifically called it *my Spirit* or *my breath.* He is the giver of life. Dead Israel was going to be restored to life and returned to its own land. The Lord added, *Then shall ye know that I the Lord have spoken it, and performed it.* Alive and free and happy at home, the people of Israel would know that God had promised to do what they thought impossible, and had done it. He always keeps His promises, and that is part of the convincing evidence that He is the Lord.

HOPE FOR NEW LIFE

Four-year-old Maron Kadosh was dying of liver disease. If a liver transplant operation could not be arranged, she had no hope for life. But her father was a poor, laboring man, and he had no way of acquiring the one hundred thousand dollars needed for such an operation.

An appeal was made for donations in her native land of Israel. Enough was given for Maron and her mother and doctor to fly to London for tests. When the 450 other passengers on her flight discovered that she was on the plane, they "passed the hat." Cash, pledges, and checks were given. One anonymous English businessman wrote a check for twenty-four thousand dollars. The total collected was seventy-two thousand dollars! A flight of desperation had become a journey of hope for Maron Kadosh!

The people of Israel were without hope, exiled in a strange land. They had sinned against God, and their present condition was God's punishment upon them. Their spirits were low; their national identity had died. But God promised to raise them to new life as a people and return them to their land.

When our sins bring despair and depression, we need to hear the word of the Lord. He tells us that there is forgiveness and new life in Christ. There is hope for resurrection!   —C. R. B.

Conclusion

"Thine, O Lord, is the greatness, and the power, and the glory, and the victory, and the majesty: for all that is in the heaven and in the earth is thine; thine is the kingdom, O Lord, and thou art exalted as head above all" (1 Chronicles 29:11). So said David, king of Israel. He himself was a powerful king. He had brought his country from weakness to power and glory. But he knew the source of all power (1 Chronicles 29:12, 13). He knew the Lord.

A. "Ye Shall Know"

The nation of Israel was dead, its people buried in captivity. But God was going to revive the nation and plant it again in its ancient homeland. When that would happen, He said, "Ye shall know that I am the Lord" (Ezekiel 37:13).

They should have known that all along. Ever since He liberated them from Egypt, bringing them through the Red Sea on dry land (Exodus 14), they should have known that He was the Lord. Their ancestor Abraham believed God and obeyed Him, and Abraham was blessed. From that time on, all the children of Abraham should have known that God was the Lord. But even after He brought them back from Babylon, they did not follow Him faithfully forever. They became rebellious again, and in A.D. 70 the Romans smashed Jerusalem and scattered all the people much as the Babylonians had done in 586 B. C. Not till this present century was there again a nation of Israel in the ancient homeland—and even now many of that nation do not know that God is the Lord.

Shall we call them slow learners? Then what of the rest of the world? The record of God's dealing with Israel is plain for all to read, but millions do not know that He is the Lord. Even those who do not read the record have God's testimony constantly before them "in that he did good, and gave us rain from heaven, and fruitful seasons, filling our hearts with food and gladness" (Acts 14:17). Creation itself is a powerful witness to the Creator, and there is no excuse for those who do not know that God is the Lord (Romans 1:18-23).

And what of us who know the Lord? He has trusted us to take His word to all the world and every creature (Mark 16:15). What is our excuse?

B. Promise and Performance

"Then shall ye know that I the Lord have spoken it, and performed it, saith the Lord" (Ezekiel 37:14). God announces events in advance, and that is assurance that He is the Lord.

He told Adam that disobedience would bring death, and it did (Genesis 2:17; 5:5). He said He would bring a flood of waters on the earth, and He did (Genesis 6:13—7:24). Only those who believed God and obeyed Him were secure in the deluge. God promised to make a great nation of Abraham (Genesis 12:1-3), and even today that nation lives to show that He did it. In the days of Abraham God said He would rescue His people from bondage (Genesis 15:12-14), and Exodus tells that He did it. Our text brings us one of God's promises to rescue His people from Babylon, and Ezra records that He did it.

God promised to send a Redeemer. In the fullness of the time He sent His Son (Galatians 4:4, 5). That Son promised that He would die and rise again (Matthew 16:21), and He did it (Mark 15, 16). In parable and plain statement He said He will come again (Matthew 25). Rest assured that He will do it.

MAYBE TODAY. A minister posted those words at the front of the auditorium for all to see. He gave no explanation, even when he was questioned. Each person in the congregation was left to interpret the words for himself.

Maybe today you will take a hot meal to a family whose cook is sick. Maybe you will do a bit of housecleaning in a house not your own, or mow a lawn or rake the fallen leaves. Or maybe today you will be too busy to help anyone in need. Maybe today you will read a story to or will play with a lonely child—or maybe you will be in a hurry and leave him lonely. Maybe today you will have a word of encouragement for someone who is lost—or maybe you will not.

Maybe today Jesus will come. Will you be glad to see Him?

C. Double Demonstration

A study of Ezekiel shows that God had two ways of demonstrating that He was the Lord.

First, God showed himself in punishment. When the people of Israel were recklessly wicked, polluting their whole land with their crookedness, He promised disaster; and He added, "Ye shall know that I am the Lord that smiteth" (Ezekiel 7:9). No less than fifteen times in the book of Ezekiel we see a promise of catastrophe coupled with the declaration, "Ye shall know that I am the Lord." God does punish evil, not always quickly, but He does it thoroughly.

Still we cannot say that every disaster is God's punishment. The book of Job upsets that idea. Job was a good man, and his terrible affliction was the work of Satan, not God. When disaster strikes, we may ask ourselves if we deserve it; but if honest examination in the light of God's Word shows that we do not, then we need not blame ourselves or God for the disaster.

To Israel, God had a second way of showing that He was the Lord. He revealed himself in blessing. When Israel was dead and the people were captives, helpless and hopeless, God promised them freedom and prosperity and joy. And He added, "Ye shall know that I am the Lord" (Ezekiel 36:8-11; 37:12, 13).

Still, we cannot say that prosperity is always God's reward for the righteous. God gives sunshine and rain to the evil as well as to the good (Matthew 5:45). A crooked farmer may use these gifts capably and get rich.

Then how could Israel know, either in disaster or in blessing, that God was the Lord? In God's dealing with Israel, the convincing fact was that He announced disaster or blessing in advance. He said He was going to bring the Babylonians to destroy Israel (Jeremiah 25:8-11), and He did it (Jeremiah 39:1-9). He said He would free the captives from Babylon in seventy years (Jeremiah 29:10), and He did it (Ezra 1). He said not only, "Ye shall know that I am the Lord," but also, "Ye shall know that I the Lord have spoken it, and performed it" (Ezekiel 37:13, 14).

God says He "hath appointed a day in the which he will judge the world in righteousness by that man whom he hath ordained" (Acts 17:31). When He does it, there will be no doubters. Every knee will bow, "of things in heaven, and things in earth, and things under the earth;" and every tongue will "confess that Jesus Christ is Lord, to the glory of God the Father" (Philippians 2:9-11).

D. Prayer

O God, we do know that You are the Lord. Thank You for keeping Your promises through the centuries. Thank You for rescuing us from sin and death. Thank You for the bright promise of eternal life and joy. Gratefully we dedicate our lives to You. Help us to be faithful, we ask in Jesus' name.

E. Thought to Remember

God is the Lord.

Learning by Doing

This page contains an alternate lesson plan emphasizing learning activities. Classes desiring such student involvement will find these suggestions helpful.

Learning Goals

After this lesson a student will be able to:
1. Describe Ezekiel's vision of dry bones.
2. Explain the meaning of Ezekiel's vision.
3. Express appreciation to God for the new life he experiences (or can experience) in Christ.

Into the Lesson

Write the following sentence on small pieces of paper, one word per piece. "Hope springs eternal in the human breast." Scramble the pieces and place them in an envelope. Make an envelope for each three people in the class.

As the class members arrive, form groups of three. Ask each group to unscramble the words in the envelopes. After a group has unscrambled the statement, the members should decide whether or not they agree with the statement, and why.

Allow adequate time for most groups to unscramble the statement. Then take a few moments to let the class members discuss whether or not they agree with the statement.

Make the transition into the Bible study by stating that this lesson will deal with the issue of hope and life.

Into the Word

Read aloud the text for today. Use the material in the "Lesson Background" section to provide a setting for the lesson. Emphasize the question asked in Ezekiel 37:3.

Ask the class members to work in pairs to re-read the text and answer the following questions. (You may want to have these questions printed for them to follow.)
1. What do the dry bones represent? (See verse 11.)
2. What promise of God is recorded in verses 5 and 6?
3. What was the purpose of God's promise as stated in verse 6?
4. Describe what happened when Ezekiel prophesied as instructed.
5. What promise of God is recorded in verses 12-14?
6. Summarize the teaching of this section of Scripture in a sentence or two.

Allow the pairs six to eight minutes to answer the questions. Then work through the questions, allowing class members to respond. You may need to provide additional information from your study to aid your class's understanding of this text, but use what you can from the students' responses. Be sure to make a clear summary statement at the conclusion.

As we have seen, today's text revealed through vivid imagery that God was going to bring Israel back from the dead; He was going to give new life to His people after their time in captivity. They would return to their homeland and once again be His people. Assign the following Scriptures for the same pairs to study: Ephesians 2:1-7; 1 Corinthians 15:17-22, 55-57; Revelation 22:1-7. Ask them to decide how these verses compare with the text from Ezekiel that we have studied today. After a few minutes, spend time showing how these Scriptures indicate something about the new life promised by God through His Son Jesus.

Into Life

Use the following brief case studies to lead a full-class discussion of the meaning of hope.

1. Jane's husband died last winter after a long illness. One week ago today, her seventeen-year-old daughter was killed in an automobile accident. Jane says to you. "Make sense out of this for me." How will you respond? How would today's lesson help Jane?

2. Tom just lost his job without warning. He has been a loyal employee of the company for many years, but new owners have decided to go with younger employees who are better educated than Tom. Tom is depressed and concerned that he won't be able to find a suitable job in the future. How would today's lesson help Tom?

3. Bill and Linda recently became Christians. Their adult lives have been lived in total disregard for Christian values and concerns. Now that they have become Christians, they sometimes worry about their sinful past. How would today's lesson help Bill and Linda?

Ask, How does today's Bible lesson help you in your daily Christian quest? Let the pupils suggest ways the text ministers to them. List their suggestions on the chalkboard. After two or three minutes, summarize the list. Close the session by encouraging the students to express their thanks to God for His redeeming power and for new life in Christ.

Let's Talk It Over

*The questions on this page are designed to encourage review of the lesson
Scriptures and to promote discussion of the lesson by the class. The answers
provided are only discussion starters. Let your class talk it over from there.*

1. What does it mean, Biblically, for a person to "hope"?

In the popular usage of the term, to hope means to desire. For example, if a person says, "I hope it rains," he implies that he wants it to rain, he desires that it rain. That usually doesn't mean the person confidently expects it to rain. But the Biblical term means precisely that—confident expectation. As Christians, we have the hope of our bodily resurrection. (1 Thessalonians 4:13-17). This implies our confident expectation that God will raise us from the dead just as He did Jesus, not simply that we wish it to happen. Biblical hope is based on God's character—His reliability, the fact that He does as He promises. The Biblical record and the experience of Christians confirm that God always keeps His word!

2. How important is hope to individuals?

Hope provides a reason for living, for hanging on, in the most desperate situations. If *all* hope is gone, a person will give up on life. Human beings have a tremendous capacity for hope and will cling to even the smallest thread of hope. Even dying persons need to have hope: of life after death; of a medical breakthrough that could mean a cure for a fatal illness; of the possibility of finding meaning and/or a witness to others in the experience; of a miraculous survival—any or all of these expressions of hope will meet the need of the dying. Living or dying, people need to hope. The wonderful message of the gospel is that God has filled mankind's need for hope by sending His Son into the world. Through His atoning death and subsequent resurrection, we have the hope of eternal life. This hope is the anchor of the soul (Hebrews 6:19).

3. How significant is despair in the experience of a person?

Despair may be seen as the direct opposite of hope. The Danish philosopher Soren Kierkegaard wrote an entire book on despair, entitling it *The Sickness unto Death*. Despair, in the final analysis, is the utter loss of hope, thus the sickness unto death, with no reason to go on. Despair is the final bottomless pit into which one falls after traveling the road of disappointment, and even discouragement, but these three "D's" are causally linked.

4. In what ways may some contemporary congregations be compared to Ezekiel's vision?

Church growth research indicates that many contemporary congregations are dying or are already dead. Like Ezekiel's valley, they are full of dry bones—spiritual skeletons with little or no life in them. These congregations continue to conduct services and to maintain many hallowed traditions, but they enjoy neither vitality nor growth. How tragic, that a church God intended, and empowered, to grow and thrive should become like Ezekiel's vision! When God's people return to Him in humility and sincerity, and open their hearts to His Spirit, even a dying church will experience the infusion of new life from above.

5. What is the distinct difference in the portrayal of the Holy Spirit in the Old and New Testaments?

In the Old Testament, God's Holy Spirit is always depicted in terms of power—as with wind or breath (which energizes). In Ezekiel 37, God's Spirit empowered the inanimate carcasses to live and function. In the New Testament, the Holy Spirit is viewed essentially as a person, rather than power. Thus Jesus referred to the Spirit as "He," not "it." In John 16:7-15 the Holy Spirit is referred to exclusively as a person. In the Godhead, three *persons* are identified: the Father, the Son, and the Holy Spirit.

6. Cite some significant ways in which the new life in Jesus Christ is truly "new."

In Christ, we have a new relationship to the following: (1) God. We are no longer rebels, alienated from God, but we are reconciled to Him as His children. (2) The past. Sins are forgiven, guilt is gone. (3) The present. The divine love permeates all of life. (4) The future. It is bright with hope, the "confident expectation" of what God will do. (5) Ourselves. The alienation within our deepest self is resolved; healing and wholeness occur. (6) Others. Sin separates people from each other. Newness is seen in the sense of "family," of belonging, and of vital fellowship that now exists among God's people.

The Triumph of God's Kingdom

LESSON SCRIPTURE: Daniel 2.

PRINTED TEXT: Daniel 2:31-36, 39-44.

Daniel 2:31-36, 39-44

31 Thou, O king, sawest, and behold a great image. This great image, whose brightness was excellent, stood before thee; and the form thereof was terrible.

32 This image's head was of fine gold, his breast and his arms of silver, his belly and his thighs of brass,

33 His legs of iron, his feet part of iron and part of clay.

34 Thou sawest till that a stone was cut out without hands, which smote the image upon his feet that were of iron and clay, and brake them to pieces.

35 Then was the iron, the clay, the brass, the silver, and the gold, broken to pieces together, and became like the chaff of the summer threshingfloors; and the wind carried them away, that no place was found for them: and the stone that smote the image became a great mountain, and filled the whole earth.

36 This is the dream; and we will tell the interpretation thereof before the king.

. . . .

39 And after thee shall arise another kingdom inferior to thee, and another third kingdom of brass, which shall bear rule over all the earth.

40 And the fourth kingdom shall be strong as iron: forasmuch as iron breaketh in pieces and subdueth all things: and as iron that breaketh all these, shall it break in pieces and bruise.

41 And whereas thou sawest the feet and toes, part of potters' clay, and part of iron, the kingdom shall be divided; but there shall be in it of the strength of the iron, forasmuch as thou sawest the iron mixed with miry clay.

42 And as the toes of the feet were part of iron, and part of clay, so the kingdom shall be partly strong, and partly broken.

43 And whereas thou sawest iron mixed with miry clay, they shall mingle themselves with the seed of men: but they shall not cleave one to another, even as iron is not mixed with clay.

44 And in the days of these kings shall the God of heaven set up a kingdom, which shall never be destroyed: and the kingdom shall not be left to other people, but it shall break in pieces and consume all these kingdoms, and it shall stand for ever.

GOLDEN TEXT: The God of heaven [shall] set up a kingdom . . . and it shall stand for ever.—Daniel 2:44.

Visions of God's Rule
Unit 2. Daniel: Through Oppression to Victory (Lessons 5-7)

Lesson Aims

After this lesson students should be able to:
1. Briefly describe Nebuchadnezzar's dream and tell what it meant.
2. Identify the four great empires pictured by the image the king saw in his dream.
3. Give allegiance to the kingdom that will last forever.

Lesson Outline

INTRODUCTION
    A. Captivity in Three Phases
    B. Lesson Background
I. DREAM (Daniel 2:31-35)
    A. Great Image (vv. 31-33)
    B. Great Victory (vv. 34, 35)
       Nothing but Dust Remains
II. EXPLANATION (Daniel 2:36-44)
    A. Mighty Kingdoms (vv. 36-40)
    B. Mixed Kingdoms (vv. 41-43)
    C. Mighty Victory (v. 44)
       Consuming Zeal
CONCLUSION
    A. God Knows
    B. God Tells
    C. Prayer
    D. Thought to Remember

Display visual 5 from the visuals/learning resources packet and let it remain before the class throughout this session. It is shown on page 45.

Introduction

After four lessons from the book of Ezekiel, we turn to Daniel for the next three studies. This group of three lessons is entitled "Through Oppression to Victory." The people of God were oppressed in Babylon, but that was not the end of the story.

A. Captivity in Three Phases

Remember the three phases of the Jews' captivity by Babylon:

Phase one. About 606 B.C. Nebuchadnezzar subdued Judah and took a few captives, including Daniel. A Jewish king was left to rule in Jerusalem and pay tribute to Babylon, but after some years he rebelled.

Phase two. About 597 B.C. Nebuchadnezzar took ten thousand captives, including Ezekiel. Again he left a Jewish king to rule Judah and pay tribute, but after some years this king also rebelled.

Phase three. About 586 B.C. Nebuchadnezzar destroyed Jerusalem and took most of the remaining people to Babylon, where they stayed for fifty years.

We have had four lessons from the book of Ezekiel. The first two had their setting in phase two of the captivity. Ten thousand Jews were captives in Babylon, and Ezekiel was God's prophet among them. Lessons 3 and 4 belong to phase three of the captivity. Jerusalem was only a heap of rubble, and most of the Jews were captives in Babylon.

Turning now to the book of Daniel, we drop back to an earlier time—phase one of the captivity. Chapter 1 records that Daniel and other promising young Jews were taken to Babylon to be given the best possible education so they might be advisers to the king. By the special favor of God, the young Jews were the most brilliant of students.

B. Lesson Background

Daniel 2:1-30 gives the background of our text. King Nebuchadnezzar had a dream that troubled him greatly. Calling the most eminent scholars of Babylon, he demanded an explanation of it. "Tell thy servants the dream," the scholars said, "and we will show the interpretation." But the king demanded that they tell him both the dream and the meaning of it.

"The thing is gone from me," said the king. Some students take this to mean that he had forgotten the dream and wanted the wise men to tell what it was. Other students think the king remembered the dream, but was testing the ability of his magicians and sorcerers. If they could tell him what he had dreamed, he would believe that they could tell him what it meant. According to this view, "The thing is gone from me" meant "The order has been given by me and will not be changed. Tell me both the dream and the meaning, or off with your heads!"

The scholars protested that it was impossible for anyone to tell him what he had dreamed, but the angry king ordered all the wise men of Babylon to be killed. By this time Daniel and some other bright young Jews were counted among the wise men. The king's servants came to get them to be slain along with the rest.

Daniel was able to get the slaughter postponed while he and his friends prayed that God would reveal the dream and its meaning to them. Then Daniel went to the king. The wise men were right, he said. It was true that no man on earth could do what the king asked. But Daniel added, "There is a God in heaven that revealeth secrets." God had revealed dream and meaning to Daniel, and our text records how Daniel told them to Nebuchadnezzar.

I. Dream
(Daniel 2:31-35)

Daniel described the dream as vividly as if he had seen it himself. Indeed he had, for God had revealed it to him in a vision (v. 19). But he told the king about it in words.

A. Great Image (vv. 31-33)

31. Thou, O king, sawest, and behold a great image. This great image, whose brightness was excellent, stood before thee; and the form thereof was terrible.

The following verses show that the image was in the shape of a man and was made of various kinds of metal. Verse 31 shows that it was remarkable in three ways: First, it was *great*; it was big. We can easily imagine that it towered above the king, many times as tall as he was. Second, its *brightness was excellent.* Perhaps it was polished to reflect the sunlight in the dream, or perhaps it was brilliant with a light of its own. Third, its *form* or appearance *was terrible*, awesome, frightening. Nebuchadnezzar, a notable warrior, was not easily frightened. But he was deeply troubled (vv. 1, 3) by this huge and dazzling statue.

32, 33. This image's head was of fine gold, his breast and his arms of silver, his belly and his thighs of brass, his legs of iron, his feet part of iron and part of clay.

A fourth feature of the image was the different metals it was made of. Proceeding downward from the golden head, each metal was less valuable, but harder and stronger. Strongest of all was iron, but at its lowest extremity its strength was diluted by a mixture of clay.

B. Great Victory (vv. 34, 35)

34. Thou sawest till that a stone was cut out without hands, which smote the image upon his feet that were of iron and clay, and brake them to pieces.

The huge statue came tumbling down! *A stone was cut out without hands:* this was no act of man; it was God's doing. The stone smashed the feet of the image, *and brake them to pieces.*

35. Then was the iron, the clay, the brass, the silver, and the gold, broken to pieces together, and became like the chaff of the summer threshing floors; and the wind carried them

away, that no place was found for them: and the stone that smote the image became a great mountain, and filled the whole earth.

Not only the feet, but the whole terrible image was pulverized by the active stone. Big as the image was, it was beaten into bits so tiny that they were gone with the wind, scattered so they could never be collected. The big, brilliant, frightening image simply ceased to exist. But the stone that smashed it grew and grew till it *became a great mountain, and filled the whole earth.*

NOTHING BUT DUST REMAINS

Built on the crumbling remains of Babylonia (where Daniel prophesied), the Persian Empire was to become one of the great empires in world history. Its greatest monarch, Darius, came to the throne by murdering his predecessor. Darius reigned over an empire that covered an area two-thirds as large as the forty-eight contiguous United States.

The Persian Empire fell to Alexander the Great in 330 B.C., as he was building an even greater empire. Then came the Romans, who showed the ancient world what armed might could accomplish.

All of these empires and many others enjoyed no more than momentary success. Despite their might, nothing but dust remains of them today. This should help us to put things into perspective. The kingdoms of this earth have never found the secret to lasting power. Only God possesses that, and He will bring low all who seek such power for themselves. Those who trust God can rest safely in the knowledge that He holds all of history in His hand.   —C. R. B.

II. Explanation
(Daniel 2:36-44)

If the king was testing the scholars of Babylon by demanding that they tell him what he had dreamed, Daniel was the only one who was able to pass the test. He described the dream clearly and vividly. Nebuchadnezzar then was confident that he could tell the meaning of it also.

A. Mighty Kingdoms (vv. 36-40)

36. This is the dream; and we will tell the interpretation thereof before the king.

Daniel had already explained to the king that he himself had no wisdom to interpret the dream; but that God had given the dream to tell Nebuchadnezzar what was going to happen in the future, and so God had revealed the meaning of it to Daniel to be passed on to the king (vv. 27-30).

37, 38. Thou, O king, art a king of kings: for the God of heaven hath given thee a kingdom, power, and strength, and glory. And wheresoever the children of men dwell, the beasts of the field and the fowls of the heaven hath he given into thine hand, and hath made thee ruler over them all. Thou art this head of gold.

These verses are left out of the printed text, but we include them here because they carry the beginning of the explanation. The golden *head* of the image represented Nebuchadnezzar, the absolute ruler of a great empire. His word was law to all the *kings* and people of the empire, and even to the animals and birds. But Nebuchadnezzar had this power only because God the supreme ruler had given it to him.

39. And after thee shall arise another kingdom inferior to thee, and another third kingdom of brass, which shall bear rule over all the earth.

The kingdoms that were to come later are not named in Daniel's explanation, but now history of later times identifies them for us. Sixty-some years after this revelation was given, a coalition of Medes and Persians conquered the Babylonian Empire and added it to their own. This Medo-Persian Empire is represented by the silver chest and arms of the image in the king's dream. The two arms are a fitting suggestion of the two nations, Media and Persia, that combined to capture Babylon. This kingdom was *inferior* to Nebuchadnezzar's. It was not inferior in power, for it was strong enough to defeat Nebuchadnezzar's successors. Neither was it inferior in the size of its territory, for it included the vast area of Media. But the Medo-Persian government was inferior in the quality of the king's rule. Cyrus was the top man, but he was not such an absolute monarch as Nebuchadnezzar had been. We see a sample of the limitation of authority in Darius, a subordinate of Cyrus, who took over Nebuchadnezzar's Babylonian kingdom (Daniel 5:30, 31). Darius' power was limited in two ways. First, once a decree was made, it could not be repealed even by the one who made it (Daniel 6:15). Second, Darius was subject to pressure by his subordinates (Daniel 6:6-9). In all the Medo-Persian Empire there was no

tyrant with such complete authority as Nebuchadnezzar had in Babylon.

The golden head represented Nebuchadnezzar and his empire, and the silver arms represented the Medo-Persian Empire. The belly and thighs of brass represented *another third kingdom of brass.* This was the empire of Greece, headed by Alexander the Great. He overthrew the Medes and Persians about 300 B.C., more than two hundred years after they conquered Babylon. This brass kingdom was overwhelming in power, but inferior in the quality of rule. Alexander was head man while he lived, but he died young. The empire later was divided among four of his generals, and in time some of the divisions engaged in war between themselves. Thus the government was even more scattered than that of the Medes and Persians. In the original text the word *belly* in verse 32 is plural, the upper and lower viscera. These two bellies and the two thighs suggest the fourfold division of Alexander's kingdom.

40. And the fourth kingdom shall be strong as iron: forasmuch as iron breaketh in pieces and subdueth all things: and as iron that breaketh all these, shall it break in pieces and bruise.

The fourth kingdom, following Alexander's Greek Empire, would be notable for its power. It would be *strong as iron.* History shows that this was a good description of the Roman Empire, which smashed the remnants of Alexander's empire in the first century before Christ. As iron is stronger than gold or silver or brass, the Roman Empire was stronger than any before it. But as iron is less precious than gold or silver or brass, the Roman Empire was farther from the pure one-man rule of Nebuchadnezzar. Strictly speaking, Rome was a republic rather than a kingdom when it smashed the remnants of Alexander's empire. Not till later (27 B.C.) did Octavian proclaim himself emperor.

B. Mixed Kingdoms (vv. 41-43)

41. And whereas thou sawest the feet and toes, part of potters' clay, and part of iron, the kingdom shall be divided; but there shall be in it of the strength of the iron, forasmuch as thou sawest the iron mixed with miry clay.

The iron empire of Rome would not be smashed by an empire stronger still, but it would be weakened by division. History records the rivalry between the eastern part of the empire and the western part even while *the strength of the iron* remained—a rivalry suggested by the two iron legs of the image. But the *clay* mixed with *iron* in *feet and toes* suggested growing weakness.

42. And as the toes of the feet were part of iron, and part of clay, so the kingdom shall be partly strong, and partly broken.

The two feet of the image ended in separate *toes*, suggesting that the Roman Empire finally would be divided into fragments, into many small nations. In these would be some of the strength of iron along with some of the weakness of clay. Some students go so far as to point out ten modern nations represented by the ten toes: Britain, France, Spain, Italy, and Greece on one foot; Turkey, Syria, Iraq, Arabia, and Egypt on the other. Such precise identification is doubtful because there are other nations in the area once ruled by Rome: Rumania, Yugoslavia, Bulgaria, and Albania in Europe; Morocco, Algeria, Tunisia, and Libya in Africa; Lebanon and Jordan in Asia. Perhaps the toes should be taken to mean many nations rather than exactly ten.

43. And whereas thou sawest iron mixed with miry clay, they shall mingle themselves with the seed of men: but they shall not cleave one to another, even as iron is not mixed with clay.

In the toes of the image the iron and clay were *mixed* and yet they were *not mixed*. That is, they existed together, but still remained separate instead of blending into one homogeneous mass. Some students think the iron represents nations ruled by kings, while clay represents democracies, nations ruled by the people. However, Daniel's description seems to indicate that each toe had in it both iron and clay. In many nations the monarchy is mixed with democracy. The power of kings is limited or nearly lost; representatives of the people are the actual rulers. Also in any nation, monarchy or republic, there are iron people and clay people, hawks and doves, warmongers and peaceniks. There are those who want to increase the army and navy for national defense, and there are those who agitate for disarmament. There is tension, sometimes antagonism, between the iron people and between the clay people.

C. Mighty Victory (v. 44)

44. And in the days of these kings shall the God of heaven set up a kingdom, which shall never be destroyed: and the kingdom shall not be left to other people, but it shall break in pieces and consume all these kingdoms, and it shall stand for ever.

This is the meaning of the stone that smashed the image in Nebuchadnezzar's dream. The stone cut out without hands represents a kingdom established by God, not man. *In the days of these kings* represented by iron and clay God will *set up a kingdom, which shall never be destroyed*

visual 5

as were the kingdoms of Babylon, Medo-Persia, Greece, and Rome. Neither shall that kingdom be *left to other people*, and the kingdoms of Babylon, Medo-Persia, Greece, and Rome were taken over by other people. This points certainly to the kingdom of God, or the kingdom of heaven, as it often is called. This triumphant final kingdom is not of this world (John 18:36). It belongs to the poor in spirit (Matthew 5:3), to those who are born of water and of the Spirit (John 3:5), who become as little children (Matthew 18:3), who do the will of the Heavenly Father (Matthew 7:21). The kingdom is for those who have the fortitude to endure much tribulation (Acts 14:22), those who have too much determination to turn back (Luke 9:62).

Obviously such a kingdom is not for everyone. Entrance is hard for a rich man (Matthew 19:23, 24) and impossible for those who prefer a life of sin (1 Corinthians 6:9, 10; Galatians 5:19-21; Ephesians 5:5).

The kingdom of God is to be sought above all else (Matthew 6:33). It is worth any sacrifice that can be made (Matthew 13:44-46).

In the days of iron Rome, God sent His Son into this world to redeem men for a kingdom not of this world. God's Son will come again to separate the redeemed from the lost, to gather His people into His kingdom for eternity (Matthew 25:31-46). It seems most probable that He will come in the days of the toes of iron and clay, the days of those many nations that have come from the Roman Empire. Most certainly He will come. Maybe today.

When Jesus comes, the kingdoms of the world will be no more. They will be pulverized like the huge image of Nebuchadnezzar's dream (v. 35). God's kingdom will *consume* them. "The kingdoms of this world are become the kingdoms of our Lord, and of his Christ; and he shall reign for ever and ever" (Revelation 11:15). The kingdom eternal will preserve all that is glorious and honorable in the nations of the world, but nothing that is unworthy (Revelation 21:26, 27). For those who oppose the Almighty there is a lake of fire (Revelation 20:15).

Whose side are you on?

CONSUMING ZEAL

An editorial cartoon showed two middle-aged businessmen looking out the office window. In the street below, a throng of young people were rioting in favor of some political cause. One businessman observed, "The youth are revolting." The other agreed, "They certainly are!"

Hot-blooded zeal and steadfast commitment to a principle seen clearly in black and white are the province primarily of the young. The ability to make allowance for viewpoints that differ from one's own is a gift usually reserved for those who have weathered a few of life's storms. There is some good to be said about both approaches to life.

Daniel prophesied of kingdoms whose mixtures of strength and weakness would result in the demise of each. Individuals, governments, churches, businesses, and organizations of all types in this present world seem to be mixtures of both good and bad characteristics.

God seems willing to put up with these contradictory combinations in all of us for now. However, the time will come when His zeal will consume all that is not pure and true. Then His holy reign shall begin and continue forever.

—C. R. B.

Conclusion

In the book of Daniel there is much that puzzles us, but there is nothing that puzzles God. He not only knows all the hidden things that are happening; He also knows what will happen in centuries to come. He shows His knowledge by telling of future things. He knows what will happen, and in various ways He makes things happen.

A. God Knows

"Then the king made Daniel a great man, and gave him many great gifts, and made him ruler over the whole province of Babylon, and chief of the governors over all the wise men of Babylon" (Daniel 2:48). Why was the king so generous? Because he was confident that Daniel had truly explained the meaning of his dream. How could he be so sure of that? Daniel told him what his secret dream was, and therefore he was sure Daniel could tell the meaning of it.

We have more reason to believe what Daniel said. From our point of view, we can see that most of what he predicted has happened. Three mighty empires that had not yet come were pictured in the image of Nebuchadnezzar's dream. Now they have come and gone. We know his prophecy was true.

Daniel made it clear that he himself had no

Home Daily Bible Readings

Monday, Sept. 25—Who Can Interpret the King's Dream? (Daniel 2:1-11)
Tuesday, Sept. 26—Daniel, Daniel, He's the Man! (Daniel 2:12-24)
Wednesday, Sept. 27—God Alone Can Make it Clear (Daniel 2:25-30)
Thursday, Sept. 28—Simple Choice: Worship Idols or Die (Daniel 3:1-7)
Friday, Sept. 29.—Three Who Said, "No Way!" (Daniel 3:8-15)
Saturday, Sept. 30—The Heat's On (Daniel 3:16-25)
Sunday, Oct. 1—God's Kingdom is Forever (Daniel 3:26—4:3)

wisdom or magic that could predict the future. "But there is a God in heaven that revealeth secrets" (Daniel 2:28). He revealed to Daniel the secret dream and meaning of it. Through Daniel He revealed them to Nebuchadnezzar and to us. In the same way He revealed that His kingdom will demolish all the kingdoms of the world and stand forever. We can depend on that.

B. God Tells

God does not tell all He knows, but He tells us all we need to know about things beyond our sight. Fortunately, we are not limited to what we can find out by ourselves. We know that God created the heaven and the earth—and us. Knowing that, we can reason that it is best for us to do what He wants us to do, and God confirms that conclusion. From His Word we know that the wages of sin is death; but the gift of God is eternal life through Jesus Christ our Lord" (Romans 6:23). We know that Jesus died to redeem us, and that "he that believeth and is baptized shall be saved" (Mark 16:16). We call Jesus our Lord, but we know that saying so is not enough. We must also do God's will (Matthew 7:21). We know Jesus is coming to welcome His people into the kingdom prepared for them, and we know His people are those who faithfully serve Him (Matthew 25:31-36).

C. Prayer

Our Father and our God, we know that nothing is hidden from You, not even the most secret thoughts and intents of our hearts. Help us then to keep our thoughts and motives pure.

D. Thought to Remember

"There is a God in heaven that revealeth secrets" (Daniel 2:28).

Learning by Doing

This page contains an alternate lesson plan emphasizing learning activities. Classes desiring such student involvement will find these suggestions helpful.

Learning Goals

After this lesson, a student will be able to:

1. Describe King Nebuchadnezzar's dream and tell what it meant.

2. Identify the four great empires pictured in the king's dream.

3. Acknowledge that God is in control of the affairs of the world.

4. State allegiance to the kingdom that will last forever.

Into the Lesson

As the class members arrive, give each a copy of the puzzle below.

Decode the Message

See if you can decode this message relating to today's lesson. You will have to decide what letter each symbol represents. Your only clue is that the message is found in today's printed text.

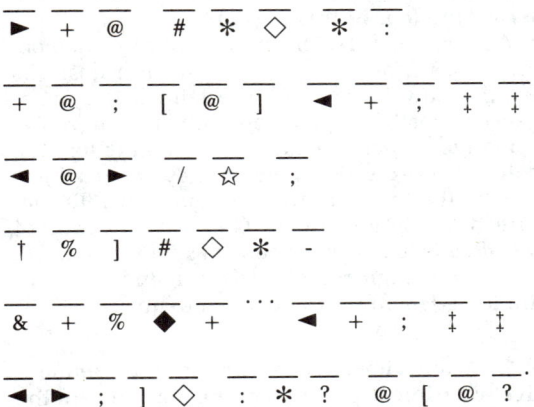

Your students obviously will have difficulty solving the puzzle. After a brief time, give each a copy of the decoding key shown immediately below and let them solve the puzzle. (The message is from Daniel 2:44).

A (;), C (◆), D (◇), E (@), F (:), G (#), H (+), I (%), K (†), L (‡), M (-), N (]), O (✳), P (☆), R (?), S (◄), T (►), U (/), V ([), W (&).

Ask the class, Would you rather solve a puzzle with or without a key? Why? Discuss briefly.

Make the transition into the Bible study section of your lesson by stating that today's text describes an ancient monarch's puzzling dream that needed to be interpreted. With God's help, the prophet Daniel was able to decode the dream's message.

Into the Word

Provide the background for the lesson by using the material in "Lesson Background." Then have someone read the text aloud. Guide the students through the text by using the following questions. Let the class members answer the questions. Add material from your study, if it is necessary to explain the text more fully.

1. Describe what Nebuchadnezzar saw in his dream (vv. 31-35).

2. What/who does the head of gold represent (vv. 36-38).

3. What/who do the breast and arms of silver represent? (You may need to explain that it represented the Medo-Persian Empire, which succeeded Nebuchadnezzar's empire.)

4. How would the kingdom represented by silver compare with the one represented by the head of gold (v. 39)? (Be sure to explain how it was inferior.)

5. What/who do the belly and thighs of brass represent? (You may need to explain that they represented the empire of Greece, headed by Alexander the Great.)

6. What/who do the legs of iron and the feet of iron and clay represent? (You may need to explain that they represented the Roman Empire.)

7. What do verses 41, 42 indicate about the fourth kingdom? (It would be weakened by division and finally would be divided into fragments.)

8. What is the kingdom mentioned in verse 44? What is its nature? (This is the kingdom of God, brought to pass by Christ's coming. It is everlasting.)

Into Life

The prophecy of Daniel contains a great deal that we don't fully understand. But it is clear that God is in control of history and the church. What does this tell us about the God whom we serve?

Continue the discussion by asking, How will this lesson help you this week? List the ideas suggested.

Let's Talk It Over

The questions on this page are designed to encourage review of the lesson Scriptures and to promote discussion of the lesson by the class. The answers provided are only discussion starters. Let your class talk it over from there.

1. What are some of the ways people attempt to find out what the future holds in store for them?

Many people resort to astrology, fortune tellers, palm readers, seances, tarot cards, and psychics in an attempt to look into the future. You name it, they'll try it. The people of Israel were specifically instructed not to engage in similar practices (see Deuteronomy 18:9-14). To attempt to consult with spirits of divination, witches, etc. was an act considered abominable by God. Now, as then, the people of God are to trust the leading of His Holy Spirit, not the spirits of the dead.

2. Why does the future hold so much fascination for so many people?

The feeling persists with some people that if they could know, or just have some idea of, their future, they could more completely control their own destiny. They feel that if they could know what the future held for them, they would be able to make both the mental and emotional preparation for it. We who are Christians do not need to know the details of the future, because we have the firm conviction that almighty God, our Heavenly Father, holds the future in His hands. The assurance that the Lord of life knows what lies ahead, knows what is best for us, and is in complete control, grants stability and serenity to all of those who trust Him. It is enough to know that He continues to be with us and will provide for us—come what may in the future.

3. What are some reasons for the current interest in prophecy?

(1) Some students of prophecy see signs of the "end times" in current history; for example, in events in the Middle East. Elaborate interpretations have been worked out involving Russia, the Common Market, Israel, Egypt, the Arabs, and the United States. (2) Times of great immorality have provoked great interest in prophecy, expressing the psychological dynamic of escapism (the desire to leave the world when you can't cope with it). Interest in prophecy today focuses almost totally on the last days, the end times, the wrap-up of human history. (3) In

church history, periodic cycles of obsessive interest in prophecy have regularly surfaced and then vanished.

To make observations 2 and 3 about prophecy may seem to some not to take Biblical prophecy seriously. In reality, these observations call for us not to take people's *interpretations* of the details of Biblical prophecy too seriously. History books are strewn with detailed interpretations that were false and illusory. It seems that many Christians would rather pour their intellectual and emotional energies into interpreting prophecy than in the task of evangelizing the lost or engaging in a caring ministry to needy people around them.

4. The Bible pictures God's relationship to people with expressions such as "the kingdom of God" and "the kingdom of heaven." What are some of the important implications of the term *kingdom* in this regard?

A kingdom differs from a republic or a democracy. In a kingdom, the king *alone* rules. His word is law. Laws are not established by consensus, nor by popular opinion, nor by representative bodies. Residents in the kingdom are called "subjects." That means they are in subjection to the king's power and authority. To picture our relationship to God, the concept of *kingdom* is just as valid today as it ever was. He is the sovereign ruler in His kingdom, and we are to be His loyal and obedient subjects.

5. When viewing the chaotic and competitive relationships among the nations of the world today, what reasons do Christians have for optimism?

Christians can confidently face the chaos and competition in evidence in the world today for the following reasons: (1) God's assurance that He is in control of human history (no nation nor group of nations is in control); (2) God's assurance that His kingdom will stand forever (remember today's Golden Text); (3) the record of history that *all* human powers wax and wane (Babylon, Medo-Persia, Greece, and Rome); (4) the record of history that God's prophecies are accurately fulfilled (notice the exact fulfillment of Nebuchadnezzar's dream).

God Acts to Deliver His People

LESSON SCRIPTURE: Daniel 7.

PRINTED TEXT: Daniel 7:13, 21-27.

Daniel 7:13, 21-27

13 I saw in the night visions, and, behold, one like the Son of man came with the clouds of heaven, and came to the Ancient of days, and they brought him near before him.

. . . .

21 I beheld, and the same horn made war with the saints, and prevailed against them;

22 Until the Ancient of days came, and judgment was given to the saints of the Most High; and the time came that the saints possessed the kingdom.

23 Thus he said, The fourth beast shall be the fourth kingdom upon earth, which shall be diverse from all kingdoms, and shall devour the whole earth, and shall tread it down, and break it in pieces.

24 And the ten horns out of this kingdom are ten kings that shall arise: and another shall rise after them; and he shall be diverse from the first, and he shall subdue three kings.

25 And he shall speak great words against the Most High, and shall wear out the saints of the Most High, and think to change times and laws: and they shall be given into his hand until a time and times and the dividing of time.

26 But the judgment shall sit, and they shall take away his dominion, to consume and to destroy it unto the end.

27 And the kingdom and dominion, and the greatness of the kingdom under the whole heaven, shall be given to the people of the saints of the Most High, whose kingdom is an everlasting kingdom, and all dominions shall serve and obey him.

GOLDEN TEXT: The Ancient of days came, and judgment was given to the saints of the Most High.—Daniel 7:22.

Lesson Aims

After this lesson a student should be able to:

1. Briefly describe Daniel's dream and tell what it meant.

2. Declare his confidence in the final victory of God's people.

3. Promise to be faithful to God.

Lesson Outline

INTRODUCTION
    A. Struggle for Power
    B. Lesson Background
I. DREAM (Daniel 7:13, 21, 22)
    A. The Son of Man (v. 13)
        The Ancient of Days
    B. Conflict (v. 21)
    C. Victory (v. 22)
        An Invincible Foe
II. EXPLANATION (Daniel 7:23-27)
    A. Conflict (vv. 23-25)
    B. Victory (vv. 26, 27)
CONCLUSION
    A. Oppression
    B. Victory
    C. When?
    D. Prayer
    E. Thought to Remember

Display visual 6 from the visuals/learning resources packet and let it remain before your class throughout this session. It is shown on page 53.

Introduction

King Nebuchadnezzar of Babylon was a capable administrator as well as a powerful warrior. As he added country after country to his empire, he brought the brightest young men of each country to be trained in Babylon and to become his advisers. Thus he surrounded himself with men who not only were the best minds of his empire, but also knew the thinking and customs and prejudices of the different countries that were included in the empire. With such advisers he could more wisely rule his wide domain.

Daniel was one of the bright young men brought from Judah. Soon he distinguished himself by explaining to the king a dream that had stumped the older wise men of Babylon, as we saw in last week's lesson. Thereupon Nebuchadnezzar made Daniel chief of the wise men and governor of a province. Probably Daniel held that favored position as long as Nebuchadnezzar lived.

A. Struggle for Power

After Nebuchadnezzar's death, there was a struggle for power. His son ruled briefly, but a brother-in-law killed him and took the throne. This man lived only a few years, and soon afterward his son was murdered by a group of conspirators. Nabonidus then emerged as emperor. His son Belshazzar, a general in the army, in time was installed as king of the province of Babylon. Even as king he was subject, of course, to his father, the emperor.

We come now to an event in the first year of Belshazzar's rule (Daniel 7:1). Probably this was sixty years after Daniel explained Nebuchadnezzar's dream, and neither Nabonidus nor Belshazzar yet recognized Daniel's greatness.

B. Lesson Background

The first part of Daniel 7 describes a dream of Daniel. Out of the sea came four great beasts, one after another: a lion, a bear, a leopard, and a terribly destructive beast that is not named. This furious beast had ten horns, but another horn appeared and displaced three of them. Then God, "the Ancient of days," sat in judgment. The fourth beast was destroyed.

"One of them that stood by" in the dream explained the meaning of it. The great beasts represented kings or kingdoms. Each was to rule in its turn, but finally they would lose their power and "the saints of the Most High shall take the kingdom, and possess the kingdom for ever, even for ever and ever" (v. 18).

This revelation seems parallel to the one given through Nebuchadnezzar's dream many years earlier. It portrayed the same great empires of Babylon, Medo-Persia, Greece, and Rome. Like the toes of the image in the king's dream, the ten horns of the fourth beast represented the many nations that would come from the Roman Empire. Each dream revealed that God would set up an everlasting kingdom for His people.

Our printed text brings us some of Daniel's dream, and then some of the explanation.

I. Dream (Daniel 7:13, 21, 22)

First we look at the climax of the dream. Verses 2-8 describe the four beasts. Verses 9-12 tell how God judged them and ended their rule. Then came the ruler whose rule will never end.

A. The Son of Man (v. 13)

13. I saw in the night visions, and, behold, one like the Son of man came with the clouds of heaven, and came to the Ancient of days, and they brought him near before him.

What Daniel saw was *in the night visions,* in a dream he had at night when he was sleeping in bed (vv. 1, 2). *One like the Son of man* came into the dream. *The Son of man* indicates a human being; but readers of the New Testament know it was the name that Jesus often used for himself, and this one like the Son of man surely is Jesus, the Son of God as well as the Son of man. In the dream He *came with the clouds of heaven,* and we know that one day all the world will see Him "coming in the clouds of heaven with power and great glory" (Matthew 24:30). In the dream He came to the Ancient of days. That was God, sitting on His throne of judgment (vv. 9-12). *Ancient* does not mean that He is weak and frail as many old men are. It means that He is older than all the earthly kingdoms He judges. He is older than days and nights on earth, more ancient than the world itself. He is eternal. As Daniel's vision showed Him on the throne, He was served by a thousand thousands of angels (v. 10). Perhaps some of them escorted the Son of man and brought him near before God on the throne. Verse 14 adds that the Son of man was given the rule over all the world and forever.

The Ancient of Days

By the time most people reach fifty-five or sixty years of age, they are as old as their grandparents were when they thought their grandparents were *very* old people! Most children have probably said more than once, "Grandma, tell me what it was like in the 'olden days.'"

It is hard for a child to imagine what it was like before there were television sets, microwave ovens, computers, air conditioning and many other modern conveniences. Thus, in order to put his own life experience into an understandable perspective, a little boy wants his grandfather to tell him about what gave life meaning and coherence a half-century ago when he was the same age as the inquisitive child.

We are the same way with God, the "Ancient of days," the one who has lived forever. Our powers of imagination are not sufficient to envision what it was like before the world began, nor can we supply a satisfactory meaning to life without divine help. Yet the human race keeps stumbling in the dark, searching for meaning while doubting that there is any, unwilling to ask our spiritual "Grandfather" for help in discerning what life is all about. However, when

---

How to Say It

BELSHAZZAR. Bel-*shazz*-er.
NABONIDUS. Nab-o-*nye*-dus.
NEBUCHADNEZZAR. *Neb*-you-kad-*nez*-er (strong accent on *nez*).

---

we do turn to God, we discover life's purpose and obtain insight into the issues that we find so perplexing.

—C. R. B.

B. Conflict (v. 21)

21. I beheld, and the same horn made war with the saints, and prevailed against them.

Verses 15-18 record that Daniel asked the meaning of the dream and was given an explanation in general terms. Then he asked specifically about the fourth beast of the dream. That beast had ten horns, which we suppose represented the many nations, not necessarily exactly ten, that came from the Roman Empire. In verse 21 *the same horn* is the eleventh horn, the one that overthrew three of the ten (vv. 8, 20). If we conclude that the ten are not necessarily exactly ten, perhaps it is as reasonable to conclude that the three are not necessarily exactly three, but that they are some of the many nations that came from the empire. But what is the eleventh horn, the one that overthrew three of the ten?

Is it some Roman emperor who defeated three rivals for the throne?

Is it the Moslem power that conquered Arabia and Syria and Egypt?

Is it the Roman Catholic Church that dominated several nations of Europe?

Is it the Protestant power that took some European nations from the Catholic Church?

Is it the Communist power that more recently took over the nations of eastern Europe?

Is it some power that has not yet appeared on the world scene, but is yet to come?

There is an old saying that history repeats itself, and it is well known that a prophecy of Scripture may have more than one fulfillment. Is it possible that the victory of one horn over three pictures several different events in history?

Whatever power this horn represents, it is one that *made war with the saints,* the people of God, *and prevailed against them* in some degree and for some time. This is true of some Roman emperors and of the Moslems. Some Protestants have charged that it is true of the Roman Catholic Church, and some Roman Catholics have charged that it is true of Protestants. Certainly Communism is opposed to Christianity.

C. Victory (v. 22)

22. Until the Ancient of days came, and judgment was given to the saints of the Most High; and the time came that the saints possessed the kingdom.

Whatever power may oppose God's people, and whatever success it may have for a time, the final *judgment* will be against it. *The Ancient of days*, the Eternal, the Lord God Almighty, will rescue His *saints* and will welcome them into His *kingdom* for eternity.

AN INVINCIBLE FOE

In December, 1957, and January and February, 1958 sharks killed five swimmers and maimed two others at beaches along the Indian Ocean coast of the South African province of Natal. Fear of these ferocious fish overpowered the tourist industry in the area. But today, tourism is a multi-million-dollar-a-year business along that coast, and swimmers and surfers confidently frolic in the waters.

Humans have regained control of the coastal waters by placing huge nets in the sea approximately five hundred yards off shore. Sharks entering the area are captured at the rate of about 1250 a year. Seldom is anyone attacked now.

Like swimmers in shark infested waters, Christians sometimes are helpless before the forces of evil in this world. It seems at times that wickedness is invincible. But then comes the Ancient of days, our God who will be victorious over all. Let us not be discouraged, because from time to time God acts to balance the evil with good, and ultimately He will destroy the power of evil totally.
—C. R. B.

II. Explanation (Daniel 7:23-27)

As we have seen, Daniel dreamed that he asked a bystander to explain what he was seeing in his dream, and the bystander explained (vv. 16-18). Daniel then asked specifically about the fourth beast of the dream and he told more specifically about what he had seen (vv. 19-22). Now we come to some further explanation by the bystander.

A. Conflict (vv. 23-25)

23. Thus he said, The fourth beast shall be the fourth kingdom upon earth, which shall be diverse from all kingdoms, and shall devour the whole earth, and shall tread it down, and break it in pieces.

Thus he said. The bystander introduced in verse 16 now gave the following explanation.

The fourth beast seems to represent the Roman Empire. It was *diverse*, different, *from all kingdoms*. It was not very different in its way of conquest. The earlier empires also ruthlessly devoured other nations and smashed whatever stood in their way. But the Roman nation was different in its form of government. It was a republic rather than a monarchy in the time of its great expansion. *The whole earth* does not mean the entire globe as we know it now. The word used in the original language can mean either *earth* or *land*. Here the translation might be *shall devour all the land*, or *shall devour the whole country*. A few centuries after the time of Daniel the Romans did gobble up all the territory bordering on the Mediterranean Sea, plus much of Europe to the north. *Tread it down, and break it in pieces* is a figurative way of describing the ruthless way the Roman troops subdued it.

24. And the ten horns out of this kingdom are ten kings that shall arise: and another shall rise after them: and he shall be diverse from the first, and he shall subdue three kings.

The ten horns of the fourth beast are identified as *ten kings that shall arise*. If there are ten kings there must be ten kingdoms, though neither kings nor kingdoms are named. Then *another shall rise after them*. This is another king with his kingdom, the one represented by the eleventh horn of the dream. *He shall be diverse from the first*. How is this eleventh king different? We are not told. One suggestion is that his interest is primarily religious rather than political. This is true of Moslems and Catholics and Protestants. Communists may claim to oppose all religion, but as a matter of fact their anti-religion is about as religious as any they denounce. Their faith is in themselves rather than God, but it is still faith. *He shall subdue three kings.* In various ways, Moslems, Catholics, Protestants, and Communists have all done this.

25. And he shall speak great words against the Most High, and shall wear out the saints of the Most High, and think to change times and laws: and they shall be given into his hand until a time and times and the dividing of time.

Now we see that this mysterious eleventh horn, the conqueror of three others, not only will fight against God's saints (v. 21) but also will speak against God himself. This gives some weight to the supposition that his interest is primarily religious rather than political. Neither Moslems nor Catholics nor Protestants will plead guilty to speaking against God, though their foes may accuse them of it. Communists quite openly speak against God, but that does not necessarily make them the only fulfillment of this prophecy. Some humanists, for example, are no less open in their denial of God; and some students suggest that humanists are even now in the process of taking over nations of western Europe and North America. And who knows what forces may oppose God in the future?

Any tyrant or nation that will take a stand against God will be likely to *change times*, abolishing the Lord's Day and other religious holidays and making any changes in the calendar that he wishes. He will feel equally free to change *laws*, both those of God and of men.

This person or nation opposed to God and His people will be allowed to have some success for *a time and times and the dividing of time*. Many students think this cryptic expression means a year plus two years plus half a year: that is, three and a half years or forty-two months. But that is such a short time in world history that we wonder if the expression has another meaning. Some students suggest that each day of the stated time represents a year of actual time. As the ancients reckoned it, a month was the actual time from new moon to new moon, which is nearly thirty days. Forty-two such months make 1260 days, so it is supposed that the anti-God power will continue for 1260 years. This is far from certain, of course. *A time* is not necessarily a year. It may be a week or a month. *Times* is not necessarily two. It may be three or four or ten. And there is nothing in our text to tell us that each day represents a year. Until we have further information, let's admit our ignorance. We do not know who the anti-God power is. We do not know when his dominion began or will begin. We do not know how long it lasted or will last.

B. Victory (vv. 26, 27)

26. But the judgment shall sit, and they shall take away his dominion, to consume and to destroy it unto the end.

Whoever or whatever is hostile to God and His people, and however long his power shall last, it is not forever. A time of *judgment* is coming. The hostile force is doomed.

27. And the kingdom and dominion, and the greatness of the kingdom under the whole heaven, shall be given to the people of the saints of the Most High, whose kingdom is an everlasting kingdom, and all dominions shall serve and obey him.

The Most High is Jehovah, the Lord God Almighty. His *kingdom is an everlasting kingdom*. Last week's lesson assured us that it "shall break in pieces and consume all these kingdoms, and it shall stand for ever" (Daniel 2:44). Now our present study soars to the same exalted height. The rule of our God is unlimited and unending. Saints are people set apart, dedicated, devoted.

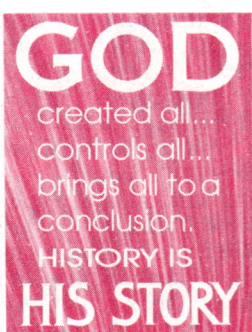

visual 6

GOD created all... controls all... brings all to a conclusion. HISTORY IS HIS STORY

The saints of the Most High are the people who are committed to the living God, the ruler of Heaven and earth. They have a share in His rule, in *the greatness of the kingdom under the whole heaven*. They are "the children of God: and if children, then heirs; heirs of God, and joint-heirs with Christ" (Romans 8:16, 17).

Conclusion

This is the second of three lessons from the book of Daniel. The group of three is entitled "Through Oppression to Victory." We can see three great thoughts developing in these lessons: (1) The people of God may be oppressed; (2) Their final victory is certain; (3) We cannot predict the time of final victory.

A. Oppression

Oppression may be good for people. Sometimes it is God's chastening. It is designed to make people better, and it actually does make them better if they allow it to. "Now no chastening for the present seemeth to be joyous, but grievous: nevertheless, afterward it yieldeth the peaceable fruit of righteousness unto the which are exercised thereby" (Hebrews 12:11).

This lesson has its setting in the time when God's chosen people were oppressed by Babylon. That was allowed because God's people had been ignoring Him and doing wrong (Jeremiah 25:1-9). In oppression, some of the people turned again to the Lord. When Persia conquered Babylon and set God's people free, those who went back to the homeland were devoted to Jehovah (Ezra 3).

Since Christ came to save His people from their sins, those who follow Him are God's people. From the beginning they were oppressed. Their leaders were jailed and beaten (Acts 5:40). Stephen was stoned to death (Acts 7:59, 60). Other believers were driven out of Jerusalem (Acts 8:1). James was killed (Acts 12:1, 2). Paul was whipped five times by Jewish authorities and three times by Gentile courts. Once he was stoned and left for dead (2 Corinthians 11:24, 25; Acts 14:19). Throughout the great Roman Empire, oppression of Christians continued until the Emperor Constantine ended it in A.D. 313.

When oppression ended, the church became corrupt. Favored by the emperor, Christianity was fashionable. Sophisticated city people became Christians, at least in name. But the sophisticated folk were more interested in following the fashion than in following Jesus, and the church became worldly.

Jesus had warned against that very thing. If the salt loses its savor, He said, "it is thenceforth good for nothing, but to be cast out, and to be trodden under foot of men" (Matthew 5:13). By the seventh century the church in Syria and Egypt had lost its savor, its distinctive Christian character. So it was trodden under foot by the conquering Moslems, who dominate those areas to this day.

In the free world, we Christians have been free from oppression for a long time. Are we all keeping our savor? Are we strongly upholding the Lord and spreading His word? If the time comes when we are not different from the rest of the world, we can expect oppression to be back.

B. Victory

The oppressor of God's people may be mighty with chariots and horsemen or with tanks and hydrogen bombs, but he is doomed. "They shall take away his dominion, to consume and to destroy it unto the end."

The saints of the Most High may be unarmed in a military sense. But they have the whole armor of God (Ephesians 6:10-18). If we put it on and use it well, our victory is certain. "The kingdom and dominion, and the greatness of the kingdom under the whole heaven, shall be given to the people of the saints of the Most High, whose kingdom is an everlasting kingdom, and all dominions shall serve and obey him."

It is sad to see atheistic Communism in charge of eastern Europe, Cuba, Ethiopia, and other countries. It is sad to know that some nations close their borders to the gospel of salvation. It is sad to see church leaders make their own rules, denying the authority of God and the Bible. It is sad that some television preachers are reckless with contributors' money, reckless in their own way of living, reckless with the truth. But there is a city eternal that is closed to anything that defiles, anything abominable, anything false; and that city is open wide to those who are registered in the Lamb's book of life (Revelation 21:27).

C. When?

When people are oppressed, it is natural for them to ask, "How long?" When we are fighting the good fight of faith and the odds against us seem overwhelming, it is natural to ask, "When will it be over?"

Such questions are easier to ask than to answer. In our text and other Scriptures, the assurance of final victory is plain, but the time of that victory is not so easily seen. Oppression by Babylon was to continue for seventy years. God made that very plain (Jeremiah 25:11). Not so plain is the prophecy of "a time and times and the dividing of time." Who can point out the beginning and end of those times?

Some of us can remember when respected teachers assured us that Jesus would come with final victory in 1914. Others set the time at 1927, and some chose 1972. We lose confidence in such self-appointed prophets, but we cling to confidence in the prophets appointed by the Almighty. Victory is sure. We know that. The time of victory is just as sure, but it is known only to God (Matthew 24:36).

We do not know when the battle will be over, but we know when we are to put on the whole armor of God and fight the good fight of faith. The time is now.

D. Prayer

Father, thank You for all You have told us in Your perfect Word. You have not told us all You know, but we rejoice in Your plain promises. In return, we promise to be faithful to You until the final victory is won.

E. Thought to Remember

We can't lose, if we trust Jesus and do our best.

Home Daily Bible Readings

Monday, Oct. 2—Daniel Defies the King (Daniel 6:1-13)

Tuesday, Oct. 3—Daniel is Thrown to the Lions (Daniel 6:14-23)

Wednesday, Oct. 4—Daniel's Vision by Night (Daniel 7:1-12)

Thursday, Oct. 5—Daniel's Dream of Four Beasts (Daniel 7:15-20)

Friday, Oct. 6—The Ram and the He-Goat (Daniel 8:1-14)

Saturday, Oct. 7—Daniel Receives the Vision's Meaning (Daniel 8:15-26)

Sunday, Oct. 8—Redeemed and Restored (Isaiah 43:14-21)

Learning by Doing

This page contains an alternate lesson plan emphasizing learning activities. Classes desiring such student involvement will find these suggestions helpful.

Learning Goals

After examining Daniel's vision, which is recorded in Daniel 7:13-27, the pupil will be able to:

1. Describe the details of Daniel's dream.
2. Explain what Daniel's dream meant.
3. Acknowledge that God's people will experience final victory.
4. Thank God for the victory of His people.

Into the Lesson

As the class members arrive, give each a card or sheet of paper with the following sentence on it: "When I think of oppression and trouble, I respond by—" Ask the students to complete the sentence in as many ways as they can in the time allotted. They may also discuss their responses with those sitting near them.

Allow five to seven minutes for the students to complete the sentences and talk with others. Then ask the class members to share some of their responses with the entire group. Probe to see if you can get several different kinds of responses.

Make the transition into the Bible study section by stating that oppression and trouble are not what we would seek. Yet, Christians who suffer for their faith have hope for ultimate victory.

Into the Word

Use the material in the "Lesson Background" section to provide a setting for this lesson and to link it to last week's lesson. Then have someone read Daniel 7:13-27 aloud.

Explain that Daniel 7:14-20 is not included in the printed text for today's lesson. Ask the students what parallels they see between Daniel 2:31-34 and 7:15-18. (Review Nebuchadnezzar's dream of the gold, silver, brass, and iron image, the stone that pulverized it, and what it meant. Mention that Belshazzar was a Babylonian king, but that the Medo-Persian Empire would soon conquer Babylon.)

Help the students work their way through the printed text by using the following questions. You will likely need to fill in details garnered from your study.

1. Who is the Son of man whom Daniel saw (v. 13)?
2. Verse 20 indicates an eleventh horn com-

ing up upon the head of the fourth beast. What did this horn do (v. 21)?

3. When did this action stop (v. 22)?
4. List the specific actions of the eleventh horn mentioned in verse 25.
5. What will happen to this great power (v. 26)?
6. What kingdom will ultimately triumph (v. 27)?
7. What are the major lessons to be learned from this text? (Be sure that these three are mentioned: (1) the people of God may be oppressed; (2) their victory is certain; (3) we do not know the time of final victory.)

Into Life

Develop a discussion to apply the Bible material to our lives. Use the questions below to help elicit discussion.

1. In what ways may oppression and trouble be good for God's people? Can you cite some Scriptures to support your answer? (James 1:2-12, 1 Peter 1:3-9, and Hebrews 12:1-11 provide insight.)
2. How can Christians who are not persecuted for their faith maintain a strong faith and witness?
3. How do you respond to this statement: "History has no meaning or direction"?
4. How does the hope of the final victory of God's people help a person remain faithful in the midst of trouble and opposition?
5. Cite some examples from your own experience when the promise of the victory of God's people helped you to endure.
6. When will the final victory occur? See Matthew 24:36-44.
7. What is the danger in setting dates for the final victory?
8. In view of the fact that we do not know the date for the final victory of God's people, how does this text help us in the meanwhile? What actions should characterize our lives while we wait for the final victory to occur?

To conclude the lesson, divide the class into groups of three or four. Have each student take a minute to tell his group how today's text has helped him. Then let each group have a time of prayer, during which each person expresses his thanks to God for the victory that is promised to those who follow Him.

Let's Talk It Over

The questions on this page are designed to encourage review of the lesson Scriptures and to promote discussion of the lesson by the class. The answers provided are only discussion starters. Let your class talk it over from there.

1. What are some ways of viewing human history in terms of purpose and meaning?

There are three dominant ways of viewing human history in this regard. Briefly, they are as follows: (1) History has no meaning or purpose. There is no pattern—just random events in a meaningless montage. (2) History follows a circular pattern. As the old adage maintains, "History repeats itself." There is a pattern, but with little or no meaning. (3) History is linear (this is the Biblical concept). History had a beginning, and it will have an ending. God started it, and He will end it. Throughout, He is in control. His purpose in creating the world ultimately will be fulfilled. It's helpful in remembering this third perspective to see history as His-story.

2. What are some possible results of oppression?

Oppression can produce both negative and positive results. Negative responses include the following: discouragement (Is there any hope?); impatience (How long will this last?); unfaithfulness (Why should I hang in there—for more suffering?); violence (Why should I take this lying down?).

Positive responses include these: perseverance (I will learn faithfulness and patience as God sustains me.); refining (Trouble and tribulation can be the refiner's fire that will remove my impurities and prove my faith to be genuine.); understanding (Through the eyes of faith, God will help me to find meaning and purpose even in the events and circumstances that are deemed evil); growth (Most lasting growth occurs with suffering and pain—I will grow in and through this oppression!).

3. Cite some of the privileges that the almighty God will grant to "the saints of the Most High."

In sum, the saints of God will enjoy the security and victory of His everlasting kingdom. In it they will serve and obey Him. They will also reign with Him, sharing in His dominion, They will be joint-heirs with the unique Son, Jesus Christ. What an impressive list of potential privileges for an oppressed people, once held cap-

tive to sin! 1 Peter 2:10 sums it up this way: "Once you were not a people, but now you are the people of God; once you had not received mercy, but now you have received mercy" (*New International Version.*) Talk about a "rags to riches" story, this is it!

4. What options do Christians have in the face of oppressive evil?

Four live options commend themselves to us. They are as follows: (1) Pray. Permeate each day with fervent prayer. Pray for those who are in places of authority. Pray for the perpetrators of the oppressive evil. Pray for wisdom, courage, and patience for yourself in confronting evil. (2) Be an agent of change in the environment. Be light in the darkness. Be salt that has not become tasteless. Your presence and the witness of your life can make an impact for righteousness. Live such a life in faith, trusting God to use it. (3) Work through the system to effect change. Instead of fighting the system, use it. Daniel worked from the inside to bring about God's will. (4) Lead others to Jesus Christ. Social structures are not converted, people are. And people are not converted en masse, but one by one. As people came to know Jesus and submit themselves to His transforming power, there is an increased possibility for change to occur in the systems in which they work.

5. List some of the significant examples of God's deliverance of His people.

When the world was to be destroyed by flood because of mankind's pervasive wickedness, God delivered His faithful people (Noah and his family) in the ark. When His people Israel cried out from oppressive bondage in Egypt, God delivered them with a mighty and miraculous hand. True to His promise, God delivered His people after they had experienced seventy years of captivity at the hands of the Babylonians. He restored them to their own land. Most importantly, God delivers His people from the tyranny and oppression of Satan and sin. The Lord is the "Great Deliverer." His consistent character and activity demonstrate that He is the liberator of those who are enslaved and oppressed.

Final Victory for God's People

LESSON SCRIPTURE: Daniel 12.

PRINTED TEXT: Daniel 12:1-3, 5-13.

Daniel 12:1-3, 5-13

1 And at that time shall Michael stand up, the great prince which standeth for the children of thy people: and there shall be a time of trouble, such as never was since there was a nation even to that same time: and at that time thy people shall be delivered, every one that shall be found written in the book.

2 And many of them that sleep in the dust of the earth shall awake, some to everlasting life, and some to shame and everlasting contempt.

3 And they that be wise shall shine as the brightness of the firmament; and they that turn many to righteousness, as the stars for ever and ever.

. . . .

5 Then I Daniel looked, and, behold, there stood other two, the one on this side of the bank of the river, and the other on that side of the bank of the river.

6 And one said to the man clothed in linen, which was upon the waters of the river, How long shall it be to the end of these wonders?

7 And I heard the man clothed in linen, which was upon the waters of the river, when he held up his right hand and his left hand unto heaven, and sware by him that liveth for ever, that it shall be for a time, times, and a half; and when he shall have accomplished to scatter the power of the holy people, all these things shall be finished.

8 And I heard, but I understood not: then said I, O my Lord, what shall be the end of these things?

9 And he said, Go thy way, Daniel: for the words are closed up and sealed till the time of the end.

10 Many shall be purified, and made white, and tried; but the wicked shall do wickedly: and none of the wicked shall understand; but the wise shall understand.

11 And from the time that the daily sacrifice shall be taken away, and the abomination that maketh desolate set up, there shall be a thousand two hundred and ninety days.

12 Blessed is he that waiteth, and cometh to the thousand three hundred and five and thirty days.

13 But go thou thy way till the end be: for thou shalt rest, and stand in thy lot at the end of the days.

Oct 15

GOLDEN TEXT: At that time thy people shall be delivered, every one that shall be found written in the book.—Daniel 12:1.

Visions of God's Rule
Unit 2. Daniel: Through Oppression
to Victory (Lessons 5-7)

Lesson Aims

After this lesson a student should be able to:
1. Repeat in his own words the promise of resurrection to life or to shame and contempt.
2. Thank God for revealing His limitless knowledge and power to Daniel and to us.
3. Pledge himself to seek God's kingdom without understanding all the details of it.

Lesson Outline

INTRODUCTION
  A. The Man Daniel
  B. Three Lessons From Daniel
  C. Lesson Background
  I. DISASTER AND TRIUMPH (Daniel 12:1-3)
  A. Trouble and Deliverance (v. 1)
  B. Resurrection (vv. 2, 3)
      The Reward of the Wise
 II. VEILED REVELATION (Daniel 12:5-11)
  A. Question and Answer (vv. 5-7)
  B. Sealed Words (vv. 8-11)
      Knowing the Future
III. FINALE (Daniel 12:12, 13)
  A. Blessing (v. 12)
  B. Assurance (v. 13)
CONCLUSION
  A. To Stand in Your Lot
  B. Prayer
  C. Thought to Remember

Display visual 7 from the visuals/learning resources packet and let it remain before the class. The visual is shown on page 61.

Introduction

Daniel was one of the towering figures of Israel's history, though he spent most of his life outside Israel. Let's review some highlights of his life.

A. The Man Daniel

Daniel was a youth when he was taken from Judah to Babylon (chapter 1). Not much later, when he was still a young man, he explained the king's dream of a big bright image. As a reward, he was made governor of a province and chief of all the wise men of Babylon (chapter 2). Probably he continued to hold a high place in

government as long as King Nebuchadnezzar lived.

There is no indication that Nebuchadnezzar's successors mistreated Daniel, but neither did they hold him in such high regard. When Belshazzar had a mystery to be explained, it was the queen, probably his mother, who remembered that Daniel could solve mysteries. This time the message was one of disaster. Babylon was about to fall to the Medes and Persians, Daniel said; and very promptly his prediction proved to be true (chapter 5).

Perhaps the Medes and Persians learned that Daniel had predicted their victory. They gave him a high place in their government, though he was now an old man. Probably he kept such a place as long as he lived. His position was greatly strengthened when he survived a night in a lions' den (chapter 6).

B. Three Lessons From Daniel

Two weeks ago we read how Daniel interpreted Nebuchadnezzar's dream. That was only a few years after young Daniel came to Babylon. Nebuchadnezzar dreamed of a huge and brilliant image that represented his own empire and predicted three great empires that would follow it.

For last week's lesson, we leaped over about sixty years and came to a dream of Daniel in the first year of Belshazzar (7:1). After all those years, it confirmed Nebuchadnezzar's dream, portraying the same powerful empires. The Babylonian Empire was near its end. The Medes and Persians soon would defeat and absorb it.

Now we come to the third lesson from the book of Daniel. The time was the third year of Cyrus, king of Persia (10:1), probably meaning the third year after he expanded his empire to include Babylon. Daniel now was an official high in the Persian government. But he was more than that. He was a prophet of God, and God gave him yet another revelation of great events to come.

C. Lesson Background

In the third year of Cyrus, Daniel was beside the River Hiddekel, the one we now call the Tigris. There in a vision he saw a luminous man dressed in linen (Daniel 10:1-6). This man told Daniel of future events, and the revelation was parallel to that of the king's dream of a great image and of Daniel's dream of four beasts. The empire of Babylon now had been replaced by that of the Medes and Persians. The man said there would be three more Persian kings, and then a fourth who would be richer than all of them. That fourth king would launch an attack on Greece (Daniel 11:2). The man told of a great king of Greece (Alexander the Great), who would defeat the Medes and Persians and "rule with great dominion" (11:3). But at the peak of his power this great Greek king would die, and his empire would be divided among four of his generals (11:4).

Daniel 11:5-39 then describes future struggles between the king of Syria in the North and the king of Egypt in the South. These were two of the four divisions of Alexander's empire. The Jews who had returned to their own land would be caught in the middle, dominated sometimes by Egypt and sometimes by Syria.

Daniel 11:40-45 looks as if it may be describing the continuation of this struggle between Syria and Egypt in the second century before Christ. But the phrase "at the time of the end" suggests that we now are looking far beyond that struggle. Can these verses be a description of the coming of Roman troops in the first century B.C.? Do they speak of the coming of the British in World War I? Do they foretell some invasion that is still in the future? Can they speak of the gathering of armies for the great battle of Armageddon? (Revelation 16:12-16). That would bring us to "the time of the end."

I. Disaster and Triumph (Daniel 12:1-3)

Daniel 11:40-45 indicates that a power from the North was to conquer many nations and establish himself "in the glorious holy mountain," Mount Zion, Jerusalem. "Yet he shall come to his end, and none shall help him." Our text goes on with the prophecy of things to come.

A. Trouble and Deliverance (v. 1)

1. And at that time shall Michael stand up, the great prince which standeth for the children of thy people: and there shall be a time of trouble, such as never was since there was a nation even to that same time: and at that time thy people shall be delivered, every one that shall be found written in the book.

With Daniel 11:40-45 in the background, *that time* must be "the time of the end" (11:40), the time when a furious conqueror will take his place in Jerusalem, but will "come to his end" (11:45). Then *shall Michael stand up* to take part in the conflict. Probably this is "Michael the archangel," who is mentioned in Jude 9. He has been named twice as a helper of the shining man who was instructing Daniel (Daniel 10:13, 21). He is *the great prince*, the outstanding leader. The term *archangel* indicates a leader of angels, and Revelation 12:7 pictures Michael leading

his angels in battle. This mighty one *standeth for the children of thy people:* in time of need, he rises to help Daniel's people, God's people. This prophecy points to a time when his help will be needed as never before, for *there shall be a time of trouble* more terrible than ever before. *At that time* Michael will be on hand, perhaps with uncounted legions of angels, and *thy people shall be delivered*. Daniel's people were the people of Israel, but the promise is not necessarily limited to literal Israel. In our time, we who have faith in Christ are "children of Abraham" and "the Israel of God" (Galatians 3:7; 6:16). Those who will be delivered are further described as *every one that shall be found written in the book*. That could be the book of Israel's census; but since we are thinking of "the time of the end," our thoughts leap to Revelation 21:27, which records that final deliverance and glory are reserved for those "which are written in the Lamb's book of life."

B. Resurrection (vv. 2, 3)

2. And many of them that sleep in the dust of the earth shall awake, some to everlasting life, and some to shame and everlasting contempt.

Now it becomes more certain that this prophecy points to that hour when Christ will call, and "all that are in the graves shall hear his voice, and shall come forth; they that have done good, unto the resurrection of life; and they that have done evil, unto the resurrection of damnation" (John 5:28, 29). This is the time of resurrection and judgment, the judgment set forth plainly in Matthew 25:31-46.

3. And they that be wise shall shine as the brightness of the firmament; and they that turn many to righteousness, as the stars for ever and ever.

How *wise* it is to "fear God, and keep his commandments"! (Proverbs 9:10; Ecclesiastes 12:13, 14). Looking at the great earth and greater sky, the wise can know the almighty Creator and stand in awe of "his eternal power and Godhead" (Romans 1:20). Searching the Scriptures, the wise can see the holiness of God, the justice of God, the mercy of God. Against the background of God's glory, the wise can see the darkness of their own faults and sins. They can come to Jesus for forgiveness. Cleansed and purified, they can be forever bright as the sunlit sky, gleaming as the stars of the night.

THE REWARD OF THE WISE

Albert Schweitzer was one of the most famous men of this century. He was an excellent musician, a respected philosopher, and a physician. At the time of his death in 1965, there were few people who were better known for either their abilities or their humility.

In 1913, Schweitzer was thirty-eight years of age, a time in life when most men are just beginning to realize some of the rewards of their long years of professional preparation. But it was then that Schweitzer renounced wealth and prestige and headed to Africa as a missionary. He set up a hospital in an abandoned chicken coop.

When asked on one occasion if he was happy in spite of his sacrifice, he said, "I have found a place of service, and that is enough happiness for anyone."

The "parallelism" that is so typical of Hebrew expression tells us in this verse that the wise are those who lead others to do right. Our present reward is the satisfaction that comes from knowing we are doing what is right and are teaching others to do it also.

Daniel says another reward awaits us, as well: we shall shine as the stars in the heavens. This is far better than even the well-deserved earthly acclaim of one like Albert Schweitzer!—C. R. B.

II. Veiled Revelation (Daniel 12:5-11)

Verse 4 is not included in our printed text, but it carries a thought that becomes plain to us as we study the book of Daniel. The glowing man in linen said, "But thou, O Daniel, shut up the words, and seal the book, even to the time of the end." In the literal sense, the book of Daniel has been an open book through the centuries. But some of its message is sealed so we cannot discover it "even to the time of the end." We shall understand its prophecies more perfectly when they are fulfilled. A tremendous revelation is given to Daniel and to us, but a veil is draped over it. Through the veil we see the outline of truth, but some of the details are hidden for now.

A. Question and Answer (vv. 5-7)

5. **Then I Daniel looked, and, behold, there stood other two, the one on this side of the bank of the river, and the other on that side of the bank of the river.**

Daniel was beside the River Hiddekel, the Tigris, when he saw this vision (10:4). Now he saw two persons standing, one on each side of the river.

6. **And one said to the man clothed in linen, which was upon the waters of the river, How long shall it be to the end of these wonders?**

We have been reading what Daniel was told by a shining man clothed in linen (10:5, 6). That

man *was upon the waters of the river.* Perhaps this is better translated *above the waters.* The man in the vision probably was suspended in the air above the water and between the two men on the two sides of the river. One of them asked him, *How long shall it be to the end of these wonders?* We are not told who the two were, but they may be a symbol of you and me. Isn't their question the one asked by every student of prophecy? When will all these things happen? How long will it be to the end of them? We would like to have the dates stated plainly.

7. **And I heard the man clothed in linen, which was upon the waters of the river, when he held up his right hand and his left hand unto heaven, and sware by him that liveth for ever, that it shall be for a time, times, and a half; and when he shall have accomplished to scatter the power of the holy people, all these things shall be finished.**

Now the veil falls over the revelation. The words are plain, but the message is not. Perhaps the time of the end was fixed so surely that the man above the river could declare it with an oath, but still we cannot mark it on the calendar. *It shall be for a time, times, and a half.* Recall the comments on a similar expression in last week's lesson, Daniel 7:25. How long is *a time?* Does *times* mean two times, or more than two? Are these times to be counted from the time the prophecy was given, or from the time when the king of the North will come like a whirlwind (11:40)? When the king of the North *shall have accomplished to scatter the power of the holy people, all these things shall be finished.* In ancient times, the people of Israel were *the holy people,* God's chosen. The Babylonians scattered their power in 586 B.C., years before this prophecy was given. The Romans would scatter it again in A.D. 70, centuries after this prophecy was given. But now in the twentieth century there is again a nation of Israel in its ancient homeland. Is some force from the North going to scatter its power at a time we cannot anticipate? Are we to understand that *all these things shall be finished* immediately when the power of the holy people is scattered, or will the finishing events begin at that time, and possibly continue for *a time, times, and a half*? And we must remember that we Christians are now *the holy people*. Is our power to be scattered before the end of these things? The veil is thick over the revelation of time. It reminds us of the words of Jesus about the time of the end in Matthew 24:36.

B. Sealed Words (vv. 8-11)

8. And I heard, but I understood not: then said I, O my Lord, what shall be the end of these things?

Here is some consolation for us who do not understand what we are reading. Daniel didn't understand it either. Passing over the question of time, he asked about the outcome of all these events. The word *Lord* does not necessarily mean that the shining man was God himself. Often *lord* was used as we use *sir*—a term of respect to someone we honor.

9. And he said, Go thy way, Daniel: for the words are closed up and sealed till the time of the end.

Go thy way. The word to Daniel might be put like this: "Never mind about that, Daniel. Just go on about your business." It was useless to ask for further information. These words were *closed up and sealed*, hiding their meaning *till the time of the end*. When that time comes, the prophecies that puzzle us will be made clear.

KNOWING THE FUTURE

Wanting to know the future is a universal human trait. On one occasion, Jesus' disciples asked Him, "Is this the time when Israel will regain her national sovereignty?" Jesus rebuffed their misplaced curiosity (Acts 1:6, 7).

Psychics, and various fortune-tellers have long preyed upon this desire of people. Those whose curiosity is not strong enough to lead them in such bizarre pursuits may still be enticed by the predictions found in tabloids that line the supermarket checkout stands.

Many Christians today are fascinated with prophecy and fall prey to preachers who preach only "prophetic" messages. Perhaps there is no harm in wondering about what God will do in the future, but far more important is knowing what He wants us to do in the present, and doing it. Rather than speculating about "end-time" events, we should hear God's words to Daniel: "The words are closed up and sealed till the time of the end."

—C. R. B.

10. Many shall be purified, and made white, and tried; but the wicked shall do wickedly:

and none of the wicked shall understand; but the wise shall understand.

Before the end comes, *many shall be purified, and made white*, by coming to Jesus and having their sins forgiven. *Tried* by temptations, they will resist. *But the wicked shall do wickedly*, rejecting the call of Jesus. *None of the wicked shall understand.* How can they? "The fear of the Lord is the beginning of wisdom" (Proverbs 9:10). Those who defy God and cling to selfish and sinful ways can make no sense of God's revelation. *But the wise shall understand.* Some devout Christians are dismayed by this. Failing to understand Daniel's prophecy, they conclude that they are not wise. So they go looking for some wise man to explain all the mysteries of Daniel for them. But Daniel himself did not understand all that he wrote (v. 8). Some of his words are "closed up and sealed" (v. 9). Even the wise will not understand all that is written "till the time of the end" (v. 9). We know more than Daniel did about the Greek and Roman Empires that came after his time. But we need not reproach ourselves because we do not know more than he did about the things that are to come after our time. If we know and treasure his writings, we shall understand them better in God's own time.

11. And from the time that the daily sacrifice shall be taken away, and the abomination that maketh desolate set up, there shall be a thousand two hundred and ninety days.

Again the words are plain, but the message is veiled. When was *the daily sacrifice . . . taken away*? When was *the abomination that maketh desolate set up*? Antiochus Epiphanes, a Syrian monarch who ruled Palestine, tried to wipe out the Jewish religion. He defiled the temple, destroyed the Scriptures, and forbade the worship of Jehovah. He ended *the daily sacrifice* at the temple, and *the abomination that maketh desolate* is commonly and reasonably taken to mean his work. But that was in the second century before Christ. In Jesus' own teaching, He indicated that this abomination was yet to come

visual 7

(Matthew 24:15-18). It came with the onslaught of Roman troops in A.D. 70. They destroyed the temple, and *the daily sacrifice* was *taken away* again. If the Jews now in charge of Jerusalem ever restore *the daily sacrifice*, may it not be *taken away* yet another time? If we are looking at a prophecy that has been fulfilled twice and may be fulfilled again, from which fulfillment shall we count *a thousand two hundred and ninety days?* If "a time, times, and a half" (v. 7) means three and a half years, we are now seeing another way of saying the same thing. A lunar month was counted as thirty days. Twelve such months do not make a full year, so sometimes a thirteenth month was added to a year. Three and a half years have 1290 days if one of the years has thirteen months. But are these the same 1290 days that we read about in verse 7?

III. Finale
(Daniel 12:12, 13)

Is the last part of Daniel 12:4 being fulfilled in our time? Certainly many are going to and fro, and knowledge is being increased. We need not doubt that there are some wise among us (12:3). But over some parts of Daniel's prophecy the veil is heavy, and we may well be skeptical when someone claims to know more than Daniel did about events that are still in the future. We shall have to wait and see.

A. Blessing (v. 12)

12. Blessed is he that waiteth, and cometh to the thousand three hundred and five and thirty days.

Now what days are these that number 1335? They are 45 days, a month and a half, more than the 1290 days mentioned in verse 11. But again the veil descends. Perhaps no one now can tell us when those days begin and end, but we can wait and see. *Blessed is he that waiteth*, he who keeps his faith and unfailing trust, his goodness intact, till he comes to the end of these days.

B. Assurance (v. 13)

13. But go thou thy way till the end be: for thou shalt rest, and stand in thy lot at the end of the days.

Go thou thy way. This is good advice for us as well as for Daniel. Go on about your business: do the will of your Father who is in Heaven; seek first His kingdom and His righteousness; stand fast; acquit yourselves like men; go into all the world and preach the gospel to every creature. Don't worry about what is hidden behind the veil. Fight the good fight of faith and finish your course on earth. Then *thou shalt rest*,

for it is appointed to man once to die. But that is not the end. You will be raised from the dead to *stand in thy lot at the end of the days.* One's *lot* is that which is allotted to him, that which he receives. Faithful Daniel could expect a glorious lot when he came to the end of the days.

Conclusion

Not for Daniel only is there a lot at the end of the days. For everyone who obeys the Lord as king and trusts Him as Savior there is a lot, an inheritance, a place in the Father's house. If you have been born of water and of the Spirit (John 3:5) you have been born "to an inheritance incorruptible, and undefiled, and that fadeth not away" (1 Peter 1:3-5).

A. To Stand in Your Lot

"Make every effort to add to your faith goodness; and to goodness, knowledge; and to knowledge, self-control; and to self-control, perseverance; and to perseverance, godliness; and to godliness, brotherly kindness; and to brotherly kindness, love. . . . For if you do these things, you will never fall, and you will receive a rich welcome into the eternal kingdom of our Lord and Savior Jesus Christ" (2 Peter 1:5-11, *New International Version*).

B. Prayer

Almighty God, thank You for revealing to us Your unlimited wisdom and power and for showing us the way of salvation. By Your grace may we walk in that way all of our lives.

C. Thought to Remember

"Seek ye first the kingdom of God" (Matthew 6:33).

Learning by Doing

This page contains an alternate lesson plan emphasizing learning activities. Classes desiring such student involvement will find these suggestions helpful.

Learning Goals

After examining Daniel 12:1-13, a student will be able to:

1. Identify the outcome of the faithful and the wicked at the end of time.

2. Acknowledge that one doesn't need to know all of the details of the end time in order to serve Christ.

3. Thank God for providing us assurance of final victory.

Into the Lesson

Prepare copies of the Word Find below. As your students arrive, give each one a copy.

Word Find

Eighteen words from Daniel 12:1-13 are hidden below. See how many you can find. The words are *awake, blessed, book, contempt, delivered, end, everlasting, holy, knowledge, life, linen, Michael, purified, shame, sleep, trouble, wicked, wise.*

```
E V E R L A S T I N G X
K N W E O N E N I L M T
N S L E E P M O M A I E
O S A A W A K E U S C N
W H A N W S S F N S H D
L A M O M I A I O L A E
E M A M A M S L E E E I
D E R E V I L E D T L F
G X S N B L E S S E D I
E L B U O R T M T S U R
C U A C O N T E M P T U
H O L Y K W I C K E D P
```

Allow the students several minutes to work on this. Let those who have found words come to the front of the class and circle those words on a master puzzle you have prepared.

Make the transition into the Bible study section by stating that this is our third lesson taken from the book of Daniel, each with the theme of the victory of God's people.

Into the Word

Develop a brief lecture using the material from the "Introduction" section. Outline Daniel's life, review the two previous lessons, and present the background for this lesson. Then have someone read Daniel 12:1-13 aloud.

Divide the class members into pairs. Ask them to find the answers to the following questions based on today's text.

1. What promise is given to God's people in verse 1?

2. What is the promise in verse 2? Read John 5:28, 29; 1 Thessalonians 4:16, 17; and Revelation 20:11-15 for information from the New Testament about this promise.

3. What is the promise given in verse 3?

4. According to this text, what are some of the events that will occur before God's final victory?

5. What is the promise to those who wait?

6. On the basis of this text, how important is it that God's people understand all of the details of the end times?

Allot five minutes for the students to find the answers to the questions. Then work through the questions one by one, allowing each of the students to provide as much information as they can. Be prepared to add details from your study to add clarification when needed.

Into Life

Continue exploring the text by using the following questions to develop discussion.

1. What is the value of this prophecy of Daniel for God's people today?

2. How can a follower of God be sure that he can be a recipient of the promises mentioned in Daniel 12? (Be sure that the class members touch upon the importance of obedience in matters of salvation and daily living.)

3. How does 1 Peter 1:3-5 provide further assurance to the Christian that these promises will be fulfilled?

4. Second Peter 1:5-11 lists the kind of effort that a Christian should make in order to receive a rich welcome into the eternal kingdom. List these. Define each. Illustrate each.

Give each person a small sheet of paper with the following sentence on it: "As I consider the three lessons of Daniel, I am _____

_____ and I commit myself to demonstrate my thankfulness in these ways: _____

_____."

After the students have had time to complete the sentence, ask several to share what they are thankful for. Ask others to share what they will do to demonstrate their thankfulness.

Let's Talk It Over

The questions on this page are designed to encourage review of the lesson Scriptures and to promote discussion of the lesson by the class. The answers provided are only discussion starters. Let your class talk it over from there.

1. What does the eye of faith see in a time of great trouble?

The eye of faith sees the reality of the existence of trouble, but essentially sees what lies beyond. God stands above and beyond the present trouble. Deliverance lies beyond—no trouble experienced by God's people lasts forever. The eye of faith affirms that the sun will shine after the storm. This is not naive optimism. It is confidence in God's promise that He will deliver His people. Second Corinthians 4:17, 18 reminds us, "For momentary, light affliction is producing for us an eternal weight of glory far beyond all comparison, while we look not at the things which are seen, but at the things which are not seen; for the things which are seen are temporal, but the things which are not seen are eternal" (*New American Standard Bible*).

2. How important is endurance to human endeavors? To the Christian life?

In the final analysis, endurance is all that counts. Starting a task without finishing it is of little import. All of us have friends or acquaintances who are eager starters, but they seldom, if ever, "endure to the end." The Christian life may be compared to a marathon. It is not a brief dash for a finish line. It is a grueling, up-and-down-hill, taxing, long-distance race that requires tremendous endurance. Completing the race means running the entire twenty-six-plus miles. Revelation 2:10 records the words of Jesus, who commands faithfulness to the finish line, and promises a reward to those who complete the race: "Be thou faithful unto death, and I will give thee a crown of life."

3. What is the difference between modesty and humility?

Modesty assesses moderately one's gifts and accomplishments. Humility carries with it the idea of submission to another. Humility causes a Christian to acknowledge the *source* of his gifts and accomplishments, to give the credit and glory to God. One can be modest without being humble. Modesty is a virtue; humility is a greater virtue. Daniel provides an excellent example of humility. In all of his accomplishments

(many and significant!) he attributed everything to the power of God. He did more than moderately assess his gifts and accomplishments; he gave God all the glory for them. Note in today's lesson: *God* gives the victory. Although His people will share with Him in the final victory, the victory is *His!*

4. What quality about the victory God gives His people is most crucial?

It is that that victory is *final.* Along the way, God's people will experience defeats. God's assurance through His prophet is about culmination and completion: in the end, He will give them the victory! Notice the last verse of the book of Daniel: "But as for you, go your way to the end; then you will enter into rest and rise again for your allotted portion at the end of the age" (Daniel 12:13 *New American Standard Bible*).

Contemporary Christianity can learn from Daniel. In some quarters, "triumphalism" is rampant—that characteristic of trumpeting nothing but all of the daily triumphs and victories in Jesus. Testimonies are given in abundance, implying to those who have been defeated that "super Christians" experience nothing but victory along the way. How out of touch with reality! Examine the record of the great prophets of the Old Testament (Jeremiah, for example) and you will notice they suffered resistance, rejection, and at times failure. But the ultimate success of their cause was certain. It is the same today. Christians also will experience suffering, rejection, and failure, mixed with victories. But the ultimate reality is—God brings *final* victory!

5. What appropriate response may Christians make to the declaration that the present generation is "the terminal generation"?

Daniel was perplexed about when the end would come, and the fulfillment of all the prophecies in his vision. God, in effect, said to him, "Daniel, that's not for you to know. Go your way, be faithful, continue to wait and work. When the time comes, you'll enter into your reward." An appropriate response for Christians today is to affirm God's advice to Daniel.

The Need for Watchfulness

LESSON SCRIPTURE: 1 Thessalonians 4, 5.

PRINTED TEXT: 1 Thessalonians 4:13—5:11.

1 Thessalonians 4:13-18

13 But I would not have you to be ignorant, brethren, concerning them which are asleep, that ye sorrow not, even as others which have no hope.

14 For if we believe that Jesus died and rose again, even so them also which sleep in Jesus will God bring with him.

15 For this we say unto you by the word of the Lord, that we which are alive and remain unto the coming of the Lord shall not prevent them which are asleep.

16 For the Lord himself shall descend from heaven with a shout, with the voice of the archangel, and with the trump of God: and the dead in Christ shall rise first:

17 Then we which are alive and remain shall be caught up together with them in the clouds, to meet the Lord in the air: and so shall we ever be with the Lord.

18 Wherefore comfort one another with these words.

1 Thessalonians 5:1-11

1 But of the times and the seasons, brethren, ye have no need that I write unto you.

2 For yourselves know perfectly that the day of the Lord so cometh as a thief in the night.

3 For when they shall say, Peace and safety; then sudden destruction cometh upon them, as travail upon a woman with child; and they shall not escape.

4 But ye, brethren, are not in darkness, that that day should overtake you as a thief.

5 Ye are all the children of light, and the children of the day: we are not of the night, nor of darkness.

6 Therefore let us not sleep, as do others; but let us watch and be sober.

7 For they that sleep sleep in the night; and they that be drunken are drunken in the night.

8 But let us, who are of the day, be sober, putting on the breastplate of faith and love; and for a helmet, the hope of salvation.

9 For God hath not appointed us to wrath, but to obtain salvation by our Lord Jesus Christ,

10 Who died for us, that, whether we wake or sleep, we should live together with him.

11 Wherefore comfort yourselves together, and edify one another, even as also ye do.

GOLDEN TEXT: Let us not sleep, as do others; but let us watch and be sober.
—1 Thessalonians 5:6.

Visions of God's Rule
Unit 3. 1 and 2 Thessalonians:
The Coming of the Lord (Lessons 8, 9)

Lesson Aims

After studying this lesson a student should be able to:

1. Tell in his own words what our text tells about the second coming of Jesus.

2. Tell what the text says to do while we wait for Jesus to return.

3. Mention one thing he will do this week to apply this lesson.

Lesson Outline

INTRODUCTION
- A. Paul the Prophet
- B. Paul and the Thessalonians
- C. Lesson Background
- I. THE COMING OF JESUS (1 Thessalonians 4:13-18)
  - A. Hope (v. 13)
    - *Those Who Have No Hope*
  - B. Resurrection (vv. 14-16)
  - C. Transformation (v. 17)
  - D. Comfort (v. 18)
- II. THE TIME OF HIS COMING (1 Thessalonians 5:1-3)
  - A. Surprise (vv. 1, 2)
  - B. No Escape (v. 3)
- III. THE TIME OF OUR WAITING (1 Thessalonians 5:4-11)
  - A. Children of Light (vv. 4, 5)
  - B. Be alert (vv. 6-8)
    - *Prepare for His Coming*
  - C. The Outcome (vv. 9-11)
CONCLUSION
- A. Jesus Is Coming
- B. What Are We Doing?
- C. Prayer
- D. Thought to Remember

Display the map (visual 8) from the visuals/ learning resources packet, and refer to it as you present the material in sections B and C of the Introduction below. It is shown on page 69.

Introduction

We now have passed the midpoint of our three-month study entitled "Visions of God's Rule." In past lessons we have seen how God revealed His message in mystical visions re-corded by two of His prophets, Ezekiel and Daniel. Now we come to a later prophet, Paul.

A. Paul the Prophet

Usually we call Paul an apostle, and he was. But he was also a prophet, as was each of the other apostles of Jesus. A prophet is a spokesman for God, one who teaches God's will authoritatively and infallibly. Paul saw the Lord in a blinding vision that changed his life (Acts 9:1-19). Thereafter he was directed by the word of the Lord, and faithfully gave it to others. Sometimes an angel brought him a message (Acts 27:23, 24). Sometimes the Holy Spirit guided him (Acts 16:7, 8), or directions came in a vision (Acts 16:9, 10). Sometimes the Lord himself stood by him and spoke (Acts 23:11). In such ways Paul received God's messages so plainly that he could write God's own commandments (1 Corinthians 14:37). This lesson focuses on a message about Christians who have died and about our Lord's triumphant return to earth.

B. Paul and the Thessalonians

Thessalonica was an important city in Macedonia, the northern part of Greece. Paul came there on his second missionary journey. He preached the gospel so powerfully that both Jews and Gentiles turned to the Lord. This aroused the envy of Jews who were not convinced, and they organized a riotous protest. To quiet the disturbance, Paul moved on to Berea (Acts 17:1-10). This flight followed the instructions Jesus had given to earlier preachers (Matthew 10:23), and perhaps to Paul himself.

The envious enemies in Thessalonica followed Paul to Berea and stirred up a riot there too. Again Paul moved on; but his companions, Silas and Timothy, stayed for a while to guide the new Christians in Berea. When Paul reached Athens, he sent word for those two to join him.

Paul was busy teaching in Athens (Acts 17:16-34), but he was concerned about the Christians back in Thessalonica. They were in the midst of the enemies who had driven him out, and he had not had time to give them much training in the Christian way. When Silas and Timothy came, Paul sent Timothy to help the Thessalonians. Perhaps he sent Silas to Philippi where he had taught before going to Thessalonica. In any case, Paul was left alone in Athens (1 Thessalonians 3:1-5).

After some time Paul moved on to Corinth (Acts 18:1). He was there when Timothy came with good news from Thessalonica. Paul was delighted to hear that the Christians there were still faithful in spite of opposition (1 Thessalonians 3:6-8).

C. Lesson Background

While in Corinth, Paul wrote his first letter to the Thessalonians to express his appreciation of their loyalty, and to give them further teaching. Our text brings us a bit of that teaching.

I. The Coming of Jesus (1 Thessalonians 4:13-18)

We all know Jesus is coming again. But nineteen hundred years have passed since He left, and some of us have fallen into the habit of thinking that more centuries surely will pass before He returns. That is dangerous. Jesus said no one on earth knows when He will return, but clearly He taught that we had better be expecting Him at any time (Matthew 24:36—25:13).

The Thessalonian Christians really were looking for Jesus to come back any minute. Opposed and slandered and ridiculed and persecuted, they found courage in the assurance that all of that soon would be over. Jesus would come in triumph, and their faith would be vindicated.

A. Hope (v. 13)

13. But I would not have you to be ignorant, brethren, concerning them which are asleep, that ye sorrow not, even as others which have no hope.

Living in persecution and sustained by the hope of Jesus' coming, the Thessalonians had a double reason for grief when a loved one died. First, they missed the familiar presence. Second, the loss was more tragic because the loved one would not be there to see Jesus come with victory and vindication. In Thessalonica, Paul had not taught much about what happens to the dead. Now he was going to give some teaching to lighten sorrow and increase hope. It is fitting for Christians to think of the dead as *asleep*. Jesus so spoke of some whom He was about to restore to life (Matthew 9:24; John 11:11-13). Paul wrote in the same way of dead Christians, for they too will be restored to life.

THOSE WHO HAVE NO HOPE

Many people have written about their prison-camp experiences during time of war.

Victor Frankl, who was later to become well-known as a psychiatrist, used his imprisonment by the Nazis as a learning experience and has since written thoughtfully about the human condition. He tells of prisoners who would hoard the few items they received in their occasional Red Cross packets. They would hold onto their chocolate bars, for example, thinking that tomorrow or the next day they would be hun-

grier than today. Or perhaps, at some point in the future, they could barter the chocolate for something they needed more.

They would do this as long as they had hope. But when hope was gone, they would eat the candy or give it away, since in their hearts they believed there was no "tomorrow" for them. Soon after this, they invariably would die.

Hope is a powerful force in our lives. It changes the way we respond to others and to life's crises. When a loved one dies, our Christian hope injects a different quality into our grieving process. Our grief is appropriate, but it is tempered by the knowledge that even death, our final enemy, has been conquered by Jesus Christ, our Lord.   —C. R. B.

B. Resurrection (vv. 14-16)

14. For if we believe that Jesus died and rose again, even so them also which sleep in Jesus will God bring with him.

Jesus did rise from the dead. That fact is so well-established that it cannot be doubted. See Paul's review of the evidence in 1 Corinthians 15:3-8, or read it in the closing chapters of the four Gospels and the opening of Acts. Resurrection not only is possible; it is an accomplished fact. Our belief in that fact gives us the assurance that God will raise all of Jesus' people, too.

15. For this we say unto you by the word of the Lord, that we which are alive and remain unto the coming of the Lord shall not prevent them which are asleep.

Prevent is here used with its original meaning, *come before*. If we are still living on earth when Jesus comes again, we will not in any way get ahead of the Christians who have died. They will not miss any of the glory and joy of His coming. This is not a theory or Paul's opinion. Paul the prophet wrote *the word of the Lord*.

16. For the Lord himself shall descend from heaven with a shout, with the voice of the archangel, and with the trump of God: and the dead in Christ shall rise first.

Jesus will not come secretly. He will come with a call that will literally wake the dead. Elsewhere it is written that He will come in the clouds with power and great glory, and "every eye shall see him" (Mark 13:26; Revelation 1:7). Dead eyes then will be dead no longer. *The dead in Christ shall rise first* and will see His glorious coming as well as any who have not died.

C. Transformation (v. 17)

17. Then we which are alive and remain shall be caught up together with them in the clouds, to meet the Lord in the air: and so shall we ever be with the Lord.

When Jesus appears in glory, the dead Christians will be alive again (v. 16). Together with the Christians still living, they will be lifted up from the earth *to meet the Lord in the air.* In another letter, Paul adds that those who have not died will be changed, "in a moment, in the twinkling of an eye." He does not describe what the changed bodies will look like, but says they will be immortal and incorruptible (1 Corinthians 15:51-54). Then all of Christ's people will *ever*, eternally, *be with the Lord.*

D. Comfort (v. 18)

18. Wherefore comfort one another with these words.

Some of the Thessalonians had lost loved ones, and their grief was greater because those dear ones had not lived to see Jesus come with victory and vindication for His people. *These words* from Paul could end that greater grief. Those who had died were not missing anything except the trouble and persecution of the present time. They would not miss the triumph of Christ's coming, for at His arrival they would be as alive as they had ever been.

II. The Time of His Coming (1 Thessalonians 5:1-3)

When will Jesus come? On that point our text confirms what past lessons have taught from the prophecies of Daniel, and what Jesus himself taught (Matthew 24:36). No one on earth knows the time of His coming. Even the angels of Heaven do not know.

A. Surprise (vv. 1, 2)

1. But of the times and the seasons, brethren, ye have no need that I write unto you.

On this particular point Paul had taught the Thessalonians thoroughly while he was with them. There was no need to write about it now, but in the next two verses he gives a short review of what he had taught.

2. For yourselves know perfectly that the day of the Lord so cometh as a thief in the night.

We do not know when *a thief in the night* will come, and we do not know when *the Lord* will come. That is what this verse says. Jesus will not come with a dishonest purpose as a thief does.

B. No Escape (v. 3)

3. For when they shall say, Peace and safety; then sudden destruction cometh upon them, as travail upon a woman with child; and they shall not escape.

Jesus will come when people of the world are going about their worldly business (Matthew

---

How to Say It

BEREA. Beh-*ree*-uh.
MACEDONIA. Mass-eh-*doe*-nee-uh.
PHILIPPI. Fih-*lip*-pie or *Fil*-ih-pie.
SILAS. *Sigh*-luss.
THESSALONICA. *Thess*-uh-lo-*nye*-kuh
(strong accent on *nye*; *th* as in *thin*).

24:37-41). Those who have accepted His redemption and devoted their lives to Him will be lifted up to be with Him forever (1 Thessalonians 4:17), but some have defied His will and scorned His redemption. To them His coming will mean *sudden destruction* in everlasting fire (Matthew 25:41). They are compared to *a woman with child.* She knows her labor is coming. If she is wise, she gets ready for it, though she does not know exactly when it is coming. So everybody ought to know Jesus is coming, and everybody ought to get ready to meet Him, though nobody knows when He will come. Those foolish ones who are not prepared for His coming shall meet *sudden destruction*, and *they shall not escape.* It will be too late.

III. The Time of Our Waiting (1 Thessalonians 5:4-11)

The Thessalonian Christians had turned away from idols "to serve the living and true God; and to wait for his Son from heaven" (1 Thessalonians 1:9, 10), and so have we. The Bible tells little about when He will come, but it tells much about what we are to do while we are waiting.

A. Children of Light (vv. 4, 5)

4. But ye, brethren, are not in darkness, that that day should overtake you as a thief.

Many people close their eyes to the light of truth and live in darkness. Unless their eyes are opened, the day of the Lord will come to them *as a thief*, unexpected and not prepared for. But we Christians have our eyes open. We see the clear promise of Jesus' coming, and we prepare for it. If He comes today, we are ready.

5. Ye are all the children of light, and the children of the day: we are not of the night, nor of darkness.

We are *the children of light.* By the light of God's truth we have been born again, born of water and of the Spirit, so that we are citizens of God's kingdom (John 3:3-6) and members of God's family (John 1:12). Therefore, we have great privileges, and we have also great responsibilities, as the following verses indicate.

B. Be Alert (vv. 6-8)

6. Therefore let us not sleep, as do others; but let us watch and be sober.

Watch. The Greek word means to be awake, alert, vigilant. As children of light we have work to do. Let's not go to sleep on the job. Let's *be sober.* Our usefulness in God's kingdom is lost if we get drunk on alcohol or if we are intoxicated by worldly pleasure or profit or power. Both sleep and drunkenness handicap *others* who are not enlightened by the truth of God.

7. For they that sleep sleep in the night; and they that be drunken are drunken in the night.

Night is the usual time for sleeping and for drunken reveling. This pictures the state of those who live in the dark night of ignorance about God and His Word. They are sound asleep to their opportunities to serve God. They are intoxicated with worldly pleasure or profit.

8. But let us, who are of the day, be sober, putting on the breastplate of faith and love; and for a helmet, the hope of salvation.

We Christians are daytime people, busy about the Lord's work. We do not go to sleep on the job. We avoid intoxication of all kinds. The devil assails us with his fiery darts of temptation, but we have protective armor. We are kept safe by our *faith* in Christ, who is with us in all our earthly trials. We have *love* for God that leads us to do His will, and *love* for our fellowmen that leads us to help them in any way we can. We have *the hope of salvation*, the hope of that great day when our Lord will save us from all the troubles of earth, even from death itself, and will give us "an inheritance incorruptible, and undefiled, and that fadeth not away" (1 Peter 1:4). Such a hope protects us against every temptation of worldly gain, and pleasure.

PREPARE FOR HIS COMING

A couple of years ago someone broke into a home in a California town. He took nothing from the home, but he made the bed, washed the dishes, took out the trash, folded the laundry, stacked the newspapers, and hung up new drapes at the window!

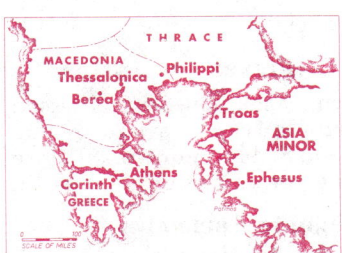

visual 8

The intruder left a note saying, "Dear Sir, I hope you don't mind. I cleaned your house. Don't worry. I won't take anything because my father is a Duke in Spain. Don't worry. I'll clean your house as long as you live here. (Signed) Prince Eddie." The intruder turned out to be a twelve-year-old mentally-retarded neighbor boy. He had noticed that the flowers outside were not being watered and thought perhaps some help was needed on the inside also.

If the homeowner had known a neighbor was coming, he would not have had such a messy house. When the Lord returns, He also will come when we least expect Him. But then it will be too late to do anything about the disorder in our lives. Christ came the first time to help us put our lives in order. When He comes again, it will be to see if we have used His help to do it.

—C. R. B.

C. The Outcome (vv. 9-11)

9. For God hath not appointed us to wrath, but to obtain salvation by our Lord Jesus Christ.

God's wrath must fall on the drunken (v. 7)— on the riotous and defiant sinners. More than that, God's wrath must fall on those who are asleep (v. 7)—on the apathetic, the indifferent, those who ignore God's call and do not care about truth or right. But we Christians are called of God; we are His chosen people. God *hath not appointed us* to be among the sleepers and drunkards who must feel His wrath. He has chosen us *to obtain salvation by our Lord Jesus Christ.* This is the outcome to which God has called and appointed us. We want to live up to His appointment, to do what He has chosen us to do. That is why we must be wide awake, alert, on guard, and protected by the armor of faith, love, and hope (vv. 6, 8). We must be so vigilant that Satan can neither entice us into sin nor lull us into lethargy.

10. Who died for us, that, whether we wake or sleep, we should live together with him.

We should live together with him! This is another way of describing the outcome to which God has called us. In this verse those who *sleep* are those who die (4:13) to be raised when Jesus comes again (4:15, 16). Those who *wake* are those who live on earth till Jesus comes (4:15). All of us who are faithful, *whether we wake or sleep,* will be caught up to be with the Lord (4:17). This outcome means a lot to Jesus—so much that He *died for us* in order to bring us to *live together with him.* How tragic it will be if we go to sleep on the job and fall short of that outcome! Christ's death then would be in vain, and it would be our fault. But we are not in darkness (v. 4). We are the "children of light, and the

Home Daily Bible Readings

Monday, Oct. 16—Signs of the End (Matthew 24:1-14)

Tuesday, Oct. 17—Beware of False Christs (Matthew 24:15-28)

Wednesday, Oct. 18—Coming of the Son of Man (Matthew 24:29-35)

Thursday, Oct. 19—Watch and Be Ready (Matthew 24:36-51)

Friday, Oct. 20—Parable of Wise and Foolish Maidens (Matthew 25:1-13)

Saturday, Oct. 21—Parable of the Talents (Matthew 25:14-30)

Sunday, Oct. 22—Parable of the Judgment (Matthew 25:31-46)

children of the day" (v. 5). We are alert to resist all the wiles of Satan and we will follow the Lord to eternal glory.

11. Wherefore comfort yourselves together, and edify one another, even as also ye do.

Comfort is a word of power. Students of Latin recognize its origin instantly. *Com* means *with; fortis* means *strong.* By being with each other we make each other strong. The devil is both alluring and threatening. We must be strong to resist him steadfastly. We find strength in being together with those who share our faith. In modern usage, *comfort* most often means to console someone who is grieving, but the word really has a larger meaning. Some recent translations of the Bible recognize this larger meaning by reading *encourage one another* instead of *comfort yourselves.*

Edify means *build up.* We build one another in knowledge by teaching God's Word and discussing how to apply it in our lives. For this reason we regularly attend Sunday school. We build one another in courage and strength by supporting and helping and praising. Do any of the brethren get discouraged because we fail to appreciate their efforts? Do hard workers ever want to quit because no one will help them? We build up our leaders by our high esteem and faithful following (vv. 12, 13). Our leaders are strong and capable and energetic, but we must not forget that they need our help as much as we need theirs. If any brethren are inclined to fall, we build them up by warning them (v. 14a). Perhaps this is where we shirk our duty most often. No one likes to "warn them that are unruly." If any are weak in their thinking or acting, we build them up by our help and support (v. 14b). We build up one another by being patient rather than exasperated (v. 14c), no matter how

exasperating some of our brethren may be. We build up one another by setting a good example of right living (vv. 15-22). How we need builders instead of wreckers.

Even as also ye do. The Thessalonian Christians were already doing what Paul told them to do, and so are we, But it is good to be reminded to keep it up. The devil is strong and tricky and always near. If we drop the armor of faith and love and hope (v. 8), we may get drunk before we know it—drunk with alcohol, drunk with greed, drunk with anger—and so we may blunder into saying and doing things we will be ashamed of when we are sober again. And if we are not tempted to get drunk, the devil may croon a lullaby and lure us into sleep. It's easy and comfortable just to do nothing for our Lord and our brethren. Let's be wide awake, alert to every opportunity to do good (Galatians 6:10).

Conclusion

Two parts are easily seen in this lesson: (A) Jesus is coming; (B) What are we doing? The two are very different, but they are very closely related.

A. Jesus Is Coming

Jesus is coming. Paul proclaimed that "by the word of the Lord." We can count on it. In the meantime, it makes little difference whether we live or die, for at His coming all His people will be alive. Thereafter, they will live with Him forever. Our dying cannot keep us from meeting Him in the air and enjoying everlasting life in His presence, but our living can.

B. What Are We Doing?

The pull of the world is strong. If we forget that Jesus is coming to take us to a better world, we may drift into worldly ways—selfish ways, or even malicious ways. Or we may drift into neutral ways, not doing anything very bad, but not doing anything very good either. How can we keep from drifting?

1. Keep our eyes open. Be alert. Watch.
2. Polish our armor—faith and love and hope.
3. Help one another.

C. Prayer

Father in Heaven, thank You for this lesson that sounds an alarm to keep us awake and active in Your kingdom. So bless our work that we shall be neither idle nor unfruitful.

D. Thought to Remember

Jesus is coming.

Learning by Doing

This page contains an alternate lesson plan emphasizing learning activities. Classes desiring such student involvement will find these suggestions helpful.

Learning Goals

After studying 1 Thessalonians 4:13—5:11, a student will be able to:

1. List the major events that the text indicates will occur at the time of the Lord's return.

2. Identify what the text says that believers should do while they wait for Jesus to come.

3. Decide how he will build others up as we prepare for Jesus' coming.

Into the Lesson

Write the following sentence on the chalkboard or on a sheet of newsprint.

"If Jesus returned today, I—"

As the class members arrive, give them paper and pencil and ask them to complete the sentence. Then have them share their responses with two or three other class members.

After you have allowed about five minutes for this, call the group together. Let several volunteers share their responses with the entire group.

Make the transition into the Bible study section by stating that today's lesson provides guidelines for our behavior while we await Jesus' return.

Into the Word

Present the material in the Introduction section to provide a background for this study. Then have someone (with whom you have arranged previously) read the Scripture passage.

Divide the class into groups of four or five. Assign each group one of the tasks below. (If you have more than three groups, assign the same task to more than one group. However the groups should work independently.)

Group 1. Read 1 Thessalonians 4:13-18. Do the following:

1. Paul mentions certain events that will occur when Jesus returns. List them in the order given in these verses. (The Lord will descend from Heaven with a shout and the sound of a trumpet; the dead in Christ shall rise first; those believers who are still alive on earth will be caught up to meet Christ in the air; all shall live with Him forever.)

2. Why did Paul give this information to the Thessalonian Christians? (To lessen their sorrow over the death of loved ones, and to strengthen their hope of eternal life with Christ.)

3. What are believers to do while they await Jesus' return? (They are to comfort one another.)

4. Why is this information important for Christians today? (It comforts and strengthens us as it did the first-century Christians.)

Group 2. Read 1 Thessalonians 5:1-3. Answer the following:

1. When will the Lord return? (No one knows.)

2. On the basis of these verses, how may the return of the Lord be described? (It will come as a surprise; it will be a time of destruction for those who do not believe.)

3. Why is this information important for Christians today? (It provides assurance of Jesus' return; it encourages us to be persistent in our life of faith.)

Group 3. Read 1 Thessalonians 5:4-11. Then answer the following questions:

1. What should believers do as they await Christ's return? (Watch; be sober; put on the breastplate of faith and love; keep the hope of salvation; comfort one another; edify one another.)

2. What is God's desire for us? (That we should live forever with Him.)

3. Why is this information important for Christians today? (It gives us directions for positive action as we await Christ's return.)

Allow five minutes to complete the tasks. Then lead a general discussion based on the questions assigned to each group.

Into Life

Continue the discussion using the following questions to guide it.

1. Why does "the word of the Lord" given to Paul here contain only sketchy details regarding Jesus' return? How would we respond if we were told exactly when Jesus would return?

2. What is the major focus of this text? (Point out that it is for us to be alert to our opportunities for service, and to help one another as we wait for Christ to come.)

3. What steps can we take to be alert? To help one another? How do all of these things help us to be prepared for Jesus' return?

Call attention to the sentence the students completed at the beginning of class. Then have them complete this sentence: If I knew Jesus would come today, I would—

Let's Talk It Over

The questions on this page are designed to encourage review of the lesson Scriptures and to promote discussion of the lesson by the class. The answers provided are only discussion starters. Let your class talk it over from there.

1. Although there is much that we do not know about the return of the Lord Jesus, Scripture does give some indications of the manner of it. What are some of them?

Here are the descriptions the Bible gives concerning the second coming of the Lord: (1) He will come swiftly. His appearance will be sudden, as labor comes to a pregnant woman (1 Thessalonians 5:3). Jesus declared, "I am coming quickly" (Revelation 22:12 *New American Standard Bible*). (2) He will come unexpectedly, like a thief in the night (1 Thessalonians 5:2), or like the master of a house who, having taken a long journey, may return in the evening, at midnight, at dawn, or in the morning (Mark 13:34, 35). (3) He will return openly. Every eye will see Him (Revelation 1:7), both the resurrected dead and those still living. (4) He will return gloriously. He will come in the clouds with great power and glory (Mark 13:26). (5) He will come triumphantly. All things shall be in subjection to Him (1 Corinthians 15:24-28). (6) His coming will be conclusive. The filthy will be sealed in their filthiness, and the righteous in their righteousness; there will be *no* changes in human condition or destiny (Revelation 22:11, 12).

2. List some ways we can minister to a person who grieves due to the death of a loved one.

We can minister in the spirit of Christ in the following ways: (1) Be there. Your sensitive presence with the bereaved counts most. People worry about saying the right words at such a time, but the non-verbal expressions of sympathy usually means more than the verbal. The presence, the arm around the shoulders, the quiet listening, mean so much! (2) Provide services. One who grieves often needs tangible help—transportation, child care, food carried in, provision of housing for out-of-town guests, etc. (3) Write notes. The handwritten, personal note conveys the message, "I'm thinking of you, I care about you, I'm praying for you. You are not forgotten in your loss." (4) Follow up. With the "thinning of the crowd," when relatives and friends have all returned to their own daily patterns of living, maintain *contact* and *concern*. As the attention given at the time of death and the funeral subsides, a grieving person often feels deserted.

3. What is the source of greatest comfort in bereavement?

To us who are Christians, there is no question about it—it is our hope (confident expectation) of the resurrection and life after death. As Paul reminds us, "If we have only hoped in Christ in this life, we are of all men most to be pitied" (1 Corinthians 15:19 *New American Standard Bible*). In the soaring passage featured in today's lesson, 1 Thessalonians 4:13-18, Paul points to the ultimate purpose of resurrection and life after death—"so shall we ever be with the Lord. Wherefore comfort one another with these words" (v. 18). Intimations of immortality and belief in life beyond the grave lie deeply imbedded in the collective unconscious of the human race. (Note, for example, the burial practices of the ancient Egyptians and the American Indians.) But only in Jesus Christ is the hope for life after death certified. Our resurrection is sure, because God the Father raised Jesus from the dead and promised that all who are His shall also be raised to life. Oh, great hope!

4. Cite some ways in which we can edify one another.

Basically, we edify each other by sharing resources. These resources are of various kinds. (1) Intellectual. We share truths and insights, formally and informally. We teach and admonish one another. (2) Relational. We share ourselves by being true and loyal friends, ministering to each other appropriately. The fellowship of the body of Christ functions in this way. (3) Emotional. We give support and encouragement. Encouragement may well be the most vital expression of edification. *Everyone* needs encouragement, especially in time of weakness or crisis. The ministry of encouragement builds up brethren, and everyone can be an encourager! (4) Spiritual. All of the preceding are spiritual in nature, but here we refer to such matters as praying for others in private and worshiping with them in public. Intercessory prayer and corporate worship feed us. (5) Material. We edify others by providing for their tangible needs, either through service, money, or other gifts. People are built up when they realize that others care and will share—tangibly, personally, lovingly.

Challenged to Stand Firm

LESSON SCRIPTURE: 2 Thessalonians 2, 3.

PRINTED TEXT: 2 Thessalonians 2:1-15.

2 Thessalonians 2:1-15

1 Now we beseech you, brethren, by the coming of our Lord Jesus Christ, and by our gathering together unto him,

2 That ye be not soon shaken in mind, or be troubled, neither by spirit, nor by word, nor by letter as from us, as that the day of Christ is at hand.

3 Let no man deceive you by any means: for that day shall not come, except there come a falling away first, and that man of sin be revealed, the son of perdition;

4 Who opposeth and exalteth himself above all that is called God, or that is worshipped; so that he as God sitteth in the temple of God, showing himself that he is God.

5 Remember ye not, that, when I was yet with you, I told you these things?

6 And now ye know what withholdeth that he might be revealed in his time.

7 For the mystery of iniquity doth already work: only he who now letteth will let, until he be taken out of the way.

8 And then shall that Wicked be revealed, whom the Lord shall consume with the spirit of his mouth, and shall destroy with the brightness of his coming:

9 Even him, whose coming is after the working of Satan with all power and signs and lying wonders,

10 And with all deceivableness of unrighteousness in them that perish; because they received not the love of the truth, that they might be saved.

11 And for this cause God shall send them strong delusion, that they should believe a lie:

12 That they all might be damned who believed not the truth, but had pleasure in unrighteousness.

13 But we are bound to give thanks always to God for you, brethren beloved of the Lord, because God hath from the beginning chosen you to salvation through sanctification of the Spirit and belief of the truth:

14 Whereunto he called you by our gospel, to the obtaining of the glory of our Lord Jesus Christ.

15 Therefore, brethren, stand fast, and hold the traditions which ye have been taught, whether by word, or our epistle.

Oct 29

GOLDEN TEXT: Stand fast, and hold the traditions which ye have been taught. —2 Thessalonians 2:15.

Visions of God's Rule
Unit 3. 1 and 2 Thessalonians:
The Coming of the Lord (Lessons 8, 9)

Lesson Aims

After this lesson a student should be able to:

1. Tell in his own words what the lesson text teaches about the falling away and the man of sin.

2. Tell what we ought to do in the face of speculation about things not made clear in the Bible (2 Thessalonians 2:15).

3. Tell what difference the expectation of Christ's return makes in his own life.

Lesson Outline

INTRODUCTION
 A. Two Letters
 B. Lesson Background
I. COMING EVENTS (2 Thessalonians 2:1-4)
 A. Jesus' Coming (vv. 1, 2)
    The Day Has Not Come
 B. Other Events (vv. 3, 4)
II. THE WICKED ONE (2 Thessalonians 2:5-12)
 A. Restraint of the Wicked One (vv. 5-7)
 B. End of the Wicked One (vv. 8, 9)
 C. Victims of the Wicked One (vv. 10-12)
    A Desire to Be Deceived
III. THE SAVED (2 Thessalonians 2:13-15)
 A. Chosen (v. 13)
 B. Called (v.14)
 C. Standing Firm (v. 15)
CONCLUSION
 A. Ready Now!
 B. Stand Firm
 C. Prayer
 D. Thought to Remember

Display visual 9 from the visuals/learning resources packet at the beginning of the session and refer to it at appropriate times during your lesson presentation. The visual is shown on page 76.

Introduction

Paul, Silas, and Timothy ran into trouble again and again. At Philippi, Paul and Silas were beaten and locked up and officially invited to get out of town (Acts 16:11-40). *(Refer to the map used in last week's lesson.)* At Thessalonica, an unofficial riot made it advisable for them to leave. Some of the rioters followed them to Berea, so Paul moved on again (Acts 17:1-14).

A. Two Letters

Paul was anxious about the new Christians he had left in Thessalonica. He had not been there long enough to give them all the teaching they needed. Were they remaining faithful? When He could, Paul sent Timothy to help and encourage them (1 Thessalonians 3:1-3). Timothy came back with good news. The new Christians in Thessalonica were faithful in spite of opposition (1 Thessalonians 3:6-8). Paul wrote his first letter to the Thessalonians to express his appreciation and to give them further teaching and encouragement. Our lesson last week was from a portion of that letter—a promise that Jesus would come and gather His people, living and dead, to live with Him forever.

Did the bearer of that letter stay in Thessalonica for a while and then come back with more news? Did Timothy make another visit there? Did some other traveler bring news to Paul? We do not know, but it seems evident that he heard about the Thessalonians in some way, and then wrote them a second letter. This week we have a part of that second letter for our study.

B. Lesson Background

Paul was thankful for the continuing faithfulness of the Thessalonians. He assured them that they would be rewarded and their enemies would be punished at Jesus' return (2 Thessalonians 1). He then went on with some other teaching about Jesus' coming and some other future events.

I. Coming Events (2 Thessalonians 2:1-4)

We know Jesus will come, but we do not know when. Therefore, two mistakes are often made. First, many people suppose that Jesus' coming is so far in the future that we need not be concerned about it. People making that mistake will be taken by surprise when He comes (1 Thessalonians 5:3). Second, some people suppose Jesus' coming is so near that we need not be concerned about anything else. People making that mistake sometimes have left jobs or businesses, confident that Jesus will come before they run out of money; but they have been disappointed. It seems that some of the Thessalonians were making that second mistake, and Paul wrote to correct it.

A. Jesus' Coming (vv. 1, 2)

1. Now we beseech you, brethren, by the coming of our Lord Jesus Christ, and by our gathering together unto him.

Instead of that little word *by*, other versions have *concerning* or *with regard to*. Both in his former letter and in this one, Paul has taught that Jesus will come and gather us to himself. Now he has a request to make in connection with that coming event

2. That ye be not soon shaken in mind, or be troubled, neither by spirit, nor by word, nor by letter as from us, as that the day of Christ is at hand.

Paul begged the Thessalonians not to be "all shook up" by the idea that Jesus was coming that very week, or month, or year. Paul mentioned three ways in which such an idea might be spread: (1) *By spirit*. In those days there were prophets who really did speak by the Holy Spirit (Acts 11:27, 28). But there were also false prophets moved by their own spirits, not by God's Spirit. Christians must not believe everything they heard (1 John 4:1). Paul said they should not be upset by any spirit that claimed Jesus would surely come very soon. (2) *By word*. Anyone excited by the prospect of Jesus' coming would be likely to spread the excitement by word of mouth. Perhaps the Thessalonians, or some of them, misinterpreted the teaching Paul himself had given when he was in Thessalonica. Perhaps they said his word indicated that Jesus would come back very soon. (3) *By letter as from us*. Paul's first letter might be misinterpreted and used to support the idea that Christ would come soon (1 Thessalonians 4:13-18). But Paul did not say *letter from us*. He said *letter as from us*. Some students think there may have been another letter supposed to be from Paul, but really written by someone else—a letter saying more plainly that Jesus was coming very soon. No matter how it might come, that teaching was not dependable.

THE DAY HAS NOT COME

What is it about predictions of the future that captivates so many people? The world is full of gullible people and of those who are willing to mislead them. Unfortunately, many Christians fit into the former category and some apparently fit into the latter.

One of the most striking examples of this phenomenon in modern times is found among the followers of Charles Taze Russell (1852-1916). He claimed that God had rejected all existing churches, and so he began the Jehovah's Witnesses. Furthermore, he predicted that 1914 was the year when the end of the world would come with the completion of the roll of the 144,000 elect. Other leaders have predicted different dates for the end, and they have been shown to be just as erroneous as Russell.

How to Say It
BEREA. Beh-*ree*-uh.
PHILIPPI. Fih-*lip*-pie or *Fil*-ih-pie.
SILAS. *Sigh*-luss.
THESSALONICA.   *Thess*-uh-lo-*nye*-kuh (strong accent on *nye; th* as in *thin*).

Paul wrote to Christians who were being similarly deceived. Apparently their example was not sufficient warning for the followers of Russell and others like him. We should be watchful, expecting the Lord's return, but also expecting the presence of false prophets who would deceive us.

—C. R. B.

B. Other Events (vv. 3, 4)

3. Let no man deceive you by any means: for that day shall not come, except there come a falling away first, and that man of sin be revealed, the son of perdition.

For once we see a teaching that Jesus would not come that very week or that very month. Of course, the teaching applied only to that time; it does not say He will not come this week or this month, or even today. But Paul pointed out two events that would happen before Jesus' return.

First, there would be *a falling away*, an apostasy. There would be false teachers, iniquity would increase, the warm love of many Christians would cool off (Matthew 24:11, 12). This prediction has been fulfilled in many Christians and many churches past and present. The prediction may refer to a greater falling away still in the future, but we cannot be sure of this.

Second, before Christ's coming *that man of sin* would *be revealed*. He would be *the son of perdition*, which means he was doomed to be defeated and destroyed. Already there have been many men of sin inside and outside the church. Perhaps a more horrible one is yet to come, but here again we cannot be sure.

4. Who opposeth and exalteth himself above all that is called God, or that is worshipped; so that he as God sitteth in the temple of God, showing himself that he is God.

The man of sin will try to usurp the place of God himself. That much is plain, but still we have problems with this verse. Will this usurper declare in plain words *that he is God*, or will he just try to take the authority that belongs to God? Will he take his seat in a literal temple like the one that used to stand in Jerusalem, or does *the temple* here mean the church? (1 Corinthians 3:16). Is the man of sin literally a man such as Hitler or Stalin, or is this a reference to a principle or movement such as Nazism or Communism? Has this prophecy already been fulfilled in one of the Roman emperors, in the Roman church, in Protestant churches, in Islam, in Nazism, in Communism? Or is the man of sin some man or principle yet to be revealed? Perhaps the prophecy is obscure because it would not be good for us to know when Jesus will come. This letter told the Thessalonians that He would not come as soon as some of them expected, but it does not tell us that He will not come today.

II. The Wicked One (2 Thessalonians 2:5-12)

The falling away would be a disaster, and so would the temporary triumph of the man of sin. But these were being restrained when Paul wrote. He does not tell us how long they were to be restrained. Knowledge of the times and seasons belongs to God (Acts 1:7).

A. Restraint of the Wicked One (vv. 5-7)

5. Remember ye not, that, when I was yet with you, I told you these things?

With this letter Paul was reminding the Thessalonians of what he had taught them while he was with them in person. He had told them about the falling away and the man of sin that would come before the return of Jesus.

6. And now ye know what withholdeth that he might be revealed in his time.

When Paul wrote this, something or someone was restraining the progress of apostasy or of the man of sin so that the evil would not become apparent before the time when God chose to allow it. The Thessalonians knew what was restraining, because Paul had told them while he was among them. We do not know, because he has not told us.

7. For the mystery of iniquity doth already work: only he who now letteth will let, until he be taken out of the way.

In this verse, *let* means the same as *withhold* in verse 6. In fact, the very same word is used in the Greek text. It means to hold down, hold back, restrain, hinder, or prevent. Already at work was the evil that later would be plainly seen in the falling away and in the man of sin. When Paul wrote, however, the evil was working mysteriously, under cover. It was restrained by someone or something. Not having all the information the Thessalonians had, we cannot identify the one who was restraining. Many suggestions have been made, but we cannot be sure any one of them is correct: (1) False teaching and ungodly living were at work in the church, but were held back by the presence and influence of Paul and other apostles. (2) Evil persecution of the church was being fomented in the Roman Empire, but was held back by Emperor Claudius and moderate advisers in the government. (3) Church leaders already were grasping for worldly power, but were held back by the power of the empire. Only after the empire disintegrated could the pope become a worldly tyrant. (4) The spirit of rebellion has always been working in the church, but it was kept in check by the apostles, then by the empire, then by the pope and his organization; but finally it broke out in Martin Luther, a priest who rebelled. (5) There have always been people who would be lawless tyrants if they could, but the forces of law and order held them in check through centuries until those forces were so weakened that a Stalin or a Hitler could have his way. When so many possibilities are suggested, we can hardly be sure of any of them. If we had been there to hear what Paul taught when he was in Thessalonica, perhaps the mystery would be solved. But as it is, we do not know who was restraining the power of evil when Paul wrote this letter; we do not know when that restrainer was or will be taken out of the way; we do not know who the man of sin is or when he appeared or will appear.

B. End of the Wicked One (vv. 8, 9)

8. And then shall that Wicked be revealed, whom the Lord shall consume with the spirit of his mouth, and shall destroy with the brightness of his coming.

That Wicked must be the same man of sin described in verses 3 and 4. At some time, we don't know when, the restraining force will be taken away, and he will stand up arrogantly to declare that he is God (v. 4). We do not know how long he will be allowed to continue that blasphemy, but we know how it will end. Jesus will come, and *that Wicked* will disappear. Probably it is better to translate *the breath of his mouth* instead of *the spirit of his mouth*. Just a puff of breath, or perhaps just a word spoken

visual 9

with His mouth, will be enough to *consume* the arrogant man of sin. Jesus will come in the clouds "with power and great glory" (Matthew 24:30), and *that Wicked* will vanish into oblivion before *the brightness of his coming.*

9. Even him, whose coming is after the working of Satan with all power and signs and lying wonders.

This tells more about the man of sin. Calling himself God, he will try to imitate what Jesus did at His first coming. Jesus did God's work with power, signs and wonders. The man of sin will do Satan's work with the power of pretended signs and wonders, with fake miracles.

C. Victims of the Wicked One (vv. 10-12)

10. And with all deceivableness of unrighteousness in them that perish; because they received not the love of the truth, that they might be saved.

Here we can translate *deceit* instead of the awkward word *deceivableness.* The first part of the verse continues to tell about the man of sin. He does Satan's work with every kind of deceit that wickedness can devise. The rest of the verse tells about the victims of the man of sin. With his wicked deceit he fools *them that perish.* Why are they so easily fooled? It is not merely that they did not receive the truth. Their problem is deeper. They did not hold and cherish *the love of the truth.* If they really loved the truth, it would be harder to lead them astray. But when people like falsehood better, it is not hard to convince them that the false is true. But the result is fatal: they *perish.* They need to love and find and cherish the truth *that they might be saved.*

11. And for this cause God shall send them strong delusion, that they should believe a lie.

For this cause, because they have no love for truth, but prefer falsehood, God lets them have what they want. Of course, God himself does not provide *a strong delusion.* He cannot lie (Titus 1:2). The way God sends delusion is simply by getting out of the way and letting Satan's delusion reach those who want it. If we love the truth, God gives it to us. If we reject the truth and prefer to believe a lie, God does not protect us from the lie we prefer.

12. That they all might be damned who believed not the truth, but had pleasure in unrighteousness.

That they all might be damned. This is the result of choosing to believe a lie rather than the truth. Why do people make that fatal choice? Because they have *pleasure in unrighteousness.* They like to do wrong. They think it is fun, or they make money by it, or doing as they please gives them a feeling of power.

A DESIRE TO BE DECEIVED

In Montreal, on a summer's evening in 1977, a supposed psychic gave a convincing demonstration of his psychic power to a believing and astounded audience. During the first half of the program, he performed feat after feat of paranormal mental power.

Following the intermission, the psychic came back onstage without his disguise and revealed himself to be a magician, newspaper columnist, and debunker of psychic charlatans. Many in the audience were enraged. Having paid good money to be fooled, they demanded to be fooled! They did not want to hear the truth about how they had been duped.

The "New Age" is all the rage, with its belief in reincarnation, "channelers," mediums, and other aspects of parapsychology. Not all magicians are charlatans, of course; most are merely entertainers. But if someone claims to have access to psychic "truth," we must beware!

The Bible has been true all along. Many people prefer deception to the truth. They would rather follow Satan and his deceivers than to follow Christ, who alone can tell us the truth about life now and life hereafter.   —C. R. B.

III. The Saved
(2 Thessalonians 2:13-15)

It is sad that some choose to believe a lie and be damned because they like to do wrong. But on the other hand, there is joy in knowing that some choose to believe the truth and be saved. Such were the Thessalonian Christians; and such are we, if we faithfully follow Jesus.

A. Chosen (v. 13)

13. But we are bound to give thanks always to God for you, brethren beloved of the Lord, because God hath from the beginning chosen you to salvation through sanctification of the Spirit and belief of the truth.

It was proper and right for Paul to thank God for the Christians in Thessalonica, and for all Christians everywhere. And why should he thank God for them? *Because God hath from the beginning chosen you to salvation.* Some students take this to mean that Christians were chosen from the beginning of their Christian life, but it seems more probable that they were chosen from the beginning of creation. Compare Ephesians 1:4. As God was making the plan of the universe, He was making also the plan of salvation, choosing those who would be saved according to that plan. Of course, that does not mean He was designating you or me or any one individual to be saved regardless of what that individual might do. Rather, He chose for salvation all those who would believe the truth and live by it. The Thessalonian Christians were among those chosen, and so are we if we are sincere Christians. Our *salvation* is accomplished *through sanctification of the Spirit and belief of the truth.* To be sanctified is to be set apart, dedicated. When we become Christians, the Holy Spirit sets us apart from the world, dedicates us to the service of God. This is possible because we believe the truth and want to live by it. When we accept God's truth and begin to obey it, we receive the gift of the Holy Spirit who sanctifies us (Acts 2:38).

B. Called (v. 14)

14. Whereunto he called you by our gospel, to the obtaining of the glory of our Lord Jesus Christ.

The *gospel* Paul preached was the means God used to call the Thessalonians and us to salvation. *Gospel* means *good news.* Paul's gospel was the good news of Christ, who died to atone for our sins and rose to bring life and immortality to light. When we hear the call of the gospel and answer by believing the truth and obeying it, we are saved. By becoming Christians and faithfully following Jesus, we not only bring *glory* to Him, but also obtain for ourselves a share of His glory (Colossians 3:4).

C. Standing Firm (v. 15)

15. Therefore, brethren, stand fast, and hold the traditions which ye have been taught, whether by word, or our epistle.

We must take our stand on the truth we believe, and refuse to be moved by any persuasion, any enticement, any threat, or any persecution. We must *hold the traditions* Paul taught the Thessalonians by *word* when he was with them and by *epistle* when he wrote to them.

Conclusion

A. Be Ready Now!

Be ready now! That is the repeated emphasis of Bible teaching about Jesus' return. He may come today. It would be a great mistake to conclude that the man of sin is yet to come, and therefore Jesus cannot come for a long time. "In an hour that ye think not"—that is just when Jesus will come (Matthew 24:44).

We cannot assign the falling away and the man of sin to some future time. The information we have is too indefinite. Some have fallen away in every generation since Christianity began, and there have been arrogant men of sin

without number. Perhaps Paul's prediction already has been fulfilled over and over. The first century was not yet over when John wrote, "Even now are there many antichrists; whereby we know that it is the last time" (1 John 2:18). The "last time" has continued for nineteen centuries, but it will end—perhaps today.

God alone knows when Christ will come (Matthew 24:36). But you and I know the time for us to be ready is today, and we know that the way to be ready is to live uprightly in the Lord.

B. Stand Firm

The Thessalonians were shaken by the idea that Jesus might come at any minute. In our time, indeed He may! We need to be alert, but not shaken. The way to be ready for His coming is not to neglect our daily work, but to do it diligently and well. Stand firm!

The Thessalonians were persecuted, and so are many Christians now. If our persecution is only the scorn of some who think they are more enlightened, we need to meet it with patience and faith (2 Thessalonians 1:4). Stand firm!

Perhaps our greatest danger is that we will become careless about the things we learn from the Bible, and drift away from them. Stand firm!

C. Prayer

O God our Father, You have loved us and given us everlasting consolation and good hope through grace. Now strengthen our hearts and establish us in every good word and work (2 Thessalonians 2:16, 17).

D. Thought to Remember

Stand firm!

Home Daily Bible Readings

Monday, Oct. 23—Hold Fast to Your Confession (Hebrews 10:19-25)
Tuesday, Oct. 24—Confidence, Endurance, and Promise (Hebrews 10:32-39)
Wednesday, Oct. 25—The Fruit of Discipline (Hebrews 12:3-11)
Thursday, Oct. 26—Do the Works of Faithful People (Hebrews 13:1-6)
Friday, Oct. 27—Follow Christ Faithfully (Hebrews 13:7-16)
Saturday, Oct. 28—Prayer and Thanksgiving for Faithful People (2 Thessalonians 1:3-12)
Sunday, Oct. 29—Confidence in the Lord (2 Thessalonians 3:1-5)

Learning by Doing

This page contains an alternate lesson plan emphasizing learning activities. Classes desiring such student involvement will find these suggestions helpful.

Learning Goals

After studying 2 Thessalonians 2:1-15, a student should be able to:

1. List characteristics mentioned in these verses regarding the end times.

2. Identify the proper conduct of a Christian in the face of speculation about things not made clear in the Bible.

3. Explain what difference the expectation of Christ's return makes in the life of a Christian.

4. Determine how he will stand firm until Christ's return.

Into the Lesson

Before the class members arrive, place this statement on the chalkboard or a sheet of newsprint: "Jesus is coming soon." Divide your students into groups of four in the order in which they enter the classroom. Ask each group to read the statement and respond to it. They may respond in any way they wish. Tell them to make both rational and emotional responses. Allow the groups four or five minutes to complete this. Then lead a general sharing time.

Make the transition into the Bible study section by stating that today's lesson attempts to clarify how Christians should regard this statement.

Into the Word

Establish the setting for this lesson by presenting the thoughts in the Introduction section of the commentary material. Then develop the lesson by leading the students through the text with the following questions:

1. What encouragement did Paul give the Thessalonian Christians to counteract the teaching that the return of the Lord was upon them? (vv. 1, 2). (They were not to be shaken or troubled.)

2. What two events must occur before Christ comes? (v. 3). (There will be a falling away from Christ, and the man of sin will be revealed.)

3. How will the man of sin behave? (vv. 4, 9). (He will oppose God; he will try to usurp the place of God; he will exalt himself to be worshiped; he will try to imitate what Jesus did at His first coming.)

4. What was happening in regard to the man of sin at the time that Paul wrote? (vv. 5-7). (The man of sin was being hindered by someone or

something, which Paul had earlier revealed to the Thessalonians, but which he has not revealed to us. In his comments under these verses, the lesson writer lists some of the suggestions that have been made regarding the identity of the evil that was at work and that which was restraining it. Mention these at this time.)

5. What will happen to the evil one when Jesus appears? (v. 8). (He will be overthrown and will vanish into oblivion.)

6. How long will the evil one work before Jesus comes? (We do not know.)

7. What are the characteristics of those who believe the evil one? (vv. 10-12). (They neither love nor believe the truth; they have pleasure in unrighteousness.)

8. What will be the end of those who follow the evil one? (They will be condemned to perdition with him.)

9. What do verses 13 and 14 say about those who are saved? (They are God's chosen; they are set apart to God's service through the Holy Spirit; they believe the truth; they are called by the gospel; they are share the glory of the Lord Jesus Christ.)

10. What should Christians do until Christ's return? (v. 15). (They are to stand firm; they are to hold on to the truth of God.)

Into Life

Make the transition into the application by stating that the Bible clearly teaches that Jesus will come again. While we wait for His coming, we are to remain firm in Him in spite of the evil one who would tempt us to abandon God. How can we remain firm while we wait?

Divide the class members into their original groups of four. Have each group use this text, and others with which they are familiar, to write a plan for standing firm as we wait. Encourage them to put their instructions in recipe terms. Allow four or five minutes for this. Then let the groups share their work.

Ask, What difference does the expectation of Christ's return make in your life as you live day by day?

Summarize the discussion by pointing out that we can depend upon the fact that Jesus will return. Let us at all times be prepared for His coming.

Let's Talk It Over

The questions on this page are designed to encourage review of the lesson Scriptures and to promote discussion of the lesson by the class. The answers provided are only discussion starters. Let your class talk it over from there.

1. What causes people to be deceived easily?

There are several reasons why people can be deceived easily. (1) They don't love the truth (2 Thessalonians 2:10). Ardent devotion to truth provides a shield against deception. (2) They are getting what they want—and God allows them to fulfill their wishes (2 Thessalonians 2:11). False teachers and demagogues know how to dupe people: they tell people what they want to hear and/or what panders to their egos and selfish interests. (3) They find great pleasure in wickedness underneath a veneer of religion and respectability (2 Thessalonians 2:12).

2. What is the function of tradition?

Tradition is the handing down of a pattern of action or thought from one generation to another. Traditions may be good or bad, depending on their validity. People may abuse traditions by worshiping them or by canonizing them as divine law. Tradition is shunned in some circles because it is equated with that which is extra-or anti-Scriptural. However, Paul calls for Christians to hold to the traditions taught by the apostles (2 Thessalonians 2:15). These traditions are valid and necessary because of their divine source. It is the role of tradition to preserve that which is important. How crucial it is for the tradition of Christ to be handed down from generation to generation! That tradition preserves not just what is important, but that which is essential to life.

3. Paul urges Christians to stand firm in their convictions based on God's Word. What will help us to do that?

There are at least four actions we can take that will help us to stand firm. (1) We can feed regularly from the truth. Truth is the antidote to error, which could lead to our falling away. (2) We can be alert to false teaching and subversive influences. Paul warns about being deceived, and of the danger of apostasy. (3) We can associate regularly with others who stand firm. Being a "lone ranger" feeds vulnerability and weakness. Maintaining vital relationships with others who share our convictions and goals gives us strength. (4) We can consistently put into practice the truth we possess. This behavior reinforces the firmness of our stand.

4. Paul mentioned three sources by which the Thessalonians might be confused concerning the second coming of the Lord. What were they?

In 2 Thessalonians 2:2 Paul reveals three unhealthy and erroneous influences that could cause such confusion. The first is suggested by his use of the word *spirit*. The disturbance could come by a spirit, that is, the spirit of a false teacher not guided by the Holy Spirit. The second arises out of the term *word* or *message*. Misinterpretations, misapplications, and distortions of Paul's teachings could be spread throughout the church. The third erroneous influence is seen in his use of the term *letter*. This would most likely refer to a spurious letter, purporting to be from Paul, claiming that the day of the Lord was right at hand. Any one or all of these could be the cause of misunderstanding.

5. Why do good causes meet with resistance?

Satan never rests—he continually is at work fomenting resistance. And the forces of evil are entrenched, fighting righteousness to the death. The light exposes the darkness, and the darkness tries to put it out. Sometimes good causes meet resistance from *good* people, because they are reluctant to undergo the sacrifice and suffering that is involved.

6. If it is not the will of God that any should perish (see 2 Peter 3:9), why doesn't He save everyone?

Heaven is going to be a happy place. Every person who is there will be there because he wants to be. Can you imagine the man who opposed the will of God throughout his life on earth finding himself in a situation where everyone is called on voluntarily and joyfully to worship the God whom he has rejected? How could such a person be happy? God wants everyone to be saved, but He will not force salvation on anyone. Everyone must make his own decision to be with the Lord.

The Redeeming Lamb

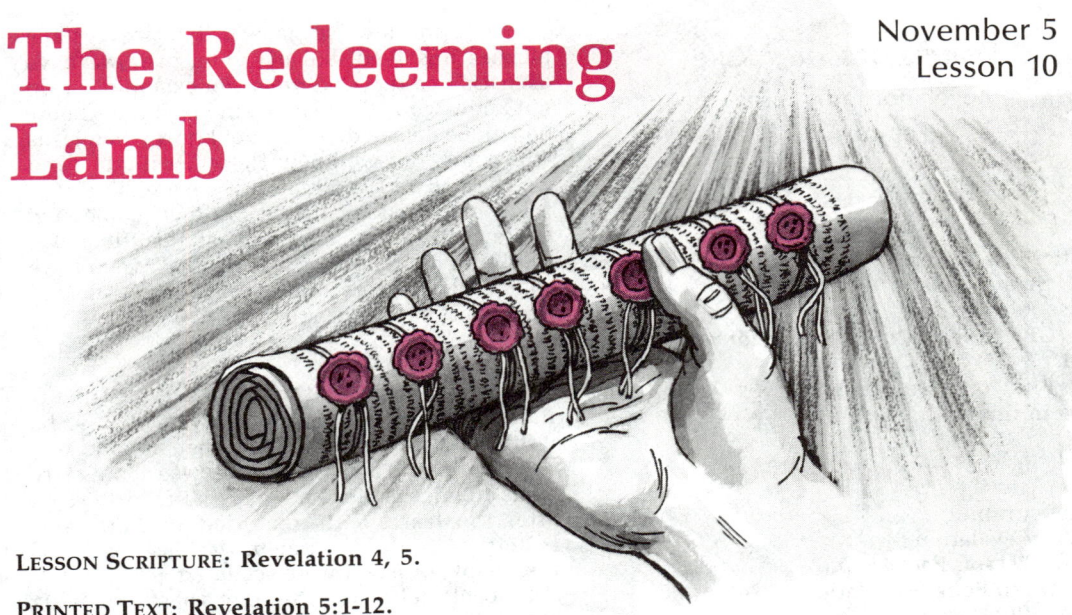

LESSON SCRIPTURE: Revelation 4, 5.

PRINTED TEXT: Revelation 5:1-12.

Revelation 5:1-12

1 And I saw in the right hand of him that sat on the throne a book written within and on the back side, sealed with seven seals.

2 And I saw a strong angel proclaiming with a loud voice, Who is worthy to open the book, and to loose the seals thereof?

3 And no man in heaven, nor in earth, neither under the earth, was able to open the book, neither to look thereon.

4 And I wept much, because no man was found worthy to open and to read the book, neither to look thereon.

5 And one of the elders saith unto me, Weep not: behold, the Lion of the tribe of Judah, the Root of David, hath prevailed to open the book, and to loose the seven seals thereof.

6 And I beheld, and, lo, in the midst of the throne and of the four beasts, and in the midst of the elders, stood a Lamb as it had been slain, having seven horns and seven eyes, which are the seven Spirits of God sent forth into all the earth.

7 And he came and took the book out of the right hand of him that sat upon the throne.

8 And when he had taken the book, the four beasts and four and twenty elders fell down before the Lamb, having every one of them harps, and golden vials full of odors, which are the prayers of saints.

9 And they sung a new song, saying, Thou art worthy to take the book, and to open the seals thereof: for thou wast slain, and hast redeemed us to God by thy blood out of every kindred, and tongue, and people, and nation;

10 And hast made us unto our God kings and priests: and we shall reign on the earth.

11 And I beheld, and I heard the voice of many angels round about the throne, and the beasts, and the elders: and the number of them was ten thousand times ten thousand, and thousands of thousands;

12 Saying with a loud voice, Worthy is the Lamb that was slain to receive power, and riches, and wisdom, and strength, and honor, and glory, and blessing.

Nov 5

GOLDEN TEXT: Worthy is the Lamb that was slain to receive power, and riches, and wisdom, and strength, and honor, and glory, and blessing.—Revelation 5:12.

Visions of God's Rule
Unit 4. Revelation: A Message of Hope
(Lessons 10-13)

Lesson Aims

After this lesson a student should be able to:

1. Briefly describe John's vision and the praise John heard.

2. Give at least three reasons for praising the Lord.

3. Find one way to bring his daily living more in line with God's will.

Lesson Outline

INTRODUCTION
   A. Revelation
   B. Lesson Background
I. CLOSED BOOK (Revelation 5:1-4)
   A. Book (v. 1)
   B. Call (v. 2)
   C. No Answer (vv. 3, 4)
      The Mystery of the Future
II. WORTHY LAMB (Revelation 5:5-7)
   A. The Announcement (v. 5)
      The Lion of the Tribe of Judah
   B. The Lamb (v. 6)
   C. The Lamb and the Book (v. 7)
III. PRAISE TO THE LAMB (Revelation 5:8-12)
   A. Beings and Elders (vv. 8-10)
   B. Angels (vv. 11, 12)
CONCLUSION
   A. Praise the Lord
   B. When to Praise the Lord
   C. How to Praise the Lord
   D. Prayer
   E. Thought to Remember

Visual 10 from the visuals/learning resources packet highlights the thoughts in the Conclusion section of the lesson. It is shown on page 83.

Introduction

For the past two months we have been engaged in a series of related studies. The whole series is entitled "Visions of God's Rule." From Ezekiel and Daniel we have seen that God rules even the heathen nations and finally will take away the power He has entrusted to them. From Thessalonians we have seen that God will crush all the anti-God forces of the world, and that Jesus will gather His people to be with Him forever.

In our studies, we have had to leave some puzzles unsolved, but over and over we have been assured that God rules. For example, we do not know who "the man of sin" is, but we know he will be defeated. We do not know when Jesus will come, but we know He will triumph, and we shall share His triumph if we are faithful.

For more visions of God's rule we come now to Revelation, the last book of the Bible. We shall find more puzzles we cannot solve, but we shall find also more assurances of God's rule and the victory of His people.

A. Revelation

The book of Revelation is placed last in our Bible, and probably it was the last book to be written. It seems most likely that its date was between A.D. 90 and 100. A.D. 90 was about sixty years after Jesus died and rose again, thirty years after the last events recorded in Acts, and twenty years after Jerusalem was destroyed and the people of Israel were scattered.

Probably John was the only apostle of Jesus still living on earth. After Jerusalem was destroyed, he lived in Ephesus and guided the Christians there and in the other cities of the area. The heathen rulers opposed Christianity, and so their displeasure fell especially on John. They made him a prisoner on a tiny island called Patmos *(see map—visual 8)*, but God set him free in spirit to see magnificent visions of events involving the whole earth, and Heaven too.

B. Lesson Background

In the first great vision of Revelation (chapters 1—3), John saw Jesus standing among the churches and sending messages to them. We bypass that vision and come to the second one, which is introduced in chapter 4. John saw an open door in Heaven, and a voice said, "Come up hither, and I will show thee things which must be hereafter."

Beyond that door John saw a dazzling vision of God on His throne, attended by twenty-four white-robed elders and four living beings resembling a lion, a calf, a man, and an eagle. John heard what the living beings were saying, and we like to think they were singing it:

Holy, holy, holy, Lord God Almighty,
   which was, and is, and is to come.

The elders also had a word or song of praise, falling down to worship the ever-living God:

Thou art worthy, O Lord,
   to receive glory and honor and power:
   for thou hast created all things,
   and for thy pleasure they are and were
      created.

We are not told who the living beings and elders are or whom they represent. It is easy to imagine that the twenty-four elders are the twelve Hebrew patriarchs and the twelve apostles, and so represent all of God's people. The four living beings may represent all of the living beings on earth, animal as well as human. God's people praise Him now, and in time to come all the creatures in the universe will praise Him (Revelation 5:13), even those who now deny Him (Philippians 2:9-11).

I. Closed Book (Revelation 5:1-4)

We are not told how long John stood awestruck before that glorious vision and listened to the resounding praise, but he understood that the song of praise was unceasing (Revelation 4:8). Then his attention was focused on one particular object, a book.

A. Book (v. 1)

1. And I saw in the right hand of him that sat on the throne a book written within and on the back side, sealed with seven seals.

Probably the *book* was a scroll, a long strip of papyrus or parchment rolled up like a roll of waxed paper in your kitchen. John had been called to see things to come (4:1), so we suppose such things were written in the book. The scroll was full, written on both sides. God held in His hand all the things that were to happen in the future. But neither John nor anyone else could see what was written. The rolled book was *sealed with seven seals*, sealed thoroughly and completely.

B. Call (v. 2)

2. And I saw a strong angel proclaiming with a loud voice, Who is worthy to open the book, and to loose the seals thereof?

The *angel* had to be *strong* to shout *with a loud voice* that could reach to the whole creation, calling for anyone anywhere to come and open the book if he was *worthy*. What would it take to make one worthy of that task? As yet we have no hint, but later we shall see what it would take.

C. No Answer (vv. 3, 4)

3. And no man in heaven, nor in earth, neither under the earth, was able to open the book, neither to look thereon.

There was no answer to the strong angel's call. In all of creation, no one was worthy to open that book. It seems better to read *no one* instead of *no man*, and some versions have that reading. Neither man nor angel could open that book. Not even one of the mystical living beings around God's throne could do it. The *King James Version* indicates that no one could even *look* at it. Some translators take this to mean that no one could look *into* it rather than *at* it. To look into the book one would have to break the seals and open it.

4. And I wept much, because no man was found worthy to open and to read the book, neither to look thereon.

John burst into tears. He had been called to see things that were to happen in the future (4:1). Now it seemed that he was not to see them after all, for no one in creation could open that book and reveal them. John *wept much* in bitter disappointment.

THE MYSTERY OF THE FUTURE

The story is told of an exhibition of paintings held in a beautiful park. The judges had narrowed the field of contestants to just two paintings that were vying for the grand prize. One was a painting of fruit so realistic that birds flew out of the trees to peck at the fruit. The other painting depicted a closed curtain with no particular beauty to it. The judges awarded the prize to the latter painting. They reasoned that the picture of fruit might attract birds, but the painting of the curtain intrigued learned philosophers.

Something about the hidden and mysterious captivates our attention. We all think we would like to see into the future, even if we have sense enough not to trust in horoscopes or crystal-ball gazers.

The apostle John tells of seeing God holding a sealed scroll, which apparently contained the account of future events. John wanted to know what was ahead, and he was saddened to find that no one could open the scroll.

To know what the future holds may seem attractive to us. But how much better off we are simply to know who holds the future in His hands!

—C. R. B.

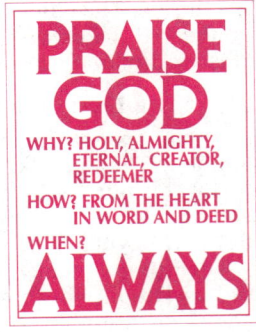

visual 10

II. Worthy Lamb
(Revelation 5:5-7)

John's disappointment and grief did not last long. Into his vision came another figure, one that had not been seen before. In all the universe, this was the one being who was worthy to open the book and disclose what was to happen in the future.

A. The Announcement (v. 5)

5. And one of the elders saith unto me, Weep not: behold, the Lion of the tribe of Judah, the Root of David, hath prevailed to open the book, and to loose the seven seals thereof.

Twenty-four elders were gathered around God's throne in the vision (Revelation 4:4). One of them comforted John with the announcement that there was someone who could open the book after all. That one was *the Lion of the tribe of Judah.* That title refers to the Christ. As a man He was *of the tribe of Judah*, the royal tribe of Israel. He was *the Lion*, the most powerful and most noble of all the kings belonging to that tribe. He was also *the Root of David.* David was the first great king from the tribe of Judah, and the Christ was heir to his throne. When used figuratively, the word *root* sometimes means the source or origin. However, it seems that the same word sometimes means a shoot or stem or branch that grows from a root. In Isaiah 53:2, for example, a root is not what is underground, but what grows out of the ground. Isaiah 11:1 describes the Christ as a rod and a Branch of Jesse (David's father), and Isaiah 11:10 describes Him as a root of Jesse. In Revelation 22:16 it seems that *root* and *offspring* may be synonyms. Some students note that the Christ was the Creator of all things (John 1:3), including David, and so *the Root of David* can mean the source of David. Christ is both God and man. As God He is David's Creator; as man He is David's descendant. This is true, of course; but in the passage we are studying, the thought seems to be that the Christ was a descendant of David and heir to his throne. The elder said He had *prevailed*, had conquered, had won a victory, and therefore He was worthy *to open the book.*

THE LION OF THE TRIBE OF JUDAH

Ancient people likened their gods to powerful animals. The lion, "king of beasts," was a favorite for this purpose. The powerful body of a lion and the head of a man are combined in the Sphinx, Egypt's most famous statue.

The Sphinx is now 4,600 years old, and is in sad condition. For thousands of years, its stone has been crumbling. Through the centuries, many attempts have been made to restore the monument, some doing more harm than good. It has had glue injected into it, mud plastered over it, and new limestone cemented onto its surface, but no final solution has been found.

In the vision given him, John saw Jesus as "the Lion of the tribe of Judah," the most powerful and noble king belonging to that tribe. Jesus the King (not just of beasts, but of all creation) has sometimes suffered from our well-meaning attempts to make cosmetic alterations to his story to make Him more like what people want. But He needs neither restoration nor alteration. We must take Him as He is, making our ideas conform to Him, and not the reverse.

B. The Lamb (v. 6)

6. And I beheld, and, lo, in the midst of the throne and of the four beasts, and in the midst of the elders, stood a Lamb as it had been slain, having seven horns and seven eyes, which are the seven Spirits of God sent forth into all the earth.

Beasts is better translated *living beings.* The four beings are described in Revelation 4:6-8. Three of them looked like beasts, but they were not bestial in intelligence, character, and ability. The four of them surrounded God's throne in the vision, and around them was the larger circle of twenty-four elders (Revelation 4:4-6). An elder had spoken of "the Lion of the tribe of Judah," but now *a Lamb* appeared between the throne and the beings and elders that encircled it. The Lamb was standing alive and well, but it appeared *as it had been slain.* We are not told just what showed that the living Lamb had once been killed, but John understood clearly that it had. Beyond a doubt the Lamb represented Christ, "the Lamb of God, which taketh away the sin of the world" (John 1:29). Students of prophecy recognize horns as a symbol of power, and seven as a symbol of completeness. The *seven horns* of the Lamb indicate that Christ has complete power (Matthew 28:18). *Seven eyes* suggest complete vision. Nothing can be hidden from the Lamb. But John adds that the eyes *are the seven Spirits of God sent forth into all the earth.* Through them the Lamb, Christ, is in touch with everything in the world. In the Bible we read often of the Spirit of God, the Holy Spirit; but in Revelation He appears sometimes

---

How to Say It

EPHESUS. *Ef*-eh-sus.
PATMOS. *Pat*-muss.

as seven Spirits (3:1; 4:5). Seven, the number of completeness, indicates that the Spirit is present everywhere, sees everything, and acts always as God wishes.

C. The Lamb and the Book (v. 7)

7. And he came and took the book out of the right hand of him that sat upon the throne.

From *the right hand* of God the Lamb *took the book* that was sealed. Chapter 6 records that He proceeded to break the seals that kept the book closed. How could a lamb do all this? Naturally we wonder, but John does not pause to tell us. Perhaps this Lamb had hands as well as feet. The figures in a vision are not so limited as things are in the material world. Remember the living beings of Revelation 4:6-8. Three of them looked like animals and one had the face of a man, but each spoke in human language and each had six wings. In such a vision, a Lamb with seven horns and seven eyes surely could have as many hands as He needed.

III. Praise to the Lamb (Revelation 5:8-12)

In Revelation 6, we read that the Lamb broke the seals of the book one by one. With the breaking of each seal, John saw a different vision. Doubtless these visions represented "things which must be hereafter" (Revelation 4:1). But before the first seal is broken, we pause to hear Heaven resounding with praise to the Lamb who can open the book.

A. Beings and Elders (vv. 8-10)

8. And when he had taken the book, the four beasts and four and twenty elders fell down before the Lamb, having every one of them harps, and golden vials full of odors, which are the prayers of saints.

Together the living beings and elders *fell down* to worship *before the Lamb.* Their *harps* symbolize praise, for the Jews used such instruments with their joyous songs of praise to God (Psalms 33:2; 43:4; 147:7; 149:3; 150:3). In a time of mourning, they hung up their harps (Psalm 137:2). Other versions have *bowls full of incense* instead of *vials full of odors.* Incense was well known as a symbol of prayer. See Revelation 8:3, 4. In the Hebrew ritual, the people prayed outside the sanctuary while a priest burned incense within. Its fragrant smoke went toward Heaven like *the prayers of saints* (Luke 1:8-10).

9, 10. And they sung a new song, saying,
Thou art worthy to take the book,
and to open the seals thereof:

for thou wast slain,
and hast redeemed us to God by thy blood
out of every kindred, and tongue, and
people, and nation;
and hast made us unto our God kings
and priests:
and we shall reign on the earth.

We saw in verse 5 that Christ could open the book because He had prevailed, had overcome, had won a victory. Now we see how He had won. He had done it by being killed, by giving His life to redeem us for God. We see also that His redemption was not limited to one nation or a few nations. He redeemed us *out of every kindred, and tongue, and people, and nation.* By His redemption He not only saved us from death, but also exalted us to be *unto our God kings and priests,* or *a kingdom and priests,* as some versions have it. When the victory of God's kingdom is complete, *we shall reign on the earth.* Of course, the redeemed will not be tyrants like the Roman emperors, but they will not be a persecuted minority as they were when John was a prisoner on Patmos. They will be triumphant and dominant. They will share God's rule, not by forcing their own way or even by forcing His way, but by unanimously and gladly doing God's will. Following different ancient manuscripts, some modern versions read *them* and *they* instead of *us* and *we* in this verse: *Thou ... hast redeemed people ... and hast made them ... kings and priests: and they shall reign.* The different reading is not important. If we are Christians, we are among those people that Christ has redeemed, we are to our God kings and priests, and we shall reign in accord with His divine will.

B. Angels (vv. 11, 12)

11. And I beheld, and I heard the voice of many angels round about the throne, and the beasts, and the elders: and the number of them was ten thousand times ten thousand, and thousands of thousands.

We have seen that God's throne was surrounded by four *beasts,* better called living beings, and then by a larger circle of twenty-four *elders.* Now we see outside of them a circle yet larger, a circle of *many angels.* This was a huge throng. *Ten thousand times ten thousand* make a hundred million, but they were not all. There were *thousands of thousands more.* The angels were simply innumerable.

12. Saying with a loud voice,
Worthy is the Lamb that was slain to
receive power, and riches, and wisdom, and
strength, and honor, and glory, and
blessing.

The countless angels added their voices to those of the elders and living beings in a grand chorus of praise to the Lamb. Because He gave His life to redeem mankind, He is worthy of all power, of every good possession, of every good attribute of character, of every word of praise.

Verse 13 adds the praise of an assembly even larger than that of countless angels. Every creature in heaven and earth and sea joined in the swelling chorus:

"Blessing, and honor, and glory, and power, be unto him that sitteth upon the throne, and unto the Lamb for ever and ever."

Then comes verse 14: "The four beasts said, Amen." So say we all: Amen!

Conclusion

John saw a mysterious book filled with writing on both sides. We suppose it told of things to come, some of which were revealed as the seals of the book were broken (Revelation 6).

But the revelation of future events began even before a seal was broken. John heard a tremendous chorus of praise rising from all the creatures of the universe. That is still to come.

John lived in Ephesus before he went to Patmos. The special goddess of Ephesus was Diana (Acts 19:23-34), but the many other deities ranged from the imaginary Jupiter to the real but ungodly emperor. Only Jews and Christians knew there was only one real God, Jehovah.

Now the people about us scorn Jupiter and Diana, but many of them scorn Jehovah as well. Still only Jews and Christians know the real God, and only Christians know His Son, the Redeemer. Still in the future is the day when every knee will bow at the name of Jesus and every

tongue will confess that He is Lord (Philippians 2:9-11). But that day will surely come. How wise it is to follow Heaven's leading and praise the Lord on earth today!

A. Praise the Lord

In John's Heavenly vision, God was praised because He is holy, because He is almighty, because He is eternal, and because He created all things (Revelation 4:8, 11). Have you praised Him today for all of those reasons?

List some created things that move you to praise the Creator: the sun that warms the earth, the tiny chrysanthemum still bravely blooming at the gate of winter. What else?

Praise God for making living creatures: the cow that builds your bones with the calcium of her milk, the cat that warms you with her purring. What else?

Praise God for people: the preacher who enlightens you with the Word of God, the baby who gladdens you with a smile. Whom else?

B. When to Praise the Lord

When do you praise the Lord? On Sunday morning at church? In your daily devotions at home? When you sit down for a meal? Around God's throne the living beings praised Him all the time. "They rest not day and night" (Revelation 4:8). Is praise in your mind continually? Do you think of God when your heart is lifted by sunlight or a flower or a smile, or when you get safely across a busy street? Do you still praise God when the sky is gray and the air is chill and the rain is falling?

C. How to Praise the Lord

Some people have honored God with their lips while their heart was far from Him (Matthew 15:7-9). Some people have called Jesus Lord without doing what He says to do (Luke 6:46). For a few minutes, forget your words of praise and think of some things you have *done* in the past week that gave praise to God. Will you dare to think also of something you have done that mutes or mars or nullifies your praise? More important, think of one thing you will do this week that will give praise to God.

D. Prayer

Holy, holy, holy, Lord God Almighty! We praise Your glory and power, O God, and we praise Your goodness and grace. How wonderful it is that You sent Your own Son as a Lamb to be slain to redeem us and bring us to life eternal!

E. Thought to Remember

Praise the Lord!

Home Daily Bible Readings

Monday, Oct. 30—A Message to Ephesus and Smyrna Christians (Revelation 2:1-11)

Tuesday, Oct. 31—A Message to Pergamum Christians (Revelation 2:12-17)

Wednesday, Nov. 1—A Message to Thyatira Christians (Revelation 2:18-29)

Thursday, Nov. 2—A Message to Sardis Christians (Revelation 3:1-6)

Friday, Nov. 3—A Message to Philadelphia Christians (Revelation 3:7-13)

Saturday, Nov. 4—A Message to Laodicea Christians (Revelation 3:14-22)

Sunday, Nov. 5—A Vision of Heavenly Worship (Revelation 4)

Learning by Doing

This page contains an alternate lesson plan emphasizing learning activities. Classes desiring such student involvement will find these suggestions helpful.

Learning Goals

After examining Revelation 5:1-12, a student will be able to:

1. Describe what John saw and heard.

2. List at least three reasons for praising the Lord.

3. Select one way to praise the Lord in his daily living this week.

Into the Lesson

Before class members arrive, write the word *praise* on the chalkboard or a sheet of newsprint. As the class members arrive, give them paper and pencil and ask them to list four or five words that they associate with the word *praise*. Have each class member interview at least two other people to find out what words they associate with praise.

After the students have had five to seven minutes to complete this, ask them to share with the class the words they have selected. Write these on the chalkboard as they call them out.

Make the transition into today's Bible study by stating that our text records John's vision of God's throne and the resounding praise given to the Lamb of God for the redemption that He has provided. What we study today should challenge and reassure us.

Into the Word

Present the material in the "Introduction" section of the commentary. Then have someone read Revelation 5:1-12 aloud to the class.

Divide the class into pairs. Give each pair a copy of the following questions and ask them to find the answers in today's text. (The answers are included for the teacher's convenience.)

1. What did John see in the right hand of God, who sat on His throne? (He saw a scroll, which had writing on both sides and was sealed with seven seals.)

2. What did the angel ask concerning it? ("Who is worthy to break the seals and open the scroll?"

3. Could any man in Heaven or earth open the scroll and look into it? (No.)

4. How did John respond? (He wept much.)

5. According to the elder who spoke, who could break the seals? (The Lion of Judah had won the victory and could break the seals and open the scroll.)

6. Who was standing in the center of the throne, surrounded by the four living beings and the twenty-four elders? (A Lamb, that is, Christ.)

7. What did each of the living creatures and the elders have? (Each had a harp and gold bowls filled with incense.)

8. What did these items represent? (Harps symbolized praise. Incense was a symbol of prayer.)

9. When the creatures and elders fell down before the Lamb, what did they do? (They sang praises to the Lamb.)

10. Why did the Lamb deserve praise? (He was worthy to break the seals of the scroll; through His death He redeemed people from every nation to God; He made these people kings and priests to serve God.)

11. What happened next? (Millions of angels joined in the song of praise to the Lamb, who is worthy to receive power, wealth, wisdom, strength, honor, glory, and praise.)

Allot six to eight minutes for this study activity. Then discuss the answers as a class.

Into Life

Each of us should follow the leading of those Heavenly beings in John's vision and praise the Lord while we live on earth. Divide the class into groups of four (combine pairs from the preceding activity), and ask each group to consider the three questions below.

1. What are some created things that move you to praise the Creator.?

2. What are some living creatures that move you to praise the Creator?

3. What persons move you to praise the Creator?

After the groups have had three of four minutes to make their lists, have them share their responses with the class.

Continue to apply the lesson by using the following questions:

1. When do you praise the Lord?

2. What are some sins in the world and in your life that mute or mar or nullify your praise of the Lord?

3. How can you praise the Lord?

Distribute small index cards to your students. Ask each to write a memo telling what he will do this week to praise the Lord.

Let's Talk It Over

*The questions on this page are designed to encourage review of the lesson
Scriptures and to promote discussion of the lesson by the class. The answers
provided are only discussion starters. Let your class talk it over from there.*

1. Why is Jesus Christ called a "lamb"?

As we read the New Testament, we see that various different metaphors are used to describe Jesus. Among them are shepherd, door, way, vine, root, and star. In today's text, He is called "Lion" in one verse and "Lamb" in the very next verse. The purpose of a metaphor is to show a likeness or an analogy between two objects that otherwise are unlike. Different metaphors are used to describe different characteristics or functions. When Jesus is pictured as "the Lamb" in John's Heavenly vision, the rich history and symbolism of the Old Testament sacrificial system is brought to mind. Under the Mosaic law, a lamb (the first and best of the flock) without "spot or blemish" was offered as a burnt offering to Jehovah every morning and every evening, while on the Sabbath two were sacrificed. Lambs formed a part of the burnt offering on many occasions throughout the year. Of particular note was the annual Passover feast. On this occasion a lamb was slain and eaten in remembrance of God's mighty redemption of His people from bondage in Egypt. All of this pointed to Jesus, who offered himself as an atoning sacrifice that we might be redeemed from bondage to sin. Thus John the Baptist described Jesus (when He came for baptism) as "the Lamb of God who takes away the sin of the world!" (John 1:29 *New International Version*) In His perfect sacrifice for sin, Jesus was "the Lamb." In John's vision (Revelation 5:6-12), Jesus is worthy to open the book because of His redeeming death as the Lamb of God.

2. What is the relationship of praise and worship?

A dust jacket on a contemporary Christian music album announces, "A celebration of worship and praise." A worship leader on a "praise tape" continually refers to "just worshiping and praising the Lord." Praise *is* worship; it is not separate from worship. More accurate expressions of the relationship between praise and worship would speak of "praise in worship" or "worship through praise." Worship is the total experience of offering reverence to God as the Divine Being. Praise, which involves the acknowledgement of the perfections of God, is one element of worship. If it is asked, "Can a person

praise God without worshiping?" the answer is no. Worship is not limited to public, corporate experience. In fact, in Romans 12:1, Paul regards worship as the living (daily) sacrifice of our lives to God. Whenever and wherever we praise God, we are involved in an act of worship, whether we have consciously designated it so, or not.

3. What is the appropriate time for praising God?

One may respond, "The appropriate time for praise is in public worship. Praise is an essential facet of worship." It is most certainly true that the time of public worship is *an* appropriate time for praising God. But the Bible does not limit our praise of God to any one particular time. On the contrary, the Bible declares that *anytime* is appropriate for praising God. Psalms 34:1 and 71:6 depict praise as being *continually* offered to God. In Psalm 61:8 David states that he will praise His name *forever*. And Psalm 22:3 says that God inhabits (or is enthroned upon) the praise of His people. What is the appropriate time to praise God? Morning, noon, and night—in good times and bad—at work, at home, at play. *Continually* praise Him.

4. What is the basis of assessing the worth of a person?

In our culture, it seems that most persons assess the worth of another on the basis of appearance or accomplishments—what the person does and how much money he or she makes. Jesus never valued anyone for looks, achievements, or possessions. A person has worth because he or she has been created in the image of God, is loved by Him, and has the potential to become a child of His (John 1:9-12; 3:16).

5. What are the implications of the statement that the Lamb had redeemed those of "every kindred, and tongue, and people, and nation"?

God's interest in the salvation of mankind is not limited. All of mankind was made in His image. All of mankind is loved by God. All of mankind is wanted by God for himself. Because of God's unwillingness for any to perish, all Christians must have the same interest in the worldwide reach of the gospel.

Provision for the Redeemed

Lesson 11

LESSON SCRIPTURE: Revelation 7.

PRINTED TEXT: Revelation 7:1-4, 9, 10, 13-17.

Revelation 7:1-4, 9, 10, 13-17

1 And after these things I saw four angels standing on the four corners of the earth, holding the four winds of the earth, that the wind should not blow on the earth, nor on the sea, nor on any tree.

2 And I saw another angel ascending from the east, having the seal of the living God: and he cried with a loud voice to the four angels, to whom it was given to hurt the earth and the sea,

3 Saying, Hurt not the earth, neither the sea, nor the trees, till we have sealed the servants of our God in their foreheads.

4 And I heard the number of them which were sealed: and there were sealed a hundred and forty and four thousand of all the tribes of the children of Israel.

. . . .

9 After this I beheld, and, lo, a great multitude, which no man could number, of all nations, and kindreds, and people, and tongues, stood before the throne, and before the Lamb, clothed with white robes, and palms in their hands;

10 And cried with a loud voice, saying, Salvation to our God which sitteth upon the throne, and unto the Lamb.

. . . .

13 And one of the elders answered, saying unto me, What are these which are arrayed in white robes? and whence came they?

14 And I said unto him, Sir, thou knowest. And he said to me, These are they which came out of great tribulation, and have washed their robes, and made them white in the blood of the Lamb.

15 Therefore are they before the throne of God, and serve him day and night in his temple: and he that sitteth on the throne shall dwell among them.

16 They shall hunger no more, neither thirst any more; neither shall the sun light on them, nor any heat.

17 For the Lamb which is in the midst of the throne shall feed them, and shall lead them unto living fountains of waters: and God shall wipe away all tears from their eyes.

Nov
12

GOLDEN TEXT: The Lamb which is in the midst of the throne shall feed them, and shall lead them unto living fountains of waters: and God shall wipe away all tears from their eyes.—Revelation 7:17.

Visions of God's Rule
Unit 4. Revelation: Message of Hope
(Lessons 10-13)

Lesson Aims

After this lesson students should be able to:

1. Tell what John saw in the vision recorded in our text.

2. Thank God that our way to Heaven is not troubled by any very great tribulation.

3. Make some special thank offering of service or of money this week.

Lesson Outline

INTRODUCTION
    A. Opening the Seals
    B. Lesson Background
I. GOD'S SERVANTS (Revelation 7:1-4)
    A. Waiting (vv. 1-3)
    B. Sealing (v. 4)
II. GOD'S PRAISE (Revelation 7:9, 10, 13, 14)
    A. The Multitude (v. 9)
        From Every Nation
    B. The Praise (v. 10)
    C. The People (vv. 13, 14)
III. GOD'S BLESSING (Revelation 7:15-17)
    A. God's Presence (v. 15)
    B. God's Care (vv. 16, 17)
        Sorrow Turns to Joy
CONCLUSION
    A. Great Tribulation
    B. Small Tribulation
    C. Checkup
    D. Prayer
    E. Thought to Remember

Display visual 11 from the visuals/learning resources packet and refer to it as you discuss the lesson text for today. It is shown on page 91.

Introduction

Last week we read about John's vision of Heaven. God on His throne handed a book to Jesus, the Lamb, while all creation sang praises. The book was closed with seven seals.

A. Opening the Seals

Chapter 6 of Revelation records what John saw as the Lamb began to open the seals. As each seal was broken, a new vision appeared. Each of the first four visions showed a horse and rider.

The first horse was white. The rider carried a bow, "and he went forth conquering, and to conquer" (Revelation 6:1, 2). There is some disagreement about this, but most students think this horseman represents either the Christ or His church or His word. It makes little difference which of these we choose, for Christ even now is conquering through His church and by His word.

It is generally agreed that the second horseman represents war, and the third represents famine, poverty, want. The fourth is plainly named as death (Revelation 6:3-8).

When the fifth seal was opened, John saw the souls of martyrs, Christians who had been killed because they held to God's word. Like many of us who are still living on earth, they were asking how long it would be until God would put a stop to injustice and give His enemies the punishment they deserved. Like us, the martyrs were not given a date (Revelation 6:9-11); but the time was coming, and the opening of the sixth seal revealed the end of the world and the terror of God's enemies in the great day of His wrath (Revelation 6:12-17).

Some students disagree with this understanding of the sixth vision. They think each vision in chapter 6 represents a period of time, and each period is to follow the one mentioned before it. If this is true, the event visualized in the beginning of chapter 7 must come after the one that closes chapter 6 and before the end of the world. Therefore they conclude that the last part of chapter 6 describes some other disturbance, not the end of the world.

It seems more probable that the visions of chapter 6 do not represent successive periods of time, but conditions continuing together through centuries of history. Ever since John saw these visions the world has been plagued with war, poverty, and death; but through the centuries, Christ and His church and His word have been conquering by winning people to the kingdom of God.

B. Lesson Background

As we see it, chapter 6 portrays conditions that were to continue from the time of John's writing to the end of the world. Chapter 7 then presents a different series of visions. Chapter 6

How to Say It

PATMOS. *Pat*-muss.
PERGAMOS. *Per*-guh-muss.
SMYRNA. *Smur*-nuh.

shows conditions in the world; chapter 7 focuses on the people of God. The first vision in chapter 7 shows what happens before the end of the world; the second one shows what happens after it.

visual 11

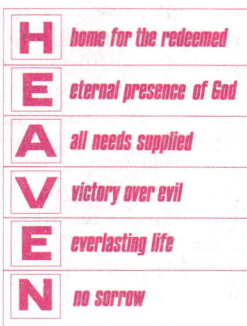

I. God's Servants (Revelation 7:1-4)

Anyone on earth could see that the world was troubled by war, poverty, and death. Anyone could see that Christians were being persecuted, even killed. But any thoughtful person could see that Christ was conquering in all this. His church was growing, spreading, turning souls from darkness to light, from the power of Satan to God. The first part of chapter 7 gives us another slant on this conquering. John's vision showed it from the viewpoint of Heaven.

A. Waiting (vv. 1-3)

1. And after these things I saw four angels standing on the four corners of the earth, holding the four winds of the earth, that the wind should not blow on the earth, nor on the sea, nor on any tree.

After these things tells us that John saw this vision after he saw those recorded in chapter 6. It does not say the vision represented an event that would happen after the events represented by the earlier visions. It seems more probable that John now was seeing something else that would go on along with war and famine and death. *The four corners of the earth* is used as we use the same expression now. It means places far away in all directions. In his vision John saw *four angels* spread afar and *holding the four winds of the earth*. As long as the angels held them, no wind could *blow on the earth, nor on the sea, nor on any tree.*

2. And I saw another angel ascending from the east, having the seal of the living God: and he cried with a loud voice to the four angels, to whom it was given to hurt the earth and the sea.

Verse 1 shows that John's vision now included the whole earth, with four angels holding the winds so that no wind could blow. Now we see that those angels were *given* the power and authority *to hurt the earth and the sea.* May we not suppose they were going to hurt them by loosing the winds they were holding? May we not suppose those winds would carry the destruction described in the end of chapter 6, the end of the world? If so, this vision reveals something else that would happen along with the war and poverty and death symbolized in chapter 6. Through centuries of war and poverty and death, the end would be delayed.

3. Saying, Hurt not the earth, neither the sea, nor the trees, till we have sealed the servants of our God in their foreheads.

The angel who came up like sunrise carried a seal that would mark God's people as His own possession (v. 2). Now the winds of destruction were to be held, delaying the end of the world until all of God's people would be marked. Compare Revelation 9:14; 14:1; 22:4.

B. Sealing (v. 4)

4. And I heard the number of them which were sealed: and there were sealed a hundred and forty and four thousand of all the tribes of the children of Israel.

John did not see the sealing; he only *heard* someone announce *the number of them that were sealed*. Perhaps the sealing continued through centuries and is continuing still. Perhaps each person receives the seal of God when he becomes a Christian, and this will go on till the winds are loosed and the world is ended.

The *number* that John heard was *a hundred and forty and four thousand of all the tribes of the children of Israel.* Shall we take *the children of Israel* literally, meaning the Jewish people? Or shall we take it figuratively, meaning Christians of all nations? In Christian teaching, followers of Jesus are "the circumcision" and "the Israel of God" (Philippians 3:3; Galatians 6:16). Is that what is meant here?

Some students think the Scripture is literal. It says these are *of the children of Israel*. It names the tribes from which they come (vv. 5-8). It gives a definite number of them, while all Christians together make up a number that cannot be counted (v. 9).

On the other hand, some think the number is symbolic. They note that twelve tribes of Israel are named in verses 5-8. Isn't it incredible, if this means literal Israel, that exactly twelve thousand are saved out of each tribe, and none at all from the tribe of Dan, which is not named here? So *a hundred and forty and four thousand* is not taken as an actual count, but as a symbol of a vast but indefinite number—the same innumerable multitude mentioned in verse 9.

Whether the number is exact or symbolic, and whether the people are Christians of Israel or Christians of all nations, these people are marked as God's own possession. They will be rescued from the catastrophes that will come at the end of the world (6:15-17). Redeemed by the blood of the Lamb, they are not among the rebels who will plead for the rocks to hide them from the Lamb's wrath.

II. God's Praise
(Revelation 7:9, 10, 13, 14)

We have been looking at a vision of the time before the end of the world (vv. 1-4). Destruction is delayed while the complete number of God's servants receive His seal. This marks them as His people, people redeemed, people to be saved when the world is destroyed. Now the scene shifts to a time after the end of the world. The scene is in front of God's throne in Heaven.

A. The Multitude (v. 9)

9. After this I beheld, and, lo, a great multitude, which no man could number, of all nations, and kindreds, and people, and tongues, stood before the throne, and before the Lamb, clothed with white robes, and palms in their hands.

The scene is the one described in chapters 4 and 5. God is on the throne. The Lamb, Jesus, is with Him. Around the throne are four living beings, twenty-four elders, and countless thousands of angels. Besides all these, John now saw *a great multitude, which no man could number.* These were human beings from all the nations of the world, the redeemed of all ages, now gathered around the throne of God. If verses 1-4 are to be taken figuratively, meaning the complete number of spiritual Israel, the Christians, then this is the same throng that was sealed before the end of the world. If verses 1-4 are to be taken literally, meaning 144,000 Jews redeemed by Christ, then they are included in this throng of people of all nations. The *white robes* signify purity and righteousness. *Palms in their hands* are not the palms of their hands. They are branches of palm trees. In ancient times, these were carried and waved in joyous celebration of victory (John 12:12, 13).

FROM EVERY NATION

On the first Christian Pentecost, Jerusalem was filled with Jewish pilgrims "from every nation under heaven" (Acts 2:5). Those on that

day who accepted Jesus as the Messiah took their newfound faith back home with them. The gospel spread throughout the Roman Empire during the first century and several centuries following.

For the next one thousand years, however, the fires of evangelism dimmed; the outreach of the gospel was limited. After the age of exploration had opened the New World and Africa and Asia to western civilization, a new missionary movement began, with William Carey (1761-1834) as its first recruit.

Following World War II, another great surge of missionary activity developed—one that still continues. Peoples in the farthest reaches of the world have been won to Christ.

Even behind the Iron and Bamboo Curtains, the church continues to grow. As the forces of evil have threatened to squelch God's message, His power has kept the church's witness alive. When the redeemed finally gather before God's throne, there will indeed be a host of people from every nation singing praises to his name, just as the Bible says.   —C. R. B.

B. The Praise (v. 10)

10. And cried with a loud voice, saying, Salvation to our God which sitteth upon the throne, and unto the Lamb.

Salvation to our God does not mean salvation is given to Him. He is the one who gives it to others. *Salvation to our God ... and unto the Lamb* means our salvation is due to them; they provide it for us. This is an abbreviated way of saying, "For our salvation we give praise to our God ... and to the Lamb." Jesus is the Lamb, who gave His life to atone for our sins and redeem us to everlasting life (John 1:29). Our God is the one who "so loved the world, that he gave his only begotten Son, that whosoever believeth in him should not perish, but have everlasting life" (John 3:16).

Verses 11 and 12 add that the angels around the throne joined in a chorus of praise to God.

C. The People (vv. 13, 14)

13. And one of the elders answered, saying unto me, What are these which are arrayed in white robes? and whence came they?

It is not recorded that John asked a question that *one of the elders answered*. Perhaps the elder responded to his unspoken wonder, or perhaps he simply responded to the vision John saw. His response was a question rather than an answer! "Who are these white-robed people, and where did they come from?"

14. And I said unto him, Sir, thou knowest. And he said to me, These are they which came out of great tribulation, and have washed their robes, and made them white in the blood of the Lamb.

John might have guessed who the people were, but he preferred to be told. When dependable revelation is available, guessing is unnecessary. The white-robed people were *they which came out of great tribulation*. This does not necessarily mean one specific short period of great tribulation. It may mean all the tribulations and trials, all the opposition and persecution of Christians through the centuries. These white-robed people endured whatever troubles they faced, and they were faithful. They were not always faultless in their living, of course. They stained their robes with sin, as everybody does. But they *washed their robes, and made them white in the blood of the Lamb.* They believed in Jesus, who shed His blood to atone for their sins. They confessed their sins and asked to be forgiven. They gave themselves wholeheartedly to Jesus and served Him faithfully. Every stain of sin was washed away in His blood, and they stood spotless before the throne.

III. God's Blessing (Revelation 7:15-17)

Two things distinguished the uncounted people who thronged before the throne of God. First, they washed their robes in the blood of the Lamb. That is, they came to Jesus and had their sins forgiven. Second, they came out of great tribulation. They endured all the opposition, persecution, reproach, and slander that was brought against them, and they remained faithful to the Savior. What was the result of their cleansing and their faithfulness? That is what John was seeing in this vision.

A. God's Presence (v. 15)

15. Therefore are they before the throne of God, and serve him day and night in his temple: and he that sitteth on the throne shall dwell among them.

While on earth, they served God in faith, believing that He was on the throne and would bring them out of tribulation in triumph. Now their faith is justified. They have come out of tribulation to see the God they did not see before, to see Him on His throne. In Heaven they *serve Him* continually, *day and night*. Part of their service is to praise Him because He has saved them (v. 10). What other service can God's people give Him in eternity? We are not told, but we can be sure their service will bring Him praise and honor. Here we read that they serve *in his temple*, the special place of His presence. This is not at all opposed to another vision in which John saw no temple (Revelation 21:22). He saw no temple because the Lord God Almighty and the Lamb are themselves the temple. That is, they are everywhere in the eternal home of the redeemed. Verse 15 of our text comes to its climax with a similar thought: *he that sitteth on the throne shall dwell among them.* God the Almighty is not only above them on the throne; He is also among them to serve them as the next two verses indicate.

B. God's Care (vv. 16, 17)

16. They shall hunger no more, neither thirst any more; neither shall the sun light on them, nor any heat.

The redeemed will never be hungry or thirsty; God will supply all their needs. Our sinning ancestors were barred from the tree of life in Eden (Genesis 3;22-24), but sinners made sinless by the blood of the Lamb will find the tree of life bearing fruit continually in the city of God (Revelation 22:2). *Neither shall the sun light on them, nor any heat.* The heat of summer was oppressive often in the Mediterranean countries where John lived, but never in the home eternal where God lives among His people. There no sun is needed, because God and the Lamb are the light (Revelation 21:23). Their light is never too little or too much.

17. For the Lamb which is in the midst of the throne shall feed them, and shall lead them unto living fountains of waters: and God shall wipe away all tears from their eyes.

Jesus is the good shepherd (John 10:11-14). On earth He was the Lamb slain to take away the sins of lost people (John 1:29); in Heaven He is the shepherd who supplies all the needs of those He has cleansed from sin. *God shall wipe away all tears*, all the anguish of great tribulation on earth; and in Heaven there will be nothing to cause another tear to flow (Revelation 21:4).

SORROW TURNS TO JOY

The fire swept rapidly through the mobile home. Neighbors raced into the trailer and found an eighty-five year-old great-grandmother unconscious on the floor. As they pulled her out and began giving her CPR, the woman's daughter ran up to them screaming, "Save my baby, save my baby!" She said her three-year-old grandson was in the burning structure.

By this time, the fire was too intense for anyone to enter the home again. When firefighters finally put out the blaze, they entered but could not find the little boy. One of the firefighters walked around to the back, surveying the damage. There he noticed two scared, wide eyes looking at him from under the trailer. He quickly pulled three-year-old Gerald Voloso from his hiding place. The boy was frightened and dirty, but unharmed.

No one knew how Gerald escaped the fire or why he hid where he did. It didn't matter: he was safe! His grandmother's tears had turned to shouts of joy.

Some day, the Lord Jesus will return for us. When He does, we will be saved from the fires of God's eternal judgment. We may not know all the answers about how we will be saved, but it won't matter: we will be safe, and our tears will be turned to shouts of joy!   —C. R. B.

Conclusion

"In the world ye shall have tribulation." Very plainly Jesus gave that warning, but He added a word of encouragement: "Be of good cheer; I have overcome the world" (John 16:33). Tribulation came soon to the apostles (Acts 5:17, 18, 40). Not much later it spread to the whole church (Acts 8:1). But in it all, the Christians remembered Jesus' encouraging word, and they kept the faith (Acts 8:4).

A. Great Tribulation

It was sixty years later when John saw the visions recorded in the book of Revelation. We have only hints of the tribulation of that time, but hints are enough to show that it was great. John was imprisoned on a tiny island (Revelation 1:9). Some of the Christians at Smyrna were about to be put in jail (Revelation 2:9, 10). A faithful witness had been killed at Pergamos, where Satan ruled (Revelation 2:13).

In the Roman Empire, many imaginary gods were worshiped, and the emperor had been exalted to the position of a god. Everyone was to worship him, and Christians were in trouble because they worshiped only the true God. But trouble with the government was only a part of their tribulation. Neighbors slandered and shunned them. They would not bow to the people's fictitious gods, so they were called atheists. In their meetings, they shared the body and blood of Jesus, so they were called cannibals. Christians had no part in the riotous heathen festivals, so they were called antisocial, haters of humanity.

B. Small Tribulation

Most of us who read this book are not in danger of jail or death because of our faith. Not many of us have ever lost a sale or a job or a friend because we are Christians. We may be unwelcome in some places because we do not care for drinking or gambling; we may meet some scorn because we oppose adultery and abortion. But our government does not oppress us because we are Christians, and most of our neighbors accept and respect us.

Because our tribulation is less, is our devotion also less? Because no great sacrifice is required of us, do we withhold even a small sacrifice?

C. Checkup

In the last week, how much time have you spent in service for the Lord or for the church? Compare it, not with the time spent earning a living, but with the time spent enjoying life—time spent in fun, recreation, loafing, watching TV. How do you rate your devotion to the Lord? Great, good, so-so, poor, bad?

How much money have you given to the Lord's work? Compare it, not with your grocery and electric bills, but with the amount spent on things you could get along without. Does it look as if you really believe that all you have belongs to the Lord?

It is not for us to be burned at the stake as some Christian martyrs have been, but it is for us to present our bodies a living sacrifice, serving God enthusiastically (Romans 12:1).

D. Prayer

Thank You, Father, for those noble Christians who kept the faith through great tribulation. Grateful because our tribulation is less, we would build a devotion no less than theirs. Help us find ways to serve You better and give more generously for Your kingdom.

E. Thought to Remember

"Be thou faithful unto death, and I will give thee a crown of life" (Revelation 2:10).

Learning by Doing

This page contains an alternate lesson plan emphasizing learning activities. Classes desiring such student involvement will find these suggestions helpful.

Learning Goals

After studying Revelation 7:1-17, the student will be able to:

1. Describe what John saw in the part of his vision recorded here.

2. List the characteristics of the redeemed in Heaven.

3. Choose a way to praise God this week through service.

Into the Lesson

Before time for class, make a scrambled verse from the words of Revelation 7:12. Do this by writing each word of the verse on a separate card or small piece of paper. Include a card that contains the Scripture reference. Scramble the pieces and place them in an envelope.

After the class members have arrived, form groups of four to six. Give each group an envelope with the scrambled verse and ask them to try to put the words in the correct order. They may use their Bibles to check the reference when they think they have succeeded.

Allot five minutes for the pupils to complete this task. Check their answers. Then make the transition into the lesson by stating that this is a key idea from today's section of Scripture.

Into the Word

At this time, present the thoughts included in the "Introduction" section of the commentary. Then have one of your class members read aloud Revelation 7:1-15.

Review the Biblical material by asking the following questions. Include thoughts garnered from your study of the lesson to help clarify this Scripture for your students.

1. Why were the angels to wait before they brought destruction to the earth? (v. 3). (To allow for the marking of the servants of God.)

2. How many people were marked with God's seal? (v. 4). (144,000).

3. Who were these 144,000 persons who were marked with God's seal? (See the comments under verse 4 in the commentary section for suggestions that have been offered.)

4. What does this marking mean? (vv. 4-8). (These people will be rescued from the catastrophes that will come at the end of the world. They will not need to plead for the rocks to hide them. See Revelation 6:12-17.)

5. What did the multitude who stood before the throne of God say? (v. 10).

6. Who were these people? (vv. 13, 14). (They were the ones who had been cleansed with the blood of the Lamb.)

7. What are the characteristics of this multitude? (vv. 15-17). (They serve God day and night; they are protected by God; they are not susceptible to hunger, thirst, or heat; the Lamb is their shepherd; God wipes every tear away from their eyes.)

Into Life

Apply this lesson to life by developing a discussion with the following questions.

1. What are the lessons for life from this passage?

2. The *Good News Bible* translates verse 9 this way: "After this I looked, and there was an enormous crowd—no one could count all the people! They were from every race, tribe, nation, and language, and they stood in front of the throne and of the Lamb, dressed in white robes, and holding palm branches in their hands." When you consider this description of the size of the crowd, how do you respond?

3. How do you respond to the statement that the people in this multitude are in the very presence of God?

4. What does this passage have to say to those who are enduring hardships in their daily lives?

5. How would you use this passage to bring comfort to those who doubt their faith when they are in distress?

6. When you think of the glories of Heaven, how does that affect how you live now?

7. Our scrambled verse was the expression of praise given to God by the angels in Heaven. How can we praise God while we are living on this earth?

8. How can our service now be a means of blessing to God? How does it prepare us for eternity with God?

9. How will you serve God this week to prepare for eternity?

Sing the hymn, "Holy, Holy, Holy," slowly and majestically to emphasize the greatness of God and our response to it. Conclude with a time of sentence prayers to praise God for what He has prepared in Heaven for the faithful.

Let's Talk It Over

The questions on this page are designed to encourage review of the lesson Scriptures and to promote discussion of the lesson by the class. The answers provided are only discussion starters. Let your class talk it over from there.

1. What implications may be seen in the fact that people from all nations were among the redeemed assembled before the throne of God?

Certainly we would think of the results of and continuing need for taking the gospel to all peoples of the earth. It could be noted further that these people were one assembly, indicating their unity of spirit and purpose. We should see this as a reminder to refuse to build barriers that separate us from other human beings.

2. What will those who have been redeemed do in Heaven?

The time-worn, distorted representation depicts the redeemed as lolling around on clouds, filling Heaven with music (mostly by strumming harps and by singing). Many people have responded to that picture negatively. They regard it as better than eternal punishment, but it doesn't offer much for all eternity.

John the Revelator gives us significant insight in chapter 7. He cites two important activities of the redeemed: worship and service. The Heavenly multitude will worship God in praise and adoration. They will serve Him continually (the meaning of "day and night" in verse 15). Worship and service give ultimate meaning to both time and eternity!

3. What can be done on earth to make people feel at home in Heaven?

Familiarity with practices and words makes us feel comfortable. People who never have spent time communing with God can hardly be expected to enjoy being in His actual presence. And if one has never served God on earth, will he be any more inclined to do so in Heaven? On the other hand, if in this life we attempt to love God with all of our hearts and do all things to the glory of Christ, perpetual worship in His presence will be a pleasurable experience. To seek first the kingdom of God on earth is to prepare for life in Heaven.

4. List some of the most distinctive differences between conditions we experience on earth and those the redeemed shall experience in Heaven.

On earth we experience pain, sorrow, and grief, but these evils will not exist in God's presence (see Revelation 21:4). On earth we hunger and thirst, but in Heaven the Lord Jesus will provide for all such needs (7:17). There will be no environmental threat, for the sun and heat will not assault us (imagine the implications of that promise to people who had suffered from the sun and heat in the Middle East!). Revelation 22:3 sums it up: "No longer will there be *any* curse" (*New International Version*).

5. Those who stood before God's throne were clothed in white robes. What are the implications of this?

The robe indicates a covering. The "white" indicates purity and righteousness. The robes of the redeemed have been washed and made white in the blood of the Lamb's sacrifice, indicating that the righteousness that is now theirs has come from what Christ has already done for them, and not as a result of their *own* goodness.

The metaphor of the people of God being clad in identifying garments (particularly robes) is used in both the Old and New Testaments. Isaiah 61:10 records, "I will greatly rejoice in the Lord, my soul shall be joyful in my God; for he hath clothed me with the garments of salvation, He hath covered me with the robe of righteousness." Revelation 3:5 affirms that he who overcomes will be clothed in a white garment. Today's chapter (7) confirms the consistent use of this metaphor.

6. In the first century, Christians suffered intense persecution for their faith. Most American Christians today, however, suffer more from stress than from sacrifices made for Christ. What are the most common major causes of stress?

Stress is caused by both external and internal factors. The external causes are clustered in three areas: pressures (such as work demand, shortage of money, disease, polluted environment); events (such as loss of relationships by death or divorce); people (for example, in marriage and family, in bureaucracies). Internally, we are stressed by excessive expectations and guilt, but most of all by attitudes and perspectives. Many times we are our own worst enemies!

The Victorious Christ

LESSON SCRIPTURE: Revelation 19, 20.

PRINTED TEXT: Revelation 19:11-16; 20:11-15.

Revelation 19:11-16

11 And I saw heaven opened, and behold a white horse; and he that sat upon him was called Faithful and True, and in righteousness he doth judge and make war.

12 His eyes were as a flame of fire, and on his head were many crowns; and he had a name written, that no man knew, but he himself.

13 And he was clothed with a vesture dipped in blood: and his name is called The Word of God.

14 And the armies which were in heaven followed him upon white horses, clothed in fine linen, white and clean.

15 And out of his mouth goeth a sharp sword, that with it he should smite the nations; and he shall rule them with a rod of iron: and he treadeth the winepress of the fierceness and wrath of Almighty God.

16 And he hath on his vesture and on his thigh a name written, King of Kings, and Lord of Lords.

Revelation 20:11-15

11 And I saw a great white throne, and him that sat on it, from whose face the earth and the heaven fled away; and there was found no place for them.

12 And I saw the dead, small and great, stand before God; and the books were opened: and another book was opened, which is the book of life: and the dead were judged out of those things which were written in the books, according to their works.

13 And the sea gave up the dead which were in it; and death and hell delivered up the dead which were in them: and they were judged every man according to their works.

14 And death and hell were cast into the lake of fire. This is the second death.

15 And whosoever was not found written in the book of life was cast into the lake of fire.

Nov
19

GOLDEN TEXT: The kingdoms of this world are become the kingdoms of our Lord, and of his Christ; and he shall reign for ever and ever.—Revelation 11:15.

Visians of God's Rule

Unit 4. Revelation: A Message of Hope

(Lessons 10-13)

Lesson Aims

After this lesson students should be able to:

1. Describe the two visions recorded in the text.

2. Explain why some people are safe from the lake of fire.

3. Specify one thing they will do this week because they are grateful for their safety.

Lesson Outline

INTRODUCTION

    A. We Won Because He Won

    B. Lesson Background

I. THE CONQUEROR (Revelation 19:11-16)

    A. The Righteous Warrior (vv. 11-13)

    B. His Armies (v. 14)

    C. His Victory and Rule (vv. 15, 16)

       The Powerful Conqueror

II. THE JUDGMENT (Revelation 20:11-15)

    A. The Judge (v. 11)

    B. The Judged (vv. 12, 13)

    C. The Condemned (vv. 14, 15)

       The Final Embarrassment

CONCLUSION

    A. The Second Death

    B. Prayer

    C. Thought to Remember

Display visual 12 from the visuals/learning resources packet. Let it remain before the class throughout the session. It is shown on page 99.

Introduction

Julie finished her homework and then curled up in an easy chair with her Bible. Much later Mom spoke to her quietly. "Julie, you have to go to school tomorrow. You'd better get to bed."

There was no response. Julie was so engrossed in her reading that she didn't even hear, but she looked up when Mom put a hand on her shoulder and shook it gently. "School tomorrow," Mom reminded. "Sleep tonight."

"Oh, sure." Julie hesitated. "Mom, can I finish this book? Just three more chapters?"

Mom looked around and called for help. "How about it, Daddy? Just three more chapters."

"It's late." Daddy frowned, but he came and

looked over Julie's shoulder. She was reading the book of Revelation. "OK," he conceded. "Finish the book, but don't start another."

Next morning Daddy grinned at Julie over his oatmeal. "Well, how did the book come out?"

Julie flashed him a radiant smile as she answered: *"We won!"*

A. We Won Because He Won

Julie got the message of Revelation. It pictures tremendous conflict, worldwide, earthshaking, agelong; but it pictures victory. There is a crown of life for everyone who is faithful unto death (Revelation 2:10). There is happiness eternal for "him that overcometh" (Revelation 2:7, 11, 17, 26; 3:5, 12, 21). We won!

But we are not alone in the conflict, nor can we win by our effort only. We won because Christ won. We can live because He abolished death and brought life and immortality to light (2 Timothy 1:10). We can stand spotless before the throne of God because we have washed our robes and made them white in the blood of the Lamb (Revelation 7:13-17).

B. Lesson Background

Last week our text ended with a vision of victory. John saw us—you and me—standing with a countless multitude before the throne to praise God and serve Him with endless joy. This lesson begins with a flashback. Again we see conflict before victory, and this time the vision focuses on Christ as the warrior and the victor. While last week's lesson ended with the joyous victory celebration of Jesus' people, this lesson ends with the dark doom of His enemies.

I. The Conqueror (Revelation 19:11-16)

The first part of chapter 19 presents a Heavenly picture similar to the one we saw last week. Earth's conflict is ended. God's enemies are defeated. Triumphant in Heaven, His people give Him praise and honor and glory.

Then our text turns back again to the time of conflict, the time before the final triumph. The fight is on, but victory is assured.

A. The Righteous Warrior (vv. 11-13)

11. And I saw heaven opened, and behold a white horse; and he that sat upon him was called Faithful and True, and in righteousness he doth judge and make war.

And I saw heaven opened. These words introduce a new vision that John saw. The vision preceding it presented a scene in Heaven, a scene of triumphant praise. But this vision shows the Heavenly warrior going forth to war, riding grandly into the conflict that will end in victory. The warrior is Jesus, who in His own time will put all His enemies under His feet (1 Corinthians 15:25). He is called *Faithful and True*. His judgment is always righteous, and His warfare is always just.

12. His eyes were as a flame of fire, and on his head were many crowns; and he had a name written, that no man knew, but he himself.

His eyes were as a flame of fire. They appeared in the same way in the first vision of Revelation (1:14). Nothing could hide from such eyes; they provided their own light to search all the dark places of earth. Their flame could not only find but also destroy all that is evil. But Jesus is like a refiner's fire (Malachi 3:2). When He has burned away all that is evil, all that is good will remain as the pure gold is left when the dross is removed in a refiner's furnace.

On his head were many crowns. Jesus is King of Kings (v. 16). All the kingdoms of the world are to become His (Daniel 2:44; Revelation 11:15). He has all authority in Heaven as well as on earth (Matthew 28:18). All enemies must fall before Him so that He can present to the Father a kingdom triumphant and perfected (1 Corinthians 15:24-28).

And he had a name written, that no man knew, but he himself. What was that name? No man knew it then, and no man knows it now. John saw it written, but even he did not know it. Very interesting and instructive are the names of this Heavenly warrior. As a baby on earth He was given the name *Jesus*, which means Jehovah is salvation or Jehovah saves (Matthew 1:21; Luke 1:31; 2:21). But in the Hebrew way of speaking, *name* did not always mean such a name as would be used in speaking to the person named. In Isaiah 9:6 "His name shall be called" is equivalent to "He shall be." Jesus is "Wonderful, Counselor, The mighty God, The everlasting Father, The Prince of Peace"; but those words are not used as names in the same way *Jesus* is. Sublimely fitting is the name *Immanuel*, God with us (Isaiah 7:14); but that is what Jesus is rather than literally what He was called by the people about Him. Four verses of our text give names of Jesus. He is Faithful and True (v. 11), The Word of God (v. 13), King of Kings, and Lord of Lords (v. 16). He also has a name or description that is known only to Him (v. 12).

13. And he was clothed with a vesture dipped in blood: and his name is called The Word of God.

Clothed with a vesture dipped in blood. This is not explained in our text. Two suggestions have

been offered: (1) This vision pictures Jesus as a conquering warrior. Some students think His vesture was dipped in the blood of His enemies. Note the graphic picture of slaughter in verses 17-21. Compare verse 15; Isaiah 63:1-3; and Revelation 14:19, 20. (2) Some students think Jesus' vesture was dipped in His own blood. His people could stand spotless in God's presence because they had washed their garments in His blood (Revelation 7:13-15). Jesus had no need of such washing because He never stained His robe with sin, but He redeemed His people by shedding His own blood, winning the victory over sin and death. Whether the garment was dipped in His own blood or the blood of His enemies, it was a symbol of His triumph.

His name is called The Word of God. The word *word* is used with various meanings. It may mean a single word like *man* or *tree* or *dish*, or it may mean a bit of news or information, as when we get word of a new baby. We use *Word* in a broad sense when we say the Bible is God's Word. It is a whole collection of His messages to us, the sum total of His communication that has been committed to writing and preserved for us. Jesus is *The Word of God* in a sense that is broader still. He is not only God's communication to us; He is also God's communicator. God's word makes God's will effective. "By the word of the Lord were the heavens made" (Psalm 33:6). "In the beginning was the Word, and the Word was with God, and the Word was God.... All things were made by him.... And the Word was made flesh, and dwelt among us.... No man hath seen God at any time; the only begotten Son, which is in the bosom of the Father, he hath declared him" (John 1:1-18).

B. His Armies (v. 14)

14. And the armies which were in heaven followed him upon white horses, clothed in fine linen, white and clean.

The armies which were in heaven. This phrase makes us think of the holy angels who will be with Jesus when He comes to judge the world (Matthew 25:31). But the armies are *clothed in fine linen, white and clean;* and some students think they are God's people who "have washed their robes, and made them white in the blood of the Lamb" (Revelation 7:14). We need not pause to debate this question, for in this vision it is Jesus who judges and makes war (v. 11). It is He who wins the victory (vv. 15, 16).

C. His Victory and Rule (vv. 15, 16)

15. And out of his mouth goeth a sharp sword, that with it he should smite the nations; and he shall rule them with a rod of iron: and he treadeth the winepress of the fierceness and wrath of Almighty God.

The conqueror's *sharp sword* is not held in His hand; it goes *out of his mouth.* His word, the truth, is all this victor needs to *smite the nations,* to make the kingdoms of the world "become the kingdoms of our Lord, and of his Christ" (Revelation 11:15). Whether we think of His rod as a shepherd's staff or a king's scepter, it is *a rod of iron.* It is a symbol of power that cannot be resisted. Before this conqueror His enemies are helpless, helpless as the grapes that are thrown into the winepress. As the grapes are trampled and crushed in the winepress, so at last shall all God's enemies be crushed.

16. And he hath on his vesture and on his thigh a name written, King of Kings, and Lord of Lords.

The great Leader of the Heavenly armies is further identified. In Revelation 17:14 we read the same title, except in reverse order. There it is applied to the Lamb. The title is most appropriate, for in the final conflict He will conquer all earthly kings and rulers.

THE POWERFUL CONQUEROR

Probably every major city in Europe and the United States has at least one statue of a great king or general in full regalia astride a powerful horse. The mighty steed may be standing nobly or pawing the air in a display of power.

The statue may be at the center of a busy traffic circle with autos, trucks, and buses noisily driving around it. Or it may be in a serene park where one can contemplate life and history. But always, the statue is larger than life—a symbol of the high regard in which the person represented by the statue was held.

However, time is not always kind to these expressions of honor for the heroes of the past. Natural erosion occurs. Vandals may deface the statue with paint. Or, if the government for which the statue was a symbol falls from favor, a rebellious populace may topple the statue.

In the Revelation given to John, our Lord is seen as a mighty conqueror astride a white horse, victorious in battle against the forces of evil. If this image were a statue, time would not erode its surface, it would never be defaced, and never be toppled in disfavor. Christ is the King of Kings and Lord of Lords forever. When all the forces of time have had their day and done their worst, he will still be the powerful conqueror.

—C. R. B.

II. The Judgment (Revelation 20:11-15)

For this lesson we bypass the first part of Revelation 20, not taking time to discuss the millennium, a thousand years in which the devil is bound and helpless. After that time he is released to go about his nefarious business for a while, but finally he must stay forever in the lake of fire (Revelation 20:1-10). The last part of our text pictures the final judgment and the doom of those who have chosen to follow the devil on earth and so must follow him to Hell.

A. The Judge (v. 11)

11. And I saw a great white throne, and him that sat on it, from whose face the earth and the heaven fled away; and there was found no place for them.

Verses 7-10 tell of earth's final conflict and the devil's fate. Now the scene shifts to Heaven. John sees God on His throne. The earth and sky we know are stained with the sins of centuries. They cannot stand in that holy presence. No doubt many people of earth wish they also could flee away, or find a place to hide (Revelation 6:15-17). But they must stay for judgment. There is no way of escape.

B. The Judged (vv. 12, 13)

12. And I saw the dead, small and great, stand before God; and the books were opened: and another book was opened, which is the book of life: and the dead were judged out of those things which were written in the books, according to their works.

Attention is focused on *the dead, small and great.* All the people who ever lived and died on earth were assembled to be judged. *And the books were opened.* No one was judged merely by the whim of the judge. The basis of judgment was a matter of record. It was *written in the books.* It is generally supposed that these books contained a record of everything that each person had done on earth, so *the dead were judged out of those things which were written in the books, according to their works.* Another possibility is that the books were the books of the Bible, God's Word. In them the right way was clearly shown. It was not necessary to write down everything a person did. That was recorded in his memory and God's. In the judgment, each person's deeds were compared with the right way shown in the books. Thus judgment was based on God's Word and a person's works. In any case, we know God's judgment was right. It was proved by the books. Even the person who was condemned could see that he ought to be condemned.

And another book was opened, which is the book of life. It seems evident that this book contained a list of the people redeemed by Christ, those who had "washed their robes, and made them white in the blood of the Lamb" (Revelation 7:13-18). Before that washing, they were stained with sin like everyone else; but their cleansing was complete. Judgment had no terror for them. No sin appeared against them either in the books or in God's memory. Every sin was blotted out (Acts 3:19). It was forgiven and forgotten, remembered no more (Jeremiah 31:34; Hebrews 8:12). If we are redeemed by the blood of the Savior, the list of our past sins will not be read in the hearing of the whole universe. They are no longer on the record. God's eraser is as good as His pen.

13. And the sea gave up the dead which were in it; and death and hell delivered up the dead which were in them: and they were judged every man according to their works.

This verse emphasizes the fact that all the people who ever lived and died were included in the throng before God's throne. Many had been lost at sea, and their bodies had never been found; but *the sea* gave them up for judgment. *Death* handed over all those it held. Instead of *hell*, recent versions read *hades*, which is merely the Greek word printed in English letters. *Hades* is a name for the place or the condition of those who have died. The main idea is that all the dead, without exception, *were judged every man according to their works.* No one, absolutely no one, escaped judgment; but those registered in the book of life were acquitted because all their sins had been taken away.

C. The Condemned (vv. 14, 15)

14. And death and hell were cast into the lake of fire. This is the second death.

In Christ's great war, the last enemy to be overcome is death (1 Corinthians 15:26). John was given a vision of the end of conflict, the final victory. Death was disposed of, never again to trouble mankind. Since people would not die any more, there would be none to go into Hades,

the place of the dead. It too was cast away. Hades is the place or condition of the dead awaiting judgment; *the lake of fire* is the destination of those condemned in the judgment. The first death, the death of the body, brings them to Hades; the lake of fire is *the second death*. Often, and properly, this is called Hell. In John's vision, death itself was put to that second and final death. Its fearsome power was ended forever.

15. And whosoever was not found written in the book of life was cast into the lake of fire.

The lake of fire is prepared for the devil and his angels (Matthew 25:41), but it will be shared by all who prefer to follow the devil instead of Jesus. The gross sinners who do evil will be there (Revelation 21:8), and so will the "nice" sinners who selfishly refuse to do good (Matthew 25:41-46). "All have sinned" (Romans 3:23). If we had nothing but our own goodness to depend on in the final judgment, all of us would be cast into the lake of fire. No one can escape that fiery fate unless he is written in the book of life. I am a sinner. I deserve the lake of fire. How then can I be enrolled in the book of life?

I can come to Jesus, confessing my sin and begging to be forgiven. If I come to Him, He will not cast me out (John 6:37). But saying He is Lord is not enough. I must show that He really is my Lord. That means I must obey Him (Matthew 7:21). I can be buried with Him in baptism for the forgiveness of my sins (Mark 16:16; Acts 2:38; 22:16). But being buried in baptism is useless unless I rise to walk in newness of life (Romans 6:4). To be baptized into Christ is to be clothed in Him (Galatians 3:27). If I say I am in Him, I had better live and act as He did (1 John 2:6). All the good I can do will never earn for me

Home Daily Bible Readings

Monday, Nov. 13—A Son Who Reflects God's Glory (Hebrews 1:1-13)

Tuesday, Nov. 14—A Servant Worthy of Worship (Philippians 2:1-11)

Wednesday, Nov. 15—The One Who Conquers Evil (Colossians 2:8-15)

Thursday, Nov. 16—Witnesses to the Resurrection (1 Corinthians 15:1-11)

Friday, Nov. 17—"If Christ Has Not Been Raised . . . (1 Corinthians 15:12-19)

Saturday, Nov. 18—The Resurrection is True! (1 Corinthians 15:20-28)

Sunday, Nov. 19—Death's Power is Destroyed! (1 Corinthians 15:51-57)

a place in the book of life. Only the gracious forgiveness of my Savior can put me there. But how can I hope to be forgiven if I keep on doing wrong instead of obeying my Savior? He gave His life to take away my sin, but His sacrifice will not avail if I keep on sinning wilfully (Hebrews 10:26-29). This does not mean I cannot be enrolled in the book unless by life is faultless. There is forgiveness for the sins of God's people (1 John 1:8, 9). At the heart of this matter is my own heart. If in my heart I want above all to do my own thing, to have my own way, to do as I please, I am on the way to the lake of fire. If in my heart I want above all to do the Lord's will, He can make me fit to be enrolled in His book of life.

THE FINAL EMBARRASSMENT

"Casey at the Bat," by Ernest Thayer, is one of the most famous American poems ever written. The sad tale of "Mighty Casey" striking out, with the resulting demise of "joy in Mudville," is known by almost every American, and certainly by every baseball fan.

One of the reasons why Casey's story is so famous may be because it reminds us all of our fear of failing and having to live with the embarrassment of it for the rest of our lives. However, there is a greater tragedy: that of failing at life and having to face the eternal consequences of not having placed one's trust in Jesus Christ for salvation.

Dying once, "at the plate" as Casey did, is not the final embarrassment. "The second death" is the Bible's description of the eternal results of sin that can never be lived down.   —C. R. B.

Conclusion

The Power of Positive Thinking. Most of us know that is the title of a famous book, whether we have read the book or not. Many of us also remember a time when everybody was humming a song that urged, "Accentuate the positive." And some whose hair is gray can recall the maxim that a popular psychologist told us to keep repeating: "Day by day, in every way, I am getting better and better."

It is good to accentuate the positive, but it is not good to ignore the negative. Salvation would not be so attractive if damnation were not so revolting. Many who walked the narrow way before us were guided by the assurance that there is a Hell to shun as well as a Heaven to seek. The Bible plainly teaches about the wrath of God (Revelation 6:15-17). "It is a fearful thing to fall into the hands of the living God" (Hebrews 10:31). Our text ends by accentuating the negative: "Whosoever was not found written in the book of life was cast into the lake of fire."

A. The Second Death

Finally someone said it out loud. At a rally for peace, an earnest young speaker declared, "Nothing is worth dying for!"

Not everyone agrees with that statement. Heroes have laid down their lives in many places and many times, confident that freedom and truth and human rights are worth dying for. Jesus also disagreed with the speaker at the rally. He thought the salvation of sinners was worth dying for.

There is a persistent idea that death is the worst thing that can happen to anyone. But the worst thing is not death—not the first death. The second death is the one to be avoided.

Jesus said, "Fear not them which kill the body, but are not able to kill the soul: but rather fear him which is able to destroy both soul and body in hell" (Matthew 10:28). He said, "Whosoever will save his life shall lose it: but whosoever will lose his life for my sake, the same shall save it" (Luke 9:24). It is foolish to give up Jesus and truth and right for the sake of a longer or pleasanter life on earth, for that life must finally be lost in any case. It is wise to lose or give or spend our life on earth to gain life in Heaven, for that life will never be lost.

The Bible does accentuate the positive. Next week we shall see a radiant picture of our eternal home. The Bible speaks briefly, but very plainly, about the second death. It is a lake of fire, as we see in our text. It is a place of torment (Luke 16:28). It is permanent, (Matthew 25:41). "The smoke of their torment ascendeth up for ever and ever" (Revelation 14:11).

Yes, there is a Hell. That is bad news to some. The good news is that no one has to go there. Jesus gave His life to open the way to Heaven. "He that believeth and is baptized shall be saved" (Mark 16:16). If anyone goes to Hell, it is by his own choice.

B. Prayer

How You have loved us, our Father! Even when we were sinners You gave Your Son for us, and He gave His life for us. In gratitude we give our lives to You and to Him. Please help us to be faithful.

C. Thought to Remember

Yes, my names' written there,
On the page white and fair.
In the book of Thy kingdom,
Yes, my names' written there.
                                —Mary A. Kidder

Learning by Doing

This page contains an alternate lesson plan emphasizing learning activities. Classes desiring such student involvement will find these suggestions helpful.

Learning Goals

After studying Revelation 19:11-16 and 20:11-15, students will be able to:

1. Describe the visions recorded in the text.
2. Explain why some people are safe from the lake of fire.
3. Express his thanks to God for deliverance from the penalty for sin.

Into the Lesson

Give each class member a sheet of paper with the following incomplete sentence on it: "When I think of the judgment, I—" Ask them to write two or three responses to the sentence. Allot one or two minutes for this. Then ask each person to compare answers with two other people. When they have done that, lead a brief sharing time with the entire group.

Make the transition into the Bible lesson by stating that today's Scripture text will help us to face the judgment with confidence.

Into the Word

Present the material in the "Introduction" section of the commentary material. Then read aloud Revelation 19:11-16 and 20:11-15.

Divide the class into groups of four to six. Let half of the groups study Revelation 19:11-16, and the other half 20:11-15. Give each group a copy of the following questions to answer.

Revelation 19:11-16

1. What images do you see when you read this text? (This is especially an image of war.)
2. What is the significance of the blazing eyes and the many crowns? (Nothing can escape Christ's judgment; all enemies will fall before Him.)
3. What is the significance of the blood on His garment? (It was a symbol and badge of His triumph.)
4. Why is the rider called the Word of God? (Perhaps it is because Jesus is God's communication and communicator to us.)
5. What is the significance of the sword that comes from His mouth? (It is a symbol of His word, the truth, which shall ultimately prevail.)

Revelation 20:11-15

1. Who appears before the throne for judgment? (All people.)
2. How is each person judged? (According to what is written in the books.

3. What happens to those whose names are not written in the book of life? (They are cast into the lake of fire.)
4. What is another description of the lake of fire? (The second death.)
5. Need Christians fear the judgment? Why? (No. Because they have been cleansed by the blood of Jesus, judgment holds no fear for them.)

After the groups have had six to eight minutes to find the answers, work through the answers as a class. Add thoughts that you have gathered from your study of the text.

Into Life

Ask, "What lessons can believers learn from these Scriptures?" List the class's suggestions.

Have the class work in the same small groups to formulate answers to the following situations. Give each group one situation to discuss.

Situation 1. Sophia tells you that she has been reading the book of Revelation and has become fearful of the final judgment because of the sins she has committed. She isn't sure that she is saved. How would you respond?

Situation 2. Lowell has become disconsolate because evil seems to reign in the world. He has recently confronted two situations that indicate to him that God is not in control of the world. How would you respond?

Situation 3. You are discussing Christianity with a business associate. He says, "Why should I become a Christian. All of the non-Christians I know seem to be doing better than many Christians. What would I gain?" How would you respond?

Situation 4. Bill is a member of a cult that denies that Jesus is the Christ. When you discuss Christianity with him, he says, "There are many paths to God. I'm as sure of eternal life as you are." How would you respond/

Allot five to seven minutes for the groups to try to answer each situation. Then let the entire class discuss each situation.

Continue the discussion by using the following questions.

1. Think back to the opening activity. After studying this text, how do you feel when you think of judgment?
2. How can we serve God in a thankful way for His deliverance to us through Jesus Christ?

Let's Talk It Over

The questions on this page are designed to encourage review of the lesson Scriptures and to promote discussion of the lesson by the class. The answers provided are only discussion starters. Let your class talk it over from there.

1. How can Jesus be called "The Word of God" when we give that title to the Bible?

In the opening segment of today's printed text, John's vision reveals Jesus Christ as the triumphant, warring king bearing the name, The Word of God (Revelation 19:13). There is no contradiction nor inconsistency in applying that appellation to both Jesus and the Bible. The Bible is the Word of God written; Jesus is the Word of God incarnate, living. Both are revelatory, disclosing the nature, character, and will of God. John also wrote the fourth Gospel, beginning that treatise with a powerful and insightful declaration, "In the beginning was the Word, and the Word was with God, and the Word was God" (John 1:1). Then he revealed that "the Word became flesh, and dwelt among us, and we beheld His glory, glory as of the only begotten from the Father, full of grace and truth" (John 1:14 *New American Standard Bible*). This prologue to the Gospel of John meshes perfectly with the Revelation of John (19:13). The *living* Word is revealed in the *written* Word (though its revelation extends beyond merely containing the record of the living Word).

2. Who constitutes the Lord's "army"?

Revelation 19:14 refers to the armies in heaven, which followed the warring king to do battle with the beast and his followers. Apparently, the army is composed of Heavenly beings. This picture is consistent with the phrase, "the Lord of hosts," by which God is characterized many times in the Old Testament. In affirming that the Lord of hosts was with His people, God's spokesmen reminded them that Heavenly armies were arrayed in support of Jehovah against the enemy.

Presently, the Lord's army also includes human participants. The New Testamanet refers to Christians as "soldiers." Military metaphors refer to the Christian life as a struggle "not against flesh and blood, but against principalities, against powers, against the rulers of the darkness of this world, against spiritual wickedness in high places" (Ephesians 6:12).

3. Why is Hell termed "the second death"?

The first death marks the end of temporal life for human beings. That death is neither final nor eternal; those characteristics are reserved for the second death, which John describes as "the lake of fire" (Revelation 20:14, 15). Eternal damnation really *is* death—it is ultimate, final, and everlasting separation from God. To be separated from God is to be cut off from life, expressed in the term *death*. Conversely, to inherit eternal life is to be forever with the living God, the source of life. The first death is not the really important one—that designation must be reserved for "the second death." Christ has already conquered death and the grave, but all who do not share in His conquest must experience an eternity of separation from God, tormented with the devil and his angels in unrelieved suffering.

4. On what bases should anyone believe that eternal damnation awaits the wicked?

First, Revelation 20:15 indicates that those who are not included in the Lamb's book of life will be cast into the lake of fire (compare verse 10). Second, when God was in flesh, in Jesus Christ, He revealed most clearly that the righteous would receive eternal life and the unrighteous eternal damnation. Read Matthew 25:31-46; Mark 9:42-48. Jesus' testimony is consistent with the other teachings in the New Testament on this subject (see, for example, Hebrews 6:4-8 and 10:26-31). Third, the character of God is consistent with this conviction. He is a *holy* God, who does not tolerate the presence of sin and impurity. Those who are not robed in His righteousness are cast out. Fourth, the Biblical principle stands that the matter of sin is not resolved until it is forgiven or punished. If forgiveness is refused, then punishment is the resultant choice.

5. Upon what bases will people be judged?

The judgment, according to everything that is written in the New Testament, will be based on two criteria. From the standpoint of mankind, judgment will be based on works done. This is not to say that one earns salvation by his works. The quality of his works will be judged according to the revealed Word. So judgment is according to what we do in response to the revelation God has given us in His Word.

New Heaven and New Earth

LESSON SCRIPTURE: Revelation 21:1—22:5.

PRINTED TEXT: Revelation 21:1-7, 22-27.

Revelation 21:1-7, 22-27

1 And I saw a new heaven and new earth: for the first heaven and the first earth were passed away; and there was no more sea.

2 And I John saw the holy city, new Jerusalem, coming down from God out of heaven, prepared as a bride adorned for her husband.

3 And I heard a great voice out of heaven saying, Behold, the tabernacle of God is with men, and he will dwell with them, and they shall be his people, and God himself shall be with them, and be their God.

4 And God shall wipe away all tears from their eyes; and there shall be no more death, neither sorrow, nor crying, neither shall there be any more pain: for the former things are passed away.

5 And he that sat upon the throne said, Behold, I make all things new. And he said unto me, Write: for these words are true and faithful.

6 And he said unto me, It is done. I am Alpha and Omega, the beginning and the end. I will give unto him that is athirst of the fountain of the water of life freely.

7 He that overcometh shall inherit all things; and I will be his God, and he shall be my son.

. . . .

22 And I saw no temple therein: for the Lord God Almighty and the Lamb are the temple of it.

23 And the city had no need of the sun, neither of the moon, to shine in it: for the glory of God did lighten it, and the Lamb is the light thereof.

24 And the nations of them which are saved shall walk in the light of it: and the kings of the earth do bring their glory and honor into it.

25 And the gates of it shall not be shut at all by day: for there shall be no night there.

26 And they shall bring the glory and honor of the nations into it.

27 And there shall in no wise enter into it any thing that defileth, neither whatsoever worketh abomination, or maketh a lie: but they which are written in the Lamb's book of life.

GOLDEN TEXT: Behold, the tabernacle of God is with men, and he will dwell with them, and they shall be his people, and God himself shall be with them.
—Revelation 21:3.

Nov
26

Visions of God's Rule
Unit 4. Revelation: A Message of Hope
(Lessons 10-13)

Lesson Aims

After this lesson students should be able to:

1. Briefly describe the holy city that John saw in his vision.

2. Briefly explain why some will live forever in the holy city while others will suffer in the lake of fire.

3. Choose the holy city as their destination and live by that choice.

Lesson Outline

INTRODUCTION

    A. Review in Ninety Seconds

    B. Lesson Background

I. THE HOLY CITY (Revelation 21:1-7)

    A. God's City (vv. 1, 2)

    B. God in His City (vv. 3-6a)

      Wanting to Live Forever

    C. God and His People (vv. 6b, 7)

II. THE GLORIOUS CITY (Revelation 21:22-27)

    A. God's Glory (vv. 22, 23)

    B. Earth's Glory (vv. 24-26)

      Honored Guests

    C. The Inglorious and the Glorious (v. 27)

CONCLUSION

    A. Two Destinations

    B. We Need Help

    C. We Choose

    D. Prayer

    E. Thought to Remember

Display visual 13 from the visuals/learning resources packet and refer to it as you present the thought in the "Introduction" section. The visual is shown on page 110.

Introduction

"Alleluia: for the Lord God omnipotent reigneth." So said a great multitude, and the sound of it was "as the voice of mighty thunderings." "The Lord God omnipotent reigneth. Let us be glad and rejoice, and give honor to him" (Revelation 19: 6, 7). This has been the theme of our studies through the past three months.

A. Review in Ninety Seconds

Can we review the lessons of three months in a minute and a half? Let's try.

In Ezekiel we saw God's rule in the present. His people were captives in Babylon because He decreed it, but even in captivity He was with them. He promised to set them free and lead them back to their own land, and He did it.

In Daniel we saw God's rule in the future. Confidently God pictured the empires, one after another, that would seem to rule the world. But "the Most High ruleth in the kingdom of men, and giveth it to whomsoever he will" (Daniel 4:25). Ultimately His kingdom "shall break in pieces and consume all these kingdoms, and it shall stand for ever" (Daniel 2:44).

In Thessalonians we saw God's rule at the end of earth's history. We shall be caught up "to meet the Lord in the air: and so shall we ever be with the Lord" (1 Thessalonians 4:17).

Revelation pictures conflict—conflict wide in the world and long in time and violent in character. But the passages chosen for our study show God triumphant, and His people share His triumph. The group of studies from Revelation is well titled "A Message of Hope."

B. Lesson Background

The book of Revelation is truly a message of hope, and yet even now some people remain without hope. In last week's lesson, we saw that some will be hopeless through all eternity. "Whosoever was not found written in the book of life was cast into the lake of fire" (Revelation 20:15). For those redeemed from the lake of fire, there is a city that is bright but not burning, a city aglow with the glory of God.

I. The Holy City (Revelation 21:1-7)

If the evils of earth have ever made us wonder who is in charge, these lessons have reassured us. "The Lord God omnipotent reigneth!" He allows evildoers to violate His will for a time because He wants them to have a chance to change from evil to good (2 Peter 3:9). In His own time He will make His rule plain to all. If this earth seems overwhelmed with evil, we "look for new heavens and a new earth, wherein dwelleth righteousness" (2 Peter 3:13). To encourage us while we wait, God gave John a vision of what is to be.

A. God's City (vv. 1, 2)

1. And I saw a new heaven and a new earth: for the first heaven and the first earth were passed away; and there was no more sea.

John saw in a vision what all of us will see in reality if we are faithful to the Savior: *a new heaven and a new earth.* We may wonder why *there was no more sea.* We like to sit on the beach and watch the ceaseless motion of the waves. We like to swim in the water or sail over its surface. We enjoy seafood. Why should there be no more sea in the better world to come? Our text gives no reason. Shall we note a few guesses? (1) The sea can be deadly. Many have perished in it. The new earth will have no such threat. (2) The sea separates people. John may have been keenly aware of this when he was imprisoned on an island and could not be with his brethren on the mainland. There will be no such barrier in the world to come. (3) Some students think the sea is a symbol of the heathen— wild, uncontrolled, in rebellion against God and His law. There will be no unbelief or rebellion in the new earth.

2. And I John saw the holy city, new Jerusalem, coming down from God out of heaven, prepared as a bride adorned for her husband.

Through the centuries from the time of Solomon to the time of Jesus, Jerusalem was the center of the world for God's chosen people. It was the place of God's special presence, symbolized by the Holy of Holies in the temple Solomon built. The rulers of Jerusalem became so godless that they demanded the crucifixion of God's Son; and the people of the area became so rebellious that they provoked the fury of Rome. Both the temple and Jerusalem were destroyed in A.D. 70. But the new and better earth will have a new and better Jerusalem. John saw it *coming down from God out of heaven:* it was not designed by human architects or erected by human builders. Since it was coming down in the vision, some students conclude that our eternal home will be on the new earth, not in Heaven. If so, it will be no less happy. God will be there, filling the place with His glory (v. 23), and righteousness will be there (2 Peter 3:13). But the vision is symbolic. *Coming down from God* may mean simply that God makes the city for us. It matters little whether it be on earth or beyond the skies. Noting that the gates are open (v. 25), some students suggest that we shall be space travelers, flashing among the galaxies at many times the speed of light. This too may be so, but it is a human fancy rather than a divine promise.

Never is a lady so beautiful as on her wedding day, and never was a city so beautiful as *the holy city, new Jerusalem ... prepared as a bride adorned for her husband.* The city was gleaming with jewels and gold, and radiant with the glory of God. Read the description in verses 9-21. In ancient times God was as a husband to Israel, and lamented because Israel was not faithful to the covenant (Jeremiah 31:31-34). In time to come the new Jerusalem will be "the bride, the Lamb's wife" (v. 9). Never again will the bride be unfaithful. This is the church, not in its present faulty condition, but perfected by the power of God.

B. God in His City (vv. 3-6a)

3. And I heard a great voice out of heaven saying, Behold, the tabernacle of God is with men, and he will dwell with them, and they shall be his people, and God himself shall be with them, and be their God.

Lovely as the city is with its gold and jewels, this is its best feature: God will live there with His people. But isn't He here with us even now? Yes, He is. He lives in His church and in each individual Christian (1 Corinthians 3:16; 6:19). But He is invisible to our mortal eyes, and all too often His presence is obscured by our faults and failures. In the new Jerusalem He will be clearly seen. No fault of ours will obscure His presence, for we then shall be faultless. When we become immortal we shall become incorruptible in every way. (1 Corinthians 15:51-53).

4. And God shall wipe away all tears from their eyes; and there shall be no more death, neither sorrow, nor crying, neither shall there be any more pain: for the former things are passed away.

God shall wipe away all tears. Whatever load of grief has been ours, He will lift it from us and set us free. We shall never grieve again, for in that Heavenly city is no cause of grief: no death, no sorrow, no crying, no pain. *For the former things are passed away.* Death has been consigned to the lake of fire (Revelation 20:14), and all our miseries are gone as well. How can this be? Shall we not grieve even in Heaven if some of our loved ones are not there? No, we shall not grieve. With God all things are possible (Matthew 19:26), and it is He who will wipe away all tears.

WANTING TO LIVE FOREVER

Six human heads and one headless body repose, frozen in liquid nitrogen at $-400\,°F$, in a laboratory in Riverside, California. Freezers operated by the same foundation in other cities contain four bodies, eight heads, two cats, and two dogs! These "suspendees," as they are called, are awaiting advances in science that supposedly will allow them to be brought to life at some time in the future. About one hundred other people pay two hundred dollars per year to have a chance to join these suspendees. (There is also a charge of $100,000 at the time of death.)

The reanimation movement—also called "cryonics"—is one of the more bizarre manifestations of the human race's deep-seated desire to escape the hand of death that eventually grasps us all.

How foolish it is to trust one's future to the whims of sinful mortals! How much surer people could be of a resurrection to new life if they would trust God, the Creator of life! —C. R. B.

5. And he that sat upon the throne said, Behold, I make all things new. And he said unto me, Write: for these words are true and faithful.

Behold, I make all things new. This summarizes what John had been seeing. Heaven and earth are new, Jerusalem is new, we are new. All of this is the work of God! *Write.* In the beginning of Revelation we read that John was instructed to write what he was about to see (Revelation 1:11). Now again he is told to write, and he can write with all confidence, *for these words are true and faithful.* The events will happen just as promised. We can depend on it.

6a. And he said unto me, It is done. I am Alpha and Omega, the beginning and the end.

It is done. All things now are made new (v. 5) in the vision, as they will be in reality. *Alpha and Omega* are the first and last letters of the Greek alphabet. What they mean here is immediately explained: *the beginning and the end.* "In the beginning God created the heaven and the earth" (Genesis 1:1). In the end of earthly history, He will make all things new.

C. God and His People (vv. 6b, 7)

6b. I will give unto him that is athirst of the fountain of the water of life freely.

Later John saw the water of life flowing in a river from the throne of God (Revelation 22:1). The meaning is plain. The living God gives life to His people, life abundant and unending; and He gives it *freely*, without cost, as a gift.

7. He that overcometh shall inherit all things; and I will be his God, and he shall be my son.

This promise is not made to everyone in the world, or even to everyone thought to be in the church. It is not for everyone who calls Jesus Lord (Matthew 7:21). The promise is made to a winner, a victor, a conqueror. *He that overcometh* is one who resists the devil and drives him away (James 4:7). He is one who refuses to give in to temptation, one who endures persecution without faltering, one who does right regardless of the cost, one who is faithful unto death. To such a winner this promise is made. Compare Revelation 2:7, 11, 17, 26; 3:5, 12, 21. Note, however, that even such a winner does not earn what is promised. He *shall inherit all things.* An inheritance is given, not earned; but it may be given with certain conditions. A father's last

will and testament may cut off one son without a cent because that son has brought shame and grief to the family, and it may bestow the entire estate on one who has pleased the father by an upright and noble life. So the New Testament of the Heavenly Father cuts off those who shame Him by rebellion or cowardice, and bestows the state on those whose heroic obedience brings honor to the family. It is a tremendous inheritance. Some versions read *these things* instead of *all things*, but these things that are mentioned are all things (v. 5). God's unique Son, Jesus, is the Father's heir (Hebrews 1:2), and God's other sons and daughters are joint-heirs with Him (Romans 8:16, 17). They do not wait for the Father to die before they receive their inheritance; they possess all things together with Him. That does not mean the heir becomes equal to the giver. The Heavenly Father is still *his God*, and he is God's *son*. God is still the provider, the giver; the heir receives blessings from Him.

II. The Glorious City (Revelation 21:22-27)

It was a huge city that John saw. If it were set down in North America, it would stretch from Hudson Bay to the Gulf of Mexico and from Maine to Montana. It it were placed in Europe, it would reach from Dublin to Moscow and from Helsinki to Crete. We admire our skyscrapers, but the new Jerusalem would tower far into outer space. It sparkled with gold and jewels, but we bypass all the brightness described in verses 9 to 21, and go on to consider the greater glory that lightened the city.

A. God's Glory (vv. 22, 23)

22. And I saw no temple therein: for the Lord God Almighty and the Lamb are the temple of it.

In old Jerusalem, the magnificent temple was the special place of God's presence, though no one actually saw Him there. New Jerusalem needs no such building, for there *the Lord God Almighty and the Lamb*, the Christ, are present in their own persons. John saw them; and when John's vision becomes a reality, all God's people will see them.

23. And the city had no need of the sun, neither of the moon, to shine in it: for the glory of God did lighten it, and the Lamb is the light thereof.

God is light (1 John 1:5). On rare occasions the radiance of His glory has been seen on earth. It filled the newly completed tabernacle in the wilderness, indicating that God made it the place of His dwelling among His people (Exodus 40:34). Likewise it filled the temple at Jerusalem when that was completed (1 Kings 8:10, 11). Once on a mountain the divine glory shone from the human body of Jesus, showing that God was within (Matthew 17:1, 2). In the new Jerusalem the divine glory fills the city with light continually.

B. Earth's Glory (vv. 24-26).

24. And the nations of them which are saved shall walk in the light of it: and the kings of the earth do bring their glory and honor into it.

All of *them which are saved* out of all the *nations* of earth will *walk in the light* of God's glory in new Jerusalem. To walk in the light is to see one's way clearly and to follow God's leading thoroughly: it is to do right (John 8:12; 1 John 1:6, 7). *The kings of the earth* like to surround themselves with as much *glory and honor* as they can. All of it that is truly glorious and honorable in the light of God will be preserved in the holy city; but no greed or cruelty, no wicked arrogance, no defiance or rebellion against God can survive.

25. And the gates of it shall not be shut at all by day: for there shall be no night there.

The open gates symbolize freedom and safety. The saved are neither shut out of the city nor imprisoned in it, and there is no need to shut the gates to keep out the unsaved. A great gulf keeps them far away from those open gates (Luke 16:26).

26. And they shall bring the glory and honor of the nations into it.

The holy city has a place for all the real *glory*, all the true *honor*, not only of the kings of earth (v. 24), but also of all the nations. Perhaps more honor will come from peasants' huts than from kings' palaces. All the glory of earth must be dim in comparison with the glory of God, but still it will be welcomed. Those who walk in the light amid earth's darkness will at last be at home in the light of God.

HONORED GUESTS

Before the light of dawn filtered into the cavernous interior of London's Westminster Abbey, the guests had begun to arrive. June 2, 1953, was to be a momentous day, the day on which Elizabeth II would become Queen of Great Britain and the head of the British Commonwealth of nations. Common people had to get there early if they were to have a seat.

The noble, mighty, wealthy, and privileged from around the world had been invited to this great event. These honored guests had special seats in prominent places reserved for them. Most ordinary citizens could only hope to find a spot on the route of the coronation parade, where they might see the new queen as she passed.

Isn't that the way it is with most important happenings in this life? It seems that ordinary people are shut out of the big events, which are made "big" because the celebrities attend.

But not in Heaven! Kings may bring their glory to it, but the true "celebrities" will be those persons whose names God has written in the Lamb's book of life. Great or small in this life, it will make no difference. They shall be the honored guests in Heaven.   —C. R. B.

C. The Inglorious and the Glorious (v. 27)

27. And there shall in no wise enter into it any thing that defileth, neither whatsoever worketh abomination, or maketh a lie: but they which are written in the Lamb's book of life.

The gates are open (v. 25), but nothing dirty can get in. Nothing shameful or false can ever enter there. All that is evil is barred by its own nature. It cannot endure the light of God. Far away across a great gulf is the lake of fire, the destination of all the ungodly (Revelation 20:15). That would be the destination of all of us if the Lamb had not given His life to redeem us. Because we have put our trust in Him and have devoted our lives to Him He has redeemed us, and purified us, and sanctified us, and written our names in His book of life. By His grace we can enter the open gates and walk in the light of God's glory forever.

Conclusion

This earth is not forever. It is going to be burned up (2 Peter 3:10). If that does not happen

Home Daily Bible Readings

Monday, Nov. 20—Sing a New Song! (Psalm 96)

Tuesday, Nov. 21—Break Forth into Praises! (Psalm 98)

Wednesday, Nov. 22—Zion's Happy Future (Isaiah 35)

Thursday, Nov. 23—God Creates Anew (Isaiah 65:17-25)

Friday, Nov. 24—Glory of the New Jerusalem (Revelation 21:9-14)

Saturday, Nov. 25—A City Beyond Description (Revelation 21:15-21)

Sunday, Nov. 26—God, Our Light and Ruler Forever! (Revelation 22:1-5)

visual 13

VISIONS
OF GOD'S RULE

EZEKIEL:
God rules now

DANIEL:
God rules the future

THESSALONIANS:
God rules the end of time

REVELATION:
God rules eternally

in this century or the next, we who are now living on the earth will leave it. What then? Where shall we go?

A. Two Destinations

God's Word pictures two destinations for those who leave this earth. There is the holy city described in our text, and there is everlasting fire prepared for the devil and his angels (Matthew 25:41). Between the two is a great gulf (Luke 16:26), but nobody lives there.

We can choose our destination, and the time to choose is now. But the choice is not one to be made once and then forgotten. It is a choice to live by as long as we live on earth.

If we decide to choose the holy city, we choose to do what God wants us to do (Matthew 7:21). We choose to believe in Jesus and to show our faith by adding virtue, knowledge, temperance, patience, godliness, brotherly kindness, and love; "for so an entrance shall be ministered unto you abundantly into the everlasting kingdom of our Lord and Saviour Jesus Christ" (2 Peter 1:5-11).

If we choose the holy city, we choose to resist the devil and drive him away (James 4:7). He is strong and threatening as a roaring lion. We must be sober and vigilant, steadfast in our resistance (1 Peter 5:8, 9). He is crafty, disguising himself as an angel of light (2 Corinthians 11:14). We must be wise as serpents and harmless as doves (Matthew 10:16).

If we choose the holy city, we choose to live by our choice as long as we are on earth. We must not get tired of doing good, for our reaping depends on our continuing (Galatians 6:9, 10). We must be faithful unto death to receive a crown of life (Revelation 2:10).

B. We Need Help

If we choose the holy city and faithfully live by that choice, then have we earned a right to the new Jerusalem? No, we are not that good. If we do all we ought to do from now on, we are still unprofitable servants (Luke 17:10). If the holy city is our chosen destination, we need help. We can't get there without it.

All of us have sinned (Romans 3:23). The wages of sin is death. If we receive eternal life instead, it is a gift, not a right (Romans 6:23). If we are saved from death, we are saved by God's grace because of our faith, not because of the good we do (Ephesians 2:8, 9).

We are not saved by doing good, but neither are we saved without doing good. In the final judgment, each person is judged by what he has done, and according to what he has done he is assigned to his destination (Matthew 25:31-46; Revelation 20:11-15). "Ye see then how that by works a man is justified, and not by faith only" (James 2:24). So our faith has a part in our salvation, and our works have a part; but nothing we have can buy a ticket to the holy city, and nothing we do can earn our way there. We each need help.

Fortunately for us, help is available. Jesus died to atone for our sins. He paid the penalty. He suffered the death that we deserve. Therefore we can be forgiven and cleansed. We can stand in judgment as spotless as if we had never sinned. Praise the Lord!

C. We Choose

We choose our eternal destination. The holy city is offered to all. "The Spirit and the bride say, Come. . . . And whosoever will, let him take the water of life freely" (Revelation 22:17). "The Lord is . . . not willing that any should perish" (2 Peter 3:9). If any perish in the lake of fire, the second death, it is by their own choice. If any survive in the holy city, it is by their own choice and God's help.

We can choose to stand up in haughty pride and say, "We need no help. No one is going to tell us what to do. We will do as we please!" That is the way to the lake of fire.

On the other hand we can devote our lives to God's service, confessing our sins and looking to Him for forgiveness. That is the way to the holy city.

The choice is ours.

D. Prayer

Using the words of the hymn writer William Williams, we pray,

"Guide me, O Thou great Jehovah,
   Pilgrim through this barren land;
I am weak, but Thou art mighty;
   Hold me with Thy powerful hand."

E. Thought to Remember

We are choosing now.

Learning by Doing

This page contains an alternate lesson plan emphasizing learning activities. Classes desiring such student involvement will find these suggestions helpful.

Learning Goals

After this study the learner will be able to:

1. Describe the holy city that John saw in his vision.

2. Explain why some will live forever in the holy city while others will suffer in the lake of fire.

3. Thank God for the final victory that belongs to those who follow Jesus.

Into the Lesson

As the class members arrive, divide them into groups of four or five. Ask each person in each group to describe the most beautiful place he has ever seen. Encourage them to be as descriptive as possible, including features such as colors, sounds, etc. Have each group select one description to be shared with the entire class.

After the groups have had a few minutes to do their work, call the class together. Let the spokesman from each group share his description.

Make the transition into the Bible study section by stating that today's text speaks of a place so beautiful that the writer could hardly find words to describe it.

Into the Word

Present the material in the "Introduction" section of the commentary. Then read aloud Revelation 21:1-7, 22-27.

Develop a guided study through the Scripture text by using the following questions.

1. What did John first see in this vision? (v. 1). (He saw a new heaven and new earth, which had replaced the old heaven and earth.)

2. What is the significance of describing the holy city, the new Jerusalem, as a bride adorned for her husband? (v. 2). (Those who are in Heaven are the church—and the church is described as the bride of Christ. See Ephesians 5; Revelation 21:9, 10.)

3. What are the characteristics of this new city? (vv. 3-6). (God lives there; there is no death or sorrow or pain; everything is new; God provides eternal life for those who are there.)

4. What is the significance of the statement that God is Alpha and Omega? (v. 6). (These are the first and last letters of the Greek alphabet. God reigned at the beginning; He will reign at the end of time.)

5. Who will enter the new city? (vv. 7, 27). (Those who have won the victory—that is, those who have claimed Jesus Christ as Savior and have followed Him faithfully. Verse 27 says that only those whose names are written in the Lamb's book of life will enter the city.)

6. Why is there no temple in the new Jerusalem? (v. 22). (None is needed since God and the Lamb are there.)

7. Describe the city (vv. 22-27). (God and the Lamb provide the light; the gates are never closed; the glory and honor of kings and nations will be brought there; nothing impure will be in the city.)

8. What is the significance of the descriptions provided in verses 22-27? (The inhabitants of the city will experience God's continuous presence; all who are there will honor and glorify God; all will enjoy freedom and safety.)

Lead the class members through the questions. Fill in gaps in their answers with information garnered from your study.

Into Life

Ask, How do you feel when you read a passage such as Revelation 21:1-7, 22-27? Let the students spend a brief amount of time responding. Then divide them into groups of four to six. Give each group one of the tasks below.

Task 1. For thirteen weeks we have studied visions of the future. Today we have considered new Jerusalem. When you think about that, how do you respond to God? Your group is to write a song that expresses your feelings to God. You may use a known tune and write new words to it.

Task 2. For thirteen weeks we have studied visions of the future. Today we have considered the new Jerusalem. When you think about that, how do you respond to God? Write a poem that expresses your feelings to God.

Task 3. For thirteen weeks we have studied visions of the future. Today we have considered the new Jerusalem. When you think about that, how do you respond to God? Write a prayer that expresses your feelings to God.

Allot ten minutes for the groups to do this. Then let each group share in turn, beginning with the poem, going next to the song (which everyone should sing), and concluding with the prayer to end the session.

Let's Talk It Over

The questions on this page are designed to encourage review of the lesson Scriptures and to promote discussion of the lesson by the class. The answers provided are only discussion starters. Let your class talk it over from there.

1. How are we to interpret John's description of Heaven?

Two approaches have persisted over the years: the *literal* and the *figurative* interpretations. Does John mean to tell the people of all centuries and cultures that Heaven is a walled city with twelve gates, and that the city is a vast cube measuring fifteen hundred miles each way? (See Revelation 21:16.) A principle that must be kept in mind as we attempt to understand John's vision is that the known is used to communicate the unknown. There is no other way to communicate the unknown. One cannot describe or define something that has no point of reference in a person's experience.

John uses the grandest and most glorious "known" (streets of gold, foundations and walls of precious gems, and gates, each of which is composed of a giant, single pearl) to communicate the unknown. He is saying, "Heaven is perfect; it is beyond anything you can imagine. To people in the twentieth century, walls and gates have little meaning or importance—they offer *no* protection against nuclear weapons and space-age technology. But to the people of John's day, walls and gates signified protection and safety. We would be wise to accept the realities that stand behind the symbolic representations. Heaven is real—more real than physical reality, difficult as that may be for us to understand. Heaven is a place, prepared by God (who is spirit) for His people, who will inhabit spiritual, glorified bodies in His presence for eternity.

2. Why is the assurance given that we will not grieve in Heaven?

In our present existence, grieving over significant losses can blight all of life's relationships and experiences. But the perfection of Heaven will not be marred by loss and grieving, by pain and tears. Most people are concerned about whether they will share Heaven with their loved ones. The revelation given to John provides insight from a different perspective. He was told that the former things have passed away (21:4): not only the losses and the grieving, but (by implication) also the focus of relationships. In Heaven, the focus will be on the divine family, the family of God, not on the former relationships that existed among family members on earth. Jesus spoke concerning this matter when He informed His adversaries that those who live in the next world will neither marry nor be given in marriage (Luke 20:27-36).

3. How will God be with people differently in Heaven than now in light of the fact that God is Spirit?

There are barriers erected by sin that now keep us from having the clearest view of God. He will be with us in spirit, but it also may be that because of our new bodies and the new heaven and new earth, we shall be much more aware of His presence. We don't really know just how it will be, but all indicators seem to point to a much closer and more readily identifiable presence.

4. What significance do you see in God's statement, "It is done"?

Even though the action of which He spoke has not taken place, the outcome of it has been determined. Once God's word has been given on a matter, the matter is considered concluded. This same principle applies to our present living. Regardless of current events or how people of the day think about a matter, if God has spoken on the subject, it is as He says it is.

5. What responsibilities belong to the present-day Christian because of the fact that Heaven is for those who have overcome?

First is the responsibility of faithfulness. Each member of the kingdom has personal responsibility for his own faithfulness. If he does not overcome the temptations to go astray, he will not enjoy the blessings of Heaven. Purity and loyalty are absolutely essential.

Also the awesome responsibility for evangelism falls upon earthly members of the kingdom. Without obedient faith no person is able to overcome. Without hearing the gospel of Jesus Christ one is not able to come to obedient faith. Because the church has been given the responsibility for evangelism, and because only those who overcome can inherit Heaven, each member of the church on earth has a part in the work of helping the other people of the world to overcome.

Winter Quarter, 1989-1990

Theme: John: The Gospel of Life and Light

Special Features

Lessons

Unit 1: Jesus Comes to His Own

Unit 2: Jesus Reveals Himself

Unit 3: Jesus Prepares His Followers

Related Resources

The following publications are offered to give more detailed help on the subjects of study presented in the Winter Quarter. They may be purchased from your supplier. Prices are subject to change.

God's Word A.D., by LeRoy Lawson. Order #11-41022, $2.95.

John (Standard Bible Studies), by Lewis Foster. Order #11-40104, $8.95.

Say Hello to Life, by Rod Huron. Order #11-41032, $2.95.

Teach With Success, Revised, by Guy P. Leavitt; revised by Eleanor Daniel. Order #18-03232, $7.95.

The Lord of Love, by LeRoy Lawson. Order #11-39941, $2.75.

The True Life, by Lewis Foster. Order #11-40047, $2.25.

You Can Teach Adults Successfully, by Ronald Davis, Mark Plunkett, Dan Schantz, Rick Shonkwiler, Mark Taylor. Order #18-03208, $2.95.

Dec 3
Dec 10
Dec 17
Dec 24
Dec 31
Jan 7
Jan 14
Jan 21
Jan 28
Feb 4
Feb 11
Feb 18
Feb 25

Thunder and Light

by Edwin V. Hayden

THERE IS NOTHING BASHFUL or shy about the Gospel according to John. It opens by asserting that the Word, later to become the man Jesus of Nazareth, was identified with God eternal and participated with Him in the creation of all things. It concludes by asserting that its writer was the "disciple whom Jesus loved," that he knew what he was talking about, and that he told the truth; also that the world itself could not contain a complete account of all Jesus said and did.

This Gospel bursts the bonds of time and space! It speaks unabashedly about God and Satan, light and darkness, life and death. It proclaims Jesus Christ as the one and only way to life eternal. It is full of paradoxes and bold comparisons as it depicts the Savior healing with a touch or withering with a word as the occasion demanded.

Thunderous Disciple

The forcefulness of John's Gospel is no wonder. This disciple whom Jesus loved was one of the "sons of thunder" (Mark 3:17), strangely suited to understand and to make understandable the infinite scope and variety of qualities he found in Jesus, the Lord of glory.

John lived near the center of the gospel facts. He had a brother James, who was probably older. They were sons of Zebedee and partners with their father in a fishing business sufficiently profitable to provide its own equipment and to hire helpers (Mark 1:19, 20). Later we learn that John kept a residence in Jerusalem (John 19:27) and that the high priest was among his acquaintances (John 18:15, 16).

By comparing Matthew 27:56 with Mark 15:40 and John 19:25 we may infer that Mary the mother of Jesus and Salome the mother of John were sisters; hence John was a first cousin of Jesus and related also to John the Baptist (Luke 1:36). It is not hard to imagine that John was brought up with some knowledge of the angelic announcements by which the births of both John the Baptist and Jesus were foretold. When, therefore, the Baptizer came preaching in the wilderness of Judea, the sons of Zebedee were prepared to take time off from their fishing in Galilee and take their place among his followers. They were also ready to accept his declaration concerning Jesus, "Behold the Lamb of God, which taketh away the sin of the world" (John 1:29, 35-40). We must admit, however, that any such family relationship as we have just inferred must have seemed less important to the apostles than it seems to us, or it would have been spelled out more plainly in the inspired record.

In any case, these earliest disciples were with Jesus when He first ministered in Galilee. They observed His first miracle and believed in His power (John 2:1-11). They did not finally leave their fishing boats and nets to become companions and learners of the Lord until some months later when He plainly called them to become fishers of men (Luke 5:1-11; Matthew 4:18-22; Mark 1:16-20).

It is not uncommon for a parent or teacher to develop a special attachment to the child or student whose liveliness breaks out most often in troublemaking. So Jesus made special companions of Zebedee's sons, whom He nicknamed *Boanerges* (sons of thunder) and Simon Peter, who frequently spoke up first and thought about it later. We find hints to justify the nickname for James and John. They were ready to call down fire on a Samaritan village where the disciples were refused a night's lodging, and John was ready with a rebuke to the unauthorized stranger who cast out demons in the name of Jesus (Luke 9:49-56). The two stirred up trouble again when they applied for top-level positions in the coming kingdom (Mark 10:35-45).

One of these who caused Jesus the most trouble became the "disciple whom Jesus loved" (John 13:23; 19:26; 20:2; 21:7, 20). Along with Simon Peter and James he accompanied Jesus on the Mount of Transfiguration, and at the raising of Jairus' daughter, and in Gethsemane, while others were kept at a distance. he was nearest of all to Jesus at the table on their final evening. John was fully prepared, then, to write, "That which was from the beginning, which we have heard, which we have seen with our eyes, which we have looked upon, and our hands have handled, of the Word of life . . . that which we have seen and heard declare we unto you, that ye also may have fellowship with us" (1 John 1:1-3).

Powerful Witness

John, who seems to have been younger than the other apostles, outlived them all, and recorded his Spirit-prompted memories of Jesus.

John's style of writing is plain, powerful, and often poetic. Many times during his long ministry he must have spoken the words he finally committed to writing for all the world to read. In speaking or writing, his purpose was the same: "That ye might believe that Jesus is the Christ, the Son of God; and that believing ye might have life through his name" (John 20:31).

We have mentioned the bold, plain contrasts that characterize John's Gospel, with its emphasis on Jesus the light, who came to dispel darkness; Jesus the way—the one way—to God; Jesus the truth that sets men free from the shackles of error and falsehood; and Jesus the life, who came to conquer death for all who in faith would receive a share in the conquest.

These contrasts, however, are not the inventions of John. They are the qualities of the One about whom John wrote. They are characteristics of the living Word, which came and dwelt among men, before they ever found their way into the written word that tells His story. The paradoxes recorded by John are the paradoxes he found in Jesus, the divine Son of God who became Son of man; full of grace and full of truth; Lord and Master and servant of all.

Distinctive Gospel

John's Gospel does, however, tell its own special story of Jesus, filling in gaps left by the other Gospel writers. Instead of Jesus' parables reported by the others, it emphasizes His more intimate teaching sessions with the apostles, His one-on-one conversations with such as Nicodemus and the unnamed woman of Samaria, and the public teaching confrontations that grew out of certain miracles.

This singular quality of John's Gospel receives full attention in our Bible-school lessons for the next twenty weeks, under the general title, "John: The Gospel of Life and Light." The material studied will be for the most part what is found in John and not in the other Gospels.

Four units are outlined:

Unit 1 (four lessons in December), "Jesus comes to His Own," presents Jesus' person and His purpose for coming into the world. It concludes with a Christmas lesson.

Unit 2 (five lessons, December 31 and January), "Jesus Reveals Himself," shows the manner and goal of Jesus' making himself known. It reveals a rising tide of resistance against Him.

Unit 3 (four lessons in February), "Jesus Prepares His Followers," points to His appointment with the cross, and shows how He instructed His disciples for their continuing ministry.

Unit 4 (seven lessons in March and April), "Jesus Lays Down His Life," deals with Jesus' trials, death, and resurrection. It concludes with an Easter lesson.

In this quarter we shall deal with only the first three units. Let us look at them a bit more closely.

Unit 1, "Jesus Comes to His Own"

Lesson 1, "Born to Bear Witness," from John 1, deals directly with John the Baptist, but presents his testimony concerning Jesus.

Lesson 2, "Born of the Spirit," from John 3, tells of Jesus' conversation with Nicodemus and reports His requirement of "birth from above."

Lesson 3, "Savior of the World," from John 4, recalls Jesus' conversation with the Samaritan woman at Jacob's well, and Jesus' mission to all peoples.

Lesson 4, "The Word Among Us," from Luke 2 and John 1, sets forth the coming of Jesus as God's Son, the eternal Word, into the world.

Unit 2, "Jesus Reveals Himself"

Lesson 5, "Jesus Reveals Himself Through Healing," from John 5, recounts the healing of a lame man on the Sabbath, resulting in controversy over Sabbath breaking.

Lesson 6, "Jesus Reveals Himself Through Scripture," from John 5 (continuing), calls forth the testimony of the words and the works of God—including the Old Testament Scriptures—to Jesus' identity as the promised Messiah.

Lesson 7, "Jesus Reveals Himself as the Bread of Life," from John 6, reviews the Lord's sermon on that subject after the miraculous feeding of the five thousand.

Lesson 8, "Jesus Reveals Himself by Setting People Free," from John 8, shows Him to be the source of freedom from sin, its power and its punishment.

Lesson 9, "Jesus Reveals Himself as the Light of the World," from John 9, tells of His healing a man blind from birth. Spiritual implications follow.

Unit 3, "Jesus Prepares His Followers"

Lesson 10, "Acceptance and Rejection," from John 12, begins with Greeks seeking Jesus, and proceeds to prediction of His death.

Lesson 11, "In the Image of the Servant," from John 13, recounts His washing of the disciples' feet, and His exhorting them to humility.

Lesson 12, "The Way, the Truth, the Life," from John 14, reports conversation following the Last Supper, with insistence on Jesus' identity with God as the only way to know Him.

Lesson 13, "Promise of the Spirit," from John 14 (continuing), brings Jesus' provision for another Companion and Advocate to sustain His disciples after His departure.

May you and your people find light and life in this study of the Gospel of John!

Why Jesus Came

by Paul McReynolds

Jesus came into the world because He was sent.

During His ministry, Jesus himself told various audiences why He came into the world. The initial reason for His coming is summarized in His words, "For I have come out of God and am present; for I have come not from myself [of my own accord] but that one [God] sent me" (John 8:42).* John 7:28 records Jesus' statement, "I have not come from myself, but the one having sent me is True." These passages clearly state that Jesus came from God. The source of Jesus' coming is critically important. In John 8:14 we see that Jesus knew both where He was from and where He was going, but His audience knew neither where Jesus was from nor where He was going. For if they had known, they would have trusted in Him. Jesus came because God sent Him.

Jesus repeatedly pointed to God as the one who sent Him. Just prior to the raising of Lazarus, Jesus prayed, "I spoke for the sake of the crowd standing around, in order that they might trust that you sent me" (John 11:42). A short time later Jesus cried out to the authorities, "The one trusting in me does not trust in me but in the one having sent me, and the one watching me watches the one having sent me" (12:44, 45).

God was the initiator for the coming of Christ, because it was God's plan to save the world through His Son. "For God loved the world so much, that he gave his only-born Son in order that everyone trusting in him might not be destroyed but might have life eternal. For God did not send the Son into the world in order that he might judge the world, but in order that the world might be delivered through him" (John 3:16, 17). God was the initiator and Jesus was the obedient Son. Jesus came down from Heaven not to do His own will but the will of God who sent Him (John 6:32). And God's will/want is clearly expressed in verse 40, "For this is the want of my Father, that everyone watching the Son and trusting in him might have life eternal." Jesus came because God sent Him.

Jesus was sent from Heaven into a corrupt, rebellious, and sinful world. If we would compare even our understanding of Heaven and this world, we would have some insight into the contrast that was set before Jesus. As Paul put it in Philippians 2:6-8, Jesus was on an equality with God, but He emptied himself and took the form of a servant and became obedient to death, even death on a cross. The contrast helps us to understand, if only slightly, the tremendous chasm that sin caused between God and His creation. The holiness of God is contrasted with the sinfulness of human beings in this world. And God sent His Son to bridge the chasm.

Jesus came into the sinful world as the light, and men loved the darkness more than the light because their works were evil (John 12:46; 3:19). The chasm between God and His people is well illustrated in John by this contrast between light and darkness. In our presentation of the good news today, we should also expect that some will want the darkness rather than the light. Another indication of the chasm between God and His people is stated by John at the beginning of his book, namely, that Jesus came to the very people who ought to have welcomed Him, and they rejected Him (1:11).

Behind the whole creation and every good thing, we must see God as the planner and initiator. After God created the world, He looked and saw that everything was good. When through man's rebellion sin entered the world, God had already made plans to reconcile the world to himself. The plan included the coming of Jesus.

God's plan included obedience—in this case, the obedience of His Son Jesus. God plans and initiates, but obedience must follow in order for His plans to be complete. Jesus came into this world to do what God wanted. He was the obedient Son. He was not like the son who, when his father asked him to work in the vineyard, said he would go and then did not go. Jesus not only came, but He performed the will of God up to and including His death on the cross. Because Jesus was tempted in all points as we are, yet was without sin, we may think that He had an easy time being obedient. But His struggle in Gethsemane revealed that He besought God if there might not be some other way to accomplish His desires. But God had planned, initiated, and sent. Difficult as His mission was, Jesus was obedient, and so should we be.

Jesus came because He was sent to die.

Several times Jesus used the expression, "My hour has not yet come" (John 2:4, 7:6, 8) to indicate that improper use of His power might touch off a premature arrest or even a rebellion. But in due time He said, "The hour has come that the Son of Man might be glorified" (12:23) and, "For this reason I have come to this hour" (v. 27). The hour was the time of His death. Jesus had come to die. It may seem strange that Jesus described His death as the time of His glorification. But it was so, because in dying He was supremely obedient to God's will.

While initially Jesus came into the world because God sent Him, the purpose for His coming was that He would die as an atonement for the sins of all people. John the Baptist made this clear when he referred to Jesus as the Lamb of God who would take away the sin of the world (John 1:29). The Hebrew picture of a lamb being killed was a picture of sacrifice for sins. Jesus referred to himself as the living bread, and He identified that bread as His flesh, which He would give on behalf of the world (6:51). Even Caiaphas, the hostile Jewish ruler, prophesied, though unknowingly, that it was expedient that one man should die on behalf of the people so that the whole nation might not be destroyed (11:49-52). In an editorial comment, John mentions this again in connection with Jesus' trial before Annas (18:14). At the trial of Jesus before Pilate it again became clear that Jesus' death would not be for His own sins. Pilate again and again declared Jesus innocent (18:31, 38; 19:6), but he finally caved in to political pressure and handed Jesus over to be crucified (19:12, 16). All of this clearly shows that Jesus came because He was sent to die on behalf of our sins.

Jesus came because He was sent to die that we might live.

When Jesus described himself as the door of the sheep, He said that all who had come before Him were thieves and robbers. Their purpose in coming was only to steal, kill, and destroy. Jesus then stated explicitly that He had come in order that all men might have life, and that they might have it abundantly (John 10:7-10). Rather than to steal, kill, and destroy, Jesus came to be killed on our behalf. It is in His death that we may have life. The implication of that statement is that apart from sharing in His death we do not have life, at least not the life that He was talking about. The abundant life is not a life that is equal to physical life. Abundant life coexists with physical life, but it goes beyond it. It is life in Christ; it is life eternal, which begins now with trust in Christ and, because of that trust, never ceases to exist. Life eternal is not a quantitative life in terms of years. Life eternal is qualitative life, that is, life in the new aeon/world/age/kingdom of God/Heaven. That life begins

with our union with Christ and does not have an end. Thou who receive Jesus' words and believe in God will not be condemned but have gone over out of death into life (5:24).

The Jews of Jesus' day thought they could find eternal life in the Scriptures, specifically by obeying the law. Jesus told them that those same Scriptures, which they were searching to find eternal life, testified of Him (John 5:39). And Jesus is the real source of life! To share this truth with everyone was John's purpose in writing his Gospel account. He testified to Jesus so that his readers of all ages would believe that Jesus is the Christ, the Son of God, and that believing they would have life in His name (John 20:31).

Life in Christ is a major theme in John's Gospel. Jesus came to give life to such persons as the woman at the well through living water, to the hungry through the living bread, and to the wandering sheep through a shepherd who cares and gives his life for them. Indeed, He gives eternal life to all who believe in Him, for He is the resurrection and the life (John 11:25).

Jesus came because He was sent to die in order that we might live. Life eternal comes through trusting in the Son. John relates the opposite of this in 3:36 when he records the words of Jesus, "But the one not obeying the Son will not see life." This passage makes clear that trusting and obedience are really parallel terms.

In one of His resurrection appearances to His apostles, Jesus said, "Just as the Father has sent me, I also send you" (John 20:21). Part of Jesus' purpose in coming, then, was to draw believers to himself and then to send them out into the sin-darkened world as partners with Him in His mission. Just as Jesus came to bring us life, we must be willing to share with others that message of abundant life.

*Scripture quotations are the author's own translations.

Answers to Quarterly Quiz on page 120

Lesson 1—1. Isaiah. 2. dove. **Lesson 2**—1. miracles. 2. water, Spirit. **Lesson 3**—1. a drink of water. 2. living water. 3. two days. **Lesson 4**—1. fear. 2. grace, truth. **Lesson 5**—1. Bethesda. 2. true. **Lesson 6**—1. love. 2. Moses. **Lesson 7**—1. bread. 2. flesh, world. **Lesson 8**—1. continue. 2. murderer. **Lesson 9**—1. light. 2. false. **Lesson 10**—1. true. 2. false. **Lesson 11**—1. true. 2. false. 3. false. **Lesson 12**—1. true. 2. true. **Lesson 13**—1. true. 2. false.

The Light of the World

by Robert Lowery

The whole world was lost in the darkness of sin;
  The Light of the world is Jesus;
Like sunshine at noonday His glory shone in,
  The Light of the world is Jesus.

Have you ever thought about how much the imagery of light enters our daily conversations? We hear someone proclaim near the end of one of life's dark times, "I can see the light at the end of the tunnel!" A person finally solves a problem after much struggle and announces, "I have seen the light!"

A preacher reminds us that as Christians we are the light of the world. From childhood to the grave, we sing songs focusing on the theme of light: "This little light of mine, I'm going to let it shine." "Let the lower lights be burning! Send a gleam across the wave!" "There's a call comes ringing o'er the restless wave, 'Send the light!' There are souls to rescue, there are souls to save, 'Send the light!'"

In our Sunday-school classes and youth group meetings, in our worship services, and in our talking to those who have not accepted Christ as Lord, we realize that our good news must reach people who are lost. Our good news "shall turn their hearts to the right"; our good news is "a story of peace and light." If the imagery of light is found so frequently in our own speaking, singing, and sharing, we should not be surprised that the imagery was a popular one in Bible times as well.

In the religious thought of the world of the New Testament, matters associated with God were often conceived in terms of light. On the other hand, the power and powers of evil and everything associated with evil were thought of in terms of darkness. The contrast between light and darkness is found, of course, in the Old Testament. Light is used on numerous occasions to represent the revelation of God. God enlightens and saves (Psalms 27:1; 36:9). His word is a light (Psalm 119:105; Isaiah 2:2-5), bringing blessing, joy, and peace to men. In contrast, darkness signifies evil, misery, and punishment (Isaiah 5:20; Psalm 88:6; Amos 5:18). But God comes to man in order to enable him to pass from darkness to light (Psalm 18:28; Isaiah 42:7).

The New Testament proclaims, especially in the Gospel of John, that the days of man's spiritual darkness are over. Jesus, the light of the world, has come.

The Gospel According to—You

No darkness have we who in Jesus abide,
  The Light of the world is Jesus;
We walk in the Light when we follow our Guide,
  The Light of the world is Jesus.

Among those who answered the call of Jesus was one named John, the beloved disciple. Near the end of his life, some sixty years after Jesus had returned to His Heavenly Father, John wrote an account of the life of Jesus. With the simplest words and in memorable images he painted a picture of Jesus. And we call it the Gospel (or the good-story) according to John.

As we study this beautiful book, Jesus is asking that each of us shall write a gospel, the gospel according to—you. What is your name? Put it in there. There is to be the gospel according to Robert and Brian, Marilyn and Rachel.

The gospel that you and I write is not to be written with ordinary pen and paper. The pen with which we write our gospel is our daily lives, and the paper on which we write is the lives of those we touch every day.

Both gospels—John's and yours—will describe Jesus in the same way: L I G H T. Why is the image of light a popular one in describing who Jesus is and what He does? When we recall the characteristics of light, the answer is obvious. Light brightens everything it touches. Darkness is dispelled by it. Light is all-pervasive. It crowns the mountaintops and finds its way into the valleys. Light reveals, uncovering hidden paths, guiding a person home.

In his Gospel account, Luke refers to Jesus as the "rising sun" (Luke 1:78)** and Matthew speaks of Him as the light that comes to save men from darkness and from the shadow of death (Matthew 4:16). Of all the New Testament authors, however, no other writer weaves the theme of light through his writings as does the apostle John. The word *light* occurs more than ninety times in the New Testament. Of those occurrences, twenty-three are in the Gospel of John, five are in 1 John, and six are in the book of Revelation, also written by John. The overwhelming majority of them describe God or Christ or their servants.

Consider again these well-known verses. John proclaims in his Gospel that in Jesus "was life, and that life was the light of men" (1:4). Jesus, the light, shines in the darkness, but the darkness does not understand it (1:5). Darkness is the antithesis of light; it is set in opposition to God. The life of which John spoke, a sharing in the life of God, must be a life of ultimate understanding. A follower of Jesus is one who has seen the light; he is the one who sees Jesus and walks in the light (see 1 John 1:7; 2:10).

Notice also that the imagery of light is used in connection with certain individuals and groups of people. John the apostle reminds us that the ministry of John the Baptist was one of giving testimony concerning the light (John 1:7, 8; 5:35). That Jesus is the light for the individual is found at the end of the account of Jesus' conversation with Nicodemus: "This is the verdict: Light has come into the world, but men loved darkness instead of light because their deeds were evil. Everyone who does evil hates the light, and will not come into the light for fear that his deeds will be exposed. But whoever lives by the truth comes into the light, so that it may be seen plainly that what he has done has been done through God" (3:19-21).

To those sympathetic to His claims and those who are hostile, Jesus is the light: "I am the light of the world. Whoever follows me will never walk in darkness, but will have the light of life" (John 8:12; see also 9:5; 11:9, 10).

As the storm clouds gathered, with the cross casting shadows on the horizon, Jesus offered another invitation to the crowds: "You are going to have the light just a little while longer. Walk while you have the light, before darkness overtakes you.... Put your trust in the light while you have it, so that you may become sons of light" (John 12:35, 36). To those who believed but were fearful of being rejected by men, Jesus offered one final reminder: "I have come into the world as a light, so that no one who believes in me should stay in darkness" (v. 46).

John's Gospel helps us to see why Jesus came to earth. All Jesus said and did revealed that God was not satisfied that men should live in darkness. This is why Paul could call on all Christians, both those at Colosse and those in today's churches, to give thanks to the Father, "who has qualified you to share in the inheritance of the saints in the kingdom of light. For he has rescued us from the dominion of darkness and brought us into the kingdom of the Son he loves, in whom we have redemption, the forgiveness of sins" (Colossians 1:12-14).

The Gospel of Light

Ye dwellers in darkness with sin-blinded eyes,
   The Light of the world is Jesus:
Go, wash at His bidding, and light will arise,
   The Light of the world is Jesus.

There is no other light apart from Jesus. In order to be rescued from darkness—from the world of ignorance, from sin, and from death—certain conditions must be met. Again, Christ, the light, is to be followed: "I am the light of the world. Whoever follows me will never walk in darkness, but will have the light of life" (John 8:12). Belief is shown by keeping His words (12:46, 47). Even though many will prefer to remain in darkness by refusing to believe in Him (1:5, 10, 11), those who believe are made children of God, children of the light (1:12, 13; 12:36).

John proclaims in his Gospel that when the Light came the shadows crept away. The story is told that in the South Sea Islands there is a monument erected to a missionary. On it are these words: "When he came, there was no light. When he left, there was no darkness." When Jesus came to earth, there was no light except for the flickering lamps of those faithful to God's revelation given through the law. When Jesus left the earth, there was no darkness, except darkness self-imposed. John's portrait of Jesus' ministry shows that wherever He went, there was no darkness at all.

The Gospel According to—You, Again

No need of the sunlight in heaven, we're told,
   The Light of the world is Jesus;
The Lamb is the Light in the City of Gold,
   The Light of the world is Jesus.

That Jesus is the light of the world is a truth that should affect you and those you meet daily. Are you writing your gospel? Is your life spelling out this simple, beautiful truth: Jesus is the light of the world?

The same John who heard and saw Jesus, the light, is the same who heard and saw the blessings awaiting those who walk in the light: "No longer will there be any curse. The throne of God and of the Lamb will be in the city, and his servants will serve him.... There will be no more night. They will not need the light of a lamp or the light of the sun, for the Lord God will give them light. And they will reign for ever and ever" (Revelation 22:3, 5).

We who have received Christ no longer stumble in spiritual darkness. Let us proclaim to those who do not know His life and love,

   Come to the Light, 'tis shining for thee;
     Sweetly the Light has dawned upon me;
   Once I was blind, but now I can see;
     The Light of the world is Jesus.

---

*"The Light of the World Is Jesus." Words by Philip P. Bliss.

**All Scripture quotations are taken from the *New International Version*.

Quarterly Quiz

The questions on this page may be used in several ways: as a pretest at the beginning of the quarter, as a review at the end of the quarter, or as a review after each lesson. The questions are based on the Scripture text of each lesson (King James Version).
The answers are on page 117.

Lesson 1

1. When the priests and Levites asked John who he was, he said he was the one spoken of by the prophet (Elijah, Isaiah, Joel). *John 1:23*
2. John testified that he saw the Spirit descend from Heaven like a _____ , which abode upon Jesus. *John 1:32*

Lesson 2

1. Because of the _____ Jesus did, Nicodemus knew that Jesus was a teacher who had come from God. *John 3:2*
2. Jesus said that a man cannot enter the kingdom of God unless he is born of _____ and of the _____ . *John 3:5*

Lesson 3

1. What request did Jesus make of a Samaritan woman at Jacob's well near Sychar? *John 4:7*
2. What did Jesus say He would have given the woman if she had asked? *John 4:10*

Lesson 4

1. On the night of Jesus' birth, the shepherds first reacted to the angel's presence with (wonder, fear, great joy). *Luke 2:9*
2. "The law was given by Moses, but _____ and _____ came by Jesus Christ." *John 1:17*

Lesson 5

1. By what pool did Jesus heal a man disabled for thirty-eight years? *John 5:2*
2. Before performing this miracle of healing, Jesus asked the man if he wanted to be made whole. (T/F) *John 5:6*

Lesson 6

1. The Jewish authorities professed allegiance to God, but Jesus said that they did not have the _____ of God in them. *John 5:42*
2. Jesus told His critics, "had ye believed _____ , ye would have believed me: for he wrote of me." *John 5:46*

Lesson 7

1. The Jews at Capernaum murmured at Jesus because He said, "I am the _____ which came down from heaven." *John 6:41*

2. Jesus said, "The bread that I will give is my _____ , which I will give for the life of the _____ ." *John 6:51*

Lesson 8

1. To those who began to believe on Him Jesus said, "If ye _____ in my word, then are ye my disciples indeed." *John 8:31*
2. Speaking of the devil, Jesus said that "he was a (deceiver, murderer, rebel) from the beginning." *John 8:44*

Lesson 9

1. Jesus said, "As long as I am in the world, I am the (light, hope, Savior) of the world." *John 9:5*
2. When Jesus directed the blind man to wash in the pool of Siloam, he replied that he had no man to take him there. (T/F) *John 9:7*

Lesson 10

1. Jesus was glorified by His humiliating death. (T/F) *John 12:23*
2. When God spoke in answer to Jesus' prayer, all the people understood the voice from Heaven. (T/F) *John 12:29*

Lesson 11

1. Jesus knew when He was going to die. (T/F) *John 13:1*
2. The disciples asked Jesus to wash their feet. (T/F) *John 13:3-5*
3. Jesus forbade His disciples to call Him Master or Lord. (T/F) *John 13:13*

Lesson 12

1. Jesus said that He was the only way to the Father in Heaven. (T/F) *John 14:6*
2. If the disciples found it difficult to believe Jesus' statement that He was one with the Father, they should have believed Him because of the works He had done. (T/F) *John 14:11*

Lesson 13

1. Love for Christ prompts us to obey Him. (T/F) *John 14:15*
2. Jesus dictated the four Gospels to His apostles before He died on the cross so that they would have a record of His teachings. (T/F) *John 14:26*

Born to Bear Witness

LESSON SCRIPTURE: John 1:6-8, 19-37; 3:22-30.

PRINTED TEXT: John 1:6-8, 19-23, 29-34.

John 1:6-8, 19-23, 29-34

6 There was a man sent from God, whose name was John.

7 The same came for a witness, to bear witness of the Light, that all men through him might believe.

8 He was not that Light, but was sent to bear witness of that Light.

. . . .

19 And this is the record of John, when the Jews sent priests and Levites from Jerusalem to ask him, Who are thou?

20 And he confessed, and denied not; but confessed, I am not the Christ.

21 And they asked him, What then? Art thou Elijah? And he saith, I am not. Art thou that Prophet? And he answered, No.

22 Then said they unto him, Who art thou? that we may give an answer to them that sent us. What sayest thou of thyself?

23 He said, I am the voice of one crying in the wilderness, Make straight the way of the Lord, as said the prophet Isaiah.

. . . .

29 The next day John seeth Jesus coming unto him, and saith, Behold the Lamb of God, which taketh away the sin of the world!

30 This is he of whom I said, After me cometh a man which is preferred before me; for he was before me.

31 And I knew him not: but that he should be made manifest to Israel, therefore am I come baptizing with water.

32 And John bare record, saying, I saw the Spirit descending from heaven like a dove, and it abode upon him.

33 And I knew him not: but he that sent me to baptize with water, the same said unto me, Upon whom thou shalt see the Spirit descending, and remaining on him, the same is he which baptizeth with the Holy Ghost.

34 And I saw, and bare record that this is the Son of God.

GOLDEN TEXT: The next day John seeth Jesus coming unto him, and saith, Behold the Lamb of God, which taketh away the sin of the world! —John 1:29.

John: The Gospel of Life and Light

Unit 1. Jesus Comes to His Own

(Lessons 1-4)

Lesson Aims

This study should equip the student to:

1. State clearly the purposes for which John the Baptist was born.

2. See clearly and state plainly his own purpose in life.

3. Accept his own measure of responsibility for making Christ known in the world.

Lesson Outline

INTRODUCTION

    A. What's the Use?

    B. John Writes About John

I. SENT FOR A PURPOSE (John 1:6-8)

II. ACKNOWLEDGING THE PURPOSE (John 1:19-23)

    A. "Who Are You?" (v. 19)

    B. "I Am Not a Great One" (vv. 20, 21)

    C. The Herald of Another's Coming (vv. 22, 23)

       Fulfill Your Role

III. FULFILLING THE PURPOSE (John 1:29-34)

    A. "He Is the Lamb of God" (v. 29)

    B. "His Is the Greater Baptism" (vv. 30-33)

    C. "He Is the Son of God" (v. 34)

CONCLUSION

    A. Success Story

    B. Prayer

    C. Thought to Remember

Display visual 1 from the visuals packet and let it remain before the class. It is shown on page 124. Display also the map (visual 14) for use throughout this lesson series.

Introduction

A. What's the Use?

"What's the use of living, anyway?"

The person who answers that question negatively, or even doubtfully, is in trouble! A distressing number of the troubled ones choose the easy way out, by suicide. Others consider it. "I just can't take it any more," they may say, citing problems, pains, and pressures as the intolerable pattern of their days.

But many of their companions face the same problems, pains, and pressures rather cheerfully, because they know what they are living

for. The big difference is not in the difficulties they face, but their reasons for facing and conquering them. They live for a purpose.

Not all purposes are good. Some are positively wicked, such as revenge or the desire to destroy personal enemies. Other purposes are selfish, such as the lust for wealth, power, pleasure, or fame. They will keep a person going, but where?

The writer of Ecclesiastes followed the self-serving purposes with remarkable success, only to conclude that they were all vain and striving after wind. He wrote at last, "Let us hear the conclusion of the whole matter: Fear God, and keep his commandments: for this is the whole duty of man" (Ecclesiastes 12:13).

Many of God's people have possessed greater assurance of a specific life purpose to which God had appointed them. These have been able to face the harshest of difficulties without flinching, because they knew the use of living.

Such a one was the prophet Jeremiah, to whom God said, "Before thou camest forth out of the womb I sanctified thee, and I ordained thee a prophet unto the nations" (Jeremiah 1:5).

Centuries later came John the Baptist, whose single life mission, foretold in prophecy and by direct revelation, was to announce and bear witness to the coming Messiah. His life-style was wholly opposite to that of the luxury-loving king described in Ecclesiastes, but it was much more satisfying. He did what God sent him to do.

B. John Writes About John

The Gospels written by Matthew, Mark, and Luke tell us about John, the son of Zebedee and brother of James, who was called from his fishing business to become an apostle of Jesus (Matthew 4:21, 22; Mark 1:19, 20; Luke 5:9-11). This John also wrote a Gospel account, some thirty years after the others wrote theirs. Nowhere in this Gospel did John mention himself by name, but usually referred to himself as the "disciple whom Jesus loved."

Matthew, Mark, and Luke wrote also about John the Baptist, son of Zechariah (Zacharias) the priest (Luke 1:5-25, 57-64), who heralded the coming Savior and prepared the people to receive Him, preaching repentance and baptizing responsive hearers (Matthew 3:1-6; Mark 1:4, 5; Luke 3:1-9). John's Gospel tells of the same ministry of the same man, saying that he made and baptized disciples, announcing the coming Messiah (John 3:22-4:1). John the apostle referred to John the Baptist simply as *John*, recognizing his prominent place in the early days of Jesus' ministry. That was in Judea and

Samaria, prior to the Lord's more notable activities in Galilee.

John's Gospel opens with a prologue (1:1-18) introducing Jesus as the eternal Word, active in creation, but coming to earth in human form as Jesus. It is interrupted briefly by reference to John the Baptist, (verses 6-8) as the man sent from God to announce the Lord's coming.

I. Sent for a Purpose
(John 1:6-8)

6. There was a man sent from God, whose name was John.

The opening verses spoke of the eternal Word, identified with God. Now to emphasize by contrast, *a man* is introduced. He was no ordinary man! Jesus later declared that "among them that are born of women there hath not risen a greater than John the Baptist" (Matthew 11:11).

This John had been *sent* as an emissary with a special mission. He was sent *from God,* who provided a special miracle that John should be born to aged and otherwise barren parents. His coming was announced by the angel Gabriel, who said that he would "be filled with the Holy Ghost, even from his mother's womb. And many of the children of Israel shall he turn to the Lord their God. And he shall go before him in the spirit and power of Elijah, to turn the hearts of the fathers to the children, and the disobedient to the wisdom of the just; to make ready a people prepared for the Lord" (Luke 1:15-17). John's very name was assigned by the angel.

So John was to introduce the Savior, not only by announcement but also by preparing the people to receive Him.

7. The same came for a witness, to bear witness of the Light, that all men through him might believe.

Witness translates the Greek word, from which comes our word *martyr*—one who suffers and perhaps dies for his faith and testimony. The more important the testimony, the greater is the danger to him who bears it.

The *Light* concerning which John testified was the eternal Word that came into the world to be the light of men (vv. 4, 5)—even Jesus. John was the first of many whose inspired testimony would extend far beyond their own time and nation, persuading hearers throughout the world to believe in Jesus.

8. He was not that Light, but was sent to bear witness of that Light.

The agent is not to be confused with the one he serves. The Lord himself would later speak of John as "a burning and a shining light" (John 5:35), but the expression He used indicates a

<table>
<tr><td colspan="2">How to Say It</td></tr>
<tr><td>NAZARETH.</td><td>Naz-uh-reth.</td></tr>
<tr><td>PHARISEES.</td><td>Fair-ih-seez.</td></tr>
<tr><td>SANHEDRIN.</td><td>San-huh-drun or San-heed-run.</td></tr>
<tr><td>ZACHARIAS.</td><td>Zack-uh-rye-us.</td></tr>
<tr><td>ZEBEDEE.</td><td>Zeb-eh-dee.</td></tr>
<tr><td>ZECHARIAH.</td><td>Zek-uh-rye-uh.</td></tr>
</table>

candle, in contrast to the all-pervasive light of midday. The difference between the greatest of men and the Man who came as the Light of the world is emphasized with insistent repetition.

II. Acknowledging the Purpose
(John 1:19-23)

Verses 9-18, not included in our printed text, continue the Gospel writer's grand introduction of the Word, which became flesh and dwelt among men. Verse 15 expresses the theme of our lesson: "John bare witness of him, and cried, saying, This was he of whom I spake, He that cometh after me is preferred before me; for he was before me." John knew that the birth in Bethlehem was not the beginning of the Messiah; it simply brought Him into the world.

A. "Who Are You?" (v. 19)

19. And this is the record of John, when the Jews sent priests and Levites from Jerusalem to ask him, Who art thou?

In the vocabulary of this Gospel, *Jews* often refers to the Jewish leaders who were hostile to Jesus (see 7:1; 9:22; 18:12-14). Here it refers to the Sanhedrin (chief priests, scribes, and elders) who were the guardians of the nation's faith. John had made such an impression that he could not be ignored by the religious leaders in Jerusalem. They wanted to know why so many hearers were going to the Jordan valley to hear him, and why so many were responding to his exhortation to change their ways and to be immersed by him in the river.

Priests performed services and offered sacrifices in the temple. *Levites* waited on the priests in their ministry and performed subordinate duties. Pharisees, as the party most interested in matters of law and Scriptural interpretation, were most prominently represented in the committee of inquiry (v. 24).

Who art thou? John could be identified very readily as the son of the priest Zechariah (Luke 1), and therefore himself a Levite. His message and his influence marked him as no ordinary man. Now the Sanhedrin wanted to examine his credentials and his authorization to deal with members of the chosen nation as though they were heathens in need of conversion.

Not many of us will have occasion to face the Pharisees' question in the same way as John did, but we all need frequently to consider our own identities. Who, after all, am I? More important, *whose* am I?

B. "I Am Not a Great One" (vv. 20, 21)

20. And he confessed, and denied not; but confessed, I am not the Christ.

Luke 3:15 indicates that some in John's audiences were wondering if he was the Messiah. John might have used his popularity with the people for his own aggrandizement, but he did not. He answered the Pharisees' question immediately, stating, "I am not the Christ." May John's example instruct anyone tempted to feel his own importance in the Lord's family.

21. And they asked him, What then? Art thou Elijah? And he saith, I am not. Art thou that Prophet? And he answered, No.

In Malachi 4:5, 6 is the prophecy, "I will send you Elijah the prophet before the coming of the great and dreadful day of the Lord; and he shall turn the heart of the fathers to the children, and the heart of the children to their fathers." The Lord himself was to say that John fulfilled Malachi's prophecy, coming in the spirit and power of Elijah (Matthew 17:10-13). But John was not, as the Pharisees' question suggested, literally Elijah reincarnated.

The Pharisees' question about *that Prophet* derived from words of Moses, found in Deuteronomy 18:15: "The Lord thy God will raise up unto thee a Prophet from the midst of thee, of thy brethren, like unto me; unto him ye shall hearken." John was not that promised prophet; Jesus was (Acts 3:22; 7:37).

C. The Herald of Another's Coming (vv. 22, 23)

22. Then said they unto him, Who art thou? that we may give an answer to them that sent us. What sayest thou of thyself?

JOHN'S PURPOSE AND OURS: TO TESTIFY TO GOD'S SON.

visual 1

Was ever a prophet so reluctant to talk about himself? The messengers had been sent to learn John's credentials—what and who he was. All they had learned so far was who he was *not*.

23. He said, I am the voice of one crying in the wilderness, make straight the way of the Lord, as said the prophet Isaiah.

John's humility was not slavish, nor even self-effacing. It was simply self-forgetful. He was denying himself in confessing his Lord. His humility was matched with an equally amazing boldness as he declared his mission.

John gave his reply in the words of Isaiah 40:3. Isaiah had called for the Babylonian captives to prepare their hearts so as to be ready when God came to rescue them from their captivity. Here John claims that he is fulfilling Isaiah's prophecy, calling the people to get ready to receive the Lord, who was coming to rescue those held captive by sin.

Note that John said he was simply *the voice*, announcing the coming of One greater than himself. The One whom the voice represented summoned the people to prepare for His coming by repenting of sin. "*I* am the voice . . . Prepare *ye* the way." No wonder the hearers seemed not to understand; it demanded too much of them. So they returned to their previous guesses: "If you are not one of those we suggested, why do you presume to demand repentance and baptism of good Jews?" They continued to focus on the messenger and ignore the message (vv. 24-28).

FULFILL YOUR ROLE

It was 1942, and the chaplain, who was newly out of Chaplain's school, was assigned to Camp Butler, North Carolina. The Commander of the post was Lieutenant General William Harrison, a Christian gentleman as well as an outstanding officer.

One Sunday morning at the appointed time for the Protestant service, no one had arrived except the chaplain and the organist. Both had agreed to call the service off since there were no worshipers. At that moment, a staff car pulled up bearing the general's insignia on the bumper, and General Harrison climbed out. The chaplain and the organist snapped immediately to attention.

"Chaplain, is there not a service at this hour?" was the General's question.

"Yes, sir, but no one has come, so I thought we might cancel it," was the chaplain's rather embarrassed reply.

"Chaplain, do you believe in the words of our Lord, 'Where two or three are gathered together, there am I in the midst'?"

"Oh, yes, sir, indeed." As he went up the steps the General said, "Then let the service begin." With a very red face, the chaplain conducted the service.

When you have a commission, faithfully fulfill its requirements. John the Baptist did just that.
—W. P.

III. Fulfilling the Purpose
(John 1:29-34)

A. "He Is the Lamb of God" (v. 29)

29. The next day John seeth Jesus coming unto him, and saith, Behold the Lamb of God, which taketh away the sin of the world!

The next day after the Jews' messengers came with their questions, Jesus came to the place where John was preaching. It had been about six weeks since Jesus had come from Nazareth and persuaded John to baptize Him. Since then, Jesus had been alone in the wilderness, fasting and enduring temptation (Matthew 3:13—4:11). Now John was able to say, "Look! this is the One I have been talking about."

The Jewish people expected their Messiah to come in power as the Lion of the tribe of Judah. John introduced a different side of the Messiah's character. His reference to the *Lamb of God* was timely, since the Passover was soon to be observed (John 2:13). At that observance, each family would slay and eat a lamb, remembering their ancestors' deliverance from the plague of death in Egypt, followed by their escape from bondage. The people were familiar also with the daily sacrifices in the temple, with a lamb sacrificed on the altar every morning and another every evening (Exodus 29:38, 39). John's reference may also have reminded the people of Isaiah's prophecy of God's suffering servant, "brought as a lamb to the slaughter, and as a sheep before her shearers is dumb, so he openeth not his mouth" (Isaiah 53:7).

Something more than the Passover was set forth in John's introduction of Jesus as the *Lamb of God, which taketh away the sin of the world.* The blood of the Passover lamb protected from immediate physical death; God's Lamb would remove sin entirely, as Isaiah had prophesied: "He was wounded for our transgressions, he was bruised for our iniquities: the chastisement of our peace was upon him; and with his stripes we are healed. . . . the Lord hath laid on him the iniquity of us all" (Isaiah 53:5, 6).

Moreover, the Passover had been effective for none but the children of Israel in Egypt; God's Lamb would bear and remove sin from the whole world—Egypt as well as Israel, and all believers on all continents for as many centuries as the world shall stand. Let all mankind everywhere behold the Lamb—get well acquainted with Him who is Savior and Lord, and King of all kingdoms forever.

B. "His Is the Greater Baptism" (vv. 30-33)

30, 31. This is he of whom I said, After me cometh a man which is preferred before me; for he was before me. And I knew him not: but that he should be made manifest to Israel, therefore am I come baptizing with water.

At the conclusion of the previous day's inquiry, the questioners from Jerusalem had asked John, "Why baptizest thou then, if thou be not that Christ, nor Elijah, neither that Prophet?" and he had answered, "I baptize with water: but there standeth one among you, whom ye know not; he it is, who coming after me is preferred before me, whose shoelatchet I am not worthy to unloose" (John 1:25-27). The reason John came baptizing with water was that Christ might be made known to Israel—and to John himself.

John was always aware of Jesus as a person. Their mothers were related, and had spent time together during their pregnancies talking about the sons who were to be born of them (Luke 1:39-57). John was six months older than Jesus and he had been preaching and baptizing for some time before Jesus came to him for baptism. Until that moment, John did not know that Jesus was the Messiah, but he was well enough acquainted with Him to know that it was more fitting for him to be baptized by Jesus than the opposite (Matthew 3:13, 14). On that occasion, however, it was revealed to John that Jesus was indeed the one for whom he had come to prepare the way (vv. 16, 17). That meant that Jesus was *before* John, both in His being with God

Home Daily Bible Readings

Monday, Nov. 27—John the Messenger (John 1:6-8)
Tuesday, Nov. 28—One Crying in the Wilderness (John 1:19-23)
Wednesday, Nov. 29—Baptizing With Water (John 1:24-28)
Thursday, Nov. 30—Spirit Come Down Like a Dove (John 1:29-34)
Friday, Dec. 1—Behold, the Lamb of God (John 1:35-39)
Saturday, Dec. 2—Sharing in Baptizing Others (John 3:22-26)
Sunday, Dec. 3—He Must Become More Important (John 3:27-30)

from eternity and in His superior standing with God and men.

Baptizing with water (in water) was a central part of John's ministry. It stirred the people to awareness of their sin and their need of a Savior. And it provided symbolic preparation for Jesus' burial and resurrection; hence also for Christian baptism.

32, 33. And John bare record, saying, I saw the Spirit descending from heaven like a dove, and it abode upon him. And I knew him not: but he that sent me to baptize with water, the same said unto me, Upon whom thou shalt see the Spirit descending, and remaining on him, the same is he which baptizeth with the Holy Ghost.

I saw the Spirit descending from heaven. Here was testimony that John was born to give. At Jesus' baptism, John saw the Spirit descend upon Jesus "in a bodily shape like a dove" (Luke 3:22), and he heard a voice from Heaven saying, "This is my beloved Son, in whom I am well pleased" (Matthew 3:17). He remembered these events clearly and affirmed them plainly, This testimony was given some six weeks after the event.

The same is he which baptizeth with the Holy Ghost. Jesus himself would do this. He repeated this promise when He was about to ascend into Heaven: "Ye shall be baptized with the Holy Ghost not many days hence" (Acts 1:5). This was fulfilled about ten days later on Pentecost (Acts 2:1-4).

C. "He Is the Son of God" (v. 34)

34. And I saw, and bare record that this is the Son of God.

Here is the climax of John's testimony to Jesus. He had heard it from Heaven, and he declared it to all the earth. Implications of divine sonship had appeared in God's Word through prophets concerning the Messiah (2 Samuel 7:14; Psalm 89:27; 2:7), but the Jews of Jesus' day had missed them. They expected a military Messiah; God sent His obedient Son. They expected a temporal Messiah; God sent His eternal Son.

The Jews had suggested high titles for John the Baptist. He rejected them all, reserving them for Jesus. But then he pronounced for Jesus a title higher than any they had mentioned. Somewhat later, the people who heard Jesus suggested again those earlier titles as being appropriate to Him, but none was high enough. It remained for Simon Peter to use again the title which John had assigned—"Son of the living God"—and be blessed for using it (Matthew 16:14-17). It is a high privilege for any of us to

join with John and with Peter in affirming that Jesus is the Son of God. It is a high purpose for which we are born—and born again.

Conclusion

A. Success Story

John's friends and disciples were concerned about his standing and reputation. He deserved the highest honor, but now the Man he had helped the most was drawing away John's followers to himself, was preaching to larger crowds than John was, and through His disciples was baptizing more people than John was (John 3:26; 4:1).

That didn't bother John a bit! May we paraphrase his reply? "You will remember that I kept saying, 'I am not the Christ.' I am as happy as the best man at a wedding. This is my whole purpose in coming onto the scene at all. The Bridegroom must increase as I decrease. Now I have accomplished what I came to do" (John 3:27-30).

So John, who was at last beheaded in prison, must be regarded as brilliantly successful, while the king who ordered his execution is remembered as a craven coward, wavering toward the wrong goal. Almost anyone can succeed if he knows what he wants and is willing to sacrifice everything else in order to attain it. Remember the successful farmer whom God called a fool, (Luke 12:20, 21). The wrong success can become the ultimate failure.

B. Prayer

You have blessed us today, O God our Father, with the success story of John, who knew what You had sent him to do in this world, and who did it. Thank You for his clear testimony to Your Son, our Savior and Lord. Led by his example, may we too be successful in doing what You would have us to do with our days. Through Jesus, Your son, amen.

C. Thought to Remember

Blessed is he who can pray with his Lord in the final hour, "I have finished the work which thou gavest me to do" (John 17:4).

Learning by Doing

This page contains an alternate lesson plan emphasizing learning activities. Classes desiring such student involvement will find these suggestions helpful.

Learning Goals

John the Baptist was probably viewed by many of his contemporaries as strange, an oddball. As we shall see, however, he was a unique man in history, one with a unique mission and unique method. In this lesson, we will:

1. Encounter John, the man, who was especially chosen to introduce the Messiah.

2. Examine his ministry for clues to his success.

3. Encourage each other to catch fire from the flame that burned in his soul.

Into the Lesson

Since John the Baptist was chosen to introduce Jesus to the world, your students can be helped to understand his role by putting themselves into a hypothetical situation of introducing Jesus. Say, "Let's pretend that Jesus, who is invisible but present in our class today, manifests himself physically, so we can all see Him. He is going to speak to our class, but one of us must give Him a proper introduction. Let's take three minutes to plan an introduction. Pair off and see what you can come up with." At the close of this time, ask several to give a one-minute introduction aloud. Then discuss what you want to accomplish with an introduction, what the purpose of an introduction is. The student book can help with this assignment.

Into the Word

The central purpose for which John the Baptist was sent from God (John 1:6) was to introduce the Christ to the world. He would do this in two ways: first, he would prepare the people's hearts to receive Christ (he would "warm up the audience," so to speak); second, he would bear witness to the credentials of Jesus (he would introduce the main speaker). John's role was unique, because the God-man whom he introduced was unique. Maybe it was because of his unique role that both Matthew and Mark paint a verbal picture of this strange man. Read Matthew 3:1-4 and Mark 1:2-6 to the class while an artist in the class (who has prepared ahead of time) draws a simple rough picture of John. The whole class can do this if they have student books. After this is completed, discuss with the class the various elements that made John distinctive. How did his looks, manner, and style arouse people's curiosity? Why didn't God use an "establishment" man, rather than John, to introduce Jesus?

All four Gospels give John's message of introduction of the Christ. Divide your class into four study groups. Give each team the assignment of summarizing the message of John the Baptist as it appears in one of the four Gospels. The four Scriptures to be studied are Matthew 3:7-17; Mark 1:7-11; Luke 3:7-18, 21-22; John 1:19-34. Give each group a sheet of paper on which to write, or you can use the student book. (This assignment can also be done individually by numbering off, one through four. Then assign the Matthew text to all number ones, the Mark text to all number twos, etc.) After five to ten minutes, have the class reassemble and ask for a scribe from each group to share their summary of John's message. Discuss these questions: How do you think you would have reacted to John's style of introducing Christ? What parts of his message would have convicted you? Would you be offended if the preacher of your congregation spoke to you the way John spoke? What factors do you think made John so effective in his mission?

Into Life

John the Baptist certainly had conviction, courage, and fire as an introducer of Jesus to the world. Those factors, along with God's blessing, are what made him successful in fulfilling the mission God gave him, though they eventually led to his physical death (Matthew 14:1-12). We who are Christians have been given an assignment similar to John's—that of introducing Jesus to people in our world. If we are to be successful in this task, we must also have conviction, courage, and fire. Conviction is firmness of faith. Courage is the willingness to risk opposition. Fire is a visible enthusiasm. Give each class member a slip of paper and ask them to rate themselves from one to ten in each of these three areas. Ask students to raise their hands indicating which is their weakest area as you call out these three needs one at a time. Starting with the *weakest* area in your class as a whole, ask students to share any insights that will help others grow in that area of weakness. Then close with "prayer pairs," praying specifically for each others' weakness.

Let's Talk It Over

The questions on this page are designed to encourage review of the lesson
Scriptures and to promote discussion of the lesson by the class. The answers
provided are only discussion starters. Let your class talk it over from there.

1. John is described as "a man sent from God." Would it be appropriate for us to think of ourselves as being sent from God, and if so, how would this be helpful to us?

Although we have not received the kind of call John did or the kind of call Moses or Jeremiah or Paul received, we are clearly a people "sent from God" when we fulfill the Great Commission. The form in which that commission is found in the Gospel of John indicates this: "Then said Jesus to them again, Peace be unto you: as my Father hath sent me, even so send I you? (John 20:21). E. Margaret Clarkson's well-known hymn based on this statement challenges us: "So send I you to labor unrewarded . . . to bind the bruised and broken . . . to bear the burdens of a world weary . . . to labor long, and love where men revile you." This is a great missionary hymn, but it is well for us to ponder the oft-repeated assertion that every Christian is meant to be a missionary. We should possess the awareness that we are sent to the people with whom we work, to the people in our neighborhood, to those with whom we share a social relationship in order to share with them the life-saving gospel of Jesus.

2. Why is it a worthwhile practice to ask ourselves occasionally, "Who am I?" or "Whose am I?"

This could be the key to a Biblical form of self-esteem. People in our society are encouraged to recognize their personal worth, dignity, and capability. If such an emphasis is separated from Biblical realities, it could lead to pride and self-glorification. From a Biblical standpoint, the question, "Who am I?" may be answered, "I am a being created in God's image" or "I am a person for whom Jesus Christ died" or "I am an individual in whom God's Holy Spirit dwells." Such statements indicate that we are precious in the sight of God, but they leave no room for excessive pride. And if, as the lesson writer notes, we also ask, "Whose am I?" the answer in the light of 1 Corinthians 3:22, 23 may be given, "All things are yours . . . and you are of Christ, and Christ is of God" (*New International Version*). To realize that we belong to Christ is to see ourselves as the recipients of an abundance of love, mercy, and privilege. And it is also to see

ourselves as owing all praise and glory and gratitude to Him who owns us.

3. Is Jesus' title, "Lamb of God," one that is likely to be understood by the unsaved upon hearing the gospel today? Why or why not?

Most hearers would be unaware of the Old Testament background of that title. And yet it still seems a universally appealing title, since it speaks of innocence, purity, and gentleness. While the wrath of God and eternal punishment in Hell are not prominent themes of sermons, lessons, and essays in our times, people still experience a sense of guilt because of their sins and a gnawing apprehension about what may result from that guilt. Some seek to ignore or dull these feelings by the use of alcohol or drugs or by throwing themselves into an unceasing pursuit of pleasure. But for those who are willing to hear, the title "Lamb of God" can generate hope that a wrathful God will also prove to be gentle when someone comes humbly to Him. Like John the Baptist, the church can announce very appropriately to a guilt-and-fear-ridden society: "Behold the Lamb of God, which taketh away the sin of the world!"

4. The lesson writer states that "it is a high privilege for any of us to join with John and Peter in affirming that Jesus is the Son of God." Why is this so?

It is a privilege just to understand that Jesus is the Son of God. For great numbers of people, many of whom regard themselves as Christians, Jesus is no more than a remarkable human being. These people are either ignorant of the Biblical evidence that points to Him as God's Son, or they choose to disregard such evidence. We should thank God for those who have taught us the facts of Jesus' life, death, and resurrection in such a way that we have been led to faith and understanding. Once we reach this understanding, we are given the privilege and responsibility of testifying to it. To affirm that Jesus is the Son of God is to state a fact that transcends in importance any of the mind-boggling discoveries of modern science; it is to announce news that is always more up-to-date and urgent than the headlines on current newspapers.

Born of the Spirit

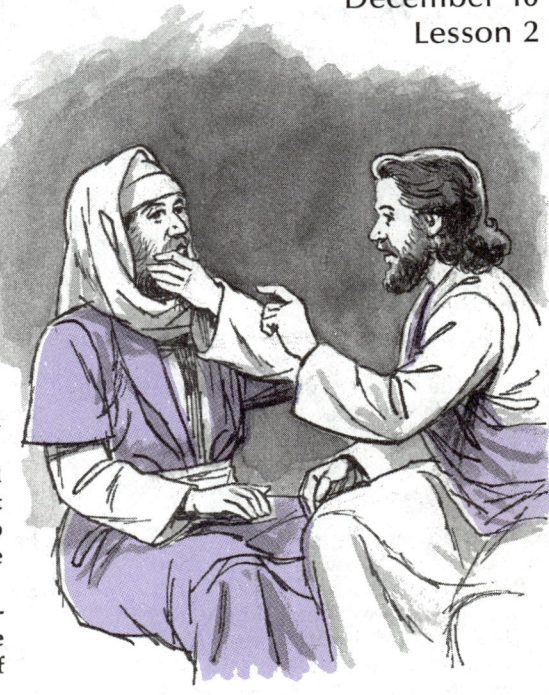

LESSON SCRIPTURE: John 3:1-21.

PRINTED TEXT: John 3:1-17.

John 3:1-17

1 There was a man of the Pharisees, named Nicodemus, a ruler of the Jews:

2 The same came to Jesus by night, and said unto him, Rabbi, we know that thou art a teacher come from God: for no man can do these miracles that thou doest, except God be with him.

3 Jesus answered and said unto him, Verily, verily, I say unto thee, Except a man be born again, he cannot see the kingdom of God.

4 Nicodemus saith unto him, How can a man be born when he is old? can he enter the second time into his mother's womb, and be born?

5 Jesus answered, Verily, verily, I say unto thee, Except a man be born of water and of the Spirit, he cannot enter into the kingdom of God.

6 That which is born of the flesh is flesh; and that which is born of the Spirit is spirit.

7 Marvel not that I said unto thee, Ye must be born again.

8 The wind bloweth where it listeth, and thou hearest the sound thereof, but canst not tell whence it cometh, and whither it goeth: so is every one that is born of the Spirit.

9 Nicodemus answered and said unto him, How can these things be?

10 Jesus answered and said unto him, Art thou a master of Israel, and knowest not these things?

11 Verily, verily, I say unto thee, We speak that we do know, and testify that we have seen; and ye receive not our witness.

12 If I have told you earthly things, and ye believe not, how shall ye believe, if I tell you of heavenly things?

13 And no man hath ascended up to heaven, but he that came down from heaven, even the Son of man which is in heaven.

14 And as Moses lifted up the serpent in the wilderness, even so must the Son of man be lifted up:

15 That whosoever believeth in him should not perish, but have eternal life.

16 For God so loved the world, that he gave his only begotten Son, that whosoever believeth in him should not perish, but have everlasting life.

17 For God sent not his Son into the world to condemn the world; but that the world through him might be saved.

GOLDEN TEXT: Verily, verily, I say unto to thee, Except a man be born again, he cannot see the kingdom of God.—John 3:3.

John: The Gospel of Life and Light
Unit 1. Jesus Comes to His Own
(Lessons 1-4)

Lesson Aims

This lesson should equip the student to:
1. Explain "birth from above" as it applied to Nicodemus.
2. Explain "birth from above" as it applies to himself or herself.
3. Share the message of Jesus that brings us new and everlasting life.

Lesson Outline

INTRODUCTION
  A. It's Radical
  B. Lesson Background
I. THE NEEDY INQUIRER (John 3:1, 2)
II. THE NEEDED NEW BIRTH (John 3:3-8)
  A. Necessity of the New Birth (v. 3)
  B. Nature of the New Birth (vv. 4-6)
  C. Mystery of the New Birth (vv. 7, 8)
III. HUMAN RESISTANCE (John 3:9-12)
  "How Can These Things Be?"
IV. DIVINE PROVISION (John 3:13-15)
  A. God's Son (v. 13)
  B. God's Sacrifice (v. 14)
  C. God's Salvation (v. 15)
V. Wrap-up and Review (John 3:16, 17)
CONCLUSION
  A. Heirs to the Kingdom
  B. Prayer
  C. Thought to Remember

Display visual 2 from the visuals packet and let it remain before the class throughout the session. The visual is shown on page 132.

Introduction

A. It's Radical

Christianity is radical. It goes to the root of the matter, whatever it is; and that's what *radical* (from the Latin *radix*) means. Jesus Christ proposes to *eradicate* (root out) sin. That requires radical provisions for the forgiveness of sins past, and radical—whole new life—conquest of sins present and future. Halfway measures will not suffice. Lovers of bland neutrality are not comfortable with the radical demands of Jesus, who requires both death to sin and also birth—new birth from above—to a new life.

In communities strongly influenced by Biblical teaching, Christianity can be made to seem comfortable—even popular. That condition has changed in the course of years as Biblical knowledge has become less widespread, and it continues to change. In times when the world seemed more friendly toward the moral aspects of Christianity and Christians could be less conspicuous, there were still some whose conversion to Christ had been notably sudden and spectacular. "Born-again Christians" became the title by which they were distinguished from their less demonstrative brethren. That distinction is fading, we think, for two very good reasons. One is the realization that the new birth from above is essential to anyone's becoming and being a Christian; hence the phrase is repetitive and inappropriate. The other reason is that confrontation with the non-Christian world has become so much a part of the Christian experience that *Christian* is sufficient to label one as being "different" and even extreme.

Radicalism is seldom comfortable. It wasn't for Nicodemus, and it isn't for most of us. Nicodemus found it hard to understand and hard to accept. So, perhaps, do we. But the rewards of accepting the radical claims of the Lord Jesus are nothing less than life itself—eternally.

B. Lesson Background

It happened during the days when the ministry of John the Baptist was waning and Jesus was developing His public ministry. That occupied about nine months, from the Passover season of one year (John 2:13) to winter, four months before the harvest (John 4:35) in the next. Jesus spent most of that time in Judea, although he was in Galilee for a while (John 2:1-12).

The influence of John was very much alive in Judea, where his preaching and baptizing were topics of excited conversation and study. His theme, "Repent ye: for the kingdom of heaven is at hand" (Matthew 3:2), became also the theme with which Jesus began His ministry (Matthew 4:17). John's demands for repentance were specific and practical, and pointed most sharply at the nation's leaders (Matthew 3:7, 8). John preached and practiced the baptism of repentance for the remission of sins (Luke 3:3), but said, "I indeed baptize you with water; but one mightier than I cometh . . . he shall baptize you with the Holy Ghost and with fire" (Luke 3:16). Jesus also came baptizing, and through the hands of His disciples He baptized more converts than John did (John 3:22; 4:1, 2). A notable difference between John's ministry and that of Jesus lay in this: "John did no miracle" (John 10:41); nevertheless his words were true and his

How to Say It

ARIMATHEA. Air-uh-muh-*thee*-uh (*th* as in thin).

CANA. *Kay*-nuh.

NICODEMUS. *Nick*-uh-*dee*-mus (strong accent on *dee*.)

PHARISEES. *Fair*-ih-seez.

SADDUCEE. *Sad*-you-see.

SANHEDRIN. *San*-huh-drun or San-*heed*-run.

predictions came to pass. Jesus came working miracles, many of which are neither described nor counted in Scripture (John 2:23). He offered the miracles as signs of His power from God (John 10:37, 38), but expressed His disappointment in those who demanded miracles and would not believe without them (John 4:48; 6:30-33).

The ingredients for theological discussion were all there: the kingdom of God (or of Heaven), long anticipated and now announced as near at hand; the nature of the kingdom, perhaps related to John's demand for a radically new way of life; water baptism and the place of the Holy Spirit as related to the new life; and finally a new and much greater prophet, establishing his credentials with miracles. Jesus, the new prophet, was in Jerusalem.

I. The Needy Inquirer (John 3:1, 2)

1, 2. There was a man of the Pharisees, named Nicodemus, a ruler of the Jews: the same came to Jesus by night, and said unto him, Rabbi, we know that thou art a teacher come from God: for no man can do these miracles that thou doest, except God be with him.

Pharisees, or "separated ones," were a party of pious and scholarly defenders of the Mosaic law, and commonly teachers in Jewish synagogues. The party was prominently represented in the committee sent to inquire about John's authority to teach and baptize (John 1:24).

Nicodemus is named on three different occasions in John's Gospel, but not elsewhere in Scripture. He spoke up in the Sanhedrin on one occasion to chide his colleagues for condemning Jesus before they heard Him (John 7:50, 51); and he joined with Joseph of Arimathea in claiming and removing the body of Jesus from the cross (John 19:38-42). In both instances, the record identifies him as having come at first to Jesus by night.

Ruler of the Jews identifies Nicodemus as a member of the ruling council, or Sanhedrin, a religious Supreme Court of seventy priests, scribes, and elders of the people.

The fact that Nicodemus came *by night* to confer with Jesus is clearly significant, but of what? Some have linked it to the statement that Joseph of Arimathea kept his discipleship secret, "for fear of the Jews" (John 19:38), and have seen a like fear controlling Nicodemus. If so, he had developed some courage before the incident recounted in John 7:50. At any rate, the night visit offered the best prospect for private, extended conversation.

Nicodemus' opening statement was genuinely complimentary, and apparently designed to introduce the question he never got around to asking—at least in words. *Rabbi*, or teacher, is a title much respected among the Pharisees. Others of them considered Jesus an ill-prepared upstart, not qualified to teach (John 7:15).

We know. Whom did that *we* include? Had Nicodemus been discussing Jesus with one or more of his colleagues? Was he in some way representative of a larger group? Some, at least, among Jewish leaders had considered and concluded, *Thou art a teacher come from God*; hence, at least a prophet qualified to explain deep questions of religion being discussed.

In John's Gospel *miracle* and *sign* are both translations of the same Greek word. In the other Gospels the word is regularly translated *sign*. Jesus' acts of divine power were signs of His identification with God, and were so accepted by Nicodemus.

Nicodemus needed something he didn't have—understanding and assurances concerning God's kingdom—and he came to the one best qualified to supply the lack.

II. The Needed New Birth (John 3:3-8)

A. Necessity for the New Birth (v. 3)

3. Jesus answered and said unto him, Verily, verily, I say unto thee, Except a man be born again, he cannot see the kingdom of God.

If Jesus' response seems abrupt and detached from Nicodemus' salutation, it is because we neglect the comment immediately preceding our lesson text: "Jesus did not commit himself unto them (the many who were convinced by His miracles), because he knew all men, and needed not that any should testify of man; for he knew what was in man." Jesus knew the mind of Nicodemus, and this itself could have become a "sign" to the Pharisee. The air was fairly crackling, though, with echoes of John's insistence that "the kingdom of heaven is at hand" (Matthew 3:2)—a theme now to be continued in the teaching of Jesus. But when would the kingdom be established? And how? And with what result? Messiah's glorious reign had been long expected. What did Jesus have to say about it?

Nicodemus' unspoken question was not to be treated lightly. The Lord's repeated *verily* (literally *amen*, or *truly*) announced a thoughtful and weighty declaration. It was to apply to all men everywhere alike. Hence Jesus spoke of the need for *a man*—any and every person—to become an entirely new person before he could *see the kingdom of God.* To see the kingdom is placed parallel to entering it.

Born again is a phrase rich with manifold meaning. The word here translated *born* (delivered in birth) means also *begotten* (generated or conceived). It can include both aspects of bringing on new life. And the word *again* translates a term that usually means *anew* or *from above.* A person cannot enter God's realm on the basis of national distinction; nor can one qualify for entrance by keeping the law more precisely. What is necessary is a recreation, a new life that has its origin not on earth but in Heaven.

B. Nature of the New Birth (vv. 4-6)

4. Nicodemus saith unto him, How can a man be born when he is old? can he enter the second time into his mother's womb, and be born?

Nicodemus' response reveals that he did not grasp Jesus' meaning. Another physical birth for a full-grown man was obviously ridiculous. Earlier, Nicodemus had indicated confidence in Jesus as an inspired teacher; now he wasn't so sure.

5, 6. Jesus answered, Verily, verily, I say unto thee, Except a man be born of water and of the Spirit, he cannot enter into the kingdom of God. That which is born of the flesh is flesh; and that which is born of the Spirit is spirit.

Jesus first specified, then explained, the spiritual order of the birth from above. It was not a physical birth—even in the line of Abraham—but it did include material as well as spiritual elements. After the death and resurrection of Jesus, and the coming of the Spirit on the great Day of Pentecost, these elements were fused into one regenerative experience, including the begetting power of the Spirit and the coming forth from the watery womb in Christian baptism. Jesus' Great Commission prescribed these two elements—the Spirit-inspired gospel to be preached and believed, and burial in water as the way of emergence into the new life of the

visual 2

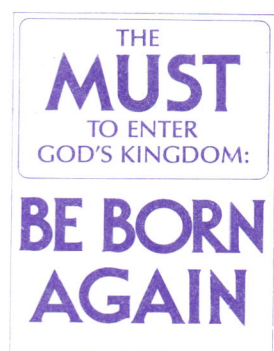

kingdom (Matthew 28:18-20; Mark 16:15, 16; Acts 2:37-41; 10:47, 48; Romans 8:3, 4). Just as fleshly birth introduced one into physical life, so the Spirit empowered birth would introduce one into the new spiritual life of God's kingdom.

C. Mystery of the New Birth (vv. 7, 8)

7, 8. Marvel not that I say unto thee, Ye must be born again. The wind bloweth where it listeth, and thou hearest the sound thereof, but canst not tell whence it cometh, and whither it goeth: so is every one that is born of the Spirit.

What Jesus had presented was only one of many marvels, most of which were accepted as commonplace. One marvel was in the night breeze that may even then have been stirring enough to draw attention. Nicodemus could easily feel it and see the leaves dance before it, but he could not name a source or destination for the wind. Just so, the one who observes the new life and power provided by God's Spirit can know its reality without being able to trace its every move.

What Jesus said to Nicodemus *(thee)* that night applied clearly to others also *(Ye)*—all the Pharisees who may have been discussing Jesus, and all persons everywhere who might ever possess an inquiring interest in the kingdom of God.

III. Human Resistance
(John 3:9-12)

9, 10. Nicodemus answered and said unto him, How can these things be? Jesus answered and said unto him, Art thou a master of Israel, and knowest not these things?

Nicodemus' response seems to have been limited to a bewildered shaking of the head, like that of the unheeding ones who later responded to Jesus' teaching about the bread of life: "This is a hard saying; who can hear it?" (John 6:60). But Nicodemus stayed around to learn more, and to realize later what the Lord had been trying to tell him all along. For now, the great counselor's bewilderment served to establish Jesus' statement that a radical change is needed in men before they can understand what the kingdom is all about. "Are you the famous teacher in Israel and yet you do not understand this?" the Lord chided. The greatest of teachers, however, are usually the first to admit how much they still need to learn. Nicodemus was still a questioner and a learner.

11, 12. Verily, verily, I say unto thee, We speak that we do know, and testify that we have seen; and ye receive not our witness. If I have told you earthly things, and ye believe not, how shall ye believe, if I tell you of heavenly things?

Jesus did not engage in trivial remarks, even in conversation with one other person. The import of what He addressed to Nicodemus went far beyond any one time, place, or person. *We speak.* The Father in Heaven, and prophets such as John the Baptist, and especially the one and only Son of God declared certainties not known to the unaided human mind.

Ye receive not. Nicodemus was not alone in his reluctance to understand and accept what Jesus taught. In fact, among his company of religious leaders he was perhaps the least resistant of all. Large numbers, on the other hand, would forever reject.

I have told you earthly things. Jesus has taken a common earthly phenomenon such as the blowing of the wind as an illustration. Yet Nicodemus is so cautious in his thinking that he is excessively slow to accept this as a basis for agreeing that the mystery of human redemption is to be expected. *If I tell you of heavenly things?* Such as He now proceeds to present—the mystery of His own divine person, the unfathomable love of God for man, His plan for man's redemption, and the eternal relationship of man with God in Heaven.

How Can These Things Be?

When Marco Polo returned from his journey to the court of the great Khans of China, his stories and those of his companions were ridiculed in medieval Europe. When they told of the splendor of the Chinese court and its palaces and of commerce being carried on with bank notes, which were not to be used in Europe until four hundred years later, they simply could not be believed. The wealth, literature, art, military might, and trade they encountered were discounted as the exaggerated reports of an enthusiastic traveler seeking fame for himself. Somehow the truth Marco Polo spoke did not fit with the concepts of the Far East held by those who heard him.

The human family has always been like that. We prefer our preconceptions to facts, and our prejudices to reality.

Nicodemus could not believe what Jesus was telling him. His question, "How can these things be?" reflected all the problems the new birth presented to his mind and tradition.

Isn't it sad that one of the greatest truths ever taught among men is still rejected because it does not conform to the experience, educational bent, or prejudice of many hearers?   —W. P.

IV. Divine Provision
(John 3:13-15)

A. God's Son (v. 13)

13. And no man hath ascended up to heaven, but he that came down from heaven, even the Son of man which is in heaven.

The first element in the birth from above is God's sending of the Son who made it possible. The Son came to earth as eyewitness to things eternal. No human could climb to Heaven to discover them. The contact had to be made from the other direction. The clause, *which is in heaven*, does not appear in the oldest manuscripts of the New Testament, hence is omitted from recent English translations. It speaks of the Lord's eternal abode, to which He returned in His ascension (Acts 1:9-11).

B. God's Sacrifice (v. 14)

14. And as Moses lifted up the serpent in the wilderness, even so must the Son of man be lifted up.

At one point during Israel's wilderness wanderings, the people complained so bitterly against God that He sent poisonous serpents among them and many died. Repentance came, and God instructed Moses to cast and erect on a pole a serpent of brass, upon which the snake-bitten people could look, and live. (Numbers 21:4-9) Jesus presented that as a prediction of His own sacrificial death on the cross. Later He said, "I, if I be lifted up from the earth, will draw all men unto me," and the Gospel writer added, "This he said, signifying what death he should die" (John 12:32, 33).

C. God's Salvation (v. 15)

15. That whosoever believeth in him should not perish, but have eternal life.

Here we see the motivation of all God's Heavenly doing. He is not willing that any should perish, but desires that all should come to repentance (2 Peter 3:9), which leads to life eternal (Acts 11:18). Here is a shift in words, but not in meaning. Up to this point Jesus had spoken of the *kingdom of God*, or of Heaven; here He spoke of *eternal life*. They are the same. God's reign is eternal, and it is life.

V. Wrap-up and Review (John 3:16, 17)

16. For God so loved the world, that he gave his only begotten Son, that whosoever believeth in him should not perish, but have everlasting life.

In this grand Golden Text of the Bible is the summary of all Jesus said to Nicodemus. The words express ultimate truth through a whole series of ultimate factors. *God* is the center of all the "heavenly things" that Nicodemus had been studying for a lifetime and had not fully understood. *Love* is the nature of God, defined here by ultimate demonstration. *The world*—specifically all humanity—encompasses the human climax of God's creation. God *gave*, as the perfect expression of His love. To the unloving and the unresponsive He gave, without the assurance that even this would bring a response. *His only begotten Son* was the one and only being to whom He was Father by a biological miracle as well as by identity in character and purpose. *Whosoever believeth in him* identifies a provision and invitation without barrier, without limit, and without compulsion. Disbelief, in the form of either doubt or disobedience (John 3:36), is the way by which the unwilling ones may escape from the acceptance of God's gift and God's presence. *Should not perish, but have everlasting life*. This marks the ultimate purpose of God and the ultimate benefit to man.

17. For God sent not his Son into the world to condemn the world; but that the world through him might be saved.

Condemn in this instance translates a word that is almost always translated *judge*, or to pass judgment. The basic meaning is that of selecting one thing over another, hence deciding. But the fact that the antonym in this verse is *to save* suggests that the Greek word used here could also have the connotation *to condemn*. But neither judgment nor condemnation was God's main purpose in sending His Son into the world. The Son came from God to bring salvation, to rescue mankind from sin and its punishment and to bring them back to God.

Conclusion

A. Heirs to the Kingdom

Scripture tells us nothing more of Nicodemus until some thirty months later when Jesus was at Jerusalem for the feast of Tabernacles and the leaders of the Pharisees sought to arrest Him. Then Nicodemus chided them, "Doth our law judge any man, before it hear him, and know what he doeth?" (John 7:51). Another six months passed before the final events of Jesus' earthly ministry. Then Nicodemus joined with Joseph of Arimathea in claiming, preparing, and wrapping Jesus' body for burial (John 19:38-42).

It was that death and burial, followed by resurrection on the third day, that provided the effective factual basis for the reign of Jesus in the kingdom He had announced. These facts also solved the mystery of the birth from above—birth of water and of Spirit—as believers identify with their Lord in a spiritual death, burial, and resurrection (Romans 6:3-5). Hearers of the gospel know more clearly now the mysteries of the kingdom concerning which Nicodemus could only listen in uncomprehending amazement. We are heirs of the kingdom!

B. Prayer

We thank You with glad humility, dear God, for spiritual pioneers like Nicodemus, who searched diligently for the truths of the kingdom that have been told so clearly to us. Thank You especially for Jesus Your Son, in whom we have available the new birth to new life—life eternal in Your kingdom. Help us, we pray, to live in a manner appropriate to children and heirs in the kingdom of Heaven. We pray in Jesus' name. Amen.

C. Thought to Remember

"For God so loved the world, that he gave his only begotten Son, that whosoever believeth in him should not perish, but have everlasting life" (John 3:16).

Home Daily Bible Readings

Monday, Dec. 4—Nicodemus' Questions (John 3:1-4)
Tuesday, Dec. 5—All Must Be Born Again (John 3:5-13)
Wednesday, Dec. 6—A New Heart (Ezekiel 36:25-28)
Thursday, Dec. 7—Christ Gives Us Eternal Life (John 3:14-17)
Friday, Dec. 8—Come Toward the Light (John 3:18-21)
Saturday, Dec. 9—Renewal in the Spirit (Titus 3:3-7)
Sunday, Dec. 10—He Who Comes From Heaven (John 3:31-36)

Learning by Doing

This page contains an alternate lesson plan emphasizing learning activities. Classes desiring such student involvement will find these suggestions helpful.

Learning Goals

"Born again" is a phrase heard today as applying to athletes and actors, salesmen and singers, politicians and preachers. It refers to a rejuvenation, a return from oblivion, a recapturing of skill, fame, fortune, and power once held. But when Jesus spoke of a person's being "born again," he was not referring to a return to former greatness but the infusion of a new, previously non-existent dimension of life. After having experienced today's lesson, your students should be able to:

1. Understand what it means to be born of the Holy Spirit.

2. Feel a deep appreciation for the inner dimension of their salvation.

3. Be ready to share with others the importance and meaning of an inner conversion.

Into the Lesson

At some time in our lives, most of us have made ourselves look foolish by something we have said. Ask your students to share one such incident from their own lives. You may want to "prime the pump" by giving them a couple of minutes to discuss it with a neighbor. Then have volunteers *briefly* share their incident with the class. These will probably be quite funny. Wrap up this activity by making the point that sometimes we ask the wrong questions or say the wrong thing because our minds and the minds of those around us are running on different tracks. We are speaking different languages. Note that in our text today Jesus and Nicodemus seemed to be talking different languages. Nicodemus didn't seem to understand what Jesus was talking about.

Into the Word

Before you read the text, ask the students to climb into Nicodemus' skin and feel how he must have felt during this exchange with Jesus, remembering that he himself was an important leader and a teacher of the law (see lesson comments on verses 1 and 2). The students are to become Nicodemus, so that they can feel what he felt. Have three students read John 3:1-17: one as narrator (John the apostle), one to read the words spoken by Nicodemus, and one to read the words of Jesus (a red-letter edition of the *New International Version* translation is

helpful for the exercise). After the reading of the text, have students respond. Ask several students, "How did you feel, Nicodemus, after this exchange with Jesus?" After the students have shared, point out that Jesus and Nicodemus were speaking different languages. Ask, "Could you give a name to the language Jesus was speaking? How about the language that Nicodemus was speaking?"

This was all very important to Jesus' point. Nicodemus could only hope to understand the kingdom of God by being born again by the Holy Spirit. The realm of the Spirit is different from the realm of the flesh (v. 6). To help students understand this new birth by the Holy Spirit, have them work in pairs to answer the following questions. You can put the questions on a chalkboard or overhead projector, print them on a sheet of paper with space to answer, or have them use their student books.

1. What does it mean to be born again?

2. Can a person be a Christian without being born again?

3. What role does water play in this new birth? (v. 5) Why?

4. What role does the Holy Spirit play in this new birth? (v. 5). why?

5. What are the evidences that a person has been born of the Spirit?

Allow ten minutes before calling this to a close, because some real thought is required here. As you have the students share some of their answers, be sure to correct misunderstandings gently, for you may find confusion in this area of the new birth. Read the lesson development carefully for answers to the questions.

Into Life

Ask for a show of hands of those who basically understand the meaning of new birth. "Volunteer" someone who has raised his hand to come to the front. Seat him in a chair across from someone who didn't raise his hand. Give this instruction: "I want you to explain to your friend here what it means to be born again." To the one who doesn't understand, say this: "You are to make it a dialogue. Ask questions about what you don't understand." If you have time, choose others to do the same. In closing, pray that God will give each person the ability to help others understand the new birth.

Let's Talk It Over

The questions on this page are designed to encourage review of the lesson Scriptures and to promote discussion of the lesson by the class. The answers provided are only discussion starters. Let your class talk it over from there.

1. A part of what Nicodemus had in mind when he came to Jesus must have been the question of how one might gain eternal life. Do most people today have a similar concern for obtaining eternal life, and if so, how can we use this concern as a means of presenting Jesus Christ to them?

While many people today seem to be almost totally caught up in the here and now, we often see evidence that thoughts of immortality are not far from their minds. An example of this is the widespread interest shown in the past few years to descriptions of after-death experiences by those who have claimed to come back to life after dying. It is safe to say that the majority of people today have at least some interest in the subject of eternal life. What we must do is to make use of those occasions when our friends and acquaintances are led by circumstances to give thought to the subject. The death of a loved one or a brush with death themselves may generate such thinking. At times like these, we need to be ready with the Bible's powerful and penetrating statements regarding eternal life and prepared with our own personal testimony of what this precious Biblical doctrine means to us.

2. Why is it vital that we emphasize that being "born again" involves being "born from above"?

The term *born again* has received prominent usage in recent years. It has often been mentioned in the national news media in connection with famous people who have claimed to have had such an experience. Some well-known individuals have spoken of themselves as being "born again" without the corresponding evidence of a life transformed and dedicated to God. Some of these people may have undergone a mere psychological or emotional crisis, which involved desperate prayer or a frantic clinging to a phrase of Scripture. Once the cause of the crisis has disappeared, the individual may resume his life much as it was before he was "born again." In contrast, when a person is "born from above," his overall outlook is changed; his values and attitudes are refashioned. He becomes an actual citizen of Heaven (Philippians 3:20), ready to live according to its standards.

3. What are some aspects of comfortable Christianity that continue to be common, and what would be the radical counterpart to each?

Many Christians still want to sit in the pew and be fed or uplifted. They may view active discipleship as a source of struggle and conflict, and may protest that they experience enough of these realities on their job or in their home. But Jesus called us to take up our cross (Matthew 16:24-26), which indicates a commitment to service that can be burdensome or painful.

Another aspect of comfortable Christianity relates to giving of money to the church and other Christian causes. In Mark 12:41-44, Jesus called His disciples' attention to the gifts being made to the temple treasury and contrasted the large gifts many "gave out of their wealth" (v. 44, New International Version) with the sacrificial offering of a poor widow. The gifts presented on a typical Sunday morning, may not represent much of a sacrifice—the givers may not suffer much discomfort in offering them. Radical Christianity involves a genuine sacrifice in terms of material things and temporal pleasures.

4. John 3:16 is such a familiar verse of Scripture to many of us that we may be inclined to overlook its grandeur. What can we do to keep our appreciation of it fresh and vibrant?

One method that may be employed to enhance one's appreciation for this verse is to substitute first-person, singular pronouns for the words *the world* and *whosoever.* Or a person may insert his own name in place of these words. This is a legitimate application, since the world that God loved and for which God gave His Son is the world of individuals like ourselves. Another way of using this verse is in making it an outline for a prayer of thanksgiving. We may thank God for loving us, for giving us His Son, for allowing us to hear the gospel that led us to belief in Jesus Christ, for the means of escaping punishment in Hell, and for the joy of eternal life now and in Heaven. Those who engage in personal evangelism will better appreciate this verse for its appeal to the spiritually hungry, as it offers God's love to those who have come to hate themselves, and it extends eternal life to those who have experienced some of the bitter foretaste of sin, death, and divine judgment.

Savior of the World

LESSON SCRIPTURE: John 4:1-42.

PRINTED TEXT: John 4:7-15, 27-29, 39-42.

John 4:7-15, 27-29, 39-42

7 There cometh a woman of Samaria to draw water: Jesus saith unto her, Give me to drink.

8 (For his disciples were gone away unto the city to buy meat.)

9 Then saith the woman of Samaria unto him, How is it that thou, being a Jew, askest drink of me, which am a woman of Samaria? for the Jews have no dealings with the Samaritans.

10 Jesus answered and said unto her, If thou knewest the gift of God, and who it is that saith to thee, Give me to drink; thou wouldest have asked of him, and he would have given thee living water.

11 The woman saith unto him, Sir, thou hast nothing to draw with, and the well is deep: from whence then hast thou that living water?

12 Art thou greater than our father Jacob, which gave us the well, and drank thereof himself, and his children, and his cattle?

13 Jesus answered and said unto her, Whosoever drinketh of this water shall thirst again:

14 But whosoever drinketh of the water that I shall give him shall never thirst; but the water that I shall give him shall be in him a well of water springing up into everlasting life.

15 The woman saith unto him, Sir, give me this water, that I thirst not, neither come hither to draw.

. . . .

27 And upon this came his disciples, and marveled that he talked with the woman: yet no man said, What seekest thou? or, Why talkest thou with her?

28 The woman then left her waterpot, and went her way into the city, and saith to the men,

29 Come, see a man, which told me all things that ever I did: is not this the Christ?

. . . .

39 And many of the Samaritans of that city believed on him for the saying of the woman, which testified, He told me all that ever I did.

40 So when the Samaritans were come unto him, they besought him that he would tarry with them: and he abode there two days.

41 And many more believed because of his own word;

42 And said unto the woman, Now we believe, not because of thy saying: for we have heard him ourselves, and know that this is indeed the Christ, the Saviour of the world.

GOLDEN TEXT: Whosoever drinketh of this water shall thirst again: but whosoever drinketh of the water that I shall give him shall never thirst.—John 4:13, 14.

John: The Gospel of Life and Light
Unit 1. Jesus Comes to His Own
(Lessons 1-4)

Lesson Aims

After this lesson students should be able to:

1. Show how the conversations of Jesus with Nicodemus and with the Samaritan woman combine to reveal Him as the Savior of all mankind.

2. Show how Jesus himself is related to the "water of life."

3. Plan some way in which he or she will act to make Jesus known as the Savior of the world.

Lesson Outline

INTRODUCTION

    A. "Just Between the Two of Us"

    B. The Samaritan Problem

    C. Lesson Background

I. THE GIFT, THE WATER OF LIFE (John 4:7-15)

    A. The Lord Accepts Help (vv. 7-9)

    B. He Offers the Gift (v. 10)

    C. He Faces Questions (vv. 11, 12)

    D. He Sustains the Offer (vv. 13-15)

       Living Water

II. THE OFFER IS REPORTED (John 4:27-29)

III. THE REPORT IS ACCEPTED (John 4:39-42)

    A. Some Believe the Telling (vv. 39, 40)

    B. Many Believe the Demonstration (vv. 41, 42)

CONCLUSION

    A. Sufficient Knowledge

    B. Prayer

    C. Thought to Remember

Display visual 3 from the visuals packet and let it remain before the class. It is shown on page 140.

Introduction

A. "Just Between the Two of Us"

Jesus did not indulge in trivial conversation. *Trivial* (from the Latin for "three ways") has come to describe the idle chatter in which two friends may engage as they linger at the point where their paths separate. "Just between the two of us" our talk may become rather irresponsible.

Not so with Jesus. Some of His most meaningful and helpful conversation occurred in one-to-one settings. In the lesson last week we studied His after-hours talk with Nicodemus; today we consider a well-side chat with a woman who came to draw water. The two events are different in many ways, but much alike in others. The settings were as different as night and day, urban and rural, Jewish center and sacred spot of the Samaritan. The persons involved were as different as man and woman, leader among the Jews and one known mostly for her many marriages. The one came deliberately to inquire from Jesus; the other met Jesus by chance, and he started the conversation. Yet, in both instances, Jesus dealt with the other person as one in need of God. To both He spoke in familiar terms about human need. Would that we followers of the Lord might learn to talk so easily, and so fruitfully of things most important to us and our friends.

B. The Samaritan Problem

Like many ancient enmities, the feud between the Jews and the Samaritans grew out of deep roots. Its early seeds were in the division of Solomon's kingdom into Judah (under his son Rehoboam) and Israel (under Jeroboam). The city of Samaria became the capital of Israel. Two centuries later the Assyrians conquered Israel and scattered its more substantial citizens throughout their land, replacing them with strangers brought in from many places (2 Kings 17:24). The result was a population mixed in nationalities and religions.

Afterward, the people of Judah were carried into captivity by the Babylonians. By the time Cyrus, the king of Persia, sent Jews back to Jerusalem to rebuild their city and their temple, the remnant Jews in the region of Samaria had made the law of Moses a dominant religious pattern among the mixed population. They still were not friendly with the Jews returning to Jerusalem, but they sought to join them in rebuilding the temple. Their offer was flatly refused, and thereafter the Samaritans did all they could to hinder all reconstruction in Jerusalem. The book of Ezra tells the story.

During the following five centuries until the time of Christ, the Samaritan religion became well established, with the five books of Moses as its only Scripture, with its temple located on Mount Gerizim, near Sychar, and with its own priesthood. Jewish disdain for all things Samaritan was well expressed in the charge hurled at Jesus in Jerusalem: "Say we not well that thou art a Samaritan, and hast a devil"? (John 8:48).

For reasons of safety as well as preference, Jews traveling between Galilee in the north and Judea in the south usually avoided Samaria, crossing the Jordan eastward through Perea.

C. Lesson Background

Jesus spent some nine months mostly in Judea, building His early ministry on the work of John the Baptist. Then King Herod arrested John. According to Josephus, the Jewish historian, John was imprisoned at Machaerus, east of the Dead Sea. Anticipating a possible move against himself, and desiring also to avoid confrontation with Pharisees resentful of His growing popularity, Jesus withdrew northward to Galilee. He chose the direct route through Samaria rather than to go through Perea, which was in Herod's domain.

His route led to Sychar, near ancient Shechem, and close by Mount Gerizim. Here was ground that Jacob had bought when he returned from his twenty years in Haran. He later conveyed the plot to Joseph for a burial place (Genesis 33:19; Joshua 24:32). On the site is a well, dug at first to a depth of more than a hundred feet. Samaritan tradition assigned to Jacob the digging and first use of the well.

Here Jesus and His disciples arrived, and he rested while His companions went into town to buy provisions. "It was about the sixth hour"— perhaps noon (by Jewish reckoning) or perhaps early evening (by Roman count). The apostle John knew and recorded this detail, not essential to the story.

I. The Gift, the Water of Life
(John 4:7-15)

A. The Lord Accepts Help (vv. 7-9)

7, 8. There cometh a woman of Samaria to draw water: Jesus saith unto her, Give me to drink. (For his disciples were gone away unto the city to buy meat.)

Jesus understood and respected the Samaritan woman, and perceived her needs, just as He had perceived the needs of Nicodemus. One may only guess why she chose this time and place to *draw water*. She may have lived or been employed nearby. She observed Jesus enough to perceive, perhaps by His clothing, or His speech, that He was a Jew. The best she could expect from such a man was polite aloofness. To the Jews, she was one of "those people." And so was He to her.

But Jesus was tired and thirsty. A mild request for a drink would not be refused. Besides, Jesus wanted to talk to this woman, and there was no better opening line than "Give me to drink." It was an honest request for needed help.

Many people are drawn to Jesus not so much by what He gives as by what He asks. In the asking, He bestows a great gift; He confers a partnership in God's enterprise.

We may wonder at the disciples' buying food in a Samaritan town (*meat* in the *King James Version* is food of any sort). Because of their disdain for the Samaritans, the Jews avoided contact with them as a matter of course. Yet commercial dealings frequently penetrated barriers that were not crossed in social or religious fellowship. Besides, Jesus desired to break down all such barriers.

9. Then saith the woman of Samaria unto him, How is it that thou, being a Jew, askest drink of me, which am a woman of Samaria? for the Jews have no dealings with the Samaritans.

The woman seems not to have been objecting to the request, but she was astonished, curious, and inquiring. The explanation, *Jews have no dealings with the Samaritans*, is interpreted in *Today's English Version*, "Jews will not use the same cups and bowls that Samaritans use." Thus it specifies the *dealings* that were involved in this circumstance. Further, it was not customary for a man to speak to a lone woman in public. Jesus' all-inclusive concern for people could not be so restricted. Human differences disappeared under His gaze. Skin color, nationality, language, cultural habits, or physical capacities melted away in the warmth of the Lord's inclusive love.

B. He Offers the Gift (v. 10)

10. Jesus answered and said unto her, If thou knewest the gift of God, and who it is that saith to thee, Give me to drink; thou wouldest have asked of him, and he would have given thee living water.

Jesus responded to the woman's need more than to her words, but in doing so He revealed why He had asked her for a drink. It was the means by which He could introduce to her the

---

How to Say It

GADARA. *Gad*-uh-ruh.

GERIZIM. *Gair*-ih-zim or Guh-*rye*-zim.

HARAN. *Hay*-run.

JEROBOAM. Jair-o-*bo*-um.

MACHAERUS. Muh-*key*-rus or Muh-*kye*-rus.

NICODEMUS. *Nick*-uh-*dee*-mus (strong accent on *dee*).

PEREA. Peh-*ree*-uh.

REHOBOAM. Re-ho-*bo*-um.

SHECHEM. *Shee*-kem or *Shek*-em.

SYCHAR. *Sy*-kar.

visual 3

DRINK THE
WATER
JESUS OFFERS
AND
NEVER
THIRST
AGAIN!

living water He desired to give. She had to become acquainted with the Giver before she could recognize the value of the gift.

Living water was something she could understand in its natural sense. It was fresh, flowing water in a supply that was not diminished by drawing from it, as opposed to water standing in a pool or cistern that could be emptied and left dry. God's messengers had spoken of His presence as living (or life-giving) water among His people. See Jeremiah 2:13. The knowledge of God was to flow out from the temple at Jerusalem as living and healing waters to all the nations (Ezekiel 47:1; Zechariah 14:8).

Again Jesus spoke of himself as the inexhaustible source of living water flowing out to the world through His followers in John 7:37, 38.

The final glory envisioned in Revelation 22:1 sounds the same theme.

If the woman had known that the tired and thirsty Jew before her was the source of God's indescribable gift of life eternal (2 Corinthians 9:15), she would have been making request of Him, and the request would have been fulfilled.

C. He Faces Questions (vv. 11, 12)

11, 12. The woman saith unto him, Sir, thou hast nothing to draw with, and the well is deep: from whence then hast thou that living water? Art thou greater than our father Jacob, which gave us the well, and drank thereof himself, and his children, and his cattle?

The woman was having trouble with Jesus' figurative language. And small wonder! Even Nicodemus, a religious leader, being already convinced that Jesus was a teacher sent from God, had faced the same difficulty in perceiving what was not material and physical (John 3:4, 9). So the woman could not think immediately of any water source beyond this well.

She respected the man before her. She addressed Him by the title that is also translated "master" or even "Lord." But she was sure that He could not do in a moment, barehanded, what

tradition assigned to the massive toil of men serving the patriarch Jacob. How many Samaritans could actually prove they had descended from Jacob is an open question, but at this tradition-hallowed place, it seemed worth a try. They all liked to picture themselves as mingling here with the family and flocks of the man who had given the chosen nation its name, Israel. So Jesus' comment seemed to violate both common sense and sacred tradition.

D. He Sustains the Offer (vv. 13-15)

13, 14. Jesus answered and said unto her, Whosoever drinketh of this water shall thirst again: but whosoever drinketh of the water that I shall give him shall never thirst; but the water that I shall give him shall be in him a well of water springing up into everlasting life.

It should have been immediately evident that Jesus was talking about a different kind of *water.* Even He would continue to experience the kind of thirst that had just caused Him to ask for a drink; and at His crucifixion He was to say through parched lips, "I thirst" (John 19:28). The woman had yet to learn of that other blessed kind of thirst recorded in Matthew 5:6.

Today's English Version translates the verse before us, "The water that I will give him will become in him a spring which will provide him with life-giving water and give him eternal life." After quoting the similar promise by Jesus in John 7:37, 38, the inspired writer explains, "But this spake he of the Spirit, which they that believe on him should receive: for the Holy Ghost was not yet given; because that Jesus was not yet glorified" (John 7:39). The time came when Jesus was glorified in being raised from the dead and finally received into Heaven. Ten days after that event the Holy Spirit came first upon the Lord's disciples, and their spokesman Simon Peter named the terms by which others might receive the Spirit (Acts 2:38). The vigorous activity of the first-century Christians in spreading the gospel demonstrated the truth of Jesus' pledge to the woman of Samaria: the water of life in Christ does enable the one who has received it to become a sharer with others, without diminishing his own supply.

15. The woman saith unto him, Sir, give me this water, that I thirst not, neither come hither to draw.

The woman liked what she heard, but she didn't hear what the Lord was saying. She simply desired to be liberated from daily trips to the well. Suppose, though, that Jesus had granted that wish in the manner that it has been granted to us, to all intents and purposes, by modern plumbing. She probably would have been content, as all too many persons are content, with the lesser blessings, and would have been left as empty and dry of spirit as she was before. The spiritual poverty of our affluent society testifies to the fact.

Jesus did not chide this woman with her lack of understanding, but suggested that she invite her husband to join the discussion. Then He revealed His awareness of her tangled domestic life, and she acknowledged Him a prophet. So she talked about places of worship, and He responded with God's hunger for worship that centers in honesty of heart rather than propriety of place. She was willing to wait for the Messiah to deal with all such prickly subjects, and He announced himself clearly as that One! The conversation had leaped and bounded to the pinnacle of revelation! (vv. 16-26).

LIVING WATER

In a January, 1986, advertisement, this rather unusual headline appeared: *If you can operate a garden tiller, you can be your own water well driller!* The article promised that all the pure, fresh water you needed for your home and garden could be yours and you would never need to pay another water bill. The cost would be just pennies a day when you drilled in your own back yard. You could have free water 365 days each year.

The advertisement promised that you could drill your own well, even if you had no experience in seeking water. Upon request, a brochure would be sent free and with no obligation.

In many arid parts of the American West, such a well would be a blessing that everyone would desire. I wonder how many in that part of our land, knowing how deep the water table may be, would venture even to send for the free brochure!

Jesus promised the Samaritan woman living water that would forever quench her thirst.

It sounded too good to be true, but she believed His words and discovered that He had an inexhaustible supply of spiritual food and drink to meet her need. It takes faith to try the impossible. The woman's faith revolutionized her life.   —W. P.

II. The Offer Is Reported
(John 4:27-29)

27. And upon this came his disciples, and marveled that he talked with the woman: yet no man said, What seekest thou? or, Why talkest thou with her?

The returning disciples must have seen in the woman's demeanor an excitement that added to their natural wonder at Jesus' breach of custom. They knew Him well enough, though, to respect His judgment and to be sure that He would tell them what they should know. Besides, what kind of questions would be suitable to the occasion? "None of them said to her, 'What do you want?' or asked him, 'Why are you talking with her?'" *(Today's English Version).* How, after all, does one go about asking God to account for His actions?

28, 29. The woman then left her waterpot, and went her way into the city, and saith to the men, Come, see a man, which told me all things that ever I did: is not this the Christ?

The woman had found at that well something far more important than a jugful of water. Whether her excitement caused her to forget the waterpot, or whether her haste persuaded her deliberately to come back for it later, it is clear that her new errand completely overshadowed the old one. She had to tell what she had found and invite others to share in the discovery.

Her report reveals the nature of her own emotional thirst. Jesus had talked about the water of life, and she hadn't understood. He had set forth the basic principle of true and acceptable worship, and she had changed the subject. He had said plainly that He was the long expected Messiah, and she didn't quite believe it. But He had respected her as a person and had asked a favor that she could grant. Most of all He had known and had revealed His understanding of *her:* "Come see a man who told me all about *me!*"

The woman's report was not limited to the *men* of the city. The word used indicates *mankind.* It seems clear that the woman was convinced Jesus was the Christ, but, instead of declaring it dogmatically she wisely asked the townspeople to decide for themselves.

III. The Report Is Accepted
(John 4:39-42)
A. Some Believe the Telling
(vv. 39, 40)

39, 40. And many of the Samaritans of that city believed on him for the saying of the woman, which testified, He told me all that ever I did. So when the Samaritans were come unto him, they besought him that he would tarry with them: and he abode there two days.

Were the citizens of Sychar naive and credulous, that they accepted so unlikely a story from so unlikely a witness? There was, in fact, some evident exaggeration in her report. Jesus had recounted only enough of her life story to convince her that He knew it all. It was clear to all hearers, though, that she was deeply moved and

Home Daily Bible Readings

Monday, Dec. 11—Baptizing Many Disciples (John 4:1-6)
Tuesday, Dec. 12—Speaking to the Samaritan Woman (John 4:7-10)
Wednesday, Dec. 13—Give Me That Water! (John 4:11-15)
Thursday, Dec. 14— Jesus as a Prophet (John 4:16-20)
Friday, Dec. 15—Jesus Revealed Himself as the Messiah (John 4:21-26)
Saturday, Dec. 16—Jesus Plans for the Harvest (John 4:31-38)
Sunday, Dec. 17—Many Samaritans Believed (John 4:27-30, 39-42)

thoroughly convinced by her experience with Jesus. Her own conviction and enthusiasm were convincing.

A considerable number accepted the woman's urgent invitation to go out to the well and see Jesus for themselves. It didn't take long to convince them that this prophet was worth a more thorough hearing. They had many questions to ask Him and He stayed and answered them.

At work here were two lasting principles. It is still true that the *invitation* and the *continued presence of friends* are major factors in almost anyone's church attendance, making a great difference in where and whether one goes to study and worship. It is also true that the abiding presence of Christ depends on the welcome extended to Him. The Samaritans invited Him to stay and He did; the citizens of Gadara later urged Him to leave, and He left (Matthew 8:34—9:1).

B. Many Believe the Demonstration (vv. 41, 42)

41, 42. And many more believed because of his own word; and said unto the woman, Now we believe, not because of thy saying: for we have heard him ourselves, and know that this is indeed the Christ, the Saviour of the world.

The woman had believed what she was saying, and she convinced some; Jesus personified what He was saying, and He convinced many. "Never man spake like this man"; so reported certain officers who were sent to arrest Jesus and came away empty-handed (John 7:46). The Samaritans were won by His words, apparently without any supporting miracles, unless His knowledge of His hearers be considered miraculous. Their confession of faith was simple and direct. It emphasized the element that brought

peculiar joy to them: the universality of the gospel. Jesus had come as *the Saviour of the world*, not merely the Jews. He had come to them—despised Samaritans—and shared with them the blessed good news from Heaven.

Even after this, however, when Jesus sent the twelve on preparatory missions in Galilee, He told them not to go "into any city of the Samaritans," but to approach only "the lost sheep of the house of Israel" (Matthew 10:5). The seed had been planted in Samaria for a later harvest. That harvest came through the evangelistic ministries of Philip, Peter, and John, some little while after the establishment of the church (Acts 1:8; 8:5-8, 14-25).

Conclusion

A. A Sufficient Knowledge

The woman who met Jesus at Jacob's well was not much of a scholar. She was well versed in prejudices and traditions, but short on understanding of abstract or spiritual matters. Yet she was aware of God, His law, and His promise of the Messiah. She knew what to look for in a prophet of God. Most significantly, she knew that God's blessings were to be shared and not hoarded. She became an important link in Jesus' total ministry.

The waterpot she left beside the well, as she hurried away with the news about Jesus, bears eloquent testimony to her conviction and conversion. Whether she did that in sheer excitement or by studied intent, she demonstrated that something more important than physical and material needs had caught her attention.

The chain of comparisons and contrasts between her and Nicodemus is thus extended. Neither of them fully understood what Jesus was trying to teach. Nicodemus went home to think it over; she ran to tell what she had learned. So the less promising of the two interviews became the more immediately fruitful one. She and her neighbors were among the first of mankind to confess Jesus openly as the Savior of the world.

B. Prayer

You, O God, have made Heaven and earth and all within them. In Your hand is the salvation of mankind, through Jesus, Your Son and our Lord. Help us to grasp anew that truth and find in it the excitement that will stir us to spread the news. We pray it in Jesus' name. Amen

C. Thought to Remember

"I will give unto him that is athirst of the fountain of the water of life freely" (Revelation 21:6).

Learning by Doing

This page contains an alternate lesson plan emphasizing learning activities. Classes desiring such student involvement will find these suggestions helpful.

Learning Goals

Some of the areas of the world in which the gospel of Christ is expanding the most rapidly have cultures that are different from our own. Yet we may find it difficult to reach across cultural barriers to bring the gospel to those who are hungriest for it. Our text today presents some valuable lessons about the cross-cultural communication of the gospel. As your students study the story of the Samaritan woman, they will be able to:

1. Examine the barriers that Christians face in converting people of other cultures to Christ.

2. Deal with their own attitudes toward people of other cultures or subcultures within our own society.

3. Make a commitment to themselves to make a new friend who is culturally different from them.

Into the Lesson

For this activity, seat your students in a circle. If that is impossible, ask them to number off around the group. Have the students speak to the persons on both sides of them in the circle (or the person with the number that is immediately higher or lower than his or her own) and share one substantive difference that they have with these persons. After two minutes at the most, go around the circle and ask each student to tell how he is different from the person on his left.

Hand every person a slip of paper (or you may use the student book for this activity) and ask them to write on it the name of a country whose culture is different from their own. Now have them find one substantive cultural difference between the people in the country they have chosen and those in their own country. After two minutes, ask several to share with the class significant cultural differences that they have noted.

Conclude by stating that these differences between individuals and cultures can present barriers to the communication of the gospel. Vastly differing cultures have walls between them which must be overcome before we can present Christ. Our text shows Jesus in action, overcoming a cultural barrier in order to introduce himself as Messiah to the Samaritan woman at the well.

Into the Word

Divide your class into three listening teams. If your class has thirty students or less, have them move chairs to sit in three discussion circles. If your class is larger, you may want to assign many smaller groups to form listening teams. Here are their assignments:

Team 1. List and describe the various cultural and personal barriers between Jesus and this Samaritan woman.

Team 2. What attitudes and feelings did Jesus possess that allowed Him to get close enough to the Samaritan woman to share with her the good news of salvation?

Team 3. What things did Jesus do that broke down barriers between himself and this Samaritan woman?

As you read aloud John 4:4-26, the teams are to listen for answers to their assignment. They may record notes in the student book or on a sheet of paper you give each group with their question. They may need up to ten minutes to discuss their assignment. Then call the class together, and have a scribe from each group discuss their results.

After this, read aloud John 4:27-42, and discuss the following questions:

1. Why was the Samaritan woman's testimony so effective to the people of Sychar?

2. Why does Jesus need to remind His disciples of an ever-present harvest (v. 35)?

3. What do you think Jesus and His disciples might have done during their two-day stay in Sychar? We are told how this event affected the Samaritans (v. 42), but how do you think it may have affected the disciples?

Into Life

Ask students to write the name of a subculture (other than their own) with which they are familiar. Now ask them to complete this sentence: "One thing that really turns me off about _____ (insert the subculture they have chosen) is that they _____." Share these with the class. Then discuss this question: "If God called you to become a witness to the very subculture you have chosen, would your attitude be a barrier? If so, how could you change it?" Ask for volunteers to befriend someone culturally different this week and report the results next week.

Let's Talk It Over

The questions on this page are designed to encourage review of the lesson Scriptures and to promote discussion of the lesson by the class. The answers provided are only discussion starters. Let your class talk it over from there.

1. The lesson writer notes that "Jesus understood and respected the Samaritan woman, and perceived her needs." Why is this an example we need to ponder in connection with evangelistic endeavors?

The question comes to mind, "Can we influence persons for Jesus Christ if we do not understand or respect them?" Perhaps we can, but it is more likely that those persons will give the gospel a fairer hearing if we show genuine interest in them and in the circumstances in which they live. Do we have difficulty respecting people of a race or nationality different from ours? Are we slow in understanding the customs, attitudes, and habits of individuals whose cultural backgrounds differ from ours? Jesus transcended such barriers and treated each individual with respect and genuine love. That should be our aim also.

2. Why is the symbol of living water an appropriate means of describing the satisfaction and refreshment of knowing Jesus?

All of us have known times of intense thirst and have experienced the sense of relief and revitalization when our thirst was satisfied. That illustrates the way Jesus can supply our deepest inner needs. We are made with a capacity for a thirst that only Jesus can satisfy. The salvation of Jesus, the friendship of Jesus, the guiding words of Jesus, the power and compassionate deeds of Jesus fill up and satisfy this tremendous craving within us. Isaiah records a beautiful invitation in connection with this: "Come, all you who are thirsty, come to the waters . . ." (Isaiah 55:1, *New International Version*). He goes on to show that God's provision for man's spiritual thirst is abundant and free, and he questions why human beings would seek instead after that which does not satisfy. So we need to recognize the thirst that is in us; we need to turn from any futile efforts to assuage it with temporal things; and we need to come wholeheartedly to Him who gives the living water and drink deeply of what He offers.

3. Why is the symbol of living water an appropriate means of describing the life and fruitfulness we receive through the ministry of the Holy Spirit?

A person who engages in farming or gardening has many opportunities to witness illustrations of how the Holy Spirit works. In a time of drought, plants wither, turn yellow or brown, and are hindered in their progress toward harvest. Then come the "showers of blessing," and in little time a transformation takes place. The plants are again green, growing, and forming fruit. In the spiritual realm, it is significant that Paul put such emphasis on "the fruit of the Spirit" (Galatians 5:22, 23). Without the ministry of the Holy Spirit, we would be barren. Much of the joy and satisfaction of the Christian life would be absent. But we need not linger long on such considerations, because the Holy Spirit has been given to us; and if we will cooperate with Him, He can make us like fields or gardens that are rich and ripe for harvest. And finally, through the power of the Holy Spirit who dwells within us, we will then be raised from the dead to live eternally with Christ (Romans 8:9-17).

4. How can we convince our friends and neighbors to attend services of the church, so that they may learn of Jesus?

What kinds of appeals do we use to convince our acquaintances that they should attend our church's services? Do we tell them what a good speaker our minister is, how well our choir sings, or how beautiful is the interior of our building? Are we eager to get them there to help us achieve a record attendance? The Samaritan woman's success in attracting her neighbors and acquaintances to Jesus resulted from her testimony that Jesus was close by and from her enthusiasm concerning how He had affected her. This is surely a key for us also. Whatever else is commendable about our church (and the features mentioned above are legitimate), the most important appeal we can present is, "Jesus Christ may be found there. We teach about Him, sing about Him, and call attention to His death and resurrection. You can recognize Him in the way our members love and serve one another. Come and see for yourself!" This will be a more convincing testimony if we can show in our own circumstances how meeting with Jesus in the church has genuinely blessed and strengthened us.

The Word Among Us

LESSON SCRIPTURE: Luke 2:8-12; John 1:1-5, 9-18.

PRINTED TEXT: Luke 2:8-12; John 1:1-5, 9-18.

Luke 2:8-12

8 And there were in the same country shepherds abiding in the field, keeping watch over their flock by night.

9 And, lo, the angel of the Lord came upon them, and the glory of the Lord shone round about them; and they were sore afraid.

10 And the angel said unto them, Fear not: for, behold, I bring you good tidings of great joy, which shall be to all people.

11 For unto you is born this day in the city of David a Saviour, which is Christ the Lord.

12 And this shall be a sign unto you; Ye shall find the babe wrapped in swaddling clothes, lying in a manger.

John 1:1-5, 9-18

1 In the beginning was the Word, and the Word was with God, and the Word was God.

2 The same was in the beginning with God.

3 All things were made by him; and without him was not any thing made that was made.

4 In him was life; and the life was the light of men.

5 And the light shineth in darkness; and the darkness comprehended it not.

. . . .

9 That was the true Light, which lighteth every man that cometh into the world.

10 He was in the world, and the world was made by him, and the world knew him not.

11 He came unto his own, and his own received him not.

12 But as many as received him, to them gave he power to become the sons of God, even to them that believe on his name:

13 Which were born, not of blood, nor of the will of the flesh, nor of the will of man, but of God.

14 And the Word was made flesh, and dwelt among us, (and we beheld his glory, the glory as of the only begotten of the Father,) full of grace and truth.

15 John bare witness of him, and cried, saying, This was he of whom I spake, He that cometh after me is preferred before me; for he was before me.

16 And of his fulness have all we received, and grace for grace.

17 For the law was given by Moses, but grace and truth came by Jesus Christ.

18 No man hath seen God at any time; the only begotten Son, which is in the bosom of the Father, he hath declared him.

GOLDEN TEXT: The Word was made flesh, and dwelt among us.—John 1:14.

Lesson Aims

This lesson should prepare the student to:

1. Show how Luke's account of Jesus' birth and John's introduction of Jesus as the eternal Word fit together.

2. Name and discuss the qualities in Jesus that prove Him to be the one and only Son of God.

3. Engage more fully in a study of the Gospel account of Jesus.

Lesson Outline

INTRODUCTION
- A. Too Full for Words
- B. Close-Up and Long-Range Pictures
- I. THE SAVIOR AND ANOINTED LORD (Luke 2:8-12)
   - A. Shepherds Were Listening (vv. 8, 9)
   - B. An Angel Announced It (vv. 10-12)
   Fear and Faith
- II. CHRIST THE ETERNAL WORD (John 1:1-5)
   - A. He Is Eternal (vv. 1, 2)
   - B. He Is Creator (v. 3)
   - C. He Is Life and Light (vv. 4, 5)
- III. CHRIST AS GOD AMONG MEN (John 1:9-18)
   - A. Rejected by Many (vv. 9-11)
   - B. Received by Some (vv. 12, 13)
   - C. Reported by Witnesses (vv. 14-16)
   - D. Revealer of God (vv. 17, 18)
- CONCLUSION
   - A. Going Home With Him
   - B. Prayer
   - C. Thought to Remember

Display visual 4 from the visuals packet and let it remain before the class. The visual is shown on page 148.

Introduction

A. Too Full for Words

"I'm just too full for words."

"I never can think of the right words to say."

Which of us has not at some time faced the frustration of not being able to find words to express some deep emotion, or some wish to console a grieving friend. Among the multiplied thousands of words in our language, there has

to be that one word in which some thoughtful person has said to another exactly what we want to say. We just can't think of it at the moment. So we may be tempted to avoid the interview altogether, or perhaps to presume on our hearer's prior knowledge of the subject, saying an empty, "You know."

The hearer may not know, even after the chosen word has been uttered. That word may not carry the same meaning to the hearer that it had for the user. The result can be confusion.

God does not indulge in you-know's. His message is affirmative and clear. The Word in which it is expressed is not always spoken; it may be a creative act, a saving miracle, or a vision. At its best it is the living Word, God's Son, expressing God's "I love you." All this has been necessary because God's thoughts are so much higher than our thoughts that we find it difficult to perceive His meaning, even in familiar terms. We tend to think only of what we would mean if we said those words, and it may not be the same at all. Very seldom, for example, can we come even close to meaning the same thing by our "I love you" that God means by His. Not words alone, therefore, but the living Word—God in human form through the person of Christ Jesus—was necessary to our understanding of God.

B. Close-Up and Long-Range Pictures

Today's lesson takes us to the Gospels of Luke and of John for two contrasting views of one fact—God's coming to earth in the person of Jesus of Nazareth to save us sinners and lead us into His presence in glory.

Luke brings his reportorial camera up close in order to record factual details. So from him we learn that Mary was visited in Nazareth by an angel who told her that she, a virgin, was to become the mother of God's Son. She went to Judea to visit her kinswoman, Elizabeth, and they talked excitedly about their common experiences in pregnancy. Later on, she went again to Judea with Joseph for enrollment in Caesar's tax lists. While there, she went into labor and bore her child in the privacy and shelter of the only maternity ward available in bustling Bethlehem. An animal's feeding trough served as her baby's bassinet.

The details were still vivid when Luke wrote his Gospel some sixty years later, and they are still vivid for as long as men shall read.

The apostle John, himself a firsthand observer of the most important events in Jesus' ministry, took another thirty years to evaluate what he had seen and heard before he wrote his gospel. What he recorded was of worldwide, eternal significance. So the setting that he chose for his

How to Say It

MESSIAH.   Meh-*sye*-uh.
MICAH.   *My*-kuh.
ZACHARIAS.   Zack-uh-*rye*-us.

account of Jesus' coming to earth was eternity itself, and creation, and timeless principles of life and death, light and darkness, truth and falsehood. Light and life and truth came from God, John knew, and they came to earth with Jesus Christ, God's Son.

I. The Savior and Anointed Lord (Luke 2:8-12)

A. Shepherds Were Listening (vv. 8, 9)

8. And there were in the same country shepherds abiding in the field, keeping watch over their flock by night.

How appropriate that the first public announcement of the Savior's birth should be made to *shepherds*, whose life task is to *save* their helpless flocks from hunger, from wandering, or from falling prey to wild beasts or human thieves! Mary had just given birth in a shelter where shepherds had probably assisted in the birth of lambs. The place was Bethlehem, where David had grown up tending his father's sheep, and then had gone on to become the kingly savior of his people from all their enemies. It was said of God that "He shall feed his flock like a shepherd" (Isaiah 40:11), and Jesus was later to refer to himself as the Good Shepherd, who knows and loves His sheep and lays down His life to save them.

9. And, lo, the angel of the Lord came upon them, and the glory of the Lord shone round about them; and they were sore afraid.

An angel (messenger) of the Lord had told Mary of Jesus' coming birth; an angel comforted Him in His agony in Gethsemane; an angel rolled the doorway stone from the tomb at His resurrection. Two Heavenly messengers attended His ascension and promised His return, when hosts of angels will attend His coming in judgment.

Overwhelming brightness surrounded the shepherds as the angel "stood by them" *(American Standard Version,)* and they were naturally amazed to the point of terror.

B. An Angel Announced It (vv. 10-12)

10. And the angel said unto them, Fear not: for, behold, I bring you good tidings of great joy, which shall be to all people.

When the angel Gabriel had appeared to Zacharias foretelling the birth of John the Baptist (Luke 1:13), and when he appeared to Mary, foretelling the birth of Jesus (Luke 1:30, 31), he had bidden them not to be afraid of good news. Great joy would indeed be the portion of those who, like Simeon and Anna in the temple at Jerusalem, spent their time in hopeful anticipation of Messiah's coming (Luke 2:25-38). The news that was first expected to bring joy to the people of Israel was here promised to bring the same joy to *all people* everywhere—shepherds and priests, Gentiles and Jews.

11. For unto you is born this day in the city of David a Saviour, which is Christ the Lord.

Just as the heir apparent in any kingdom is considered to have been born to the nation as well as to the royal family, so Christ was born *unto you*—to the shepherds, to the nation, and to all who would avail themselves of the attendant blessing.

He was *born* a red-faced, crying little baby boy! "God sent forth his Son, made of a woman, made under the law, to redeem them that were under the law, that we might receive the adoption of sons" (Galatians 4:4, 5). Born *this day*. The baby was then a few hours old.

The *city of David*, Bethlehem, was the home of David's father (1 Samuel 16:1), Micah indicated that the Messiah would come forth from that city (Micah 5:2). More could not be packed into fewer words than the angel revealed in announcing the *Saviour*, who is *Christ* the *Lord*. "Thou shalt call his name Jesus," the angel had told Joseph, "For he shall save his people from their sins" (Matthew 1:21). *Christ* is the Greek equivalent of the Hebrew *Messiah*—the anointed one, vested with divine authority with those offices to which chosen men were set apart by the application of oil to their heads—prophets, priests, and kings. *Lord* was the term of honor that might be applied in common speech to masters and owners, but was reserved in religious usage to God himself. It signifies the authority that carries with it the right to be heard, heeded, and fully obeyed.

FEAR AND FAITH

We tend to be afraid of new events, new challenges, or changes in our lives.

On October 10, 1987, my wife, Marjorie, a devout believer who trusted the Lord, faced a new demand for faith without fear. On that day she was to be tested for the possibility of liver cancer. After two cancer surgeries the year before, this was not easy.

As she lay very still in the tomblike MRI (Magnetic Resonance Imaging) machine that could

visual 4

view the hidden tissues of her body, the temptation for fear was very real.

Suddenly the words of the Christmas story came to her mind. "Fear not . . . I bring you good tidings of great joy, which shall be to all people." The shepherds had been frightened by the dazzling appearance of the Heavenly messenger sent to them. But there was no need to fear, for the message the angel delivered was the grandest message ever to fall on man's ears. A Savior had been born. His coming meant life, eternal life, to anyone who would accept Him.

For Marjorie, the fear of the new test was gone. Whatever answer it gave was all right, for in coming to Jesus she had already laid hold of the life He has promised. Faith can overcome fear.   —W. P.

12. And this shall be a sign unto you; Ye shall find the babe wrapped in swaddling clothes lying in a manger.

The angel didn't tell the shepherds to make that night journey into Bethlehem, but he knew they would, and he supplied directions. If there had been a holy glow emanating from the birthplace, or halos crowning the people there, he surely would have mentioned the fact and simplified their search. No such signs were available; only that the baby, wrapped in strips of cloth as the newborn usually were, would be found lying in a feeding trough for animals.

II. Christ the Eternal Word
(John 1:1-5)

A. He Is Eternal (vv. 1, 2)

1, 2. In the beginning was the Word, and the Word was with God, and the Word was God. The same was in the beginning with God.

"How did God get to be God?" Someone asked us not long ago, and added, "I always like to know about the beginning of things." Genesis 1 and John 1 tell us about the beginning of *things*, but God is not a thing, and He did not begin. He simply *is*. He was already there when time began, and He will be there when time ceases to be. John tells that the *Word*, who took on human nature and lived among men as Jesus of Nazareth (compare Philippians 2:5-8), was a part of the divine being always. "When all things began, the Word already was" (*The New English Bible*.)

The Word is the expression of God's mind, and the way He communicates to the minds of men. Proverbs 8:27-30 speaks of divine *wisdom* in ways similar to John's description of the Word—eternal with God and accomplisher of His creative work.

Verse 1 may be translated literally, "The Word was face to face with God (in closest association), and God was the Word." To avoid any misunderstanding, verse 2 repeats the declaration. *The New English Bible* translates it, "The Word dwelt with God, and what God was, the Word was."

B. He Is Creator (v. 3)

3. All things were made by him; and without him was not any thing made that was made.

Psalm 33:6 puts it plainly, "By the word of the Lord were the heavens made; and all the host of them by the breath of his mouth." This clearly reflects the Genesis account of creation, with its repeated expression, "God said . . ." and it came into being. Colossians 1:16 affirms the identity of Jesus Christ with that creative word: "By him were all things created. . . : all things were created by him, and for him: and he is before all things, and by him all things consist" (compare Ephesians 3:9; Hebrews 1:2).

C. He Is Life and Light (vv. 4, 5)

4. In him was life; and the life was the light of men.

Here is a clear statement bypassing all the guesses of men concerning the source of life on earth. As *The New English Bible* says it, "All that came to be was alive with his life."

The life derived from Jesus becomes the source of spiritual life and growth, and the means by which men see and follow the way, just as sunlight sustains physical life and enables physical sight. "I am the light of the world," Jesus said to His detractors (John 8:12). But some of them closed their eyes to Him.

5. And the light shineth in darkness; and the darkness comprehended it not.

Shineth is in the present tense! When the apostle wrote this inspired and inspiring summary some sixty years after Jesus departed this earth, the light of Christ was still shining, and it shines yet today. The brilliance of Jesus becomes increasingly visible in a dark world.

Comprehended translates a word that may be rendered "apprehended," or grasped. The laying hold may be mental (to understand) or physical (to arrest or overcome). In this verse, both meanings are correct. The self-darkened enemies of Jesus never did *grasp* what He was trying to teach them; and although they did accomplish His arrest and crucifixion, they could not extinguish the light He set glowing in the world. As with a candle in a cave, no amount of darkness can quench the tiniest light, but a great deal of light is needed to dispel all the darkness—of evil, and error, and hate.

III. Christ as God Among Men (John 1:9-18)

A. Rejected by Many (vv. 9-11)

Verses 6-8 introduce John the Baptist, who came to bear witness of Christ as the Light of the world, that everyone might believe in Him. John denied that he himself was the light of whom he spoke.

9. That was the true Light, which lighteth every man that cometh into the world.

The *New International Version* states the fact a little more clearly: "The true light that gives light to every man was coming into the world." John testified concerning Jesus, when Jesus was coming into the world, that is, entering His public ministry. *Lighteth every man.* This may mean that as Creator, the Word gives to each person the light of intelligence, or that as Savior, He offers the light of the gospel to all persons in all times.

10, 11. He was in the world, and the world was made by him, and the world knew him not. He came unto his own, and his own received him not.

The world owed its being to the Word, but its people did not recognize Him when He came among them. The Christmas spiritual, "Sweet Little Jesus Boy," explains the general mistreatment of the Lord, saying, "We didn't know who You was." Too many have no wish to know Him.

A significant shift in the grammar of verse 11 is perhaps best represented by reading it, "He came to that which was His own by creation, and those who were His own people, those whom He had made, did not receive Him." Mankind, represented by Israel, utterly rejected Him, with the exception of those to whom reference is made in the next two verses.

B. Received by Some (vv. 12, 13)

12, 13. But as many as received him, to them gave he power to become the sons of God, even to them that believe on his name: which were born, not of blood, nor of the will of the flesh, nor of the will of man, but of God.

Election into the family of God is made by the potential child of God, who determines for himself (or herself) whether or not he (or she) will *receive him.* Each for himself must *believe on his name*—that is, have confidence in Jesus as Lord, that what He says is true, what He does is just, and what He commands is to be obeyed. Acceptance brings from God the *right* (a better translation than *power*) to become a child of God. All of mankind are creatures of God, made in His image, and hence one family in the flesh; but the childhood status here indicated depends on the birth from above according to God's plan, by His revelation, and by His power.

C. Reported by Witnesses (vv. 14-16)

14. And the Word was made flesh, and dwelt among us, (and we beheld his glory, the glory as of the only begotten of the Father,) full of grace and truth.

This is the testimony of John the apostle, who associated most closely with Jesus in the days of His flesh. John was to write later, emphasizing that he and others saw with their eyes and handled with their hands the material person of Jesus, the Word of life. Anyone, he said, was to be known as friend or foe on his confession or denial that "Jesus Christ is come in the flesh" (1 John 1:1-3; 4:1-3).

Dwelt translates a word that indicates living in tents, hence not permanently in one place. In the days of Moses God had *dwelt* in the midst of His people in the tabernacle or tent of meeting. God's glory had filled that tent. So in Jesus, the glory of God lived and moved among men. His physical presence was for a limited time, but it allowed for the closest acquaintance. During that time the apostles *beheld*, both with their physical eyes and with their understanding, God's glory in Jesus. They saw Him in dazzling light at the time of His transfiguration (Matthew 17:1-8), and they saw the glory of His character in patience, wisdom, and power.

As the *only begotten*, the one and only representation of the Father, Jesus demonstrated the perfect balance and abundance of *grace and truth*. In Him was fulfilled the promise of Psalm 85:10: "Mercy and truth are met together; righteousness and peace have kissed each other." In Him grace was most merciful without being indulgent, and truth was most complete without being cruel.

15. John bare witness of him, and cried, saying, This was he of whom I spake, He that cometh after me is preferred before me; for he was before me.

This testimony was spoken by John the Baptist when Jesus returned from His time of temptation in the wilderness. John's preaching had contained reference to the One whose ministry would follow his in time, but would greatly excel his in authority and acceptance, because Jesus was in glory with God before He came to minister among men.

16. And of his fulness have all we received, and grace for grace.

This testimony was written by John the apostle long after the close of Jesus' earthly ministry. He and all the other apostles, plus multitudes more of believers, had drawn from the divine fullness of which Paul wrote, "In him [Christ] dwelleth all the fulness of the Godhead bodily (Colossians 2:9). In Christ they had received favor upon favor, like waves one after another washing the shore. When one devine mercy was used, another replaced it, and there was always enough. So the Christian has received, continues to receive, and will always receive from the boundless store of God's mercy in Christ Jesus.

D. Revealer of God (vv. 17, 18)

17, 18. For the law was given by Moses, but grace and truth came by Jesus Christ. No man hath seen God at any time; the only begotten Son, which is in the bosom of the Father, he hath declared him.

The previous verse, with its testimony to the embodied Word as the channel of God's boundless grace, or unmerited favor, suggested this comparison between the law and grace, Moses and Jesus. The law was *delivered* through Moses, the servant of God, to *point* the way of life; grace was *revealed* through Jesus, the Son of God, to *show* the way of life. The law dealt with

outward actions. It forbade murder and adultery, for example, and prescribed punishments for disobedience. Grace deals with inner motivation. It opposes anger and lust, for example, and provides strength to overcome them. Grace is forgiving; truth is enabling. The law said, "Do this and live"; the gospel says, "Live and do this."

Moses is described as having conversed with God face to face (Exodus 33:11; Deuteronomy 34:10), and yet his vision of God's glory was limited to seeing His "back parts" as He passed by (Exodus 33:17-23). Jesus, on the other hand, as "God's only Son, he who is nearest to the Father's heart, he has made him known" *(The New English Bible)*. "He that hath seen me hath seen the Father," Jesus declared, asserting that He is a full and sufficient revelation of God in the flesh (John 14:8-11).

Conclusion

A. Going Home With Him

Jesus "tented" for a time on earth among men in order that His friends may live eternally in Heavenly mansions with Him. That sounds beautiful, but is it what we really want? The idea of Heavenly mansions appeals to just about everyone, if he can choose his own Heaven, and design and furnish his own mansion according to his own tastes. Enthusiasm for being with the Lord Jesus as the all-dominant personality forever may be somewhat less keen. Do we really want to be with God, as He is revealed in Christ, forever? Enjoyment of that kind of intimacy requires some getting acquainted.

God has done His part in providing for the acquaintance. He has expressed himself through the living Word. What is He saying? How is He describing himself? The answer is in the Book that describes Him through what it says of His Son. We need to catch and savor every syllable of the Word. Are we listening?

B. Prayer

You have loved us, O God, with a perfect love, and have expressed that love in Your Word from Heaven—even Jesus Christ our Lord. Stir us, please, to a proper thankfulness. Open our ears to listen, open our hearts to receive, and direct our doings to deeds of praise. In Jesus' name, amen.

C. Thought to Remember

In Jesus there resides all of God's nature that could be included in human form. In Him is all of God's person that can be comprehended by the human mind. Turn your eyes upon Jesus.

Learning by Doing

This page contains an alternate lesson plan emphasizing learning activities. Classes desiring such student involvement will find these suggestions helpful.

Learning Goals

Christmas is a time when Christians worship Christ in celebration of His unique birth. In the following activities, your students will be led to:

1. Examine where the real emphasis of their Christmas celebration lies.

2. Discover in the Christmas story focal points for worshiping Christ.

3. Commit themselves to some new emphasis of worship this Christmas.

Into the Lesson

As you open the lesson time, say to your class, "Christmas is such a long-established holiday that it is filled with a variety of activities for most people. Let's examine the priorities we place on these activities. First, rate what you see as the priorities of the non-Christian or nominally-Christian person. Then estimate your own priorities as indicated by the amount of time you spend in each area. Finally, indicate what you feel a Christian's priorities ought to be. Rate each activity 1 through 8, 1 representing the highest priority." You may use the student book for this activity or print the following chart for each student. Print the Christmas activities on the left-hand side of the paper. On the right-hand side, put three vertical columns labeled: Non-Christian priorities, My priorities, and Ideal Christian priorities. (You could put the chart on the chalkboard or overhead projector and have the students write their priorities on a blank piece of paper.)

CELEBRATING CHRISTMAS

1. Purchasing, wrapping, and giving or exchanging gifts.

2. Creating a holiday environment, such as decorating the house and tree, baking, etc.

3. Parties, meals, get-togethers and their preparations.

4. Planning, preparing, and participating in worship services.

5. Kind deeds such as caroling to shut-ins, making things for shut-ins, Christmas baskets, etc.

6. Christmas cards and other communication with friends and relatives.

7. Home celebration such as family worship activities or personal devotions.

8. Myth celebration (Santa Claus, Rudolph, etc.) such as TV specials or visiting Santa.

After a few minutes of individual thought, have students discuss their results and how they felt as they were filling out the chart.

Into the Word

Our text today presents two descriptions of the coming of Christ. Luke gives us a historical account of Jesus' birth, while John delivers a theological statement on the same. Combining these accounts gives us a fuller view, the history and the meaning of the coming of Christ. Both accounts are filled with reasons for worshiping Christ. To worship ("worth-ship" in old English) is to "attribute worth." To worship God is to praise Him with words or deeds for His worthwhile attributes possessed by Jesus Christ as indicated in the passages. You may use your student books for this activity.

After giving neighbors some time to compare notes, have the class share these attributes. As they do, write them on a chalkboard, chartboard, or overhead under the title, "Why We Worship Christ at Christmas." (Hint: Some of Jesus' worthwhile attributes are revealed in the names and titles that identify Him.) Conclude by noting that when we focus on the Biblical events and explanations of the coming of Christ, there is much "food for worship" during the Christmas season.

Into Life

Let's now focus on "How We Worship Christ at Christmas." Divide your class into groups of three or four and give them this assignment: "I want you to plan a Christmas Eve worship service for a church gathering, or a family at home, or a community service in a public facility. Remember that worship is praising God in word or deed. As you plan a word of praise (such as a song or testimony) or a deed of praise (such as kneeling or lighting Christmas candles) or a combination of the two, indicate what particular attribute of Christ is being praised."

Finally, discuss with your class any unique ideas they may have thought of. How could you use any of these ideas tonight, Christmas Eve?

Spend the final moments praying that this Christmas we may focus more than ever before on the worship of Christ.

Let's Talk It Over

The questions on this page are designed to encourage review of the lesson Scriptures and to promote discussion of the lesson by the class. The answers provided are only discussion starters. Let your class talk it over from there.

1. Are there people today who are more afraid than joyous regarding the good news about Jesus, and if so, why?

Some people may be wary of the good news, because they see it as "something too good to be true." They may have already believed in a lot of different ideas and different people, only to find their faith was ill-founded. To be told that God is good, that He loves them, and that He has provided a way for them to be freed from the guilt of their sins may seem impossible to grasp. But we may respond by pointing out that the good news is anything but a fabrication of human wishfulness—it is based on historical facts attested to by eyewitnesses.

Others may fear the good news because acceptance of it requires a change in their spiritual and moral values. And they may be unwilling to face up to such change. We must demonstrate to such people that the things they are inclined to cling to are rubbish compared with the great gain that comes through accepting the good news (see Philippians 3:7-10).

2. What should our response be to the tragic statements found in John 1:10, 11?

When we read a book or view a movie in which a person is unjustly treated and rejected, we fell sympathy for that person and outrage because of the mistreatment. So strong may our feelings become that we find ourselves wishing we could somehow right the wrongs. John 1:10, 11 causes us to react in a similar way. We feel a profound sense of sympathy for Jesus, who came to earth on a mission of love and was spurned by many of those for whom He came. And although we may feel outrage toward those who effected His suffering and death, we must quickly recognize that it was because of our sins also that He died. This should cause us profound grief and should move us to the point that we will endeavor to love and serve Jesus so intensely that, if possible, we can "make up for" the terrible rejection He endured while here on earth.

3. The sense of wonder at God's coming to earth in the person of Jesus Christ sometimes seems lacking in the church. How can we make use of John's experience to cultivate it?

In his first epistle, John points out that one reason he has written is to share this sense of wonder with us. He begins, "That which was from the beginning, which we have heard, which we have seen with our eyes, which we have looked at and our hands have touched—this we proclaim concerning the Word of life" (1 John 1:1, *New International Version*). A moment later John expresses his purpose in writing this: "We proclaim to you what we have seen and heard, so that you also may have fellowship with us" (v. 3, *New International Version*). Of course, this proclamation John refers to is found in his Gospel as well as in his epistles. We do well to give considerable attention to John's Gospel, even though it is quite "deep" in places—that is just the quality that stirs us to wonder! Let us not neglect our fellowship with John. He retained through the years a very special kind of awe over the hours he spent in companionship with Jesus, and he wanted to share that with us through all of his writings.

4. Why is the prospect of eternal companionship with Jesus the most appealing feature of our Heavenly home?

The times of imperfect fellowship we have already enjoyed with Him have been the greatest of our earthly experiences. These have included the day of our receiving Him as Savior, the many occasions on which we have met with Him around His table, the precious moments when His presence has been manifested through the fellowship of believers, and many other "mountaintop experiences." We have appreciated these times, but we have surely hungered for something even better. Perhaps we have read John's testimony or the records provided by the other Gospel writers, and we find ourselves almost envying those first-century believers because of the closeness to Jesus they enjoyed. The closing chapters of Revelation thrill us with their description of gates of pearl, streets of gold, and the abundantly fruitful tree of life. But we may have long ago decided that all those other features pale in comparison to the fact that "the throne of God and of the Lamb shall be in [the city]; and his servants shall serve him: and they shall see his face; and his name shall be in their foreheads" (Revelation 22:3, 4).

Jesus Reveals Himself Through Healing

LESSON SCRIPTURE: John 4:46—5:18.

PRINTED TEXT: John 5:1-15.

John 5:1-15

1 After this there was a feast of the Jews; and Jesus went up to Jerusalem.

2 Now there is at Jerusalem by the sheep market a pool, which is called in the Hebrew tongue Bethesda, having five porches.

3 In these lay a great multitude of impotent folk, of blind, halt, withered, waiting for the moving of the water.

4 For an angel went down at a certain season into the pool, and troubled the water: whosoever then first after the troubling of the water stepped in was made whole of whatsoever disease he had.

5 And a certain man was there, which had an infirmity thirty and eight years.

6 When Jesus saw him lie, and knew that he had been now a long time in that case, he saith unto him, Wilt thou be made whole?

7 The impotent man answered him, Sir, I have no man, when the water is troubled, to put me into the pool: but while I am coming, another steppeth down before me.

8 Jesus saith unto him, Rise, take up thy bed, and walk.

9 And immediately the man was made whole, and took up his bed, and walked: and on the same day was the sabbath.

10 The Jews therefore said unto him that was cured, It is the sabbath day: it is not lawful for thee to carry thy bed.

11 He answered them, He that made me whole, the same said unto me, Take up thy bed, and walk.

12 Then asked they him, What man is that which said unto thee, Take up thy bed, and walk?

13 And he that was healed wist not who it was: for Jesus had conveyed himself away, a multitude being in that place.

14 Afterward Jesus findeth him in the temple, and said unto him, Behold, thou art made whole: sin no more, lest a worse thing come unto thee.

15 The man departed, and told the Jews that it was Jesus, which had made him whole.

GOLDEN TEXT: Jesus saith unto him, Rise, take up thy bed, and walk. And immediately the man was made whole, and took up his bed, and walked.—John 5:8, 9.

John: The Gospel of Life and Light

Unit 2. Jesus Reveals Himself

(Lessons 5-9)

Lesson Aims

This study should equip the student to:
1. Tell in brief the story of John 5:1-15.
2. Show how miracles of physical healing relate to the total ministry of Jesus.
3. Choose an act of compassion to do in Jesus' name this week.

Lesson Outline

INTRODUCTION
    A. The Forest and the Trees
    B. Lesson Background
 I. JESUS FINDS HIS PATIENT (John 5:1-6)
    A. The Occasion, a Feast (v. 1)
    B. The Place, Bethesda (vv. 2-4)
       The Need to Be Healed
    C. The Longtime Invalid (vv. 5, 6)
 II. JESUS HEALS HIS PATIENT (John 5:7-9)
    A. Catches His Interest (v. 7)
       Help Needed
    B. Commands His Participation (v. 8)
    C. Secures His Obedience (v. 9)
III. SABBATH-BREAKING IS CHARGED (John 5:10, 11)
    A. The Patient Is Accused (v. 10)
    B. The Patient Explains (v. 11)
IV. THE HEALER IS IDENTIFIED (John 5:12-15)
    A. Jesus Heals and Departs (vv. 12, 13)
    B. He Exhorts to Repentance (v. 14)
    C. The Patient Reports (v. 15)
CONCLUSION
    A. The Rest of the Story
    B. Where Are You Needed?
    C. Prayer
    D. Thought to Remember

Display visual 5 from the visuals packet. It illustrates a principal thought in the conclusion, section B. It is shown on page 156.

Introduction

A. The Forest and the Trees

It may never have happened exactly this way, but it happens in principle all too often. A wealthy philanthropist is preparing the speech with which he will dedicate the new hospital wing he has financed. He is not to be disturbed by any callers, he says, explaining, "I am much too busy with the welfare of mankind to be interrupted by people."

Here we have the opposite of the oft-noted problem, that of not being able to see the forest for the trees. Some humanitarians have a hard time seeing the trees for the forest. Humanity gets in their way of seeing a person.

Not so with Jesus. God so loved the world—the swarming billions of humanity—that He gave His only begotten Son, that whosoever—whatever insignificant individual—believes in Him might be saved from death to life eternal. God's concern for the globe-encircling forest is expressed in Jesus' care for each seedling and sapling and lightning-scarred snag in the whole stand.

While on earth, Jesus performed many healing miracles; but with one exception they are reported as being accomplished one at a time, with great consideration for the special needs of each person. He did heal ten lepers in one batch, but that experience was disappointing (Luke 17:11-19). So, in today's lesson, we read of His finding one hopeless invalid in a mass of more hopeful ones, and making the hopeless one whole. It's just like Him to do it that way!

B. Lesson Background

Today's lesson calls attention to two examples of Jesus' healing. The first, recorded in John 4:46-54, is not in our printed text. It took place soon after His encounter with the Samaritan woman at the well of Sychar. Jesus left Samaria and continued on to Cana of Galilee, where earlier He had performed His first miracle (John 2:1-11). A nobleman from Capernaum, found Jesus at Cana, nearly twenty miles away, and pled with Him on behalf of his sick son back home. Without going to the boy, Jesus assured the man that his son would be all right. Believing Jesus' word, the nobleman returned and found that the boy's sickness was conquered as of the hour when Jesus spoke.

For the second healing John takes us some eighty miles southward to Jerusalem on a festival occasion. This miracle commands our attention in this lesson.

How to Say It

BETHESDA. Beth-*thez*-duh.
CANA. *Kay*-nuh.
CAPERNAUM. Kuh-*per*-nay-um.
MORIAH. Mo-*rye*-uh.
SYCHAR. *Sye*-kar.

I. Jesus Finds His Patient (John 5:1-6)

A. The Occasion, a Feast (v. 1)

1. After this there was a feast of the Jews; and Jesus went up to Jerusalem.

John does not indicate which of the several annual feasts this was. Jesus' respect for the law would have caused Him to interrupt His Galilean ministry to attend one of the three pilgrim feasts (Passover, Pentecost, and Tabernacles); or His love for God's people could have drawn Him to be with them and serve them even at a lesser occasion. He liked to be present where the tides of human need and opportunity were most full.

B. The Place, Bethesda (vv. 2-4)

2. Now there is at Jerusalem by the sheep market a pool, which is called in the Hebrew tongue Bethesda, having five porches.

The original text has no noun following *sheep*, so the *King James Version* supplies *market* in italics. Other translations use *gate*, suggesting the *sheep gate* of Nehemiah 3:1 and 12:39. *The New English Bible* says "sheep pool." *Bethesda* signifies "house of mercy," which is appropriate to the use made of the place. Present-day visitors in Jerusalem are shown a "Pool of Bethesda," some one hundred yards north of the temple. This pool is fed by the intermittent flow of water from some sort of a siphon spring under Mount Moriah. At irregular intervals, the pool is stirred by the water flowing in below its surface. This compares with the "troubling of the water" mentioned in verses 4 and 7.

Porches, arches, or covered colonnades surrounding the pool provided shelter for the sick and crippled folk who came to be healed.

3. In these lay a great multitude of impotent folk, of blind, halt, withered, waiting for the moving of the water.

Bethesda's reputation as a place for healing drew crowds of folk who were not able to function normally. The surrounding porticoes provided a sort of hospital waiting room for these who came every day.

What were these disabled ones waiting for? Jesus' chosen patient answered that question in the words of verse 7. They anticipated a stirring movement in the water, upon which the first one entering the water would be healed. This explanation is written into the latter part of verse 3 (beginning with "waiting for" and continuing through all of verse 4). But these words are not found in the earliest manuscripts of John's Gospel, and so they are either omitted or they are inserted with explanation in the newer translations. A solid fact is that the sick folk were waiting patiently for the water to show movement.

4. For an angel went down at a certain season into the pool, and troubled the water: whosoever then first after the troubling of the water stepped in was made whole of whatsoever disease he had.

This explanation sets forth the belief of those who came for healing. On that belief they acted.

Explanatory notes such as this were sometimes written in the margins of ancient manuscripts, and were occasionally copied by later scribes as a part of the text. It seems so here.

THE NEED TO BE HEALED

Good Samaritan Hospital is a busy place. Twenty-four hours a day, doctors, nurses, medical technicians, and support staff stream in and out of Good Samaritan Hospital. Almost from its opening, additions have been made to it in an attempt to meet the medical needs of the Santa Clara Valley.

Prices are high for hospital care. A few days in the hospital can cost thousands of dollars, if surgery or special treatment is required. Still the people keep coming. Year after year the drama of disease, injury, and aging crowd the corridors and rooms of Good Samaritan. It is typical of many other hospitals in this area and all across the land.

People come to be healed. They are suffering, and there is hope in the care and treatment they receive. They want to be well.

In this regard, nothing has changed since Jesus viewed the crowd of disabled persons at the pool of Bethesda. All were crowded into those porches because they wanted to be well.

Mankind suffers from the sickness of sin. Only Jesus can provide the complete healing we need. Do we truly desire the spiritual healing that only He can provide? Do we bring others to Him for such healing also? —W. P.

C. The Longtime Invalid (vv. 5, 6)

5. And a certain man was there, which had an infirmity thirty and eight years.

Attention is focused on one invalid in the multitude. The man's *infirmity*, his disability, is not described.

6. When Jesus saw him lie, and knew that he had been now a long time in that case, he saith unto him, Wilt thou be made whole?

Jesus was making a hospital call! The Lord had come to Jerusalem for a religious festival, but this time He was not lingering in the temple as He had done almost twenty years ago (Luke 2:41-50). He was drawn instead to the place where He would encounter the greatest number of folk who might recognize their need for His help. Once there He singled out a patient whose condition was most long-lasting and hopeless. He did not need to look at medical charts; He "knew what was in man" (John 2:25).

Did the man before Him really desire healing? The question may have seemed ridiculous. We have no way of knowing how many of the nearly fourteen thousand days of his invalidism this man had spent beside the pool seeking a cure, but a flicker of desire, either in himself or in whoever brought him to the place, had to motivate his coming.

But the question is not so simple as it may seem. It could be directed to almost anyone with almost any kind of disability. Do you really want to be well? Do you want to get along without the attention, the excuses, and the lack of responsibility that come with illness? Do you really prefer the unknown risks and responsibilities of health to the familiar misery of your ailment?

Sudden cures and sudden conversions don't last very long with folk who lack the desire to be made whole. Would Jesus be wasting His time working an unwanted miracle on the man before Him? His question at least caught the man's attention, focused his mind on the possibilities, and established a circle of interest in the surrounding throng.

II. Jesus Heals His Patient (John 5:7-9)

A. Catches His Interest (v. 7)

7. The impotent man answered him, Sir, I have no man, when the water is troubled, to put me into the pool: but while I am coming, another steppeth down before me.

The man did not answer Jesus directly. Almost defensively, he offered an explanation, implying his earnest desire for healing. *I have no man . . . to put me into the pool.* If anyone had assisted this man in getting to Bethesda, that

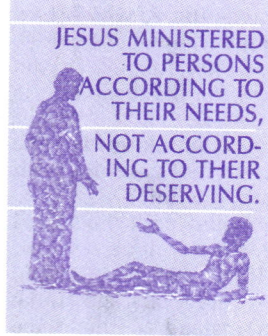

visual 5

person had not remained to assist him at the critical moment. Not totally helpless, the man was slow enough that he was left behind in every effort to reach the pool. Those who needed help the least would be most likely to get whatever help was available. It is ever thus, until some Christlike person steps in to assist.

I have no man. It is the age-long problem of human need and isolation, even in the midst of a throng. In our own time, we can reach out and touch our chosen friends without regard to distance, but the very ease of communication may leave a next-door neighbor deprived of human help and companionship. Awareness and caring are more important than distance and opportunity. Jesus knew and cared.

HELP NEEDED

Bill's body shook a little, and the sweat on his face said something was terribly wrong; but his words were, "Leave me alone. I'm OK. I'll be fine." No amount of persuasion could get Bill to a doctor, or even home to bed. A few days later, the same symptoms occurred, and his protests that he was fine were even louder. The only change in his words were, "I can handle it."

Somehow those words jogged his mother's memory, and she read an article on drug abuse. Bill's pattern of behavior fit one of those described in the magazine. When Bill next was ill, she asked him directly, "Bill, are you on drugs? Is that what's wrong with you?" He replied, "Mom, everyone uses a little. I can quit anytime."

Only after more incidents and a job loss was Bill finally ready to seek help.

One day, in a church service, Bill heard the gospel and came forward, weeping. "I want to be healed. I need Jesus," was his heartrending confession. It was neither quick nor easy, but today Bill is whole again, both physically and spiritually.

Many persons who are mired in sin want to be freed from its crippling effect, but they don't know where to turn. Our task is to find them and bring them to Jesus, the Great Physician.—W. P.

B. Commands His Participation (v. 8)

8. Jesus saith unto him, Rise, take up thy bed, and walk.

Get up! Roll up that mat you have been lying and relying on, and carry it home! Jesus said almost the same words to the palsied man who had been carried to Him (Mark 2:3-12). But that time the party had come to Jesus expecting an act of healing. This time the only suggestion of help lay in Jesus' question as to the man's desire to be made whole. He didn't even know that the one inquiring was Jesus the prophet of Nazareth (v. 13).

After thirty-eight years of helplessness, a man hearing such a command might be expected to laugh or sneer, making no effort to rise. The personality of Jesus must have had a profound influence to win the man's faith and obedience.

C. Secures His Obedience (v. 9)

9. And immediately the man was made whole, and took up his bed, and walked: and on the same day was the sabbath.

Was the man healed only as he obeyed the Lord's command? Concerning the ten lepers reported in Luke 17:11-19 we read, "As they went, they were cleansed." Here, however, there was healing that may have been sensed by the invalid before he acted: he *was made whole*. But his obedience to the Lord's command was prompt, complete, and decisive. He did exactly as he was told to do.

It almost seems as though Jesus chose deliberately to work miracles of healing on the *sabbath* in order to establish these principles: "It is lawful to do well on the Sabbath days" (Matthew 12:12), and "The sabbath was made for man, and not man for the sabbath" (Mark 2:27, 28). Yet, Jesus did the works of His Father on all days alike. The Sabbath healings became an issue only as Jesus' critics challenged them.

III. Sabbath-Breaking Is Charged (John 5:10, 11)

A. The Patient Is Accused (v. 10)

10. The Jews therefore said unto him that was cured, It is the sabbath day: it is not lawful for thee to carry thy bed.

Jews, in the vocabulary of John's Gospel, were the officers of religion in Jerusalem—the priests and the Pharisees—along with their immediate followers. When they saw the man carrying his rolled-up pallet in the street, they rebuked him for violating the Sabbath. Jeremiah (17:21) and Nehemiah (13:19) had labeled the carrying of burdens as labor forbidden by the law of Moses (Exodus 20:8-11), but it was in the context of commerce that they made the ruling. These religious officers in Jesus' day viewed this man's carrying his mat the same as if he were carrying any burden to the marketplace for trading or selling. So they made their interpretations of the law (which placed intolerable burdens on the people) equal to the words of Scripture in application. They thought that in doing so they honored God, who had given the law of the Sabbath; but their interpretations of this law obscured its merciful intent.

B. The Patient Explains (v. 11)

11. He answered them, He that made me whole, the same said unto me, Take up thy bed, and walk.

If there was guilt in the matter, it rested on someone other than the bed-carrier. He was doing as he had been instructed; and the instructor came with good credentials. He had provided the capability for the walking and the carrying; hence it was reasonable that He had a right to say how the capability should be used.

IV. The Healer Is Identified (John 5:12-15)

A. Jesus Heals and Departs (vv. 12, 13)

12. Then asked they him, What man is that which said unto thee, Take up thy bed, and walk?

Hadn't they heard what the man said about having been made whole? A person, made in the image of God, had been given perfect soundness, but that meant nothing to the faultfinders. They could see only that the Sabbath tradition had been violated and that they must find the culprit, the *man* who would dare to give instructions contrary to the law of God! Conveniently they forgot that a *man* had written their interpretation of divine law!

This verse may provide food for thought the next time we are tempted to complain about the wear and tear suffered by our church building, at the hands and feet of all those youngsters coming in from the neighborhood. If the Sabbath was made for man, what were church buildings provided for?

13. And he that was healed wist not who it was: for Jesus had conveyed himself away, a multitude being in that place.

Up to this point the longtime cripple was interested in the healing, not in the identity of the Healer. "The man who was healed had no idea who it was, for Jesus had slipped away into the crowd that was there" (*New International Version*). The Lord chose to let the facts make their own impression on the observers before He confronted His critics.

B. He Exhorts to Repentance (v. 14)

14. Afterward Jesus findeth him in the temple, and said unto him, Behold, thou art made whole: sin no more, lest a worse thing come unto thee.

We have no way of knowing how long *afterward* Jesus found the man *in the temple*. It is clear, though, that Jesus was looking for the man, and not the reverse. The man may have come to make a thank-offering for his healing, or he may simply have desired to exercise a long-denied ability to move freely among his fellow-men. In any case, Jesus had some unfinished business to carry out with His patient before He dismissed him.

Sin no more. Many readers infer that some long-ago sin had caused the man's illness. Perhaps so. Long-lasting disabilities can result from one sinful act. But the grammar of Jesus' exhortation points to habitual sinning, rather than one long-ago sin, as requiring repentance. Even invalids can be sinful in what they think, say, and do. And they need to repent, turning to God for cleansing and for power to live in fellowship with Him. Jesus had healed the man's body, and that was a significant part of His ministry; but that healing would be nullified ultimately in physical death. The more important ministry of Jesus was to heal the man's sin-sickness. The purpose of His coming, then and for as long as time shall be, was to seek and to save those who are lost.

C. The Patient Reports (v. 15)

15. The man departed, and told the Jews that it was Jesus, which had made him whole.

We are left with a lot of unanswered questions about the man before us. What was the nature of his affliction? Did it come as a result of sin on his part? After his healing, what was he doing in the temple? What was the nature of the habitual sinning he was warned to cease? How did he finally learn who Jesus was?

In conclusion, why did he hurry off to tell the religious leaders that Jesus was the one who had healed him and had commanded him to carry his pallet home on the Sabbath? Was the man smarting under the Lord's demand for repentance? Was he seeking further self-justification against the charge of Sabbath violation? Or was he sincerely bearing witness to Him who had bestowed the gift of health and wholeness, giving all possible credit where credit was due? If so, his good intentions backfired, for his report to these leaders fueled the fires of their enmity against Jesus.

Conclusion

A. The Rest of the Story

John 5:16-18, as part of our lesson but not in our printed text, tells the rest of the story. As a direct result of the healed man's testimony, Jewish officialdom plotted to kill Jesus for Sabbath violation. He responded to their charge by affirming that He would continue to do good works on the Sabbath, even as "my Father worketh." That added the more serious charge of blasphemy to the accusations against Him. It was all in the pattern of events leading to the cross, where His accusers said, "He saved others; himself he cannot save" (Matthew 27:42).

B. Where Are You Needed?

Words of Paul found in Acts 20:35 quote an otherwise-unrecorded saying of Jesus: "It is more blessed to give than to receive." So Jesus gave freely of himself, and He is most blessed.

He revealed himself in His ministry of healing. He did not inquire who was worthy to be healed, or whose healing would return benefits to Jesus and His cause. He ministered to men according to their needs, not according to their deserving. His compassion led Him to the needy ones, and His loving power made them well.

The followers of Christ reveal their likeness to Him. They do not ask, "What's in it for me?" Instead, "Where is a need I can fill, and how can I fill it?" In so doing, they find satisfaction of their own great need—the need to be needed! That is a priceless blessing to the self-giver.

C. Prayer

We thank You, Father, for the works of healing through which Jesus revealed His divine compassion and power. Give us, we pray, an increasing measure of His compassion, that we may increase also in our power to find and meet the needs of others in His name. Amen.

D. Thought to Remember

"The blind see, the lame walk, the lepers are cleansed, the deaf hear, the dead are raised, to the poor the gospel is preached. And blessed is he, whosoever shall not be offended in me" (Luke 7:22, 23).

Home Daily Bible Readings

Monday, Dec. 25—Seeking Jesus' Healing Power (John 4:43-50)

Tuesday, Dec. 26—Healing the Official's Son (John 4:51-54)

Wednesday, Dec. 27—Many Sick at the Pool (John 5:1-6)

Thursday, Dec. 28—"Pick Up Your Mat and Walk" (John 5:7-10)

Friday, Dec. 29—You Are Now Well (John 5:11-14)

Saturday, Dec. 30—My Father Is Always Working (John 5:15-18)

Sunday, Dec. 31—The Father and I Are One (John 10:22-30)

Learning by Doing

This page contains an alternate lesson plan emphasizing learning activities. Classes desiring such student involvement will find these suggestions helpful.

Learning Goals

1. The student should understand in what ways the power of Christ, as seen in His miracles, bears evidence to His divine nature.

2. The student should realize a greater sense of trust in Jesus as a firm foundation and guide for his life.

Into the Lesson

Begin by evaluating the attitudes of the students toward the miracles of Jesus and events that are called miracles today. At the present time, there is a lot of false teaching in this area that you can help correct if you can find out what your students actually think about miracles. If you are gentle and supportive of the individual, you may get a chance to help.

Let's Pretend. This activity reveals a secret desire in everyone's heart to have a miracle in his own life regarding something that he is powerless to deal with. Say, "Let's pretend that Jesus stops by your house unexpectedly today. You chat for a while, and you know there's something special about this Man; but you're still not sure He is really Christ. Sensing that, He says to you, 'I want you really to believe that I'm the Son of God, so I am going to do a miracle for you. You name it. I'll do it.' What miracle will you ask Jesus to perform?"

Miracle Inventory. After a brief discussion, have students respond individually in writing to the following inventory.

What Do You Think About Miracles?

1. What is a miracle?

2. Have you ever seen what you thought was a miracle? If so, what was it?

3. Does it take a special person to do miracles, or just anyone who has faith?

4. Are the miracles performed today the same as the miracles of the Bible? If not, how are they different?

5. What do miracles prove, if anything?

6. What is the biggest thing you don't understand about miracles?

Into the Word

Divide the students into groups of four or five. As you read the Scripture text aloud, have the students to listen for the factors that are involved in the healing of the man beside the pool of Bethesda.

Now ask the students to buzz in their small groups for a couple of minutes on what factors produced the healing of the invalid. Ask them to share their answers with the whole class.

Discuss with students the following questions. If you are using students books, you might give them a moment to jot notes in the space provided there for these questions.

1. Why was the man at the pool if he had no hope of getting to the water for healing?

2. Why did Jesus heal this man who didn't even know who Jesus was, much less believe in Him?

3. Why did Jesus slip away into the crowd?

4. What was the response of the religious leaders when they learned that this man had been healed of his infirmity?

5. Why do you think the healed man revealed Jesus' identity to the religious authorities?

6. Did Jesus deliberately choose the time (Sabbath) and the place (Jerusalem) to perform this miracle in order to confront the Jewish leaders? (See vv. 16-18.)

Into Life

Though the evidence of Jesus' miracles is weighty, some today deny them. Everyone has some kind of response to the miracles of Jesus. This activity is to probe the response of those in your class.

Three Discussion Groups. Divide your students into three large discussion groups. Assign one in each group to lead the discussion. Hand each group a slip on which is written one of the following questions:

1. What do you *think* about Christ because of His miracles?

2. How do you *feel* about Christ because of His miracles?

3. What does Christ want you to *do* because of His miracles?

After a five minute discussion, have the group leaders share results with the whole class.

In closing, emphasize that the principal purpose of Jesus' miracles was to offer evidence that He was who He claimed to be—the Son of God—and thereby to lead people to believe in Him. The work of bringing people to faith in Christ continues today, and each of us can have a part in it. Urge your students to do their part in this soul-saving ministry.

Let's Talk It Over

The questions on this page are designed to encourage review of the lesson Scriptures and to promote discussion of the lesson by the class. The answers provided are only discussion starters. Let your class talk it over from there.

1. Jesus used the Jewish feasts, and other occasions when worshipers gathered in great numbers, as times to minister. How is this an example to us?

Jesus once stated, "For even the Son of man came not to be ministered unto, but to minister, and to give his life a ransom for many" (Mark 10:45). One has the impression that in the average congregation the majority of members present on a Sunday morning are there "to be ministered unto" They are uplifted through sermon, special music, and the Lord's Supper. Indeed, we are to benefit from these elements of worship. But when the emphasis is all on "What does it do for me?" we miss an important aspect of discipleship. We should all see ourselves as being present "to minister." Going out of our way to express a word of greeting, offering assistance in finding a page in the hymnal or a Biblical passage, or simply praying that other worshipers will be strengthened or encouraged by the services are some forms our ministry can take. We also need to keep this principle in mind when we attend men's or women's meetings, or other larger gatherings.

2. Our service through the church may bring us into contact with persons who actually take a measure of satisfaction in being sick. How should we deal with them?

Such persons may cling to their illness, because it brings them attention and sympathy they would not otherwise enjoy. Being chronically ill may be their mark of distinction, and a restoration to health would create a kind of identity crisis for them. We must be understanding and patient in ministering to these people. Perhaps we could help them to focus on some strong attribute they have and to emphasize that as a mark of distinction instead. The individual may, for example, have an ability to write poetry, knit, or paint—we can concentrate on these. Perhaps we can urge him or her to perform some task for the church, such as telephoning, correspondence, repairing hymnals, working on the church history, etc. In such ways we may lead the individual to desire improved health, and that desire may itself be the key to such improvement.

3. Jesus advised the healed invalid, "Sin no more, lest a worse thing come unto thee." To what kinds of individuals today would such advice be particularly appropriate?

An obvious answer would be those who have undergone rehabilitation for drug or alcohol abuse. Of course, in some circles it would be considered improper to label such abuse as sin. But the abusers might be better served to have their behavior designated as sin rather than sickness. Jesus' advice could also be given to those who have impaired health because of poor diet, lack of rest, or failure to exercise properly. Since our body is referred to as the temple of the Holy Spirit (1 Corinthians 6:19) it is clearly sin to harm it through neglect or mistreatment. But no one, whether in good or poor physical health, should overlook the warning carried in Jesus' words to this man. This warning certainly implied that a spiritual punishment awaits a person who continues in sin and refuses to repent.

4. The lesson writer observes that Jesus "ministered to men according to their needs, not according to their deserving." Why is this an observation that we need to ponder?

We may be hasty at times to judge those who seek assistance from us. "They ought to be able to get a job and provide for themselves," we may reason, but we may not always perceive the physical and mental handicaps that hinder them from holding a job. Or we may think regarding some poor person we encounter: "He could at least make an effort to clean himself up, and if I give him something, I expect him to show a little gratitude." But it is clear that Jesus ministered to many who were unlovely and unkempt, and even though a lack of gratitude on the part of the healed disappointed Him, He did not make such gratitude a requirement for healing (see Luke 17:11-19). Even within the church, we may find individuals who appear ungrateful and who may berate us in spite of our efforts to minister to them. It would be easy for us to curtail our ministry to them because they seem neither to deserve nor to appreciate our attention. But our Lord's example indicates that we must persist in serving even those who seem unworthy of such service.

Jesus Reveals Himself Through Scripture

LESSON SCRIPTURE: **John 5:19-47.**

PRINTED TEXT: **John 5:30-47.**

**Jan
7**

John 5:30-47

30 I can of mine own self do nothing: as I hear, I judge: and my judgment is just; because I seek not mine own will, but the will of the Father which hath sent me.

31 If I bear witness of myself, my witness is not true.

32 There is another that beareth witness of me; and I know that the witness which he witnesseth of me is true.

33 Ye sent unto John, and he bare witness unto the truth.

34 But I receive not testimony from man: but these things I say, that ye might be saved.

35 He was a burning and a shining light: and ye were willing for a season to rejoice in his light.

36 But I have greater witness than that of John: for the works which the Father hath given me to finish, the same works that I do, bear witness of me, that the Father hath sent me.

37 And the Father himself, which hath sent me, hath borne witness of me. Ye have neither heard his voice at any time, nor seen his shape.

38 And ye have not his word abiding in you: for whom he hath sent, him ye believe not.

39 Search the Scriptures; for in them ye think ye have eternal life: and they are they which testify of me.

40 And ye will not come to me, that ye might have life.

41 I receive not honor from men.

42 But I know you, that ye have not the love of God in you.

43 I am come in my Father's name, and ye receive me not: if another shall come in his own name, him ye will receive.

44 How can ye believe, which receive honor one of another, and seek not the honor that cometh from God only?

45 Do not think that I will accuse you to the Father: there is one that accuseth you, even Moses, in whom ye trust.

46 For had ye believed Moses, ye would have believed me: for he wrote of me.

47 But if ye believe not his writings, how shall ye believe my words?

GOLDEN TEXT: Search the Scriptures; for in them ye think ye have eternal life: and they are they which testify of me.—John 5:39.

John: The Gospel of Life and Light
Unit 2. Jesus Reveals Himself
(Lessons 5-9)

Lesson Aims

This study should enable the student to:

1. Name the "witnesses" Jesus referred to as supporting His claims to identity with God.

2. Explain the relationship between confidence in the Bible and faith in Christ.

3. Discuss with a friend the convincing evidence that Jesus is the Son of God.

Lesson Outline

INTRODUCTION

    A. Members of the Jury

    B. The Case for the Defense

I. JESUS' WITNESSES (John 5:30-39)

    A. Not Himself Alone (vv. 30-32)

    B. John the Baptist (vv. 33-35)

    C. The Works Jesus Did (v. 36)

    D. The Father in Heaven (vv. 37, 38)

       Rejection and Loss

    E. Old Testament Scripture (v. 39)

       The Living Word

II. DESCRIBING THE OPPOSITION (John 5:40-47)

    A. Rejection of God's Love (vv. 40-42)

    B. Disregard for God's Judgment (vv. 43, 44)

    C. Disbelief of Scripture (vv. 45-47)

CONCLUSION

    A. Instructions to the Jury

    B. Prayer

    C. Thought to Remember

Display visual 6 from the visuals packet. It illustrates point I in the lesson outline. The visual is shown on page 163.

Introduction

A. Members of the Jury

We still chuckle over the old story about a man who was called in to settle an argument between two friends. One man presented his case, and the arbiter was convinced. "You are right," he said.

"Wait a minute," the other objected. "You haven't heard me yet." So he presented his case, and again the arbiter was convinced.

"You are right," he said again. This time a listening third party objected.

"These two men have flatly contradicted each other. They can't both be right." To which the arbiter responded thoughtfully, "You are right."

Anyone who has listened attentively to almost any debate or disagreement must have some sympathy for the vacillating arbiter. That is true especially of judges and juries in trials that come to court. If all the truth lay clearly with either side, there would be no trial. Only when there is conflict in the testimony does the court have to intervene. Then someone has to decide which, if either, of the litigants is telling the truth.

Today's lesson presents just such a conflict. Jesus spoke of himself as one with God and doing always the will of His Heavenly Father. The Jewish authorities said that could not be so; hence Jesus was guilty of blasphemy and deserving of death. The case involves events recorded in John 5. The reader becomes a member of the jury and must decide which claimant to believe. Both can't be equally right.

B. The Case for the Defense

The charge against Jesus was blasphemy—speech or behavior that belittle the majesty of God. This, the Jewish leaders said, Jesus had done in asserting His participation in the work of God, "Making himself equal with God" (John 5:17, 18; see also John 10:33; Matthew 26:63-66). According to the law, it was a crime punishable by death (Leviticus 24:11-16).

The conflict had begun during a festival in Jerusalem, when Jesus healed an invalid at the pool of Bethesda and directed him to pick up and carry the mat on which he had been lying. (See last week's lesson.) That happened on the Sabbath, and mat-carrying on the Sabbath was forbidden by traditional interpretation of the law. So Jesus was charged with disregard for the Sabbath. In reply, He said that He would continue to do good works on the Sabbath, even as God, His Father, continued to work in His world. That brought the accusation of blasphemy.

Jesus' continuing response to the religious leaders at the festival becomes our lesson for today. The first part of His response, found in John 5:19-29, is not in our printed text. Here, Jesus affirmed in detail His identity with the Father. He acted with the Father, He said; He was one with the Father in love and in purpose; and He was one with the Father in giving life; and He was one with the Father in judgments rendered.

The Lord continued by declaring His special relationship with men, deriving from His relationship with God. He had the right to be honored, He said, and to carry out judgment, and to give life.

Such amazing claims demanded, of course, the support of many witnesses. Those witnesses were called up, and their testimony becomes our special study for this lesson.

I. Jesus' Witnesses
(John 5:30-39)

A. Not Himself Alone (vv. 30-32)

30. I can of mine own self do nothing: as I hear, I judge: and my judgment is just; because I seek not mine own will, but the will of the Father which hath sent me.

It was impossible for Jesus to act independently or on His own initiative. As one with the Father, Jesus was bound by His very nature to do and say only those things that represented accurately the will of God. In matters of *judgment*, He accepted the Father's directives, expressing God's conclusion. Hence, the judgment was right and just, never stained by selfishness or caprice, and always authoritative (John 8:16).

The audacity of Jesus' claim still leaves us breathless. It is hard for us to imagine the shock and righteous wrath it must have stirred among His critics. Yet it has within it the fine balance of complete boldness and complete humility. There was no place for timidity in Him who spoke with divine authority; nor for boastful self-promotion in Him whose total wisdom was Heaven-supplied.

31. If I bear witness of myself, my witness is not true.

Jesus anticipated His critics' objection that His testimony concerning himself was without value because it was prejudiced, subjective, and not supported by other evidence. Thus, in saying *my witness is not true*, Jesus seems to have meant that His witness was not true *in their estimation*. On another occasion, Jesus did bear witness to himself, and He stated that His witness was true (see John 8:12-18).

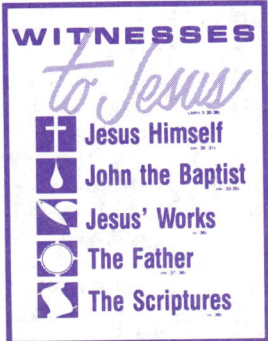

visual 6

32. There is another that beareth witness of me; and I know that the witness which he witnesseth of me is true.

This statement, cast in the present tense, has to refer to the eternally present testimony in Jesus' favor that comes from the Father and His unchanging Word. That testimony was evident even then in many spiritual and moral expressions, which the opposing party could not perceive and would not acknowledge, but were most certainly *true*. Jesus elaborates on this in verses 36 and 37.

B. John the Baptist (vv. 33-35)

33. Ye sent unto John, and he bare witness of the truth.

John the Baptist had been one voice, that the religious authorities had heard in testimony to Jesus. With John's imprisonment, that voice was now effectively stilled. Here the Lord spoke to members of the same party who had *sent* their messengers into the wilderness to inquire of John (John 1:6, 7, 19-27). They had heard the prophet's bold testimony concerning the coming One who was immeasurably greater than himself. This, John said, was the Son of God—the Lamb of God, who was to take away the sin of the world (John 1:29, 34). John's testimony was solid enough. Some who heard it became followers and even apostles of Jesus.

34. But I receive not testimony from man: but these things I say, that ye might be saved.

John's testimony concerning Jesus was true, but Jesus did not depend on the testimony from man to establish His claim. Nevertheless, in the hope that His hearers might be led to faith through the testimony of John, the Lord reminded them of it. The saving message has saving power, even when brought by imperfect men.

35. He was a burning and a shining light: and ye were willing for a season to rejoice in his light.

John the Baptist had been as a lamp in the night, lighting the way of his hearers until the sun (Son) should rise. The religious leaders had paid attention to John, and some had approved of his moral teaching. But they would not accept his testimony that Jesus was the Son of God and the one through whom salvation would come.

C. The Works Jesus Did (v. 36)

36. But I have greater witness than that of John: for the works which the Father hath given me to finish, the same works that I do, bear witness of me, that the Father hath sent me.

Here Jesus returns to the thought He introduced earlier (v. 32). The weightier testimony to

Jesus' divine identity came from the revelation of God's power in what Jesus did. By many miracles, especially of healing, Jesus fulfilled the Messianic prophecies found in such passages as Isaiah 35:5, 6 and 61:1, 2. Because of Jesus' miracles, Nicodemus recognized him as a teacher come from God (John 3:2). Jesus called attention to these miracles in His introductory sermon at Nazareth (Luke 4:18, 19) and again when assuring John the Baptist that He was indeed the promised Messiah (Luke 7:22, 23). Even at the close of His earthly ministry He made a similar appeal to His apostles: "Believe me that I am in the Father, and the Father in me: or else believe me for the very works' sake (John 14:11).

His works were not all in the nature of material signs. His entire ministry—His life, His teaching, and His moral perfection in doing the Fathers will—constituted *works* for which He had been *sent*. Only within the shadow of the cross could He pray, "I have finished the work which thou gavest me to do" (John 17:4).

D. The Father in Heaven (vv. 37, 38)

37a. And the Father himself, which hath sent me, hath borne witness of me.

John the apostle was later to write of God's witness to Jesus in the hearts of believers, "If we receive the witness of men, the witness of God is greater: for this is the witness of God which he hath testified of his Son" (1 John 5:9). At Jesus' baptism the voice from Heaven was heard saying, "This is my beloved Son, in whom I am well pleased" (Matthew 3:17). At Jesus' transfiguration the audible voice made the same declaration, adding, "Hear ye him" (Matthew 17:5). God's testimony to Jesus was found, but especially in His resurrection. He was "declared to be the Son of God with power . . . by the resurrection from the dead" (Romans 1:4).

37b, 38. Ye have neither heard his voice at any time, nor seen his shape. And ye have not his word abiding in you: for whom he hath sent, him ye believe not.

All these testimonies to Christ had been lost on the unbelievers. In Jesus, these men could have heard and seen God (John 14:24; 2 Corinthians 4:4), but they chose not to receive the revelation God gave to them. They had misinterpreted and misapplied the prophetic revelations; and they had even attributed Jesus' mighty works to demons. All the lines of God's communication led to Christ. By rejecting Him, the unbelievers removed all meaning from what they themselves held and taught.

Ye believe not. Faith in God and His Christ involves responsibilities that many folk are not willing to accept. So they "discover" flaws in the gospel message, creating reasons to reject it. But as one has said, "Many more folk are kept from faith by cold feet than by cold facts."

REJECTION AND LOSS

"No thanks. I don't need any help," Tim said. The young man did look big and strong, but the fall over the low cement wall had left him flat and with one leg twisted under him.

The passersby moved away, and his companion tried to help him up. Suddenly, with a moan of anguish, Tim collapsed on the ground. It took quite an effort, but his friend managed to help him into their car and drive him home.

Tim's parents took him to the emergency room of the hospital, and x-rays showed a break just below the knee. Lengthy surgery was required, during which a metal splint had to be fastened to the bone with screws. A painful recovery under heavy sedation followed.

The surgeon told the parents that by refusing help right after the fall and by trying to walk with his friend's inadequate support, Tim had caused unnecessary damage that would take weeks to heal properly.

Jesus knew the hurt that would come to His people for rejecting Him and His teaching. Not only that, their loss would be irretrievable.

Do we reject Jesus because of a false sense that we are all right, when our need is really immediate and desperate?   —W. P.

E. Old Testament Scripture (v. 39)

39. Search the Scriptures; for in them ye think ye have eternal life: and they are they which testify of me.

The final witness to be called in support of Jesus' claim was the very Book the scribes were using to condemn Him. A legitimate and probably better translation of this verse would read. "Ye search (study, examine, and pore over) the Scriptures." The scribes by long study had made themselves expert in the words of Scripture and their interpretation. They loved the Book, but they overlooked and rejected the reason for which the Book was written.

In them ye think ye have eternal life. A rabbinic saying was this: "He who has gotten to himself words of the Law hath gotten to himself the life of the world to come." How wrong! The condition of eternal life is more than the mere possession of and examination of the Scriptures.

They testify of me. After his first meeting with Jesus, Philip went and found Nathanael and said, "We have found him, of whom Moses in the law, and the prophets did write" (John 1:45). Jesus described His sufferings as fulfillment of what was written in the law of Moses, and in the prophets, and in the psalms, concerning Him (Luke 24:44). As demonstrated by the unbelieving Jews, it is all too easy to know the words, but miss the message.

THE LIVING WORD

"There's an Epidemic With 27 Million Victims and No Visible Symptoms."

That headline was designed to catch the eye and hold the attention.

The article that followed was startling. In our nation, which has one of the best educational systems in the world, there are twenty-seven million persons who cannot read or write. To these persons, the world of literature, newspapers, magazines, and the Bible is closed.

Where people cannot read, the story of Jesus, the living Word, must be told and retold. This is one of the great challenges to missions. The task becomes easier when the Scriptures are translated into the people's language, and they are taught to read.

Let us not, however, confuse possession of the Scriptures with possession of the life God offers. The Scriptures lead us to Christ, the living Word. Only if He dwells within us do we have eternal life.

The Jews had the written Word of God, and they could read it. But because of their prejudice and pride, they refused to accept its testimony concerning the Christ, who alone could give them the life they desired.   —W. P.

II. Describing the Opposition
(John 5:40-47)

A. Rejection of God's Love (vv. 40-42)

40. And ye will not come to me, that ye might have life.

Jesus had been affirming and supporting His claim to oneness with the Father. Now He named the evils that prevented the unbelievers from accepting the evidence. First was their own perverse *will.* They had determined not to acknowledge Jesus as Messiah, even though He was the only source of the real life for which they had searched in the Scriptures that bore witness to Him! The whole tragic situation is summarized in John 1:11: "He came unto his own, and his own received him not."

41, 42. I receive not honor from men. But I know you, that ye have not the love of God in you.

A key word in this part of the discourse is *honor* or *glory*—the ultimate splendor that Christ shared with the Father before the world was (John 17:5). *Honor* is also the appropriate recognition of that splendor—the respect due to

Jesus as one with the Almighty. Jesus' claims had been supported by Heaven's testimony, so He possessed an eternal splendor that did not depend on honor bestowed by human beings. When, however, men did render suitable respect to Him, He accepted it not for himself but for the Father to whom it belongs (see Mark 9:37).

But I know you. Jesus did not need to be told the thoughts or the character of those whom He addressed (John 1:47-50; 2:24, 25). The men present before Him lived by a set of values totally opposed to those of Jesus. They cared more for popularity with their peers than they did for pleasing God. Whatever love for God they possessed, it was not their inmost motivation.

B. Disregard for God's Judgment
(vv. 43, 44)

43. I am come in my Father's name, and ye receive me not: if another shall come in his own name, him ye will receive.

A principal cause for Jesus' rejection by these leaders was the very fact that He had come in the Father's name, and citing the Father's recommendation. They said this was blasphemous. But in future years they would fulfill His prophecy many times by attaching themselves to self-proclaimed messiahs who would come to them with no credentials from Heaven. Nor is the church free from this charge. The apostle Paul wrote strong rebuke to the Corinthians for their gullible acceptance of self-promoting professionals in religion (2 Corinthians 11:19, 20). Even now the world follows religious leaders of many persuasions who dominate the flocks they profess to feed, but fleece them instead for their own advantage.

44. How can ye believe, which receive honor of one another, and seek not the honor that cometh from God only?

It is impossible to maintain faith in God when one is constantly seeking the approval of other persons—thus indicating dependence on them —more than the approval of God. Jesus said that persons who do even good and religious deeds to gain the approving attention of their fellowmen cannot expect any reward beyond what they first sought—the approval of men (Matthew 6:1-6; compare John 12:42, 43; Romans 2:29).

Men cannot give the kind of *honor that cometh from God only.* They can give flattery and praise and riches and power, all of which seem pleasant for a time; but they cannot give the approval of a good conscience. All their gifts are left behind at moving day, the time of transition from this world to the next. Those persons who steadfastly seek the honor that God bestows, will find priceless treasures in this world (Matthew 19:29) and will enjoy eternal companionship with the Father whose smile they have sought.

C. Disbelief of Scripture (vv. 45-47)

45. Do not think that I will accuse you to the Father: there is one that accuseth you, even Moses, in whom ye trust.

Even for His enemies, Jesus is the advocate and not the prosecutor. He seeks not their condemnation, but their salvation (John 3:17; 1 John 2:1); hence He warns, rebukes, and exhorts, trying to prepare them for the judgment they must face. When, however, they reject Him as their advocate, they are left without defense or defender to face the accusations of the law.

These men set their hopes on Moses. Once, they scoffed at a man who spoke up for Jesus, "Thou art his disciple; but we are Moses' disciples" (John 9:28). How, then, could Moses become their accuser? Principally because Moses was the giver and administrator of law, and law by its very nature cannot forgive the lawbreaker. "By the deeds of the law there shall no flesh be justified in [God's] sight," wrote Paul, "for by the law is the knowledge of sin" (Romans 3:20). He cited the purpose of the law, "that sin by the commandment might become exceeding sinful" (7:13). The law could command and condemn, but it could not save. It could do no better than point to the Savior whom God would send.

46, 47. For had ye believed Moses, ye would have believed me: for he wrote of me. But if ye believe not his writings, how shall ye believe my words?

The scribes had made a thorough study of Moses' words, but they had not paid much attention to Moses' message. The most direct and notable in Moses' testimony is from Deuteronomy 18:15-19. The apostles showed this to be a clear prediction concerning Jesus (Acts 3:22, 23; 7:37).

Besides direct prediction, the writings of Moses abound in types and figures—directives concerning priesthood, sacrifices, and celebrations—pointing to their perfect fulfillment in the Christ. The New Testament book of Hebrews has been called a partial elaboration on the Christology of Moses.

The Jewish leaders claimed to be followers of Moses (John 9:28) and to accept anything written by him. The facts, however, spoke differently, for they refused to accept what he had written about Christ. How then could they be expected to believe the Prophet against whom they were prejudiced from the beginning?

Conclusion

A. Instructions to the Jury

The witnesses have been heard. The evidence is in. The Advocate has presented His case, charging His opponents with stubborn prejudice. One thing more is necessary before the jury retires to consider its verdict. The presiding judge must instruct the jury in points of law relating to the facts before them.

We are members of the jury faced with Jesus' claims to messiahship. We must be instructed in one important element besides the facts revealed in the Gospels. Now the Lord takes the place of the judge, asking us to relate the law to the facts. He reveals himself through Scripture, showing what *kind* of Messiah He had to be.

That is what Jesus did in conversation with His disciples after His resurrection: "Beginning at Moses, and all the prophets, he expounded unto them in all the Scriptures the things concerning himself.... Then opened he their understanding, that they might understand the Scriptures, and said unto them, Thus it is written, and thus it behooved Christ to suffer, and to rise from the dead the third day" (Luke 24:27, 45, 46). Now we are ready to decide.

B. Prayer

We marvel at Your mercy, O God, maker and ruler of all, that You have provided the way for us to know You, first through the words of Scripture and then through Your living Word, Jesus. Help us more fully to believe His words and to believe completely in Him. Amen.

C. Thought to Remember

"If they hear not Moses and the prophets, neither will they be persuaded, though one rose from the dead" (Luke 16:31).

Home Daily Bible Readings

Monday, Jan. 1— A Son With God's Authority (John 5:19-24)

Tuesday, Jan. 2—An Executor of God's Judgment (John 5:25-29)

Wednesday, Jan. 3—A Testimony of John the Baptist (John 5:30-35)

Thursday, Jan. 4—A Servant Sent by God (John 5:36-39)

Friday, Jan. 5—A Rejected Giver of Life (John 5:40-47)

Saturday, Jan. 6—A Prophet, Greater Than Moses (Mark 7:1-13)

Sunday, Jan. 7—A Savior for the World (Romans 5:6-11)

Learning by Doing

This page contains an alternate lesson plan emphasizing learning activities. Classes desiring such student involvement will find these suggestions helpful.

Learning Goals

Many people today find it hard to accept an idea unless they have convincing evidence that it is true. This lesson should help each of the students to:

1. Identify the basis for their faith in Jesus Christ.
2. Understand the broad evidences presented by Jesus that He was the Son of God.
3. Share with unbelievers the evidence that Jesus is the Messiah.

Into the Lesson

Ask students to complete individually a survey about the origins of their faith. (You may use the student book or a copied sheet for this activity.)

The Origins of My Faith. Check three of the most important reasons why you believe in Jesus Christ.

____ Christian parents
____ A Christian minister
____ Reading the Bible
____ A Christian friend
____ Other relatives
____ Godly lives of Christians
____ Studying the evidence
____ Afraid of Hell
____ Why not?
____ Other _____

After about three minutes, read the list aloud, asking for a show of hands of those who checked each area. Tally the results on the chalkboard and discuss the relative importance of these factors. Then point out how many people believe in Christ without really studying the evidence. Ask, "What are the potential dangers for a Christian who has never studied the evidences for his faith?"

Into the Word

Divide your class into five study teams. (Larger classes should form more than one team for each area of study, with no more than four or five on a team.) Each group is assigned one area of evidence to discuss. Say, "Jesus gives five witnesses to convince the Jewish leaders that He was the Son of God. As I read John 5:30-47, listen for Jesus' witnesses."

Read the text aloud. Give each team a copy of the comments found in the lesson treatment (I.

A. through E. in the outline) that relates to their witness. Now ask the teams to read their section and write out a summary of the evidence that their witness gives to the messiahship of Jesus. (You may use the student books for this activity.)

WITNESSES FOR JESUS' DEFENSE

1. Jesus himself (vv. 30, 31).
2. John the Baptist (vv. 33-35).
3. Jesus' works (v. 36).
4. The Father (vv. 37, 38).
5. Old Testament Scripture (v. 39).

After about seven minutes, ask each group to explain the evidence of their witness to the whole class. Allow the rest of the class to ask questions regarding this evidence. Be prepared to step in and supplement the knowledge of the reporting group.

Now ask the class how they would view the relative importance of each of these lines of evidence. What is the most convincing to them? To the unbeliever?

Discuss what other evidences there may be to the validity of Jesus' claims. For example, someone might note that His teachings actually work when applied consistently in a Christian's life, bearing witness to their truthfulness and therefore to His claims.

Into Life

Ask, "If all this is true, what ought we to do?" Discuss the importance of strengthening believers in their faith and letting unbelievers know the strong evidence on which the Christian faith is built.

Conclude by encouraging students to memorize Jesus' five witnesses so they may share them with others. To do so, have each group make up a phrase that helps them to remember H-J-W-F-S (Himself, John, Works, Father, Scripture). For example, "*Heaven's Joys Wait For Saints.*" (They can use their student book for this activity.) Afterward, drill the class to see if they are indeed memorizing the five points. You can also have them state in their own words the nature of the evidence that the witnesses bear.

Ask each group to pray together for each person to find someone with whom to share these evidences.

Let's Talk It Over

The questions on this page are designed to encourage review of the lesson Scriptures and to promote discussion of the lesson by the class. The answers provided are only discussion starters. Let your class talk it over from there.

1. Some unbelievers have charged that Jesus was either a clever charlatan or the victim of extreme delusions. How does today's lesson text disprove these charges?

Webster defines *megalomania* as "a mania for great or grandiose performance." This accurately describes some of those religious leaders of past and present who have proved to be something other than "spiritual giants." These leaders have trafficked in the spectacular, and they have generally tended to exalt themselves instead of the God they profess to serve. In contrast, Jesus' declaration, "I seek not to please myself but him who sent me" (John 5:30, *New International Version*) is indicative of the way He turned the focus of glory onto the Father. One sees in Jesus a becoming humility rather than an overbearing pride, a spirit of submission to the Father's will instead of the exaltation of His own will. It is true that Jesus' miracles were often spectacular events. But at no time did He use the excitement resulting from the miracle as a means of self-exaltation.

2. How can Jesus' fulfillment of Old Testament prophecy provide a testimony solid enough to impress modern man?

Here is an approach to faith in Jesus Christ that should appeal to an age that demands tangible, verifiable evidence to support claims. Old Testament passages such as Psalm 22, Isaiah 53, and others can be set alongside the Gospel accounts and we can see for ourselves the numerous points at which Jesus fulfilled prophecies hundreds of years old. The facts point compellingly to the truth that Jesus' birth, ministry, death, burial, resurrection, and ascension were predicted in detail long before the events actually occurred. Jesus said of the Old Testament Scriptures, "They are they which testify of me" (John 5:39), and the burden of proof lies on those who would seek to deny the accuracy of that statement.

3. When Jesus told the Jews, "Ye will not come to me, that ye might have life" (John 5:40), we seem to catch a glimpse of the inner pain He felt over their rejection of Him. How can a declaration such as this help us in our evangelistic efforts?

It is certainly not a misapplication to say that Jesus feels similar pain over all who reject Him today. This may help us to remember that everyone we encounter is of concern to Jesus. Sometimes we may be troubled by the thought that we are imposing on others or that we are endeavoring to force our views on them by seeking to influence them for Christ. But Jesus' declaration reminds us of how foolish it is, how tragic it is, to reject the One who can give us eternal life. To offer others such a free gift, and even to urge it upon them, is hardly a matter of imposing. When our efforts to evangelize are rejected and perhaps even ridiculed, we need not feel personally repudiated. Like our Lord, we have offered the greatest possible benefit, and the only reason to feel pain is that those who reject Jesus are spurning what can enrich their present lives and prepare them for the even greater riches of eternity.

4. What are some ways in which the desire for human approval keeps people from coming to Christ today?

Those individuals whose jobs bring them into association with people of the intellectual or scientific community may feel the pressure of some who disparage Christianity as an emotional, irrational kind of viewpoint. Though attracted to Jesus Christ, they may resist the idea of becoming Christians for fear they will be regarded as anti-intellectual or lacking in objectivity. Also, there seems at times an effort on the part of unbelievers to brand Christianity as a "white man's religion." When people of other races express an interest in Christian faith, they run the risk of being regarded as traitors to their own people. Among young people peer pressure is a particularly strong factor in determining personal decisions. Sometimes teenagers must wrestle with the likelihood of rejection and ridicule from their peers when they contemplate becoming Christians. It is likely, of course, that nearly every Christian has made his or her decision to follow Christ in the face of some disapproval from family members, friends, schoolmates, fellow workers, etc. For some people, this disapproval is a more powerful force; but for all, Jesus' demand to love Him first and foremost is applicable (Matthew 10:31).

Jesus Reveals Himself as the Bread of Life

LESSON SCRIPTURE: John 6.

PRINTED TEXT: John 6:35-51.

John 6:35-51

35 And Jesus said unto them, I am the bread of life: he that cometh to me shall never hunger; and he that believeth on me shall never thirst.

36 But I said unto you, That ye also have seen me, and believe not.

37 All that the Father giveth me shall come to me; and him that cometh to me I will in no wise cast out.

38 For I came down from heaven, not to do mine own will, but the will of him that sent me.

39 And this is the Father's will which hath sent me, that of all which he hath given me I should lose nothing, but should raise it up again at the last day.

40 And this is the will of him that sent me, that every one which seeth the Son, and believeth on him, may have everlasting life: and I will raise him up at the last day.

41 The Jews then murmured at him, because he said, I am the bread which came down from heaven.

42 And they said, Is not this Jesus, the son of Joseph, whose father and mother we know? how is it then that he saith, I came down from heaven?

43 Jesus therefore answered and said unto them, Murmur not among yourselves.

44 No man can come to me, except the Father which hath sent me draw him: and I will raise him up at the last day.

45 It is written in the prophets, And they shall be all taught of God. Every man therefore that hath heard, and hath learned of the Father, cometh unto me.

46 Not that any man hath seen the Father, save he which is of God, he hath seen the Father.

47 Verily, verily, I say unto you, He that believeth on me hath everlasting life.

48 I am that bread of life.

49 Your fathers did eat manna in the wilderness, and are dead.

50 This is the bread which cometh down from heaven, that a man may eat thereof, and not die.

51 I am the living bread which came down from heaven: if any man eat of this bread, he shall live for ever: and the bread that I will give is my flesh, which I will give for the life of the world.

Jan
14

GOLDEN TEXT: Jesus said unto them, I am the bread of life: he that cometh to me shall never hunger; and he that believeth on me shall never thirst.—John 6:35.

John: The Gospel of Life and Light

Unit 2. Jesus Reveals Himself

(Lessons 5-9)

Lesson Aims

This study should enable the students to:

1. Quote from today's Scripture three statements made repeatedly by Jesus.

2. Compare Jesus, the bread of life, with the manna supplied to the children of Israel.

3. Name a way in which they will make Jesus a greater part of their daily lives.

Lesson Outline

INTRODUCTION

    A. It's Basic

    B. Coming Back for More

I. GOD SENT LIVING BREAD (John 6:35-40)

    A. "You Haven't Seen What Is Before You" (vv. 35, 36).

    B. This Is God's Program (vv. 37,38)

    C. God's Program Is for Eternal Life (vv. 39, 40)

II. HE DIDN'T! YES, HE DID! (John 6:41-46)

    A. "Jesus Is Only One of Us" (vv. 41, 42)

    B. "You Must Respond to God" (vv. 43, 44)

    C. "You Must Accept God's Teaching (vv. 45, 46)

III. THIS BREAD NOURISHES FOR EVER (John 6:47-51)

    A. "I Am the Bread of Life" (vv. 47, 48)

    B. The Heaven-sent Bread Is for Ever (vv. 49, 50)

    C. "You Must Eat of Me" (v. 51)

    Famine Relief

CONCLUSION

    A. The Breaking of Bread

    B. Prayer

    C. Thought to Remember

Display visual 7 from the visuals packet and let it remain before the class. It is shown on page 172.

Introduction

A. It's Basic

When the Christian Hospital was opened at Mashoko in Southern Rhodesia (now Zimbabwe), the staff served their patients a well-balanced diet prepared in a well-equipped kitchen. But the African patients ate little and fared poorly. They had good appetite, though, for the familiar *sadza*—a simple dish of cooked corn meal—which their relatives brought occasionally to them in the hospital. Finally, the hospital administrators set aside their sophisticated equipment and menus, replacing them with huge pots in which they cooked up *sadza* enough for everybody. Patients' appetites and resultant conditions improved dramatically on the familiar basic fare.

Not surprisingly, then, when Jesus presented himself as God's gift on which His people must be sustained for life eternal, He spoke in terms of familiar, basic food: "I am the bread of life."

This was only the first of many *I am's* in which the Lord spoke of himself as a familiar basic necessity in some vital human experience. John's Gospel records them for us: "I am the light of the world"; "I am the door (of the sheepfold)"; "I am the good shepherd"; "I am the resurrection, and the life"; "I am the way, the truth, and the life"; "I am the true vine".

These all bear on the general topic of our present unit of five lessons. "Jesus Reveals Himself." Three of the five deal with the manner or means by which Jesus revealed himself—through healing (Lesson 5), through Scripture (Lesson 6), and by setting people free (Lesson 8). Today's study and Lesson 9 deal with what Jesus revealed himself to be—the bread of life and the light of the world.

B. Coming Back for More

Six months to a year passed from the time of last week's lesson to the miraculous feeding of the five thousand, which is recorded in the opening verses of John 6. During this time, Jesus conducted His great Galilean ministry. The feeding of the five thousand marked the close of this ministry. Today we study a part of a discussion that took place on the following day—Jesus' sermon on the bread of Life.

Leaders in the throng that enjoyed their fill of fish sandwiches that afternoon would have made Jesus their king, whether He wished it or not, but He disappeared alone among the surrounding hills. In the evening, His disciples set out by boat across the lake toward Capernaum. On the way a storm caught them, and Jesus came to them, walking on the sea. Receiving Him into the ship, they came safely to land (vv. 15-21).

They were followed the next day by a crowd from the previous gathering who demanded to know *when* Jesus had reached Capernaum. The Lord changed the subject to *why* they had followed Him, "not because ye saw the miracles, but because ye did eat of the loaves, and were filled." He added the exhortation on which He expanded through the following discussion: "Do not work for food that spoils, but for food that endures to eternal life, which the Son of Man will give you" (v. 27, *New International Version*). The Galileans wanted to know how they might earn God's marvelous bounty, and Jesus replied, "This is the work of God, that ye believe on him whom he hath sent" (vv. 22-29).

That pricked the crowd into revealing their true interest: "What miraculous sign then will you give that we may see it and believe you? . . . . Our forefathers ate the manna in the desert; as it is written: He gave them bread from heaven to eat" (vv. 30, 31, *New International Version*). A challenge was evident in their question.

Jesus' answer announced at least five corrections. (1) Not Moses but God had given the manna. (2) Moses was God's servant; Jesus is God's Son. (3) The *true bread* coming down from Heaven is quite different from the material manna. (4) That gift was in the distant past; this is now and continues as nourishment for life eternal. (5) That was for *you*, the children of Israel; this is for the whole world, including you (vv. 32, 33).

Comprehending only that Jesus offered some wonderful, continuing bounty, they put in their order: "Lord, evermore give us this bread" (v. 34). The crowd was eager to enlist Jesus for their purposes. They had not yet considered committing themselves to Him for God's purposes. Our printed text picks up the story at this point.

I. God Sent Living Bread (John 6:35-40)

A. "You Haven't Seen What Is Before You" (vv. 35, 36)

35. And Jesus said unto them, I am the bread of life: he that cometh to me shall never hunger; and he that believeth on me shall never thirst.

The questioners had asked for bread. Jesus said in effect, "If you but knew it, I am what you are looking for, and infinitely more. I am the living bread, the vital, active, sustaining gift of God. I am the bread that gives life, not only for the present day, but also for the boundless stretch of tomorrows." Jesus does not merely bestow the gift; He is the gift that is bestowed.

"He who comes to me will never go hungry, and he who believes in me will never be thirsty" *(New International Version)*. These two clauses mean much the same thing, repeated for poetic emphasis, but they offer more than repetition. *Coming* to Christ and *believing* in Him are both parts of the same voluntary commitment. One is active and self-giving—approaching, surrendering; the other is passive and receptive—trust-

ing, committing, confident. The reward is as promised to those who hunger and thirst after righteousness (Matthew 5:6); they are filled, never again to suffer lack.

36. But I said unto you, That ye also have seen me, and believe not.

Seeing is not always believing. These folk had seen the mighty miracles of Jesus, demonstrating His unity with the Father; but as He had *said* earlier, their interest was in filling themselves with free food (v. 26).

God's messengers have frequently found themselves addressing folk who have eyes but do not see, and have ears but do not hear (Ezekiel 12:2). Even at the conclusion of His earthly ministry, Jesus had to rebuke His own best friends, "Have I been so long time with you, and yet hast thou not known me?" (John 14:9).

The Lord's critics in Capernaum were blinded by something worse than human limitation, however. The evidence was there, but it did not convince men whose minds were tuned to a totally different wave length. They would have been glad to accept His gifts as they perceived them, but on their own terms. Himself and His program they could do without—or so they thought.

B. This Is God's Program (vv. 37, 38)

37. All that the Father giveth me shall come to me; and him that cometh to me I will in no wise cast out.

As a businessman might convey to his son the enterprise into which he has invested his life and fortune, so God the Father bestows upon Jesus the hearers who come with receptive and responsive hearts. The purpose and program of the Father and the Son are inseparably joined.

Jesus will never drive away anyone who comes to Him. We cannot forget, though, the young ruler who came to Jesus and then saddened both himself and the Lord by turning and departing (Mark 10:17-22). Defectors from the Lord's reign will not be forced to stay in His kingdom.

38. For I came down from heaven, not to do mine own will, but the will of him that sent me.

Two grand themes are repeated like a refrain. Jesus was sent from God in Heaven; and He will not separate himself from the purpose and the

---

How to Say It

CAPERNAUM.   Kuh-*per*-nay-um.
EMMAUS.   Em-*may*-us.
GOLGOTHA.   *Gahl*-guh-thuh.

program of the Father. It was not possible, therefore, for Him to negotiate any compromise with alternative purposes and programs of men. We can accept Christ or reject Him. We cannot change Him.

C. God's Program Is for Eternal Life (vv. 39, 40)

39. And this is the Father's will which hath sent me, that of all which he hath given me I should lose nothing, but should raise it up again at the last day.

Four themes are sounded in this verse. The first two we have heard before: God sent Jesus, and God's will must be done. Two are introduced here for the first time: the preservation of those whom God had given to Jesus (v. 37) and their being raised at *the last day* when Jesus will come again in judgment.

God's will for mankind—the "work" by which men may please God—is that they believe on Jesus, the Son whom He sent into the world (vv. 28, 29). Not only the salvation, but the preservation, of believers is most important to Him (1 Peter 1:3-5). Even Jesus, however, would not keep by force the one who was determined to depart. Judas was such a one. Just before the Lord's crucifixion He prayed, "Those that thou gavest me I have kept, and none of them is lost, but the son of perdition; that the Scripture might be fulfilled" (John 17:12).

As a new theme, the raising up of Jesus' followers at the last day is sounded with the utmost insistence here and in verses 40, 44, and 54. None must be allowed to forget this great contrast between the wilderness manna and the living Bread sent down from Heaven. The *living* that the Son of God makes possible is for ever!

40. And this is the will of him that sent me, that every one which seeth the Son, and believeth on him, may have everlasting life: and I will raise him up at the last day.

Familiar themes again: the will of God, faith in the Son, everlasting life, and resurrection.

THE LORD
CAME DOWN FROM
HEAVEN ABOVE,
THE LIVING BREAD
TO BE.
AND ALL WHO COME
TO HIM AND EAT
WILL LIVE
ETERNALLY.

visual 7

"The Lord is . . . not willing that any should perish, but that all should come to repentance" (2 Peter 3:9). *Seeing* and *believing* are inseparably linked again in God's program for man's redemption. Jesus' critics in Capernaum had seen Him, but had not believed (v. 36). They came under the sad summary of John 1:5, 11: "The light shineth in darkness; and the darkness comprehended it not. . . . He came unto his own, and his own received him not."

II. He Didn't! Yes, He Did! (John 6:41-46)

A. "Jesus Is Only One of Us" (vv. 41, 42)

41, 42. The Jews then murmured at him, because he said, I am the bread which came down from heaven. And they said, Is not this Jesus, the son of Joseph, whose father and mother we know? How is it then that he saith, I came down from heaven?

Here was another parallel to the situation in the wilderness when the children of Israel ate manna from Heaven. They murmured or grumbled about it (Numbers 11).

The critics at Capernaum complained at Jesus' saying He was the Bread of life. He couldn't possibly have come from Heaven. They knew He came from the family of Joseph in Nazareth. The neighbors in Nazareth had raised the same objection when He told them He was the fulfillment of Isaiah's Messianic prophecy (Luke 4:16-24; Isaiah 61:1-3).

None of the objectors knew or believed that Jesus was not the son of Joseph, but was the Son of God, which we know from Luke 2 and Matthew 1. Jesus did not make public the facts of His birth from a virgin; He did continue to affirm that God had sent Him. He had indeed grown up among the common folk in Galilee, where He should have been most admired for His spotless character, but He was not (Luke 4:24).

B. "You Must Respond to God" (vv. 43, 44)

43, 44. Jesus therefore answered and said unto them, Murmur not among yourselves. No man can come to me, except the Father which hath sent me draw him: and I will raise him up at the last day.

The grumblers had been talking not to Jesus, but about Him. Nevertheless, He knew their objections and told them to stop grumbling among themselves. Then He dealt with the real reason for their unbelief, and it had nothing to do with His boyhood background. It dealt rather with the Father, whose glory He had shared before He became a boy. They simply were not much attracted to God!

As a loving Father with His child, God had dealt with Israel (Hosea 11:1-4). He had wooed them and warned them through the law and the prophets. They had often sought to appease Him, but seldom really to please Him. If through their long history the chosen people were not drawn to God, how could they now be interested in the Son, who bore His image?

God continues to woo through the gospel, seeking to *draw* mankind. "God was in Christ, reconciling the world unto himself.... Now then we are ambassadors for Christ, as though God did beseech you by us ... be ye reconciled to God" (2 Corinthians 5:19, 20).

Again we hear the promise: those who are drawn to God, and so come to the Son, who bears His image, will be raised up to enjoy the divine companionship forever.

C. "You Must Accept God's Teaching" (vv. 45, 46)

45. It is written in the prophets, And they shall be all taught of God. Every man therefore that hath heard, and hath learned of the Father, cometh unto me.

This is a variation on the theme of verse 44. God draws men to himself by revealing His nature, His commands, His way of life; and this is done through inspired messengers such as the prophets. Isaiah 54:13 sets forth the proportion that men are taught about God: by hearing and learning they make up their minds to give their lives to the doing of His will. The reason these Jews were refusing to hear God's final messenger was that they had not learned of God as they should have through the prophets.

46. Not that any man hath seen the Father, save he which is of God, he hath seen the Father.

Those to whom Jesus spoke could not expect to be drawn to God by any miraculous vision of Him. They must give heed to God's Son, who was "with God" (John 1:1) before He "was made flesh" (v. 14).

III. This Bread Nourishes for Ever (John 6:47-51)

A. "I Am the Bread of Life" (vv. 47, 48)

47, 48. Verily, verily, I say unto you, He that believeth on me hath everlasting life. I am that bread of life.

The Lord's double *verily* introduces a sober and weighty pronouncement. This is the focus of the whole discussion—not new, but emphasized.

He that believeth on me. The manuscript evidence for the words *on me* is not strong, so they are omitted from most translations. The faith of which Jesus spoke, however, was belief and trust in Him, the *person* present before His hearers. It was not faith in faith itself, or even faith in an essentially good moral universe. Jesus had said repeatedly that men were to believe in, trust in, and come to the One whom the Father had sent into the world. The personal emphasis is repeated in the following positive identification: "*I am that bread of life.*"

The assurance of life eternal is for the here-and-now. The believer in Christ *has* life as a present possession, not to be wrested from him. We are to live in Him now, and act like it now!

B. The Heaven-sent Bread Is for Ever (vv. 49, 50)

49. 50. Your fathers did eat manna in the wilderness, and are dead. This is the bread which cometh down from heaven, that a man may eat thereof, and not die.

Jesus' critics had said, "Our fathers did eat manna in the desert.... He gave them bread from heaven to eat" (v. 31). True! That bread from Heaven sustained the multitude through the years of their wandering. But all but two of the adults who left Egypt died before the nation came into the promised land! The bread that Jesus now offered was very different in that it was sustenance for the spirit, eternal. It would not, prevent physical death and decay, but concerning it, Jesus would declare, "I am the resurrection, and the life: he that believeth in me, though he were dead, yet shall he live: and whosoever liveth and believeth in me shall never die" (John 11:25, 26).

C. "You Must Eat of Me" (v. 51)

51. I am the living bread which came down from heaven: if any man eat of this bread, he shall live for ever: and the bread that I will give is my flesh, which I will give for the life of the world.

By repetition and restatement, the Lord established the foundation of His teaching; and then, by adding new truth, gradually He built so His words could not be forgotten, even when they were not wholly understood. Bread. Living bread. Sent from Heaven. He was it!

Now we hear again that the bread must be eaten if it is to provide nourishment. It must be ingested, digested, and assimilated into the body. With some reason we say that a person *is* what he eats. The believer in Christ is to feed himself on Jesus, mentally, emotionally, and spiritually. He must live on Christ, so Christ may live in him and say with the apostle Paul, "Christ liveth in me: and the life which I now live in the flesh I live by the faith of the Son of God" (Galatians 2:20).

Jesus' final declaration is both new and shocking: "The bread which I shall give for the life of the world is my flesh" (Revised Standard Version.) The Lord had been speaking in figurative terms concerning himself as living bread for life eternal. But this reference to *flesh* gives the whole discussion a physical and material turn. Now also He speaks in the future tense of a gift yet to be conveyed. And again He labels His gift as to the whole world rather than to Israel alone (v. 33). There was much here that His immediate audience could not understand and certainly was not ready to accept.

The Word was made flesh, John said, and dwelt among men (1:14). Jesus was to *give* that fleshly self in His death on the cross. That fleshly self was also to be symbolized and memorialized in the *bread* of the Lord's Supper, concerning which Jesus said, "Take, eat; this is my body" (Mark 14:22). The Upper Room and Golgotha have provided to us the key to understanding what Jesus said that day at Capernaum. He has given the flesh He said He would give for the life of the world—for our lives. It is for us to come in faith, to take and eat, filling and nourishing ourselves daily with Him, for life eternal.

Famine Relief

Famine in our world has been headline news for several years. The pictures of starving children, shriveled crops, refugee food camps, and the dying all touch our hearts and make us generous givers for famine relief. We feel responsible for the food supply required.

Tons of grain pour from the bounty of our land to help relieve the hunger. Agencies of government and church come into the devastated areas with medical and food supplies to preserve life and lessen disease and suffering. Volunteers go and care for the hurt of those in need.

We do not want to see people die needlessly, and the children touch our hearts most.

Jesus understood the need for bread. He knew that hunger must be satisfied or death would result. He declared himself to be "the bread of life." Without Him, no one can live and be in spiritual health.

We ourselves must eat and then share Him with others, if we would overcome the famine for the Word of God that engulfs our world. The emergency is real, and we have the remedy. Will we give that men might live?   —W. P.

Conclusion

A. The Breaking of Bread

Luke 24:13-35 tells that on the afternoon of His resurrection day Jesus walked, unrecognized, with two disciples to Emmaus, where He accepted their invitation to eat with them and was recognized at last "in breaking of bread." He, the Bread of life, had broken bread to feed the thousands in Galilee, and He had broken bread to establish His memorial Supper. The church was to recognize and remember Him regularly in meeting to break bread (Acts 2:41-47; 20:7; 1 Corinthians 10:16, 17; 11: 23-29). The phrase points to three practices, all closely related to Jesus, the Bread of life. First is material and spiritual—communion in the Lord's Supper. The second is material and social—eating together in Christian fellowship. The third is spiritual and social—proclaiming, teaching, learning, and encouraging one another concerning Jesus Christ, God's Heaven-sent Bread of life eternal. If we are to come with good appetite to these sessions of spiritual nourishment, we shall need vigorous exercise between times through our daily walk and service in Jesus' name.

B. Prayer

We thank You, God, for Jesus, the Bread from Heaven, whom You sent to give us life eternal. May we have good appetite to learn of Him, to nourish ourselves with His Spirit, and to share Your bountiful Gift with our hungry neighbors. We pray it in His name. Amen.

C. Thought to Remember

"The bread that I will give is my flesh, which I will give for the life of the world" (John 6:51).

Learning by Doing

This page contains an alternate lesson plan emphasizing learning activities. Classes desiring such student involvement will find these suggestions helpful.

Learning Goals

We live in a time that may well qualify for Charles Dickens' description, "It was the best of times. It was the worst of times." In a time of unprecedented prosperity, the unquenched thirsting of people's souls causes them to turn to drugs, alcohol, gangs, and other self-destructive behaviors, in an attempt to find satisfaction. Therefore, this lesson will help a student:

1. Understand the nature of the spiritual longing that is within human beings.

2. Encounter Jesus as the ultimate answer to the yearnings of the soul.

3. Risk believing in Jesus for any areas of unmet needs.

Into the Lesson

Turn the class's focus upon people's unmet needs. Remind them that all of us have needs that are not completely met. To identify some of these, give each student a slip of paper and ask them to write what they consider to be the greatest unmet need in their lives. Request total candor, and assure students that no one will know what anyone else writes (no names on slips, please). Have them fold their papers before you collect them all.

Read several of these, and ask students to comment on the following aspects of each:

1. The nature of the need (physical, social, mental, or spiritual).

2. The most common way that worldly people might meet that need.

3. The way that the committed Christian might meet that need.

Point out that when Jesus refers to himself as "the bread of life," He is claiming the role of a "need meeter." As bread is the answer to hunger (v. 35), Jesus is the answer to our deepest yearnings. Note the contrast between human efforts at meeting our own needs and how Jesus meets our needs. Say, "Jesus reveals himself to mankind, not only through His healing power (lesson 5) and through Scripture (lesson 6), but also by His ability to meet their deepest needs."

Into the Word

Divide the class into discussion groups of four or five students each. Ask them to listen, as you read aloud John 6:35-51, for any ways in which Jesus is like bread. Read the text.

Now ask them to discuss the following questions in their groups. Give each student a copy of the questions, or have them use their student books.

1. In what ways is Jesus like bread?

2. What is the greatest hungering that a person faces in life?

3. What miraculous sign did Jesus give just prior to our text (John 6:1-15) to prove that He was capable of meeting their needs?

4. In what way were the people seeking to have their needs met by Jesus? (v. 34).

5. How did Jesus promise to meet their needs? (vv. 37-40).

6. How does spiritual security affect a person's inner yearnings?

7. Jesus had been referring to himself in spiritual terms as bread for eternal life, when suddenly in verse 51 he turned the hearers thoughts in another direction. To what was He referring? How did this meet their needs?

8. How does a person get this bread of life?

Take about twenty minutes for this study before having groups share their results.

Into Life

Remind your students that in order to have Jesus meet our needs, we have to risk some things. Ask the small groups to make a list of these risks. (For example, *loneliness*—a person may risk loneliness if he or she breaks off friendships with those who are spiritually destructive.)

After five minutes, have someone from each group share with the class the risks they have identified. Record these on the chalkboard.

Now ask the groups to make a second list of the steps that a person must take in order to have Jesus meet his or her need. (For example, *prayer*—a person will have to be in constant communication with God in order to make such a change.)

After five minutes, ask the group to share their results. Record these on the chalkboard so that students may write down any ideas that did not occur to them in their own small group.

Finally, have each individual identify in his or her small group one need they would be willing to turn over to Jesus this week. Ask that after sharing these commitments, each group join together in prayer for one another.

Let's Talk It Over

The questions on this page are designed to encourage review of the lesson Scriptures and to promote discussion of the lesson by the class. The answers provided are only discussion starters. Let your class talk it over from there.

1. What does the title "bread of life" indicate about the kind of satisfaction Jesus can bring to our souls?

All of us have known occasions when our hunger for food was quite intense. How satisfying it was when at last we sat down at the table and ate heartily of the food that was prepared! This may also describe the circumstances under which we accepted Jesus as our Savior. We may have been aware of an emptiness within our lives and had tried unsuccessfully to satisfy it through education, recreation, or participation in a worthy cause. But it was when we experienced Jesus' salvation and came to know Him as Lord and Friend that the emptiness was genuinely filled. And we have found since then that while material prosperity, physical pleasure, and social contacts provide a measure of satisfaction, the only enduring, ever-refreshing satisfaction comes through our continuing communion with Jesus.

2. Why is it important that we cooperate with Jesus in His efforts to preserve us as believers?

The New Testament indicates that it is our responsibility to work in harmony with God's power within us to achieve holiness of life and fruitfulness in service. Thus Paul wrote to the Colossians, "To this end I labor, struggling with all his energy, which so powerfully works in me" (Colossians 1:29, *New International Version*). This blending of human effort with divine power is presented also in Philippians 2:12, 13, where Paul urges believers to "continue to work out your salvation with fear and trembling" and then says that "it is God who works in you to will and to act according to his good purpose" *(New International Version)* If we wait idly, even prayerfully, for God to transform us into dynamic Christians, we will be disappointed. But when we step out boldly in faith with the aim of achieving a purer, more godly life and the goal of accomplishing effective service for Christ, we find that divine power at work within us. If we stand still and make no effort to strengthen our spiritual lives, we run the danger of stagnation and loss. But if we are active and growing and appropriating God's power, we preserve the freshness and effectiveness of our faith.

3. It seems a very human tendency to limit Jesus, to confine Him according to our prejudices or our imperfect knowledge of Him. How can we overcome this tendency?

We should learn from the Jews' inclination to limit Jesus when they grumbled, "Is not this Jesus, the son of Joseph, whose father and mother we know? How is it then that he saith, I came down from heaven?" (John 6:42). We must keep in mind that Jesus is greater than any of our theories or opinions about Him, and He is beyond what we are able to conceive with our finite minds. It is difficult to understand how Jesus could be both God and man and how the divine and human natures blended within Him. But we should not deny or attempt to explain away these realities simply because we do not understand. Our human comprehension also falls short of grasping just how Jesus' death atones for our sin or how His lifeless body was restored to life on resurrection morning. But again, we must accept with our understanding that which is given through clear testimony and compelling evidence, and then we must accept by faith those truths about our Lord that transcend our ability to comprehend.

4. The lesson writer refers to the church's programs of teaching, preaching, and other learning activities and says, "If we are to come with good appetite to these sessions of spiritual nourishment, we shall need vigorous exercise between times through our daily walk and service in Jesus' name." What kinds of exercise can best build up our spiritual appetite?

An informal Bible-study group, in which members are encouraged to participate by offering personal insights into Scripture, would be one. When we have an opportunity to share the good things we discover in our personal study of the Bible, it is likely to increase our hunger for further discoveries. The Christian who teaches a Bible class will expend much in the way of spiritual resources on the task and will soon feel the need to replenish those resources through further study. The task of evangelism similarly enhances our appetite, since different people whom we approach will raise different questions or problems, and we will be drawn to the Bible to find answers.

Jesus Reveals Himself by Setting People Free

LESSON SCRIPTURE: John 8:12-59.

PRINTED TEXT: John 8:31-47.

John 8:31-47

31 Then said Jesus to those Jews which believed on him, If ye continue in my word, then are ye my disciples indeed;

32 And ye shall know the truth, and the truth shall make you free.

33 They answered him, We be Abraham's seed, and were never in bondage to any man: how sayest thou, Ye shall be made free?

34 Jesus answered them, Verily, verily, I say unto you, Whosoever committeth sin is the servant of sin.

35 And the servant abideth not in the house for ever: but the Son abideth ever.

36 If the Son therefore shall make you free, ye shall be free indeed.

37 I know that ye are Abraham's seed; but ye seek to kill me, because my word hath no place in you.

38 I speak that which I have seen with my Father: and ye do that which ye have seen with your father.

39 They answered and said unto him, Abraham is our father. Jesus saith unto them, If ye were Abraham's children, ye would do the works of Abraham.

40 But now ye seek to kill me, a man that hath told you the truth, which I have heard of God: this did not Abraham.

41 Ye do the deeds of your father. Then said they to him, We be not born of fornication; we have one Father, even God.

42 Jesus said unto them, If God were your Father, ye would love me: for I proceeded forth and came from God; neither came I of myself, but he sent me.

43 Why do ye not understand my speech? even because ye cannot hear my word.

44 Ye are of your father the devil, and the lusts of your father ye will do: he was a murderer from the beginning, and abode not in the truth, because there is no truth in him. When he speaketh a lie, he speaketh of his own: for he is a liar, and the father of it.

45 And because I tell you the truth, ye believe me not.

46 Which of you convinceth me of sin? And if I say the truth, why do ye not believe me?

47 He that is of God heareth God's words: ye therefore hear them not, because ye are not of God.

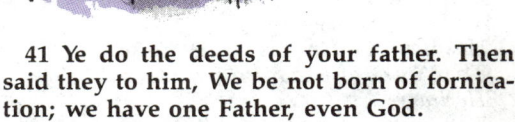

Jan
21

GOLDEN TEXT: Ye shall know the truth, and the truth shall make you free.—John 8:32.

> *John: The Gospel of Life and Light*
> Unit 2. Jesus Reveals Himself
> (Lessons 5-9)

Lesson Aims

This study should prepare the student to:

1. Describe the *freedom* that Jesus promises and provides for His faithful followers.

2. Explain why unbelievers cannot have this freedom.

Lesson Outline

INTRODUCTION
  A. What Is Freedom?
  B. What Is Truth?
  C. Conflicting Viewpoints
I. TRUTH AND FREEDOM (John 8: 31-36)
  A. Freedom in Truth (vv. 31-33)
     Abiding
  B. Freedom in the Son (vv. 34-36)
II. TEST OF TWO FAMILIES (John 8:37-47)
  A. Heads of the Houses (vv. 37, 38)
  B. The Works of Abraham (vv. 39, 40)
     Heritage
  C. The Love of God (vv. 41-43)
  D. The Project of the Devil (vv. 44, 45)
  E. Not Attuned to God (vv. 46, 47)
CONCLUSION
  A. The Rest of the Story
  B. Prayer
  C. Thought to Remember

Display visual 8 from the visuals packet. Let it remain before the class throughout the session. The visual is shown on page 180.

Introduction

A. What Is Freedom?

Freedom is a word that is highly regarded and widely used in our world. It describes a condition so precious that men will fight to achieve it and will die in order that others whom they love may have it. But there is wide disagreement as to what freedom is and just how it may be achieved.

Bondage is generally understood to be the opposite of freedom; hence we talk most easily about freedom *from* the forces that bind, such as prison or slavery. We think almost automatically of Israel's forced servitude in Egypt and the miracles by which God set them free.

For a full generation, however, Israel's material condition was not greatly improved. They were not *freed* from pain, or from fear, or from a considerable degree of hunger, hard labor, and disease, as well as death. In fact, there were times when they longed for the familiar servitude and diet of Egypt.

What they did have more fully were the *affirmative* freedoms to make choices and act responsibly on them—to choose what they would do to earn a living, to think and to express their thoughts, and above all to worship God according to the revelation He had given them.

Large elements of freedom were written into the law of God given through Moses. Slavery and debtors' loss were not avoided, but Sabbath years and years of Jubilee protected against permanent involuntary servitude.

A large part of the Messiah's mission was to set men free from various kinds of bondage: "The Lord hath anointed me to preach good tidings unto the meek; he hath sent me to bind up the brokenhearted, to proclaim liberty to the captives, and the opening of the prison to them that are bound; to proclaim the acceptable year of the Lord" (Isaiah 61:1, 2). At the outset of Jesus' ministry, He chose this passage to describe His purpose (Luke 4:16-21). As His ministry developed, however, it became increasingly evident that the freedom He came to provide was wider, deeper, and infinitely more lasting than loosing a paralytic from his rigidity, a leper from the restrictions associated with his disease, or even a widow from her grief.

B. What Is Truth?

Along with *freedom*, *truth* is a word much used and highly touted, but without any total agreement as to its meaning. That was demonstrated most clearly in Jesus' conversation with Pilate. Pilate asked if Jesus was a king, and the Lord answered affirmatively: "To this end was I born, and for this cause came I into the world, that I should bear witness unto the truth. Every one that is of the truth heareth my voice." To which Pilate responded, "What is truth?" He didn't wait for an answer (John 18:37, 38).

To the Christian, truth resides in Jesus, the Son of God. To the Communist, truth is whatever may advance the Communist cause. To the scientist, truth is what he learns from his experiments. To the humanist, truth is what most glorifies Man. Perhaps we may generalize by saying that each interpreter regards as truth whatever conforms best to the values or authority he regards as supreme.

Obviously, then, the words of Jesus—"Ye shall know the truth, and the truth shall make you free"—are subject to being lifted out of context and expounded in many different ways. Hence this is a favorite text with many folk who know or care very little about Scripture in general. The big question for the honest inquirer is, "What did Jesus mean by these words when He said them?"

C. Conflicting Viewpoints

Disagreements as to the meaning of such words as *truth* and *freedom* are not new. They seethe throughout the events recorded in John 7 and 8, and they boil over in the conclusion of chapter 8. So enraged were the Jewish leaders at Jesus that they would have ignored the authority of Rome and stoned Jesus to death, but He removed himself from their sight and presence.

The occasion was the feast of Tabernacles celebrated in October, about six months before Jesus' death. Jesus lingered in Galilee, then went up to Jerusalem for the feast privately. Even before His arrival, He was the subject of much discussion and disagreement both among the Jewish people and among their leaders. Once there, He began to teach publicly in the temple, rebuking the leaders for their rejection of Him. When they sent soldiers to arrest Him, they returned empty handed, themselves enthralled by His teaching. He announced himself as the water of life and the light of the world, and predicted that before long He would be going where His enemies could not find or reach Him.

Opinions about Jesus ranged from open, determined, and murderous hatred (John 7:1, 25) to various levels of faith and acceptance: "Many of the people believed on him and said, When Christ cometh, will he do more miracles than these which this man hath done?" (John 7:31). Even among those He most directly challenged, "As he spake these words, many believed on him" (8:30).

At that point, our printed text begins.

I. Truth and Freedom
(John 8:31-36)

A. Freedom in Truth (vv. 31-33)

31. Then said Jesus to those Jews which believed on him, If ye continue in my word, then are ye my disciples indeed.

Almost immediately, the belief of these Jews began to turn to antagonism toward Jesus, as is seen in verses 33 and 37. Some think that the entire group of believers mentioned in verse 30 turned from Him. Others feel that the defectors were a smaller group within that number. We note that those mentioned in verse 30 "believed

on" Jesus. In verse 31, Jesus addressed those Jews "who had believed him" (*New International Version*. The word *on* does not appear in the Greek text of this verse.) Perhaps some had accepted Jesus' statement of messiahship, but did not trust Him as Lord. That is, they had been mentally persuaded that He was the Messiah they had longed for, but they did not wholeheartedly surrender themselves to Him.

If ye continue. Not the beginners in a race, but those who finish, are rewarded. *Remain, abide,* and *endure* are other translations of the word for *continue.* The believer is not only to hold the truths that Jesus has revealed; he is to make them his permanent residence. His doing so becomes the mark of his genuine and total discipleship. This is the necessary foundation for the knowledge and freedom yet to be mentioned.

ABIDING

We don't use the word *abide* much anymore. It carries the meaning of remaining stable or fixed, and suggests the concept of steadfastness, which we need to develop in our lives.

Grandfather Carson was a master carpenter who put in long work days. His joy was in completing a job and hearing the approval of his clients. Nothing came from his shop that was not first class, and his reputation provided him with all the employment he needed.

Someone asked Mr. Carson why he always used the best materials and was so painstaking with his work. His answer is worth noting.

"When I was a boy apprenticing for the trade, the man who taught me said, 'George, when you begin a job, stay with it. Abide until you can know in your heart and mind that it has been well done.' I've always kept that in mind, and I never leave a task until I feel I would be proud to be the owner of my construction."

Jesus said, "If you abide in My word, you are My disciples indeed" (John 8:31, *The New King James Version*).

In a generation characterized all too much by a lack of commitment, Jesus' followers will be known by their unwavering adherence to His teachings.   —W. P.

32. And ye shall know the truth, and the truth shall make you free.

The *truth*, here as throughout the Bible, resides in the being of God. It is the word of God, addressed to mankind. It is the living Word, embodied in Jesus, the way, the truth, and the life (John 14:6). It is the teaching of Jesus, expressing His person in words.

To *know* is to receive and accept information, as one knows history or geography, making it the basis for action. To *know* is also to enjoy a

visual 8

vital and intimate acquaintance, as one knows a friend or member of his family. The two aspects become one when applied to knowing God's truth. We know His truth by obeying it, doing it (John 3:21), walking in it (3 John 3, 4).

Truth in Christ makes one free negatively and affirmatively. He is no longer in bondage to sin, its guilt, its power, and its condemnation. He is no longer in bondage to self, greed, pride, and ambition. He is no longer in bondage to the opinions of men shaping him to their molds by frowns or applause. Instead, he can look with hope to the future and shape his path toward it. Drawn by love of God and his fellowman, he can choose the way of service and peace (Galatians 5:13-15). He can pray jubilantly, "I will walk at liberty: for I seek thy precepts" (Psalm 119:45).

33. They answered him, We be Abraham's seed, and were never in bondage to any man: how sayest thou, Ye shall be made free?

Jesus' hearers resented the implication that they were slaves and not free men. Their pride in their physical descent from Abraham was such that they resisted any suggestion of spiritual flaws.

Of course, the nation had been in bondage to Egypt, Babylon, Persia, and Syria, and even now was ruled by Rome. Even so, the descendants of Abraham had never accepted the dominion of their conquerors or cooperated in spirit with them. They had maintained a sense of superiority to their oppressors because of their unique position as God's covenant people (Genesis 17:7). How, then, dared this Galilean suggest they needed any freedom He could give?

B. Freedom in the Son (vv. 34-36)

34. Jesus answered them, Verily, verily, I say unto you, Whosoever committeth sin is the servant of sin.

Jesus' hearers claimed that they had never been enslaved, but He responded that everyone who commits sin, that is, who is living a life of sin, is in bondage to sin. It is a bondage that worsens with each sin committed, and from which no one, by his or her own power, can escape. Jesus made it clear that His definition of freedom and slavery was not limited to matters of outward and material constraint.

35, 36. And the servant abideth not in the house for ever: but the Son abideth ever. If the Son therefore shall make you free, ye shall be free indeed.

By His response in the preceding verse, Jesus pictured His hearers as slaves in chains. He now slightly alters His thought to speak of another aspect of slavery. A slave may work in His master's house and thereby enjoy certain privileges for awhile; but he is not a permanent member of the family and can be cast out whenever the master is displeased with him. Not so a son. His family relationship is as long as life, and he will inherit his portion of the estate.

By this, Jesus drew a contrast between the Old Covenant and the New, which He had come to establish. The Old Covenant was soon to be done away. No longer would a person enjoy special privileges simply by being born a Jew. Freedom from all that enslaves would come only through the Son of God.

The real freedom God's Son came to give was ultimately freedom from sin and all that goes with it. And that kind of freedom can come from no other source.

II. Test of Two Families (John 8:37-47)

A. Heads of the Houses (vv. 37, 38)

37. I know that ye are Abraham's seed; but ye seek to kill me, because my word hath no place in you.

Jesus acknowledged the Jews' physical descent from Abraham, but He pointed to their determined effort to destroy that seed of Abraham through whom God had promised to bless all mankind (Genesis 12:1-3; Galatians 3:8, 16-19).

Ye seek to kill me. Their plot to that purpose was known and discussed in the temple and throughout Jerusalem (John 7:1, 25).

As a river bed clogged with debris will prevent the free flow of the stream in its channel, so these people gave Jesus' message *no place* to work within them. And having rejected the message, they saw only one way to make themselves comfortable. That was to destroy the irritating messenger.

38. I speak that which I have seen with my Father: and ye do that which ye have seen with your father.

Jesus was revealing in words what He had learned in God's presence; His critics were revealing in action what they had learned from a very different source. Here are introduced two households, two sets of children, two styles of language and thought. One was divine, the other diabolic.

B. The Works of Abraham (vv. 39, 40)

39, 40. They answered and said unto him, Abraham is our father. Jesus saith unto them, If ye were Abraham's children, ye would do the works of Abraham. But now ye seek to kill me, a man that hath told you the truth, which I have heard of God: this did not Abraham.

Jesus had not yet named the *father* whose influence was reflected in His critics' behavior, but they were rather sure He did not mean Abraham. Therefore they asserted again their relationship to the "father of the faithful." But their actions belied their words. They might be descendants from Abraham, but they were not his *children*. Otherwise they would act like it. Abraham was especially for going where God directed, doing what God commanded him to do, and dealing unselfishly with his fellowmen. No family resemblance to Abraham could be found in Jesus' critics.

Especially unlike Abraham was the Jewish leaders' plot to destroy Jesus for His offense in setting God's truth before them. Abraham, by contrast, had always been sensitive to God's word of instruction or command, whether by vision, or by angel, or by mankind. Most memorable is his hospitality to three strangers who came as men but delivered the message of angels (Genesis 18; Hebrews 13:2). Abraham-like conduct would have respected Jesus' truth from God, even if Jesus had been as they supposed, only a *man.*

HERITAGE

Mother-daughter look-alike advertising was the real "in" thing not long ago. On our TV screens would appear two lovely women, obviously related, and we were invited to decide which was the mother and which was the daughter. Sometimes we could not do it, because the two were so similar in facial features and they were wearing the same type of clothing, hair style, etc. In some cases, even their speech and walk were alike. One seemed to be the clone of the other.

The truth that always came to mind was that because they were mother and daughter, the younger woman had inherited much of the looks and traits of the woman who gave her birth.

We do bear the image of our forebears. We should, because we are their children.

Jesus applied this thought to the spiritual realm. The religious leaders who opposed Jesus claimed that they were Abraham's children, but Jesus declared that they were false sons because they did not act in the character of Abraham.

As children of God through faith in His Son, do our lives reflect His character?   —W. P.

C. The Love of God (vv. 41-43)

41. Ye do the deeds of your father. Then said they to him, We be not born of fornication; we have one Father, even God.

By now the Jewish critics perceived that Jesus referred to a spiritual heritage rather than a physical one. They knew the Old Testament figure of the spiritual family, with Israel the bride of Jehovah, and with idolatry regarded as unfaithfulness in marriage. They were not about to admit any such irregularity. They were not illegitimate children of idolatry. They were sure that God was the only head of their spiritual family. Perhaps they even emphasized the *we* in their denial of illegitimacy, suggesting that Jesus' own ancestry, physical or spiritual, was suspect. They were ready to charge Him with being a Samaritan—virtually a mongrel—and being possessed with a devil (John 8:48).

42. Jesus said unto them, If God were your Father, ye would love me: for I proceeded forth and came from God; neither came I of myself, but he sent me.

There is something radically wrong with a family that is not characterized by love among its members. In the family of God, it is not only wrong but impossible. One cannot love God and hate His children. Jesus was and is God's Son, having come to earth from the presence of God, not on His own initiative, but as directed by the Father. He was the obedient Son. Their hatred of Him belied their claim to be God's children.

43. Why do ye not understand my speech? even because ye cannot hear my word.

Jesus' question was accompanied by its own answer. The words, expressions, and parables of Jesus did not get through to the understanding of his hearers because the subject matter—the message or word—was beyond their spiritual capacity. They were not in "hearing distance" of the truth that makes men free.

D. The Project of the Devil (vv. 44, 45)

44. Ye are of your father the devil, and the lusts of your father ye will do: he was a murderer from the beginning, and abode not in the truth, because there is no truth in him. When he speaketh a lie, he speaketh of his own: for he is a liar, and the father of it.

Here for the first time Jesus clearly identified the spiritual father of His adversaries.

The lusts of your father. Satan's ambition concerning Jesus was to destroy Him, to nullify His plan for the salvation of mankind, and thus to keep the world in bondage to himself. These Jewish leaders were acting like obedient children on the business of their father, the devil.

A murderer from the beginning. Even in the Garden of Eden, Satan arranged the entrance of death into the world. He did his first murderous work by inciting Cain to kill his brother. Now he was inciting Jesus' enemies to plot and arrange His death. Satan's murderous career continues in every person he can persuade to hate his brother (see 1 John 3:8, 15).

He is a liar. Beginning with his lie to Eve (Genesis 3:1-5), Satan has waged a relentless campaign against the truth—especially the saving truth of the gospel. When he lies he is speaking in character, for *there is no truth in him.*

45. And because I tell you the truth, ye believe me not.

Jesus had come from the Father to reveal man's sinful condition and God's plan of salvation. But these prideful leaders, who were following the leading of the father of lies, rejected the *truth* when Jesus presented it to them.

E. Not Attuned to God (vv. 46, 47)

46. Which of you convinceth me of sin? And if I say the truth, why do ye not believe me?

Convinceth means convicts. A courtroom lawyer conducting a cross-examination will often seek to discredit a witness by showing him to be a person less than upright and dependable. No such procedure could be used against Jesus. No whisper of moral failure could be raised against

Him. His faultless goodness became a significant theme in the preaching of the first-century church (2 Corinthians 5:21; Hebrews 4:15).

The Jews could not convict Jesus of sin. Necessarily, therefore, He spoke the truth. If they could find no untruth in what He said, why did they still reject it?"

47. He that is of God heareth God's words: ye therefore hear them not, because ye are not of God.

Here is the Lord's answer to His enemies' claim and to His own question. These people were not as they claimed to be, children of God. That is why they rejected His message, even though it was God's truth. Children of the devil would rather be bound in flattering deceit than freed in humbling truth. (See John 3:19, 20.)

Conclusion

A. The Rest of the Story

John 8:12-30 includes several paragraphs of discussion in which certain of Jesus' hearers came to some level of faith in Him and His words. Our printed text makes it plain that certain of these "believers" withered under the bright light of His continued teaching. They couldn't stand the test. The closing paragraphs of the chapter reveal even more intense conflict.

Fortunately, however, there is another side to the story. Some of these early believers grew in their faith, and some who were neutral or even antagonistic to Jesus at the time were later convinced by His death, resurrection, and ascension into Heaven. They were among those who, on the Day of Pentecost, responded to the gospel message, saying, "Men and brethren, what shall we do?" On that occasion they heard the liberating truth, "Repent, and be baptized every one of you in the name of Jesus Christ for the remission of sins, and ye shall receive the gift of the Holy Ghost.... Save yourselves from this untoward generation" (Acts 2:37-40).

Three thousand responded on that day, and millions have responded since then to the offer of freedom that comes through the truth of God.

B. Prayer

Open our hearts, we pray, dear God, to receive, believe, and live according to the truth that is in Christ Jesus. May we be given grace and courage to share this liberating truth with others who, like ourselves, are sin-bound slaves without it. In Jesus' name, amen.

C. Thought to Remember

"If the Son therefore shall make you free, ye shall be free indeed" (John 8:36).

Learning by Doing

This page contains an alternate lesson plan emphasizing learning activities. Classes desiring such student involvement will find these suggestions helpful.

Learning Goals

All of us have experienced the frustration of falling victim to a sin of which we had previously repented. We have experienced the binding power of sin and Satan. Some finally say, "What's the use?" They give up and give in. It is vital for your students to find renewed hope in the power of Jesus Christ to set them free from sin. Therefore, this lesson will help your student to:

1. Identify any frustrations they may have experienced (or are experiencing) in overcoming sin in their lives.

2. Understand how they may avail themselves of the power of Christ to overcome sin.

3. Experience a new sense of hope in areas of personal frustration and failure.

Into the Lesson

Begin the session with a sin survey. Ask your students to look over a list of categories of sin that you have written on the chalkboard or overhead projector. (You may use the student book for this activity, if you prefer.) Tell students that you would like a show of hands to determine which of these sins they think is the biggest problem for non-Christians. Ask them to vote for three. Count the number of votes for each sin, and put the number to the *left* of each sin. Then circle the sins that rank first, second, and third, and indicate their ranking.

Now ask students to vote for the three sins they think are the biggest problems among Christians. Record the votes to the *right* of each sin. With a different color of chalk or marker, circle and rank the top three sins that Christians fall to. Here are the categories of sin in this Sin Survey: adultery, gossip, pride, lying, materialism, slander, lust, dishonesty, selfishness, hatred, stealing, swearing, hypocrisy, jealousy, discord, violence, drunkenness, partying, rebelliousness.

Talk about how and why sin problems are the *same* for Christians and non-Christians. How and why are they *different?*

Ask the students to look over the list of sins and to themselves identify the sin that has been the most difficult for them to conquer. Don't dwell on this activity, but don't skip it. It is important for the students to recognize their own need for this lesson.

Into the Word

Before reading the Scripture, note that this teaching of Jesus is directed to those who had come to some level of faith in Him (John 8:31). As you read aloud John 8:31-47, have your students listen for any reasons why sin has such a powerful hold on some people's lives. (The *New International Version* is particularly good on this passage.)

Now have the students break into groups of four or five and discuss the following questions. You may either distribute copies of them or use the student book.

Free at Last

1. In this text, what indication does Jesus give as to why sin seems to have such a grip on some people's lives?

2. Jesus gives three steps to freedom in verses 31 and 32. List them:

    a. (hold to His teaching)

    b. (know the truth)

    c. (the truth sets a person free)

3. How does sin make slaves of people (v. 34)?

4. How did Abraham find victory over sin (vv. 39, 40; see Romans 4:3)? How can we make his victory our victory?

5. If knowing the truth sets a person free from sin, why isn't everyone who hears delivered (v. 43)?

6. Is it possible to overcome sin before being born into the family of God (v. 44)?

7. How does being in the family of God help a person to overcome sin (v. 47)?

Once the groups have discussed these questions, let the whole class discuss question 2. Why does commitment (holding to Jesus' teaching) come before insight (knowing the truth)?

Into Life

Ask the class if anyone feels more guilty now than when he or she first came to class. How did Jesus' audience feel after hearing His teaching on this occasion? (See vv. 48, 52a.)

Say, "Whenever we are reminded of our moral failures, we have a tendency to feel guilty. But Jesus came to set us free from sin *and its guilt*. Do any of you have any idea how we can relieve any guilt we may feel from our failures?" Allow time for discussion, and then close the session with prayer.

Let's Talk It Over

The questions on this page are designed to encourage review of the lesson Scriptures and to promote discussion of the lesson by the class. The answers provided are only discussion starters. Let your class talk it over from there.

1. As the lesson writer points out, "truth" means something different to people who hold to various philosophies and religions. How does this fact create confusion in our society?

When we Christians declare that "truth resides in Jesus, the Son of God," we recognize that we do not need to twist the truth in order to advance Jesus' cause. Truth is absolute, and truthfulness and forthrightness on our part are consistent with it. However, in certain philosophies of our time, truth is regarded as relative, and whatever advances "the cause" is considered true and legitimate. We are familiar with this as a working principle of the communist world, but it is also an increasing problem in our own society. And so it seems that some government officials and political candidates see lying or manipulating the truth as a legitimate tactic. The view that truth is relative and that lying is legitimate is hardly restricted to political leaders. Others in our society protect or advance their interests by the clever use of lies or half-truths. And each such incident erodes the ties of mutual trust and respect that help to hold our society together. The judgment of God given through the prophet Isaiah applies here: "Woe unto them that call evil good, and good evil" (Isaiah 5:20).

2. "Everyone who sins is a slave to sin" (John 8:34, *New International Version*). Why do we need to emphasize this fact in our evangelistic endeavors?

In our society, we glory in our liberty. We also glory in our intelligence, our resourcefulness, and determination to succeed. And yet many in our society are slaves, and that enslavement is manifest. Some are clearly enslaved by the sin of greed, others by the sin of sexual lust, still others by the sin of addiction to alcohol or drugs. The list goes on. To emphasize this in our evangelistic efforts is to puncture the pride that keeps the multitudes from coming to Christ. If we are not smart enough or strong enough or persistent enough to throw off the shackles of our enslavement, then where shall we look to find liberation? When people come to the point of facing this dilemma, we can be ready to answer, "If the Son therefore shall make you free, ye shall be free indeed" (John 8:36).

3. The Jews' hatred of Jesus proved that God was not their Father. How does this apply to hatred within the church?

The apostle John wrote, "He that saith he is in the light, and hateth his brother, is in darkness even until now" (1 John 2:9). Some Christians justify their ill feelings toward a brother or sister by complaining that the other person has done them some terrible wrong. Or they may deceive themselves by insisting that they do not harbor personal hatred, but that they "hate the other person's ways." If we hold any harsh and bitter feelings toward a fellow Christian, we need to recognize it as a grievous sin, pray for forgiveness, and pray as well for hatred to be transformed into love. Another aspect of this matter is that Jesus commanded love of enemies (Matthew 5:43-48). Christians may be tempted to hate the atheists, humanists, and others who attack their faith and the moral values, but here again hatred is an unthinkable response. Jesus did not allow the taunts and brutalities of His enemies to destroy His love for them, and neither should we allow the attacks of unbelievers to turn our love to hatred.

4. "You belong to your father, the devil, and you want to carry out your father's desire" (John 8:44 *New International Version*). Why do we need to put particular emphasis on this statement of Jesus in our preaching and other evangelistic endeavors?

So many people today scoff at the idea of a personal devil that Christians may be tempted to remain silent about him. The devil and his angels have been made such a source of humor that few people are inclined to take him seriously. It is probable that Satan wants it that way. Jesus' words provide a blunt reminder of the fact that all persons belong to one of two spiritual fathers. Either they have been reconciled to God through Jesus Christ and are enjoying fellowship with their Heavenly Father, or they are living under the authority of the devil and doing his bidding. Some people may feel that they occupy neutral ground, but Jesus' statement is one among several Biblical references that show neutrality is not possible. We should not hesitate to speak out about Satan's reality and the very real control he exercises in human lives.

Jesus Reveals Himself as the Light of the World

LESSON SCRIPTURE: John 9.

PRINTED TEXT: John 9:1-11, 35-41.

John 9:1-11, 35-41

1 And as Jesus passed by, he saw a man which was blind from his birth.

2 And his disciples asked him, saying, Master, who did sin, this man, or his parents, that he was born blind?

3 Jesus answered, Neither hath this man sinned, nor his parents: but that the works of God should be made manifest in him.

4 I must work the works of him that sent me, while it is day: the night cometh, when no man can work.

5 As long as I am in the world, I am the light of the world.

6 When he had thus spoken, he spat on the ground, and made clay of the spittle, and he anointed the eyes of the blind man with the clay,

7 And said unto him, Go, wash in the pool of Siloam, (which is by interpretation, Sent.) He went his way therefore, and washed, and came seeing.

8 The neighbors therefore, and they which before had seen him that he was blind, said, Is not this he that sat and begged?

9 Some said, This is he: others said, He is like him: but he said, I am he.

10 Therefore said they unto him, How were thine eyes opened?

11 He answered and said, A man that is called Jesus made clay, and anointed mine eyes, and said unto me, Go to the pool of Siloam, and wash: and I went and washed, and I received sight.

. . . .

35 Jesus heard that they had cast him out; and when he had found him, he said unto him, Dost thou believe on the Son of God?

36 He answered and said, Who is he, Lord, that I might believe on him?

37 And Jesus said unto him, Thou hast both seen him, and it is he that talketh with thee.

38 And he said, Lord, I believe. And he worshipped him.

39 And Jesus said, For judgment I am come into this world, that they which see not might see; and that they which see might be made blind.

40 And some of the Pharisees which were with him heard these words, and said unto him, Are we blind also?

41 Jesus said unto them, If ye were blind, ye should have no sin: but now ye say, We see; therefore your sin remaineth.

Jan 28

GOLDEN TEXT: I am the light of the world.—John 9:5.

John: The Gospel of Life and Light
Unit 2: Jesus Reveals Himself
(Lessons 5-9)

Lesson Aims

A study of this lesson should equip the student to:

1. Report in brief outline the events recorded in John 9.

2. Compare and contrast the two kinds of blindness, physical and spiritual.

3. Name some important things he can see clearly only because of Jesus.

Lesson Outline

INTRODUCTION
  A. Light and Vision
  B. Lesson Background
  I. BESTOWING PHYSICAL SIGHT (John 9:1-7)
  A. Respect for the Blind Man (vv. 1-3)
  B. Respect for the Opportunity (vv. 4, 5)
  C. Accomplishing the Miracle (vv. 6, 7)
     No Hesitation!
 II. CONFIRMING THE MIRACLE (John 9:8-11)
  A. The Person Identified (vv. 8, 9)
  B. The Procedure Reported (vv. 10, 11)
III. BESTOWING SPIRITUAL SIGHT (John 9:35-38)
  A. Compassion to the Outcast (v. 35)
  B. Identifying the Giver of Light (vv. 36, 37)
  C. Accepting Confession and Worship (v. 38)
     "Lord, I Believe"
 IV. REJECTING THE GIFT (John 9:39-41)
  A. Reversing the Roles (v. 39)
  B. Removal of Mercy (vv. 40, 41)
CONCLUSION
  A. What Do You See?
  B. Prayer for Sight
  C. Thought to Remember

Display visual 9 from the visuals packet. Let it remain before the class throughout the session. It is shown on page 187.

Introduction

A. Light and Vision

The first recorded utterance of God was, "Let there be light" (Genesis 1:3). And the light that came into being at His word made possible the life that He afterward created—every green thing that grows and provides food for animal life and for mankind. Life is impossible without light.

But to mankind God gave eyes to make other uses of light. They are thus made able to go, and to find, and to do, and to learn, and to enjoy beauty. Those who have not useful eyes must depend heavily on others who can see. Light is of limited use to those who do not have vision, but vision is of no use at all without light.

Messianic prophecy makes repeated reference to giving sight to the blind: (Isaiah 35:5; see also 29:18 and 42:7). Fulfillment of these prophecies is found in the life and ministry of Jesus. John 1:1-5 introduces the creative Word of God as the "light of men" who became flesh and "dwelt among us" (John 1:14). Jesus announced himself as "the light of the world" (John 8:12). He introduced His ministry in terms of Isaiah's prophecy, with emphasis on "recovering of sight to the blind" (Luke 4:18; 7:21, 22). The Gospels describe half a dozen miracles in which Jesus healed the blind. No other one affliction is so often specified.

Jesus' ministry as the Light of the world could not be limited, however, to half a dozen or even half a thousand gifts of physical sight. He recognized and combatted an even more devastating spiritual blindness—the blindness shutting out the light of God. That is His necessary ministry to all of us. And to us, as well as to those who saw Him in the flesh, He proved His power to open the eyes of the soul by opening the eyes of the body.

B. Lesson Background

The event in this lesson took place in Jerusalem, probably on the final Sabbath of the feast of Tabernacles, six months before the Lord's crucifixion. The tense controversy noted in last week's lesson ended with Jesus' withdrawal from the murderous wrath of the Jewish leaders.

Later, Jesus was making His way, with His disciples, in a public area when he encountered a blind man. The blind man probably was seated at an entrance to the temple where he could encounter worshipers as they came and went (compare Acts 3:1, 2). What followed provides a most vivid narrative—the entire ninth chapter of John. Our printed text includes the beginning and end of the story. The interim verses, 12-34, focus on the problems faced by the man after he

---

How to Say It

GIHON.   *Gye*-hahn.
SILOAM.   Sy-*lo*-um.

was healed, and may be dealt with only briefly. The entire narrative presents Jesus vividly as the Light of the world, making life and vision available to all, and establishes His claim by giving a full-grown man his first glimpse of sunlight.

I. Bestowing Physical Sight
(John 9:1-7)

A. Respect for the Blind Man (vv. 1-3)

1. And as Jesus passed by, he saw a man which was blind from his birth.

We do not really need to know the time, the place, or the circumstances. What the Gospel writer considered worth telling was that Jesus *saw a man* and recognized an opportunity to serve. He saw not only the outward appearance of a blind beggar, but also the man's lifelong predicament. He saw, too, the personality that would respond to the relief of his darkness, both physical and spiritual, with grateful faith, perceptive understanding, and steadfast courage.

2. And his disciples asked him, saying, Master, who did sin, this man, or his parents, that he was born blind?

How did the disciples know that the man had never seen? Perhaps he had announced it in his plea for alms. They expected Jesus, however, to know what mortal men can only guess at—what moral failure brought on this punishment. They assumed along with multitudes in all ages, that any affliction must be caused by some specific sin (compare Acts 28: 3, 4). We know that sin brought hardship and death into the world, and that God does visit some sins of parents on their children and grandchildren (Exodus 20:5). Experience shows that some sins, such as fornication, drug abuse, and brawling bring disasters to the sinner. Yet it is equally true that many afflictions, illnesses, and accidents are suffered without relation to sin or sinning, and that many saints of God have been afflicted specifically *because* they were saints. The adversary, Satan, prince of darkness, is really behind it all.

3. Jesus answered, Neither hath this man sinned, nor his parents: but that the works of God should be made manifest in him.

The Lord made it plain that in this instance the blindness did not result from any specific sin. Jesus' present concern was not with the *cause*, but with the *result*, of the affliction. He would ask, not who is to blame, but how can God be glorified through the experience?

The always-pertinent question is, How can I use this experience to build up my own faith and glorify God? The difficult or tragic event may prove to be the eye-opener needed to help us see Heaven.

B. Respect for the Opportunity (vv. 4, 5)

4, 5. I must work the works of him that sent me, while it is day: the night cometh, when no man can work. As long as I am in the world, I am the light of the world.

There was one program to which the Lord would tolerate no interruption. That was His commitment to doing the will of God, from whom He had come, and to whom He would soon return. He knew that the *day* of His ministry on earth was already in its afternoon hours. What He was to do must be done promptly.

Later translations quote Jesus as saying, "We must work . . ." Was He thinking of working in concert with the Father who had sent Him, or was He including the disciples in the obligation to participate with Him in His ministry? If the latter, it harmonizes with His invitation, "Take my yoke upon you" (Matthew 11:29) and His promise to obedient disciples, "Lo, I am with you" (Matthew 28:20).

The work-ending *night* of which He spoke was His forthcoming death and departure from earth. Until then, "I am the world's light as long as I am in it" (Phillips translation). We hesitate even to consider the depth of darkness that would settle on the earth if the light of Christ, reflected in His disciples and radiated through His gospel, should ever be removed.

Just as Jesus had to accomplish the works of God before His day on earth ended, so must we who are His followers. For each of us, the night of death comes when all opportunity to work for the Master ceases.

C. Accomplishing the Miracle (vv. 6, 7)

6. When he had thus spoken, he spat on the ground, and made clay of the spittle, and he anointed the eyes of the blind man with the clay.

Jesus' words were followed with deeds. The patient could not see the procedure; others could. Why Jesus chose to heal the man in this manner, we are not told. The spittle mingled with the dust of the ground became a kind of salve, which the man could feel as it was applied to his sightless eyes (v. 11). The touching

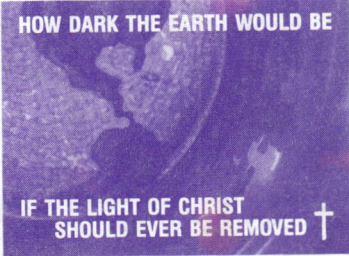

HOW DARK THE EARTH WOULD BE

IF THE LIGHT OF CHRIST SHOULD EVER BE REMOVED †

visual 9

of his eyes with it must have been designed to awaken faith in the blind man.

To the Jewish leaders, however, this act carried a different message. Their tradition forbade working with clay or anointing eyes for healing on the Sabbath, and this took place on the Sabbath (v. 14).

7. And said unto him, Go, wash in the pool of Siloam, (which is by interpretation, Sent.) He went his way therefore, and washed, and came seeing.

The man had evidently heard Jesus' conversation with His disciples, but not until now was he addressed directly. There was no question or explanation; only a terse command: "Go wash in the pool called *Sent*." The One who was *sent* from God (v. 4) was now *sending* a blind man a distance of a quarter to a half mile to *wash* the mud from his eyes in a pool whose waters were *sent* to it through an aqueduct from the spring of Gihon. The directive was not convenient for the man, but his obedience was prompt and without question. He *went* the distance and *washed* as directed, and *came* away *seeing*. Where did he go from the pool? Some translations say he "came home." At least his parents (v. 20) and neighbors learned promptly of his healing.

No one supposed or supposes that the healing was accomplished by mud or by water, any more than that the salvation of believers in Christ is accomplished by physical cleansing in Christian baptism (1 Peter 3:21) In both instances, the Light of the world works His own cleansing through the obedience of faith.

No Hesitation!

The little fellow got out to the end of the high dive, looked down, gave a little bounce, stopped, and backed onto the security of the tower.

"Go ahead, jump. The water's fine," came the encouraging cries from companions in the pool below. Once more the lad got out on the board and again backed off. This time there were no encouraging cries from below. Engrossed in their own pleasure in the pool, his friends had forgotten about him.

For over an hour the boy ventured out on the board and then retreated to the tower again. It was obvious that he did not want to climb back down the steps and admit defeat.

Finally, almost in desperation, he walked to the end of the board, closed his eyes, and jumped in. Immediately he was up laughing and shouting in joy over his accomplishment and joining in the fun of the others already in the pool.

When Jesus directed the blind man to "wash in the pool of Siloam," the man obeyed without hesitation; and he was blessed immediately.

Like the boy on the high dive, we miss many blessings when fear keeps us from doing what Jesus asks us to do.   —W. P.

II. Confirming the Miracle (John 9:8-11)

A. The Person Identified (vv. 8, 9)

8. The neighbors therefore, and they which before had seen him that he was blind, said, Is not this he that sat and begged?

The man seems to have returned first to his home community, causing much amazement among folk who had known him more or less well. His customary behavior had given way to a whole new personality. Not sitting disconsolately and begging, he was moving confidently. His glad appreciation of the world around him gave him a different appearance.

9. Some said, This is he: others said, He is like him: but he said, I am he.

They talked *about* him and disagreed, some affirming his identity, others not at all sure. Then they talked *with* him and learned the truth. Even so, the religious leaders doubted until they went to his parents to confirm it (v. 19).

B. The Procedure Reported (vv. 10, 11)

10, 11. Therefore said they unto him, How were thine eyes opened? He answered and said, A man that is called Jesus made clay, and anointed mine eyes, and said unto me, Go to the pool of Siloam, and wash: and I went and washed, and I received sight.

The central fact of the miracle was clear to everyone: this man, blind from birth, was now seeing clearly. How did it happen?

His replay is a masterpiece of brief and accurate, facts-only reporting. It began with a *man* whose name he had heard, but concerning whom he knew very little. It continued with what that man did and said; then what the blind man did in response; "And then I could see!"

This report he repeated, steadfastly and consistently, under merciless interrogation by the Pharisees (vv. 13-34). The interrogations involved *him* first (vv. 3-17), then *his parents* (vv. 18-23), then *him* again (vv. 24-34). Rather than yielding to pressure and softening his testimony about Jesus, he did some clear reasoning from the facts and strengthened it. He concluded that this Man called Jesus was a prophet (v. 17), and that He was sent from God (v. 33).

The healed man's growing conviction brought him into increasing conflict and difficulty. He accepted that, knowing the religious authorities' earlier warning that anyone who confessed Jesus as the Messiah would be put out of the synagogue (v. 22). And that is exactly what happened (v. 34), leaving him without religious fellowship, or community support, or social acceptance. The healed man paid a price for his faithfulness.

III. Bestowing Spiritual Sight (John 9:35-38)

A. Compassion to the Outcast (v. 35)

35. Jesus heard that they had cast him out; and when he had found him, he said unto him, Dost thou believe on the Son of God?

The Jews cast the man out of the temple; the Lord of the temple found him! How long it took, or where he was found, we are not told. But soon he learned that in losing the supportive fellowship of men, he had cast himself upon the supportive fellowship of the Messiah. But first he needed to know the Messiah for himself.

Dost thou believe on the Son of God? Jesus customarily referred to himself as the Son of man, and so it appears here in several of the oldest Greek manuscripts and most of the newer English translations. In any case, the man understood the sublime meaning of Jesus' words.

The Lord's question is basic to any Christian experience. If one believes, trusts, and follows Jesus, he can learn later anything he needs to know; but without this basic conviction and commitment, all other knowledge is unavailing.

B. Identifying the Giver of Light (vv. 36, 37)

36, 37. He answered and said, Who is he, Lord, that I might believe on Him? And Jesus said unto him, Thou hast both seen him, and it is he that talketh with thee.

Did the man know from the voice of this questioner that He was the man called Jesus who had healed him? If so, he had already confessed Him as a prophet and a righteous man in whom God had worked for his healing. In any case, his reference to *Lord* in this instance probably has the force of *Sir*—an address of respect but not of worship. (The Greek word used here can mean either "lord" or "sir.") He obviously knew something of the messianic promises, and he wanted to know more. "Tell me so that I may believe in him" *(New International Version)*. He was eager to learn, and he was willing to believe.

Jesus' reply is marvelous for its tender compassion and its dignity. The third-person references, *him* and *he*, rob it of any boastfulness, but it is totally clear (compare John 4:26).

C. Accepting Confession and Worship (v. 38)

38. And he said, Lord, I believe. And he worshipped him.

This time there was no question as to the meaning attached to *Lord*. The One who had seen and understood his plight, had given him the dignity of participation in his own miraculous healing, had opened the blind eyes and given spiritual sight, and had sought his company when others cast him out—that One now revealed himself in direct and friendly conversation as the long-awaited Messiah! None could have *worshipped* with a heart more full of grateful love than this man kneeling before Jesus.

Be it noted that Jesus readily accepted the worship that the apostles were later to reject (Acts 10: 25, 26; 14:11-15). Jesus and His worshiper both knew that He was not just another man. He was and is the Light of the world.

How much did the man understand and believe? Enough to confess his Lord. He was a learner. His faith had developed swiftly under the most difficult circumstances. Whatever he knew, that was enough for acceptance now, and he would keep on learning.

"LORD, I BELIEVE"

The hunt was on. It was not a matter of life or death. It was the simple search for the lost shirt.

June's directions were explicit. "John, I ironed that shirt just this morning, and it is hanging in your closet." Another hurried search by John proved fruitless.

In desperation, John rushed into the kitchen and told June that she could not have put the shirt in his closet, because it was not there.

Resignedly, June left her meal preparation, walked quickly into the bedroom, opened the closet door, reached in and brought out the shirt. Without a word, she laid it on the bed.

Later John sheepishly came in to apologize and to ask, "Why couldn't I see that shirt." He was amazed at Junes' reply. "You didn't want to. You had already decided it wasn't there."

It's difficult to see what we don't want to see. The healed man immediately said, "Lord, I believe." He had experienced Jesus' power and his mind was open concerning Jesus' claims. The Pharisees had already made up their minds about Jesus, and so they could not even see the obvious. Are you blind or seeing?   —W. P.

IV. Rejecting the Gift (John 9:39-41)

A. Reversing the Roles (v. 39)

39. And Jesus said, For judgment I am come into this world, that they which see not might see; and that they which see might be made blind.

Judgment—the separation of mankind into contrasting groups according to the different ways they have chosen—is the unavoidable result of Christ's coming. The Light of the world reveals things and people for what they are.

The purpose of Jesus' coming into the world was not judgment and condemnation, but salvation. Some, rejected His salvation and so brought condemnation on themselves (John 3:17-19).

Human resistance to divine truth has been so prevalent that it seems at times as though the messenger's purpose was to confuse, harden, and condemn the hearers (Isaiah 6:8-10; Matthew 13: 11-17). The same teaching, however, does convince and convert some, bringing them salvation. That is infinitely better than to leave the whole company of mankind untouched and unsaved.

The situation immediately before Jesus was typical. The blind beggar and the critical Pharisees were witnesses to the same facts. The one accepted and believed; he received sight, both physical and spiritual. The others refused to acknowledge any need, assuming they already possessed all light and truth. So they became increasingly hard and bitter in closing their eyes to the light Jesus came to bring.

B. Removal of Mercy (vv. 40, 41)

40. And some of the Pharisees which were with him heard these words, and said unto him, Are we blind also?

At this time in Jesus' ministry *some of the Pharisees* or their messengers were usually within hearing distance of Jesus, hoping to "catch him in his words" (Mark 12:13). This time they were stung by Jesus' suggestion that they might be blind. They were God's chosen ones; certain that they could never be blind!

41. Jesus said unto them, If ye were blind, ye should have no sin: but now ye say, We see; therefore your sin remaineth.

If the Pharisees had been *blind*, that is, truly incapable of perceiving the light, the spiritual truth, that Jesus had been revealing, no charge could have been brought against them. But they claimed that they could *see*. They were confident that they were the guides of the blind, a light to those who were in darkness, and instructors of the foolish (see Romans 2:19, 20). Therefore, they had no excuse for rejecting the light that Jesus brought them. They confirmed their own condemnation when they rejected divine mercy. They chose darkness when they closed their eyes against the Light of the world.

Conclusion

A. What Do You See?

In the light of Jesus' rebuke to those who say, "We see," one may be hesitant to admit seeing anything. It need not be so if, like the unnamed blind man, we first see and admit our own need of light, and come in faith and obedience to Him who is the Light of the world.

That man saw Jesus! It was the most important part of his new experience. None of us can do better than to fix our attention on Jesus and make Him the center of a continuing and increasingly enthusiastic study. It would be most tragic if any of us should become a careless, uncomprehending part of the world to which the Light has come (John 1:4, 5).

A profitable part of our seeing will be to follow Jesus' gaze, to see what He saw, in the way He saw it. He saw people and their needs, as He saw the man who was blind from birth. We must never be unseeing or indifferent to those whom God loves and Christ died to save. Jesus saw an opportunity to serve a man and so to glorify God; to save a man and so to please God. God's light is in the world. Let's greet it and glory in it.

B. Prayer for Sight

We would see You, our Father, and in the light of Your countenance we would see what You see, in the way You see it. May we reflect Your light, that we may be a part of Your ministry of light to the world. In Jesus' name, amen.

C. Thought to Remember

There are none so blind as those who will not see.

Learning by Doing

This page contains an alternate lesson plan emphasizing learning activities. Classes desiring such student involvement will find these suggestions helpful.

Learning Goals

There are many things that can blind a person to the truth of who Jesus is. In today's text, Jesus uses the condition of a person's physical blindness to teach us about people's spiritual blindness. This lesson will help your students to:

1. Recall any areas where they have grown to new insights about Jesus the Christ.

2. Examine their own prejudices that would keep them from receiving the full light of Jesus.

3. Distinguish between facts and opinions so that they may be firm in the facts of the gospel and flexible in their opinions about the gospel.

Into the Lesson

As you begin this lesson, you will explore with your students how their views about Jesus have changed through the years. Ask them to work individually on completing the following sentence: *"I used to see Jesus as—, but now I see Jesus as—"* You may use the student book for this activity or make copies of these incomplete statements and distribute them. Ask students to go way back, maybe even before their conversion, to identify areas in which their understanding of Jesus has changed. After about two minutes of individual work, ask students to share how their view of Jesus has changed.

Now ask them to share what factors have been most significant in bringing about their change in thinking about Jesus. These may include such things as people, special events, personal experiences, or studying the Bible.

Into the Word

Today's lesson is a story that occupies the whole ninth chapter of John. It is best to study the whole chapter to get the force of Jesus' teaching. Do this in a dramatic fashion by assigning parts to be read by a cast of characters. You will need to give out the following assignments; narrator, disciple, Jesus, blind man, blind man's neighbors (2), Pharisees (2), blind man's parents.

For this dramatic reading, *The Living Bible* is an excellent choice in capturing a natural flow in the conversation. You can give each participant a copy of *The Living Bible* to follow. It would be helpful if you would make these assignments a week ahead so that the characters could rehearse their parts for greatest dramatic effect. It should take about six minutes to read this chapter.

Break into groups of four or five and discuss the following questions:

1. Often Jesus healed people who sought Him in faith. On this occasion, Jesus chose to heal a man who apparently neither sought healing nor had faith in Him at the time. Why did Jesus heal this blind man? What were the results?

2. What prevented the Pharisees from accepting the implications of Jesus' ability to perform such a miracle?

3. Why did the man who was healed become so frustrated with the Pharisees?

4. Describe the feelings of the healed man after he was excommunicated from the synagogue. How do you think his parents felt?

5. Jesus said that, as a result of His coming into the world, the blind would see (v. 39). Who are these blind? How do they come to see?

6. Jesus said that, as a result of His coming into the world, those who see will become blind (v. 39). Who are these who see? How do they become blind?

Into Life

The Pharisees possessed certain prejudices that kept them blind to who Jesus was. (See question 2 above.) Ask each small group to think of one prejudice that keeps people today from believing in Jesus. After two minutes, ask each group to share their prejudice with the whole class. Then say, "When we began, we asked you to share an area in which your view of Jesus had changed. What prejudices kept you from seeing Jesus as you now do?"

Now ask the students, "How would the Pharisees' opinions of Jesus have differed if they had been willing to accept the truths about Jesus revealed in His ability to perform miracles?" After discussing this briefly, go on to discuss the importance of our believing the facts of the gospel. Ask, "What are the *facts* of the gospel?" (Those events that are testified to by reliable eyewitnesses.) Discuss how it would affect our non-Christian friends' opinions about Jesus, if we convinced them about the *facts* of the gospel. Say, "Prejudices are opinions that are not disciplined by facts. What can we do to keep our prejudices from blinding us to truth?"

Close with prayer in your small groups.

Let's Talk It Over

The questions on this page are designed to encourage review of the lesson
Scriptures and to promote discussion of the lesson by the class. The answers
provided are only discussion starters. Let your class talk it over from there.

1. Personal afflictions can be valuable teaching tools. Why do we need to keep that in mind when we pray for ourselves and others?

We are inclined to be like Paul in his struggle with the famous "thorn in the flesh." He related that he asked the Lord three times to take it away from him (2 Corinthians 12:8). But the Lord showed Paul that it was meant to have a teaching and molding influence in his life. When we or someone dear to us suffers illness, financial reverses, or some other personal crisis, we naturally ask the Lord to remove the painful, trying circumstances. But we need to pray with equal vigor that the Lord will teach us whatever lessons may be learned through the experience, that He will shape us through our sufferings into what He wants us to be, and that he will help us to glorify Him through our response to the trial. When we are praying for friends who are not Christians, we will want to ask God to awaken them through their sufferings to their need for salvation.

2. Jesus expressed a sense of urgency when He said, "I must work the works of him that sent me, while it is day: the night cometh, when no man can work" (John 9:4). How can we develop a similar sense of urgency regarding Christian work?

The Psalmist prayed, "So teach us to number our days, that we may apply our hearts unto wisdom" (Psalm 90:12). It is wise for us to take inventory of the remaining days or years we may have on earth and to plan how we may best use them to achieve worthwhile, godly goals. The sobering exhortation in Ecclesiastes expresses a related sentiment: "Whatsoever thy hand findeth to do, do it with thy might; for there is no work, nor device, nor knowledge, nor wisdom, in the grave, whither thou goest" (Ecclesiastes 9:10). Although our knowledge of the risen Christ prevents our sharing in the gloominess of this viewpoint, we can profit from the practical counsel. While we have earthly life, strength, and opportunity, we need to employ our resources in doing something significant for the glory of God. Jesus knew that the "night" of His death was fast approaching, and He was concerned that He use well the hours of "day" that yet remained. Our "day" is also rapidly passing, and we must not procrastinate or waste time if we are to finish the work God wants us to accomplish.

3. When asked if he believed in the Son of man, the man who had received his sight answered, "Who is he, Lord, that I might believe on him?" (John 9:36). Why is this a particularly appealing request?

If only we Christians could lead the lost people we encounter to make such a request, how eager we would be to fulfill that request! We would be thrilled if a friend or acquaintance were to speak to us in words similar to those penned by Catherine Hankey: "Tell me the story softly, with earnest tones and grave; remember I'm the sinner whom Jesus came to save." But too often we encounter indifference or ridicule or outright hostility from those with whom we seek to share the gospel. They may point to the coldness or exclusiveness or lovelessness of the church as a reason for their lack of interest. Perhaps if we could demonstrate the same kind of compassion that Jesus demonstrated, we might cause more people to make earnest inquiry about Him whom we represent.

4. Why should we be careful about saying, "I see," as the Pharisees did, in regard to spiritual matters?

One is reminded of Paul's statement, "If any man think that he knoweth any thing, he knoweth nothing yet as he ought to know" (1 Corinthians 8:2). We must recognize the incompleteness of our knowledge and avoid the attitude that says, "I already know everything I need to know." Of course, there are clear truths we have learned that can never be subject to change. Among these are the deity of Christ, the fact of His atoning death for our sins, the reality of His bodily resurrection, and the necessity of coming to Him with penitent, obedient faith. But in matters of interpretation where legitimate differences of opinion exist, we dare not become too rigid in rejecting other people's views and advocating our own. The psalmist said, "Open thou mine eyes, that I may behold wondrous things out of thy law" (Psalm 119:18). May that spirit be evident in our prayers and in our conversations with fellow Christians.

Acceptance and Rejection

LESSON SCRIPTURE: John 12.

PRINTED TEXT: John 12:20-36a.

John 12:20-36a

20 And there were certain Greeks among them that came up to worship at the feast:

21 The same came therefore to Philip, which was of Bethsaida of Galilee, and desired him, saying, Sir, we would see Jesus.

22 Philip cometh and telleth Andrew: and again Andrew and Philip tell Jesus.

23 And Jesus answered them, saying, The hour is come, that the Son of man should be glorified.

24 Verily, verily, I say unto you, Except a corn of wheat fall into the ground and die, it abideth alone: but if it die, it bringeth forth much fruit.

25 He that loveth his life shall lose it; and he that hateth his life in this world shall keep it unto life eternal.

26 If any man serve me, let him follow me; and where I am, there shall also my servant be: if any man serve me, him will my Father honor.

27 Now is my soul troubled; and what shall I say? Father, save me from this hour: but for this cause came I unto this hour.

28 Father, glorify thy name. Then came there a voice from heaven, saying, I have both glorified it, and will glorify it again.

29 The people therefore that stood by, and heard it, said that it thundered: others said, An angel spake to him.

30 Jesus answered and said, This voice came not because of me, but for your sakes.

31 Now is the judgment of this world: now shall the prince of this world be cast out.

32 And I, if I be lifted up from the earth, will draw all men unto me.

33 This he said, signifying what death he should die.

34 The people answered him, We have heard out of the law that Christ abideth for ever: and how sayest thou, The Son of man must be lifted up? who is this Son of man?

35 Then Jesus said unto them, Yet a little while is the light with you. Walk while ye have the light, lest darkness come upon you: for he that walketh in darkness knoweth not whither he goeth.

36a While ye have light, believe in the light, that ye may be the children of light.

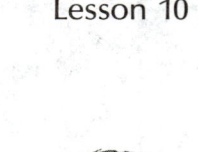
Feb
4

GOLDEN TEXT: If any man serve me, let him follow me; and where I am, there shall also my servant be; if any man serve me, him will my Father honor.—John 12:26.

John: The Gospel of Life and Light
Unit 3. Jesus Prepares His Followers
(Lessons 10-13)

Lesson Aims

This study should equip the class member to:

1. Explain the parable of the wheat seed (v. 24).

2. Answer the objections of those who say they can't accept as Lord one who died as a criminal.

3. Name important decisions in which he has been influenced by Jesus' example and teaching.

Lesson Outline

INTRODUCTION

   A. Remarkable Interviews

   B. Time of Turmoil

I. INQUIRERS (John 12:20-22)

II. LIFE IS FOUND THROUGH DEATH (John 12:23-28a)

   A. In the Hour of Sacrifice (v. 23)

   B. In the Grainfield (v. 24)

   C. Among Disciples (vv. 25, 26)
     Service and Honor

   D. In Jesus (vv. 27, 28a)

III. GOD PROVIDES FOR LIFE (John 12:28b-36a)

   A. Words of Encouragement (vv. 28b-30)

   B. Fact of Judgment (v. 31)

   C. Christ's Death for All (vv. 32-34)
     Exaltation

   D. Light for the Way (vv. 35, 36a)

CONCLUSION

   A. Reviewing the Interview

   B. Prayer of a Follower

   C. Thought to Remember

Display visual 10 from the visuals packet and let it remain before the class. The visual is shown on page 196.

Introduction

A. Remarkable Interviews

Have you been involved recently in an interview—one of those face-to-face consultations on which an enterprise, a career, or a reputation may depend? They usually involve asking and answering questions prepared beforehand.

There is the business interview, involving chiefly the parties present, and dealing with questions like these: Should I employ you (or work for you)? Should I accept, or reject, the enterprise you represent? Will you buy what I am selling?

Then there is the "news interview," designed to give or to gain information to be published. A friendly, accepting interviewer will usually encourage the person before him to say what he wants to say, in the way that is most acceptable. An unfriendly, rejecting interviewer, will try to get his victim to say what the interviewer wants to hear, and will seek to dominate the interview for that purpose.

Jesus' ministry on earth was punctuated with remarkable interviews. Accepting hearers asked questions in order to learn; honest inquirers tested Him with honest questions; curious questioners came seeking to satisfy their curiosity; and rejecting critics framed captious questions carefully to trap Him in His answers.

The Lord's consistent policy with them all was to convey eternal truth. Sometimes He answered plain questions plainly. Sometimes He seemed to ignore a question, but told a story in which the answer became evident. Sometimes His reply dealt not with the immediate question, but with some underlying need or thought that He perceived behind the words. Sometimes He answered a question with a question, claiming for himself the right to have His own questions answered. Sometimes He simply declined to reply.

The account in today's lesson opens with the arrival of some strangers seeking an interview with Jesus. His response was so indirect that it has puzzled Bible readers to this day. Some say He simply refused the interview. Others say He granted it, but it was unrecorded. Still others hold that the following paragraphs record a presentation of what the strangers wanted and needed to know. In any case, we must admit that the Lord Jesus was a fascinating, instructive, and probably difficult subject for a remarkable interview.

B. Time of Turmoil

Six tumultuous months had passed since the feast at which Jesus had healed the man born blind. He spent most of that time teaching in areas safely removed from Jerusalem, where official determination to destroy Him grew more bitter daily. When He came as near as Bethany to raise Lazarus from the grave, His disciples feared for His life. Jesus was talking more often and more plainly about His approaching death, and that disturbed His apostles. He had claimed, with convincing demonstrations, that He was the Jews' long-promised Messiah. But what kind of Messiah would allow himself to be killed by the leaders of His own people?

At last Jesus chose the time for final confrontation, and entered Jerusalem amid public acclaim on the first day of the week before the Passover. It is now called Palm Sunday. The next day He further infuriated the temple officers by driving their tradesmen out of the sacred precincts. At evening He withdrew to relative safety among friends at Bethany.

There followed a busy day of teaching, discussion, and tension in the temple as pilgrims gathered from all over Jewry for the Passover, seeking to see and hear this prophet from Nazareth whose name and fame were on every tongue. The frustrated Pharisees complained, "Behold, the world is gone after him" (v. 19).

I. Inquirers
(John 12:20-22)

20. And there were certain Greeks among them that came up to worship at the feast.

Many Greek nationals lived in Galilee and Decapolis, where Jesus had done much of His teaching and healing. Coming in touch with the Jews around them, some of them had been drawn to the worship of one God. Becoming converts and proselytes to Judaism, such nationals would go *up to worship at the feast* in Jerusalem, although they did not enjoy the full temple privileges of Israelites (compare Acts 10:22; 13-43; 18:7). The gospel of Christ was yet to be preached to all men, with Gentiles brought into the kingdom just as the Jews were, by obedient faith in Jesus as Lord (Romans 1:16).

21, 22. The same came therefore to Philip, which was of Bethsaida of Galilee, and desired him, saying, Sir, we would see Jesus. Philip cometh and telleth Andrew: and again Andrew and Philip tell Jesus.

Bethsaida ("house of fishing") cannot be certainly located, but seems to have been a fishing village near Capernaum on the northern shore of Galilee. There among Greek neighbors, Philip and Andrew (brother of Simon Peter) had been given Greek names (John 1:44).

Upon inquiry, the Greeks probably learned that two of the disciples of Jesus had Greek names, so they approached one of them thinking that their request might be favorably received. The Greeks' desire to see Jesus was no idle curiosity that could be satisfied by having Him pointed out in a crowd. They wanted an interview with Him. Philip, sensing some seriousness in their request, included his friend and townsman—the efficient contact man, Andrew (John 1:41; 6:8, 9)—in the errand. The Greeks

would probably have done as well by approaching Jesus directly, but they did not know it. Neither do multitudes of our friends and neighbors, who need our help to encourage their acquaintance with the Lord.

II. Life Is Found Through Death
(John 12:23-28a)

A. In the Hour of Sacrifice (v. 23)

23. And Jesus answered them, saying, The hour is come, that the Son of man should be glorified.

To whom did Jesus direct this answer? To Philip and Andrew? To the inquiring Greeks? To all whom He was teaching in the temple? To the whole world? Yes, to the whole world, with special point to the inquirers present.

The coming of the *hour*—the climax of Jesus' ministry on earth—was a subject repeatedly on His lips. Until that *hour*, He would not allow himself to be taken (John 7:6, 8, 30; 8:20). Now that time was arriving. He was meeting His lifelong appointment with the cross.

Son of man was Jesus' chosen term of reference to himself. He had come from the Father to sacrifice himself for the lost world. There was glory in the sacrifice, as it marked the accomplishment of the purpose for which He had come. It also marked His triumph over every self-interest, worldly influence, and all temptations, including the temptations of friendly voices trying to dissuade Him from His goal.

The visible side of Christ's glory—His resurrection—was yet to come, but that depended on the completion of His sacrifice.

B. In the Grainfield (v. 24)

24. Verily, verily, I say unto you, Except a corn of wheat fall into the ground and die, it abideth alone: but if it die, it bringeth forth much fruit.

In His preceding statement, Jesus introduced the thought that the time of His death was near. By means of the illustration in this verse, He showed that His death was necessary if there was to be a harvest of souls saved for eternity. If a kernel of grain, any kind of grain, is stored and protected, it remains alone and does not accomplish what God intended for it. But if it is

---

How to Say It

BETHSAIDA. Beth-*say*-uh-duh.
CAPERNAUM. Kuh-*per*-nay-um.
GETHSEMANE. Geth-*sem*-uh-nee.

visual 10

THE WAY OF **DEATH** **IS** THE WAY TO **LIFE**

planted in the ground, the grain decomposes, it dies, but from it much fruit comes forth. So, Jesus was saying, He must die in order that others might have life.

C. Among Disciples (vv. 25, 26)

25. He that loveth his life shall lose it; and he that hateth his life in this world shall keep it unto life eternal.

Here is the application of the seed grain principle to one's own experience. Like the grain of wheat withheld from its divine purpose and kept in storage, the person who refuses to yield to God and to give himself in His cause meets ultimate destruction. Holding life most dear, the selfish person actually destroys himself in the very acts that he considers self-preservation. On the other hand, love of God and one's fellowman leads to joyous service in which self is sacrificed, but eternal life is gained.

The Bible uses the word *hate* in three ways. One is bitter malice or hostility, as one might hate his worst enemy. You don't do that to your *life*. Another is aversion or abhorrence, as God hates sin. That doesn't fit here, either. The third is a relative disregard, contrasted with total absorption in some greater love. This is what Jesus commands in Mark 8:35. The apostle Paul rejoiced in finding life as Jesus directed; gladly he released every material asset in order to claim the hope of eternal life in Christ (Philippians 3:7-16).

26. If any man serve me, let him follow me; and where I am, there shall also my servant be: if any man serve me, him will my Father honor.

The Phillips translation expresses it well: "If a man wants to enter my service, he must follow my way." Jesus let it be known that the way to fellowship and service in His company was open to all. If the inquiring Greeks were interested in becoming His disciples, they must know that it demanded more than private interviews. It required open commitment to Him and His way.

Jesus' way led to the cross; and the disciple of Jesus must "deny himself, and take up his cross, and follow" Jesus (Matthew 16:24). That is the hard part. The reward is that the follower enjoys the company of Jesus on the journey, comes with Jesus to His destination, and shares with Jesus in His glory. To follow Jesus is the whole duty of the disciple; to be with Jesus is the whole reward. (See John 14:2, 3; 17:24; 1 Thessalonians 4:17.) He who shares in the service of Christ will share also in His glory—glory given by the same Father who honors the Son.

SERVICE AND HONOR

The woman was obviously looking for a special name. She slowly made her way down the long, black marble monument. Suddenly she stopped. Then, slowly, she reached out her hand to one name. All the others were important, but this one was special. It was the name of her son. She traced the letters with her fingers. The tears began to flow, though there was no sound of crying. Her eyes closed in memory or perhaps in prayer. After some minutes had passed, she turned and walked slowly away.

John had died in Vietnam. He was just out of high school, and all life seemed before him; but it ended on a battlefield. John had followed the command of his officer and had died with him in the action that had been ordered.

Here, at the Vietnam Memorial in Washington, D. C., our nation honors those who fell in the "forgotten war." It may have been unpopular, but it will never be forgotten by the families and friends of those servicemen whose names are inscribed on that memorial wall.

The commands Jesus gave His followers lead to Calvary, and there they must be willing to die with Him before honor will be theirs. The names of the faithful will be written in the book of life, and Heaven will be their reward.   —W. P.

D. In Jesus (vv. 27, 28a)

27, 28a. Now is my soul troubled; and what shall I say? Father, save me from this hour: but for this cause came I unto this hour. Father, glorify thy name.

Now is my soul troubled. Jesus was not here indulging in mere academic discussion. He was talking about His death—crucifixion—soon to be endured. Even Jesus could not endure that without a struggle (Hebrews 4:15). Involved was not only indescribable torment to the body, but also the disgrace and anguish of sin bearing. John's Gospel does not tell of the Lord's agony in Gethsemane (Mark 14:33-35), but this passage expresses much of the same turmoil in Jesus' spirit.

What shall I say? What words could express His feelings? In fact, which among several conflicting sentiments should find expression? *Father, save me from this hour.* Several translations present this as part of the question that precedes it: "What shall I say? Shall I say, 'Father, save me from this hour'?" (that is, from the suffering that lay ahead). He did pray thus in Gethsemane, but with the provision that it be possible within the purpose of God. This time He canceled the thought immediately: "No, it was for this very reason I came to this hour" (*New International Version*).

The sharp conflict between dread and commitment was resolved swiftly in favor of commitment, with a fervent prayer that God would complete His work, even at the cost of Jesus' death: *Father, glorify thy name.*

III. God Provides for Life (John 12:28b-36a)

A. Words of Encouragement (vv. 28b-30)

28b. Then came there a voice from heaven, saying, I have both glorified it, and will glorify it again.

Scripture tells of three occasions on which God spoke audibly to His Son on earth. In every instance Jesus' coming death was involved. At Jesus' baptism, a dramatic symbol of death, burial, and resurrection, God said, "Thou art my beloved Son, in whom I am well pleased" (Mark 1:11). On the mount of transfiguration, where Jesus talked with Moses and Elijah about His coming death, the Father said, "This is my beloved Son: hear him" (Luke 9:30, 31, 35). On this occasion the Father assured His Son that the divine name had been *glorified* through the life and ministry of Jesus. He would glorify His name through Jesus' death and resurrection. He would glorify it to the ends of the earth through the proclamation of the gospel, Christ returns in final glory with His angels to judge the world and receive His own.

29, 30. The people therefore that stood by, and heard it, said it thundered: others said, An angel spake to him. Jesus answered and said, This voice came not because of me, but for your sakes.

Three differing interpretations were given to the message. Some attributed the sudden noise to natural coincidence without special meaning, though the very sound must have been impressive, coming at the very moment Jesus addressed His Father in Heaven. Other's regarded it as the voice of a Heavenly messenger speaking to Jesus. But Jesus said the greater purpose was to build faith and courage in the listeners present. They needed both, in the face of events to come. We, too, need to be assured that God is glorified and will be glorified in Christ!

B. Fact of Judgment (v. 31)

31. Now is the judgment of this world: now shall the prince of this world be cast out.

The final judgment at the end of the world was (and is) at some unnamed future time. But the events of the hour then at hand would provide the basis for that judgment. Even at that hour, though, some observers had ranged themselves stubbornly in opposition to Jesus, and so had already judged themselves unworthy of the light and life He came to give (compare Acts 13:46).

Satan is *the prince of this world* in the sense that he had seized control of those deluded humans who are God-rejecting, self-centered, and sin-bound (2 Corinthians 4:4; Ephesians 6:12). Satan's doom was sealed at Calvary. The carrying out of the sentence against him was delayed, but it is sure.

C. Christ's Death for All (vv. 32-34)

32, 33. And I, if I be lifted up from the earth, will draw all men unto me. This he said, signifying what death he should die.

Jesus had already compared His being *lifted up* with the elevated display of the brazen serpent in the wilderness by Moses (John 3:14; compare John 8:28). The present statement was a clear reference to Jesus' being raised from the ground on the cross, and it was so understood by His hearers (v. 34). The cross is the means by which He would *draw* followers from Satan to himself. The magnetic force of the cross is exerted upon *all men*; but just as some material substances do not respond to the influence of a magnet, so some persons remain unmoved by the sacrifice of Christ. Yet the urgent invitation is extended through all time to all persons everywhere.

Exaltation

In Northern California, prior to World War II, and in many cities and towns in later years, one of the great events of the winter season was the raising of the city's Christmas tree.

The tree selected was usually a tall, perfectly formed fir. It was displayed either in the town square or in the center of the main street crossing in the town. When it was up and the lights installed, there was a ceremony to formally signal the beginning of the holiday season. The big moment came when the star, symbolizing the guiding light that led the Wise-men to Jesus, was turned on.

Those days are gone. Traffic is imperiled by a tree in the center of busy crossroads. Angry people, who do not want Jesus honored at Christmas, complain, protest, or wage legal battles to keep Him from being exalted in public.

Men may take Jesus out of Christmas, but they cannot take Him down from the cross. That tree is lifted over all history. It marks the moment of sacrifice for our sins. By His death, Jesus draws us to himself and from sin's death penalty. Because of Jesus' obedience in death, "God also hath highly exalted him" (Philippians 2:9).

—W. P.

34. The people answered him, We have heard out of the law that Christ abideth for ever: and how sayest thou, The Son of man must be lifted up? who is this Son of man?

These words represent the gist of what came from many voices. This time it was not religious officialdom speaking, but the common folk. They understood that Jesus claimed to be the Christ, and that Jesus was talking about His being lifted up in death. Yet they had heard from the teaching of the Scriptures that the Christ would remain forever. They probably had passages in mind such as Psalm 110:4; Isaiah 9:7; Ezekiel 37:25; and Daniel 7:14. Interpreting these passages literally to mean that the Messiah would rule on earth forever as king of the Jews, they could not understand how Jesus could be the Christ and yet die.

D. Light for the Way (vv. 35, 36a)

35, 36a. Then Jesus said unto them, Yet a little while is the light with you. Walk while ye have the light, lest darkness come upon you: for he that walketh in darkness knoweth not whither he goeth. While ye have light, believe in the light, that ye may be the children of light.

Again the Lord controlled the interview, not answering questions as they were asked, but saying what His questioners needed to hear. The answer to their question, however, was implicit in what He said: the Son of man stood before them and was with them for a very short time yet. He had no leisure to satisfy their curiosity or to indulge now in needless controversy. That would come all too soon. For now, He would go on teaching in preparation for His departure.

He had announced himself as the light of the world, and He had repeatedly warned of His coming death. Now He put the two together and advised, Go as far as you can in learning God's truth while the light is still available. Night will come all too soon, and you won't be able to see where you are going. Put your trust in the light while you have it. Go boldly where it leads. Absorb the light; make its qualities your own, so you will come to reflect and resemble that light. Then it may be said of you, "Ye are the light of the world" (Matthew 5:14-16).

That is the blessing of those who accept Christ as the light of life. The rejecters, walking in darkness, stumble along in the way that seems most easy, but always leads downward, toward destruction.

Conclusion

A. Reviewing the Interview

We are left wondering what happened to the Greeks who came seeking an interview with Jesus. Did they find what they sought?

If they desired time to be with Him alone, there is no evidence of their being granted it. He had come to give His life for sinners, and He would complete His mission. If they sought to know more of Jesus' methods and ministry—His character and His kingdom—they were instructed briefly but thoroughly. His was, and is, a worldwide, inclusive kingdom, a costly and a demanding kingdom, a kingdom with rewards as limitless as God. The interview of the day was open, and published for all to read.

B. Prayer of a Follower

We thank You, Father, for Your Son Jesus, our Lord, our Light, and our Leader. We have not always followed Him closely or consistently, and we have sometimes lost our way. Forgive us, and build within us that grateful love and trust that will fix our attention on Him, His sacrifice, and His way, amen.

C. Thought to Remember

To follow Jesus is the whole duty of the disciple; to be with Jesus is the whole reward.

Learning by Doing

This page contains an alternate lesson plan emphasizing learning activities. Classes desiring such student involvement will find these suggestions helpful.

Learning Goals

Ours is a complicated world in which there are a large variety of factors that bear upon our choices. Basic to all our choices is the necessity of choosing a foundation on which to operate our lives. Jesus calls on His disciples to make a basic choice of commitment to follow Him. In this lesson, students will:

1. Discover the importance of making wise decisions in life.

2. Learn what are the most important decisions they must address in life.

3. Commit themselves to making decisions that have desirable consequences.

Into the Lesson

Decisions, Decisions, Decisions. Ask students to write down answers to the following:

1. List the three most important decisions that a person must make in life.

2. What was the hardest decision you had to make this week? Did you make the right choice?

3. What was the hardest decision you *ever* made?

Copy these on paper or use the student books. After about four minutes, ask students to share their answers, unless they consider them too personal. In your discussion of question 1, bring out (1) a person's relationship with God, (2) the choice of a mate, and (3) the selection of a vocation. Point out that many decisions are difficult, and we sometimes make mistakes. But in the long run, our decisions will tend to be right if we have made the right decisions about the most important things. We could call these basic decisions, "foundational decisions." Our text looks at these foundational decisions.

Into the Word

Say, "the Greeks in our text were looking for a special audience with Jesus. Their purpose was to evaluate Him further. Jesus used this occasion, just three days before His death, to stress that the time was past for evaluating—it was now time to choose. Jesus was choosing to die for them, and now they must choose whether or not they would live for Him."

Now read aloud John 12:20-36a from the *New International Version* for this study.

Note that in this passage there are three levels of choosing that Jesus asks His disciples to do.

1. Heart choices, v. 25. We must choose *attitudes* that elevate Christ and humble ourselves.

2. Hand choices, v. 26. We must choose *actions* that advance the lordship of Christ.

3. Head choices, vv. 35, 36a. We must choose *knowledge* that is in keeping with the truth revealed by Jesus Christ.

Give each student a sheet of paper on which you have written Jesus. Or you may use the student books for this assignment. Divide the class into groups of four or five, and ask them to list choices that Christians must make in order to commit their hearts, hands, and heads to Jesus.

After fifteen minutes, discuss together what the class considers to be the most important of the heart, hand, and head choices they have discovered. Some basic *heart* choices may include: the elevation of the needs of others above self; focusing on Heavenly rewards rather than earthly rewards; loving those who mistreat us rather than retaliating. Some basic *hand* choices may include: giving time to use our abilities for the church each week; helping those in need; offering financial assistance for Christ's work. Some basic *head* choices may include: daily Bible reading; regular prayer for courage to apply Christ's teachings to our lives; discussing with mature Christians matters that we don't understand about our spiritual life.

Into Life

Say, "A decision is judged by its ultimate consequences. There are three ways in which we learn to make right choices based on their consequences:

1. The Bible gives us many insights into the consequences of our choices.

2. Some consequences are learned from the choices we have seen other people make.

3. Some consequences we learn from trial and error."

Ask every person in your small groups to share one wrong decision for which they have had to pay the consequences. Have them share what lesson they may have learned from that situation. Do not share these results with the whole class, because they may be too personal to share comfortably with the larger group. Instead, ask the small groups to pray together that God will help them to learn to make right choices.

Let's Talk It Over

The questions on this page are designed to encourage review of the lesson Scriptures and to promote discussion of the lesson by the class. The answers provided are only discussion starters. Let your class talk it over from there.

1. There is an emphasis in Christian literature today on the importance of self-esteem. How does this fit with Jesus' statement that one should hate one's own life?

Many people seem to hate themselves in a way that is foreign to Jesus' teaching. They hate their bodies, because they view themselves as being ugly or weak. They hate their personalities, feeling that they are mentally inferior and socially unbecoming. They hate their environment, being ashamed of the shortcoming of their home and family. These people have such a negative view of themselves that they tend to expect failure, rejection, and disappointment. Jesus intended that we "hate" ourselves in the sense of putting our allegiances to Him ahead of the human inclination to seek our own pleasure or convenience. Each person needs to have a certain level of self-esteem and that self-esteem is proper if it leads us to see ourselves as persons of worth because we are made in God's image, we are objects of God's love, and we are guided and protected by Him. But a self-esteem that leads to a self-centered life or to an excessive level of self-sufficiency likewise is opposed to what Jesus taught.

2. John 12:27, 28a suggest there was turmoil in Jesus' spirit as the time for His suffering on the cross drew nearer. How are the question and statement in these verses of practical value to us?

It is reassuring to see that Jesus grappled with temptation to sidestep His duty, because we also experience a similar struggle. We may feel guilty that we sometimes think of relinquishing our responsibilities within the church or that occasionally we find the thought appealing to cast aside even our domestic duties and occupational obligations. But such temptations are a natural reaction to the pain and pressure we must endure at times in fulfilling our tasks. It is of utmost importance that we respond to such temptations as decisively as Jesus did. He did this again in Gethsemane when He prayed, "O my Father, if it be possible, let this cup pass from me: nevertheless, not as I will, but as thou wilt" (Matthew 26:39). We can surely profit from His example of determination to fulfill the task given Him.

3. When Jesus said that the prince of this world would be driven out, it was one of many Biblical statements regarding the certainty of Satan's destruction. Why do we need to give attention to such statements today?

Recent years have witnessed the production of many books and films focusing on the devil's power. Satanic cults, as well as various occult practitioners, receive a great deal of publicity in the news media. It is remarkable that our generation, so much noted for scientific and technological advancements, has become so Satan conscious. But on the other hand, it could be said that some of the evils that have accompanied our scientific progress (such as, the destructive potential of nuclear weapons, the development of more efficient methods of abortion, the threat of loss of privacy and of depersonalization in the computer age) have made human beings more aware of our capacity for the kind of evil that the devil represents. Therefore, we take comfort in knowing that "the reason the Son of God appeared was to destroy the devil's work" (1 John 3:8, *New International Version*). No matter how strong Satan is represented as being, no matter how pervasive the power of evil may appear to be, our Lord Jesus Christ is the conqueror of both.

4. The message of the crucified Christ possesses a drawing power, as Jesus indicated in John 12:32. Why is this an important fact to keep in mind in our evangelistic labors?

Paul wrote to the Corinthians, "For I determined not to know any thing among you save Jesus Christ, and him crucified" (1 Corinthians 2:2). We might say that Paul was depending on the drawing power of the cross, and so should we. It is tempting to center our evangelistic approach on either the woes of the non-Christian life or the benefits of the Christian life. If our church offers a variety of programs and activities, we may be inclined to put our emphasis on these. But these approaches fail to put first things first. A person must first come face-to-face with Christ's death and resurrection. Then, having responded in faith and obedience to those realities, one can concentrate on enjoying the advantages of the church and the Christian life.

In the Image of the Servant

LESSON SCRIPTURE: John 13:1-30.

PRINTED TEXT: John 13:1-17.

John 13:1-17

1 Now before the feast of the passover, when Jesus knew that his hour was come that he should depart out of this world unto the Father, having loved his own which were in the world, he loved them unto the end.

2 And supper being ended, the devil having now put into the heart of Judas Iscariot, Simon's son, to betray him;

3 Jesus knowing that the Father had given all things into his hands, and that he was come from God, and went to God;

4 He riseth from supper, and laid aside his garments; and took a towel, and girded himself.

5 After that he poureth water into a basin, and began to wash the disciples' feet, and to wipe them with the towel wherewith he was girded.

6 Then cometh he to Simon Peter: and Peter saith unto him, Lord, dost thou wash my feet?

7 Jesus answered and said unto him, What I do thou knowest not now; but thou shalt know hereafter.

8 Peter saith unto him, Thou shalt never wash my feet. Jesus answered him, If I wash thee not, thou hast no part with me.

9 Simon Peter saith unto him, Lord, not my feet only, but also my hands and my head.

10 Jesus saith to him, He that is washed needeth not save to wash his feet, but is clean every whit: and ye are clean, but not all.

11 For he knew who should betray him; therefore said he, Ye are not all clean.

12 So after he had washed their feet, and had taken his garments, and was set down again, he said unto them, Know ye what I have done to you?

13 Ye call me Master and Lord: and ye say well; for so I am.

14 If I then, your Lord and Master, have washed your feet; ye also ought to wash one another's feet.

15 For I have given you an example, that ye should do as I have done to you.

16 Verily, verily, I say unto you, The servant is not greater than his lord; neither he that is sent greater than he that sent him.

17 If ye know these things, happy are ye if ye do them.

Feb
11

GOLDEN TEXT: Verily, verily, I say unto you, The servant is not greater than his lord; neither he that is sent greater than he that sent him.—John 13:16.

John: The Gospel of Life and Light
Unit 3. Jesus Prepares His Followers
(Lessons 10-13)

Lesson Aims

This lesson should equip students to:

1. Relate in brief the facts set forth in John 13:1-17.

2. Tell how we avail ourselves of Jesus' spiritual cleansing.

3. Identify, and commit themselves to, acts of service meeting current human needs.

Lesson Outline

INTRODUCTION
    A. The Passover
    B. The Persistence of Pride
    C. The Washing of Feet
I. THE SETTING FOR SERVICE (John 13:1-3)
    A. Persistent Love (v. 1)
    B. Betrayal (v. 2)
    C. End of a Sojourn (v. 3)
II. THE ACT OF SERVING (John 13:4, 5)
    A. Equipped to Serve (v. 4)
    B. Active in Service (v. 5)
III. A RESPONSE TO SERVICE (John 13:6-11)
    A. Facing Objection (vv. 6-8a)
    B. Gaining Acceptance (vv. 8b, 9)
    C. The Cleansing Offered (vv. 10, 11)
IV. APPLYING THE LESSON (John 13:12-17)
    A. Presenting the Question (v. 12)
    B. Providing the Example (vv. 13-15)
        Learning Through Example
    C. Establishing Authority (v. 16)
    D. Call to Action (v. 17)
        Do As I Do
CONCLUSION
    A. A Ruling Servant
    B. A Servant's Prayer
    C. Thought to Remember

Display visual 11 from the visuals packet and let it remain before the class. The visual is shown on page 203.

Introduction

A. The Passover

John 13 introduces events on the eve of Jesus' crucifixion during the Jews' passover season.

Beginning with the Israelites' deliverance from bondage in Egypt, the Passover has been a major celebration for annual observance. Exodus 12 details God's instructions to Moses in Egypt, commanding each Hebrew family to slay a perfect yearling lamb and mark the doorposts and lintel of their house with its blood, so the death angel would *pass over* that house on the way to slaying the firstborn in every household of the Egyptians. The event was to be reenacted every year in a week-long family festival of "unleavened bread". At the passover meal, bitter herbs and unleavened bread were to be eaten, along with roast lamb, recalling the bitterness of bondage and the haste with which the Israelites finally departed from Egypt.

The Passover means much to Christians. John the Baptist announced Jesus as the "Lamb of God, which taketh away the sin of the world (John 1:29), and Paul declared that "Christ our passover is sacrificed for us" (1 Corinthians 5:7), indicating that His atonement supersedes and does away with the Old Testament sacrificial system.

Jesus said of His final passover with His disciples, "With desire I have desired to eat this passover with you before I suffer" (Luke 22:15). Details are found in Matthew 26:17-30; Mark 14:12-26; and Luke 22:7-38. Jesus made use of the Passover to share an intimate, meaningful occasion with His spiritual family and to establish His own memorial feast, which we call the Lord's Supper. In this, His church would forever observe His sacrifice as God's Lamb given for the sin of the whole world.

John's Gospel does not describe the supper itself, either in any detail as the Passover or in reference to Jesus' memorial ordinance. Instead, it dwells on the Lord's instructive words and actions during the evening.

B. The Persistence of Pride

This occasion gave Jesus one last opportunity to deal with a problem that had plagued His disciples during most of his earthly ministry. That was ambitious pride. They had argued among themselves as to which of them was the most important. Only recently James and John had requested high offices in His coming kingdom, and the others had keenly resented their presumption (Matthew 20:20-28; Mark 10:35-45). Jesus had rebuked them all, insisting that service, not position or power, was to be respected in His kingdom. He told them that "even the Son of man came not to be ministered unto, but to minister, and to give his life a ransom for many" (Mark 10:45).

Yet even as the twelve gathered for the supper that night, "there was also a strife among them, which of them should be accounted the greatest" (Luke 22:24). Jesus answered again, "He that is greatest among you, let him be as the younger; and he that is chief, as he that doth serve" (Luke 22:26).

C. The Washing of Feet

Guests arriving on foot with only shoe soles tied on with thongs to protect against mud, grit, and grime, were customarily welcomed into a home with the comfort of a foot bath. Abraham had welcomed guests that way, and so had Lot, Laban, and Joseph (Genesis 18:4; 19:2; 24:32; 43:24). By the time of Christ, a system of foot-washing procedures had developed by which the relative social status of the guests might be recognized. Most honored guests' feet were washed by a servant. Others washed their own feet with water provided.

As Jesus and His disciples gathered to eat the Passover meal, the common service of foot-washing seems to have been overlooked. The disciple who was the host to Jesus and His disciples had thoughtfully provided water and a basin and towel for their use in washing their feet. With a fine sense of propriety, he seems to have retired from the scene to leave the details of their personal preparation for an evening of comfort to their own desires. The disciples, too busy with other matters, not only did not wash their own feet, but did not think to offer this loving service to Jesus, their Master, as He entered the room.

I. The Setting for Service (John 13:1-3)

A. Persistent Love (v. 1)

1. Now before the feast of the passover, when Jesus knew that his hour was come that he should depart out of this world unto the Father, having loved his own which were in the world, he loved them unto the end.

The warm and friendly tender love in which Jesus held these companions of the past three difficult years seems to have grown with the difficulties. The city of Jerusalem was becoming increasingly crowded as "many went out of the country up to Jerusalem before the passover, to purify themselves" (John 11:55). The time of Jesus' ministry to such folk was drawing swiftly to an end as the *hour* of His return to God approached. He had spoken clearly and would continue to speak of that time: "I came forth from the Father, and am come into the world: again, I leave the world, and go to the Father" (John 16:28).

The Lord was keenly aware of problems awaiting His disciples after His departure. Be-

visual 11

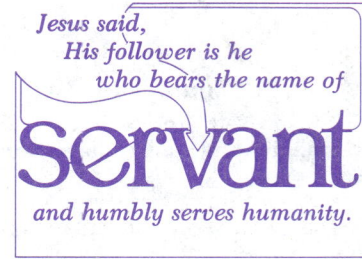

Jesus said, His follower is he who bears the name of **Servant** *and humbly serves humanity.*

fore this evening was over He would pray, "I have manifested thy name unto the men which thou gavest me out of the world: thine they were, and thou gavest them me.... I pray for them . . . for they are thine" (John 17:6-9). Jesus' love for these men was not only *to the end* of His days on earth, but also *to the end*, or fullest capacity, of His love.

B. Betrayal (v. 2)

2. And supper being ended, the devil having now put into the heart of Judas Iscariot, Simon's son, to betray him.

Judas' plot to betray Jesus to the nation's religious leaders was already accomplished. Satan had planted evil in Judas' heart, and Judas had let it grow. Matthew 26:3-5, 14-16; Mark 14:10, 11; and Luke 22:3-6 provide the details.

The prophet Ezekiel had warned that the good man who abandons goodness and turns to evil will die in his sin, and his former goodness will be forgotten (Ezekiel 33:13). This is tragically true of Judas, whom Jesus chose as an apostle, but who is remembered only as betrayer and devil (John 6:70). *Simon*, his father, is not otherwise known.

What happened next took place "during supper" (*American Standard Version*) rather than after it was ended. It was probably shortly after the quarrel among the apostles about "which of them should be accounted the greatest" (Luke 22:24).

C. End of a Sojourn (v. 3)

3. Jesus knowing that the Father had given all things into his hands, and that he was come from God, and went to God.

Small persons, unsure of their worth and their standing, sometimes engage in ridiculous displays of pomp and cruelty in an effort to impress their peers. Not so with Jesus. Fully aware of His divine nature and glory, and wholly assured of the authority conveyed to Him by the Father, Jesus could express His love in the humblest of service. His brief stay on earth was about to be concluded with the most godlike service and sacrifice.

II. The Act of Serving
(John 13:4, 5)

A. Equipped to Serve (v. 4)

4. He riseth from supper, and laid aside his garments; and took a towel, and girded himself.

Shocked amazement engrave every movement in the memory of John and the other apostles, as Jesus arose from His reclining position at the table, deliberately removed His outer robe, found the towel that had been provided, and wrapped it around His waist in the manner of a slave preparing for duty. A guilty conscience must have smitten them as they watched Him. Peter may have been remembering this moment as he wrote thirty years later, exhorting Christians, "Be clothed with humility" (1 Peter 5:5).

B. Active in Service (v. 5)

5. After that he poureth water into a basin, and began to wash the disciples' feet, and to wipe them with the towel wherewith he was girded.

The water, the basin, and the towel were available in the room for anyone who might have wished to use them. None had thought to do so until this moment. The servant Lord had no difficulty in reaching the diners' feet, which trailed off the back of the couches on which they reclined in Roman fashion at the table. We are not told which disciple was first to receive this service. Judas?

This was clearly not a habitual act on Jesus' part. Neither was it contrived. These men were in need. Their feet were soiled and needed washing. Their eyes were dim and needed to be opened to the folly of their prideful ambition. Jesus acted to meet both the physical and the spiritual needs of those He loved.

III. A Response to Service
(John 13:6-11)

A. Facing Objection (vv. 6-8a)

6-8a. Then cometh he to Simon Peter: and Peter saith unto him, Lord, dost thou wash my feet? Jesus answered and said unto him, What I do thou knowest not now; but thou shalt know hereafter. Peter saith unto him, Thou shalt never wash my feet.

Peter probably put into words what others of the apostles were thinking as Jesus approached them with basin and towel. *Dost thou wash my feet?* The pronouns *thou* and *my* are emphatic. To Peter it seemed incredible that hands that had touched blind eyes and healed them and

had lifted the dead back to life, should now wash the grime from *his* feet.

Thou knowest not now. There was more to the event than appeared on the surface. There was an object lesson not yet understood; and there was the symbol of spiritual cleansing. The apostles would gain some understanding before the evening was over; they would understand more with God's Spirit after Jesus' teachings were already stored in the apostles' memory for understanding only after Jesus' death and resurrection (see John 2:22; 12:16).

"Never at any time will you wash my feet" *(Today's English Version)*. It would be hard to frame a rejection stronger than this. Peter wanted to be respectful and loyal to Jesus, but according to Peter's view of respect and loyalty.

B. Gaining Acceptance (vv. 8b, 9)

8b, 9. Jesus answered him, If I wash thee not, thou hast no part with me. Simon Peter saith unto him, Lord, not my feet only, but also my hands and my head.

Christian humility does not *begin* with rendering service. It begins with overcoming pride enough to acknowledge a need, and then accepting gratefully what is needed, according to the judgment of the giver.

"Unless you let me wash you, Peter, you cannot share my lot" *(Phillips translation)*. There is obviously much more to the cleansing offered by Jesus than the removal of material soil. The blood of Jesus Christ, God's son, cleanses us from all sin, we are told (1 John 1:7), and again, "Christ also loved the church, and gave himself for it; that he might sanctify and cleanse it with the washing of water by the word" (Ephesians 5:25, 26). If Jesus does not cleanse us, we have no cleansing.

Not my feet only. With his characteristic impetuous enthusiasm, Peter asked for more than was offered. If fellowship with his beloved Lord was involved, he wanted all of it!

C. The Cleansing Offered (vv. 10, 11)

10, 11. Jesus saith to him, He that is washed needeth not save to wash his feet, but is clean every whit: and ye are clean, but not all. For he knew who should betray him; therefore said he, Ye are not all clean.

Assuming that the disciples had bathed before leaving their quarters, they would now need only to remove the soil of travel from their feet to be wholly acceptable. None present needed a bath.

Deeper than this surface meaning, of course, is the thought of spiritual cleansing. The conversation about bathing the whole body and then washing the soiled members—then turning to spiritual cleansing—suggests the acts associated with Christ's cleansing from sin. Sins are washed away when one turns to God in sincere faith, repentance, and baptism (Acts 2:38; 22:16), so that repetition of this act is unnecessary. For the removal of the stain of an offense committed afterward, Peter exhorted, "Repent therefore of this thy wickedness, and pray God, if perhaps the thought of thine heart may be forgiven thee" (Acts 8:22).

Ye are clean, but not all. By these words, Jesus revealed that He knew one was present who was not cleansed as the other eleven were.

IV. Applying the Lesson (John 13:12-17)

A. Presenting the Question (v. 12)

12. So after he had washed their feet, and had taken his garments, and was set down again, he said unto them, Know ye what I have done to you?"

Jesus put on again the garments He had laid off, and then resumed His place among the disciples reclining at the table. At last He broke the tense silence, not with the explanation the disciples expected, but with a question that demanded an explanation from them. "Do you know what I have just done to you?" Why, yes. He had washed their feet, and they were puzzled and uneasy, as John the Baptist had been when Jesus came to him for baptism (Matthew 3:14). There must be more to the matter than appeared on the surface.

B. Providing the Example (vv. 13-15)

13. Ye call me Master and Lord: and ye say well; for so I am.

Jesus had not laid off His authority when He exchanged His business suit for work clothes. Towel-wrapped and kneeling at their feet, He was still their Teacher, instructing them. He was still their Lord, directing them.

14, 15. If I then, your Lord and Master, have washed your feet; ye also ought to wash one another's feet. For I have given you an example, that ye should do as I have done to you.

The Teacher's object lesson was driven home by plain application and exhortation. While they had been bickering and scrambling for places of honor, they had left the simplest acts of

courtesy unattended. Each seems to have thought himself too important to render menial service. But their Lord and Master served! If they were truly His followers, they would walk in the way He led (compare 1 Peter 2:21).

Through the ages there have been some who have interpreted this passage to mean that churches ought to include foot-washing ceremonies in their public meetings. Jesus' meaning must be sought in the example of the church as it was guided by the apostles, who themselves were led by the Holy Spirit. From the Scripture we learn that the Holy Spirit never led the church into any such practice. But when guests arrived in the saints' homes with tired and grimy feet, the saints washed them, along with providing other items of hospitality (1 Timothy 5:10). The principle that is enunciated here, however, the principle of humility and service, is one that is eternal. In every act of humility and every act of submission, as we seek to do God's will in serving one another, we carry out the injunction that Jesus gave His apostles in that upper room.

LEARNING THROUGH EXAMPLE

"Do it again, please. I can't see how to do it." The request came from a grandson struggling to learn to tie his own shoes.

After several more demonstrations and instructions from Grandpa, Josh finally got his shoes tied. The tie wasn't secure enough to stay in place very long. Most caring adults would be tempted to say, "Here let me help you," and then stoop down to do it for the little boy.

The key to good teaching by example is explanation, demonstration, encouragement to practice, and then applause for a job well done. We can learn by hearing or reading instructions. But most of us learn better when we are shown.

Jesus washed the disciples' feet. When He was finished, He instructed them to serve one another as He had done to them. His greatest demonstration of humble service for others would be seen in just a few hours as He, the sinless one, gave His life for the sins of the world.

We are God's children. Our maturing in faith comes as we allow Jesus to teach us and as we follow the example He has given of humble service to others.   —W. P.

C. Establishing Authority (v. 16)

16. Verily, verily, I say unto you, The servant is not greater than his lord; neither he that is sent greater than he that sent him.

Here was the solemn pronouncement to conclude the discussion. Jesus the Lord was not above rendering service—even menial service—where there was need. Would any of His followers claim to be greater than He? They were His apostles (messengers), soon to be sent with His message to the entire world. Were they prepared to challenge His authority as to where they would go or what they would preach? "But every one that is perfect shall be as his master" (Luke 6:40). And that includes serving, with the spirit in which Jesus served.

D. Call to Action (v. 17)

17. If ye know these things, happy are ye if ye do them.

The Phillips translation says, "Once you have realized these things you will find your happiness in doing them." What *things?* That Jesus was their Teacher, and they must learn from Him; that Jesus was their Lord, and they must obey Him; that He was their example, and they must follow Him; that His way demanded humility rather than self-promotion; that they were to serve more than to be served; and that self-sacrifice, rather than self-indulgence or even self-protection, was the law of life with Him.

But awareness was not enough. Until they came to do what they knew, the knowing would bring only an uneasy conscience, frustration, and condemnation. At this point, the twelve must have heard echoes of the Lord's parable concluding the Sermon on the Mount: He who hears and does may be compared to a wise man, who built carefully a lasting house; he who hears but fails to do will be compared to a fool, who built carelessly for destruction (Matthew 7:24-27). James repeated the message to be hearers and doers of the word and concluded, "He being not a forgetful hearer, but a doer of the work . . . shall be blessed in his deed" (James 1:22, 25). Such a person will enjoy a blessed wholeness of mind, spirit, purpose, and accomplishment, and will have an approving conscience and fellowship with God.

Do As I Do

One of the favorite childhood games is "Follow the Leader." For small children it is a delightful game. A leader simply goes where he wants to go, and all the rest of his playmates follow in his steps. The laughter at stumbling and failing is all part of the fun of the game. When the children are a little older, the leader tries to go places and do things that will be hard to follow. Among youths, the game can be used in developing sports skills.

In one sense, most of the activities of living are related to "following the leader." Unfortunately, if the leader is evil, mistaken, or misin-

formed, the results of such leadership can be a disaster. We read examples of this every day.

In the game of life, we must learn to follow Jesus as our leader. If we do, we will find fulfillment and happiness in this life, and He will lead us safely home to Heaven. And what is more, our lives will point others to Him so that they too may follow.

—W. P.

Conclusion

A. A Ruling Servant

Jesus did not spend all His time washing His disciples' feet. The need for it had probably never risen before that night when He so greatly amazed the twelve. The same loving, serving spirit had been expressed in His teaching and healing and feeding the multitudes—and occasionally permitting others to row the boat in which He rested. He refused to rebuke Mary for leaving Martha to serve in the kitchen while Mary absorbed His teaching (Luke 10:38-42). He would serve, and He would have His followers serve, where the service was most needed, most important, and best suited to the purposes and the glory of God. The Lord would always serve, but that Servant was always Lord.

B. A Servant's Prayer

Teach us, please, almighty God, to serve You and Your people as we ought, having learned from the words and the works of our Lord Jesus. Help us to see what is needed where we live, and to give ourselves gladly in meeting that need. In Jesus' name we pray. Amen.

C. Thought to Remember

"I am among you as he that serveth" (Luke 22:27).

Learning by Doing

This page contains an alternate lesson plan emphasizing learning activities. Classes desiring such student involvement will find these suggestions helpful.

Learning Goals

Some have too much pride to help others. Some have too much pride to receive help from others. Both attitudes must be overcome if a person is to grow to spiritual maturity. In this lesson, your students will:

1. Explore attitudes that keep a person from being humble.

2. Discover the connection between acts of serving others and the overcoming of selfish pride.

3. Commit themselves to an act of service that is humbling for them to do.

Into the Lesson

After an opening prayer, divide immediately into small groups of *four only*. Ask the students to share with the group what they consider to be the most humbling experience in their life. After five minutes, give each group a copy of the following questions, which help focus on the reason why we are sometimes humbled by life's experiences. These questions are also in the student books.

YOUR MOST HUMBLING EXPERIENCE

1. What qualities in you did this experience reveal?

2. What did others see in you that you did not want them to know?

3. Did you feel embarrassed by this incident? Why?

4. Was this experience ultimately good for you or bad for you?

5. In what ways can life's humbling experiences be helpful for our development?

After about seven more minutes of discussion in small groups, share with the glass the importance of receiving humbling experineces in life as lessons from the Lord. Note that through these experiences, God breaks down our pride, helps break down barriers, and keeps us vulnerable and thus approachable.

As you prepare to open the Bible text, say, "In John 13:1-17, we have one of Peter's more humbling experiences. Through it, Peter and the other disciples were taught a great lesson in developing a servant-spirit."

Into the Word

Give to one student a red-letter edition of the Bible. You read the black type, and ask the person to read the red-lettered print. It is most helpful if you can give out this assignment before class so that the student can practice reading of the Word. Read John 13:1-17.

After the text is read, ask the groups of four to share with each other their observations on how the people in this story felt. Have one student in each group reflect on Jesus' feelings, one on Peter's feelings, one on the disciples' feelings, and one on Judas' feelings. Give them five minutes to discuss these feelings in their groups. Then have the whole class share their insights. This will give students an opportunity to tell how people react to humbling circumstances. Ask, "How could such an act as washing another's feet teach Jesus' disciples to be humble servants of Christ?"

Into Life

Footwashing was not a religious observance when Jesus did it, nor does Scripture indicate that He designed it to become one. It was a non-religious act of humble service in accordance with the customs of that day. Ask students, "What non-religious acts of humble service to day would compare with footwashing in Jesus' time?" Allow a few minutes for students to brainstorm this idea. As ideas are given, have students record the modern-day parallels to footwashing on a sheet of paper or in their student books.

Ask each student to select the one parallel that would be hardest for him or her personally to perform. In small groups, have them discuss the following questions:

1. Why do you suppose this service might be difficult for you?

2. Is it harder for you to serve someone else or to have someone else serve you? Why?

3. What could it possibly teach you if you were to perform this act of service?

4. Would you ever be willing to perform this act of service if called on to do so?

Close by asking the students to identify in their groups one act of service they will commit themselves to do this week. Since service is a response to a need, it may be important for the students first to identify an already-known need. Ask small groups to commit these deeds to mutual prayer and support throughout the week, as well as in closing today.

Let's Talk It Over

The questions on this page are designed to encourage review of the lesson Scriptures and to promote discussion of the lesson by the class. The answers provided are only discussion starters. Let your class talk it over from there.

1. In what ways is the church troubled with the problem of ambitious pride? How can we deal with it?

It is sad but true that some have sought offices of leadership, not for the primary purpose of serving, but for the power and prestige they felt the offices carried. In women's groups, in choirs and on committees, power struggles sometimes take place. Ministers may attempt to impose their opinions or programs on the church out of an ambition for prestige among their peers. But it is not profitable to single out certain groups or individuals and assume the problem is limited to them. Jesus' attitude of servanthood is often lacking throughout the church, and too many members are jealous of their rights and prerogatives. Each of us needs to give constant prayerful attention to Jesus' remarkable counsel: "Whoever wants to become great among you must be your servant, and whoever wants to be first must be slave of all. For even the Son of Man did not come to be served, but to serve, and to give his life as a ransom for many" (Mark 10:44, 45, *New International Version.*)

2. Some think that each of the apostles seated at the Passover table waited for one of the others to perform the humble service of foot-washing. And then Jesus took the initiative! Why is taking the initiative in service so significant in the church today?

How may church members wait for someone else to take the initiative in performing simple services? How many operate on the principle, "If another member will lead the way, I will welcome our visitors; if someone else will volunteer for that committee or that special project, I will join him"? We might be amazed to know how many worthy programs fail, how much time is wasted, how many opportunities are lost, because no member will take the initiative. Jesus led the way in rendering service to others. The church needs people who will boldly step out when there is an opportunity to serve and will see that service through to completion. Perhaps Paul's counsel to slaves at Colosse is applicable here: "Whatever you do, work at it with all your heart, as working for the Lord, not for men" (Colossians 3:23, *New International Version*).

3. The lesson writer describes Peter's reaction when Jesus prepared to wash his feet: "To Peter it seemed incredible that hands that had touched blind eyes and healed them and had lifted the dead back to life, should now wash the grime from *his* feet." How can contemplating the hands of Jesus aid us in making *our* hands instruments of ministry?

Jesus' hands may have been rough from years of toiling in the carpenter's shop, but He used them tenderly and gently. They were employed in providing food for multitudes and touching the blind and other sick persons to heal them. It may be instructive to think of the ways we use our hands. Are they often clenched as fists? Do they frequently feature the intimidating pointed finger? Are they waved as a gesture of disdain toward a person with whom we disagree? Jesus' hands challenge us to find ways of employing our hands to comfort, to encourage, to welcome, to instruct. It should be our aim to make our hands object lessons of the love of Jesus as they minister to the needs of others.

4. What are some ways in which Christians may need to humbly accept the service of others, so that they in turn may learn to serve?

Young Christians should be made aware that the leaders of the church are willing to answer their questions and aid them in working through the problems that may have resulted from their conversion to Christ. They must cultivate the humility that will enable them to admit their misconceptions, doubts, temptations, etc. When church members are ill, suffer a death within their family, or encounter a financial crisis, they should not be hesitant to accept the assistance that their spiritual brothers and sisters offer them at such times. Sometimes members let pride or embarrassment keep them from accepting. Another situation in which service must be accepted is in connection with public worship services. One occasionally hears of Christians who prefer to come into the assembly unobtrusively, worship, then leave as hurriedly as possible. These people need to see they are hurting themselves and others by neglecting contacts with fellow believers who can serve them by greeting them, inquiring as to their well-being, and offering them encouragement.

The Way, the Truth, the Life

LESSON SCRIPTURE: **John 13:31—14:14.**

PRINTED TEXT: **John 14:1-14.**

John 14:1-14

1 Let not your heart be troubled: ye believe in God, believe also in me.

2 In my Father's house are many mansions: if it were not so, I would have told you. I go to prepare a place for you.

3 And if I go and prepare a place for you, I will come again, and receive you unto myself; that where I am, there ye may be also.

4 And whither I go ye know, and the way ye know.

5 Thomas saith unto him, Lord, we know not whither thou goest; and how can we know the way?

6 Jesus saith unto him, I am the way, the truth, and the life: no man cometh unto the Father, but by me.

7 If ye had known me, ye should have known my Father also: and from henceforth ye know him, and have seen him.

8 Philip saith unto him, Lord, show us the Father, and it sufficeth us.

9 Jesus saith unto him, Have I been so long time with you, and yet hast thou not known me, Philip? he that hath seen me hath seen the Father; and how sayest thou then, Show us the Father?

10 Believest thou not that I am in the Father, and the Father in me? the words that I speak unto you I speak not of myself: but the Father that dwelleth in me, he doeth the works.

11 Believe me that I am in the Father, and the Father in me: or else believe me for the very works' sake.

12 Verily, verily, I say unto you, He that believeth on me, the works that I do shall he do also; and greater works than these shall he do; because I go unto my Father.

13 And whatsoever ye shall ask in my name, that will I do, that the Father may be glorified in the Son.

14 If ye shall ask any thing in my name, I will do it.

GOLDEN TEXT: Jesus saith unto him, I am the way, the truth, and the life: no man cometh unto the Father, but by me.—John 14:6.

John: The Gospel of Life and Light
Unit 3. Jesus Prepares His Followers
(Lessons 10-13)

Lesson Aims

After this lesson students should be able to:
1. Quote John 14:1 and 6.
2. Give reasons for a solid conviction that Jesus Christ is one with God the Father.

Lesson Outline

INTRODUCTION
  A. Follow the Leader
  B. A Great Storm
 I. "TRUST ME!" (John 14:1-4)
  A. "Peace, Be Still!" (v. 1)
  B. Welcome Home (vv. 2-4)
    A Prepared Place
 II. "I AM THE WAY" (John 14:5-7)
  A. "How Can We Know?" (v. 5)
  B. One Access to God (vv. 6, 7)
    One Way
III. "I AM ONE WITH GOD" (John 14:8-11)
  A. "Show Us the Father" (v. 8).
  B. "I Have Shown the Father" (vv. 9, 10)
  C. Believe What You See (v. 11)
IV. "I WILL HEAR YOUR PRAYER" (John 14:12-14)
  A. "You Will Do My Work" (v. 12)
  B. "I Will Do What You Request" (vv. 13, 14)
CONCLUSION
  A. A Great Calm
  B. A Believer's Prayer
  C. Thought to Remember

Display visual 12 from the visuals packet and let it remain before the class. The visual is shown on page 211.

Introduction

A. Follow the Leader

"Can you tell me how to get to the nearest hospital?" You and your wife are on vacation and find yourselves in a strange city when your wife becomes suddenly ill.

The friendly stranger at the service station replies, "I could tell you, or I could show you a map, but you would have a hard time following directions. I'm going in that direction. I'll lead you there." He knows the way through a maze of streets and traffic, and he keeps you in sight by frequent glances in his rearview mirror. You concentrate on following close enough to avoid being cut off by traffic and suddenly changing signals at busy intersections. You reach your destination in good time, thanks to good leading and good following.

There is, however, a still better way. Sensing a real emergency, the stranger says at the onset, "Leave your car here and get in with me. I'll take you there." And he does.

In somewhat similar fashion, our Lord Jesus makes himself available to bring us safely through life. We've never traveled this way before, and would be lost without guidance. He knows the way—He laid out the city!—and He keeps a watchful eye as we follow His instructions and His example. But we must do our part by keeping our eyes on Him, lest we be distracted and cut off by other traffic. There is a still better way—to let Him be the driver as we travel with Him. Thus we can come increasingly to say, "For me to live is Christ," and "Christ liveth in me" (Philippians 1:21; Galatians 2:20).

This week we join the apostles of Christ in pleading, "Explain it to us" and "Show us"; then in hearing the Lord say, "I'll do better than that. I'm the way; I'll take you there."

B. A Great Storm

On one occasion Jesus and the apostles were in a boat on the Sea of Galilee, "and there arose a great storm of wind, and the waves beat into the ship." On that occasion the Lord commanded the winds and the turbulent sea, saying, "Peace, be still," and "there was a great calm." Then He addressed His frightened friends, "Why are ye so fearful? how is it that ye have no faith?" (Mark 4:37-40). Troubled waters were quieted immediately at the voice of their Maker. Troubled spirits yielded more slowly to the appeal for trustful faith.

The same calming assurance is found in John 14:1-14, a beloved passage that has brought Jesus' "Peace, be still" to troubled folk in all kinds of circumstances. The passage has, in fact, been so readily adapted to our own stormy seasons that we may fail to measure its special meaning to those men to whom it was addressed.

The winds of circumstance were indeed buffeting those men that night. They were still shaken by Jesus' foot-washing object lesson in humility, and were shocked by the announcement that one of them would betray Him to His enemies. John 13:31-38 summarizes other troublesome news-breaks. Jesus was going to be "glorified," and He was going where they could not follow Him now. He was evidently talking again about imminent death. Peter wanted to follow Him anyhow, even to the grave. But Peter was told that before this night was over he would deny, three times, that he even knew Jesus!

The apostles didn't fully realize that their Master was buffeted by winds of circumstance far worse than any they felt. He faced rejection by His people and abandonment by His friends as He underwent the indescribable agonies of crucifixion, bearing the guilt of the world and the rejection of Heaven. He could avoid it all if He chose, but that would mean abandoning the Father's will and the work He came to do. But in the midst of it all Jesus expressed concern for others, and never pity nor complaint for himself.

I. "Trust Me!"
(John 14:1-4)

A. "Peace, Be Still" (v. 1)

1. Let not your heart be troubled: ye believe in God, believe also in me.

Let not your heart be troubled. Quit being worried, agitated, upset, or distressed—stirred into a turmoil by present and coming afflictions. How, though, can you avoid it?

Believe—trust in God; and *believe*—trust in the Son of God present with you. The repeated *believe* can be either a statement of fact—"ye believe"—or an exhortation—"believe ye." A *continuing* trust is indicated: never let go of your faith in God and in His Son!

The rest of the passage emphasizes an appeal for trust in Jesus as being *one* with the eternally trustworthy Father. To distrust Jesus, then, is to distrust God himself.

B. Welcome Home (vv. 2-4)

2. In my Father's house are many mansions: if it were not so, I would have told you. I go to prepare a place for you.

The apostles had left their homes and families to follow Jesus, and they had sometimes wondered whether they would be left homeless at His departure (Matthew 19:27-29). They needed to have no such fear. The Father will not so neglect His children. There are dwelling places for all in His home.

For the evening when this was spoken, Peter and John had been sent ahead to prepare the place for celebrating the Passover (Luke 22:8). So now Jesus assured them that in His death He was going ahead to prepare a suitable dwelling for each of His own. The Lord had already told His disciples, "If any man serve me, let him follow me; and where I am, there shall also my

visual 12

JESUS WENT TO PREPARE A HOME IN HEAVEN FOR YOU. ARE YOU GETTING READY TO LIVE THERE?

servant be" (John 12:26). It was not an idle promise, and here it is repeated.

Imagination balks at any effort to describe the Lord's preparation for His people, but the most important element is named in His next words.

3. And if I go and prepare a place for you, I will come again, and receive you unto myself; that where I am, there ye may be also.

The Lord came again into the presence of His apostles after the resurrection, but that was for a temporary visit. At His ascension six weeks later, angels renewed the promise made here. (See Acts 1:11.)

That promise became a prominent theme in the apostles' preaching and writing: "The Lord himself shall descend from heaven with a shout, with the voice of the archangel, and with the trump of God: and the dead in Christ shall rise first: then we which are alive and remain shall be caught up together with them in the clouds, to meet the Lord in the air: and so shall we ever be with the Lord" (1 Thessalonians 4:16, 17).

4. And whither I go ye know, and the way ye know.

Jesus had said that He was going away and that others could not presently come with Him (John 7:34; 13:33). If the disciples' understanding of His goal was unclear, they ought to have known the way in which He would reach it. He had told them that He was to suffer, be rejected, and die, and that His death would be a ransom for many. The example of His life also should have caused them to understand that His way was by spiritual processes and not by secular triumphs.

A PREPARED PLACE

Sam and Trish's house had just been completed in a new subdivision. They were to be married in three weeks, and the house was finished at exactly the right time. They had signed the contract on the house just a few days before Trish's parents came to visit, and the young couple proudly showed them the lovely home.

There was only one catch. They still had to wait to see if their resources were sufficient to make the high monthly payments on the house. They believed that they should qualify, and the SOLD sign on the home indicated they would. It would be a blow to them both, if they found out just before the wedding that their chosen home would not be theirs!

Jesus' promise is that He is coming again to receive to himself all who have found life in Him. Such persons can rest assured that a home awaits them in Heaven.

Some believe that by their own goodness they are preparing a home for themselves in the next life. These will be disappointed to discover that Jesus is the one who prepares those dwelling places. We must meet His terms. In faith, accept Him as your guarantee for the future and obey Him today, so you will not be disappointed when He comes.   —W. P.

II. "I Am the Way"
(John 14:5-7)

A. "How Can We Know?" (v. 5)

5. Thomas saith unto him, Lord, we know not whither thou goest; and how can we know the way?

Even the disciples were handicapped by a temporal and materialistic conception of the kingdom. Thomas now added his voice to that of Peter (John 13:36) and asked the question that must have been on the minds of all. Things once so difficult to understand become clear when the veil of the earthly kingdom idea is removed, and we see the spiritual nature of the kingdom and the corresponding redemptive work of Christ.

B. One Access to God (vv. 6, 7)

6. Jesus saith unto him, I am the way, the truth, and the life: no man cometh unto the Father, but by me.

Anyone who knows Jesus knows the *way* to where He is going, because He is the *way!* He is more than a sure guide; He is the access road. Earlier, Jesus had called himself the door to the sheepfold for the Father's flock, saying, "By me, if any man enter in, he shall be saved, and shall go in and out, and find pasture" (John 10:9). Hebrews 10:20 speaks of our access to God by "a new and living way, which he [Christ] hath consecrated for us, through the veil, that is his flesh." It is only natural that His cause came to be designated "the way" (Acts 9:2; 19:9, 23; 22:4; 24:14, 22).

Christ is *the truth.* Certainly His words are true, but this goes much deeper. Christ is the

truth personified. Christ did not have to search for the truth. He affirmed directly, for He himself was the truth. He had identified himself previously as the truth that sets men free (John 8:31-36).

Christ as *life* is a dominant theme in this Gospel. In his introductory lines, John said of the living Word, "In him was life, and the life was the light of men" (1:4). Jesus' own statements are even bolder. "I am the resurrection, and the life," He told a grieving Martha (11:25). And on this night before He was to die He would pray, "Thou hast given him [the Son] power . . . that he should give eternal life. . . . And this is life eternal, that they might know thee the only true God, and Jesus Christ, whom thou hast sent" (John 17:2, 3). He is more than the life giver; He is the life that is given!

Jesus' declaration in this verse is the basic fact on which God's saving gospel is built, and it cannot be diminished without self-destroying. It was so understood by the apostles. "Neither is there salvation in any other," Peter declared, "for there is none other name under heaven given among men, whereby we must be saved" (Acts 4:12). The Christ who came from the Father and returned to reign with the Father is eternally one with the Father, and is himself the only access to the Father's presence.

7. If ye had known me, ye should have known my Father also: and from henceforth ye know him, and have seen him.

Jesus' most intimate friends still didn't really know Him! But these words of rebuke to them become words of promise to any who will take Him fully at His word, will make Him the center of their being, and will thus come to know God for time and for eternity. "No man hath seen God at any time; the only begotten Son, which is in the bosom of the Father, he hath declared him" (John 1:18). "Blessed are they that have not seen, and yet have believed" (John 20:29).

ONE WAY

Our family always enjoyed coming to Hope Gardens, a beautiful park on the island of Jamaica. The lovely trees, shrubs, and flowers made it a delight at any season of the year. In winter the poinsettias grew to over ten feet in height and were a mass of flame red or light white-lemon contrasted against the green lawns, azure sky, and towering Blue Mountains.

But the attraction for the children and many adults was the intricate maze that had been developed over many years. It was of impenetrable hedge, more than head high, that prevented any shortcuts in working toward the well-hidden center. A wrong turn would bring one to a dead-end, and careful retracing of steps was necessary to find the right path again. It was quite an accomplishment to make it into the center and then out again. There was only one way it could be done. All other paths proved to be false leads. Reaching the clearly marked center was the only reward for success.

Life is something like that Hope Gardens maze. Most of us have taken paths that seemed right, only to discover they were dead ends. The retracing of our steps was painful and slow.

To know God is the supreme good of man's existence. Jesus is the one Way to the Father. Don't miss God's way!   —W. P.

III. "I Am One With God" (John 14:8-11)

A. "Show Us the Father" (v. 8)

8. Philip saith unto him, Lord, show us the Father, and it sufficeth us.

Again one of the apostles responded with a question brought forth by the Lord's previous statement. Thomas had asked for a road map to satisfy his reason; Philip wanted a photograph to satisfy his curiosity. Both seem to have been thinking in material terms.

B. "I Have Shown the Father" (vv. 9, 10)

9. Jesus saith unto him, Have I been so long time with you, and yet hast thou not known me, Philip? he that hath seen me hath seen the Father; and how sayest thou then, Show us the Father?

For three years Jesus had been in close daily contact with the band of apostles (*you* is plural), and they had seen Him deal with all kinds of people under all kinds of circumstances. Yet at least one of them (*thou* is singular) had failed to perceive in Him the spiritual identity He came to reveal. Philip was surely not the only one who was looking for a God who would sit for a portrait, despite Jesus' insistence that "God is a Spirit" (John 4:24). But Philip asked, and Philip was answered.

Jesus had dealt with this matter before, saying to His detractors, "If ye had known me, ye should have known my Father also," and "He that seeth me seeth him that sent me" (John 8:19; 12:45). The apostle Paul summarized the truth when he wrote, "In him [Christ] dwelleth all the fulness of the Godhead bodily" (Colossians 2:9). The spiritual attributes of God were all there, but in human form; and that form prevented many from seeing the nature of God. They were looking at God and did not know it.

10. Believest thou not that I am in the Father, and the Father in me? the words that I speak unto you I speak not of myself: but the Father that dwelleth in me, he doeth the works.

Some frustration is evident in the Lord's recognition that His closest friends did not understand or fully accept His most insistent teaching—His oneness with God. He could not quote, as did the ancient prophets, saying, "Thus saith the Lord." He, as God with a human body and a human voice, was himself saying what he wanted to say to accomplish what He wanted to do. The words Jesus spoke were God's words; the works He did were God's works. More than that He could not do, to make God visible to human eyes.

C. Believe What You See (v. 11)

11. Believe me that I am in the Father, and the Father in me: or else believe me for the very works' sake.

Jesus had never lied to these men, nor in any way deceived them. By now they ought to take Him at His word. Further, He had demonstrated divine power by doing what none but God could do. Jesus' miracles impressed Nicodemus to say, "We know that thou art a teacher come from God: for no man can do these miracles that thou doest, except God be with him" (John 3:2). Shortly before this final Passover, Jesus had challenged the unbelieving Jews, saying, "If I do not the works of my Father, believe me not. But if I do, though ye believe not me, believe the works; that ye may know, and believe, that the Father is in me, and I in him" (John 10:37, 38).

There were other works of God seen in Jesus: at least as remarkable as the physical miracles: the spotless life in a sin-drenched world, the selfless life in a selfish world, the compassionate life in a heartless world. So Jesus would say to us as He did to the twelve, "If you can't go all

Home Daily Bible Readings

Monday, Feb. 12—A New Commandment—The Way of Love (John 13:31-35)

Tuesday, Feb. 13—The Way to God's House (John 14:1-6)

Wednesday, Feb. 14—The New and Living Way (Hebrews 10:19-22)

Thursday, Feb. 15—Moses' Request for Communion (Exodus 33:17-23)

Friday, Feb. 16—Knowing Christ Is Knowing God (John 14:7-11)

Saturday, Feb. 17—Love, the Key to Knowing God (1 John 4:7-12)

Sunday, Feb. 18—God Leads in Love (1 John 4:13-21)

the way in a mature faith, then go as far as your best observation will take you, and hold on there until more complete observations lead you farther."

IV. "I Will Hear Your Prayer" (John 14:12-14)

A. "You Will Do My Work" (v. 12)

12. Verily, verily, I say unto you, He that believeth on me, the works that I do shall he do also; and greater works than these shall he do, because I go unto my Father.

I go unto my Father. These words link the promises in this verse with the ones spoken in verses 1-4. All these promises are made possible by Jesus' going to the Father. These promises are important, introduced with the emphatic *verily, verily.* They are conditional, given to none but those who follow His first exhortation, "Believe . . . in me" (v. 1).

The works that I do shall he do also. This suggests a second dimension to the statement, "I go to prepare a place for you." Jesus' departure created a vacancy here for the apostles to fill by carrying on His work. He had come to seek and to save that which was lost; they would make His salvation available to the lost through their preaching. They would even establish their ministries by certain miracles of healing, as Jesus had done; but they would know that they were not God, and they would resist any suggestion of superhuman status (see Acts 3:12-16; 10:25, 26; 14:8-18).

The *greater works* mentioned by Jesus were certainly not miracles greater than His. The greater works were in the scope of their evangelistic labors, with their moral and spiritual influence over men and nations. Not until Jesus departed and the Holy Spirit came was there even a complete gospel to proclaim in all its power. Pentecost with its three thousand converts, and the missionary outreach of Paul and his co-workers, were not possible until Jesus returned to the Father.

B. "I Will Do What You Request" (vv. 13, 14)

13, 14. And whatsoever ye shall ask in my name, that will I do, that the Father may be glorified in the Son. If ye shall ask anything in my name, I will do it.

This promise, like the previous one, is addressed to those who have exercised a persistent and consistent trust in the Father as revealed in His Son. Their trust in His wisdom and His way will lead them to follow Him, even when the following is contrary to every human impulse.

Previously, Jesus had invited His followers, "Ask, and it shall be given you; seek, and ye shall find; knock, and it shall be opened unto you" (Matthew 7:7). One must, however, ask in faith (Matthew 21:22), and he must be in right relationship with his fellowmen (Matthew 6:14). All of this is involved in the employment of Jesus' *name*—His person and purpose—in making request.

During the rest of the evening's conversation with the apostles, Jesus expanded on the invitation to give His *name* priority in their praying (John 15:7, 16; 16:23, 24). In saying *that will I do,* Jesus made it plain that He became the *doer* in response to prayer, and not simply the bearer of messages to a higher authority (see Acts 7:59; 9:14, 21; 1 Corinthians 1:2). To prevent any misunderstanding, the Lord established His promise with a final brief repetition: *I will do it.*

Conclusion

A. A Great Calm

The troubled spirits of the apostles did not yield as promptly to the words of Jesus as the troubled waters of Galilee had yielded when He said, "Peace, be still." In time, however, they did yield, and it could be said finally that among them "there was a great calm." The Lord's words *to* the apostles were fulfilled *in* the apostles. Convinced at last by Jesus' resurrection, and empowered at Pentecost and afterward by the Holy Spirit, they preached with confident boldness as Jesus had preached; they endured opposition and affliction with patient serenity; they continued undaunted through amazing obstacles; and they even went to death without flinching. They had found and followed the way to the Father; they had committed themselves wholly to the truth of Christ; and they had accepted a share in life eternal through Him. That same serenity has been enjoyed by millions of saints through the ages, and it is still available to all mankind on the same terms, through Jesus Christ our Lord who is eternally the Way, the Truth, and the Life.

B. A Believer's Prayer

Lord, I believe; please help my unbelief! I acknowledge You as the Way; help me to follow more closely. I confess You as the Truth; help me to declare You more faithfully. I yield myself to You as the Life; help me to live in You more completely, now and always. Amen.

C. Thought to Remember

Jesus has answered the hard questions. We need to hear, believe, trust, and follow Him.

Learning by Doing

This page contains an alternate lesson plan emphasizing learning activities. Classes desiring such student involvement will find these suggestions helpful.

Learning Goals

We will feel more comfortable when we know about our future. Most people find a way to afford some kind of insurance, because it gives them an assurance about their future. In a day when the insurance business is booming, the greatest insurance of one's future is still the assurance Jesus gives to those who truly believe in Him. Therefore, your students need to:

1. Examine the assurance that they have of their own future security.

2. Feel at peace if they have placed their future in Jesus Christ as Lord.

3. Discipline their minds with the firm assurance that a blessed existence awaits all believers.

Into the Lesson

After opening with prayer, ask students to brainstorm on all the kinds of insurance policies that are available. Write on a chalkboard or overhead projector one-word answers as quickly as they can name them (for example, life, fire, health, earthquake, auto, etc.). Ask students not to comment on any type of insurance that is mentioned, because this will interrupt the free flow of ideas. Now, ask students to work with a neighbor and come up with what they think are the three most important of all the insurance policies listed on the board. Give them a couple of minutes to work on this before asking them to share with the class what they chose and why. Finally, connect *insurance* with *assurance* by pointing out that the purpose of insurance is to give assurance. Say, "The most important insurance policies to us are the ones that give us the most assurance." Ask how many have enough insurance to make them feel assured about their future. How much more would it take? Say, "The trouble with any insurance policy is that it can give only limited assurance, no matter how large the policy reads." Discuss why that is true.

Draw the conversation around to the ultimate source of assurance about the future—Jesus Christ. Discuss why that is true. (Because He is eternal.)

Into the Word

Jesus offers believers an insurance policy with only three clauses in it. Write them on the chalkboard. They are:

1. I Am the Way
2. I Am the Truth
3. I Am the Life

Divide your class into *listening teams* of three students each. If possible, ask each group of three to move their chairs together so they are sitting in a circle knee-to-knee.

As you read the Scripture text aloud, one on each team will listen for anything it says about how Jesus is the *way*, one will listen for what it means that Jesus is the *truth*, and one will listen for insights into Jesus as the *life*. If possible, read from a modern translation. Ask the teams to share their insights together in their group of three. Then have students share their results with the class.

Into Life

Ask students to conduct the following "Soul Search." Either copy the following questions on slips of paper to hand out, or have the class use their student books. Allow students about ten minutes of quiet time to record their answers to the questions.

SOUL SEARCH

1. Have I come to the place in my spiritual life where I'm sure that if I were to die tonight I would wake up in Heaven with Jesus?

2. Do I allow my heart to be troubled about the future? How? Why?

3. Am I more concerned about my future in this life or my future in the life to come?

4. Even though I accept Jesus as the truth, are there areas of doubt with which I am still struggling?

5. Am I experiencing the life of Jesus to the full, as He intends?

6. If I may ask for anything in the name of Jesus (vv. 13, 14), what can I ask for right now that will help me find a rich assurance as to my future?

Discuss with students how this soul search made them feel. "What areas of insecurity did this reveal in you?"

Gently ask if anyone felt uncomfortable or uncertain about question 1. This opens the door for you to explain the covenant of faith with Jesus Christ and how we may enter it.

Discuss the questions as time permits, always drawing the students away from discouragement toward renewal and commitment.

Let's Talk It Over

The questions on this page are designed to encourage review of the lesson Scriptures and to promote discussion of the lesson by the class. The answers provided are only discussion starters. Let your class talk it over from there.

1. "Ye believe in God, believe also in me" (John 14:1). Both of these references to believing could be translated as exhortations. Some people protest that it does no good to command or exhort them to believe—they feel they are unable to develop a firm faith in God. How may we answer them?

Of course, some will use this as a way of excusing themselves from commitment to Christ. But others can readily identify with the father of the demon-possessed son in his cry, "I do believe; help me overcome my unbelief!" (Mark 9:24, *New International Version*). In connection with that same incident, Jesus spoke to His disciples about the potential of "faith as a grain of mustard seed" (Matthew 17:20). That suggests that faith is a spiritual attribute that a person may grow. Paul points us to the environment in which that growing may take place, when he says, "Faith cometh by hearing, and hearing by the word of God" (Romans 10:17). If we encounter those who are sincerely interested in growing a healthy faith, we can direct them to center their thoughts on the Word of God, and to dedicate themselves to fulfilling God's will as they learn it there.

2. Why is it helpful to think of Heaven as a place Jesus is preparing for us?

In spite of the description of the new Jerusalem in Revelation 21 and 22, some Christians are uncertain as to the superiority of Heaven over earth and lack a strong sense of anticipation at dwelling there. But a comparison of the prepared earth with the prepared Heaven is an aid to correcting this. Genesis 1 describes God's preparation of the earth for human habitation. Sin marred the excellency of the original creation, but it is still true that the earth is marvelously suited to supply what we need in terms of climate, food, clothing, shelter, rest, and beauty. It should be clear, therefore, that the prepared Heaven will also be ideally arranged so as to satisfy every need we shall feel in the resurrected state. Jesus put special emphasis on the most important aspect of this preparation: we shall be where He is; we shall have fellowship with Him. Somehow it will be possible for all the saints of all the ages to have access to their glorious Savior.

3. The apostles were slow to recognize that Jesus was God in human form. Many people today have difficulty acknowledging Jesus as deity. How can these today benefit from the apostles' experience?

We may think it was easier for the apostles to resolve this question. Since they witnessed Jesus' miracles, they enjoyed a form of evidence that we possess only secondhand. But they were acquainted with the human side of Jesus much better than we are. They saw Him eat, drink, sleep, and even weep as a human being. To imagine that this flesh-and-blood companion was the almighty God in human form must have been a staggering thought. We can trace their struggle in the Gospel accounts. We hear them say in awe and perplexity after the stilling of the storm, "What manner of man is this, that even the winds and the sea obey him!" (Matthew 8:27). We hear Peter declare, "Thou art the Christ, the Son of the living God" (16:16), and yet immediately afterward Peter was unaware of the implications of that statement. Even after the resurrection, the apostles struggled to believe that Jesus had power to conquer death, until He showed himself to them and they knew that He was alive. We today can find convincing evidence of the deity of Christ by examining the apostles' experiences.

4. Jesus promised His apostles that they would do "greater works" than he had done. Does this promise extend to us also? If so, in what ways is it true?

It has been said that Jesus apparently never traveled far from home. Today, evangelists travel all over the nation and sometimes to foreign lands. That is one example of "greater works." Jesus did not write a book, whereas today Christian writers communicate Biblical truths to millions by means of the printed word. In a sense, any Christian who influences another person to receive Jesus as Savior is performing a greater work, since the gospel of salvation was not yet complete and the plan of salvation could not yet be announced when Jesus spoke those words. Perhaps one reason Jesus made this promise was to spur us to use every legitimate tool available to accomplish the greater work of winning many souls to Him.

Promise of the Spirit

February 25
Lesson 13

LESSON SCRIPTURE: John 14:15-31.

PRINTED TEXT: John 14:15-27.

Love EXPRESS
itSel/ in OBEdiENce
and loBediencE
pRovE Reality
of Love

John 14:15-27

15 If ye love me, keep my commandments.

16 And I will pray the Father, and he shall give you another Comforter, that he may abide with you for ever;

17 Even the Spirit of truth; whom the world cannot receive, because it seeth him not, neither knoweth him: but ye know him; for he dwelleth with you, and shall be in you.

18 I will not leave you comfortless: I will come to you.

19 Yet a little while, and the world seeth me no more; but ye see me: because I live, ye shall live also.

20 At that day ye shall know that I am in my Father, and ye in me, and I in you.

21 He that hath my commandments, and keepeth them, he it is that loveth me: and he that loveth me shall be loved of my Father, and I will love him, and will manifest myself to him.

22 Judas saith unto him, not Iscariot, Lord, how is it that thou wilt manifest thyself unto us, and not unto the world?

23 Jesus answered and said unto him, If a man love me, he will keep my words: and my Father will love him, and we will come unto him, and make our abode with him.

24 He that loveth me not keepeth not my sayings: and the word which ye hear is not mine, but the Father's which sent me.

25 These things have I spoken unto you, being yet present with you.

26 But the Comforter, which is the Holy Ghost, whom the Father will send in my name, he shall teach you all things, and bring all things to your remembrance, whatsoever I have said unto you.

27 Peace I leave with you, my peace I give unto you: not as the world giveth, give I unto you. Let not your heart be troubled, neither let it be afraid.

GOLDEN TEXT: The Comforter, which is the Holy Ghost, whom the Father will send in my name, he shall teach you all things, and bring all things to your remembrance, whatsoever I have said unto you.—John 14:26.

John: The Gospel of Life and Light
Unit 3. Jesus Prepares His Followers
(Lessons 10-13)

Lesson Aims

This lesson should prepare the student to:

1. Explain the relationship between the close of Jesus' earthly ministry and the coming of the Holy Spirit.

2. Show how Jesus' promises concerning the Holy Spirit related specifically to the apostles, and explain what that means to us.

Lesson Outline

INTRODUCTION
   A. On Hand as Needed
   B. No Stranger
 I. REQUEST AND PROVISION (John 14:15-17)
   A. Basis for Provision (v. 15)
   B. Abiding Advocate (vv. 16, 17)
      Companion and Guide
 II. RETURN AND INDWELLING (John 14:18-20)
 III. REQUIREMENT FOR FELLOWSHIP (John 14:21-24)
   A. Requirement Stated (v. 21)
   B. Question and Restatement (vv. 22, 23)
   C. Recognition of Authority (v. 24)
 IV. BEQUESTS (John 14:25-27)
   A. Teacher and Reminder (vv. 25, 26)
   B. Peace! (v. 27)
      A Gift From God
CONCLUSION
   A. Promise Fulfilled
   B. Prayer
   C. Thought to Remember

Display visual 13 from the visuals packet and have it remain before the class. It is shown on page 219.

Introduction

A. On Hand as Needed

"Tarry ye here, and watch with me. . . . What, could ye not watch with me one hour?"

"No man stood with me, but all men forsook, me. . . . Notwithstanding the Lord stood with me, and strengthened me."

Jesus in the garden of Gethsemane (Matthew 26:38, 40) and Paul facing trial before Caesar in Rome (2 Timothy 4:16, 17) had a common need and a common problem. Each needed the sup-portive presence of a trustworthy companion in his time of testing, and neither was able to find it in his friends. Paul had one great advantage, however. The Lord who faced His agony alone was present to sustain Paul! "The Lord stood with me."

The friend alongside may sometimes serve best by simply being there without saying or doing anything. Such a friend is still a source of strong personal support in carrying a part of whatever load we bear.

Teachers, athletic coaches, and trainers, as well as counselors, preachers, and parents, provide instruction, guidance, and encouragement every day. For special needs there are physicians, nurses, therapists, and attorneys to lend their training and experience to reduce the severity of emergencies.

Throughout His ministry, Jesus had stood with His disciples in almost every imaginable circumstance. As teacher He had instructed, directed and encouraged; as attorney-advocate He had pled their case before the bar of Heaven; as friend He had given them patient support in their faltering efforts to serve. Now that relationship was coming to an end. He was going to leave them, but not without warning or without provision for another to stand with them in their daily doings, their afflictions, and their emergencies. His Spirit would be with them in ways infinitely more substantial than mere memory or lingering influence. He had walked among them as God in the flesh. So now another manifestation of God would be present among them and within them to continue doing for them what He had done.

B. No Stranger

The active, enabling, instructive Spirit of God, here promised by Jesus, was no stranger to God's people. He had been a factor in the divine economy from the beginning, when "the Spirit of God moved upon the face of the waters" in the creative order (Genesis 1:2). Bezaleel, the principal craftsman and instructor in building the tabernacle under Moses, was "filled . . . with the Spirit of God" to possess many skills (Exodus 31:3). Joshua, Moses' successor, was "a man in whom is the spirit" to equip him for his task. (Numbers 27:18). The "spirit of the Lord came upon" Gideon to assemble and lead Israel (Judges 6:34), and Nehemiah said that God testified against the sinful nation "by thy Spirit in thy prophets" (Nehemiah 9:30).

The Holy Spirit was active in the life of Jesus. His very birth came through the activity of the Holy Spirit (Matthew 1:20). At Jesus' baptism the "Holy Ghost descended in a bodily shape like a dove upon him" (Luke 3:22), and the Spirit then led Him into the wilderness for a period of temptation (Matthew 4:1; Mark 1:12). At the beginning of His public ministry, Jesus said in the words of Isaiah 61, "The Spirit of the Lord is upon me, because he hath anointed me to preach the gospel to the poor" (Luke 4:18). And Hebrews 9:14 speaks summarily of "Christ, who through the eternal Spirit offered himself without spot to God."

The words of our text are the words spoken by Jesus immediately after assuring His disciples He was the one way of access to the Father, that He and the Father are one, and that those who had seen Him had seen the Father (John 14:1-14). We continue with Jesus' teaching to His apostles in that final evening fellowship, which began with the Passover supper and concluded in the Garden of Gethsemane.

I. Request and Provision (John 14:15-17)

A. Basis for Provision (v. 15)

15. If ye love me, keep my commandments.
Love—the selfless desire to do good to another —is the identifying characteristic of God and His people. God so loved the world that He gave His Son; Jesus loved so greatly that He laid down His life, even for those who hated Him. He commanded His disciples to love one another, as He had loved them. But He had not said anything about their loving Him. Could it be assumed that they did? Here was a test. If they loved Him, they would do as He directed them to do. They would live according to His teachings. *Commandments* in this instance are precepts and instructions rather than legal decrees. The disciples' obedience, as the expression of love, is the condition on which they were to receive the promise about to be given.

B. Abiding Advocate (vv. 16, 17)

16. And I will pray the Father, and he shall give you another Comforter, that he may abide with you for ever.
An earlier note had explained, "The Holy Ghost was not yet given; because that Jesus was not yet glorified" (John 7:39). The time for the giving was now at hand because the glorification was about to take place. *Pray* in this instance is the request of the Son to the Father, rather than the supplication of the creature to the Creator. The Father would send someone else to be teacher, encourager, companion, and friend that Jesus had been to the apostles.
Comforter means one who sustains or lends strength to another. The Greek word here means literally one called alongside—called to the assistance of another. It is variously translated "Advocate," "Counselor," and "Helper." It never would be necessary for this other sustainer and guide to go away from His friends as Jesus was about to go.

Romans 8:26 records some ways the Spirit would help the followers of Christ: "the spirit also helpeth our infirmities: for we know not what we should pray for as we ought: but the Spirit itself maketh intercession for us with groanings which cannot be uttered."

17. Even the Spirit of truth; whom the world cannot receive, *Belived* **because it seeth him not, neither knoweth him: but ye know him; for he dwelleth with you, and shall be in you.**
Jesus had just identified himself with the truth: "I am . . . the truth." He then described the Holy Spirit as the *Spirit of truth.* He expanded on this, saying, "When the Comforter is come, whom I will send unto you from the Father, even the Spirit of truth . . . he shall testify of me" (John 15:26).

The world cannot receive, or accept, the Spirit of truth any more than it could receive, or apprehend, the light that shone in its darkness (John 1:4, 5). Rejecting out of hand anything not evident to its physical senses, the materialistic world renders itself incapable of perceiving the Spirit's testimony.

But ye know him. The disciples were reminded that they did know the Spirit. When they went forth two by two and performed many miracles, it was by the power of the Holy Spirit. But they were to have a more intimate fellowship as the Spirit would live in their hearts.

COMPANION AND GUIDE

Wherever you saw Bill Sawyer you saw his companion also. At every street crossing, in the lobby of the bank, at the grocery store—Bill was never alone. Somehow it was a reassuring sight to see Bill and Trevor making their way down the sidewalk side by side.

Bill lost his sight due to an auto accident. He underwent weeks of hospitalization and the necessary rehabilitation process. Then one day

✝ DIVINE
Although Jesus went away,
He is with us yet today.
Through His Spirit we may know
God's loving presence here below.
Father, Son, and Spirit will
Come to us our hearts to still.
COMFORT

visual 13

Trevor came into Bill's life. Trevor was a trained guide dog, and an instant bonding took place between the two of them.

With Trevor, Bill was able to get around with confidence, and soon he was back in his office carrying on the business that had seemed doomed when he lost his sight.

Though Trevor could not talk, his warning growl would alert Bill to possible danger or difficulty. His companionship at all hours became an indispensable part of Bill's life. It was good to see them together and to know that Bill was able to live a renewed, active life through Trevor's presence.

We were once blind in sin. God has given us a constant companion, one who speaks to us in the Word to all areas of our lives. The Holy Spirit is that companion, that helper.

We must allow Him to enter our lives before we can truly see. Does He live in you? —W. P.

II. Return and Indwelling (John 14:18-20)

18. I will not leave you comfortless: I will come to you.

In leaving the disciples, the Lord did not abandon them. The Greek here may be translated, "I will not leave you orphans." *I will come unto you.* Jesus would return to the apostles in His resurrection body, and He would return for all to see Him at the end of the world. But His promise here is linked to the coming of the Spirit. The unity of Father, Son, and Spirit in the Godhead is such that it was not necessary for Him to distinguish one from the other. In the Spirit's coming, Christ would be continually with His own, according to the promise recorded in Matthew 28:20.

19. Yet a little while, and the world seeth me no more; but ye see me: because I live, ye shall live also.

The world seeth me no more. On this very night, Jesus would allow himself to be taken by His enemies, and in a matter of hours they would crucify Him. The world would seemingly have its way. Then the world would see Him no more until the second coming, when every eye will see Him (Revelation 1:7).

Ye see me. The disciples, however, would see Jesus literally following the resurrection, and by the eye of faith after the coming of the Holy Spirit on the Day of Pentecost. At that time the apostolic message was, "This Jesus hath God raised up, whereof we all are witnesses. Therefore being by the right hand of God exalted, and having received of the Father the promise of the Holy Ghost, he hath shed forth this, which ye

now see and hear" (Acts 2:32, 33). Being continually aware of Jesus' living presence, the apostles would know that His living assured them of endless life. Jesus' unending life is the sure basis for life to all those who believe in Him.

20. At that day ye shall know that I am in my Father, and ye in me, and I in you.

That day. On Pentecost, with the outpouring of the Holy Spirit, the disciples would more fully understand the spiritual unity that had always existed between God the Father and Jesus the Son. And they would also come to realize the wonderful unity of the disciple with his Lord.

III. Requirement for Fellowship (John 14:21-24)

A. Requirement Stated (v. 21)

21. He that hath my commandments, and keepeth them, he it is that loveth me: and he that loveth me shall be loved of my Father, and I will love him, and will manifest myself to him.

Many have heard and known the teachings of Christ. Presumably this includes most of those who now live in "Christian" communities, churches, and families. But that is not the test of acceptance. The test lies in *keeping*, that is, obeying or *doing*, what Jesus has said. This shows the believer's love for his Lord. Linked with the words of verse 15, this indicates that love expresses itself in obedience, and obedience proves the reality of love.

Does God really love only those who lovingly obey His Son? Does He not love the whole world? (John 3:16). Is not His love like the sunshine and rain that come equally upon all? Yes! But just as men erect barriers to protect themselves against sunshine and rain, so do the disobedient ones shut themselves off from receiving divine love. God's love gets through and blesses those who love and obey God. To them Jesus is able to *manifest* himself. They alone are really able to see and understand Him as beloved Friend. To others He is forever a stranger.

B. Question and Restatement (vv. 22, 23)

22. Judas saith unto him, not Iscariot, Lord, how is it that thou wilt manifest thyself unto us, and not unto the world?

The traitor, Judas Iscariot, had already left the upper room (John 13:30). The Judas mentioned here was otherwise known as Thaddeus or Lebbeus (Matthew 10:3). It seems that he was still thinking in political terms and was asking in effect, "What has happened to the Messianic kingdom that You should keep Your messiahship secret from everybody but us?"

23. Jesus answered and said unto him, If a man love me, he will keep my words: and my Father will love him, and we will come unto him, and make our abode with him.

Judas had not understood Jesus' statement (v. 21), which dealt with a spiritual, not a political, revelation. Those to whom Jesus would manifest himself would be those who, when hearing His gospel, would respond to Him in love and obedience. In view here is a disciple's intimate fellowship with Christ as he walks with Him through the years. "Anyone who loves me will heed what I say" (*The New English Bible*).

Then Jesus added a great promise, *We will come unto him, and make our abode with him. Abode*, in this instance, translates the same word that is rendered, *mansions* in verse 2. Just as dwellings in Heaven are prepared to receive believers into the presence of God, so the loving and obedient hearts of believers become dwelling places for the Father and the Son. This on earth is a preview of Heaven, where "the tabernacle of God is with men, and he will dwell with them, and they shall be his people, and God himself shall be with them, and be their God" (Revelation 21:3).

C. Recognition of Authority (v. 24)

24. He that loveth me not keepeth not my sayings: and the word which ye hear is not mine, but the Father's which sent me.

In this discussion, Jesus has shown that (1) those who love Him will keep His teachings, and (2) those who obey Jesus' teachings reveal their love for Him. It follows that the person who does not love Jesus will not keep His words. But to reject Jesus' words is a matter with very serious consequences, for the teachings of Jesus, both as to men's behavior and as to relationship with God, come not from any man—not even from Jesus as man—but from the eternal and unchanging God.

IV. Bequests
(John 14:25-27)

A. Teacher and Reminder (vv. 25, 26)

25, 26. These things have I spoken unto you, being yet present with you. But the Comforter, which is the Holy Ghost, whom the Father will send in my name, he shall teach you all things, and bring all things to your remembrance, whatsoever I have said unto you.

The final part of our text becomes a sort of last will and testament. What would Jesus leave to His spiritual family? First, He would supply a replacement for himself as their spiritual support—but something more practical also.

How To Say It

GETHSEMANE. Geth-*sem*-uh-nee.
ISCARIOT. Iss-*care*-e-ut.
LEBBEUS. Leh-*bee*-us.
THADDEUS. Tha-*dee*-us.

These things have I spoken unto you. I have spoken unto you, but have you listened? Have you understood? Will you remember? The disciples knew human weakness and how easy it is to forget the things we should remember. Forestalling any despair over the responsibility of preserving His many words, Jesus renewed His promise to send the Comforter, the Holy Spirit, to them.

Elsewhere we are told that the Spirit would testify of Jesus and glorify Him. Here we are told that He would become Teacher to the apostles, persuading them of what Jesus had said, and reminding them of teachings they had forgotten. He would guide them into all truth. Because this promise to the apostles was kept and fulfilled in the apostles, it could be said later that Christ's church is built solidly upon the foundation of the apostles and prophets (Ephesians 2:20). They laid the foundation by their Spirit-inspired preaching and writing—which writing becomes available to us in the New Testament. The Spirit speaks to us in the sacred writings, but for our perception and understanding of the Word, we need His presence and His help.

B. Peace (v. 27)

27. Peace I leave with you, my peace I give unto you: not as the world giveth, give I unto you. Let not your heart be troubled, neither let it be afraid.

Of all Jesus' possessions He might bequeath to His friends in parting from them, none was more valuable than His *peace*—that special and peculiar serenity that enabled Him to face temptation without faltering, to face ingratitude and opposition without bitterness, and to face even death with steadfast willingness. His was a miraculous inner calm in the midst of storm. The world has no such peace to enjoy, and none to offer. The best it can muster is a balance of power that makes enemies afraid to attack each other and so preserves an uneasy pause between conflicts.

Jesus extended a bit on His bestowal of peace: "These things I have spoken unto you, that in me ye might have peace. In the world ye shall have tribulation: but be of good cheer; I have overcome the world" (John 16:33).

The Lord had already exhorted His disciples, "Let not your heart be troubled" (John 14:1); but they needed a second admonition, saying in effect, "Quiet your troubled minds, and dismiss your persistent fears. You have a heritage of boundless, timeless peace; enjoy it!"

A GIFT FROM GOD

On August 28, 1987, students at the Diliman campus of the University of the Philippines were reported to have heard airplanes flying overhead and bombs exploding in the vicinity of the school. Later reports confirmed that this was an effort of the Philippine military to avert the attempted coup d'etat staged by discontented officers and soldiers, who said they wanted to force reform in the government.

In the days following, there were political assassinations. President Aquino was in a tight situation trying to balance all the groups vying for influence. Many leaders were calling for prayer as the key to peace.

Karen Plumb, a graduate student residing in the International Center and member of Los Gatos Christian Church, said it was the most frightening moment she had faced in her four years in the Philippines. Then she added, "Yet I felt this strange peace, because I knew that God had sent me and He would keep me. I just knew it deep down."

We long for peace, but fighting and unrest continue. The world cannot offer a lasting peace. Only Jesus can. The peace He gives His followers is the inner assurance that no matter what our situation, He is with us, and we are safe in His hands.   —W. P.

Conclusion

A. Promise Fulfilled

Jesus pursued and fulfilled His Spirit-promise to the apostles. Meeting with them after the resurrection He said, "I send the promise of my Father upon you: but tarry ye in the city of Jerusalem until ye be endued with power from on high" (Luke 24:49). Just before His ascension He added, "Ye shall be baptized with the Holy Ghost not many days hence" (Acts 1:5).

Acts 2 is the account of Pentecost, when the apostles "were all filled with the Holy Ghost, and began to speak with other tongues, as the Spirit gave them utterance" (Acts 2;4). Later chapters tell of miracles performed by the apostles under the power of the Spirit, and note that certain others, on whom the apostles laid their hands, also showed miraculous manifestations of the Spirit (Acts 8:4-24). The frequency of such miracles diminished, though, with the de-

veloping maturity of the church; and even the apostle Paul, who was the center of many miracles, found no miracles accompanying or easing his later days in prison.

That did not mean, however, that the Spirit was any less present, either with the apostles or with the saints whom they brought to Christ. Peter's promise on the day of Pentecost was clear: "Repent, and be baptized every one of you in the name of Jesus Christ for the remission of sins, and ye shall receive the gift of the Holy Ghost. For the promise is unto you, and to your children, and to all that are afar off, even as many as the Lord our God shall call" (Acts 2:38, 39). Paul urged upon the Christians at Corinth that "your body is the temple of the Holy Ghost which is in you" (1 Corinthians 6:19), and he spelled out to the Galatians the qualities that could be expected as fruit of the Spirit to dominate their life-style: "love, joy, peace, long-suffering, gentleness, goodness, faith, meekness, temperance" (Galatians 5:22). In those qualities, Jesus' promise of the Holy Spirit is still effective among His people, and will be so until He comes again.

B. Prayer

Thank You, O God our Creator, for Your Son our Lord—for His living presence in the days of His flesh, and for His living presence always through His Holy Spirit. Thank You for the sacred writings, the dependable Word written under the inspiration of the Spirit. Help us, we pray, to follow it more fully. In Jesus' name, amen.

C. Thought to Remember

God's people will always have an invisible means of support.

Learning by Doing

This page contains an alternate lesson plan emphasizing learning activities. Classes desiring such student involvement will find these suggestions helpful.

Learning Goals

Most young adults have a restless optimism that they can do almost anything they decide to do. But as years roll on, adults realize that there are many factors in their lives over which they have very little control. The promise of the presence of the Holy Spirit assures believers that God is always in control, even when things seem out of control. In today's lesson, the students will:

1. Face their own need for a source of power beyond themselves in their lives.

2. Discover the power in the abiding presence of the Holy Spirit in each believer.

3. Commit themselves to plugging into the power of the Holy Spirit in their daily lives.

Into the Lesson

After your opening prayer time, write in large letters on the chalkboard or overhead the phrase from Romans 5:6 (*New International Version*), "... while we were still *powerless*...." Say, "This refers to the helpless condition of a person outside of Christ. But even as Christians, aren't there times when we feel powerless?" Ask the students to take the following "Power Check" and to indicate the times that they feel most powerless. Make copies ahead of time and give one to each student, or you may use your students books for this exercise.

POWER CHECK

Put a check mark by those circumstances in which you feel most powerless.

When my boss hassles me

When there isn't enough money to pay the bills

When I'm held up in traffic for an appointment

When I get a poor grade in a class

When I do something stupid

When I do something I promised I would never do again

When someone I care about very much dies

When my prayers are not answered to my-satisfaction

When my children fight

When I can't get all my work done on time

When I can't seem to get over an illness quickly

All of the above

Other _____

After giving students two minutes to complete this, let them share how they feel when some of these things happen. Then say, "God has given us the Holy Spirit to deal with our weakness as human beings. Today, let's see how the Holy Spirit can help us."

Into the Word

Divide the class into groups of four or five to work on this activity. As you read the Scripture text aloud, ask students to listen for the names given to the Holy Spirit, the roles assigned to the Holy Spirit, and the results of the presence of the Holy Spirit in the believer. Give each student a sheet with the title "The Holy Spirit and You." Down the left side of the sheet put the headings "Names," "Roles," and "Results," and leave space under each heading for notes.

Names could include "Comforter" ("Advocate," "Counselor," "Helper"; see lesson treatment for verse 16); "Spirit of truth" (v. 17); "Holy Ghost" ("Holy Spirit"; v. 26).

Roles could include comforting, advocating, counseling, helping (v. 16); indwelling (v. 17): teaching, reminding (v. 26).

Results could include: obedience (v. 15); belonging (v. 18; see lesson treatment regarding "orphans"); life (v. 19); love of the Father (v. 21); peace (v. 27).

After the small groups have worked on this for fifteen minutes, have them share their results with the whole class.

Into Life

You have explored the students' needs and the power of the Holy Spirit to meet those needs. Now connect the needs with God's power. Ask the small groups to discuss this question: "In what areas of my life could the Holy Spirit provide power that I am not now allowing Him to?" Ask students to refer to their "Power Check" to determine their needs and how the Holy Spirit could meet them.

Our text seems to indicate that obedience releases the power of the Holy Spirit in the life of the believer. Obedience, as an expression of love, enables the Holy Spirit to work in our lives. Close with prayer in small groups in which the students ask God to help them become obedient followers of Christ so they may know the presence and power of the Holy Spirit.

Let's Talk It Over

The questions on this page are designed to encourage review of the lesson Scriptures and to promote discussion of the lesson by the class. The answers provided are only discussion starters. Let your class talk it over from there.

1. The Holy Spirit is called the Comforter or the "Counselor" *(New International Version)* How does the Spirit comfort and counsel us today?

The apostles and other early Christian leaders experienced the guidance of the Holy Spirit in a special, miraculous way. On Pentecost, for example, Peter and the other apostles were guided by the Counselor as they proclaimed the risen Christ publicly for the first time. Philip experienced angelic and Spirit guidance in evangelizing the Ethiopian eunuch (Acts 8:26, 29). We may feel that we don't have such clear and dramatic guidance today. But actually, through the Scriptures the Holy Spirit has given us a remarkable instrument for obtaining His comfort and counsel. When one thinks of the array of comforting statements of Jesus the Spirit has furnished us (Matthew 11:28-30; 18:20; Mark 13:31; Luke 19:10; John 6:35; 10:27-30; 14:1-6, 27, for example), it seems that we are no less blessed than the apostles. Again, when we consider the counsel the Spirit provides us by enabling us to have the Sermon on the Mount (Matthew 5-7) and many of Jesus' parables, we must say that we suffer little deprivation as far as spiritual guidance is concerned.

2. The *New International Version* translates Jesus' promise in John 14:18 in this way: "I will not leave you as orphans; I will come to you." What does this indicate about a life without the Holy Spirit's influence?

It is difficult for us to comprehend the lot of orphans in Biblical times. Orphans then may have faced the horror of being alone in a harsh, alien world. They may have become the prey of those who profited from selling children into slavery and other forms of degradation. If we were orphans in the spiritual sense, we would feel surrounded by hostile forces without any sense of contact with a strong and loving benefactor. The Holy Spirit helps us to be aware of our connection with a loving Father and a redeeming Savior, even though we are dwelling in "enemy territory." As spiritual orphans, we would be completely vulnerable to Satan's false teachings and temptations to immorality. With the Holy Spirit helping us we have wisdom and power to over come Satan's tactics.

3. How does Jesus manifest himself to us?

Some people read the New Testament and find in it nothing more than an interesting story. For them, Jesus of Nazareth is only a prominent religious leader of the past. But Christians read the same material and develop an ever-increasing intimacy with Him who is the focus of those writings. The difference is that Christians commit themselves to trusting Jesus, to loving Him, to following Him. In this way they open their hearts and minds, so that Jesus is able to fulfill His promise, "He that loveth me shall be loved by my Father, and I will love him, and will manifest myself to him" (John 14:21). Of course, some believers claim to have visions or other special revelations of Jesus. But these are not necessary, for Jesus is as real and personal to us who love Him, as though He were physically present among us. We can identify with Peter's statement: "Though you have not seen him, you love him; and even though you do not see him now, you believe in him and are filled with an inexpressible and glorious joy" (1 Peter 1:8, *New International Version*).

4. Jesus promised His peace to those who followed Him. What are some of the characteristics of this peace?

In an age in which people rely to a great extent on tranquilizers and sleeping pills in order to achieve physical and emotional calm, it is significant that Jesus was able to sleep soundly in a storm-tossed boat (Mark 4:35-41). Of course, there are times of stress in almost any person's life that could result in an occasional sleepless night. But the Christian should be able generally to claim the kind of sleep that Jesus did, the kind of which the psalmist spoke: "I lie down and sleep; I wake again, because the Lord sustains me" (Psalm 3:5, *New International Version*). Another characteristic of Jesus' peace is the fact that mistreatment by others could not destroy it. When Jesus was on trial, for example, He displayed a calmness that contrasted with the raging emotions of His enemies. Often, one harsh or critical comment from a fellow human being can virtually ruin our entire day. But with Jesus' peace, we can learn to ride those upsetting waves and maintain a more consistent serenity.

Spring Quarter, 1990

Theme: John Writes of Life, Light, and Love

Special Features

Lessons

Unit 1—John: The Gospel of Life and Light

Unit 2—Abiding in Love

Related Resources

The following publications are offered to give more detailed help for the subjects of study presented in the Spring Quarter. They may be purchased from your supplier. Prices are subject to change.

The Fourfold Gospel, by J. W. McGarvey and P. Y. Pendleton. Order #30-02884, $9.95.

Help! I've Got Problems, by Dean Dickinson. This book contains ideas and problem solutions for adult teachers and leaders. Order #14-03663, $1.95.

The Lord of Love, by LeRoy Lawson. Based on the Gospel of John, this book explains what love is and how to practice it. Order #11-39940, $2.95.

Love in Action, by Beth Holzbauer. Among many other helps, specific ideas for expressions of love are included. Order #11-39968, $3.95.

The Only Way, by Lewis Foster. Part two of a study of John's Gospel, with applications of significant spiritual concepts. Order #11-40048, $2.25.

Training for Service: A survey of the Bible, by Orrin Root, revised by Eleanor Daniel. Order #18-03211, $4.95.

Mar 4

Mar 11

Mar 18

Mar 25

Apr 1

Apr 8

Apr 15

Apr 22

Apr 29

May 6

May 13

May 20

May 27

An Aged Apostle Remembers

by John W. Wade

OLD AGE can be a lonely time, especially if one outlives his or her friends and family members. On occasion, the apostle John undoubtedly must have felt pangs of loneliness. His fellow apostles, with whom he had shared so many enlightening hours as they listened to Jesus' teaching, had all preceded him in death. We know little about John's family. His father, Zebedee, and his mother, Salome, had certainly died many years before; and John's brother, the apostle James, had been martyred by Herod Agrippa I in about A.D. 44. After the death of Jesus, John became responsible for the care of Mary, Jesus' mother, but she too must have passed from this earthly life some time before he wrote his epistle.

John certainly had many friends in the growing number of churches that stretched from Jerusalem to Rome and beyond. But new friends could not share the memories that his family and old friends could. And so John was left with his memories, memories that were quickened and sharpened by the power of the Holy Spirit. Some of those memories must have brought a twinge of remorse. For example, he may have remembered the selfish ambitions he and his brother, James, shared. As the followers of Jesus, they wanted to be sure that they would have prominent positions in His kingdom. They even enlisted the aid of their mother to plead their case with Jesus. But all their worldly ambitions had come crashing down that night at the supper in the upper room when Jesus had taken a basin of water and proceeded to wash the disciples' feet. The way to greatness was not through prominent positions but through humble service. Thoroughly chastened by the incident, John had given his life to unselfish service to others.

Other memories must have brought a smile to his lips, or even a chuckle. Perhaps he remembered on occasion the nickname Jesus had given to him and his brother James—*Boanerges.* "Sons of thunder" it meant, an appropriate title for these two impetuous and zealous followers of Jesus. Once when they had been traveling with Jesus through Samaria, the residents of a village refused to receive them. James and John, their wrath quickly aroused, wanted to call down fire from heaven to consume that unhospitable town. John could well afford to smile at that memory, for the life of the son of thunder had

been so dramatically changed that now he was called "the apostle of love."

A Loving Savior

If we had to select one word that best characterizes the lessons of this quarter, that word would be *love.* The first seven lessons of the quarter deal with aspects of the life of Jesus as recorded in the Gospel of John. These lessons conclude the study that was begun the previous quarter. The first lesson (based on John 15) is a part of Jesus' discourse with His disciples on the night in which He was betrayed. In this lesson, Jesus describes himself as a vine and His disciples as branches. Jesus emphasizes the importance of abiding in Him and bearing fruit.

Lesson 2 (John 16) deals with the subject of the Holy Spirit. While the intent of this lesson is not to describe all of the activities of the Holy Spirit, it does deal with some of His most important work. Jesus would soon be leaving His disciples and He was concerned that they might feel that He was abandoning them. To encourage them during their time of sorrow, the Spirit would come. Beyond this immediate mission of the Spirit, He would guide them into all truth. Within a short time, these men would be leaders of the newly-founded church. But they were only men, with many weaknesses. The Spirit would guide them as they preached the message of salvation to a dying world. More than that, the Spirit would also give them direction as they took pen to write the Scriptures.

In the third lesson (John 18), the drama of Jesus' trial and crucifixion begins to unfold. We see Him in the Garden as Judas betrays Him by leading the officers of the chief priests and Pharisees to His place of retreat. We see Him rebuke Peter for supposing that the kingdom of God could be advanced by the sword. Jesus' time has come, and He is ready to drink of the cup that God has prepared for Him.

The events recorded in lesson 4 (John 18) must have brought painful memories to John, for this lesson treats of Peter's denial of Jesus. We doubt that John was very critical of Peter's actions, for John was honest enough to realize that he himself might have been guilty of similar denials if he had been in Peter's situation. Even as he sorrowed, John could be thankful, for he knew that Peter had repented of his weakness and had been fully restored to God's grace.

Lesson 5 deals with Jesus' trial before Pilate (John 18). Among the many things that Jesus' trials reveal, two stand out: the hypocrisy of the religious leaders who brought false charges against him, and the cowardice of Pilate, who thought more of his own skin than he did of seeing that justice was done.

Lessons 6 and 7 deal with Jesus' death and resurrection. While we are quite familiar with the details of these events, yet these two lessons give us some insights into these events not found in the Synoptic Gospels. In teaching these two lessons, the teacher may want to call attention to those distinctive details.

Abiding in Love

The last six lessons of this quarter take us to the three epistles of John. The first five texts are selected from the book of 1 John, while the last lesson of the quarter is based on the short letters of 2 and 3 John.

Lesson 8 (1 John 1, 2) makes several important points. John begins this epistle by affirming his own testimony for the historicity of the incarnation. Apparently some heretics had been teaching that the Word, the Christ, had not really come in the flesh. John's testimony as an eyewitness exposes this kind of teaching as heresy. John further insists that talking about love is not enough. One's theology and one's life do not exist in two separate, watertight compartments. If we have fellowship with God, we must walk in the light. When we walk in the light, we can enjoy fellowship with God and also with other Christians who walk in the light.

In lesson 9 (1 John 2), John continues his warning against false teachers, whom he calls antichrists. Seemingly, these false teachers had been a part of the congregation, but when they were exposed, they had left the congregation. The point of this lesson is just as timely now as it was in the first century. False teachers seem to abound both within and without the church. Only constant vigilance can protect the flock against their ravages.

Lesson 10 (1 John 3) deals with some specific things that love involves. From the negative point of view, one who loves cannot at the same time hate. Cain is held up as a horrible example of what may happen when one hates his brother. John reminds us that one who hates his brother is just as guilty of murder as if he actually killed him. There is a positive side of love also. One who loves his brother will care for his needs.

Lesson 11 (1 John 4) deals with a perennial problem—fear. In every age man has to deal with this problem. The primitive savage lives in dread of the unknown; every shadow or unusual phenomenon forebodes danger. Civilized man in the twentieth century does not escape fear, either. He fears the known—the tremendous power of the unleashed atom that can vaporize a city in seconds. In every age, man has sought an antidote to fear: the primitive man hopes to find his amulets and rituals; the modern man in treaties and better defenses against atomic missiles. Both efforts have failed. John gives us the only answer: "There is no fear in love; but perfect love casteth out fear" (v. 18).

The theme of lesson 12 (1 John 5) is a victorious one: "This is the victory that overcometh the world, even our faith" (v. 4). One overcomes the world by believing that Jesus is the Son of God. John's message may seem narrow and exclusive in an age that prefers to blur distinctions and pretend that one set of ideas is as good as another. But John will have none of this. His formula is simple and precise. One who has the Son of God has life; one who does not have the Son does not have life.

The text for the final lesson of the quarter is both 2 and 3 John. The first point that John makes, drawn from 2 John, is that we must love one another. In 3 John, Gaius is commended because he has shown hospitality both to the brethren and to strangers. The example that Gaius set has obvious implications for all of us today.

"That Ye Might Believe"

In these four writings of John, the beloved apostle does not try to impress us with his scholarship. Nor do his writings have the poetic lilt of the psalms or some of the verses from Isaiah. His prose is simple and straightforward, and rarely do we have any question about what he is trying to communicate. While he does refute some of the false teachers who threatened the doctrinal integrity of the churches, his main purpose in writing is not to seek out heresies or defend the true faith. John's main purpose in writing is to lead his readers to faith in Jesus Christ. In the epistles (1 John 5:13) as well as in his Gospel account, he states that purpose clearly: "These are written, that ye might believe that Jesus is the Christ, the Son of God; and that believing ye might have life through his name" (John 20:31).

May you keep this thought ever before you as you come before your class this quarter. In an age when nothing seems secure, people are seeking something they can believe, an anchor they can hang on to as the swirling tides of worldy doubt and fear sweep about them. In these works of a man who lived nearly two thousand years ago, they can find the answer to their needs.

At the Cross

by Mark Krause

THE CROSS, that most Christian of symbols, has instant, worldwide identification with the cause of our Lord Jesus. Other Christian symbols (such as the fish or the dove) are not as quickly associated with Christianity by those outside the faith.

The symbol of the cross has been employed in many ways in the nearly two thousand years of Christian history.

Believers scratched crosses on the walls of catacombs and other secret meeting places. Worshipers prayed with arms outstretched to form a cross with their bodies. Christian architecture incorporated the cross in its designs, including the basic shape of many of the great European cathedrals. One cannot help but be impressed upon seeing the thousands of white crosses marking the final resting places of soldiers in military cemeteries.

Behind this remarkable symbol lies the greatest act of love the world has ever seen: the atoning death of Jesus Christ. The apostle Paul comments on this in Romans, saying, "But God shows his love for us in that while we were yet sinners Christ died for us" (5:8, *Revised Standard Version*). What an incredible thought! We are self-appointed enemies of God, and He still loves us! Paul gives us no reason for God's love; he merely makes the observation. Robert Harkness' hymn poses the questions, "Why should He love me so? Why should my Savior to Calvary go? Why should He love me so?" But no answer is given, because there is no reasonable answer. Because of rebellion in sin, we have no claim on the love of God. God is gracious and loving in spite of our sin, and that is a great mystery of the Christian faith.

Seven of this quarter's lessons will be based on the Gospel of John, culminating with John's account of Jesus' crucifixion and resurrection. John's chronicle of these events is unlike the other Gospels, yet the story is the same: it is a record of incredible love.

John, the Eyewitness

In several verses in the fourth Gospel, reference is made to "the disciple whom Jesus loved." Students of this Gospel have long identified that disciple as the apostle John, the author. In describing himself that way, John did not mean that Jesus loved him more than any of the other disciples. The designation indicated the great debt John felt to his Master. John meant to say that he, a witness of the wonders of Jesus' life, was overwhelmed by this fact: this Person loved me! Without a doubt, John's appreciation of this undeserved love permeated his preaching and teaching in the early church.

John was an intimate eyewitness of the crucifixion. When the mob seized Jesus in the Garden of Gethsemane, Peter and John followed, even into the courtyard of the high priest's house (John 18:15). There, perhaps, John heard the proceedings of the first of several trials Jesus had, a kangaroo court session led by Annas.

John stood with the women at the cross itself and received instruction from Jesus concerning the care of Jesus' mother, Mary (19:25-27). The fourth Gospel emphasizes that John was an eyewitness to the piercing of Jesus' side and that he heard the Roman soldiers' pronouncement of Jesus' death (19:33-35). There is no more qualified eyewitness to the crucifixion than the author of the fourth Gospel.

Crucifixion as a Theme in John

The careful reader of John will note that the idea of Jesus' coming death is introduced long before the final chapters. John does this by the use of several key ideas.

The Lamb of God

The introduction of the physical Jesus in the fourth Gospel comes from John the Baptizer. When he saw Jesus walking his way, John cried out "Behold, the Lamb of God, who takes away the sin of the world!" (1:29, *Revised Standard Version*). In Jewish religious thought of the first century, a lamb was a sacrificial lamb, offered for the sins of the people. Jesus was the ultimate and final sacrifice for sin. John intentionally makes this parallel in 19:36, when, in reporting that Jesus' legs were not broken during the crucifixion, he states that this was the fulfillment of Scripture. The prophecy he points to is that concerning the Passover lamb. (See Exodus 12:46; Numbers 9:12; Psalm 34:20.)

The Passover lamb was to be young and unblemished, killed in accordance with God's instructions. During the original Passover event, the blood of the young animal was smeared upon the doorposts of the Israelites' houses. This act protected those households from the final plague: death of the firstborn child. This was the last event before the liberation from Egyptian bondage of the Hebrew children.

The parallels between this and John's account of Jesus' death are too striking to be ignored. Jesus is the perfect lamb. His many trials prove not His guilt, but His innocence. His blood is smeared in Jerusalem in grisly torture and death. Jesus leads His followers through the Red Sea of death to liberation and to life eternal (John 11:25, 26).

Lifted Up

Three times in this Gospel Jesus says He would be "lifted up" (3:14; 8:28; 12:32). John clearly points out that this is a reference to the crucifixion (12:33). Notice what Jesus has to say as to the implications of this "lifting up."

First, the lifting up of Jesus on the cross is compared to the bronze serpent of Moses (3:14). This remarkable story is told in Numbers 21. The Israelites were being punished by God with a plague of poisonous snakes. Moses was instructed to make a bronze snake and to put it up on a pole. Anyone who looked at this towering serpent would be saved from certain death as a result of snakebite.

What did Jesus mean by this analogy? Simply that His being "lifted up" (crucifixion) would provide salvation for all who would look upon (believe in) Him.

Second, Jesus affirmed that the lifting up would make His identity clear (8:28). The Savior sent by God was not a ruthless conquering general or a clever political leader. He was much more than a brilliant teacher and religious guide. He was God's full expression of love for mankind. God loved us so much that He sent his Son to die!

Third, Jesus proclaimed that by being lifted up, He would draw all men to Him (12:32). What did He mean by this? Some understand this in terms of Christian preaching. If we lift Him up by communicating Him to the world, mankind will respond in faith to the gospel.

But there is more here than that. Jesus was undoubtedly talking about the impact of His death. He was looking ahead to the cruelest possible execution of the most innocent man who ever lived. The contrast is stark, yet inescapable. In Jesus' death on the cross, we see the utter inhumanity of mankind against the incomprehensible love of God. Such love is irresistible in an impersonal world starved for love, a harsh world needing a God of compassion. Such love goes beyond our wildest expectations and far beyond any rightful claims we might imagine that we have on God. Such love reaches across the centuries and draws us to God.

Lasting Results of the Crucifixion

Although it is outside the scope of the fourth Gospel, John's impression of the resurrected Christ in the book of Revelation is enlightening. In chapter 5, as Jesus (the Lamb) makes His dramatic appearance, John describes Him as "a lamb standing, as though it had been slain" (5:6 *Revised Standard Version*). From this we gain a startling glimpse into the permanent effects of the crucifixion. To be sure, Jesus is the triumphant, conquering Lamb of the book of Revelation, but the scars of His horrible death are still there. John points to this in His Gospel also, when he records that the risen Jesus appeared to the disciples and showed them the fresh scars of the nails and spear. (20:19-28).

Jesus gave himself so completely and so willingly to such unimaginable and undeserved suffering that He would never be quite the same again. While this may be difficult for us to comprehend, the personal implication for each of us is this: We are saved! God has provided a costly, yet permanent, means for our salvation!

The medieval monastic, Bernard of Clairvaux, was a deeply pious man whose love was passionately centered in God and Christ. He wrote many sermons based on the Song of Songs, because there he found a mystical expression of the love of God. When we consider the love of God, as expressed in the death of His Son on the cross, we are led with Bernard to say,

What language shall I borrow
  To thank thee, dearest friend,
For this Thy dying sorrow,
  Thy pity without end?
O make me Thine forever;
  And, should I fainting be,
Lord, let me never, never
  Outlive my love for Thee!

Answers to Quarterly Quiz

Lesson 1—1. false. 2. much fruit. **Lesson 2**—1. truth, truth. 2. joy. **Lesson 3**—1. false. 2. Caiaphas. **Lesson 4**—1. fire. 2. the cock crew. **Lesson 5**—1. fault. 2. Barabbas. **Lesson 6**—1. false. 2. one of the soldiers. 3. Joseph of Arimathea, Nicodemus. **Lesson 7**—1. the Jews. 2. Thomas. **Lesson 8**—1. darkness. 2. Jesus Christ. 3. commandments. **Lesson 9**— 1. liar. 2. ashamed. **Lesson 10**—1. we should love one another. 2. death, life. **Lesson 11**—1. true. 2. fear. 3. liar. **Lesson 12**—1. grievous. 2. liar. **Lesson 13**—1. truth. 2. true.

Abiding in Love

by Douglas Redford

A N ESSAY on the subject of love may appear to be covering an overworked, exhausted topic. Other issues await discussion and resolution by the body of Christ. Why give love additional space and attention?

Yet consider the situation of the apostle John when he penned the brief letters we call 1, 2, and 3 John. Writing near the end of the first century, the aged soldier of the cross stated that the topic of love was by no means a new one to his readers: "This is the message you heard *from the beginning:* We should love one another" (1 John 3:11, emphasis mine; compare John 2:7; 2 John 6).* John, however, did not view love as a subject that deserved to be placed on the back burner lest Christians become weary of it. The apostle regarded love (*agape*, to use the Greek term) as a burning issue when he wrote; the succeeding nineteen centuries of history have not quenched the fire.

Today we live, as did John, with a new century on the horizon. Many express concern about the church's readiness to enter the year 2000. New methods are being developed, studied, and tested to make the church the most effective instrument of evangelism possible. We are wise, however, not to neglect the "old commandment, which we too have heard from the beginning: "As I have loved you, so you must love one another. All men will know that you are my disciples if you love one another" (John 13:34b, 35).

The Condition of the World

One of the ironies of the 1980s is that in spite of the incredible means of communication at our disposal, American society is probably experiencing less genuine communication than ever before. We are surrounded with songs, sermons, and seminars about love and yet appear more confused about the subject every day.

This was certainly not always the case. When American society was essentially Biblical in its orientation, one could sense a spirit of concern and neighborliness even among unbelievers. Non-Christians came to the aid of friends in dire straits as readily as did Christians. In this regard, often the difference between the two groups was difficult to discern. But with the erosion of respect for Biblical values has come the erosion of consideration for others, which was one of the quiet but ever-dependable fruits of

such values. In its place have entered fear (1 John 4:18), isolation, and the all too common "silent agreement" by which people who have lived next to each other for years have never spoken to each other once. To paraphrase a statement from John Naisbitt's *Megatrends*, "We are drowning in a sea of communication but starving for love."

From a Christian perspective, there is a positive side to this dilemma, for it actually provides a bumper crop of opportunities for God's people to display genuine love in the midst of the counterfeits. We must be prepared to rescue the drowning and feed the starving.

The Compassion of the Savior

According to John, it is impossible to understand or experience authentic love apart from God. "Dear friends, let us love one another, for love comes from God. Everyone who loves has been born of God and knows God. Whoever does not love does not know God, because God is love" (1 John 4:7, 8).

But John goes one step further. Certainly God has demonstrated His love in a multitude of ways, and He continues to do so. John focuses on one specific, historical manifestation of God's love, without which *agape* can never be grasped. "This is how God showed his love among us: He sent his one and only Son into the world that we might live through him. This is love: not that we loved God, but that he loved us and sent his Son as an atoning sacrifice for our sins" (1 John 4:9, 10).

Thus, the epitome of love is not found in any of man's achievements, as noble as they may appear to be. *Agape*, as R. C. Trench observes, is "a word born within the bosom of revealed religion." Whatever else an individual believes about what God has done for him, without Jesus Christ he has not experienced the fullness of the Father's love for him. This is why the command to "love one another" cannot be separated from the command to "believe in the name of his Son, Jesus Christ" (1 John 3:23).

It is also why John in his writings exhibits such a passion for truth (3 John 4). The very idea that a person would declare that Jesus Christ did not come in human flesh is enough for him to be categorized as "the deceiver and the antichrist" (2 John 7). If such a basic truth is undercut, the love of Calvary is drained of its power and the church's message collapses. Indeed, there really is no reason for the church to continue.

The Commission of the Church

Beyond Our Walls

While John 3:16 capsulizes the love of God for His world, 1 John 3:16 teaches that Christians are the bridge by which the Father's love travels to a hurting world: "This is how we know what love is: Jesus Christ laid down his life for us. And we ought to lay down our lives for our brothers" (compare 1 John 4:11).

In his classic work, *My Utmost for His Highest,* Oswald Chambers makes this observation: "Jesus does not ask me to die for Him, but to lay down my life for him. . . . It is far easier to die than to lay down the life day in and day out with the sense of the high calling. We are not made for brilliant moments, but we have to walk in the light of them in ordinary ways."

With Chambers' interpretation, the idea of "laying down our lives" becomes applicable not only to martyrs or dedicated missionaries, but also to the "average Christian" whose every day can be "the Lord's day" and a powerful testimony marking him as a follower of Jesus. "If *anyone* has material possessions and sees his brother in need but has no pity on him, how can the love of God be in him?" (1 John 3:17, emphasis mine). All that is required is that the disciple of Jesus recognize a need and respond to it in a Christ-honoring way.

When Jesus spoke of the importance of love, He did so shortly after one of the most selfless acts of His ministry (John 13:34, 35). This was the washing of His disciples' feet. The most critical need facing the church today may not be new or updated tools and programs, but renewed Christians who are willing to take up the timeless tools of servanthood and help those who are in need. We should avoid entanglement in the moot question of whether the term *brothers* in 1 John 3:17 (and elsewhere) refers only to Christians. It is unmistakably clear from Jesus' Sermon on the Mount that the extension of love beyond "our own kind" distinguishes Christians from pagans (Matthew 5:46, 47).

Behind Our Walls

Can we expect to infiltrate the world with a message of love if this quality is missing in our church life? Hebrews 10:24, 25 states that one of the purposes of our gatherings is to "spur one another on toward love and good deeds." Sadly, this dimension of Christian fellowship is usually not given the attention it deserves. Frequently a congregation's witness to unbelievers is weakened, not by a serious doctrinal flaw, but by the failure to love another as Jesus commanded us. Often the problem lies in one of the aspects of love as defined by Paul in 1 Corinthians 13:4-8; that is, someone is not patient, not kind, is proud, is self-seeking, etc.

This condition is certainly not a new one, just as the commandment to love is not a new one. Indeed, such situations have troubled the church "from the beginning." John testified to the joys he experienced from the maturity and solidity of men such as Gaius (3 John 1-8) and Demetrius (v. 12). But his delight was tempered by the behavior of Diotrephes (vv. 9, 10).

It is possible that doctrinally, Diotrephes was as on target as John himself. His downfall was a very unlovely attitude, which unfortunately had become quite flagrant. Such a "frontal affront" could be dealt with only by a direct confrontation, for which John was preparing (v. 10). *Agape* demanded nothing less.

Amidst the recent wave of wrongdoing in the ranks of religious leaders, the case of Diotrephes is a timely one. Anyone in a leadership position may congratulate himself on having escaped the ruination caused by sexual misconduct or financial mismanagement. But Diotrephes' behavior and John's reaction show that one does not have to succumb to those particular temptations to be considered a dangerous religious leader. Diotrephes' passion for preeminence is still just as deadly when reproduced within any leader of any congregation.

Today the spirit of Diotrephes must be countered and overcome by the spirit of John, who himself provides a sterling example of abiding in love. Let us note that John by nature was not such a person. He and his brother James had been tagged as the "sons of thunder" by Jesus, and they demonstrated on a number of occasions how well they deserved such a label.

As he learned from Jesus, John's thunder gradually calmed. Standing at the foot of Calvary's cross, he saw the supreme demonstration of God's love for mankind. The fire that was kindled in him there burned brightly through the remainder of the first century. Even in his old age, his love for his Lord was as new as on that Galilean morning when he chose to leave his nets and follow the master.

May the church today be blessed with wise and saintly disciples, who like John refuse to "hang up" their towel and basin. May such persons provide the love and leadership so necessary to carry the church of Jesus into a new century of loyalty to the old commandment: "Love one another."

---

*Scripture quotations are from the *New International Version.*

Quarterly Quiz

The questions on this page may be used in several ways: as a pretest at the beginning of the quarter; as a review at the end of the quarter; or as a review after each lesson. The questions are based on the Scripture text of each lesson (King James Version).
Answers are on page 229

Lesson 1

1. Jesus said that His Father, as the husbandman, is interested only in removing fruitless branches from the vine. (T/F) *John 15:2*
2. Jesus said that His Father is glorified when His disciples bear _____ _____ . *John 15:8*

Lesson 2

1. Jesus told His disciples that the Spirit of _____ would guide them into all _____ . *John 16:13*
2. Jesus said the world would rejoice over His death, and His disciples would be sorrowful; but their sorrow would turn to _____ . *John 16:20*

Lesson 3

1. When the arresting party came to the Garden of Gethsemane, they called for Jesus to come out to them. (T/F) *John 18:3, 4*
2. The high priest who had stated that "it was expedient that one man should die for the people" was _____ . *John 18:14*

Lesson 4

1. Peter denied Jesus while he stood with the servants and officers around a _____ in the high priest's courtyard. *John 18:17, 18, 25-27*
2. After Peter denied Jesus the third time, what happened? *John 18:27*

Lesson 5

1. After interrogating Jesus, Pilate told the Jews assembled outside the judgment hall that he found no _____ in Him. *John 18:38*
2. The crowd demanded that Pilate release (Barnabas, Barsabas, Barabbas). *John 18:40*

Lesson 6

1. The soldiers broke Jesus' legs to hasten His death. (T/F) *John 19:33*
2. Who pierced Jesus' side, causing blood and water to come forth? *John 19:34*
3. What two men saw to the burial of Jesus' body? *John 19:38-42*

Lesson 7

1. When Jesus first appeared to the disciples, they were assembled behind closed doors "for fear of _____ _____ ." *John 20:19*
2. The first time Jesus appeared to the disciples after His resurrection, which disciple was absent? *John 20:24*

Lesson 8

1. "God is light, and in him is no _____ at all." *1 John 1:5*
2. Who does John say is our advocate with the Father? *1 John 2:1*
3. We know that we know God if we keep His _____ . *1 John 2:3*

Lesson 9

1. John asks, "Who is a _____ but he that denieth that Jesus is the Christ?" *1 John 2:22*
2. John urges Christians to abide in Christ, so that "when he shall appear, we may have confidence, and not be _____ before him at his coming." *1 John 2:28*

Lesson 10

1. What message did John say his readers had heard "from the beginning"? *1 John 3:11*
2. John said that because we love the brethren, we know we have passed from _____ unto _____ . *1 John 3:14*

Lesson 11

1. The presence of God's Spirit in us assures us that we dwell in God. (T/F) *1 John 4:13*
2. What is cast out by perfect love? *1 John 4:18*
3. If a person says, "I love God," and hates his brother, he is a _____ . *1 John 4:20*

Lesson 12

1. To love God is to keep His commandments, and His commandments are not (galling, grievous, difficult). *1 John 5:3*
2. The person who does not believe the record that God gave of His Son makes God a _____ . *1 John 5:10*

Lesson 13

1. John rejoiced greatly when he found that the children of the "elect lady" were walking in _____ . *2 John 4*
2. John praised Gaius for the hospitality he had shown to missionaries. (T/F) *3 John 5, 6*

When Love Abides

March 4
Lesson 1

LESSON SCRIPTURE: John 15:1-17.

PRINTED TEXT: John 15:1-17.

John 15:1-17

1 I am the true vine, and my Father is the husbandman.

2 Every branch in me that beareth not fruit he taketh away: and every branch that beareth fruit, he purgeth it, that it may bring forth more fruit.

3 Now ye are clean through the word which I have spoken unto you.

4 Abide in me, and I in you. As the branch cannot bear fruit of itself, except it abide in the vine; no more can ye, except ye abide in me.

5 I am the vine, ye are the branches. He that abideth in me, and I in him, the same bringeth forth much fruit; for without me ye can do nothing.

6 If a man abide not in me, he is cast forth as a branch, and is withered; and men gather them, and cast them into the fire, and they are burned.

7 If ye abide in me, and my words abide in you, ye shall ask what ye will, and it shall be done unto you.

8 Herein is my Father glorified, that ye bear much fruit; so shall ye be my disciples.

9 As the Father hath loved me, so have I loved you: continue ye in my love.

10 If ye keep my commandments, ye shall abide in my love; even as I have kept my Father's commandments, and abide in his love.

11 These things have I spoken unto you, that my joy might remain in you, and that your joy might be full.

12 This is my commandment, That ye love one another, as I have loved you.

13 Greater love hath no man than this, that a man lay down his life for his friends.

14 Ye are my friends, if ye do whatsoever I command you.

15 Henceforth I call you not servants; for the servant knoweth not what his lord doeth: but I have called you friends; for all things that I have heard of my Father I have made known unto you.

16 Ye have not chosen me, but I have chosen you, and ordained you, that ye should go and bring forth fruit, and that your fruit should remain; that whatsoever ye shall ask of the Father in my name, he may give it you.

17 These things I command you, that ye love one another.

GOLDEN TEXT: This is my commandment, That ye love one another, as I have loved you.—John 15:12.

John Writes of Life, Light, and Love
Unit 1: The Gospel of Life and Light
(John, Lessons 1-7)

Lesson Aims

As a result of studying this lesson the students should be able to:

1. Understand the setting in which Jesus gave the teaching of this lesson.

2. Desire to obey every commandment of Jesus.

3. State one way in which they will express Christian love to someone else this week.

Lesson Outline

INTRODUCTION
   A. Abiding in Him
   B. Lesson Background
I. THE VINE (John 15:1-4)
   A. The Husbandman (v. 1)
   B. Cleansing the Vine (vv. 2, 3)
       Prudent Pruning
   C. Abiding in Jesus (v. 4)
II. THE VINE AND BRANCHES (John 15:5-14)
   A. Vital Connection (v. 5)
   B. Disaster of a Broken Relationship (v. 6)
   C. Unlimited Potential (vv. 7, 8)
       Positive I.D.
   D. Abiding in Jesus' Love (vv. 9-14)
III. A NEW RELATIONSHIP (John 15:15-17)
   A. Servants Become Friends (v. 15)
   B. Jesus' Chosen Ones (v. 16)
   C. The Divine Commandment (v. 17)
CONCLUSION
   A. Dying or Living Heroes
   B. Let Us Pray
   C. Thought to Remember

Display visual 1 from the visuals packet to illustrate a principal teaching in the lesson text. It is shown on page 237.

Introduction

A. Abiding in Him

Several years ago my young son watched me as I set out several grape vines. Later, after the vines had begun to grow, I trimmed some of the branches back in order to train the vines onto wires. My son gathered some of the branches I cut and stuck them into the ground at the end of the garden. "This is my vineyard," he said.

A few days later he asked me to look at his vines. "They're all dead," he said, his voice reflecting his great disappointment. "What happened to them?" I had to explain to him that the vines that he had set out had been severed from the main vine and had no roots. Without roots to supply nourishment, they could not live.

We are like those trimmings. So long as we are attached to the vine—Jesus Christ—we will receive nourishment and we will grow. But if we allow ourselves to be severed from him, we lose our source of spiritual nourishment and we are doomed to shrivel and die.

B. Lesson Background

The teaching of Jesus, recorded in our lesson text was given shortly after His promise in last week's text that He would send the Holy Spirit to His disciples. The time was the night before Jesus was crucified. He had gathered the twelve in the upper room to share with them in eating the Passover. At some point, probably before the institution of the Lord's Supper, Jesus made it evident to Judas that He knew of his plot to betray Him. The traitor then took his leave of the group. Most scholars believe that Jesus' extended discourse with His apostles, recorded in John 15-17, occurred in the upper room. They see Jesus' description of himself as the true vine, which is included in today's lesson text, arising naturally from the fruit of the vine used in the Lord's Supper. Other scholars, however, feel that this part of Jesus' discussion occurred after they left the upper room and made their way to Gethsemane.

I. The Vine
(John 15:1-4)

A. The Husbandman (v. 1)

1. I am the true vine, and my Father is the husbandman.

In the Old Testament, Israel is sometimes depicted as a vine or a vineyard (See Psalm 80:8-18; Isaiah 5:1-7; Jeremiah 2:21; Ezekiel 15:1-6; and Hosea 10:1.) But consistently the figure is used of an undesirable vine. Perhaps in contrast to Israel, Jesus said, *I am the true vine.* To be of the children of Israel by race was not enough. One must be a branch of the true vine to find the real source of life and fruitfulness.

In this figure, God the Father is the *husbandman.* The word used here means one who tills the soil, or it may also mean a vinedresser. Both are appropriate in this situation, for one who keeps a vineyard must both till the soil and tend to the vines. In this figure, God the Father provides the nourishment and care that are necessary for growth. He also brings judgment as does the vinedresser who trims the vines.

B. Cleansing the Vine (vv. 2, 3)

2. Every branch in me that beareth not fruit he taketh away: and every branch that beareth fruit, he purgeth it, that it may bring forth more fruit.

Left to itself without attention, a vine produces a profusion of branches. Most of these branches bear no fruit, but they sap the strength of the vine. A wise vinedresser trims out these fruitless branches. While Jesus does not specify the fruit of which He is speaking, it is reasonable to identify it with those motives, attitudes, dispositions, words, and deeds that glorify God. See especially Galatians 5:22, 23. The Father recognizes those persons who bear no spiritual fruit and rejects them.

The vinedresser's work is not completed when the fruitless branches are removed. He will even trim and shape the fruitbearing branches so that they may bear more and better fruit. For the Christian this refining process is continued (see Hebrews 12:5-11).

PRUDENT PRUNING

Our church was blessed recently with a new member whose gift is horticulture. Not only does he possess a "green thumb," he is suspected to be the Green Giant! At least his skills with green-and-growing things are gigantic. And, the best part is, Ben is generously and cheerfully giving himself to the ministry of beautifying our church grounds.

One project that Ben undertook, however, puzzled me. I arrived at the church building one day to discover that the shrubs by the entrance had been severely cut back. Nothing remained but brown-barked branches, obviously shortened with a saw—very unattractive. Oh no, I thought. Ben has gotten carried away with his caretaking! Why would he destroy all the beautiful foliage on those shrubs?

In just a few weeks I saw the beneficial results of the process called "pruning." The shrubs are now fuller with green than ever before, shaped nicely by Ben's skillful hands.

Prudent pruning promotes production. If your soul seems stripped of beauty and excitement by the boredom of routine living, trust the Vinedresser. God can make your life "like a tree planted by streams of water, which yields its fruit in season and whose leaf does not wither" (Psalm 1:3, *New International Version*).

—R. W. B.

3. Now ye are clean through the word which I have spoken unto you.

The disciples to whom Jesus spoke had already been subjected to some pruning. For three years they had sat under His teaching, which had removed some of their selfishness and pride and worldly aspirations. The principles of His word would continue to change them, enabling them to produce more and better fruit. Just as the vinedresser's work must go on month after month and year after year, so the process of Christian growth to maturity is an ongoing one.

C. Abiding in Jesus (v. 4)

4. Abide in me, and I in you. As the branch cannot bear fruit of itself, except it abide in the vine; no more can ye, except ye abide in me.

Abiding in Christ means to remain in a saving relationship with Him. One cannot gain salvation on his own; it must be through the redemptive work of Jesus Christ. Our relationship with Christ is a mutual one. As we abide in Him, He will also abide in us.

It is obvious that a branch cannot bear fruit if it is separated from the vine. Neither can a person bear fruit for God when separated from Christ. In order to abide in Christ, one must be obedient to His commandments.

II. The Vine and Branches (John 15:5-14)

A. Vital Connection (v. 5)

5. I am the vine, ye are the branches. He that abideth in me, and I in him, the same bringeth forth much fruit; for without me ye can do nothing.

Jesus repeated the thought of verse 1—that He is the vine. Then He stated plainly what was implied in verses 2-4: His followers are the branches. A branch by itself is powerless to produce fruit. But if it remains connected to the vine, it is capable of bearing much fruit. We know this to be true, even if we know little of the process by which the vine utilizes soil, water, air, and sunlight to produce grapes.

Even so, our abiding in Christ provides what is needed for our growth as Christians. The Scriptures indicate in a general way how this process works, yet with our finite minds we

VISUALS FOR THESE LESSONS

The *Adult Visuals/Learning Resources* packet contains classroom-size visuals designed for use with the lessons in the Spring Quarter. The packet is available from your supplier. Order no. ST 392.

cannot understand all that is involved in this relationship. But that need not trouble us. We do not have to know all of what is involved in plant growth to enjoy the grapes that a vine produces. Nor do we need to know all of the mysteries of Christ's working in and through us to be able to enjoy the blessed fruit that it brings.

B. Disaster of a Broken Relationship (v. 6)

6. If a man abide not in me, he is cast forth as a branch, and is withered; and men gather them, and cast them into the fire, and they are burned.

Jesus next stated the consequences for those who fail to abide in Him. Such persons become fruitless; and just as a fruitless branch is cut from the vine, so will fruitless persons be severed from Christ. Such a fruitless condition most often comes as the result of many small deviations from the way of Christ over a period of time. Jesus' warning about the final disposition of those who do not abide in Him ought to cause us to take frequent inventory of our lives.

C. Unlimited Potential (vv. 7, 8)

7. If ye abide in me, and my words abide in you, ye shall ask what ye will, and it shall be done unto you.

We abide in Christ when we allow His words to abide in us. Paul echoes this when he urges the Colossians, "Let the word of Christ dwell in you richly" (Colossians 3:16). This suggests that our relationship with Christ is not just a subjective feeling but is based on vital doctrines that we receive and obey.

Jesus promised to hear and answer the petitions of those who abide in Him. Those who abide in Him live and walk in His will. Thus their petitions always reflect His will. Jesus did not promise to indulge our every whim. Nothing could be more disastrous for us than to have every wish fulfilled, whenever we wanted it. Such power would fan our greed and gluttony and focus our attention upon worldly things.

8. Herein is my Father glorified, that ye bear much fruit; so shall ye be my disciples.

God is glorified through the work of His Son (John 13:31, 32). He is also glorified through the work of the disciples of His Son. There is, perhaps, a progression in the level of fruit bearing. Verse 2 speaks of the vine that bears fruit and then bears more fruit as a result of being purged. Here we read that God is glorified when Jesus' disciples bear *much* fruit.

So shall ye be my disciples. In the bearing of fruit, in the accomplishment of work that gives glory to the Father, we show that we are disciples of the Lord who said, "My meat is to do the will of him that sent me, and to finish his work" (John 4:34).

Positive I.D.

Supplying proper identification for check cashing is an aggravation. "May I see your driver's license and a major credit card, please?" says the cashier. And we grudgingly take from our wallet the I.D.s, which are subsequently examined, registered, and approved—if one computer or another doesn't betray us by slandering our credit rating. Even automatic check-cashing cards will occasionally humiliate an honest and solvent citizen. One slip of a digit, your number doesn't compute, and you face rejection. Technology has its own unique indignities!

But strangers need to know who we are, if they are to trust us with their money and/or credit—and particularly if they are to trust us with the responsibility of leading them to "the way, the truth, and the life." The unsaved have a right to require from Christians some positive identification, some way of knowing that we are followers of Christ, as we say we are.

Jesus said that we are known by our "fruits," by our values, attitudes, and life-style. We show ourselves to be His disciples when our lives "bear much fruit," fruit of the Spirit (Galatians 5:22, 23). These qualities positively identify one as a "Jesus person." —R. W. B.

D. Abiding in Jesus' Love (vv. 9-14)

At this point in His discourse, Jesus turned from the lesson He was giving them in the figure of the vine and the branches to express His love for them.

9. As the Father hath loved me, so have I loved you: continue ye in my love.

We are not capable of understanding all that is involved in the Father's love for the Son. Even if our minds could comprehend this, our language would not have the words to express it. But the disciples had no trouble understanding the point that Jesus was making. The Father loved the Son, and in the same manner the Son shed that love upon the disciples. Jesus then encouraged them to remain in that love. Of course, Jesus would continue to love them no matter what they did, but if they strayed away from that love, they would miss the blessings that such love can bring. Judas, for example, had that very night made the decision to turn away from Jesus' love, and the consequences were dire indeed.

10. If ye keep my commandments, ye shall abide in my love; even as I have kept my Father's commandments, and abide in his love.

Once more Jesus turned to His relationship with the Father to explain His relationship with them. Throughout His life and His ministry, our Lord had been obedient to the Father. On at least two occasions, God had acknowledged this obedience by expressing His pleasure in Jesus (Matthew 3:17; 17:5). Jesus' example of obedience was a forceful one for the disciples, for they had been with Him for three years and they knew what kind of life He had lived.

11. These things have I spoken unto you, that my joy might remain in you, and that your joy might be full.

The obedience of the disciples would bring joy to Jesus. It would also bring joy to them. Those who reject Christianity because they think that it is without joy simply do not understand what Christianity is all about. God wants us to enjoy ourselves, but He knows that we can never experience that full joy so long as we rebel against Him. Our joy comes in complete self-surrender and love toward God. This surrender is rewarded in the fullness of joy that comes through being sure of our relationship with God, seeing the fruits of our service to Him, and understanding the glory that comes in God.

12. This is my commandment, That ye love one another, as I have loved you.

In verse 10 Jesus spoke of "commandments"; now He speaks of but one commandment. He is not contradicting himself, for the commandment to love is all-encompassing; every other commandment is based upon it. The commandment to love, however, poses a problem for us. How can we be commanded to love anyone? After all, one's emotions cannot be controlled with the flip of a switch or on command. But our problem comes because we think of love primarily as an emotion. The love spoken of here is *agape* love, which has been defined as "intelligent good will toward another person or toward God." Viewed in this light, we can see how one can be commanded to exercise intelligent good will toward other persons.

Jesus is the vine. Abide in Him in order to bear fruit.

visual 1

13. Greater love hath no man than this, that a man lay down his life for his friends.

Jesus did not leave His commandment hanging in midair as some kind of a lovely but impractical theory. He made it clear just exactly how that commandment could best be embodied. The greatest love that one can show to a friend is to die for him. Within hours Jesus would demonstrate an even greater love—He would die, not just for His friends, but for His enemies as well.

14. Ye are my friends, if ye do whatsoever I command you.

To be called a friend of God was a mark of rare distinction, a distinction that few ever enjoyed. Abraham was called a friend of God (James 2:23), as was Moses (Exodus 33:11). True friendship involves a sharing of common goals and values. Jesus made this clear when He pointed out that disciples are His friends if they live lives of obedience to Him.

III. A New Relationship (John 15:15-17)

A. Servants Become Friends (v. 15)

15. Henceforth I call you not servants; for the servant knoweth not what his lord doeth: but I have called you friends; for all things that I have heard of my Father I have made known unto you.

Jesus now announced to His disciples a new relationship between Him and them that had begun to develop during His ministry. On one occasion before, Jesus had referred to them as His friends (Luke 12:4). The disciples may not have caught the full implication of this earlier statement, and so Jesus gave them further insights into this new relationship.

A servant or slave—for that is what the word means—is not invited to share in the decisions that his lord may make. His only obligation is to carry out the orders of his master without questioning them. Friends are different. They share confidences with one another, and often make plans together. Jesus had been sharing with the disciples what he had been sent to earth to do, thus proving His friendship for them. Though Jesus' friends, the disciples would still be His servants, and He their Master. But they would serve Him from a higher motive.

B. Jesus' Chosen Ones (v. 16)

16. Ye have not chosen me, but I have chosen you, and ordained you, that ye should go and bring forth fruit, and that your fruit should remain; that whatsoever ye shall ask of the Father in my name, he may give it you.

Ordinarily friends choose each other because they share mutual interests or compatible personalities. But this was not the case with Jesus and His disciples. Even though the disciples had accepted His invitation to follow Him, it was He who had actually made the choice. The eleven who heard Jesus' words could think back to the occasion when Jesus had called them and many others to become His students. Then as the months had passed and they had grown spiritually, He had called them into a closer relationship, designating them apostles (Matthew 10:1-4; Mark 3:13-19; Luke 6:12-16). Although Jesus had chosen them to be His special disciples, yet they were free to reject that offer at any time. Even as Jesus spoke these words, Judas was exercising that freedom to betray Him.

And ordained you. In calling the eleven to be His apostles, He had set them apart for a very special mission. They were to be His chosen leaders in the church, which He was soon to establish. On Pentecost, only a few weeks hence, they would begin to function in this special capacity. *That ye should go.* When Jesus spoke these words, the disciples little realized their full implication. Only after the resurrection, when Jesus had given them the Great Commission, did they realize that their going meant going into the whole world.

Bring forth fruit. Jesus called and ordained the disciples, not just for the joy that their friendship might bring, but that they might bring forth fruit. *Fruit* here has reference to the souls they were to win for the Father. They would bear fruit by carrying the good news to those who had not heard it. The beginning of this mission must yet await Jesus' death, burial, and resurrection, for without this conclusion to His ministry there is no gospel. When the disciples did preach the gospel, starting at Pentecost, men and women by the thousands responded.

Repeating the idea expressed in verse 7, Jesus assured them that whatever they asked of the Father in His name would be given them. In verse 7, the condition for granting their petitions was that they abide in Him. Here it is bringing forth fruit, which amounts to the same thing. One cannot abide in Him without bringing forth fruit.

C. The Divine Commandment (v. 17)

17. These things I command you, that ye love one another.

Jesus concluded this portion of His discourse by repeating the idea expressed in verse 12. The Greek verb suggests the idea of "keeping on loving one another." In review of the jealousy and quarreling they had exhibited earlier in the evening, the commandment seems most appropriate. And in view of the persecution they would soon be facing (see verses 18-25), this commandment would be much needed.

Conclusion

A. Dying or Living Heroes

We read in the newspaper of one who sacrifices his own life to save another. We rightly applaud such heroic action. But it may be more heroic to live for another than to die for him. What about a wife who endures years of physical and mental abuse living with an alcoholic husband in the hope that he can be saved? Or a mother who without special recognition works to hold her family together and bring them up in the Christian faith? Or a husband who cares for an invalid wife, and is breadwinner, homemaker, and nurse to his family?

The heroes in the headlines gain their badge of courage in one brief moment. We do well to hold them up as examples of honorable bravery, but quiet heroes among us are also worthy of honor. Examples of both kinds of sacrificial love are needed in our "me" generation, when so many care only about themselves.

B. Let Us Pray

Dear Father, help us to realize that we can live and bear fruit only as we abide in Christ, the true vine. We pray also for your purging, painful though it might be, that we might bear even more fruit. Amen.

C. Thought to Remember

The vine can live without an individual branch, but that branch soon withers and dies without the vine.

Home Daily Bible Readings

Monday, Feb. 26—"I Am the True Vine" (John 15:1-7)

Tuesday, Feb. 27—A Call to Bear the Fruit of Love (John 15:8-17)

Wednesday, Feb. 28—A Call to Unity (Ephesians 4:1-7)

Thursday, Mar. 1—A Call to Renewal (Ephesians 4:17-24)

Friday, Mar. 2—A Call to Love and Holiness (Ephesians 4:25—5:2)

Saturday, Mar. 3—Many Gifts, One Spirit (1 Corinthians 12:4-11)

Sunday, Mar. 4—Many Members, One Body (1 Corinthians 12:12-26)

Learning by Doing

This page contains an alternate lesson plan emphasizing learning activities. Classes desiring such student involvement will find these suggestions helpful.

Learning Goals

This lesson should enable your students to:

1. List the promises, the commands, and the warnings set forth in John 15:1-17.

2. Summarize the relationship between Jesus and His believers that is taught in this text.

3. Choose a specific spiritual growth step under one of the following headings: Prayer; Bible reading; Love; Relationship with Jesus.

Into the Lesson

Bring a vining houseplant, such as an ivy, to class and display it prominently. Begin your session by talking with students about it.

Cut a leaf or a branch off the plant. Ask, "What's going to happen to this branch, now that it's removed from the vine?" (It will die!) "What role does the vine play in the health of the branch?" (The branch can't live without it!)

Say, "In today's text Jesus compares himself to a vine, us to the branches, and God to the vinedresser. As we study the text, we'll see the significance of this picture."

Into the Word

Provide worksheets with the following six headings, or write them on the chalkboard for students to copy onto blank paper:

Who Jesus is and what He does
Who God is and what He does
Who the disciples are and what they should do
Promises
Commands
Warnings

Assign each of the headings to a different section of the class. As today's Scripture is read out loud, students are to listen for phrases that belong under their assigned headings. They should jot down the phrases.

Read the Scripture out loud two or three times. Or record the text on a cassette before class, and play the tape at this time. Rotate the assigned headings so that students are listening for something new with each reading of the Scripture.

After you've done this, let students tell you what they've written under each heading. Their answers should look something like this:

Who Jesus is and what He does
Vine (vv. 1, 5)
Loves His disciples (v. 9)

Calls His disciples His friends (v. 15)
Chose His disciples and expects them to bear fruit (v. 16)

Who God is and what He does
Father (vv. 1, 8, 9)
Vinedresser (v. 1)
Cuts off fruitless branches and prunes fruit-bearing branches (v. 2)

Who the disciples are and what they should do
Remain—abide—in Christ (v. 4)
Branches (v. 5)
Obey Christ's commands (vv. 10, 14)
Love each other (vv. 12, 17)
Friends of Jesus (vv. 14, 15)
Bear fruit (vv. 5, 8, 16)
Ask of the Father in Jesus' name (v. 16)

Promises
Abide in Jesus, and He will abide in you (v. 4)
Abide in Jesus, and you'll bear fruit for Him (vv. 4, 5)
Abide in Jesus, and Your requests will be granted (v. 6)
Obey Christ's commands, and you'll remain in His love (v. 10)
You are Christ's friends, if you do what He commands (v. 14)

Commands
Remain—abide—in Christ (vv. 4, 9)
Obey Christ's commands (v. 10)
Love each other as Christ has loved you (vv. 12, 17)

Warnings
Apart from Christ you can do nothing (v. 5)
If you do not abide in Christ, you will be like a branch that is burned in the fire (v. 6)

Into Life

Discuss the following with students:

1. What does this passage say about prayer? How can verses 7 and 16 be true?

2. What does this passage say about Bible reading?

3. What does this passage say about love?

4. Write a sentence describing what a Christian's relationship with Jesus and God should be.

Display four flash cards to the class: Prayer; Bible reading; Love; Relationship. Ask, "In which of these areas could you make spiritual progress this week? Is there some specific step you could take?" Ask for volunteers to respond.

Let's Talk It Over

*The questions on this page are designed to encourage review of the lesson
Scriptures and to promote discussion of the lesson by the class. The answers
provided are only discussion starters. Let your class talk it over from there.*

1. The vine is the source of life, energy, fulfillment, and character for the branches. What are some false "vines" that persons get attached to today?

The following are points of reference that many persons allow to determine the kind of fruit they will bear: (1) tradition—some allow tradition to have more impact upon them than Jesus' teachings; (2) relationships—others permit their relationships with friends, family, clubs, etc. to affect their actions and reactions more than Jesus; (3) security—still others allow the security of position, possessions, or prestige to determine how they live.

2. The kind of fruit a vine produces is always determined by what is inside the vine. What are the characteristics inside the Vine—Jesus—that should be seen in the fruit we bear?

Jesus was innovative. He was gentle. He forgave. His outreach included the upper-uppers (Nicodemus) and the lower-lowers (the woman at the well). He had compassion for the temporary physical needs of people. He developed friendships. He did lowly services (washed feet). He made decisions for the benefit of others, not for self (the cross). He was courageous and spoke the truth.

3. Which of the above characteristics are most needed in the church today?

Forgiveness—is it possible that we have not learned how to let a person's past be his past? Lowly services—is it possible that we get caught up in doing the "important things" and neglect some of the less spectacular ministries to people, such as meeting special needs of single parents? Are we creative and innovative in our church's programming? Is our outreach into the community what it should and could be? Are the upper-uppers and the lower-lowers included? Are we brave enough to stand up and be counted for Scriptural principles when moral issues face our communities?

4. Pruning a vine cuts away excesses that drain its energy, and results in the vine's greater vitality and productivity. What are some possible areas in which our lives need pruning?

Perhaps we need to prune away the tendency to fill every idle moment with something to do, which would enable us to have more quiet time with the Lord. Perhaps we need to prune away the habit of saying something on every issue, so we can begin to listen to others more. Perhaps we need to prune away the workaholic syndrome, so we can have time to enjoy people more. Perhaps we need to prune away our pet opinions that prevent us from allowing others to express their ideas.

5. Jesus said that if we keep His commandments, we will abide in His love. What is the relationship between keeping Jesus' commandments and abiding in His love?

Whenever we keep Jesus' commandments we never hurt other people; and if we abide in His love, we will not hurt others, for real love does not do harm to others. That's why Jesus taught that loving God and one's fellowman were the two great commandments upon which all of the law and the prophets were built (Matthew 22:36-40; see also Romans 13:8-10).

6. Jesus spoke about abiding in love and having full joy. Discuss times in which your joy was heightened by acts of love.

Doesn't it happen as mothers begin to care for their newborn babies? Doesn't it happen at Christmas time when out of love we sacrificially give to others? Doesn't it happen when we are set free because out of love we forgive someone who has hurt us? Doesn't it happen when we know that we have intentionally shared attitudes or activities that have promoted happiness in others?

7. Jesus spoke about His friendship with His apostles. What can we do to strengthen the bonds of friendship in the church?

We can listen more and talk less; we can be more transparent and thus let others know we trust them; we can create space in our relationships, so that others can have friends besides us; we can allow others to have opinions without trying to force ours upon them; we can forgive; we can apologize; we can quit keeping score; we can hold confidences—never gossip; we can help make other persons feel important.

Guided by the Spirit of Truth

LESSON SCRIPTURE: John 16.

PRINTED TEXT: John 16:12-24.

John 16:12-24

12 I have yet many things to say unto you, but ye cannot bear them now.

13 Howbeit when he, the Spirit of truth, is come, he will guide you into all truth: for he shall not speak of himself; but whatsoever he shall hear, that shall he speak: and he will show you things to come.

14 He shall glorify me: for he shall receive of mine, and shall show it unto you.

15 All things that the Father hath are mine: therefore said I, that he shall take of mine, and shall show it unto you.

16 A little while, and ye shall not see me: and again, a little while, and ye shall see me, because I go to the Father.

17 Then said some of his disciples among themselves, What is this that he saith unto us, A little while, and ye shall not see me: and again, a little while, and ye shall see me: and, Because I go to the Father?

18 They said therefore, What is this that he saith, A little while? we cannot tell what he saith.

19 Now Jesus knew that they were desirous to ask him, and said unto them, Do ye inquire among yourselves of that I said, A little while, and ye shall not see me: and again, a little while, and ye shall see me?

20 Verily, verily, I say unto you, That ye shall weep and lament, but the world shall rejoice; and ye shall be sorrowful, but your sorrow shall be turned into joy.

21 A woman when she is in travail hath sorrow, because her hour is come: but as soon as she is delivered of the child, she remembereth no more the anguish, for joy that a man is born into the world.

22 And ye now therefore have sorrow: but I will see you again, and your heart shall rejoice, and your joy no man taketh from you.

23 And in that day ye shall ask me nothing. Verily, verily, I say unto you, Whatsoever ye shall ask the Father in my name, he will give it you.

24 Hitherto have ye asked nothing in my name: ask, and ye shall receive, that your joy may be full.

GOLDEN TEXT: When . . . the Spirit of truth, is come, he will guide you into all truth.
—John 16:13

John Writes of Life, Light, and Love

Unit 1: The Gospel of Life and Light
(John, Lessons 1-7)

Lesson Aims

This lesson should help students to:

1. Understand that Jesus promised to send the Holy Spirit to guide the disciples into new truths.

2. See that Jesus sometimes spoke to His disciples in veiled language in order to challenge them.

3. Find strength for life's problems by trusting in Jesus.

Lesson Outline

INTRODUCTION
    A. Called to Be Beside Another
    B. Lesson Background
I. THE SPIRIT'S COMING (John 16:12-15)
    A. To Guide Into All Truth (vv. 12, 13)
    B. To Glorify Christ (vv. 14, 15)
II. JESUS' DEPARTURE AND RETURN (John 16:16-24)
    A. The Disciples Perplexed (vv. 16-18)
       Trust Me
    B. Grief Followed by Joy (vv. 19-22)
    C. New Strength Promised (vv. 23, 24)
       Name Dropping?
CONCLUSION
    A. Into All Truth
    B. The Real Security
    C. Let Us Pray
    D. Thought to Remember

Visual 2 in the visuals packet illustrates the thoughts under the first major point in the lesson outline. The visual is shown on page 244.

Introduction

A. Called to Be Beside Another

Visiting the United States House of Representatives when a sharp debate is being waged on the floor is an enlightening experience. The Speaker presides over these debates. Even though he is a man of wide experience, he often has a difficult task keeping the debate proceeding properly. Sitting beside him is an expert in parliamentary procedure. At times, the Speaker may turn to him for advice or information. On other occasions, the expert will arise and whisper something in the Speaker's ear. As he observes the debate, he attempts to anticipate any problems that may arise and informs the Speaker to prevent difficulties.

In a similar way, the Holy Spirit worked in the lives of the disciples. Several times in John's Gospel the Holy Spirit is called *Comforter*, which translates the Greek word that means "one who is called beside a person" to assist him. Just as the Speaker is expected to rely upon his own knowledge and experience, so Jesus expected His disciples to use their knowledge and experience to make decisions regarding the life of the church, soon to be established. But Jesus knew at times they would face situations beyond their ability to handle. Then the Holy Spirit would provide the guidance.

B. Lesson Background

For several weeks, we have studied Jesus' discourse with His disciples on the night before His arrest and crucifixion. This lesson deals with another portion of that discourse.

In last week's lesson (John 15:1-17), Jesus referred to himself as the vine and to His disciples as branches. The closing verses of John 15 contain Jesus' warning that His disciples must expect persecution from the world. Even as the world would persecute Jesus, the Master, it would also persecute the disciples, His servants. This warning continues into chapter 16. But Jesus assured them that in their suffering they would not be left alone. He would send the Holy Spirit, the Comforter, to stand beside them and strengthen them through their troubles. Before the Comforter would come, it was necessary for Christ to leave them. When the comforter would come, He would reprove the world of sin, righteousness, and judgment.

I. The Spirit's Coming (John 16:12-15)

A. To Guide Into All Truth (vv. 12, 13)

12. I have yet many things to say unto you, but ye cannot bear them now.

For three years Jesus had taught the disciples. He had revealed to them many new truths and he had enlarged their understanding of many truths they had learned from their childhood up. But they had much more to learn. Learning involves not only the acquisition of information; it also involves the changing of attitudes. It is usually easier to learn facts than it is to change attitudes. The attitude of jealousy and personal ambition that the disciples had displayed in the upper room indicated that they had not understood Jesus' teaching.

Jesus knew that it takes time for a person to change his basic attitudes. That is the reason that He was willing to give them more time and to send the Holy Spirit to assist them. As teachers, we should also keep this fact in mind. At times we become impatient when a person doesn't learn as readily or change his behavior as quickly as we think he should.

13. Howbeit when he, the Spirit of truth, is come, he will guide you into all truth: for he shall not speak of himself; but whatsoever he shall hear, that shall he speak: and he will show you things to come.

The Greek word for *Spirit* is neuter, but the pronoun *he* referring to the Spirit is masculine, indicating the personality of the Spirit. We are not told the exact methods that the Spirit would use to reveal God's truth. As the New Testament revelation is unfolded, we see that He used several modes to bring truth to the disciples. We note that this revelation was not a mechanical process; but rather the disciples would be led into the truth, indicating that they were actively involved in the process. They were not to be merely computers into which data was processed and from which this same data might be retrieved later. In the process of revelation, human personality was never cancelled out.

Into all truth. The disciples would be led into all the truth necessary to establish the church and to show men and women the way of salvation. The first example of this new revelation was seen on the Day of Pentecost. This promise of the Spirit's guidance was given only to those disciples who were specially chosen to be the instruments through whom Christ would establish His church and guide it in its early years. There is no basis in this passage for persons living in a later age to claim this special blessing of the Spirit. Some claim to have received new revelations through the Holy Spirit. When these new revelations contradict what the inspired writers recorded in the Scriptures, we may safely conclude that their claims are false.

The Spirit *shall not speak of himself.* The Spirit would not speak on His own authority but would speak about the things that He would hear. Jesus spoke in similar terms when He said that He could of His "own self do nothing" (John 5:30). On another occasion He said, "I have not spoken of myself; but the Father which sent me, he gave me a commandment, what I should say, and what I should speak" (John 12:49).

He will show you things to come. These things, no doubt, would pertain to the structure and life of the church, which was soon to be established. But there is no reason to doubt that the Spirit

would also reveal events that were to come in the more distant future, even of the last things. Evidence of this is seen in 2 Peter 3:3-13 and again in the entire book of Revelation, written by John.

B. To Glorify Christ (vv. 14, 15)

14. He shall glorify me: for he shall receive of mine, and shall show it unto you.

Jesus, by His work while He was on earth, glorified the Father (John 17:4). In the same way, the Spirit through His work would glorify the Son. Among the most important works of the Holy Spirit would be bringing further revelation about the Son. That work continues as we reflect on the Spirit-inspired Word and are led into deeper understanding of Christ and His mission. *For he shall receive of mine.* The Holy Spirit would not be the source of the message He would bring; He would deliver what He received of the Son.

15. All things that the Father hath are mine: therefore said I, that he shall take of mine, and shall show it unto you.

This verse stands as further evidence of the essential unity of the Father and the Son. Specifically in this situation, that unity is expressed in the Son's mission unto the world. His life, His sufferings, His death, and His resurrection were all a part of God's plan for the redemption of the human race. The Holy Spirit would help the disciples, and all succeeding generations, to understand that.

II. Jesus' Departure and Return (John 16:16-24)

A. The Disciples Perplexed (vv. 16-18)

16. A little while, and ye shall not see me: and again, a little while, and ye shall see me, because I go to the Father.

Jesus spoke in regard to His coming crucifixion, burial, and resurrection. On three other occasions in the months preceding, Jesus had told His disciples that He would be killed and would rise again (see Matthew 16:21, 22; 17:22, 23; 20:17-19). Yet the disciples were so blinded by their own ideas about what the Messianic kingdom should be that they could not understand what He was talking about.

The latter part of this verse, *because I go to the Father,* is not found in several ancient manuscripts and thus is omitted from most modern translations.

17, 18. Then said some of his disciples among themselves, What is this that he saith unto us, A little while, and ye shall not see me: and again, a little while, and ye shall see me:

and, Because I go to the Father? They said therefore, What is this that he saith, A little while? we cannot tell what he saith.

In *a little while,* actually in just a few hours, He would be delivered up to His persecutors and crucified. From Friday afternoon until Sunday morning He would be out of their sight in the tomb. Then they would see Him again following the resurrection.

Although the disciples did not understand what Jesus was talking about, they were afraid to come right out and ask Him. Two things that Jesus said may have bothered them. They may have been concerned about the matter of *time— a little while.* How long was a little while—an hour, a day, a week? Nothing that Jesus had said seemed to offer even a hint. The other thing that puzzled them was His statement that they would not see Him and then they would see Him again. This reference to His disappearance and reappearance mystified them.

Because I go to the Father. Even though these words may not properly belong in verse 16, Jesus had uttered them previously in verse 10, and so they were on the disciples' minds. Earlier in the evening Jesus had said that He was going to the Father's house (John 14:2). They learned that there were many mansions in the Father's house, that Jesus was going there to prepare a place for them, and that they could go there to be with Him. Thomas had raised a question about where that house was and how they were to get there (John 14:5). Jesus then had indicated that the way to the Father was through Him.

TRUST ME

A father says good-bye to his small son: "I'm going to fly to Chicago for a business conference. I'll be there before you and Mom get back home from the airport. In fact, if the plane is on schedule, I'll arrive before I leave, because Chicago is in a different time zone."

The child is mystified. "Daddy, what do you mean, you'll get there before you leave?"

"Don't worry, Son. You wouldn't understand if I explained it to you. *Trust me;* I'll be back home tomorrow night."

The boy is satisfied with that, content with the promise of his father's return. He does trust his dad, even though he doesn't understand everything he says, or even why his father must leave.

The first disciples could not comprehend all that Jesus told them. He used ambiguous language because much of what He wanted to tell them was more than they could bear (v. 12). It was as if Jesus said to them, "Though you don't

understand me, *trust me;* I must leave you, but I shall return."

We today who are His disciples don't understand all that Jesus said, either. But we trust Him, and He has promised to come again. We are at peace, because in "a little while" we shall understand all the mysteries of this life and the next.

—R. W. B.

B. Grief Followed by Joy (vv. 19-22)

19. Now Jesus knew that they were desirous to ask him, and said unto them, Do ye inquire among yourselves of that I said, A little while, and ye shall not see me: and again, a little while, and ye shall see me?

Of course, Jesus knew what the disciples were whispering about among themselves. Realizing that these questions arose because they were disturbed and even depressed by His words, He sought to relieve some of their doubt.

20. Verily, verily, I say unto you, That ye shall weep and lament, but the world shall rejoice; and ye shall be sorrowful, but your sorrow shall be turned into joy.

Verily, verily I say unto you. With these words, Jesus impressed upon them the solemnity of what He was going to tell them. Shortly they would be in deep sorrow, a sorrow marked by weeping and lamenting. Of course, Jesus was speaking about their response to His crucifixion, which was only a few hours away. In contrast to the disciples, the world would rejoice, supposing that it had won a complete and final victory over Him.

But the disciples' sorrow would be short lived, for death could not claim victory over Him. Released from the bonds of death, He would rise again to bring joy to His followers (Matthew 28:8; John 20:20).

21. A woman when she is in travail hath sorrow, because her hour is come: but as soon as she is delivered of the child, she remembereth no more the anguish, for joy that a man is born into the world.

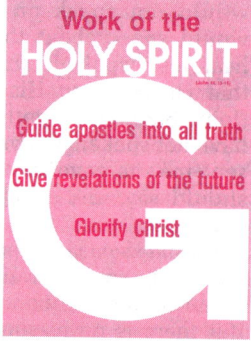

Work of the HOLY SPIRIT

Guide apostles into all truth

Give revelations of the future

Glorify Christ

visual 2

Jesus illustrated His point by using the example of a woman in childbirth. The labor pains are intense, but once the child has been born, the pains are forgotten in the joy of knowing that *a man is born into the world.* The word here translated *man* is really the word for mankind or the human race. A mother rejoices whether a boy or a girl is born.

22. And ye now therefore have sorrow: but I will see you again, and your heart shall rejoice, and your joy no man taketh from you.

Jesus reassured them that He would see them again, and when that happened, they would rejoice. At this time the disciples were sorrowful over Jesus' imminent departure (John 14:1, 27; 16:6). But all that changed when Jesus appeared among them on that first resurrection day. Some scholars think Jesus had reference to His activity in the church after Pentecost or perhaps even to His return in the final judgment. But these views seem a bit strained in the context that clearly points to the resurrection.

Many joys in this life come quickly and pass just as quickly. But the joy that Jesus promised was permanent; it could not be taken away. He did not indicate that they would never know pain or sorrow, but that tragedies in this life could never destroy the joy that He gave because it was grounded in eternity.

C. New Strength Promised (vv. 23, 24)

23. And in that day ye shall ask me nothing. Verily, verily, I say unto you, Whatsoever ye shall ask the Father in my name, he will give it you.

In that day. This expression refers to that age that would follow the resurrection.

Ye shall ask me nothing. The Greek word here translated *ask* usually means to ask a question, and that seems to be the sense in which Jesus used the word here. During His ministry, the disciples had often asked him questions. In the new age, they would no longer direct their questions to Him, for He would have returned to the Father. Instead, the Holy Spirit would be with them, leading them into all truth so that they would not need to ask any questions.

Verily, verily. As in verse 20, Jesus used this expression to impress upon the disciples the solemnity of His words that were to follow. *Whatsoever ye shall ask the Father.* Here the verb translated *ask* means to ask for or request something from someone. It is a word that is often used of prayer. Because this request is directed to the Father, it quite obviously does refer to prayer. *In my name.* The disciples were not given a blank check to pray for anything that they might desire. Rather, their requests were to be within the

framework of their relationship to Jesus. While this did, of course, limit the things for which they could pray, it also gave them a new privilege and authority in their prayers.

24. Hitherto have ye asked nothing in my name: ask, and ye shall receive, that your joy may be full.

The disciples had been encouraged to pray to the Father before (see Matthew 6:9). But up until this time they had never been invited to pray in Jesus' name. Jesus now urged them to ask in order that they might receive. This was necessary if they were to know the full joy that He had promised (v. 22). So often we do not experience this joy because we do not make requests for the things in His name that will insure that joy. In a similar vein, James wrote, "Ye have not, because ye ask not" (4:2). How tragic that the door to the Father's storehouse of blessings remains locked to us because we are not willing to use the key our Lord has given us to open it.

NAME DROPPING?

"It's not *what* you know that counts; it's *who* you know!" A case can be made for that cynical sentiment. Letters of reference often seem to carry more weight of influence than resumes that are crowded with educational credentials and work experience. Bureaucratic "red tape" can nearly always be cut if one borrows "scissors" from the right person. Sometimes the mere dropping of a name can open doors.

In the military, and in almost every other life situation, "the system" requires certain protocol for making requests and for filing appeals and grievances. Unwritten rules seem to exist, whereby "getting action" happens more quickly when requisitions are sponsored by someone whose name or title carries clout.

Though Jesus never suggested that God's favor can be secured by political manipulation, He taught that our requests should be brought to the Father in His name. Christ is our divine and perfect advocate. Friends may go to bat for us, but Jesus went to the cross for us. Requests made in His name are given top priority, according to God's will.   —R. W. B.

Conclusion

A. Into All Truth

Absolute certainty is a rare commodity. Even modern scientists are reluctant to claim that they have achieved absolute truth in any field. The so-called laws of science are but way stations on the road to truth. Scientists know that these laws are likely to be modified or even rejected by further research.

Jesus promised His disciples that when the Holy Spirit came He would guide the disciples "into all truth." Obviously, Jesus did not intend to say that the Spirit would guide the disciples into all the truths of science or history or engineering. Man is able to discover these truths on his own. The Holy Spirit, on the other hand, would bring those truths that man could not discover by himself—that is, those truths that deal with human redemption. No one can find his way to Heaven on his own. We must rely upon the map and compass that the Holy Spirit has provided in order to find our way to our eternal home.

We need to keep in mind that Jesus' promise to send the Holy Spirit to lead His followers into all the truth necessary for salvation was given to the apostles and the apostles alone. Once the Holy Spirit had led them in the founding of the church and in writing the New Testament Scriptures, this specific work of revelation was done. While the Holy Spirit continues to work in the world in many other different ways, we have no need for new or additional Scriptures.

From time to time across the centuries, men and women have arisen claiming that they have some new revelation from God. Such claims need to be evaluated in the light of the Bible and strongly rejected when they contradict the plain teachings of Scripture. The inspired writers, led by the Spirit, revealed God's plan for human redemption that was adequate and complete in the first century. There is certainly no reason to suppose that God changed His mind and/or His plan at any time since then. In the twentieth century, as in the first, man is a sinner who can be saved only through the blood of Jesus Christ. Any plan of salvation that is less than this is not enough, and any plan that requires more than this is too much.

B. The Real Security

Some time ago I had to make a trip to a large city in the East. When I arrived at the motel where I had made reservations, I thought it a bit unusual that the parking lot was surrounded by a high chain link fence topped by barbed wire. My concern grew when I was stopped at the entrance to the parking lot by a guard who demanded to see my reservation before he would let me enter. Then when I went to my room, there were three locks on the door with prominent signs urging the occupant to lock all three locks.

I must confess that the guarded parking lot and the locks on the door did not make me feel secure. Indeed, they had quite the opposite effect, and I slept rather fitfully that night. When I

Home Daily Bible Readings

Monday, Mar. 5—God Promises the Spirit (Joel 2:23-29)
Tuesday, Mar. 6—We Will Not Suffer Alone (Matthew 10:16-25)
Wednesday, Mar. 7—Jesus Promises the Spirit (John 15:18-27)
Thursday, Mar. 8—The Work of the Spirit (John 16:5-15)
Friday, Mar. 9—Jesus Promises Peace (John 16:25-33)
Saturday, Mar. 10—The Spirit Is Our Witness (Romans 8:11-17)
Sunday, Mar. 11—First Fruits of the Spirit (Romans 8:18-27)

---

checked out the next day, I asked the clerk why there were three locks on the door. He replied, "Mister, if you lived around here, you wouldn't ask a question like that!" I can assure you that I was glad that I didn't have to spend another night there.

What's the point of relating this incident? It illustrates how foolish it is to trust in things, whether they be locks or nuclear missiles, to bring security. It is ironic that as we multiply them, we often multiply our anxiety. In today's text, Jesus addressed the issue of security. In verse 22, He told His disciples that they would soon have joy, a joy that came from trusting in Him, a joy that no one could take from them. In the closing verse of this chapter, Jesus made it quite clear that the disciples could expect trials in this world—"in the world ye shall have tribulation." But as painful as this would be, they need not be overwhelmed. He then gave the reason for this assurance—"Be of good cheer; I have overcome the world."

C. Let Us Pray

Dear Heavenly Father, we thank you that You sent the Holy Spirit to guide the disciples into all truth. We further thank You that truth has been preserved for us in the Scriptures. Give us the wisdom to study the Scriptures and to apply these truths to our lives so that we might know the joy that You have promised to those who have placed their trust in You. In Jesus' name we pray, amen.

D. Thought to Remember

Jesus has promised us that by trusting in Him we can know a joy that passes understanding, that thrives in the midst of afflictions, and that cannot be taken away from us.

Learning by Doing

This page contains an alternate lesson plan emphasizing learning activities. Classes desiring such student involvement will find these suggestions helpful.

Learning Goals

After this lesson students should be able to:

1. List the assurances in John 16:12-24 that Jesus gave to comfort the disciples.

2. Decide what assurance these truths can bring to believers today.

3. Choose one personal insecurity to trust more fully to God.

Into the Lesson

Write the following letters on the chalkboard before the students arrive:

C U S T Y I E R

Ask class members in groups of four to try unscrambling the letters. When each group thinks it has successfully unscrambled the word, they should open an envelope containing a sheet on which you've written the following: *Congratulations! The word is* security.

1. Ask each person in your group to share the following: Something that gave me a great sense of security as a child. Each person should spend no more than thirty seconds answering.

2. How do people in our society seek security?

A. As a group, quickly list as many answers to this question as you can.

B. After you feel your list is complete, mark the three items on the list that are sought most often by people you know.

C. Discuss the items you've marked. Is security actually found in these things?

After about eight minutes, let the small groups share with the whole class. You needn't spend much time with number 1. But take at least enough time to hear the top three items from each group's list under number 2.

Into the Word

Use the "Lesson Background" section to give the setting for this lesson.

Tell students, "Today's text, which is a part of Jesus' discourse to His disciples, contains both 'good news' and 'bad news' for them. As you read today's Scripture, decide which statements would seem good to the disciples, and which would seem bad to them."

Ask students to use the printed text in the student book. Or they may mark their own Bibles or a copy of the text that you have duplicated before class. Beside each verse in the text, they should mark either "G" ("good news"),

"B" ("bad news"), or "G & B" ("good" and "bad news"). Students may work individually or in the already-formed groups.

After a few minutes, let students report. Their findings will resemble this list: *Good News:* verses 13-15, 23, 24; *Bad News:* verses 12, 17, 18; *Good and Bad News:* verses 16, 19-22.

Ask students to help you make a list on the chalkboard of the good news to the disciples that is contained in this passage. Items include:

1. The Holy Spirit would guide them into all truth (vv. 13-15).

2. After Christ's death would come His resurrection (vv. 16, 19).

3. Their grief at His death would turn to joy at His resurrection (v. 20).

4. No one would be able to take away their joy (v. 22).

5. Their requests would be granted by the Father (vv. 23, 24).

Discuss with students: "How does each of these statements lead to good news for believers today?" List the basic principles of your discussion on the chalkboard. Your list will look something like this:

1. The Bible is true.

2. Christ really *is* the Son of God.

3. Because He lives, we can live also.

4. He is the author of joy that is untouchable by the world.

5. Our prayers are answered by God.

Into Life

Tell students, "At the beginning of today's class session, we discussed the ways many people seek security. We saw how inadequate many of these resources are. Let's briefly think about insecurity. What are some concerns that may make people feel insecure today?"

Write this list beside the five principles above. After some discussion and listing, ask students, "How do the statements from our list of principles speak to these insecurities?"

Ask class members, "Have we mentioned something that causes you to feel insecure? How do the truths of today's lesson bring you reassurance or new confidence?"

Conclude your class session with sentence prayers. Challenge members to thank God for the provisions of security that have been listed. Their prayers should be personal and specific.

Let's Talk It Over

The questions on this page are designed to encourage review of the lesson Scriptures and to promote discussion of the lesson by the class. The answers provided are only discussion starters. Let your class talk it over from there.

1. Jesus talked with His disciples about his imminent death. What is there about death that causes us to be reluctant to face it?

While we want to go to Heaven, we also want to stay on this earth as long as possible to see our children and grandchildren grow up. We also want to be of service to God here and continue to grow in Christlikeness. Since we who are still alive obviously have not yet experienced death, it remains an unknown to us; and that reality haunts us.

2. What does it mean to make requests of the Father "in the name of Jesus"?

Our requests are not made "in the name of Jesus" simply by including these words in our petition. We ask in Jesus' name when we ask for the kinds of things He would ask for. We ask in His name as His representatives. We ask in His name when we ask in a manner characteristic of Jesus—unselfishly, for the benefit of others, for God's glory and for the enlargement of God's kingdom on earth.

3. Jesus knew that His disciples would have sorrow when He died. Why does death of a loved one bring sorrow to us, even though we know that there will be a resurrection and we will be reunited with them?

Sorrow comes with separation. In families where love prevails, there is sorrow mixed with joy when children leave home for college or the military service. When one of our children marries and enters into that very natural separation from us, there is sorrow mixed with joy. Whenever we visit our loved ones whom we haven't seen for quite a while, there is some sorrow when we must leave to return home. Sorrowing over the death of a loved one does not mean we do not have faith; rather, it is an indication of the preciousness of the relationship that has been broken.

4. Part of the joy the disciples would experience after Jesus left would be the presence of the Comforter (v. 7). How is the Holy Spirit a Comforter to us, and how does His presence bring us joy?

The Holy Spirit is the presence of the Father and the Son abiding in us (John 14). He helps us to overcome the world and its temptations (1 John 4:4). Through His presence we know we are in Christ, not temporarily but eternally; He leads us to life and peace; He intercedes for us when we don't know how to pray (Romans 8). If we follow His leading, as manifested through Jesus' specially chosen disciples, we know we will be in the truth (John 16:13). What a comfort to have such a compassionate strength and guide within! What joy we can derive from being victorious in our daily lives because of the Holy Spirit's work within us!

5. Jesus told the disciples that they would be sorrowful, but that their sorrow would be turned into joy. Does joy sometimes come *after* pain or suffering in life? Give examples.

Jesus himself mentioned the example of childbirth (v. 21). The joy of giving birth to a child causes a woman to forget the anguish she experienced. Sometimes after a husband and wife have gone through a difficult period in their marriage, their relationship is stronger and happier than before. Experiencing physical suffering or hardship helps us appreciate good health that much more.

6. What did Jesus mean when He said that his disciples would have joy that no man could take from them? How can we have that kind of joy?

Jesus was referring specifically to the joy the disciples would experience when, three days following His crucifixion, He would show himself alive to them. When they saw that He had been raised from the dead, they would begin to understand that Jesus had complete power over death. Then His statements about going to the Father and preparing a place for them there would have tremendous meaning. They would realize that if evil men should persecute and even kill them, Christ's power would raise them to eternal life also. This understanding would bring them overwhelming joy, a joy that evil men could not in any way take from them. We who are Christ's have the same hope of life after death, and we share these disciples' joy. It is an internal, abiding, eternal joy that rests not on outward circumstances or situations, but rather on what Christ has done for us.

Jesus Is Betrayed and Arrested

LESSON SCRIPTURE: John 11:47-53; 18:1-14.

PRINTED TEXT: John 18:1-14.

John 18:1-14

1 When Jesus had spoken these words, he went forth with his disciples over the brook Cedron, where was a garden, into the which he entered, and his disciples.

2 And Judas also, which betrayed him, knew the place: for Jesus ofttimes resorted thither with his disciples.

3 Judas then, having received a band of men and officers from the chief priests and Pharisees, cometh thither with lanterns and torches and weapons.

4 Jesus therefore, knowing all things that should come upon him, went forth, and said unto them, Whom seek ye?

5 They answered him, Jesus of Nazareth. Jesus saith unto them, I am he. And Judas also, which betrayed him, stood with them.

6 As soon then as he had said unto them, I am he, they went backward, and fell to the ground.

7 Then asked he them again, Whom seek ye? And they said, Jesus of Nazareth.

8 Jesus answered, I have told you that I am he: if therefore ye seek me, let these go their way:

9 That the saying might be fulfilled, which he spake, Of them which thou gavest me have I lost none.

10 Then Simon Peter having a sword drew it, and smote the high priest's servant, and cut off his right ear. The servant's name was Malchus.

11 Then said Jesus unto Peter, Put up thy sword into the sheath: the cup which my Father hath given me, shall I not drink it?

12 Then the band and the captain and officers of the Jews took Jesus, and bound him,

13 And led him away to Annas first; for he was father-in-law to Caiaphas, which was the high priest that same year.

14 Now Caiaphas was he, which gave counsel to the Jews, that it was expedient that one man should die for the people.

GOLDEN TEXT: No man taketh [my life] from me, but I lay it down of myself.
—John 10:18.

Lesson Aims

This lesson should cause each student to:

1. Understand that Jesus accepted the cross as a part of God's plan for Him.

2. Feel revulsion at the act of treachery that led to Jesus' betrayal.

3. Resist personal temptations to betray Jesus.

Lesson Outline

INTRODUCTION
    A. Sellout
    B. Lesson Background
I. JUDAS' ARMED APPROACH (John 18:1-3)
    A. Retirement to an Olive Grove (v. 1)
    B. Judas and the Officers (vv. 2, 3)
II. JESUS' SOLITARY STAND (John 18:4-9)
    A. Jesus' Question (v. 4)
      Premeditated Sacrifice
    B. Reply and Response (vv. 5, 6)
    C. The Disciples Protected (vv. 7-9)
III. PETER'S RASH REACTION (John 18:10, 11)
    A. Peter's Defense (v. 10)
    B. Jesus' Response (v. 11)
      Defending God
IV. HEARING BEFORE THE HIGH PRIEST (John 18:12-14)
    A. Jesus Arrested (v. 12)
    B. Jesus Taken to Annas (v. 13)
    C. Caiaphas Identified (v. 14)
CONCLUSION
    A. All We Are Traitors
    B. Let Us Pray
    C. Thought to Remember

Visual 3 in the visuals packet illustrates the scene in the Bible text for this lesson. The visual is shown on page 252.

Introduction

A. Sellout

The name *Judas* signifies a traitor. Theologians and psychologists have argued about Judas' motives in betraying Jesus. Some have maintained that he acted out of jealousy, feeling that he had been forced to play second fiddle to some of the other disciples. Others have felt that

Judas betrayed Jesus to cover up his stealing from the funds that he kept for the disciples (John 12:6). Others have ingeniously attempted to exonerate Judas, saying that he acted in the hope of forcing Jesus to confront the religious power structure and establish His kingdom immediately. This theory depicts Judas as a man with good motives whose only mistake was in using bad judgment! But Judas' sordid behavior gives the lie to this theory.

We are appalled to think that one of the disciples who lived and worked with Jesus for three years—three years in which he saw Jesus perform miracles and acts of loving concern—could then sell out His Master to His enemies. But we need not travel back two thousand years to witness such behavior. All we have to do is look around. On every hand are persons who betray Jesus or turn their backs upon Him. For that matter, we don't even have to look around to find examples of this kind of betrayal. All we have to do is look into our own hearts. What we see is likely to be humbling.

B. Lesson Background

In the previous two lessons, we have considered portions of Jesus' farewell discourse with His disciples. This discourse was followed by His great intercessory prayer for them, which is recorded in John 17. Whether this prayer took place in the upper room or at some point along the way to the Garden of Gethsemane is not completely clear. If the upper room was in the southwestern part of Jerusalem, as tradition holds, then it is likely that the route to the garden would have taken them through the temple area. If this was the case, the temple area would have been an appropriate place for Jesus to have uttered this prayer. After finishing His prayer, He then would have passed through the gate in the eastern wall of the city that led down to the Brook Kidron.

I. Judas' Armed Approach (John 18:1-3)

A. Retirement to an Olive Grove (v. 1)

1. When Jesus had spoken these words, he went forth with his disciples over the brook Cedron, where was a garden, into the which he entered, and his disciples.

These words refers back to the intercessory prayer in chapter 17. The road from the gate in the eastern wall of the city descends steeply down to the *brook Cedron* (most modern versions spell it "Kidron"). The valley of the Kidron separated the city from the Mount of Olives to the east. Water runs through the valley only during the winter, and then only after a heavy shower. Crossing the Kidron, Jesus and His disciples entered a *garden*, or "grove" or "orchard" as some translate it. Both Matthew and Mark tell us that Jesus and the disciples went to the Mount of Olives when they left the upper room. They also identify the place where they went as Gethsemane, which means "oil press" (Matthew 26:30, 36; Mark 14:26, 32). From this information, it is logical to suppose that it was to an olive grove on the Mount of Olives that Jesus led His disciples.

B. Judas and the Officers (vv. 2, 3)

2. And Judas also, which betrayed him, knew the place: for Jesus ofttimes resorted thither with his disciples.

Perhaps the owner of this garden was a follower of Jesus and had given Him and His disciples permission to use it as a camping site on their visits to Jerusalem. It may be that they had stayed there for at least a couple of nights during this week (see Luke 21:37; 22:39). Judas would have been with the group on the occasions when they had used the garden, and so he could have easily led the soldiers and temple guards there on this night.

3. Judas then, having received a band of men and officers from the chief priests and Pharisees, cometh thither with lanterns and torches and weapons.

The word here for *band* means a Roman cohort, a body of six hundred soldiers. It is not likely that the entire cohort would have been used, since a small detachment would have been adequate for the job. But still, the band must have been rather large. In order to use Roman soldiers for this operation, the religious leaders would have received the permission of Pilate, the Roman governor. This shows that Pilate had some knowledge of Jesus before He stood before him (see Matthew 28:18, 19).

The Romans soldiers were accompanied by *officers from the chief priests and Pharisees*. These were temple guards sent by the Jewish authorities. They were armed—carrying swords and clubs—and lighting their way with lanterns.

How to Say It

ANNAS. *An*-nus.
CAIAPHAS. *Kay*-uh-fus or *Kye*-uh-fus.
CEDRON. *See*-drun.
GETHSEMANE. Geth-*sem*-uh-nee.
KIDRON. *Kid*-ron.
MALCHUS. *Mal*-kus.

The lanterns were covered oil lamps, and the torches were rods or poles with an oil-soaked rag wrapped around them, which would burn when ignited. It strikes us as rather ironic that under the light of a full moon they would need lanterns and torches to find the Light of the world.

II. Jesus' Solitary Stand (John 18:4-9)

A. Jesus' Question (v. 4)

4. Jesus therefore, knowing all things that should come upon him, went forth, and said unto them, Whom seek ye?

John does not tell us about Jesus' agony in the garden. That agony was now past, and it had been replaced with calm resolution. Those who came to take Jesus probably expected Him to be hiding in some darkened corner of the garden. Little did they anticipate that He would come out to meet them. The way from the garden to the cross Jesus knew very well, even before He traveled it. With divine foreknowledge, He could see the trials, the scourging, the final, excruciating agony of the cross. Rather than fleeing or taking cover in the garden, He *went forth* from the relative darkness among the trees and stepped into the open to meet His captors.

Although it is mentioned in all three of the Synoptic Gospels (Matthew 26:49; Mark 14:45; Luke 22:47), John does not tell about Judas' betrayal of Jesus with a kiss. Apparently this occurred before Jesus identified himself to them (v. 6). After Judas had kissed Jesus as a part of the prearranged signal, Jesus then asked whom they sought.

PREMEDITATED SACRIFICE

The crew of *Challenger*, the ill-fated shuttle craft that exploded just seconds after lift-off, risked and lost their lives to bring America closer to the conquest of outer space.

Countless soldiers have risked and lost their lives to defend freedom around the world.

Police officers and firemen risk their lives regularly to protect citizens from crime and disaster. Many of them lose their lives in the line of duty.

Some of God's best ambassadors have risked their lives to take the gospel to hostile hearers, and more than a few have died while fulfilling their mission.

We admire and honor those who have risked and lost their lives while serving others.

To Jesus, however, belongs the greater glory. He not only *risked* His life for us, He *gave* it. Others realize that their work and service might jeopardize their personal welfare and existence.

Jesus knew that His supreme sacrifice was a *certainty.* Knowing full well the cross lay before Him, He set His course for Calvary. He determined to fulfill His mission, and He knew the price He would have to pay. "Greater love hath no man than this. . . ."   —R. W. B.

B. Reply and Response (vv. 5, 6)

5. They answered him, Jesus of Nazareth. Jesus saith unto them, I am he. And Judas also, which betrayed him, stood with them.

Several in the crowd spoke up. Not only did they mention His name, they also included His hometown in order to make sure of His identity. It is even possible that the commander of the soldiers had written orders specifically identifying Jesus as a man from Nazareth.

Briefly and to the point, Jesus identified himself: *I am he.* His coming out to meet them and His forthright identification of himself thus rendered Judas' kiss unnecessary. John then tells us that Judas was standing with the mob. That he was standing with the crowd is but further evidence that Satan now had complete control over his life. The crowd that one stands with often affords an excellent clue as to who controls his life.

6. As soon then as he had said unto them, I am he, they went backward, and fell to the ground.

Were the soldiers simply startled by Jesus' stepping forward so boldly to identify himself? This certainly would be unusual behavior for one being arrested. Or did Jesus in His action exhibit His deity in such an impressive fashion that the men were overwhelmed? The latter seems more appropriate. We know that Jesus could have called twelve legions of angels to protect himself (Matthew 26:53). He chose instead to reveal but a glimpse of the vast power He possessed.

C. The Disciples Protected (vv. 7-9)

7. Then asked he them again, Whom seek ye? And they said, Jesus of Nazareth.

Sprawling backward from Jesus, the troops had completely lost their dignity. But Jesus remained completely calm and poised as He repeated His question. Persons who have placed their lives completely in the hands of God can face difficult situations, even death, with serenity and calm assurance.

8. Jesus answered, I have told you that I am he: if therefore ye seek me, let these go their way.

Jesus reminded them that He had already answered their question. Perhaps Jesus had them repeat the answer so that there would be no question that He, and He alone, was the object of their search. Once this was impressed upon them, Jesus then requested that they allow the disciples to go. Even though He knew that He faced death in a few hours, His immediate concern was for His disciples' welfare, not His own.

9. That the saying might be fulfilled, which he spake, Of them which thou gavest me have I lost none.

Jesus spoke similar words about His disciples on more than one occasion, and we can't be certain which occasion John refers to. (See John 6:39; 10:28; or 17:12.) These verses primarily refer to the disciples' spiritual, rather than to their physical, welfare. Yet, if they had been seized by the mob and subjected to torture, they may very well have suffered a severe spiritual setback. Later on, they did suffer physical affliction at the hands of the authorities without compromising their faith. But Jesus knew that they were not yet ready to face such an ordeal. And does not God deal with us in the same way, not allowing us to be tempted beyond our capacity? (See 1 Corinthians 10:13.)

III. Peter's Rash Reaction (John 18:10, 11)

A. Peter's Defense (v. 10)

10. Then Simon Peter having a sword drew it, and smote the high priest's servant, and cut off his right ear. The servant's name was Malchus.

This incident is mentioned in all four of the Gospel accounts (Matthew 26:51, 52; Mark 14:47; and Luke 22:50, 51). Only John mentions both Peter and the servant, Malchus, by name. It may be that both were still alive when the other Gospels were written and their names were omitted to avoid embarrassment. Just a short time before, the disciples had two swords among them (Luke 22:38). Apparently Peter had one of them. It was probably a short sword, the kind used by soldiers. Peter's action here fits his

visual 3

reputation for being impetuous. Further, he had boasted earlier in the evening that he would stand beside Jesus even if all the others abandoned Him (Matthew 26:33; Luke 22:33). Now he had to make good on his boast.

Peter's action seems extremely rash in view of the odds against him. But people who act emotionally often don't look at the odds logically. Peter's action was foolish for another reason. Jesus had asked the officers to let the disciples go, but Peter's attack could have put them in jeopardy.

B. Jesus' Response (v. 11)

11. Then said Jesus unto Peter, Put up thy sword into the sheath: the cup which my Father hath given me, shall I not drink it?

It is likely that Jesus first ordered Peter to put up his sword and then turned to restore the ear of Malchus. Jesus could have given several good reasons for not resorting to violence at this time. The most obvious reason is that the disciples were hopelessly outnumbered and would have quickly been overwhelmed. A second reason is the truism recorded in Matthew 26:52: "All they that take the sword shall perish with the sword." Incidents of terrorism in our times illustrate how true this maxim is. Each act of violence seems only to inspire other acts of violence that lead to an escalating spiral of destruction and suffering.

But the real reason for Jesus' refusal to allow Peter to defend Him was that such action would have thwarted His whole purpose for coming to earth. Only a short time before, Jesus had prayed that the cup, that is, His suffering on the cross, might pass away. Yet God's plan for human redemption could be carried out only through the death of Jesus, and so He was unswervingly resolved to drink that cup to the very dregs, no matter how bitter they might be. Even after three years of Jesus' teaching, Peter had not really grasped the fact that Jesus' death was at the very heart of the gospel.

DEFENDING GOD

Though not always one hundred percent successful, Secret Service personnel are appointed the task of protecting our president and other government VIPs from anyone who would harm them in any way. When an attempt was made on the life of former President Reagan, the quick response of the Secret Service men at his side clearly thwarted an assassination. Such protection is important for the powerful, the rich, and the famous. Dignitaries and celebrities often need someone to come to their rescue and/or defense.

Jesus, however, did not need bodyguards. And He certainly did not desire that His friends resort to physical violence to protect or defend Him. "Put your sword away!" He said to Peter. At any stage of His Passion, Christ could have called thousands of angels to rescue Him from His enemies. But He chose rather to suffer whatever pain and indignities were necessary for the will of God to be fulfilled. His arrest, His trial, and His crucifixion were all part of God's plan to redeem mankind. Jesus would not allow His enemies, or His *friends*, to interfere with that plan.

Though we are Christian soldiers, God hardly needs us to wield swords in His defense. We are not commissioned to *protect* Christ, but to *proclaim* Christ.   —R. W. B.

IV. Hearing Before the High Priest (John 18:12-14)

In the remaining verses the scene moves from Gethsemane, on the slopes of the Mount of Olives, back into the city, where Jesus was given a preliminary hearing before Annas.

A. Jesus Arrested (v. 12)

12. Then the band and the captain and officers of the Jews took Jesus, and bound him.

The Roman soldiers and the temple guards seized Jesus, probably at the command of the captain. The captain was a high-ranking officer (the Greek word means the commander of a thousand), indicating that those in charge did not look upon Jesus as just a common criminal. They *bound him*, not that there was any likelihood He would try to escape, but as an effort to humiliate Him publicly. John does not mention what happened to the disciples. Matthew 26:56 and Mark 14:50 tell us that they all forsook Him and fled. Peter and John, recovering from their initial fright, followed Him at a distance (Luke 22:54; John 18:15).

B. Jesus Taken to Annas (v. 13)

13. And led him away to Annas first; for he was father-in-law to Caiaphas, which was the high priest that same year.

Annas had become high priest in A.D. 6, but had been deposed by the Romans in A.D. 15. Although he no longer officially held the office, he is sometimes referred to as the high priest by Luke (Luke 3:2; Acts 4:6). In spite of the Roman action, the Jews probably continued to refer to him as high priest. Although technically Caiaphas, his son-in-law, was high priest, Annas still wielded much of the power inherent in the office. This appearance at night before Annas was a preliminary hearing, held while the members of the Sanhedrin were being assembled for a more formal trial. This hearing was held in the palace of Caiaphas (Matthew 26:57, 58), where apparently Annas lived with his son-in-law.

C. Caiaphas Identified (v. 14)

14. Now Caiaphas was he, which gave counsel to the Jews, that it was expedient that one man should die for the people.

In a parenthetical statement, John identifies Caiaphas for his readers. This verse refers to what took place in a meeting of some of the religious authorities some time before the Passover (see John 11:45-53). These authorities had met to discuss Jesus' growing popularity among the people. They feared that the turmoil surrounding His ministry might bring the Roman government down upon them. In that meeting, Caiaphas had coldly and cynically recommended that Jesus be killed, arguing "that it is expedient for us, that one man should die for the people, and that the whole nation perish not" (John 11:50). The assembled leaders had agreed with Caiaphas, and from that time forth, in total disregard for justice, they had sought some way to have Jesus silenced. Caiaphas had one thought in mind when he uttered the words recorded in John 11:50. In reporting them, John indicated that there was a far deeper meaning. Jesus would indeed die for the people, but as the sacrificial lamb of God, not as a person murdered for political expediency.

Conclusion

A. All We Are Traitors

Traitors are universally despised. The Brutuses, the Judases, the Benedict Arnolds of history are in every society loathed and rejected—and for good reason. They are guilty of two sins. Their first sin is feigning friendship and loyalty while all the time they are planning their evil deed. Thus they are guilty of hypocrisy. Their second sin is the actual betrayal itself.

A betrayal is always hard to understand. What kind of a person will turn on his benefactor, will bite the hand that feeds him? Through the mind and heart of the traitor run motives that honest men cannot comprehend. Various theories have been put forth to try to explain Judas' actions. But when all of these are examined, he still remains guilty of a heinous crime. Not only did he act maliciously, he carried out his plot despite many efforts on Jesus' part to turn him aside from his wicked deed.

Yet even Judas' depravity was not total. When he finally came to realize the enormity of what he had done, he tried to undo it by returning the blood money. When he realized that he had been used by the religious leaders, and that there was no way he could gain Jesus' release, he was so overwhelmed by remorse that he could not live with himself, and so he went out and took his own life.

But even as we condemn Judas, we are also pointing the finger of guilt at ourselves. Of course, we don't deliberately conspire with Jesus' enemies to betray Him. Our betrayals are more subtle, less obvious. We betray Him when we fail to take advantage of our opportunities to share the good news with others. We betray Him when our own business becomes more important than the King's business. We betray Him when we are stingy with the possessions He has given us. We betray Him when foolish pride or jealousy keeps us from using our talents for Him. We betray Him when racism or prejudice causes us to become respecters of persons.

But fortunately, our acts of treason need not lead us to suicide, either physical or spiritual. Jesus stands ready and willing to forgive our failures, if we turn to Him in repentance. Further, He has promised to give us strength to avoid future failures.

B. Let Us Pray

We thank You, Heavenly Father, that Jesus did not flee from the mob but went forward to meet them, knowing that His death on the cross was necessary for our salvation. In His name we pray. Amen.

C. Thought to Remember

In a garden man first sinned; in another garden a big step was taken to relieve many of the burdens of sin.

Home Daily Bible Readings

Monday, Mar. 12—One Death for the Many (John 11:45-53)
Tuesday, Mar. 13—Betrayer at Work (Luke 22:1-6)
Wednesday, Mar. 14—Preparing the Passover (Luke 22:7-13)
Thursday, Mar. 15—The Passover Meal (Luke 22:14-23)
Friday, Mar. 16—The Sign of True Greatness (Luke 22:24-30)
Saturday, Mar. 17—"It is Enough" (Luke 22:31-38)
Sunday, Mar. 18—Prayer of Surrender (Luke 22:39-46)

Learning by Doing

This page contains an alternate lesson plan emphasizing learning activities. Classes desiring such student involvement will find these suggestions helpful.

Learning Goals

Lead each student to do the following:

1. Compare and contrast the sins of Judas and Peter.

2. Analyze the relationship to God of each of the following (as seen in John 18:1-14): Judas, Peter, the arresting crowd, and Jesus.

3. Name one way he or she can be more like Jesus as He is seen here.

Into the Lesson

Slowly read each of the following agree/disagree statements to your class members. After each statement, poll the class to see how many agree with it, and how many disagree.

1. Sin that occurs outside the church is more damaging to the church than sin that occurs within the church.

2. When we obey God's will, success follows.

3. Even though we have right motives, our actions may be sinful.

Write the words *sin* and *obedience* on the chalkboard. Tell students, "These are the issues that today's lesson considers. We will look at what happens when people sin and what may happen after obedience. We'll have the chance to decide how obedient our life-style really is."

Into the Word

Explain the "Lesson Background" to your students. Then lead them to explore today's text. One way to do this, and to communicate the drama of today's event to them, is to share today's printed text with a *dialogical reading.* You'll need three readers: The Narrator, Jesus, and The Crowd. Give each of these readers a copy of the printed text that you've marked ahead of time with the appropriate sections that they are to read. (The Narrator reads the verses of narration. Jesus reads only the words that Jesus spoke. The Crowd reads only the words spoken by the crowd.) Ask the rest of your students to listen carefully as the story is read aloud for them.

Then divide the students into groups of three or four. Use *one* of the following activities for their small-group Bible study:

"Point-of-view Paraphrase." Students should retell the story of today's text from the perspective of one of the following: The crowd, Judas, Peter, or Jesus. Each group should choose a different character, and the members of each group should work together to write down one paraphrase for the group.

"Here's How I'd Describe Him. . . ." Each group should make three columns on a sheet of paper: Judas, Jesus, Peter. Under each name they should write adjectives that describe this person in this passage. (Possibilities include: *Judas:* devious, sneaky, treacherous; *Jesus:* steady, in control, purposeful, calm; *Peter:* impetuous, aggressive, impulsive.)

Allow groups several minutes to work. Then ask each group to report to the whole class. After they have shared, discuss with the class:

1. Why did Judas behave as he did here?

2. Why did Peter behave as he did here?

3. What is the common denominator in the behavior of Judas and Peter? (Each took matters into his own hands. Each man's methods were opposed to Jesus' ways.)

Into Life

Discuss with students:

1. What actions can we see around us to match the treachery of Judas? Who in our society is blatantly undermining the cause of Christ?

2. What actions have we seen that match the impulsiveness of Peter? Have you ever known someone who brashly acted on behalf of Christ in a way that Christ would not approve?

3. How can each of these approaches be dangerous or damaging?

4. What persons living today may fit into one of the following categories:

The crowd—seeking strength in the world instead of in the will of God.

Jesus—calmly pursuing God's will in spite of how the world misunderstands or persecutes.

Judas—openly confronting or contradicting the will of God.

Peter—trying to do God's will, but without success, perhaps in a way that's not pleasing to Him.

5. What must the people you've thought about do to become more like Jesus as we see Him here?

6. Which of the characters are you most like today? What one thing must you do to become more like Jesus as we see Him here?

Challenge all students to do what they must do to be more like Jesus.

Let's Talk It Over

The questions on this page are designed to encourage review of the lesson Scriptures and to promote discussion of the lesson by the class. The answers provided are only discussion starters. Let your class talk it over from there.

1. In the midst of our busy, rush-aholic, go-aholic, and belong-aholic world, what are some ways we can get away to a "garden spot," as did Jesus, to commune with God?

We can get up a few minutes earlier each morning and spend some time alone with God. We can use some of our "dead" time for a garden experience. Some examples of "dead" time are the time we spend driving back and forth to work, waiting in line, waiting in a doctor's office, etc. We can turn off the television for one-half hour each evening to meditate on God's Word privately or with our families. We can designate the Lord's Day to really be His day. On that day we can worship and devote a greater amount of time to meditating on spiritual matters.

2. When betrayed, what practical help can a person in the church receive from the recorded actions and attitudes of Judas against Jesus?

The Christian can take consolation in the fact that when he is betrayed by trusted brethren he is not suffering something that Christ did not experience. Jesus knows how the sin of betrayal hurts, and the realization that Jesus understands goes far in bringing comfort to the faithful servant. It is also helpful to know that if Jesus didn't foster faithfulness in the heart of every worker, we are not apt to do so either. So if someone does betray your faith in him, don't blame yourself unnecessarily. Examine the facts carefully to make sure you are not at fault, and once assured that you are not the betrayer, walk courageously in the Lord.

3. Peter reacted irrationally when he found himself in a tense situation. Give examples of irrational reactions that some church members make in tense situations in the church today.

Some persons may decide to fight; others may take flight. Some may fight by lashing out verbally against a brother or sister in Christ, or by trying to discredit those who oppose them. If the opposing party is a leader in the church, they may try to have the person removed from that position. Others may take flight by quitting the church or withdrawing from an activity or withholding their offerings from the church.

4. Jesus told Peter to put his sword into the sheath. What are some ways in which we can put our sword of revenge into the sheath?

We can decide not to let the sun go down upon our anger, but instead seek reconciliation with those who injure us. We can decide to govern our tongues and speak words that benefit others instead of words that harm them. We can decide to be stewards of what we know about others—refusing to pass on information about them that might damage their reputation. We can decide that if we have a right to our opinions, other people have a right to theirs; and we won't divide the church over those opinions. We can decide to treat others the way we would like for them to treat us—whether they ever do or not. We can decide to allow the Holy Spirit, instead of our human spirit, to control our actions.

5. Jesus protected His disciples when He asked His captors to let them go free. What are some ways that we can protect one another in the church today?

We can look for the best in people and talk about that to others. We can go in private to people who are in sin, and in a spirit of gentleness, seek to restore them to spiritual health. We can forgive those who have sinned against us; we can determine not to permit their offense to become public knowledge. We can protect the dignity of others by giving financial help when there is need, without causing them to feel uncomfortable receiving it.

6. Peter reacted violently in attempting to defend Jesus from His enemies. Many in our society today react with violence when they feel that someone has wronged them. What do you think are some causes for this violent behavior?

Reading materials, television, movies, even the news reports of the day are filled with acts of violence—violence that results in making a point, promoting a cause, or moving things along. It is often depicted as the approved way of venting anger and frustration. People who fill their minds with such pictures and words and who accept such a philosophy will tend to do violent acts.

Peter Denies Knowing Jesus

LESSON SCRIPTURE: John 18:15-27.

PRINTED TEXT: John 18:15-27.

John 18:15-27

15 And Simon Peter followed Jesus, and so did another disciple: that disciple was known unto the high priest, and went in with Jesus into the palace of the high priest.

16 But Peter stood at the door without. Then went out that other disciple, which was known unto the high priest, and spake unto her that kept the door, and brought in Peter.

17 Then saith the damsel that kept the door unto Peter, Art not thou also one of this man's disciples? He saith, I am not.

18 And the servants and officers stood there, who had made a fire of coals, for it was cold; and they warmed themselves: and Peter stood with them, and warmed himself.

19 The high priest then asked Jesus of his disciples, and of his doctrine.

20 Jesus answered him, I spake openly to the world; I ever taught in the synagogue, and in the temple, whither the Jews always resort; and in secret have I said nothing.

21 Why askest thou me? ask them which heard me, what I have said unto them: behold, they know what I said.

22 And when he had thus spoken, one of the officers which stood by struck Jesus with the palm of his hand, saying, Answerest thou the high priest so?

23 Jesus answered him, If I have spoken evil, bear witness of the evil: but if well, why smitest thou me?

24 Now Annas had sent him bound unto Caiaphas the high priest.

25 And Simon Peter stood and warmed himself. They said therefore unto him, Art not thou also one of his disciples? He denied it, and said, I am not.

26 One of the servants of the high priest, being his kinsman whose ear Peter cut off, saith, Did not I see thee in the garden with him?

27 Peter then denied again; and immediately the cock crew.

GOLDEN TEXT: Then saith the damsel that kept the door unto Peter, Art not thou also one of this man's disciples? He saith, I am not.—John 18:17.

John Writes of Life, Light, and Love

Unit 1: The Gospel of Life and Light
(John, Lessons 1-7)

Lesson Aims

After studying this lesson, a student should:

1. Realize that even strong and courageous persons may sometimes act in a cowardly manner.

2. Be sympathetic and understanding toward those who fail under pressure.

3. Take steps to prepare himself or herself for times of crisis.

Lesson Outline

INTRODUCTION
    A. No One Ever Knew
    B. Lesson Background
 I. FEAR OVERCOME (John 18:15, 16)
    A. Following at a Distance (v. 15)
    B. Favor Requested (v. 16)
 II. PETER'S FIRST DENIAL (John 18:17, 18)
    A. Accusation and Denial (v. 17)
    B. At the Fire of the Enemy (v. 18)
        Uncommon Cold
 III. JESUS BEFORE ANNAS (John 18:19-24)
    A. Leading Questions (v. 19)
    B. Lawful Reply (vv. 20, 21)
        Nothing in Secret
    C. Loathsome Act (vv. 22, 23)
    D. Led Away to Caiaphas (v. 24)
 IV. PETER'S REPEATED DENIALS (John 18:25-27)
    Of Chickens, Roosters, and Other Fowl
CONCLUSION
    A. Avoiding Temptation
    B. Let Us Pray
    C. Thought to Remember

Introduction

A. No One Ever Knew

It's an old story, but it is fitting for this lesson. A young man had taken a summer job in a lumbering camp. The young man's minister, who was well aware of the reputation of these lumber camps, took the young man aside and began to give him some advice that would help him keep his faith in the face of these temptations. "They are likely to give you a hard time," he said, "when they find out that you are a Christian. But the Lord will help you stand fast in your faith."

At the end of the summer, when the young man returned, the minister was interested in how he had fared. "Did you have any problems in the camp because you were a Christian?"

"Oh, no, sir," came his reply. "I never had a bit of trouble. No one ever found out that I was a Christian!"

The young man had at least that much in common with Peter—under pressure, he denied his Lord. For that matter, don't we all share his guilt?

B. Lesson Background

The text for this lesson follows immediately that of last week's lesson. As we saw, Judas led the Roman soldiers and the temple guards to where Jesus was in the garden with His disciples. The armed guard then arrested Jesus, bound Him, and brought Him to Annas for a hearing. At that point, all the disciples forsook Jesus and fled (Matthew 26:56; Mark 14:50).

I. Fear Overcome
(John 18:15, 16)

A. Following at a Distance (v. 15)

15. And Simon Peter followed Jesus, and so did another disciple: that disciple was known unto the high priest, and went in with Jesus into the palace of the high priest.

Peter had stood ready to defend Jesus, drawing his sword and using it with deadly intent. But when Jesus had made it clear that His kingdom was not to be advanced by physical violence, Peter had been filled with doubt and fear. Bewildered by the turn of events, he and the other disciples had fled. But Peter did not go far before he overcame his fright and turned to follow Jesus and the officers at a distance (Matthew 26:58; Mark 14:54).

Peter was accompanied by *another disciple*, whom most commentators take to be John. As the author of this Gospel, John was reluctant to name himself. We see this reticence on another occasion, when John identifies himself as the "disciple whom Jesus loved" (John 21:7, 20).

Jesus was taken to the palace of Caiaphas, the high priest. It seems that Annas and his son-in-

How to Say It

ANNAS. *An*-nus.
CAIAPHAS. *Kay*-uh-fus or *Kye*-uh-fus.
MALCHUS. *Mal*-kus.
SANHEDRIN. *San*-huh-drun or San-*heed*-run.

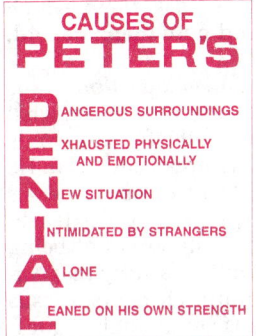

visual 4

CAUSES OF PETER'S DENIAL

DANGEROUS SURROUNDINGS

EXHAUSTED PHYSICALLY AND EMOTIONALLY

NEW SITUATION

INTIMIDATED BY STRANGERS

ALONE

LEANED ON HIS OWN STRENGTH

law Caiaphas lived in different wings of the same building. Probably these wings were arranged about an open courtyard. John, because he was known by the high priest, was allowed to enter with Jesus. We are not told the nature of the connection between John and the high priest.

B. Favor Requested (v. 16)

16. But Peter stood at the door without. Then went out that other disciple, which was known unto the high priest, and spake unto her that kept the door, and brought in Peter.

Seeing that his companion had been stopped at the gate, John went back and spoke to the gatekeeper. John was known by her also, and so he was able to get Peter into the courtyard. But, alas, as it turned out he did Peter no favor in getting him admitted. It only subjected him to temptation.

II. Peter's First Denial (John 18:17, 18)

A. Accusation and Denial (v. 17)

17. Then saith the damsel that kept the door unto Peter, Art not thou also one of this man's disciples? He saith, I am not.

We are not told where John went after Peter entered the palace. It is speculated that he crossed the courtyard and went to the room where Jesus' hearing was held, leaving Peter alone. Peter then walked through the arched passage that led to the courtyard and there joined the servants and guards around a fire (v. 18).

We can only guess what caused the gatekeeper to become suspicious about Peter. Were his actions uneasy? Did his facial expression give him away? or did his association with John, a known disciple, arouse her suspicions? Whatever it was, the girl approached Peter, looked at him closely, and asked if he were not one of Jesus' disciples (Luke 22:56). The question

caught Peter off guard. Unprepared for the challenge, he not only denied Jesus but lied in doing so. Satan still uses this tactic. He knows that mature Christians can often resist him if they have time to get their defenses set. And so he attacks at a time and place they least expect it.

It is ironic that Peter, only a short time before, had boasted that he would never deny Jesus, even if all the other disciples did. And yet he fell. Peter was aware of his strengths. He had been willing to face an armed mob and even die for his Lord. Yet he was not aware of his weaknesses.

B. At the Fire of the Enemy (v. 18)

18. And the servants and officers stood there, who had made a fire of coals, for it was cold; and they warmed themselves: and Peter stood with them, and warmed himself.

Early in the spring the nights can be quite chilly in Jerusalem, so it is not surprising that the servants and the officers of the temple guard who were assembled in the courtyard needed a fire. It was a charcoal fire, perhaps in a brazier. It would not provide a great deal of heat, unless the people were huddled closely about it. Peter would have been wiser to have kept to the shadows around the side of the courtyard, but he was never one to seek the easy or safe way.

UNCOMMON COLD

John Stossell, investigative reporter for ABC-TV's 20/20 program, on assignment submitted to some unusual scientific experiments, testing the human body's reactions to cold. Stossell sat in a tank of ice water until his body temperature was reduced to incredibly low levels.

The human body compensates for cold temperatures with shivering. Shivering is our bodies' involuntary reaction to cold that increases circulation and produces body heat.

The human spirit also reacts to cold—the cold of non-acceptance, the cold of loneliness and fears, the cold of belonging to an unrespected minority. Peter's fragile spirit reacted to disillusionment and uncertainty by "joining the crowd." He was afraid that being known as a disciple of Christ might bring ridicule, imprisonment, or even death. So, he warmed himself by fraternizing incognito with unbelievers, shrinking from public confession of faith, and finally denying any association with Christ.

Our spirits too sometimes shiver in the cold of aloneness, doubts, and cynicism. We are tempted to warm our souls at the fires of uninvolvement and compromise. If we yield to such temptation, we may be spiritually scorched, seared by our own apostasy.   —R. W. B.

III. Jesus Before Annas
(John 18:19-24)

A. Leading Questions (v. 19)

19. The high priest then asked Jesus of his disciples, and of his doctrine.

The man here designated as the high priest was Annas, the father-in-law of Caiaphas. Although Caiaphas was the official high priest, Annas was the ruling spirit of the Sanhedrin, the Jewish high council. Only after Annas had finished with Jesus was He sent to Caiaphas.

We are not told the exact nature of Annas' questions, but probably he was trying to gather evidence to be used against Jesus when He was tried before the Sanhedrin. Annas had already made up his mind that Jesus would be found guilty. He was just looking for information that might be twisted and used against Jesus.

Annas asked first about Jesus' disciples. He may have wanted to know who the twelve were in order that they could be arrested also. But if this had been the case, they could have been arrested in the garden. It is more likely that he was interested in finding out just how extensive Jesus' following was beyond the twelve. He really wanted to know how many dedicated followers Jesus had.

Annas' other questions concerned Jesus' teaching. He asked these questions in the hope of getting Jesus to say something incriminating. Obviously, the high priest knew what Jesus had been teaching. For some time the religious leaders had sent spies to observe Jesus and report back on what He was saying and doing (see John 11:46). Just a few days before Jesus' arrest, many of the religious leaders had argued furiously with Him in the temple (Matthew 21:23—22:46).

B. Lawful Reply (vv. 20, 21)

20. Jesus answered him, I spake openly to the world; I ever taught in the synagogue, and in the temple, whither the Jews always resort; and in secret have I said nothing.

Jesus addressed His reply only to the question about His doctrine. Unless they were able to prove that His doctrine was false, He had every right to have disciples. From the very beginning, Jesus' ministry had been open and public. He had taught where the people gathered—in the synagogues and in the temple—and all were welcome to hear Him. While it is true that Jesus had on occasion taught the twelve disciples in private, yet He had never taught anything in private for the purposes of concealment (see Matthew 13:10, 11; 10:27).

21. Why askest thou me? ask them which heard me, what I have said unto them: behold, they know what I said.

In refusing to answer Annas' question, Jesus let him know that He understood exactly what he was up to. Jesus was not going to utter words that could be used against Him at a later trial. He challenged the high priest to call up witnesses to testify in an open court regarding His teaching. In refusing to testify, Jesus was not being uncooperative; He was simply insisting that Annas follow proper procedure. Of course, Jesus knew that honest witnesses could not bring testimony that would incriminate Him. It is quite likely that some of the officers then guarding Jesus had heard Him teach. Annas chose not to call on any of them for testimony. Without coaching from the high priest, their testimony would not have been adequate to convict Jesus.

NOTHING IN SECRET

"I've Got a Secret" was a popular TV show for several seasons in the fifties. A panel of celebrities attempted to guess the "secret" of the guest/contestant by asking a limited number of questions. Usually the secret was some unusual occupation or achievement.

Secrecy is fascinating to human nature. Little children delight in knowing a secret. Kids form secret clubs, spend hours in secret hiding places, and daydream secret fantasies.

Adults like secrets, too. Fraternities, lodges, and secret-sister societies abound. We seem to have a penchant for classified information. Many cults and religious sects thrive on the secrecy of their initiatory rites, worship ceremonies, and unorthodox doctrines.

The church was never intended to be a secret society. Though Jesus taught his followers to give offerings in secret, pray in secret, and fast in secret (Matthew 6:1-18), He commissioned us to tell the whole world the glorious mysteries of the gospel. He spoke "openly to the world," and so should we. To His disciples Jesus said, "The knowledge of the secrets of the kingdom of heaven has been given to you" (Matthew 13:11, *New International Version*). "Therefore go and make disciples of all nations" (28:19, *New International Version*).   —R. W. B.

C. Loathsome Act (vv. 22, 23)

22. And when he had thus spoken, one of the officers which stood by struck Jesus with the palm of his hand, saying, Answerest thou the high priest so?

While there is no indication that the high priest ordered Jesus to be struck, yet the temple guard who hit Him must have sensed that Annas would approve of his action. No doubt this underling saw this as a means of currying favor with the high priest. The man's action seems all the more despicable when we realize that Jesus' hands were tied so that He could not ward off the blow. The officer hit Jesus with the palm of his hand, more of a stinging slap than a bruising blow with a fist. Its purpose was not so much to bring physical harm as to humiliate Jesus.

23. Jesus answered him, If I have spoken evil, bear witness of the evil: but if well, why smitest thou me?

Even a common criminal would not have deserved the treatment Jesus received. Yet Jesus, who was innocent, was physically mistreated and humiliated even before His trial had begun. In His response, He reminded the court that His rights had been violated. But Annas and his associates were not interested in a fair trial; they were, instead, bent on murder. Jesus' behavior before Annas is typical of His behavior in His other hearings. He meekly accepted the mistreatment, but His behavior called attention to the injustice of the whole process.

D. Led Away to Caiaphas (v. 24)

24. Now Annas had sent him bound unto Caiaphas the high priest.

Annas had failed in his efforts to discover any evidence that might be used against Jesus in additional trials. When he saw the futility of further questioning, he sent him on to Caiaphas, who was the official high priest. However, the hearing before Annas had given the members of the Sanhedrin time to assemble at the high priest's palace. If, as it seems, Annas and Caiaphas occupied the same house, then Jesus was probably taken just across the courtyard to another room.

IV. Peter's Repeated Denials (John 18:25-27)

The denials of Peter are recorded in all four of the Gospel accounts. It seems that John counts the denials differently than Matthew, Mark, and Luke. He omits what they count as the second denial, and splits into two denials what they count as the third.

25. And Simon Peter stood and warmed himself. They said therefore unto him, Art not thou also one of his disciples? He denied it, and said, I am not.

John now turns the narrative back to Peter who was trying to ward off the night chill by standing close to the fire. The maid at the gate may have shared her suspicions about Peter with the others in the courtyard. Or Peter's speech may have betrayed him, for Mark tells us that the people standing nearby recognized that he was a Galilean by his speech (14:70). In any event, Peter was challenged once again.

Peter did not attempt to turn the question aside or hedge in his answer. His denial was emphatic: "I am not!" Peter was not given to compromise or quibbling. Whatever he did, he did emphatically. He was emphatic in his affirmation of Jesus (Matthew 16:16); he was just as emphatic in his denials.

26, 27. One of the servants of the high priest, being his kinsman whose ear Peter cut off, saith, Did not I see thee in the garden with him? Peter then denied again; and immediately the cock crew.

This questioner was a relative of Malchus, the man whose ear Peter cut off, and he had been present when Peter had wielded his sword. He was almost certain that Peter was the man he had seen. And so he asked his question expecting an affirmative answer: "I saw you in the garden with him, didn't I?"

Peter may have been taken by surprise the first time he was questioned, but this time he should have been prepared, for an hour or more had passed since his first denial (Luke 22:59). But realizing that this revelation could lead to his own arrest, Peter panicked. Once more he blurted out his denial. Matthew and Mark both report that Peter punctuated his denial by cursing and swearing (Matthew 26:74; Mark 14:71).

The words were scarcely out of Peter's mouth before the cock crowed. That shrill cry must have reechoed to the very bottom of Peter's heart. Just at that moment, Jesus, who was being led from Annas to Caiaphas, turned and looked at Peter (Luke 22:61). A hot iron laid across his bare chest could not have brought Peter more pain than this look of Jesus. While John does not report Peter's subsequent action, the synoptic Gospels all tell us that he went out and wept bitterly (Matthew 26:75; Mark 14:72; Luke 22:62).

OF CHICKENS, ROOSTERS, AND OTHER FOWL

Who knows when cowards began to be called "chicken"? Actually, this slang term is a shortened version of *chicken-hearted* and *chicken-livered*, both of which mean "timid, fearful, or cowardly." Pullets in particular fit that description—thus, the label for humans of similar temperament.

Name-callers seem to delight in using "fowl language." A "goose" is someone who is silly, simple, and stupid—or someone who is at least *acting* silly, simple, and stupid. A "turkey" was at first a slang name for a theatrical production that was a failure. More recently, anyone acting like a goose might be called a turkey.

Simon Peter, on his night of denial, acted like a chicken. His behavior was cowardly. He was suddenly timid and fearful. Though his cowardice should not be excused, it can be understood by chicken-hearted Christians everywhere. (And they are everywhere, aren't they?)

Though Peter was a chicken in crisis, he was certainly no goose, nor a turkey. When the rooster crowed, he repented. Then he soared like an eagle.   —R. W. B.

Conclusion

A. Avoiding Temptation

Visual 4 in the visuals packet illustrates the points contained in this section.

A study of Peter's denials of Jesus raises several points worthy of our consideration. First of all, his denials came when he was alone. He had been with John when he entered the courtyard of the residence of Caiaphas. But in some way, he had become separated from John. At least there is nothing in the narrative to indicate that John was present to witness the denials. The devil knows that we are usually weaker when we try to go it alone. For that reason, he often works to isolate us when he tempts us.

Earlier in His ministry, when Jesus sent out His disciples, He sent them out two by two. Paired up they could strengthen one another, supplement each other's efforts, and together provide a united front against temptation. Today we often find strength and support in the fellowship of a congregation. That is one reason why regular attendance at worship is so important.

Second, Peter got into trouble because he was in the camp of the enemy. We may debate whether he ever should have gone there in the first place. But even granted that he had a right to be there, he should have taken precautions to protect himself in a situation that he knew was certain to be hazardous. As Christians, we need to recognize that there are some places, persons, and situations that we ought to avoid. Satan tries to get us into situations where we are tempted to compromise our convictions.

The third mistake Peter made was to trust in his own strength. Earlier that evening he had boasted that he would never betray Jesus. In the garden, he had shown his courage when he drew his sword to protect Jesus, even though he was hopelessly outnumbered. He was confident that that kind of courage would stand him in good stead even in the courtyard of the high priest. What he didn't realize was that physical courage and moral courage are not the same.

Home Daily Bible Readings

Monday, Mar. 19—"You Are the Christ" (Matthew 16:13-23)
Tuesday, Mar. 20—Invitation to Discipleship (Matthew 16:24-28)
Wednesday, Mar. 21—Denying the Denial (Matthew 26:31-35)
Thursday, Mar. 22—The Ordeal in Gethsemane (Matthew 26:36-46)
Friday, Mar. 23—Where Did Everybody Go? (Matthew 26:47-56)
Saturday, Mar. 24—Following—At a Distance (Matthew 26:57-68)
Sunday, Mar. 25—The Agony of Failure (Matthew 26:69-75)

Satan works on us in the same way. He leads us to trust in our own strength to be able to face temptation and escape unscathed. We need to realize that we are no match for Satan and his bag of tricks. If we are to escape serious temptation, we need to trust in the Lord's strength, not our own.

One other factor entered into Peter's denials. He was physically and emotionally fatigued by the time he reached the courtyard. Jesus and the disciples, for the few days prior to this, had been going at a pace that was physically exhausting and emotionally draining. No one performs at his best under such conditions. Peter may have thought that it didn't make any difference, but it did. When we are tired, our resolve is weakened and our ability to respond is limited. When we are in that condition, we ought especially to avoid situations that place us under great temptation.

From Peter's denials, then, we can learn these important lessons: (1) we should not try to go it alone; (2) whenever possible, we should avoid those situations that are spiritually dangerous; (3) we should depend upon the Lord's strength, not our own; and (4) we should not take on big risks when we are tired.

B. Let Us Pray

Dear God, give us the wisdom to be alert to all the subtle ways that we can be tempted to deny Jesus. Then give us the strength to resist those temptations. In Jesus' name we pray. Amen.

C. Thought to Remember

To pray against temptation, and yet rush into it, is to thrust your fingers into the fire, and then pray that they might not be burned.

—Thomas Secker

Learning by Doing

This page contains an alternate lesson plan emphasizing learning activities. Classes desiring such student involvement will find these suggestions helpful.

Learning Goals

This lesson will help students:

1. List the negatives and the positives behind Peter's behavior as recorded in John 18:15-27.

2. Isolate factors that may undermine their own loyalty to Christ.

3. Determine how to overcome these challenges to their own consistent Christian walk.

Into the Lesson

Distribute blank sheets of paper to students and begin the class session with this assignment: "Write at the top of your paper, *Three Principles That Guide My Life.* These can be words, such as *honesty, purity, industry.* Or they may be phrases, such as, *Work hard. Love your family. Obey God.*" Students should do this privately.

Now ask students to draw a simple chart on their paper. At the left of the chart is a vertical line, numbered from 0 to 10 in even steps from bottom to top. Across the bottom of the chart is a horizontal line, numbered from 10 to 1 in even steps, from left to right. The vertical scale represents levels of consistency, from totally inconsistent at the bottom to completely consistent at the top. The scale across the bottom represents years, from ten years ago at the left through the present day at the right.

Students are to evaluate how well they have lived their lives by the principles they have written on their sheets. Have their lives been totally consistent with their principles through the years? On the graph they should rate their consistency for each of the last ten years and then connect the dots to form a line graph.

Students may be willing to share what factors in those years affected their consistency. Maybe they were not Christians for all of that time. Maybe a friend or relative made a difference. Maybe they can pinpoint the times when their prayer habits were or weren't in place.

Tell students that this self-study may help them to look afresh at the experience of Peter at the time of Christ's arrest and trial. He was not consistent with his principles, either.

Into the Word

Divide the class into two teams. Each is to study today's printed text and then finish a sentence. The sentence for Team 1 is "I read this story and condemn Peter, because ..." The sentence for Team 2 is "I read this story with compassion for Peter, because ..." Let the students on each team work in groups of four.

Team 1 may list items such as these:

He repeatedly denied His Lord.

He tried to protect his own skin.

He passed up valuable opportunities to tell the truth about Jesus.

Even though he had spent three years in the presence of Jesus, he lacked faith.

Team 2 may list items such as these:

He nearly entered the very place where Jesus was being tried.

His courage was further magnified by the fact that the other disciples had all fled in fear.

Peter *tried* to act on his vows of loyalty.

Give students about ten minutes for this. Then have them share with the whole class.

Into Life

Ask students to pretend that they've been asked to write a devotional meditation for the back of your church's Sunday bulletin. It is to be based on today's text. What thoughts would they use if the *topic* for the devotion were "Loyalty—Wherever You Are"? What thoughts would they include if the topic were "The Challenge to Complete Consistency."

Have students discuss this in the groups that formed the study teams above. After several minutes discuss their ideas as a whole class.

Ask students to name items for two lists that you will make on the chalkboard: "Places Where It's *Easy* to Be Loyal to Christ"; "Places Where It's *Difficult* to Be Loyal to Christ."

Students should number a blank sheet of paper from one to four. This will be a private "Consistency Check" for students as you ask them to write answers to the following questions:

1. What is the biggest challenge to complete consistency in your Christian walk?

2. In what place do you find the greatest stumbling block?

3. Is there one person who, more than anyone else, causes you to stumble?

4. What can you do?

After the last question, suggest that perhaps students may want to seek the counsel of a Christian friend. Perhaps there is a situation that they can simply determine to avoid.

Let's Talk It Over

The questions on this page are designed to encourage review of the lesson Scriptures and to promote discussion of the lesson by the class. The answers provided are only discussion starters. Let your class talk it over from there.

1. How may we evaluate Peter's actions through the entire night of Jesus' betrayal and arrest?

Peter was brave in that he was willing to fight physically for Jesus. He exercised a measure of bravery in following Jesus after his arrest. Peter's problems came because of too much confidence in himself and too little understanding of what Jesus' kingdom was designed to be and do. Peter's intentions and actions were those of a man who wanted to do right but hadn't adequately prepared himself to do it.

2. The servant girl who was the gatekeeper at the high priest's palace recognized Peter as one of Jesus' disciples. What are some ways in which people today may know that we are Jesus' followers.

We show that we are Jesus' followers by the actions and attitudes that we manifest each day. A few examples are these: by refusing to listen to or participate in any kind of obscene talk, by our modest dress, by walking out on embarrassing movies, by refusing to allow other activities to interfere with our corporate worship. People will take notice if we do not retaliate in kind when we are mistreated. By helping when people have special needs, we can demonstrate Jesus' spirit of love and concern for others.

3. What are some ways in which we can deny that we know Jesus today?

Of course, we can deny the Lord in the same way Peter did—by refusing to acknowledge that we are followers of Jesus. We can also deny that we know Jesus by our life-style. We can deny that we know Jesus by what we love and what we hate. We can deny that we know Jesus by how we spend our money. We can deny Jesus by not standing up for what He would stand up for. It has been said if we don't stand for something, we will fall for anything.

4. Peter must have felt very pressured when he succumbed to the temptation to deny Jesus. What are some of the pressures we face that can cause us to turn away from Jesus?

Here are just a few: the values and activities of our peers—(everyone is doing it); the prevailing materialistic view of success, the work ethic, and leisure; the philosophy that says we ought to do whatever feels good; the subtlety of the feeling that "little" sins are okay—("I can get by with a little sin"); our arrogance in thinking we can subject ourselves to the media's portrayals of violence, immorality, and unethical behavior without being affected by it.

5. What kind of commitment must Christians make to arm ourselves against making the kind of denial Peter made?

It must be a commitment of the will, one that involves a total commitment of the person's life. The kind of commitment that is dangerous is the one based purely on emotion. When emotion runs thin, so does that kind of commitment.

6. What universal principle does Satan use in tempting people?

His tactic is to hit a person where he is the most vulnerable. Satan doesn't waste time attacking us where we are strongest. He knows our weaknesses and that is where he casts his darts.

7. Jesus was not judged fairly when He stood before Annas. In what ways are people misjudged today?

One of the most common ways to misjudge people is by considering only their outward appearance: the length or style of hair, the kind of clothes worn, the color of their skin. Sometimes a person is judged unfairly, simply because he or she comes from a certain geographical area or a particular neighborhood. Let us take care that we do not judge others on such factors.

8. When the cock crowed, Peter remembered the prophetic words of Jesus that he would deny his Lord three times that very night. How may we be reminded that we may be denying Jesus?

Our own conscience can be our crowing cock. But the cock may also crow for us through the counsel of Christian friends, the preacher's sermon or this lesson. The Word of God is a crowing cock for all of us. It is like a mirror, which allows us to see ourselves against God's perfect standard. In whatever way we hear it, the cock is letting us know that we are doing wrong.

Tried and Condemned

LESSON SCRIPTURE: John 18:28—19:16.

PRINTED TEXT: John 18:28-40.

John 18:28-40

28 Then led they Jesus from Caiaphas unto the hall of judgment: and it was early; and they themselves went not into the judgment hall, lest they should be defiled; but that they might eat the passover.

29 Pilate then went out unto them, and said, What accusation bring ye against this man?

30 They answered and said unto him, If he were not a malefactor, we would not have delivered him up unto thee.

31 Then said Pilate unto them, Take ye him, and judge him according to your law. The Jews therefore said unto him, It is not lawful for us to put any man to death:

32 That the saying of Jesus might be fulfilled, which he spake, signifying what death he should die.

33 Then Pilate entered into the judgment hall again, and called Jesus, and said unto him, Art thou the King of the Jews?

34 Jesus answered him, Sayest thou this thing of thyself, or did others tell it thee of me?

35 Pilate answered, Am I a Jew? Thine own nation and the chief priests have delivered thee unto me: what hast thou done?

36 Jesus answered, My kingdom is not of this world: if my kingdom were of this world, then would my servants fight, that I should not be delivered to the Jews: but now is my kingdom not from hence.

37 Pilate therefore said unto him, Art thou a king then? Jesus answered, Thou sayest that I am a king. To this end was I born, and for this cause came I into the world, that I should bear witness unto the truth. Every one that is of the truth heareth my voice.

38 Pilate saith unto him, What is truth? And when he had said this, he went out again unto the Jews, and saith unto them, I find in him no fault at all.

39 But ye have a custom, that I should release unto you one at the passover: will ye therefore that I release unto you the King of the Jews?

40 Then cried they all again, saying, Not this man, but Barabbas. Now Barabbas was a robber.

GOLDEN TEXT: Jesus answered, Thou sayest that I am a king. To this end was I born, and for this cause came I into the world, that I should bear witness unto the truth. —John 18:37.

Lesson Aims

After studying this lesson a student should:
1. Have a better understanding of Jesus' trial.
2. Recognize some of the social and political forces that work to thwart justice.
3. Be able to list attitudes that can lead to a betrayal of Jesus today.

Lesson Outline

INTRODUCTION
    A. A Dirty Brown Color
    B. Lesson Background
I. JESUS BROUGHT TO PILATE (John 18:28-32)
    A. Concern About Defilement (v. 28)
    B. Charges Against Jesus (vv. 29, 30)
       File Your Charges
    C. Constrained by Law (vv. 31, 32)
II. JESUS ON TRIAL (John 18:33-37)
    A. Questions (vv. 33-35)
    B. Response (vv. 36, 37)
       Simply Out of This World
III. DECISIONS (John 18:38-40)
    A. Pilate Declares Jesus Innocent (v. 38)
    B. The Crowd Chooses Barabbas (vv. 39, 40)
CONCLUSION
    A. No Fault in Him
    B. Let Us Pray
    C. Thought to Remember

Display visual 5 from the visuals packet and let it remain before the class throughout this session. The visual is shown on page 269.

Introduction

A. A Dirty Brown Color

Years ago at a county fair I was enthralled by chameleons, which were being sold at one of the concessions. This little lizard has the unusual ability to change the color of its skin to the color of its surroundings. My brother and I bought one and took it home.

This little reptile brought us a great deal of entertainment. We would place it on a background of one color and within a few minutes it would begin to take on that color. Then we would put it on another color and it would

change again. But even the chameleon has its limits. Once I put a newspaper in the bottom of its cage. I excitedly watched to see if it would begin to look like a printed page, but all that it did was turn to a dirty brown color.

Some people resemble chameleons in that they can take on the color of any situation in which they find themselves. Pilate was one of those persons. Undoubtedly this ability helped him make his way up the Roman bureaucracy ladder to high office. But like the chameleon, his ability had limits. Faced with making a decision about Jesus, he found himself in a situation with which he could not cope. Torn between his Roman commitment to justice and the Jews' demands for Jesus' life, he made a compromise that showed his true colors—a dirty brown.

B. Lesson Background

Last week's lesson concluded with Jesus being led from a preliminary hearing before Annas to a hearing before the Sanhedrin, presided over by Caiaphas. It was at this point that Jesus looked at Peter, causing Peter to realize that he had betrayed his Master. John mentions this second hearing, but he does not give us any details about it. They are recorded in Matthew 26:57, 59-68; Mark 14:53, 55-65; Luke 22:54, 63-65. After daybreak, this same body met once again (Luke 22:66-71; Matthew 27:1; Mark 15:1). Their purpose was to gather evidence that could become a basis for formal charges. When they asked Jesus if He was the Christ, He did not deny it, but He refused to give them a direct answer because He knew they would not believe Him. They also asked Him if He was the Son of God. His answer gave them grounds for charging Him with blasphemy, a charge that could bring the death penalty under Jewish laws. Once they had this information, they were ready to take Jesus to Pilate, the Roman governor.

I. Jesus Brought to Pilate (John 18:28-32)

A. Concern About Defilement (v. 28)

28. Then led they Jesus from Caiaphas unto the hall of judgment: and it was early; and they themselves went not into the judgment hall, lest they should be defiled; but that they might eat the passover.

After the Sanhedrin had decreed that Jesus should die, He was led to the judgment hall, or praetorium, which was the official residence of the governor. Many scholars believe that this was in the fortress of Antonia, a castle-like structure located at the northwest corner of the temple area.

Jesus and His accusers arrived at the judgment hall early in the morning. The Jewish leaders had a specific reason for being there early. They wanted to be certain that Jesus' conviction and execution could be carried out before evening, when the Sabbath began.

According to the teachings of the rabbis, a Jew who entered a Gentile home became ceremonially unclean. This would have barred them from the ceremonies of the Passover feast, so they remained outside the judgment hall. Notice the irony involved in this. The religious leaders were exceedingly scrupulous about observing the details of their ceremonial law, even at the very time they were conspiring to violate the moral law by arranging for Jesus' execution.

B. Charges Against Jesus (vv. 29, 30)

29. Pilate then went out unto them, and said, What accusation bring ye against this man?

Pontius Pilate had been appointed governor of Judea in A.D. 26, and he served for ten years before he was removed. During this period, he had gained a reputation for being quite brutal in his efforts to rule over the Jews. On one occasion he had aroused a very serious controversy with them by bringing into the city troops bearing their military standards with busts of the emperor upon them. Protesting that these were idolatrous, the people had staged a massive demonstration. On another occasion Pilate had given orders to attack some Jews while they were at worship (Luke 13:1). The Jewish leaders hated and distrusted Pilate. But since the Romans reserved for themselves the right to exercise the death penalty, the Jewish leaders had to obtain Pilate's judgment against Jesus in order to have Him executed.

Being aware of the stubborn prejudice of the Jews regarding entering a Gentile home, Pilate went outside to them and called on them to make their charges against Jesus.

30. They answered and said unto him, If he were not a malefactor, we would not have delivered him up unto thee.

The Jews' reply to Pilate's question bordered on arrogance. It was as if they were saying, "We constitute the highest court in Israel, and we have already found this man to be guilty. Your inquiry into this matter isn't necessary. Just do what we have decided must be done with Him."

FILE YOUR CHARGES

A certain preacher invited all the men of his community to a special meeting where he promised to give them an opportunity to register their complaints against the church. Twelve-hundred men showed up, and several aired their objec-tions to Christianity. The preacher made a list as the men voiced their criticisms.

"Church members act no differently than non-members." "Ministers don't practice what they preach." "The church patronizes the rich and ignores the poor." "Christians don't seem to believe the Bible anymore."

Twenty-seven charges were filed against Christianity. When the men were finished, the preacher read the list, then wadded the paper and threw it on the floor. He said, "Friends, you have criticized church members, preachers, the Bible, and public worship—but you have not said one word against my Master!"

Then in a brief testimony, he preached to them Jesus, the sinless Son of God. When he extended an invitation to accept Christ as Savior, forty-nine men stepped forward.

Pilate found no fault in Jesus. The charges brought against Him were unfounded and false. Christ was tempted, but sinless. His church is not perfect, but forgiven.   —R. W. B.

C. Constrained by Law (vv. 31, 32)

31. Then said Pilate unto them, Take ye him, and judge him according to your law. The Jews therefore said unto him, It is not lawful for us to put any man to death.

Obviously the governor did not have time to hear every case that might arise among the Jews. Because they had presented no formal charges, Pilate assumed that their complaint against Jesus involved matters that they, within the bounds of their law, could deal with. So, he attempted to dismiss the case. Faced with Pilate's rejection of their case, they had to provide more information. Their intention had never been for Pilate to try the case. They had already tried Jesus and condemned Him to death. All they wanted Pilate to do was sign the execution order. This was necessary, for while they could pass the death sentence, they could not carry out capital punishment.

32. That the saying of Jesus might be fulfilled, which he spake, signifying what death he should die.

Something much more significant than Roman law was at work. Earlier in His ministry, Jesus had predicted that He would be crucified (John 3:14; 12:32, 33). Jewish execution was ordinarily by stoning, and so if the Jews had executed Jesus, it would not have been by crucifixion. Ironically, the method of execution that the Jewish leaders were forced to demand made possible the fulfillment of Jesus' prediction. This is but another illustration of how God can use the anger of His enemies to carry out His purposes.

II. Jesus on Trial
(John 18:33-37)

A. Questions (vv. 33-35)

33. Then Pilate entered into the judgment hall again, and called Jesus, and said unto him, Art thou the King of the Jews?

Luke informs us that the Jews brought three charges against Jesus (23:2). He was accused of perverting the nation, forbidding the Jewish people to pay taxes to the Romans, and claiming that He was a king. Taken together, these charges meant that Jesus was stirring up rebellion against Rome in order to establish himself as the ruler of an independent Jewish nation.

The Jewish leaders brought these charges because they knew they would catch the attention of Pilate. Their real charge against Jesus—blasphemy because He had made himself the Son of God—would not carry much weight with the governor. The Romans were quite willing to allow a great deal of religious freedom among their subject peoples so long as their practices did not disrupt the peace or challenge Rome's rule. But for someone to claim that he was a king was an act of subversion that Rome would not tolerate. Pilate, therefore, went inside the judgment hall and summoned the prisoner to be brought in so he might question Him.

34. Jesus answered him, Sayest thou this thing of thyself, or did others tell it thee of me?

Jesus did not answer Pilate directly, but countered with a question of His own. He was not trying to avoid the question, but He wanted to make certain that Pilate would understand His answer when He gave it. As a Roman, Pilate would naturally think in terms of a physical kingdom, and so if Jesus answered "yes" to Pilate's question, then Pilate would misunderstand Him. For that matter, Jesus' own disciples misunderstood His teachings about the kingdom. They too were looking for a physical kingdom (Acts 1:6). In raising His question, Jesus was asking whether Pilate had carefully thought the matter through or whether he was merely repeating the charges he had heard from the Pharisees and Sadducees.

35. Pilate answered, Am I a Jew? Thine own nation and the chief priests have delivered thee unto me: what hast thou done?

Pilate responded with obvious contempt. He certainly was not a Jew, and he had no reason to conclude, as did these Jewish leaders, that Jesus wanted to be a king. After all, Pilate reminded Jesus, the Romans had nothing to do with the whole affair. It was Jesus' own people, the Jews, led by the chief priests, who had brought Him for judgment. Pilate knew that these leaders had brought Jesus to him because of envy (Mark 15:10). He wanted to know what Jesus had done to cause these rulers to reject Him.

B. Response (vv. 36, 37)

36. Jesus answered, My kingdom is not of this world: if my kingdom were of this world, then would my servants fight, that I should not be delivered to the Jews: but now is my kingdom not from hence.

Jesus returned to Pilate's earlier question. To answer whether or not He was a king, Jesus had first of all to explain to Pilate the nature of His kingdom. Certainly Jesus did not look like a king or act like one in the usual sense. Jesus' kingdom was *not of this world*, that is, His power did not come from worldly sources. Earthly kings fought or led their armies into battle to defend their kingdoms. The clearest evidence that Jesus' kingdom was different was that He did not encourage or even allow His subjects to fight in order to protect Him from the Jews. Just a few days earlier, thousands of them had escorted Jesus into Jerusalem, crying, "Blessed is the King of Israel that cometh in the name of the Lord" (John 12:13). Pilate certainly knew about this. No doubt many of the people would have been eager to join in armed rebellion, but Jesus had kept the peace.

The truth Jesus related here is hard for men to accept or understand. Because Jesus' kingdom is not of this world, some have concluded that it has nothing to do with this world. Nothing could be further from the truth! This physical world was created by God, and Jesus' kingdom was also created by God to redeem this world. To withdraw from the world because Christ's kingdom is Heavenly is to miss the redemptive purpose God has for the church.

Some, forgetting that Christ's kingdom is not of this world, have at times resorted to worldly methods to advance it. The Crusades offer a good example of the use of military force to help the cause of the kingdom. We today are under

---

How to Say It

ANNAS. *An*-nus.

BARABBAS. Buh-*rab*-us.

CAIAPHAS. *Kay*-uh-fus or *Kye*-uh-fus.

PHARISEES. *Fair*-ih-seez.

SADDUCEES. *Sad*-you-seez.

SANHEDRIN. *San*-huh-drun or San-*heed*-run.

constant temptation to use the methods of the world to win victories for His kingdom.

37. Pilate therefore said unto him, Art thou a king then? Jesus answered, Thou sayest that I am a king. To this end was I born, and for this cause came I into the world, that I should bear witness unto the truth. Every one that is of the truth heareth my voice.

It seems evident from Pilate's next question that he did not really grasp what Jesus was talking about. Words about a spiritual kingdom simply did not make sense to a Roman, who was conditioned to think in worldly terms. Pilate would have been right at home in the intellectual climate of today's world. We too live in an age that rejects spiritual values for material ones.

Jesus turned Pilate's question into an affirmation: "You have said that I am a king. You are quite correct. I am a king." Jesus then went on to point out that He was not a king by being born into a royal family or because of some political quirk of fate. Jesus was born into the world for no other purpose than to be a king. He left the halls of Heaven with the explicit purpose of claiming the throne that only He could occupy. He humbled himself by entering the world through the natural birth process. Everything that He had done on earth was to establish himself as king over His kingdom.

As king, His mission was to bear witness to the truth that God had made provisions for the salvation of the human race. His mission was not to rule over vast territories or preside over the imperial court as did the Roman emperor. His kingship consisted in bearing witness to God's gracious offer of salvation. The subjects of King Jesus were not those who had been born in His realm or who had been subjected to His rule by military conquest. His subjects were and still are those who believe and accept the salvation He came to offer.

SIMPLY OUT OF THIS WORLD

Herschel Ford once published a sermon with that title. The purpose of the sermon was to point up the wonderful nature of the works of God, the extraordinary quality of the spiritual life. He wrote of God's plan for salvation, the gift of God's Spirit, the revelation of God's Word, God's answers to prayer, the joy of doing God's work, and the promise of God's Heaven. Those topics can only be described in terms of supernatural wonder and awesome providence. Such realities are "other-worldly," beyond the realm of ordinary experience.

That's what Jesus spoke of when He said, "My kingdom is not of this world." His reign is spiri-

visual 5

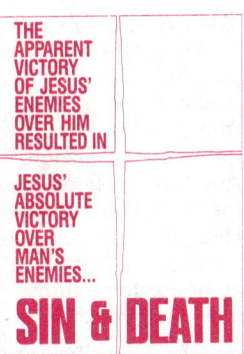

THE APPARENT VICTORY OF JESUS' ENEMIES OVER HIM RESULTED IN

JESUS' ABSOLUTE VICTORY OVER MAN'S ENEMIES...

SIN & DEATH

tual, beyond the limits of earth-bound existence. Pilate's power was puny by contrast.

The church is the evidence of Christ's kingdom on earth. All obedient believers around the world and through the ages are included. It is immense and powerful beyond imagination. It is glorious and redemptive; it is secure and radiant. The church of Jesus Christ is simply out of this world!

—R. W. B.

III. Decisions
(John 18:38-40)

A. Pilate Declares Jesus Innocent
(v. 38)

38. Pilate saith unto him, What is truth? And when he had said this, he went out again unto the Jews, and saith unto them, I find in him no fault at all.

For centuries, concerned and sincere persons have raised and struggled to answer the question that Pilate asked Jesus. What, indeed, is the nature of truth? How do we test it? How do we distinguish it from falsehood? What are the implications of truth in our lives? But it is doubtful that Pilate felt any of these concerns when he raised his question. His question seems to have been a cynical rejection of the whole issue, the words of a man who had long since abandoned any interest in searching for truth. In a sneering tone, he seems to have been signaling his dismissal of Jesus' case as a matter of little moment. The tragedy of the situation was that the answer to his question stood before him, for Jesus embodied the ultimate Truth of the universe.

However, Pilate had learned one thing from his interrogation of Jesus—Jesus was not guilty of any crime. It was readily apparent to Pilate that Jesus offered no threat to the Roman government. Going back outside to the waiting crowd, Pilate announced his verdict. He was honest enough to tell the Jews that he found no fault in Jesus, but he lacked the courage to release Him.

Upon hearing Pilate's verdict, the crowd, controlled by the chief priests and the rulers of the people, cried out the more fiercely against Jesus. It was then that Pilate learned that Jesus was from Galilee. Seizing on this as an opportunity to avoid the responsibility for the case, Pilate sent him to Herod, who had come to Jerusalem for the Passover. Herod and his soldiers mocked Him and, placing a royal robe about him, sent Him back to Pilate (Luke 23:6-12). Verses 39 and 40 of our text tell of Jesus' final appearance before Pilate after He was returned from Herod.

B. The Crowd Chooses Barabbas
(vv. 39, 40)

39. But ye have a custom, that I should release unto you one at the passover: will ye therefore that I release unto you the King of the Jews?

Apparently new crowds of people by this time had joined those standing in front of the judgment hall. Among them must have been some friends of Jesus, for they reminded Pilate of his custom of releasing a prisoner at the Passover (Mark 15:6-8). Pilate seized upon this as an opportunity to set Jesus free. He nominated two candidates for release, Barabbas and Jesus (Matthew 27:17). Mark 15:9 and the verse before us indicated that he hoped they would ask for the release of Jesus.

40. Then cried they all again, saying, Not this man, but Barabbas. Now Barabbas was a robber.

The last thing Pilate expected was that the crowd would demand the release of Barabbas, a man who was not only a robber but an insurrectionist and a murderer (Luke 23:19). Pilate did not realize that the chief priests and elders had outsmarted him by persuading the crowd to demand Barabbas (Matthew 27:20). How tragic that the crowd chose a criminal instead of the Prince of Peace! And how ironic that the Jewish leaders unwittingly made a decision that ultimately carried out God's will!

Conclusion

A. No Fault in Him

The Jewish leaders during Jesus' trials did everything they could to find a legal basis to bring charges against Him. They brought false witnesses to testify against Him, but their testimony proved contradictory and worthless. When it was all over, they still did not have any evidence that he was guilty of any crime or sin. Pilate heard the charges brought against Jesus and, after examining Him, declared that he could find in Him no basis for condemnation. The multitude, whipped into a frenzied mob, demanded His blood, but without ever charging him with a crime. Though none of these—the leaders, Pilate, or the mob—could find any fault in Him, yet they all rejected Him.

Through the centuries, this same pattern has been repeated. Religious leaders, philosophers, politicians, the multitudes—all have acclaimed or acknowledged the moral perfection of Jesus. No one has proposed a moral standard higher than His. Yet even as these have found no fault in Him, most of them have not been willing to surrender themselves to Him.

Even today, none have found any fault in Him. For one even to hint that Jesus was less than morally perfect is to reveal that that person has not examined the record or has deliberately perverted that record. Yet most of those who would not think of speaking ill of Jesus are still unwilling to surrender their lives to Him.

The leaders of Israel, Pilate, and the crowd all faced a choice when Jesus was on trial: to seek that which is temporary or that which is permanent, the approval of men or the approval of God. In rejecting Jesus, they chose the former in each instance. Which will we choose?

B. Let Us Pray

Dear God, our hearts are moved as we see the envy of the religious leaders and the cowardice of Pilate that resulted in Jesus being crucified. May we learn from their examples to avoid these sins. Father, help us acknowledge our own sins that were just as responsible for Jesus' death. Forgive us these sins. Amen.

C. Thought to Remember

Jesus did not come to defend traditions; He was sent to His death by men who did.

Home Daily Bible Readings

Monday, Mar. 26—Shared Suffering (1 Peter 4:12-19)

Tuesday, Mar. 27—Through Pain to Blessing (Hebrews 12:3-11)

Wednesday, Mar. 28—Obedient to the Death (Philippians 2:1-11)

Thursday, Mar. 29—The Death of Judas (Matthew 27:1-5)

Friday, Mar. 30—Jesus Before Pilate (Matthew 27:11-19)

Saturday, Mar. 31—Pilate Hands Jesus Over (Matthew 27:20-26)

Sunday, Apr. 1—The Soldiers Mock Jesus (Matthew 27:27-32)

Learning by Doing

This page contains an alternate lesson plan emphasizing learning activities. Classes desiring such student involvement will find these suggestions helpful.

Learning Goals

As students participate in today's session, they should accomplish the following:

1. Survey all four Gospels to gain a complete picture of all the trials of Jesus before His crucifixion.

2. Compare these trials with the way people may relate to Jesus today.

3. Consider ways they themselves may have rejected Jesus.

Into the Lesson

Write the words *Jesus on Trial* on your chalkboard before class. To begin the class, ask students, "Can you think of ways Jesus has been put on trial by our society?" Be ready with some examples of your own to start their thinking. Give them sixty seconds to discuss this in pairs, and then discuss with the whole class.

Tell students that our study of Christ's life leads us today to examine the trials that led to His death. Tell them, "We will try to see how Jesus' actual trials compare with the way men and women are trying Him today."

Into the Word

Give each student a copy of the following outline. Or make a poster or overhead transparency to display before the class:

THE TRIALS OF JESUS

Trial One
John 18:12-14, 19-23

Trial Two
Matthew 26:57, 59-68
Mark 14:53, 55-65
Luke 22:54, 63-65
John 18:24

Trial Three
Matthew 27:1
Mark 15:1
Luke 22:66-71

Trial Four
Matthew 27:2, 11-14
Mark 15:2-5
Luke 23:1-5
John 18:28-38

Trial Five
Luke 23:6-12

Trial Six
Matthew 27:15-26
Mark 15:6-15
Luke 23:13-25
John 18:39—19:16

Tell students that today they will look at the Biblical record of all the trials of Jesus. Divide them into groups of about four and ask them to look up the Scriptures listed under each heading and to answer the following questions for each trial:

1. Before whom was Jesus tried? (Answers— one: Annas; two: Caiaphas; three: the Sanhedrin; four: Pilate; five: Herod; six: Pilate again.)

2. Who were His accusers?

3. What was the attitude of His judge?

4. What defense did He offer?

5. What was the outcome?

6. Did Jesus get a fair trial here?

It will be beneficial for students if they have time in their small groups to answer the questions about all six trials. If you do not have time for this, assign each of your small groups one or two of the trials. Students can take notes on the trials they have not studied as they hear their classmates report.

Into Life

After you have established the facts of all the trials, help students see the significance of the trials. To do this, lead them to answer the following discussion questions:

1. How were Jesus' accusers and judges like each other? How were they different?

2. How was their attitude or relationship to Jesus like the way some people in our day feel about Him?

3. How is Jesus sometimes put on trial by Christians?

4. Suppose today's study were your first serious introduction to Jesus. What could you learn about Him from this text alone?

Read, from the conclusion of the first lesson plan, the section entitled "No Fault in Him." (You may want to have a class member prepared ahead of time to read this. Or you could even tape record this section before class.)

Ask students, "As we've considered these trials of Jesus today, have you thought of ways you yourself have rejected Him?" Close the class session with guided prayer.

Let's Talk It Over

The questions on this page are designed to encourage review of the lesson Scriptures and to promote discussion of the lesson by the class. The answers provided are only discussion starters. Let your class talk it over from there.

1. Decisions made in the political arena (the Pilates of our day) can hinder or help the Christian cause. When should Christians run for political office?

That depends partly on the conscience of the individual Christian. Christians are both citizens of Heaven in an eternal sense and citizens on earth in a temporary sense. We are to be salt, light, and leaven here on earth. A Christian should express his citizenship in a way that will accomplish as much good as possible. We are to express our Christianity in the communities in which we live. It is certainly not wrong for us who are Christians to run for political office; however, those who do so should be qualified and competent.

2. At Jesus' trial, Pilate asked of Jesus' enemies, "What accusation do you bring against this man?" How may we use this question?

That would be a good question to ask someone who does not accept Jesus as the Messiah. It would also be a good question to ask someone who refuses to have anything to do with the church. We could mention to that person that Jesus himself instituted the church. Admittedly, problems sometimes arise in the church, and that is simply because the church is made up of fallible human beings. But what fault may be found in Jesus? If none, then surely He is worthy of our celebration of Him and worship of Him in the context of the church He established.

3. Should Christians today bring any issue to politicians to settle?

Of course. Christians are to use the political system just as much as anyone else. At the time Paul was being falsely accused before the provincial governor, he did not hesitate to appeal to Caesar. Those who occupy positions of political authority are to be God's servants for rewarding the good and punishing the evil (Romans 13:3, 4).

4. Because political authority has been instituted by God, does that mean every politician is God's choice and is thus God's servant or minister?

Of course not. Political authority is part of God's design for maintaining law and order on earth, but the specific person who occupies a position of authority may be perverted and not God's choice at all. A good example of that would be Hitler. All politicians should understand that they occupy positions of responsibility that God ordained for the purpose of serving Him by rewarding the good and avenging the wrong. When those in high position use their power for perverse purposes, they bring upon themselves the judgment of God.

5. When (if ever) should Christians disobey a political order?

It is proper for us who are Christians to disobey a political order if that order directly violates a clear command that God has given us in His Word. (See Acts 4:18-21.) But we should not disobey as if the governing authorities were our enemies. If we do disobey such an order, we should take without complaint whatever consequences come as a result. We should pray for our rulers, so that the laws they enact will promote godliness and honesty in the citizenry and will enable us to live quiet and peaceful lives (1 Timothy 2:1, 2). We should always do what is morally right (1 Peter 2:13-17).

6. As Christians, how should we react when we are unfairly accused?

We should do as Jesus did—state simply and clearly the truth, realizing that we cannot control another person's judgment or actions. But we should not allow another person's actions to control our reactions. When we do, that other person is in control of us whether we realize it or not. All we can do is control ourselves. When Jesus was reviled, He did not revile in return. He uttered no threats, but entrusted himself to God (1 Peter 2:23). Consequently, Jesus was victorious over His accusers—even though the final victory came after much pain.

7. Often it is said that all of us, not just those Roman soldiers, put Jesus on the cross. What do you think?

Our sins, as much as those of every other person who ever lived, were the reason Jesus went to the cross. We did not drive the nails into His body; but if we were not sinners, He would not have had to die.

Death and Burial

LESSON SCRIPTURE: John 19:17-42.

PRINTED TEXT: John 19:28-42.

John 19:28-42

28 After this, Jesus knowing that all things were now accomplished, that the Scripture might be fulfilled, saith, I thirst.

29 Now there was set a vessel full of vinegar: and they filled a sponge with vinegar, and put it upon hyssop, and put it to his mouth.

30 When Jesus therefore had received the vinegar, he said, It is finished: and he bowed his head, and gave up the ghost.

31 The Jews therefore, because it was the preparation, that the bodies should not remain upon the cross on the sabbath day, (for that sabbath day was a high day,) besought Pilate that their legs might be broken, and that they might be taken away.

32 Then came the soldiers, and brake the legs of the first, and of the other which was crucified with him.

33 But when they came to Jesus, and saw that he was dead already, they brake not his legs:

34 But one of the soldiers with a spear pierced his side, and forthwith came there out blood and water.

35 And he that saw it bare record, and his record is true; and he knoweth that he saith true, that ye might believe.

36 For these things were done, that the Scripture should be fulfilled, A bone of him shall not be broken.

37 And again another Scripture saith, They shall look on him whom they pierced.

38 And after this Joseph of Arimathea, being a disciple of Jesus, but secretly for fear of the Jews, besought Pilate that he might take away the body of Jesus: and Pilate gave him leave. He came therefore, and took the body of Jesus.

39 And there came also Nicodemus, which at the first came to Jesus by night, and brought a mixture of myrrh and aloes, about a hundred pound weight.

40 Then took they the body of Jesus, and wound it in linen clothes with the spices, as the manner of the Jews is to bury.

41 Now in the place where he was crucified there was a garden; and in the garden a new sepulchre, wherein was never man yet laid.

42 There laid they Jesus therefore because of the Jews' preparation day; for the sepulchre was nigh at hand.

GOLDEN TEXT: When Jesus therefore had received the vinegar, he said, It is finished: and he bowed his head, and gave up the ghost.—John 19:30.

John Writes of Life, Light, and Love
Unit 1: The Gospel of Life and Light
(John, Lessons 1-7)

Lesson Aims

As a result of studying this lesson, each student should:

1. Have a greater appreciation for what Jesus' suffering and death meant for us.

2. Be able to share with others the facts of Jesus' death and burial as recorded in the Gospel of John.

Lesson Outline

INTRODUCTION
   A. "The Way of the Cross Leads Home"
   B. Lesson Background
I. JESUS' DEATH (John 19:28-30)
   A. Request for a Drink (v. 28)
   B. Jesus Given Vinegar (v. 29)
   C. "It Is Finished" (v. 30)
     The Fulfillment of Finishing
II. JESUS' DEATH MADE SURE (John 19:31-37)
   A. Concern About the Sabbath (v. 31)
   B. Thieves' Legs Broken (vv. 32, 33)
   C. Jesus' Side Pierced (v. 34)
   D. John's Testimony (vv. 35-37)
III. JESUS' BURIAL (John 19:38-42)
   A. The Body Removed (v. 38)
   B. Preparation for Burial (vv. 39, 40)
   C. The Garden Tomb (vv. 41, 42)
     Closet Christians
CONCLUSION
   A. "I Thirst"
   B. Let Us Pray
   C. Thought to Remember

Display visual 6 from the visuals packet and let it remain before the class. The visual is shown on page 277.

Introduction

A. "The Way of the Cross Leads Home"

On the outskirts of London a large white cross stands at an important intersection. One day in the heart of London a policeman came upon a small boy standing on a corner, who was crying his heart out.

"What's the matter, son?" asked the policeman.

"I'm lost," sniffled the lad.

"Where do you live?"

"I don't know."

"But if we don't know where you live, how can we help you get home?"

"Well, if you can get me to the big white cross, I can find my way home from there!" This little lad had learned that the way of the cross leads home.

We need to learn that same truth on a higher, spiritual level. Our human minds will never be able to fully understand the meaning of Christ's cross. We know that it meant suffering and death for Jesus. We know that it brought a death of shame. We know that it was a stumbling block for the Jews and foolishness for the Greeks. But we still have not plumbed the depths of the theological meaning of the cross. One thing we know for sure, however, is that the way of the cross leads home to the home that awaits us in Heaven!

B. Lesson Background

Last week's lesson concluded with Pilate offering the crowd the choice of having Jesus or Barabbas released unto them. Much to Pilate's dismay, the mob chose Barabbas. But Pilate was still unwilling to order Jesus' execution. Instead, he ordered Jesus scourged. After the soldiers had placed a crown of thorns on Jesus' head and placed a purple robe about Him, Pilate presented Him to the crowd with the assurance that he still found no fault in Him. Apparently Pilate hoped that the crowd, seeing Jesus in such a pitiful state, would feel some sympathy for Him and relent in their demand that He be crucified.

Pilate miscalculated the antagonism that the mob held for Jesus. Led by the chief priests and officers, they arose to a frenzy in their cry, "Crucify Him, Crucify Him!" But in spite of this, Pilate still sought to release Him. The Jewish leaders, however, would have none of this. They argued that if he let Jesus go, he was no friend of Caesar. The implied threat was that they would see to it that Caesar heard all about this incident if Pilate released Jesus. Pilate was not courageous enough to stand against such a threat, and so he finally turned Jesus over to them to be crucified.

I. Jesus' Death (John 19:28-30)

In the verses immediately preceding the printed text, John tells that Jesus was crucified between two thieves at "the place of a skull" or "Golgotha" in Hebrew. Pilate had placed on the cross above Jesus the inscription "Jesus of Nazareth the King of the Jews." The chief priests objected to this title, but Pilate, who had been bullied to his limit by them, refused to change it. As Jesus hung dying on the cross, the Roman soldiers gambled for his garments. In spite of humiliating indignities and excruciating pain, Jesus still thought of His mother, commending her to the apostle John for care.

A. Request for a Drink (v. 28)

28. After this, Jesus knowing that all things were now accomplished, that the Scripture might be fulfilled, saith, I thirst.

Both Matthew and Mark tell us that Jesus was given a drink, but only John tells us that He asked for it. Jesus had been on the cross for six hours. The loss of blood and the severe shock of His suffering would cause intense thirst. Jesus knew that the end of His terrible suffering was at hand. He had drunk the cup of agony to its very dregs, and now He could take a bit of relief by assuaging His thirst. John tells us that this action marked the fulfillment of prophecy. The Scripture referred to may be either Psalm 22:15 or Psalm 69:21.

B. Jesus Given Vinegar (v. 29)

29. Now there was set a vessel full of vinegar: and they filled a sponge with vinegar, and put it upon hyssop, and put it to his mouth.

The *vinegar* was a cheap sour wine, probably brought by the soldiers for their own use during their long duty at the cross. Previously Jesus had refused "wine mingled with myrrh" (Mark 15:23), which was given to reduce the pain of crucifixion. At that point, Jesus did not want to deaden the pain of His death, but intended to bear it fully for the sins of man. Now, however, Jesus could accept the drink because it contained no pain killer and because His suffering was almost completed.

A sponge was soaked in the liquid and it was raised to His parched lips on the stalk of a hyssop plant. Several plants bear this generic name, making it impossible to identify precisely the plant that was used.

C. "It Is Finished" (v. 30)

30. When Jesus therefore had received the vinegar, he said, It is finished: and he bowed his head, and gave up the ghost.

Once he had received the drink of vinegar, Jesus uttered His final words. Both Matthew and Mark report that He cried with a loud voice and gave up the ghost. The vinegar may have cleared His mouth and throat so that He could utter these words loudly and clearly. Luke tells us that Jesus' final words were, "Father, into thy

hands I commend my spirit" (23:46). There is no contradiction. John just gives us additional information that Luke did not report. Jesus' words, "It is finished," would quite logically accompany the words that Luke records.

It is finished. These words mean more than just the fact that Jesus' life was completed. Jesus was saying that His earthly ministry was fulfilled. While it is true that He still had to be placed in the tomb and rise again on the third day, yet the shedding of His blood, His sacrificial death that made the atonement possible, had been completed. Once this was accomplished, He *gave up the ghost.* It is important to note that He *gave up* His life; it was not taken from Him. Earlier He had talked of voluntarily giving His life: "No man taketh it from me, but I lay it down of myself" (John 10:18).

THE FULFILLMENT OF FINISHING

Visiting the pyramids in Egypt is an awesome experience. The logistics of such constructions are staggering. A vast number of workers were involved, many of whom labored all of their lives on the project and never saw its completion. They never experienced the grand fulfillment of a moment when they could say with relief and satisfaction, "It is finished!"

It is important to the human attitude toward work of any kind, that the end of it be in sight. The longer it takes to complete a task, and the more difficult the labor is, the greater the sense of accomplishment when the job is complete.

Even before the foundations of earth were laid, Jesus was assigned the work of redemption. He anticipated the cross from that time until finally He came to earth in the flesh to dwell among us. In His death, the work was completed. So, His cry of relief and victory: "It is finished!"

If we are faithful Christians until we die, we can realize the fulfillment sensed by Paul when he wrote, "I have finished my course, I have kept the faith" (2 Timothy 4:7).   —R. W. B.

II. Jesus' Death Made Sure (John 19:31-37)

A. Concern About the Sabbath (v. 31)

31. The Jews therefore, because it was the preparation, that the bodies should not remain upon the cross on the sabbath day, (for that sabbath day was a high day,) besought Pilate that their legs might be broken, and that they might be taken away.

How ironic that the religious leaders were so concerned about keeping the details of the law even while they were committing murder! Deuteronomy 21:23 states that anyone executed should not "remain all night upon the tree." Such a one was considered accursed of God, and the land would be defiled if the body were to remain thus exposed. The Jews had an additional concern because it was *the preparation*, that is, Friday, the day before the Sabbath. And this was no ordinary Sabbath. It was the Sabbath of the feast of Passover, *a high day.*

Once more the Jewish leaders had to come before Pilate with a request, that the legs of the men on the crosses be broken and that they be removed from the crosses. This brutal custom of the Romans added to the shame and torment of the victim, even though it hastened death.

B. Thieves' Legs Broken (vv. 32, 33)

32, 33. Then came the soldiers, and brake the legs of the first, and of the other which was crucified with him. But when they came to Jesus, and saw that he was dead already, they brake not his legs.

Given the urgency of the situation, Pilate probably immediately ordered the deed to be carried out. The legs of the two thieves were broken first, but when they turned to Jesus and found that He was already dead, they did not break His bones. Some have surmised that the treatment that Jesus had suffered during His trial (including the terrible scourging) had so weakened His body that He died first. But John has already told us the reason for His early death: He had knowingly and deliberately given up His life.

C. Jesus' Side Pierced (v. 34)

34. But one of the soldiers with a spear pierced his side, and forthwith came there out blood and water.

A Roman soldier under orders was not likely to take any chances. In order to make certain that no life remained in Jesus' body, one of the soldiers thrust his spear into Jesus' side. Only John reports this incident. John's Gospel was written after the other three Gospels, and by that time some were raising doubts that Jesus had actually died. It may be that John mentions this in order to refute this early heresy.

Both blood and water came from the wound. Physiologists and physicians have written dozens of treatises about this phenomenon in order to explain it. There is no general agreement about which hypothesis best explains the evidence, but, of course, that doesn't really matter. John reported what he saw, and that is what is important. From his testimony we can be sure that Jesus was most certainly human and that He most certainly died.

D. John's Testimony (vv. 35-37)

35. And he that saw it bare record, and his record is true; and he knoweth that he saith true, that ye might believe.

While John narrates this in the third person, it is evident that he is referring to himself as the witness. Courts recognize that the surest testimony comes from a competent eyewitness who was in a position to have observed the event in question. John met all of these requirements. He was an eyewitness, he was in a position to observe the event, and certainly he was competent.

That ye might believe. John's purpose in writing his Gospel is stated here and again in 20:31. His intent was that persons come to believe that Jesus Christ is the Son of God, and thereby receive eternal life through Him.

36. For these things were done, that the Scripture should be fulfilled, A bone of him shall not be broken.

Exodus 12:46 and Numbers 9:12 specify that none of the bones of the Passover lamb should be broken as it was prepared for the Passover meal. At the very beginning of Jesus' public ministry, John the Baptist had identified Him as the "Lamb of God, which taketh away the sin of the world" (John 1:29). Further, the apostle Paul indicates that the Passover lamb was a type of Christ when he says, "Christ our passover is sacrificed for us" (1 Corinthians 5:7). Thus, when the soldiers left Jesus' legs unbroken, the Old Testament Scripture was literally fulfilled in Him. This fulfillment of Scripture is recorded by John so that our faith may be strengthened.

37. And again another Scripture saith, They shall look on him whom they pierced.

John shows that the piercing of Jesus' body was the fulfillment of another Scripture (Zechariah 12:10). Those who witnessed this last act of desecration heaped upon Jesus may be divided into at least three groups: the religious leaders or their representatives, who rejoiced in it; the Roman soldiers, who probably looked upon it as

---

How to Say It

ARIMATHEA.   Air-uh-muh-*thee*-uh.
BARABBAS.   Buh-*rab*-us.
DOCETISM.   Doe-*set*-iz-um.
GOLGOTHA.   *Gahl*-guh-thuh.
NICODEMUS.   *Nick*-uh-*dee*-mus (strong accent on *dee*).
SANHEDRIN.   *San*-huh-drun or San-*heed*-run.

nothing more than part of the day's work; and the followers of Jesus, who agonized over it. Even in our day we may discern similar groupings: some who oppose Jesus and vehemently reject all that He stands for; many, perhaps the majority, who are neutral, having no strong feelings about Him either way; and His followers, who seek to obey Him.

III. Jesus' Burial
(John 19:38-42)

A. The Body Removed (v. 38)

38. And after this Joseph of Arimathea, being a disciple of Jesus, but secretly for fear of the Jews, besought Pilate that he might take away the body of Jesus: and Pilate gave him leave. He came therefore, and took the body of Jesus.

Joseph is mentioned in all three of the other Gospel accounts. He was a rich man (Matthew 27:57), an honorable counselor (Mark 15:43), and a good man and a member of the Sanhedrin (Luke 23:50, 51). The location of Arimathea is not known for certain, although some place it about twenty miles northwest of Jerusalem.

Joseph had been a disciple of Jesus, but he had not revealed that fact *for fear of the Jews.* He had good reason to fear the religious leaders. Even without resorting to physical threats, they had several weapons of coercion at their disposal. They could have expelled him from the Sanhedrin; they could have expelled him from the synagogue; or, if he had been in business, they could have boycotted him.

Although Joseph may have been timid earlier about expressing his feelings toward Jesus, he now threw those restraints aside and boldly approached Pilate for permission to bury the body. We are not told the reason for Joseph's change in sentiment, but several factors may have contributed to it. He may have been appalled at how unjustly Jesus had been treated during his trials; he may have been disgusted at the hypocrisy of the chief priests and scribes; or he may have been exasperated by their arrogance.

Most of the twelve had fled, and Mary was so overwhelmed by grief that she could not make arrangements for the burial. Since no one else had asked for the body, Pilate, after making certain that Jesus was dead (Mark 15:44, 45), gave Joseph permission to take the body.

B. Preparation for Burial (vv. 39, 40)

39, 40. And there came also Nicodemus, which at the first came to Jesus by night, and brought a mixture of myrrh and aloes, about a hundred pound weight. Then took they the body of Jesus, wound it in linen clothes with the spices, as the manner of the Jews is to bury.

Joseph did not have to carry out this painful task alone. He was assisted by Nicodemus, who, like Joseph, was a member of the Sanhedrin (John 3:1, 2). On one occasion Nicodemus had spoken out in defense of Jesus before the chief priests and Pharisees (John 7:50-52). It seems certain that the two men had cooperated in making burial arrangements even before Jesus died, for each brought only a part of the items necessary for burial. Nicodemus brought the spices; Joseph brought the linen cloths (Mark 15:46) and provided the tomb (Matthew 27:60).

Myrrh is a resinous substance exuded from the branches of certain plants that grow in the Arabian Desert. It was one of the gifts brought to Jesus at His birth by the Wise-men. Aloe was a fragrant powdered wood, imported from the East. A substantial amount of these two items was used—*a hundred pound weight,* or about seventy-five pounds by our standards. The two men may have been assisted by servants in transporting the spices and the linen to the grave site. There, as the linen strips were wound around the limbs and the body, the spices were strewn in generously.

C. The Garden Tomb (vv. 41, 42)

41, 42. Now in the place where he was crucified there was a garden; and in the garden a new sepulchre, wherein was never man yet laid. There laid they Jesus therefore because of the Jews' preparation day; for the sepulcher was nigh at hand.

Two sites are usually suggested for the crucifixion and burial. The Church of the Holy Sepulcher in the northwestern part of old Jerusalem is one of these. The other is the so-called Garden Tomb north of the Damascus Gate on the north side of the city. At the latter location, tourists will be shown a rock-hewn tomb that is quite ancient and certainly resembles the type of tomb used in Jesus' day. But there is no clear evidence that this is actually the tomb where His body was laid. Nearby is a rugged outcropping of rock that resembles a skull. Guides point this out as

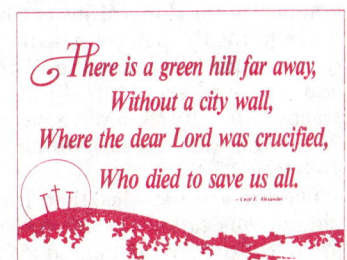

There is a green hill far away,
Without a city wall,
Where the dear Lord was crucified,
Who died to save us all.

visual 6

the place of the crucifixion. Even if the scholars are not able to settle the question about the exact place where these events took place, the important thing to keep in mind is that they did.

The tomb was a new one that had never been used before. No decay or decomposition had ever touched it, thus it was a most fitting resting place for Jesus' body. Furthermore, it was situated conveniently near the place where the crucifixion occurred. Joseph and Nicodemus had to complete their work in a hurry, for it was *the Jews' preparation day*, that is, Friday, and the Sabbath was rapidly approaching (Luke 23:54). Once they had prepared the body and placed it in the bomb, they "rolled a great stone to the door of the sepulchre, and departed" (Matthew 27:60).

CLOSET CHRISTIANS

Coming "out of the closet" seems to be a social phenomenon peculiar to the last quarter of this century. We see it demonstrated by those in differing groups—from "gays" admitting their homosexuality, to politicians acknowledging extra-marital affairs. Motivations vary, but many who reveal such secret sins hope to win "points" for *honesty*—with voters, fans, and the public at large.

And modern citizens *do* tend to forgive "up front" sinners more quickly than they forgive hypocritical Christians. Most people despise those who pretend to be righteous. Followers of Jesus Christ who keep their discipleship secret are not highly regarded either.

When the body of Jesus needed proper burial, Nicodemus and Joseph of Arimathea "came out of the closet." They had secretly received His teaching and followed Him "afar off," but finally their faith had to be declared.

Do we keep our commitment to Christ secret? Do we sign our promises to God: "Anonymous"? If so, isn't it time we came out of the closet?   —R. W. B.

Conclusion

A. "I Thirst"

The Gospel of John goes to great lengths to emphasize the deity of Jesus Christ. In the prologue to his Gospel, John writes, "In the beginning was the Word, and the Word was with God, and the Word was God." But John also stresses Jesus' humanity. A few verses later, he writes, "And the Word was made flesh, and dwelt among us."

One of the heresies that plagued the early church was called Docetism. Docetists, by one argument or another, denied that the Son of God really came in the flesh. Some of them said that what appeared to be a human being was actually a phantom, some kind of a ghostly figure. Others, unwilling to accept the fact that the Son of God could die, held that the divine element left the body of Jesus at the crucifixion.

John portrays the crucifixion in enough detail to make it clear that Jesus suffered terrible agony on the cross just as any other human being would. Jesus' cry, "I thirst," illustrates one example of that suffering. The loss of blood and shock from the beating He had taken would bring on a burning thirst. Nothing better illustrates His humanity than His anguished cry for a drink.

In our day, the skeptics are more likely to question Jesus' deity than His humanity. The result is that we are inclined to defend His deity so strenuously that we neglect his humanity. Let us never forget that the Son of God came in a human body and that He experienced hunger and thirst and pain just as we do. More important, in that human body He "was in all points tempted like as we are, yet without sin" (Hebrews 4:15).

B. Let Us Pray

Dear Father, may our hearts be touched by Jesus' sufferings on the cross. Help us to realize even more fully that His sufferings came because of our sins. May we ever keep that in mind as we pray for forgiveness. In His name, amen.

C. Thought to Remember

There is a green hill far away,
  Without a city wall,
Where the dear Lord was crucified,
  Who died to save us all.
                            —CECIL F. ALEXANDER

Home Daily Bible Readings

Monday, Apr. 2—"The King of the Jews" (John 19:17-22)

Tuesday, Apr. 3—The Crucifixion (John 19:23-27)

Wednesday, Apr. 4—"Weep Not for Me" (Luke 23:26-31)

Thursday, Apr. 5—A Prayer for Forgiveness From the Cross (Luke 23:32-38)

Friday, Apr. 6—A Promise of Life From the Cross (Luke 23:39-43)

Saturday, Apr. 7—Jesus Dies (Luke 23:44-49)

Sunday, Apr. 8—Jesus Is Buried (Luke 23:50-56)

Learning by Doing

This page contains an alternate lesson plan emphasizing learning activities. Classes desiring such student involvement will find these suggestions helpful.

Learning Goals

Lead students to accomplish the following:

1. List key characters and facts in the story of Jesus' death and burial as recorded by John.

2. Reflect on the meaning of Jesus' death for us today and thank God for His marvelous gift.

Into the Lesson

Ask students to discuss in small groups, "When was the first time *grief* became something more than just a word to you?" Allow three minutes for this, then briefly discuss it as a whole class. The events that are recorded in today's lesson text brought grief to many who observed them. Although they stir feelings of grief in us as well, ultimately these events can lead us to joy.

Into the Word

Choose one, two or three of the following Bible-study ideas this week.

What did he do? When did he do it? Put the following list of characters on your chalkboard, but not in the order shown. Beside them write the list of actions (one action per character), but mix those up too. Ask students to study today's text to discover what each of the characters did, and then arrange the characters and their actions in the correct chronological order. (This activity is in the student book.)

1. Jesus (said "I thirst").

2. Soldiers (broke the legs of the malefactors and pierced Jesus' side with a spear).

3. Joseph of Arimathea (asked Pilate for permission to take the body of Jesus).

4. Nicodemus (brought spices to the tomb).

5. Joseph of Arimathea and Nicodemus (wrapped the body of Jesus in cloths with spices and buried Him).

Did Jesus really die? Ask students to suppose they are talking with someone who believes that Jesus didn't really die on the cross. How does this text alone prove this person wrong?

Background reports. During the week before class, ask four students to prepare a two-minute report for today's class session. Each of them should be assigned one of the following:

Joseph of Arimathea,
Nicodemus,
crucifixion,
day of preparation.

Have the students give these reports before you examine the text itself.

Whom does this describe? Which phrase from the list of descriptions (a-j) below fits each of the characters in the first list? (Have students work in pairs and begin with John 19:17 for this exercise.) This activity is found in the student book. You may want to prepare this as a worksheet to distribute to students (omit the answers shown).

1. Jesus (h)
2. Pilate (e)
3. Soldiers (b)
4. Three Marys (j)
5. John (a)
6. Jesus (c)
7. Soldiers (d)
8. A soldier (f)
9. Joseph of Arimathea (i)
10. Nicodemus (g)

a. Generally thought to be "the disciple whom Jesus loved."

b. Gambled for the garment of our Lord.

c. His thirst was quenched just before His death.

d. They broke two of three pairs of legs.

e. Named Jesus as King of the Jews.

f. His spear pierced the side of our Lord.

g. He brought spices for Jesus' burial.

h. He humbly endured shame and pain.

i. He asked Pilate for Jesus' body.

j. They stood close, watching the crucifixion.

Into Life

Lead students to explore the significance of Jesus' crucifixion. Before class, put each of the following sentences on slips of paper, making enough slips for half of your class members. Give a slip to every other student.

In pairs, students are to reflect on the death and burial of Jesus. What would they say to a person who said what is written on their slip? You may want to compose more sentences.

• Why have a whole lesson on the *death* of Jesus? Isn't this kind of depressing?

• I don't see why Jesus had to *die.* Couldn't God have worked out salvation some other way?

• My sin is too great. God won't forgive something as awful as I've done.

• This is an interesting fact from history, but nothing more.

Let's Talk It Over

The questions on this page are designed to encourage review of the lesson Scriptures and to promote discussion of the lesson by the class. The answers provided are only discussion starters. Let your class talk it over from there.

1. Jesus said that we should take up our cross daily and follow Him. How may we imitate in our daily lives the attitudes Jesus displayed at the time of His crucifixion?

Even while suffering intense pain, Jesus was concerned about others, particularly His mother. We should be "other-oriented." Jesus had been cruelly mistreated. He could have called down legions of angels to get revenge; but He refused to do so. There are times when we are tempted to take revenge; but to take up our cross is to reach out with grace not to respond with verbal or non-verbal violence. Jesus forgave, and forgiveness is a part of our cross bearing. We may find it relatively easy to forgive a person who hurts us unintentionally, but it is tough to forgive a person who plans to do something that he or she knows will hurt us. And it is more difficult still if that person rejoices in hurting us. That is precisely what happened to Jesus on the cross, yet he said, "Father, forgive them."

2. When Jesus said, "It is finished," He was making it clear that He had reached the intended goal of His life. What is the value of our having goals in life?

Psychologists today are telling us that what we are is determined more by the goals we have for the future than by what has happened in our past. Thus it is extremely important to have a purpose that is bigger than we are and that comes out of unselfishness. Only when people have a purpose toward which they aim their lives will they go through all sorts of difficulties in order to say, "It is finished. We have accomplished our goal." The Pilgrims on the *Mayflower* endured the rigors of that voyage because they had a goal—they desired the religious freedom that would be theirs in the new world. Much of the restlessness and boredom that many persons experience today stems from the fact that they do not have definite goals in life. At this point, it would be appropriate to discuss some of the goals that we should establish in keeping with Christ's purpose for us.

3. There are a number of evidences in our lesson Scripture that prove the reality of Jesus' death. Why is the reality of the death of a loved one difficult for most persons to accept?

We find death difficult to accept because we are reluctant to let go of our loved ones. Also, few of us are really ready to deal with death when it comes. We do believe that all of us are mortal, but somehow we still feel that we might escape this reality. Consequently, prior to accepting the reality of the death of a loved one, many persons go through the cycle of reactions that include shock, disbelief, anger, and a kind of numbness or unreality. But these reactions are therapeutic and help us to accept the reality of a major loss in our lives. Readjustments are required, but with Christ's comforting presence and the help of His people, they can be made.

4. Joseph of Arimathea offered a tomb, and Nicodemus brought a mixture of myrrh and aloes to provide for Jesus' burial. What are some things we can do for a person who is sorrowing over the death of a loved one?

A grieving person needs our shoulder more than anything else. Few words we say during the initial days of bereavement are remembered. One of the most important things we can do is to simply show up and be there for awhile. It is also important to allow the bereaved to talk about the deceased loved one and their relationship together. It is also important to allow that person to weep. Notice that neither Joseph nor Nicodemus asked, "Is there anything I can do?" Many who have suffered the death of a loved one are in a state of shock and do not know what needs to be done. There are some things you know you can do—just do them. Carry in a meal, mow the lawn, call the relatives, etc.

5. The authorities of Jesus' day destroyed His body. In what ways can we destroy people today—not their bodies, but their spirits?

We can kill the spirits of people by neglecting them, ignoring them, or belittling them. We can destroy their spirits by not noticing their accomplishments and by not giving them encouragement and recognition for what they are doing. All of us want to feel appreciated and to feel that what we are doing is making some kind of difference. We can destroy the human spirit by not allowing a person to be unique, by trying to control that person, or by trying to make that person be like ourselves.

Resurrection and Faith

LESSON SCRIPTURE: John 20.

PRINTED TEXT: John 20:18-31.

John 20:18-31

18 Mary Magdalene came and told the disciples that she had seen the Lord, and that he had spoken these things unto her.

19 Then the same day at evening, being the first day of the week, when the doors were shut where the disciples were assembled for fear of the Jews, came Jesus and stood in the midst, and saith unto them, Peace be unto you.

20 And when he had so said, he showed unto them his hands and his side. Then were the disciples glad, when they saw the Lord.

21 Then said Jesus to them again, Peace be unto you: as my Father hath sent me, even so send I you.

22 And when he had said this, he breathed on them, and saith unto them, Receive ye the Holy Ghost:

23 Whosesoever sins ye remit, they are remitted unto them; and whosesoever sins ye retain, they are retained.

24 But Thomas, one of the twelve, called Didymus, was not with them when Jesus came.

25 The other disciples therefore said unto him, We have seen the Lord. But he said unto them, Except I shall see in his hands the print of the nails, and put my finger into the print of the nails, and thrust my hand into his side, I will not believe.

26 And after eight days again his disciples were within, and Thomas with them: then came Jesus, the doors being shut, and stood in the midst, and said, Peace be unto you.

27 Then saith he to Thomas, Reach hither thy finger, and behold my hands; and reach hither thy hand, and thrust it into my side; and be not faithless, but believing.

28 And Thomas answered and said unto him, My Lord and my God.

29 Jesus saith unto him, Thomas, because thou hast seen me, thou hast believed: blessed are they that have not seen, and yet have believed.

30 And many other signs truly did Jesus in the presence of his disciples, which are not written in this book:

31 But these are written, that ye might believe that Jesus is the Christ, the Son of God; and that believing ye might have life through his name.

GOLDEN TEXT: Jesus saith unto him, Thomas, because thou hast seen me, thou hast believed: blessed are they that have not seen, and yet have believed.—John 20:29.

John Writes of Life, Light, and Love

Unit 1: The Gospel of Life and Light
(John, Lessons 1-7)

Lesson Aims

As a result of studying this lesson each student should:

1. Have a better understanding of Jesus' resurrection as recorded in the Gospel of John.

2. Experience a growing joy in the meaning of the resurrection for his or her life.

3. Share the joy of the resurrection with others.

Lesson Outline

INTRODUCTION
  A. A Dead Prophet or a Living Savior?
  B. Lesson Background
I. JESUS APPEARS TO THE DISCIPLES (John 20:18-23)
  A. Mary Magdalene's Report (v. 18)
  B. Behind Locked Doors (v. 19)
  C. Identity Established (v. 20)
  D. Commission Given (vv. 21-23)
II. JESUS APPEARS AGAIN (John 20:24-29)
  A. Thomas' Unbelief (vv. 24, 25)
      Too Good to Be True
  B. Jesus' Appearance (v. 26)
  C. Invitation and Response (vv. 27, 28)
  D. Jesus' Blessing (v. 29)
      Seeing Is Believing?
III. JOHN'S PURPOSE IN WRITING (John 20:30, 31)
CONCLUSION
  A. "So Send I You"
  B. Let Us Pray
  C. Thought to Remember

Display visual 7 from the visuals packet to illustrate the theme of this lesson. The visual is shown at the bottom of this page.

Introduction

A. A Dead Prophet or a Living Savior?

A Moslem and a Christian were discussing their respective faiths. "We Moslems have a distinct advantage over you Christians," said the Moslem. "We can journey to Mecca and see the tomb where our prophet, Mohammed, is buried. You Christians don't have any place you can point to as the place where your prophet is buried."

"My friend," responded the Christian, "I can't think of a better way to illustrate the difference between our two faiths. You honor a dead prophet, and we worship a living Savior!"

Christianity is unique among the religions of the world for this very reason. We worship One who was crucified, who was buried, but who arose from the grave victorious over death. Jesus' resurrection stands at the very heart of our faith. If Jesus did not rise from the grave, then our hope in Him is false, and as Paul observes, "We are of all men most miserable" (1 Corinthians 15:19).

But John's Gospel, as do the other Gospel accounts, assures us that our hope is not in vain. In our lesson text, John gives us some solid historic evidence that we "might believe" and that believing, we "might have life through his name."

B. Lesson Background

Last week's lesson closed with Joseph of Arimathea and Nicodemus laying Jesus' body in the tomb. Had the account ended at that point, there would be no gospel, no good news. But we can rejoice that the Gospel of John does not end with chapter 19. There is more, and it is good news—the best news of all—Jesus lives!

Joseph and Nicodemus, faced with the onset of the Sabbath the day Jesus died, could only partially prepare the body for its final interment. They and other of Jesus' followers had to wait through Saturday until early Sunday morning before they could finish this task. Chapter 20 picks up the account at this point.

Early on that Sunday morning several of the women who had been followers of Jesus carried spices to the tomb in order to finish preparing the body for its final burial. John, however, mentions only Mary Magdalene. When she saw that the tomb was empty, she ran to report this to Peter and John, who then ran to the tomb. When they confirmed her report that the tomb was indeed empty, they left, returning to the place where they had been staying.

When they left, Mary remained beside the tomb, weeping in her grief. It was then that

visual 7

Jesus appeared to her. At first, she did not recognize Him, but as soon as she knew that it was He, her grief was swept away in a flood of joy. Once she had recovered from the shock of seeing Jesus alive, He sent her to tell the other disciples the good news.

I. Jesus Appears to the Disciples (John 20:18-23)

A. Mary Magdalene's Report (v. 18)

18. Mary Magdalene came and told the disciples that she had seen the Lord, and that he had spoken these things unto her.

When Jesus sent Mary to carry the good news to the others, she did not hesitate. Her joy gave wings to her feet as she ran to the place where they were meeting. Her message was simple and to the point: "I have seen the Lord!" Mark indicates that the disciples refused to believe Mary (Mark 16:11). Still in a state of shock from their grief, they found the word she brought too good to be true.

B. Behind Locked Doors (v. 19)

19. Then the same day at evening, being the first day of the week, when the doors were shut where the disciples were assembled for fear of the Jews, came Jesus and stood in the midst, and saith unto them, Peace be unto you.

The same day is the day of Jesus' resurrection. Evening had come, and it was probably already dark. Earlier in the day Jesus had made several appearances: to Mary Magdalene, to the other women (Matthew 28:9, 10), to the two on the road to Emmaus (Luke 24:13-35), and to Peter (Luke 24:34; 1 Corinthians 15:5). But reports of these appearances had not brought all of the disciples to the point where they believed that Jesus had arisen. Anxious and perplexed as they were, it is not surprising that they met to find some answers to the strange and unusual reports they had been hearing. Their place of meeting is not identified, although many commentators believe that it was in the upper room where they had celebrated the Passover with Jesus.

When the doors were shut. The outside gate or door that opened into the courtyard along with the door to their room were closed. The word translated *shut* may mean "locked" or "bolted," and some modern versions so translate it. The reason the disciples took those precautions was *for fear of the Jews.* After the way the religious leaders had treated Jesus, the disciples had good reason to believe they might be the next victims of persecution.

Into this tense situation suddenly Jesus came. Scholars have debated how it was possible for Him to do this. Some suppose that Jesus' resurrection body was changed, that it was no longer subject to the usual laws of nature. But there is nothing in the Scriptures to indicate that His body was transformed. We need to remember that Jesus had unlimited power over nature. This had been demonstrated earlier in His ministry through His miracles. Now it was demonstrated in His ability to appear wherever He chose. For example, when He appeared to the two on the road to Emmaus, His identity was hidden from them. Then, when His conversation with them was finished, He vanished from their sight (Luke 24:13-31). Locked doors posed no problem for the Creator and Master of the universe!

Jesus' first words to the assembled disciples were words of assurance: *Peace be unto you.* This was and still is a common greeting among Jewish people, but in this case it was more than just a casual greeting. It was given to bring assurance to troubled hearts, hearts that had been torn by doubt and plagued by fear. Jesus knew their need and ministered to it.

C. Identity Established (v. 20)

20. And when he had so said, he showed unto them his hands and his side. Then were the disciples glad, when they saw the Lord.

Jesus' greeting should have brought peace to the hearts of those in the room, but He knew that they would have lingering doubts. Luke 24:36-45 gives a more detailed account of Jesus' efforts to reassure them. There we read that the disciples were terrified and thought that Jesus was a spirit. Then He showed them His hands and feet trying to convince them that a spirit did not have flesh and bones. Still they refused to believe "for joy." Next Jesus asked for food, and when He had eaten it, they seemed finally to be convinced that it really was Jesus.

John gives us an abbreviated account, mentioning only that Jesus showed them His hands and His side. Apparently He showed them the marks where the nails pierced His hands and the spear pierced His side. This seemed to satisfy them, for they began to rejoice *when they saw the Lord,* that is, when they finally recognized that He who stood before them was not only alive but was the exalted Lord.

D. Commission Given (vv. 21-23)

21. Then said Jesus to them again, Peace be unto you: as my Father hath sent me, even so send I you.

Once again the Lord reassured the disciples with the words, *Peace be unto you.* But these words were more than just reassurance; they were to prepare them for the commission He was about to give them. The Father had sent the Son into the world to proclaim the message of salvation. In His prayer, recorded in John 17:18, Jesus had made reference to this mission and that it would be passed on to His disciples. Now the time had come to put this commission into effect. The disciples would meet hatred, opposition, and violence as they presented God's truth. Jesus wished for His people a peace like His own (John 14:27), a peace that would abide with them even in the midst of conflict.

22. And when he had said this, he breathed on them, and saith unto them, Receive ye the Holy Ghost.

The commission that Jesus had just extended to those in the room was too great and too important for them to begin alone and on their own. Power for their mission would be supplied by the Holy Spirit, or "Holy Ghost," as the King James Version has it. Jesus had promised this before (John 16:7-15), and He would promise it again before leaving His disciples and returning to Heaven (Acts 1:8). It is quite clearly recorded that the Spirit did come to the apostles soon after Jesus returned to Heaven (Acts 2:1-4). Jesus' breath on the disciples while He was with them was a fitting symbol of the Spirit He would send after His departure (John 16:7).

23. Whosoever sins ye remit, they are remitted unto them; and whosoever sins ye retain, they are retained.

This verse, along with Matthew 16:19, has engendered no little controversy across the centuries. Roman Catholics have held the view that Peter was given the "keys of the kingdom of heaven," which gave him the power to forgive sins, and that this authority was then passed on to his "successors," the members of the priesthood. Others have held that the authority to forgive sins resides in officers of the church or in church councils.

To understand this verse, we must look at it in its context. Jesus had just given a commission to His followers. The parallel passage in Luke gives us more details of what this commission involved: "It behooved Christ to suffer, and to rise from the dead the third day: and that repentance and remission of sins should be preached in his name among all nations, beginning at Jerusalem" (Luke 24:46, 47). It is clear, then, that the remission of sins would be accomplished through the preaching of the good news, not through some priestly power or ecclesiastical activity.

When Jesus' followers preached the good news, people repented. Faith in Jesus Christ and repentance were the prerequisites for the forgiveness of sins. The first application of this commission came on the day of Pentecost, when Peter proclaimed, "Repent, and be baptized every one of you in the name of Jesus Christ for the remission of sins" (Acts 2:38).

II. Jesus Appears Again (John 20:24-29)

A. Thomas' Unbelief (vv. 24, 25)

24, 25. But Thomas, one of the twelve, called Didymus, was not with them when Jesus came. The other disciples therefore said unto him, We have seen the Lord. But he said unto them, Except I shall see in his hands the print of the nails, and put my finger into the print of the nails, and thrust my hand into his side, I will not believe.

The name *Thomas* means "twin," as does its Greek equivalent, *Didymus*. What little we know about him comes from a couple of references, both of them in John. John 11 tells of the illness and subsequent death of Lazarus in Bethany of Judea. When Jesus prepared to go to His friend, His disciples, knowing that the Jewish leaders in Judea were plotting to kill Him, tried to restrain Him. But Thomas, with a dedication that would lead him even to face death with his Lord, said, "Let us also go, that we may die with him" (11:16). The other mention of Thomas came in the upper room. Jesus had just informed His disciples that He must leave them, but that they would follow. Thomas, clearly perplexed by Jesus' statement but still wanting information, asked, "Lord, we know not whither thou goest; and how can we know the way?" (John 14:5).

The picture that emerges is of a man who is dedicated to the Lord, but who is also a hard-headed realist. He wants facts before he acts. If this is an accurate picture of Thomas, then it seems hardly fair to call him "Doubting" Thomas. He is a person who would be right at home in our scientific, no nonsense age.

We do not know why he was absent when Jesus first appeared to the other disciples. Whatever the reason, he stubbornly refused to believe the testimony of the others. Stubborn and practical man that he was, he insisted that he have the same experience as they. He did not refuse to believe; rather, he insisted that he would believe only under certain conditions.

TOO GOOD TO BE TRUE

Consumer advocates give this advice to those who receive tempting direct-mail advertisements: "If it seems too good to be true, it usually is!" Something-for-nothing promises are suspect; unusual "bargains" often have hidden costs; the quality of surprisingly inexpensive products is often *not surprisingly* shoddy and cheap. Suspicion and doubt are natural and proper reactions to such incredible offers.

The response of Thomas to the resurrection reports was typical. His faith was not necessarily weaker than that of any other apostle; they all at first disbelieved the women's report. Thomas was cautious, as they all were, when he heard news that seemed too good to be true. The others now believed on the basis of evidence that Thomas had not yet experienced. Later, when he was confronted with the living presence of Christ, he too believed.

Skepticism is fine, even virtuous, when reading junk-mail offers. Buyer beware! But the eyewitness testimony to the resurrected Lord should leave no doubt in anyone's mind that He lives. Unbelievers disregard the facts, blind themselves to the evidence, and thus reject the Savior. Christians, on the other hand, have the "hope of glory" (Colossians 1:27), the salvation of their souls (1 Peter 1:8, 9).   —R. W. B.

B. Jesus' Appearance (v. 26)

26. And after eight days again his disciples were within, and Thomas with them: then came Jesus, the doors being shut, and stood in the midst, and said, Peace be unto you.

One week later, the disciples were once again assembled, presumably in the same room. Why Jesus delayed a whole week before appearing again we do not know. Perhaps it was in order to give the disciples time to discuss the Scriptures He had explained to them, and time to convince Thomas. Just as before, Jesus suddenly appeared in their midst even though the doors were locked. Again He gave the same greeting to reassure them and to allay their fears.

C. Invitation and Response (vv. 27, 28)

27. Then saith he to Thomas, Reach hither thy finger, and behold my hands; and reach hither thy hand, and thrust it into my side; and be not faithless, but believing.

Jesus did not berate Thomas for his lack of faith. Instead, He answered every one of his demands. Thomas wanted to see and touch, and that was Jesus' invitation to him. Thomas was one of the apostles who were specially chosen to be witnesses unto Jesus (Acts 1:8). Thomas and the others were not to give hearsay evidence; they were to tell what they had seen. Whatever proof Thomas asked, Jesus was ready to give. Thomas and the other apostles must be convinced without a doubt so that we may be thoroughly convinced by their testimony.

28. And Thomas answered and said unto him, My Lord and my God.

We are not told whether Thomas actually put his hands into the nail prints or not. Seeing Jesus and hearing Him speak may have made additional proof unnecessary. His response shows overwhelming conviction. He was sure.

My Lord and my God. This is the most profound confession anyone can make in regard to Jesus Christ. Thomas accepted Jesus not only as Lord and Master of his life, but as God! This is no casual statement, made at the the moment of great emotion. If so, Jesus would not have given it His unreserved approval.

D. Jesus' Blessing (v. 29)

29. Jesus saith unto him, Thomas, because thou hast seen me, thou hast believed: blessed are they that have not seen, and yet have believed.

Thomas' faith was based on physical evidence. In that, he was no different from the other disciples, who also struggled with unbelief until Jesus appeared to them. Some see Jesus' response as a question: "Have you believed only because you have seen me?" This would suggest that Jesus was administering a mild rebuke of Thomas's unbelief. It seems better, however, to take it as a statement of Jesus' approval that Thomas had now come to believe.

Blessed. This is the same word that Jesus used in pronouncing the Beatitudes in the Sermon on the Mount. Thus Jesus pronounced a special blessing on those, who, though not seeing Him, yet would believe in Him on the basis of the testimony of others. Included were many in Jesus' own day who were never privileged to see the risen Lord. But thanks be to God, this blessing has extended to every generation that has lived since then, and it includes us today.

SEEING IS BELIEVING?

Millions of TV viewers watched David Copperfield make the Statue of Liberty disappear a few years ago. Many had seen the same magician "vaporize" a 747 airplane several months before that. Copperfield is an illusionist par excellence. He can cause us to believe we have seen what we have not really seen.

How to Say It

DIDYMUS. *Did*-uh-mus.
EMMAUS. Em-*may*-us.
MAGDALENE. *Mag*-duh-leen or Mag-duh-*lee*—nee.

Our senses have ways of fooling us. A rigid object appears to bend just where it enters a container of water; train rails seem to converge where the tracks meet the horizon; jet trails sometimes look as though they are vertical when in reality they are horizontal.

In spite of optical illusions, many folk still insist; "Seeing is believing." But seeing is *not* believing. *Faith* is believing. Faith is based on evidence; it is psychological certainty arising out of contemplation of *facts*, not illusions.

Thomas was led to credible conviction and concrete commitment by examining the facts of Jesus' resurrection: he stood in Jesus' presence; he spoke with Him; he was invited to touch Him. Because of the testimony of Thomas and the others, we may believe in Christ and be "certain of what we do not see" (Hebrews 11:1, *New International Version*).   —R. W. B.

III. John's Purpose in Writing (John 20:30, 31)

30. And many other signs truly did Jesus in the presence of his disciples, which are not written in this book.

John did not attempt to record everything Jesus did and taught. He was not attempting to write an exhaustive biography. Since John wrote his Gospel some years after the three other Gospels had been written, he did not even repeat many of the events they recorded. We may wish that he had written more, but guided by the Holy Spirit, he wrote what was necessary for us.

31. But these are written, that ye might believe that Jesus is the Christ, the Son of God; and that believing ye might have life through his name.

John wrote to present Jesus as the Christ, the divine Son of God, in order to bring people to faith in Him. He did this through citing many of the signs connected with Jesus' ministry: the changing of the water to wine, the feeding of the five thousand, the opening of the eyes of the man born blind, and, most important, the resurrection. And those who believe have now and will continue to have eternal life in His name.

Conclusion

A. "So Send I You"

The son of God came into the world to suffer, to die, to be raised again in order that mankind might have the opportunity to enjoy everlasting life. Jesus entrusted that message to His disciples. God might have chosen to send His Son back into the world for every generation, but He didn't. He could have chosen to send angels to carry the message of salvation, but He didn't. He could have chosen to give the good news by special revelation to every member of the human race, but He didn't. Instead, through His divine wisdom, He chose to make every Christian a messenger to the lost world.

Some Christians have carried that message to distant lands or different cultures as missionaries or evangelists. Others, have supported missionaries and evangelists through their prayers and their financial contributions. Both are necessary if the message of eternal life in Jesus Christ is to be taken into all the world.

One amazing fact about the church revealed in the New Testament was its rapid growth. It quickly burst out of the confines of Jerusalem and the Jewish nation, and soon established beachheads in every province of the Roman Empire and beyond. That remarkable expansion was not accomplished by professional missionaries, but by Christians who took Jesus' commission seriously. They had good news—Jesus was victorious over death—and they shared it wherever they went.

What is your congregation doing to spread the word? What are *you* doing to help?

B. Let Us Pray

We thank You, Father, that Your Son triumphed over death and the grave. We thank You that Jesus appeared to witnesses who were convinced that He had been raised from the dead. Because of their testimony, we may believe, and have eternal life. Amen.

C. Thought to Remember

We see in the risen Christ the end for which man was made, and the assurance that the end is within our reach.   —B. F. WESTCOTT

Home Daily Bible Readings

Monday, Apr. 9—Who Ever Heard of Such a Thing? (Luke 24:1-12)

Tuesday, Apr. 10—What Happened? (John 20:1-10)

Wednesday, Apr. 11—I Have Seen the Lord! (John 20:11-18)

Thursday, Apr. 12—We Had Hoped He Was the One . . . (Luke 24:13-21)

Friday, Apr. 13—Don't You Understand? (Luke 24:22-27)

Saturday, Apr. 14—He Is the One! (Luke 24:28-35)

Sunday, Apr. 15—We Were Bursting With Joy! (Luke 24:36-53)

Learning by Doing

This page contains an alternate lesson plan emphasizing learning activities. Classes desiring such student involvement will find these suggestions helpful.

Learning Goals

Because students participate in today's class session, they should be able to accomplish the following:

1. Survey John 20:18-31 to discover how the resurrection brings peace, purpose, pardon, and proof.

2. Choose at least one of these as a "gift" they would like to receive and at least one as a "gift" they would like to give.

Into the Lesson

1. What is one thing you have *given* this year at Easter?

2. Do you give more at Easter or Christmas? Why?

After a very short time, about three minutes, discuss these questions with the whole class, allowing volunteers to share their answers. Tell the class, "Although we think of gift-giving more at Christmastime, we know that Christ gave us something wonderful with His resurrection. Today's text will show us what He gave."

Into the Word

Use the following questions to lead your students in an all-class discussion. Tell them that together you'll explore this text to discover "the gifts of Easter." Write each "gift" (signified by Roman numerals, below) on the chalkboard as you discuss it together.

I. Peace (vv. 19, 20)

1. What was the attitude of the disciples before Jesus appeared? Why?

2. What transformation took place in their attitude?

3. Even though Christ's words, "Peace be unto you," were a common greeting in that part of the world, what significance may they have had for the disciples?

4. The word *peace* has several dimensions:

• It is a *diplomatic* term. Although there was, of course, no declaration of war, in a sense the disciples were at war. How? (They were afraid of their enemies, the Jews.) How are Christians today at war with the world? How does Christ provide peace in spite of our clashes with the world's values?

• It is a *theological* term. Think of some ways the disciples had been in conflict with the purposes and plans of Christ. How do Christians sometimes seem to want to squeeze God into their own box? What about our culture at large? What faulty attempts do many make to establish peace with God?

• It is an *emotional* term. Why were the disciples afraid? What causes people today to be afraid and uneasy as the disciples were? How does Christ bring peace to quell the fears in our lives today?

II. Purpose (vv. 21-23)

1. What was to be the mission of the disciples from this time forward?

2. How was their mission different from ours? How is ours similar?

3. How should the Christian's mission mirror Christ's? (Refer to the following Scriptures for statements from Christ about His purpose on earth: Matthew 20:28; Luke 4:43; 19:10; John 10:10).

III. Proof (vv. 24-29)

1. What stereotype of Thomas is usually presented? How does this stereotype contrast with the pictures of Thomas we see in these Scriptures: John 11:16; 14:5?

2. What did Thomas seek? How did Jesus respond? Why did Jesus respond to Thomas' requests as He did? What significance is there for us in this incident?

IV. Pardon (vv. 30, 31)

1. Why did John write his Gospel?

2. What is the natural outgrowth of belief?

Into Life

Divide the students into pairs again. Ask them to survey the four main headings above that you have written on the chalkboard. Have them share with each other:

1. The gift I find most surprising.

2. The gift I'd most like to receive.

3. The gift I'd most like to give.

If you have time you may wish to allow volunteers to share their responses with the entire class.

It would be good to end today's lesson with a musical challenge. Secure a tape or record of some contemporary or classic song or anthem that speaks of the resurrection. Play it at the end of class, challenging students to think of the gift from this list that they would like to give or receive.

Let's Talk It Over

*The questions on this page are designed to encourage review of the lesson
Scriptures and to promote discussion of the lesson by the class. The answers
provided are only discussion starters. Let your class talk it over from there.*

1. We often criticize Thomas for not believing the report of the other disciples regarding Jesus' resurrection, but there was something positive about his position that we should apply in our lives. Discuss what that was.

Thomas was willing to stand up against the crowd. He would not allow their position to become his position just so he could fit in. He would not pretend about his belief. His faith in Jesus was not to be secondhand. He was honest and transparent. It is interesting that when Jesus met Thomas, He did not criticize him for his unbelief. Because Thomas was sincerely searching, he grew in both knowledge and faith. How many times do we clam up in a Sunday-school class and not admit it when we are puzzled about a teaching? The tragedy is that unless we get our questions out into the open, we may never be exposed to the evidence or explanation that can help us.

2. For some reason, Thomas was absent the first day of the week when Jesus first showed himself alive to the assembled disciples—He missed Jesus. What do we miss when we absent ourselves from the assembling of God's people on the first day of the week?

We miss the reinforcement of our assurance that Jesus is alive and well. We miss the reminder that Christ died and arose for us. We miss the visual reminder that the church is made up of people just like us—that there is diversity amid the unity. Few of us have it all together. We miss a whole community of believers singing and praying together. We miss the preaching of God's Word for man's world. We miss the Lord's Supper and the reassurance it gives us that Christ died for the forgiveness of our sins and that we don't have to continue living in guilt. We miss the presence of Christ—that very special dimension.

3. Three times in our text Jesus said, "Peace be unto you." In what areas in our lives today do we need peace?

We need peace with God. We need to know that He is not angry with us, but rather, by His grace, we are saved through His love. We need peace with ourselves. Too often we live in despair, overcome with guilt. Because we are in Christ, we have been freed from that; in Him there is no condemnation. We need peace with our past. We need to recognize that in Christ the past is eliminated; God will never bring it up to us again. We need peace with our future, to be assured of where we are going. We are going to Heaven; we are going to live with God. We have an undefiled inheritance that is reserved for us; our name is on it. We need peace with our surrounding circumstances. We need to recognize that when things go wrong, it is not because God is angry. Nothing can separate us from the love of God. We need peace with our brothers and sisters in Christ.

4. Where the disciples were assembled, the doors were shut because of their fear of the Jews. What doors in our lives do we shut because of our fears? What can we do to open them?

We shut doors to close relationships because we fear being hurt. We shut doors to witnessing as we should because we fear rejection or failure. We shut doors to fulfilling our potential because we fear that our efforts won't be accepted or they won't be good enough. We shut doors to intimacy with God because we fear total surrender to Him. We shut doors to opportunities because we fear the unknown. Fear is cured when we trust God fully, when we truly believe that He has our best interests at heart and is in control of our lives and the whole universe.

5. John wrote this Gospel to promote belief in Jesus Christ as God's Son. What can we do today to promote this same belief?

We can maintain an intimate relationship with Christ ourselves so that our countenance, our attitudes, our words, our actions, reflect the purity of Christ. Then we can specifically and intentionally tell others about the Christ that we know so well; our words will be backed up by our lives. We can pray and support financially those who spend all of their time preaching and teaching that gospel in our communities and in other countries. We can continue to grow and mature in our own understanding of what that belief means in our lives, and we can support and encourage our Christian brothers and sisters in their Christian walk.

Forgiveness and Fellowship

April 22
Lesson 8

LESSON SCRIPTURE: 1 John 1:1—2:17.

PRINTED TEXT: 1 John 1:1—2:6.

1 John 1:1-10

1 That which was from the beginning, which we have heard, which we have seen with our eyes, which we have looked upon, and our hands have handled, of the Word of life;

2 (For the life was manifested, and we have seen it, and bear witness, and show unto you that eternal life, which was with the Father, and was manifested unto us;)

3 That which we have seen and heard declare we unto you, that ye also may have fellowship with us: and truly our fellowship is with the Father, and with his Son Jesus Christ.

4 And these things write we unto you, that your joy may be full.

5 This then is the message which we have heard of him, and declare unto you, that God is light, and in him is no darkness at all.

6 If we say that we have fellowship with him, and walk in darkness, we lie, and do not the truth:

7 But if we walk in the light, as he is in the light, we have fellowship one with another, and the blood of Jesus Christ his Son cleanseth us from all sin.

8 If we say that we have no sin, we deceive ourselves, and the truth is not in us.

9 If we confess our sins, he is faithful and just to forgive us our sins, and to cleanse us from all unrighteousness.

10 If we say that we have not sinned, we make him a liar, and his word is not in us.

1 John 2:1-6

1 My little children, these things write I unto you, that ye sin not. And if any man sin, we have an advocate with the Father, Jesus Christ the righteous:

2 And he is the propitiation for our sins: and not for ours only, but also for the sins of the whole world.

3 And hereby we do know that we know him, if we keep his commandments.

4 He that saith, I know him, and keepeth not his commandments, is a liar, and the truth is not in him.

5 But whoso keepeth his word, in him verily is the love of God perfected: hereby know we that we are in him.

6 He that saith he abideth in him ought himself also so to walk, even as he walked.

Apr 22

GOLDEN TEXT: If we walk in the light, as he is in the light, we have fellowship one with another, and the blood of Jesus Christ his Son cleanseth us from all sin.
—1 John 1:7.

John Writes of Life, Light, and Love
Unit 2: Abiding in Love
(1, 2, and 3 John, Lessons 8-13)

Lesson Aims

As a result of studying this lesson, each student should:

1. Understand that one cannot claim to know God while continuing to disobey His commandments.

2. Appreciate more fully that through Jesus Christ we may have forgiveness of sin.

3. Mention one way in which he or she will be more obedient to Christ in the daily walk of life.

Lesson Outline

INTRODUCTION
    A. "The Truth Is Not in Us"
    B. Lesson Background
I. JOHN'S WITNESS (1 John 1:1-4)
    A. John's Qualifications (vv. 1, 2)
    B. John's Purpose in Writing (vv. 3, 4)
II. JOHN'S MESSAGE (1 John 1:5—2:2)
    A. God Is Light (v. 5)
    B. Fellowship in the Light (vv. 6, 7)
    C. The Reality of Sin (vv. 8-10)
    D. God's Remedy for Sin (2:1, 2)
      Sin and Forgiveness
III. TESTS OF TRUE KNOWLEDGE (1 John 2:3-6)
    A. Obedience to God's Commands (vv. 3-5)
    B. Walking as Jesus Walked (v. 6)
      Stepping in the Light
CONCLUSION
    A. No More Sin
    B. Let Us Pray
    C. Thought to Remember

Display visual 8 from the visuals packet and let it remain before the class. The visual is shown on page 292.

Introduction

A. "The Truth Is Not in Us"

Years ago in a village in the Scottish highlands lived a strange man. Among his idiosyncracies was the coat he always wore. The front of his coat was covered with large patches, each patch marked with a sin of one of his neighbors. On the back of the coat was one very small patch, which represented the man's own sin.

Through this unusual garment, this man was emphasizing the sins of others while trying to deny his own sins or at least keep them out of sight. We may smile at the man's strange behavior, but the truth is we are all a little like that. We tend to emphasize the sins of others while denying or at least downplaying our own. John had a comment for this kind of behavior: "If we say that we have no sin, we deceive ourselves, and the truth is not in us."

B. Lesson Background

Today's lesson is the first of six based on 1, 2, and 3 John. The previous seven lessons in this quarter's study climaxed in Jesus' resurrection. The resurrection has far-reaching implications. It shows that Jesus is not just an ancient teacher of morality, but that He is who He claimed to be—the Son of God. If we believe in Jesus and accept Him as Lord and Savior, our relationship to God is changed. We become His children, members of His family. This, in turn, leads to a change in our relationship with our fellowmen. The word *love* best characterizes this new relationship, hence the title for this unit: "Abiding in Love."

Just as the author of the Gospel of John does not explicitly identify himself, so the author of these three epistles is not identified by name. The author of 1 John makes it clear that he was an eyewitness [of Jesus during His ministry] (1 John 1:1, 2). Certainly the apostle John met this qualification. The writer of 2 and 3 John refers to himself as "the elder" (2 John 1 and 3 John 1). If these letters were written late in the first century, as certainly seems to be the case, then John the apostle would have had good reason to refer to himself as "the elder," since he would have been well advanced in years.

By the end of the first century, certain heresies had begun to make their appearance within the church. John wrote in order to protect the flock from these deceivers. But amid all of his warnings, he never ceased to admonish the people to demonstrate their faith by their love.

I. John's Witness (1 John 1:1-4)

A. John's Qualifications (vv. 1, 2)

1, 2. That which was from the beginning, which we have heard, which we have seen with our eyes, which we have looked upon, and our hands have handled, of the Word of life; (for the life was manifested, and we have seen it, and bear witness, and show unto you that eternal life, which was with the Father, and was manifested unto us.)

Even though 1 John is often referred to as a letter or an epistle, it does not begin like the epistles of Paul. For one thing, the writer is not identified by name. Further, the destination of the letter is not mentioned. Yet it is clear from the book that John had a personal relationship with those to whom he was writing.

The life John saw was the life of Jesus Christ. He carefully explains the basis for the testimony he is bringing. John and other witnesses had not only heard Jesus, but they had seen Him and touched Him as well. Some feel that John was so explicit in stating the basis for his testimony in order to refute the teachings of the Docetists. This group taught that Christ never really came in the flesh, or that which people took for a human body was really a ghost or a phantom. But a ghost or a phantom could not pass the rigid tests mentioned here. John and the others had frequent contacts with Jesus over an extended period of time. There was no way that they could be mistaken or fooled. In the Gospel of John, the apostle affirmed the incarnation just as emphatically: "The Word was made flesh, and dwelt among us" (1:14).

John bore witness to the historic Jesus. Jesus was indeed a human being, but as *the Word of life*, He existed prior to the incarnation. He had lived eternally with the Father. This is restating what is set forth in the prologue of the Gospel of John: "In the beginning was the Word, and the Word was with God, and the Word was God" (1:1). (See also John 17:5.)

B. John's Purpose in Writing (vv. 3, 4)

3. That which we have seen and heard declare we unto you, that ye also may have fellowship with us: and truly our fellowship is with the Father, and with his Son Jesus Christ.

John's purpose in witnessing about Christ was in order for his readers to have fellowship with himself and other Christians. The word here translated *fellowship* means to share or to have something in common. Whatever else Christians may or may not have in common, we share a common belief that Jesus is the Christ, the Son of the living God. The only way that a person can come to hold that belief is for someone to bear witness to that fact. That is exactly what John was doing.

John shared his faith with us through his writings, so that ultimately we may all come to share *with the Father, and with His Son Jesus Christ.* Thus we not only share eternal life (v. 2; see John 17:3; 20:31) but we also become children of God and joint-heirs with Christ (Romans 8:16, 17). He is heir of all things (Hebrews 1:2), and that is the inheritance we share.

4. And these things write we unto you, that your joy may be full.

Some manuscripts have "our joy" instead of *your joy*, and so it is translated that way in several modern translations. Either translation makes good sense. John may have written that if we have fellowship with God, our joy will be full. What could possibly give more joy than to share what God has in store for us?

On the other hand, John may have been writing about his own joy. As an apostle and overseer of the church, he would certainly rejoice whenever he saw anyone move into a loving relationship with the Father. Paul called the Philippian church his "joy and crown" because they had so faithfully served the Lord (Philippians 4:1). John himself repeats these sentiments in 3 John 4: "I have no greater joy than to hear that my children walk in truth." Any Christian who has a sincere love for his fellow Christians will experience the same emotion.

II. John's Message (1 John 1:5—2:2)

A. God Is Light (v. 5)

5. This then is the message which we have heard of him, and declare unto you, that God is light, and in him is no darkness at all.

John did not concoct the message that he was sharing. Rather, he was declaring the message he had heard from Christ. In our day, when we hear so many different and conflicting religious messages, we ought to test them to determine whether they come from Jesus Christ.

God is light. He is not *a* light, nor is He *the* light; by His very nature He *is* light. Light symbolizes purity and holiness and that describes God's very essence. One function of light is to provide illumination. God provides illumination to the mind of man by revealing to him His will.

In him is no darkness at all. Light and darkness cannot exist side by side. When light shines, darkness vanishes. It is clear that John is using

---

How to Say It

CAESAREA PHILIPPI. Ses-uh-*ree*-uh Fuh-*lip*-pie or *Fil*-uh-pie.

CAPERNAUM. Kuh-*per*-nay-um.

DOCETISTS. Doe-*set*-ists.

GNOSTICISM. *Nahs*-tih-*siz*-im (strong accent on *Nahs*).

GNOSTICS. *Nahs*-tiks.

PARACLETE. *pair*-uh-kleet.

the contrast between light and darkness in an ethical sense. If light represents purity, then in God there can be no darkness, which represents evil and corruption.

B. Fellowship in the Light (vv. 6, 7)

6. If we say that we have fellowship with him, and walk in darkness, we lie, and do not the truth.

John now makes a practical application of the fact that light and darkness are incompatible.

No compromise is possible between the demands of God for holiness and the call of the forces of darkness that lead to worldliness. Some may deceive themselves into supposing that they can serve two masters—that they can have fellowship with God, who is light, and at the same time have fellowship with darkness—but this is an impossibility. Some may even convince themselves that their acts of worldliness are not really sinful. But John doesn't waste time arguing this point. He quite bluntly calls them liars!

7. But if we walk in the light, as he is in the light, we have fellowship one with another, and the blood of Jesus Christ his Son cleanseth us from all sin.

It is impossible to have fellowship with God if we walk in darkness, that is, in sin. But the good news is that if we walk in the light, that is, if we continually believe and obey the truth of God as revealed in Christ, we can enjoy fellowship with those who are also walking in the light.

But we are frail, and, despite our best efforts, come short of the glory of God. Since this is the case, we might be led to suppose that we cannot enjoy this promised fellowship. The latter part of the verse, however, solves the problem. In our own strength we cannot live a sinless life; but our deficiency is overcome because *the blood of Jesus Christ his Son cleanseth us from all sin.* Because Jesus died for us on the cross, we are cleansed and can live with confidence before God and with our fellowmen. The blood of Jesus establishes and maintains our fellowship with the all-holy God of light.

C. The Reality of Sin (vv. 8-10)

8. If we say that we have no sin, we deceive ourselves, and the truth is not in us.

Satan has always been the great deceiver. He deceived Adam and Eve in the garden, and he has succeeded in deceiving every generation since then. He may lead us to believe that we are without sin by having us compare our life with the life of some obvious, blatant sinner. He never encourages us to compare our life to that of Jesus Christ. In the *we* of this verse, John finds

himself as well as other Christians guilty of transgressing God's will. The battle between, the spirit and the flesh is constant. The spirit is not always victorious. In Romans 7:14-25, the apostle Paul writes of his own struggles.

9. If we confess our sins, he is faithful and just to forgive us our sins, and to cleanse us from all unrighteousness.

Our case is not hopeless. If we walk in the light, yet transgress, sincere confession and desire for forgiveness gain the ear and heart of the merciful and forgiving Father. (See Matthew 6:12; Acts 8:18-24.) We can have the assurance that our sins are forgiven because of God's very nature. *He is faithful.* He has promised to forgive our sins, and we know that He will keep His promise. He is also *just.* At first glance, we might raise a question at this point. After all, justice would seem to require that we pay the full price for our sins. The glorious truth is that the price has already been paid! In His death, Jesus Christ met the demands of justice for us, and so God can forgive our sins and still not compromise His standards of justice.

10. If we say that we have not sinned, we make him a liar, and his word is not in us.

In verse 8 John insisted that those who claim they have no sin are deceived. Now he affirms that they are guilty of something even worse—they are making God out to be a liar. Such an attitude makes it quite clear that such persons do not have His word in them.

D. God's Remedy for Sin (2:1, 2)

1. My little children, these things write I unto you, that ye sin not. And if any man sin, we have an advocate with the Father, Jesus Christ the righteous.

In the previous verses, John has affirmed that all have sinned and that all continue to commit sins. Here he indicates that he is writing these warnings about sin so that they may *not* sin. *My little children.* These are the words of a pastor, a faithful shepherd, who loves his flock and is

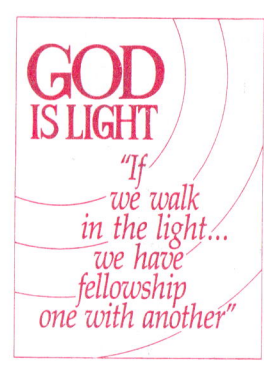

GOD IS LIGHT

"If we walk in the light... we have fellowship one with another"

visual 8

concerned about them. Since they had sinned in the past and they continued to sin, they might feel that their situation was hopeless. But John's words were reassuring. Even though he urges them not to sin, he adds that if they do, they *have an advocate with the Father*. The word here translated *advocate* is the Greek word *paraclete*. In John's Gospel it is used of the Holy Spirit as the Christian's helper and is translated "Comforter" (14:16, 26; 15:26; 16:7). Literally, the word means "one who is called alongside" for the purpose of helping. In this verse, it is translated *advocate* because it refers to Jesus Christ, who is like a lawyer, pleading our case before the Father. The *New International Version* conveys this idea in translating it this way: "We have one who speaks to the Father in our defense—Jesus Christ, the Righteous One."

2. And he is the propitiation for our sins: and not for ours only, but also for the sins of the whole world.

Jesus Christ is more than an advocate who pleads our case before the Father. He is the *propitiation*, the atoning sacrifice, for our sins. Through His death on the cross, our sins are covered and the restoration of friendship between man and God is made possible. First John 4:10 tells us that because of God's love for sinful man, Jesus was sent into the world for the purpose of being the propitiation for our sins. He is, thus, both the lawyer who defends us before God and the sacrificial lamb who pays the price for our sins.

SIN AND FORGIVENESS

Browsing in libraries and bookstores is a favorite pastime. Even the titles of books are fascinating. Consider the pattern of these classics: *Advise and Consent; The Rise and Fall . . . (of either the Roman Empire or the Third Reich); Crime and Punishment.*

Some recent translations and paraphrases of the Bible are marketed under contemporary titles, such as *The Way* or *Good News*. Other possibilities come to mind. Perhaps *Sin and Retribution* would catch the Bible-buyer's eye.

If Bible bindings are going to carry popularized titles, however, *Sin and Forgiveness* would be more accurate. God's justice and His wrath against wickedness are definitely emphasized in Scripture, but the major thrust of Biblical content is the *good* news of salvation. Sin is a fact of life, a universal flaw in human character, but forgiveness is available through Christ. The real plot of the Bible's story centers in the Savior, who offers redemption to "the whole world."

Sin and Forgiveness is a title that truly describes the key topics of the "Sacred Oracles."

But the Book by any other name is still God's word, divine revelation.   —R. W. B.

III. Tests of True Knowledge (1 John 2:3-6)

A. Obedience to God's Commands (vv. 3-5)

3. And hereby we do know that we know him, if we keep his commandments.

By the second century a strange heresy called Gnosticism threatened the church. Among other things, Gnostics claimed a special, esoteric knowledge of God, a knowledge not readily available to ordinary Christians. This heresy not only led to spiritual snobbery, but it also often led to wanton living. It may very well be that some early forms of Gnosticism were already evident when John wrote this epistle.

If so, John does not refute it by complicated arguments based on philosophy or theology. Instead, he points to a more obvious way to test whether one really knows God. When we obey God's commandments, we demonstrate to any who observe that we truly know Him. This test is by no means out of date or out of fashion. It still is applicable. In suggesting this test, John is echoing what the Master had said earlier: "By their fruits ye shall know them" (Matthew 7:20).

4. He that saith, I know him, and keepeth not his commandments, is a liar, and the truth is not in him.

In this verse, John gives us the negative side of the same test. John doesn't mince any words in his denunciation. If a person claims that he knows God and yet refuses to obey Him, that person *is a liar*.

5. But whoso keepeth his word, in him verily is the love of God perfected: hereby know we that we are in him.

After rejecting the heretical notion that one can know God in some mystical way, John now shows that the Christian can know that he is in God. When one keeps God's word, that is, keeps His commandments, the love of God is perfected or made complete in him. The expression *love of God* can mean God's love for the Christian or the Christian's love for God. The latter seems more appropriate here. God's love, after all, is already perfect toward us. It is *our* love that needs to become mature and complete.

B. Walking as Jesus Walked (v. 6)

6. He that saith he abideth in him ought himself also so to walk, even as he walked.

To make sure that no one misunderstands his point, John states it in yet another way. A person who claims to abide or live in God ought to live as Jesus did. While John does not specifically mention Jesus, in the context it is obvious that John intends that we pattern our lives after the life of Christ. One of the reasons why Jesus came in the flesh was to show us what God is like and to encourage us to strive to be more like Him.

STEPPING IN THE LIGHT

Thousands have walked where Jesus walked. Tours of the "Holy Land" are commonplace these days, with more people traveling to more places more frequently than ever before. It is exciting to see Jerusalem from the Mount of Olives, to visit the site of Herod's temple, to stand on the bank of the Jordan River. One can also trace the steps of Christ in Galilee—by the sea, to the ruins of ancient Capernaum and Caesarea Philippi, even to the mountains where the Master taught and was transfigured.

As thrilling as it is actually to walk paths and streets that Jesus walked during His earthly ministry, the daily disciplines of walking (*living, speaking, acting, and reacting*) as He did provide far greater excitement and longer-lasting satisfaction.

John describes the Christian walk in terms of obedience, truth, and love. Knowing Christ and abiding in Him will issue in a life-style that reflects the attributes that characterized His person, His preaching, and His perfection.

Physical educators recommend walking as a most beneficial, non-strenuous exercise. For Christians, walking with Jesus is the only way to spiritual health and happiness.   —R. W. B.

Conclusion

A. No More Sin

The word *sin* has gone out of style. In earlier generations, a preacher or an evangelist could thunder out the term with such force that his hearers outwardly shuddered and inwardly began a self-examination that often led to tearful repentance. But no more. Sins have become "social maladjustments" or "minor indiscretions." Homosexuality is not considered a sin by society, but an "alternate life-style." Marital infidelity is no longer adultery but an "open marriage." Alcoholism is now a "disease" to which no moral responsibility may be attached. Of course, our culture still opposes a few transgressions. Being overweight, if not quite a sin, is likely to meet considerably more social disapproval than even many flagrant sins.

God's Word forbids certain types of behavior. Giving them names that society finds more acceptable does not change the nature of those practices. Calling evil "good" is a form of self-

deception and a denial of sin. This, was the kind of behavior that John so strongly condemned. When we engage in the subtle denial of sin, we are, as John said, liars—clever, sophisticated liars, but liars nevertheless.

What can we do to change this dangerous situation into which we have drifted? We must begin by holding our own lives up to the light of the Scriptures and facing the consequences of that examination. Once we have purged our own lives, then we will be ready to help others. We need not be harsh or judgmental as we speak to others, but, we dare not compromise the truth revealed in the Scriptures.

But even as we clearly set forth the teaching of God's Word concerning the reality of our sin, let us always, in a spirit of love, share the remedy that God has provided for our sin. In His great love, He sent His Son into the world to be the atoning sacrifice for the sins of all mankind. Only as we yield our lives fully to Him can we be free from sin's possession and its penalty.

B. Let Us Pray

Dear God of Light, teach us to shun the darkness and walk in the light. Show us our sins, and then give us the courage and the maturity to turn away from them. Grant us the cleansing that comes through the blood of Jesus Christ and let us know the rich fellowship that comes when we walk in the light. Teach us Your commandments and show us how to obey them, knowing that we have an Advocate pleading our case before You when we fail. In His name we pray. Amen.

C. Thought to Remember

Our sense of sin is in proportion to our nearness to God.   —Thomas D. Bernard.

Home Daily Bible Readings

Monday, Apr. 16—Love God, and Teach God's Word (Deuteronomy 6:4-9)
Tuesday, Apr. 17—Love God, and Serve God Faithfully (Deuteronomy 10:12-21)
Wednesday, Apr. 18—"Love Your Enemies" (Matthew 5:43-48)
Thursday, Apr. 19—Two Great Love Commandments (Mark 12:28-34)
Friday, Apr. 20—Love, Forgive, and Live in Peace (Colossians 3:12-17)
Saturday, Apr. 21—Love and Bless All People (1 Peter 3:8-12)
Sunday, Apr. 22—Lovers Live in the Light (1 John 2:7-17)

Learning by Doing

This page contains an alternate lesson plan emphasizing learning activities. Classes desiring such student involvement will find these suggestions helpful.

Learning Goals

Participating in this lesson, students should:

1. List the key teachings from today's text.

2. Apply those teachings to case studies representing contemporary problems.

3. Identify real people who need to respond to at least one of these teachings.

Into the Lesson

Before class write the following sentences on a sheet and make photocopies:

1. I don't want to be with those people at church anymore. We used to be friends, but now we don't seem to speak the same language.

2. Pray every day? That's a wonderful idea, but after ninety seconds, I've run out of things to pray about. I can't honestly say I have much of a prayer life. God seems so far away.

3. You mind your business and I'll mind mine. Don't tell me my actions are sinful when you've got such obvious problems in your life. I know I'm not perfect, but who is? My relationship with God is just fine, thank you.

4. Jesus Christ may have been a wonderful teacher, but you can't convince me He was anything more than that.

5. I can't come back to church, because I've sinned too terribly. There's no hope for anyone who's done what I've done. I can't face God, and I can't face my Christian friends.

Cut some of the sheets into strips so that each strip has a different sentence. Give each student a sentence. Ask students to divide themselves into pairs and to decide:

1. On a scale of one to five, how real is the "problem" on your paper? (One means, very unrealistic; five means, "I actually know someone who feels this way.")

2. On a scale of one to five, how easy is this "problem" to answer? (One means, "I don't have any idea how to answer this"; five means, "Here's my answer, and I'm sure it's complete.")

Have the pairs discuss these questions and their statements for three or four minutes. Then spend another five minutes discussing with the whole class. Tell class members that we'll come back to these sentences later in the session.

Into the Word

Write these words on your chalkboard: Life, Fellowship, Light and Darkness, Sin and For-

giveness. Tell students these are the issues considered in today's text. Have each pair from the first activity find another pair so that you have groups of four. Ask the groups to survey today's printed text to see what the Scripture says about each of the above words or pairs of words. Give students about ten minutes to make their lists under each heading. Then discuss as a class.

Their lists should look something like this:

Life

1:1, 2: John had intimate, physical contact with the Word of life.

1:2: This life is eternal life.

Fellowship

1:3: We are united in fellowship by our common belief about Jesus.

1:6: Our fellowship with God is interrupted by our sin.

1:7: Obedience to Christ unites us to each other.

2:3-6: The fact that we know (have fellowship with) God is affirmed by our obedience to Him.

Light and Darkness

1:5: God is light; in Him is no darkness.

1:6: If we're walking in darkness, we're not in fellowship with God.

1:7: If we walk in the light, we have fellowship with each other.

Sin and Forgiveness

1:6: Sin separates us from God.

1:8, 10: No one is without sin.

1:9: God will forgive the sins of Christians when they confess them to Him.

2:1: All that John wrote about sin should keep us from sinning.

2:1, 2: Christ is the bridge uniting us with God; He is the defender who secures our forgiveness.

2:3, 4: We're lying if we pretend to know God but do not obey Him.

Into Life

After discussing the Biblical text, return to the sentence-problems considered at first. Distribute a sheet with all five sentences to every class member. In groups, or as a class, consider how today's text speaks to each problem.

Ask class members: "Is there someone you know who needs to understand what this passage teaches? Is there some truth in this passage you need to fully realize yourself?"

Let's Talk It Over

The questions on this page are designed to encourage review of the lesson Scriptures and to promote discussion of the lesson by the class. The answers provided are only discussion starters. Let your class talk it over from there.

1. Of what value is it to us to say that Jesus Christ was "from the beginning"?

Although Christianity is relatively new on earth, it is not new in Heaven. God had planned for Christ, Christianity, and Christians from before creation. Isn't it wonderful to know that God has wanted us to be in His family that long? To know that Christ was from the beginning is also to say that Christianity is not simply the result of the events that transpired in any culture, or the appearance in history of some human superstar. Christianity is not manufactured, but *God*ufactured. Jesus was beyond history, and yet He came to history because of His love for us.

2. When visitors come to the worship services of our congregation, how may we show them that we want them to "have fellowship with us"?

We could begin to show it in the church parking lot. Do we have a special place for visitors to park? That would communicate to them that they are welcome. We could sit toward the middle of the pew so that others do not have to climb over us to find a place to sit. We could have a special greeting time for visitors without embarrassing them. We could send them cards or phone them during the week to let them know we were glad they were there, and would like for them to return.

3. How is Christian fellowship expressed?

The word *fellowship* means a sharing. It stresses that we have a commonness. Fellowship is a caring activity. It is not just being together in the same place at the same time. Fellowship is Christ in people benefiting people in Christ.

4. What practical application can we draw from the truth that if we have fellowship with God, we do not walk in darkness?

We may respond to the invitation to come to Christ while the congregation sings the song "Just As I Am," but we are not to remain as we are. We are to be constantly changing into Christlikeness. God does not save us *in* our sins, but *from* our sins. The idea that we can fellowship with God and continue to live without any regard for His wishes must be abandoned. God will affect both what we say and what we do.

5. What advantage do Christians who sin have over non-Christians who sin?

As Christians we have an advocate, someone who intercedes for us before the Father; that person is Jesus Christ. Because we have received Christ, we are the children of God (John 1:12). Being in God's family, we can relate to our loving Father as erring children; non-Christians are not in His family and will relate to God as outsiders. Christians possess the privilege of prayer—asking and receiving forgiveness.

6. To whom should we confess our sins?

We should confess first of all to God, because He is the one who is the most hurt. Then we need to confess our sin to the person against whom we have sinned, *provided* that such a confession will not damage or hurt that person. There are some situations in which it is better not to reveal our sin to a person, for that other person's own well-being.

7. What does keeping God's commandments have to do with really knowing God?

To really know God is to love Him. And to love God is to respect what He respects, and to want to please Him. It is to want His desires to be met. We keep His commandments, not out of fear because He terrorizes us, but out of respect because we are in awe of Him. To really know God is to know that His commandments are *always* for our benefit.

8. Why does the Christian life involve fellowship with other people? Isn't fellowship with God enough?

God has created us to need each other in addition to needing Him. We see that in newborn infants. No baby can live long without the help of people. God ministers to us through people. He puts His Spirit in us so that He can minister through us to others. In the Garden of Eden, Adam had fellowship with God. But even with that, God said, "It is not good that man should be alone." The first person ever created needed another person. To deny that is to deny our created nature.

Knowing and Abiding

LESSON SCRIPTURE: 1 John 2:18-29.

PRINTED TEXT: 1 John 2:18-29.

1 John 2:18-29

18 Little children, it is the last time: and as ye have heard that antichrist shall come, even now are there many antichrists; whereby we know that it is the last time.

19 They went out from us, but they were not of us; for if they had been of us, they would no doubt have continued with us: but they went out, that they might be made manifest that they were not all of us.

20 But ye have an unction from the Holy One, and ye know all things.

21 I have not written unto you because ye know not the truth, but because ye know it, and that no lie is of the truth.

22 Who is a liar but he that denieth that Jesus is the Christ? He is antichrist, that denieth the Father and the Son.

23 Whosoever denieth the Son, the same hath not the Father: [but] he that acknowledgeth the Son hath the Father also.

24 Let that therefore abide in you, which ye have heard from the beginning. If that which ye have heard from the beginning shall remain in you, ye also shall continue in the Son, and in the Father.

25 And this is the promise that he hath promised us, even eternal life.

26 These things have I written unto you concerning them that seduce you.

27 But the anointing which ye have received of him abideth in you, and ye need not that any man teach you: but as the same anointing teacheth you of all things, and is truth, and is no lie, and even as it hath taught you, ye shall abide in him.

28 And now, little children, abide in him; that, when he shall appear, we may have confidence, and not be ashamed before him at his coming.

29 If ye know that he is righteous, ye know that every one that doeth righteousness is born of him.

Apr 29

GOLDEN TEXT: If that which ye have heard from the beginning shall remain in you, ye also shall continue in the Son, and in the Father.—1 John 2:24.

John Writes of Life, Light, and Love

Unit 2: Abiding in Love
(1, 2, and 3 John, Lessons 8-13)

Lesson Aims

As a result of studying this lesson each student should:

1. Understand that John calls anyone who denies the Father and the Son an antichrist.

2. Be ready to guard the true faith against those who would deny it.

3. Be able to discern ways by which persons deny Bible truths today.

Lesson Outline

INTRODUCTION
  A. Know Thyself
  B. Lesson Background
I. A WARNING FOR THE LAST TIMES (1 John 2:18, 19)
  A. Antichrists Are Present (v. 18)
    The Last Hour
  B. Some Have Deserted the Faith (v. 19)
II. GOD'S PROTECTION AGAINST DECEPTION (1 John 2:20-27)
  A. The Anointing of the Holy One (v. 20)
  B. Knowing the Truth (v. 21)
  C. Antichrists Identified (vv. 22, 23)
  D. Abiding in Truth (v. 24)
  E. The Promise of Eternal Life (v. 25)
  F. Confidence in Their Faith (vv. 26, 27)
III. EXHORTATION TO FAITHFULNESS (1 John 2:28, 29)
  A. Abide in Him (v. 28)
    The King Is Coming
  B. Do Right (v. 29)
CONCLUSION
  A. Knowing and Feeling
  B. Knowing and Doing
  C. Let Us Pray
  D. Thought to Remember

Display visual 9 from the visuals packet to illustrate a main teaching of this lesson. The visual is shown on page 301.

Introduction

A. Know Thyself

"Know thyself!" said Socrates to the youth of ancient Athens. And, following his own advice, he gave his life to a pursuit of knowledge. Other philosophers joined in this pursuit, and as a result Athens was regarded as the intellectual center of the ancient world. Yet Athens, like her less intellectually inclined neighbors, eventually fell into ruin. Her vaunted brilliance could not save her.

Are we then to suppose that intellectual activities are useless, that one might just as well remain ignorant? Not at all. Athens' problem was not that she gave priority to mental activities, but that she turned in the wrong direction in seeking knowledge. Socrates supposed that man possessed within himself all that he needed to reach the intellectual heights. Little did he realize that man within himself does not have the tools to plumb the depths of his own soul. Further, even if he had those tools, his own sinfulness would keep him from using them adequately. Blinded as he is by his own pride, man alone can never find truth.

Thus, we must look outside ourselves to find the ultimate truth that God would have us to follow. That is the point that John makes in this lesson. We must look to God's revelation to find that truth, and we must allow ourselves to be led by the Holy Spirit as we seek God's will for our lives.

Many Greek philosophers held that knowledge is virtue. John does not make that mistake. To know, to understand is not enough. God is not satisfied with us until His truth is reflected in changed lives and changed relationships.

B. Lesson Background

Last week's lesson was first in our study of 1 John. In chapter 1, John warned Christians against certain heresies that were beginning to appear within the church. In today's lesson, we see John enlarging upon that warning, pointing out to his readers that knowledge revealed to them through the Holy Spirit provides a good defense against the seducers and gives strength to abide in the Father and the Son.

Two thousand years of church history have passed, and we have learned many lessons from this history. Yet John's message is just as needed today as it was in the first century.

I. A Warning for the Last Times (1 John 2:18, 19)

A. Antichrists Are Present (v. 18)

18. Little children, it is the last time: and as ye have heard that antichrist shall come, even now are there many antichrists; whereby we know that it is the last time.

Little children. John addresses his readers not condescendingly but lovingly as would a parent or a dedicated teacher. *It is the last time.* Literally, John wrote that it was the last "hour." His readers may have understood this to mean that the end was very near. Verse 17, which states that the "world passeth away," would tend to reinforce this idea. However after nineteen hundred years we are in a position to understand this differently. We can see that John meant that the last period of the world's history had begun. God views time differently than we do. For Him, a thousand years is as a day and a day as a thousand years (2 Peter 3:8).

As evidence that the last hour is at hand, John points out the presence of antichrists. At some point in the past they had been taught that before Christ's return an "antichrist" must first come. This prophecy, John indicates, had been amply fulfilled, for there were already many antichrists on the scene. The word *antichrist* is used only by John in the New Testament. There has been much scholarly debate about what John meant by this term. Its most obvious meaning is *anyone who opposes Christ.* John himself defines it in verse 22 as anyone who denies the Father and the Son.

THE LAST HOUR

I am seated across from a man whose doctor says his death is imminent. Any day, any hour, he could draw his last breath. His spiritual condition is uncertain. I probe his thoughts. "How is it between you and God?"

"So, so," he gestures. He claims to be a believer, and was baptized as a youth, but he's not a "church man." He hasn't worshiped publicly for decades. He seems to be a respected citizen, and well-loved by family and friends. Even youngsters, teenagers, come to visit him. Obviously he is a good, moral man.

But now it's his last hour—he is anticipating the universal appointment with death. I have been called to his home to offer Christian comfort and reassurance. Though he doesn't say so, I suspect this dying man wishes he had honored spiritual priorities more consistently as he walked carelessly through life. If he had lived as if *each* hour might be his last, he would not now be so anxious about his eternal destiny.

The faith of the first-century Christians had about it a sense of urgency. They were con-

---

How to Say It

GNOSTICISM. *Nahs*-ti-siz-im.
NICODEMUS. *Nick*-uh-*dee*-mus. (strong accent on *dee*).

---

vinced that Christ's return was imminent. They also knew that martyrdom was a very real possibility for any courageous Christian. Have we lost that quality of faith that is sure He may return at any moment?
—R. W. B.

B. Some Have Deserted the Faith (v. 19)

19. They went out from us, but they were not of us; for if they had been of us, they would no doubt have continued with us: but they went out, that they might be made manifest that they were not all of us.

They went out from us. John indicates that at some point in the past those whom he designates as antichrists had left the church. *But they were not of us.* Inwardly, these persons were not really united with us. At one time these apostates had made the true confesson (either sincerely or otherwise) and had been admitted into the fellowship of the congregation. But now they had shown their true colors and had left. The true test of discipleship is to remain in the fellowship of the congregation. Their breaking of that fellowship was clear indication that they were not true disciples.

This test can still be applied today. An apostate can remain within the fellowship of true believers, where his false teachings are a disruptive force. While he remains within the congregation, he may argue that he is true to the faith. But when he leaves, his apostasy becomes evident to all. Of course, not everyone who leaves a congregation is guilty of apostasy. On occasion the faithful may be forced out by the apostates or heretics. (See 3 John 10.)

II. God's Protection Against Deception (1 John 2:20-27)

A. The Anointing of the Holy One (v. 20)

20. But ye have an unction from the Holy One, and ye know all things.

Faithful Christians have a protection against the false teachers. They have received an anointing from the Holy One, who is Christ, the Holy One of God (Mark 1:24; Acts 3:14). Some feel that the unction of the Holy One is some special blessing from the Holy Spirit that gave them insights of truth that were denied to others. That interpretation doesn't seem likely. If those who had left the congregation were involved in some form of Gnosticism, they would have been the ones claiming a subjective experience of truth denied to others. John would hardly have suggested that the best way to combat a subjective feeling was with another subjective feeling. This anointing of the Holy One seems rather to refer to an objective truth. In verse 14, John refers to the word of God that was abiding in them. Clearly he had reference to the apostolic message, which was inspired by the Holy Spirit, and which they had heard and hidden in their hearts.

In the twentieth century, as well as in the first century, there is no better protection against heresies and apostasies than the Word of God, the Scriptures. But we must study that Word, we must hide it deep within our hearts if it is to protect us against all the fads and false teachings of our day.

B. Knowing the Truth (v. 21)

21. I have not written unto you because ye know not the truth, but because ye know it, and that no lie is of the truth.

The persons to whom John was writing did not need further teaching in the truth. John was confident that they possessed the knowledge necessary to discern the truth from lies. Clearly John did not, like some modern theologians, take the position that truth is relative. Truth and falsehood stand at opposite poles. Man, relying upon his feelings and his own intellect, may not be able to distinguish between truth and falsehood. But armed with the Scriptures, a Christian would be able to tell the difference. John's words may have been designed to give reassurance to those who doubted their ability to discern truth.

C. Antichrists Identified (vv. 22, 23)

22, 23. Who is a liar but he that denieth that Jesus is the Christ? He is antichrist, that denieth the Father and the Son. Whosoever denieth the Son, the same hath not the Father: [but] he that acknowledgeth the Son hath the Father also.

Persons who succumb to heretical lies usually have trouble keeping the truth in other areas of their lives. The central truths of the Christian faith form a solid foundation upon which one can develop a consistent life-style. But once any of these central truths are denied, then consistency becomes impossible. It is not possible to test every aspect of a person's life to determine if he is a true believer. All we have to do is see whether he holds these foundational truths. This is the point that John was making.

At the very heart of the Christian faith is the doctrine that Jesus is the Christ, the Son of the living God. Every Christian must make this confession. If a person cannot in honesty make this confession, then he cannot be a Christian, no matter how many other admirable attributes he may possess. Anyone who says he is a Christian and denies that Jesus is the Christ is a liar. Indeed, such a person is an antichrist!

John also makes the point that we cannot break these truths up into pieces and accept some parts and reject other parts. For example, one cannot have the Father (that is, affirm a belief in God) while denying His Son. Truth is of one whole piece, and it is lost if it is fragmented. The opposite of this is that if one acknowledges the Son, he also has the Father.

D. Abiding in Truth (v. 24)

24. Let that therefore abide in you, which ye have heard from the beginning. If that which ye have heard from the beginning shall remain in you, ye also shall continue in the Son, and in the Father.

The way for them to avoid becoming antichrists was to allow the word of God to abide in them. They had first heard the word proclaimed by the apostles or by those who came from the apostles. Later they had access to the Word in written form. John reminded them that the way to be safe was to remain faithful to what they had *heard from the beginning*. Other New Testament writers also stressed the importance of holding fast to the original truths. In writing to the Galatians, Paul warned against accepting any other gospel. Anyone, whether he be a man or an angel, who brought another gospel was accursed (Galatians 1:8, 9). Jude urged his readers to "earnestly contend for the faith which was once delivered unto the saints" (Jude 3).

Across the centuries, millions of words have been written to define and explain that true faith. These writings have often helped people come to a better understanding of that faith. Yet none of these writings carries the authority of the Scriptures. They do not constitute what was *heard from the beginning*. The Bible and the Bible alone can give us the guidance that John recommended for his "little children."

E. The Promise of Eternal Life (v. 25)

25. And this is the promise that he hath promised us, even eternal life.

Apparently John is referring to promises that Jesus had made during His ministry. We are likely to think of eternal life as the Christian's home in Heaven, which awaits in the future. But Jesus also spoke of eternal life as something one can possess here and now. On one occasion Jesus said, "He that believeth on the Son hath everlasting life" (John 3:36). He expressed the same idea in John 6:47. It is clear that Jesus was saying that eternal life begins here and now. We can as Christians begin to taste some of the joys and blessings that we will receive in a far larger measure in the future life. That idea seems to fit in very well with the context here. Continuing in the Son and in the Father (v. 24) is necessary to the fulfillment of this promise.

F. Confidence in Their Faith (vv. 26, 27)

26. These things have I written unto you concerning them that seduce you.

In these two verses, John summarizes the warning he has just given them. But now he adds another element. The enemies of the truth, those who denied that Jesus was the Christ, had gone out from them, had become apostates. But they were not content just to leave. They were attempting to mislead others. This is the usual practice of heretics and apostates. Once they have accepted false doctrine, they are usually not content just to leave and practice their doctrine among themselves. They seek to seduce as many others as they can to follow them in their wayward paths.

27. But the anointing which ye have received of him abideth in you, and ye need not that any man teach you: but as the same anointing teacheth you of all things, and is truth, and is no lie, and even as it hath taught you, ye shall abide in him.

As we have seen in verse 20, this anointing refers to the Spirit-inspired Word, which they had learned and stored in their hearts. Because they had this Word in their hearts, they did not need any further teaching. John did not mean to suggest that they could dispense with all their teachers. After all, John himself was doing a great deal of teaching in this epistle. What he meant was that they did not need any teaching from the false teachers.

The Word that they had received through the Spirit-inspired apostles provided a standard by which they could measure all other teachings. So long as they obeyed the Word, they would abide in Him. Some take this last clause, *ye shall abide in him*, to be imperative. Thus John was urging them to abide in Him, not just stating that they would abide in him.

Christianity is a historic religion. It deals with events that happened in history, not in some mythical past. Thus its truths can be passed on from person to person in objective statements.

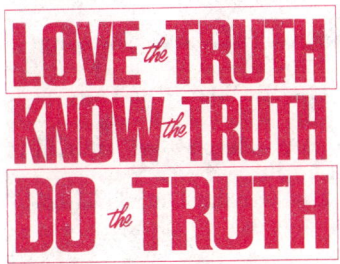

visual 9

Since this is so, the best defense against false teachings is a constant reference to the objective Word, not one's subjective feelings. We, like the apostle John, must do all that we can to encourage people to study the Word of God and abide in it.

III. Exhortation to Faithfulness (1 John 2:28, 29)

A. Abide in Him (v. 28)

28. And now, little children, abide in him; that, when he shall appear, we may have confidence, and not be ashamed before him at his coming.

The best protection against false teachers is to remain in Christ. To remain in Christ means not only to remain true to His teachings but to apply those teachings to our lives. The final test of faithfulness must always be measured by fruitful lives.

John now presents a compelling reason for Christians to abide in Christ. Christ will appear—He is coming back! John urges his readers to abide in Christ so that they may have *confidence* when He comes. This confidence arises from their trust in Him and His promises. Because of Christ's sacrificial death, Christians can come before the throne of grace with boldness (Hebrews 4:16; 10:19). They can experience this same boldness when He returns.

Those who have not remained in Him will be *ashamed*. The clear implication is that Christ's return will involve judgment, a doctrine that is affirmed in other passages of Scripture. John's emphasis is positive, but he is careful to remind his readers that there is a negative side to our Lord's return.

THE KING IS COMING!

The Roman Catholic Church spent $20 million preparing for the pope's visit to America in 1987. His itinerary and schedule were planned to the minute, with no detail overlooked. Security precautions were maximized, and news media people were prepared to capture each moment with film, print, and broadcast commentary.

It is not surprising that such ado accompanied the travels of the pope. He is a religious celebrity, a leader of fame and power. To Roman Catholics, such elaborate preparations for his coming seem most appropriate.

Christians live in anticipation of the return of Christ, the Son of God. We should be occupied with daily preparations for His coming. He is far more than a mere man who has been elected to high position. He is the Savior of the world, exalted by God to glory and honor. He is King of kings and Lord of lords! No sacrifice should be spared in getting ready for His coming. Will you be *ashamed* or *confident* when He appears?

—R. W. B.

B. Do Right (v. 29)

29. If ye know that he is righteous, ye know that every one that doeth righteousness is born of him.

Although in verse 28 John has spoken of Jesus, it seems best to understand that in the verse before us he is thinking of God the Father. In other references in this epistle, John indicates specifically that we are born of God (see 3:1, 9; 4:7; 5:18). This reference to birth reminds us of Jesus' conversation with Nicodemus that to enter the kingdom of God, he must be born again (John 3:3). At least one implication of this figure is that one who is born into a family will bear certain family resemblances. It follows then that since God is righteous, those who are born into His kingdom will bear the marks of righteousness.

A note of caution must be inserted here. One might draw the conclusion from John's words that anyone whose life displays works of righteousness has been born of God. From the context, it seems clear that John does not intend such an interpretation. The point he is making is that those who are born into the family of God will live righteously.

Conclusion

A. Knowing and Feeling

The Scriptures plainly teach that Christians are led by the Holy Spirit. But not everyone agrees as to how that leading takes place. It is not unusual to hear a person say that the Holy Spirit led him to make a certain decision or to take a certain action. When asked how he knows that the Spirit was leading him, he is likely to respond that he has a feeling in his heart that he is following the leading of the Spirit. Since feelings are subjective, one can hardly deny that another had a feeling. One can, however, raise questions about interpretations of feelings. Some time ago a friend of mine had a feeling of tightness in his throat and chest, and intense pain in his chest that ran down his left arm, and other symptoms that convinced him that he was having a heart attack. He was rushed to the hospital and given a thorough examination with surprising results. They found not a bit of evidence of a heart attack, but they did find a badly inflamed gall bladder. My friend felt

with absolute certainty that he was having a heart attack. Fortunately in this case, his feelings had misled him. A more objective diagnosis found the real problem.

We cannot separate our faith from our feelings, but we must take care that our feelings don't dominate our actions. We have a standard—the Scriptures—as a guide for our spiritual lives. That is what John meant when he wrote that we have an "unction from the Holy One," which allows us to "know all things." He was speaking of the Word, which had come to them through inspired men. We have that same Word. Let us learn to use it wisely to accomplish God's will in our lives.

B. Knowing and Doing

We are encouraged to study God's Word and to learn its content. But simply to know the truth is not enough. To be pleasing to God, we must also do the truth. We must move the truths we learn from the head to the heart, where they will change our will, and then to the hands, where they will change our actions. That's what John meant when he wrote that "every one that doeth righteousness is born of him."

C. Let Us Pray

Dear Father, create a love in our hearts for Your holy Word. May its teachings protect us against the false teachings that threaten us on all sides. May its precepts guide us and encourage us to walk in the paths of righteousness. In Jesus' name we pray. Amen.

D. Thought to Remember

Know thyself, but also know what God's will is for your life.

Home Daily Bible Readings

Monday, Apr. 23—An Appeal for Unity (1 Corinthians 1:10-17)

Tuesday, Apr. 24—God's Wisdom Revealed in Christ (1 Corinthians 1:18-25)

Wednesday, Apr. 25—Christ, the Source of our Wisdom (1 Corinthians 1:26—2:5)

Thursday, Apr. 26—The Marks of Wisdom (2 Timothy 2:20-26)

Friday, Apr. 27—The Marks of Folly (2 Timothy 3:1-9)

Saturday, Apr. 28—Teach the Truth (1 Timothy 4:1-10)

Sunday, Apr. 29—Live the Truth (1 Timothy 4:11-16)

Learning by Doing

This page contains an alternate lesson plan emphasizing learning activities. Classes desiring such student involvement will find these suggestions helpful.

Learning Goals

As a result of studying this lesson, students should be able to:

1. Discover and list at least three truths from 1 John 2:18-29 for dealing with false teaching today.

2. Choose a specific way of applying at least one of these truths to their lives this week.

Into the Lesson

Ahead of time, make four posters, each with one of these four responses printed on it in large letters: STRONGLY AGREE, AGREE, DISAGREE, STRONGLY DISAGREE. Mount them at the four corners of your classroom. Use the following agree/disagree statements to begin today's class session. As you read each of the sentences aloud, class members should stand by the poster that represents their feeling about the sentence.

1. False teaching isn't much of a problem for most Christians I know.

2. Most Christians feel prepared to answer those persons claims who deny the deity of Christ.

3. The best way to protect yourself against false teaching is to attend church several times a week.

4. The best way to protect yourself against false teaching is to study every cult and sect in order to analyze its errors.

5. The best way to protect yourself against false teaching is to become thoroughly familiar with what the Bible says about Jesus.

6. The best way to protect yourself against false teaching is to ask the preacher for help whenever you hear some questionable doctrine.

Into the Word

Read 1 John 2:26 aloud. Then read the whole printed text aloud as the class listens to discern the false teaching that was threatening the Christians whom John addressed. (Some were saying that Jesus was not the Christ—v. 22.) Ask, "How does John describe the person who teaches this wrong idea?" (Liar. Antichrist.) "What does John say about the one way to know God?" (We can relate to God only through the Son—v. 23.)

Tell the class that at first glance this Scripture may seem difficult to understand. There are a number of terms and ideas that need clarifica-

tion. Read the whole printed text aloud again, slowly. On note cards or paper that you have distributed to the students, they should write down any questions they have about the text. Gather and group these questions. While you're doing this, ask a class member to read the text aloud to the class a third time. On a second note card, class members should jot down truths from the text for people to live by today.

You should probably anticipate questions such as these:

Who is the antichrist? (Anyone who denies the Father and the Son—v. 22.)

What does John mean by "anointing"? (See the commentary under verses 20 and 27.)

What is the last hour? (The Christian age, the last era of time before Jesus returns and time shall be no more.)

If students do not write down all the following truths from this text, add any that they missed. Write the truths on the chalkboard.

• We must learn the truth, and use it to combat falsehood (vv. 20, 21).

• Anyone who denies that Jesus is the Christ is a liar (v. 22).

• The only way to God is Jesus (v. 23).

• We must cling to the truth about Christ (v. 24).

• Christ brings us eternal life (v. 25).

• We must remain in Christ (vv. 24, 27-29).

• We must continue His righteousness (vv. 28, 29).

Into Life

Ask students to look again at the truths on the chalkboard. With these in mind, what are some examples of false teachings or false teachers who threaten the church today?

List answers on the chalkboard. Examples may include any of the cults. Any group or any teacher that denies that Jesus is the only Son of God is false and dangerous. Such a denial is the one constant among all the cults.

Ask students, in pairs, to think of at least two implications of each of the truths. Assign a different truth to each pair. Ask class members to write down the truth, followed by its implications. For example, "We must cling to the truth about Christ, therefore (a) read our Bibles daily, and (b) we should compare every religious teaching with what the Bible reveals."

Let's Talk It Over

The questions on this page are designed to encourage review of the lesson Scriptures and to promote discussion of the lesson by the class. The answers provided are only discussion starters. Let your class talk it over from there.

1. The word *antichrist* literally means against Christ. How does the coming of antichrists to Christians help prove that Jesus is the Christ, the promised Messiah?

Antichrists would never have come toward the end of the first century had the Messiah himself not already come. People would not have taken a stand against the Messiah if the existence of the Messiah were not a fact. The fact that antichrists came adds evidence to the fact that the authentic Messiah preceded them. The fact that antichrists were confronting Christians adds evidence to the fact that Christians had recognized and were following the authentic Messiah.

2. What characterizes an antichrist in our society today?

An antichrist is someone who denies that Jesus is the Messiah. Such a person may simply deny the divinity of Jesus. An antichrist may also instigate and promote both attitudes and actions that are diametrically opposed to Jesus' way of acting. Groups that promote pornography and homosexuality are antichrists. They may verbally affirm the divinity of Jesus, but they do not do the will of Jesus. A person could be an antichrist either by denying the reality of Jesus as the Messiah or by denying the eternal character of Jesus. To be against what Christ stands for is to be *anti*-Christ.

3. Some Christians try to label other Christians as antichrists. What is the danger of doing that?

It is one thing to be against Christ; it is quite another to hold opinions that differ from those of other Christians. We must understand that followers of Christ may differ in opinions about some matters, because we are at different levels of maturity in the family of God. That should not surprise us, if we understand how any family works. To claim that anyone who differs from us is not accepting the inspiration of Scripture or the deity of Jesus and thus is an antichrist is mere sectarianism. That will divide the family of God; it comes too close to claiming that one person's understanding of Scripture is infal-

lible, while everyone else's is erroneous. We must understand that the term *antichrist* refers to just one kind of person—the person who denies that Jesus is the Christ. A person may be in error in his understanding of Scriptural teaching without being an antichrist, but he cannot be in error about the deity of Jesus without being an antichrist.

4. John makes it plain that we must confess our sin (1 John 1:9) and God's Son as Messiah (2:22, 23). What is the relationship of those two confessions for us?

Those two confessions are directly related to each other. If we do not confess our sin, we presume that we have no need for the Son of God. If we do not confess Jesus as the Son of God, we have no remedy for our sin problems. To confess Jesus is to acknowledge that we need a Savior. However, the "lip confession" must be coupled with the "life commitment." That's what abiding in the Son is all about.

5. When John says that the anointing we have received abides in us and we have no need for anyone to teach us (v. 27), does he mean that we should not listen to any human teachers at all?

No, of course not. If that were true, then all of the other New Testament writings that deal with teaching one another would be invalid. Teaching is one of the gifts of the Holy Spirit. John himself could not be writing this to Christians if he meant that they could receive no teaching through a human vessel. In this context, he is saying that we should not be willing to listen to *just* anyone. We should be careful when we select those whom we will allow to teach us. We should not listen to teaching that violates the commitment and character of Jesus himself. We have a responsibility to test the teachers (4:1). The first test is the teacher's acknowledgement of Jesus as the divine, perfect Messiah from God. If a teacher doesn't acknowledge that, then do not listen to his teaching. He is an antichrist who would like to deceive you. There is too much at stake to be playing games and following the teachings of people just because they are smooth, persuasive orators.

Love and Hate

LESSON SCRIPTURE: 1 John 3:11-24.

PRINTED TEXT: 1 John 3:11-24.

1 John 3:11-24

11 For this is the message that ye heard from the beginning, that we should love one another.

12 Not as Cain, who was of that wicked one, and slew his brother. And wherefore slew he him? Because his own works were evil, and his brother's righteous.

13 Marvel not, my brethren, if the world hate you.

14 We know that we have passed from death unto life, because we love the brethren. He that loveth not his brother abideth in death.

15 Whosoever hateth his brother is a murderer: and ye know that no murderer hath eternal life abiding in him.

16 Hereby perceive we the love of God, because he laid down his life for us: and we ought to lay down our lives for the brethren.

17 But whoso hath this world's good, and seeth his brother have need, and shutteth up his bowels of compassion from him, how dwelleth the love of God in him?

18 My little children, let us not love in word, neither in tongue; but in deed and in truth.

19 And hereby we know that we are of the truth, and shall assure our hearts before him.

20 For if our heart condemn us, God is greater than our heart, and knoweth all things.

21 Beloved, if our heart condemn us not, then have we confidence toward God.

22 And whatsoever we ask, we receive of him, because we keep his commandments, and do those things that are pleasing in his sight.

23 And this is his commandment, That we should believe on the name of his Son Jesus Christ, and love one another, as he gave us commandment.

24 And he that keepeth his commandments dwelleth in him, and he in him. And hereby we know that he abideth in us, by the Spirit which he hath given us.

GOLDEN TEXT: Hereby perceive we the love of God, because he laid down his life for us: and we ought to lay down our lives for the brethren.—1 John 3:16.

John Writes of Life, Light, and Love

Unit 2: Abiding in Love
(1, 2, and 3 John, Lessons 8-13)

Lesson Aims

This lesson should help your students:

1. Understand that those who love God are likely to be hated by the world.

2. Develop greater love for one another.

3. Decide on at least one thing each will do in the coming week to show love toward others.

Lesson Outline

Display visual 10 from the visuals packet. It highlights a thought about love, which is the central thought of this lesson. The visual is shown on page 310.

Introduction

In last week's lesson, we saw that John warned his readers against false teachings. He identified as an antichrist anyone who denied the Father and the Son. To protect themselves against these false teachings and teachers, John urged his readers to rely upon the knowledge they had received through the Word. If they would allow this Word to abide in them, they would remain safe in the Father and the Son.

In today's lesson, John turns to the theme of love and hate. Using the example of the sacrificial death of Christ, he urges his readers to love one another. This admonition follows logically from his emphasis on sound doctrine. Sound doctrine ought to issue in a life of love and service. This message is still not out of date. Some emphasize doctrine and fail to apply it to their lives. Others neglect doctrine and stress good works. Neither position measures up to the standard that John sets in 1 John 2 and 3.

I. Love One Another (1 John 3:11-15)

A. An Old Message (v. 11)

11. For this is the message that ye heard from the beginning, that we should love one another.

This verse is a logical continuation of John's statement in verse 10. There he makes the point that our lives reveal whether we are children of God or children of the devil. One test of our status is whether we love one another. Anyone who does not love others is not of God.

In saying that Christians must love one another, John was not introducing some new teaching. This was a part of the good news they had heard *from the beginning*. This phrase may refer to the first preaching of the gospel to the specific readers John was addressing, or it may refer to Jesus' teaching during His ministry (John 13:34, 35; 15:12, 17).

B. A Negative Example (v. 12)

12. Not as Cain, who was of that wicked one, and slew his brother. And wherefore slew he him? Because his own works were evil, and his brother's righteous.

To make his point more obvious, John gives an example of what Christians should not do. Both love and hate have consequences. The overt act of murder has its origin in the hatred one holds in his heart. Cain's violent act against his brother (see Genesis 4) is a perfect example of this.

In verse 8 of this chapter John states that one who commits sin (in the context he means one who habitually lives in sin) is "of the devil." Here he identifies Cain as one of those persons—*who was of that wicked one*. Cain slew his brother because he had surrendered his life to Satan. Paul states it this way: "Know ye not, that to whom ye yield yourselves servants to obey, his servants ye are" (Romans 6:16). As a servant of Satan, Cain's *works were evil*. We do not know all of the circumstances about Cain's actions to know in what way they were evil. Perhaps he had brought his offering to God grudgingly, while Abel had brought his gladly. Seeing that God accepted Abel's sacrifice but rejected his own, Cain became envious of his brother.

Envy can become a cancer, growing and gnawing away at a person's spiritual vitals. For example, when the religious leaders demanded that Jesus be crucified, Pilate was keen enough to see that it was "for envy they had delivered him" (Matthew 27:18). This would lead us to believe that Cain's act was not sudden or impulsive. Rather it sprang from hatred that Cain had harbored and had allowed to grow in his heart.

C. The Hatred of the World (v. 13)

13. Marvel not, my brethren, if the world hate you.

John now addresses his readers as *my brethren* rather than as "little children," as he had done in earlier verses. Just as Cain, whose actions were evil, hated Abel, so the world, because its actions are also evil, will hate Christians. The mark of the world is hatred; the mark of the Christian is love. Jesus had earlier warned his followers to expect this kind of treatment: "If the world hate you, ye know that it hated me before it hated you. If ye were of the world, the world would love his own: but because ye are not of the world, but I have chosen you out of the world, therefore the world hateth you" (John 15:18, 19). Many in the early church had already felt this hatred of the world in violent fashion.

It may seem strange that the world would hate Christians, especially when Christians desire nothing more than to love and help those about them. One reason may be that people of the world see something in the lives of Christians that they don't have. Unwilling to pay the price to achieve it, they turn instead to jealousy and envy. Another reason that worldly people hate Christians is that the godly lives of Christians stand in judgment upon the lives of the wicked. Christians are not always aware of just how forceful a life dedicated to righteousness can be in witnessing to and convicting those who walk worldly paths.

These verses remind us of another reason why the world hates Christians. Children of the world are actually children of the devil (v. 10), and their father cannot tolerate anything righteous or decent. And so he seeks to destroy it or pervert it.

DEFENSIVE OFFENDERS

Why do "underachievers" pick on straight-A students? Why do lazy workers harass hard-working employees? Why do carnal-minded hypocrites ridicule Christians who honestly try to be good? Why did Cain kill Abel?

The answer is the same in every case: "Because his own works were evil, and his brother's righteous."

If your children or grandchildren are "peak performers," don't be surprised if they are picked on by classmates who earn just average grades or below. If you strive for excellence in your work, don't be surprised if goof-offs shun you, or even threaten you. If you observe speed laws, if you insist on Sunday worship, even when on vacation trips, and if you refuse to watch R-rated movies—don't be surprised if less-conscientious Christians laugh at your convictions. You can expect the world (and the *worldly*) to resent your pursuit of holiness.

Wrongdoers hate those who do good. To rationalize and justify their own laziness, selfishness, dishonesty, and sinfulness, people ostracize, persecute, and attack those who are industrious and generous, those who possess integrity and morality. The guilty are shamed by the presence of innocence; the wicked are condemned by the proofs of righteousness.

—R. W. B.

D. Message of Life (vv. 14, 15)

14. We know that we have passed from death unto life, because we love the brethren. He that loveth not his brother abideth in death.

As far as John is concerned there are but two categories of existence—life and death. These two categories are quite distinct; a person cannot be part of both at the same time. Nor is there some kind of a half-way house between the two that one may occupy.

We have here one criterion by which we can determine whether we have crossed the frontier between death and life. Death is separation from God, a state of alienation from Him who is the source of being. Life is union with God through Christ. "He that hath the Son hath life; and he that hath not the Son of God hath not life" (1 John 5:12). Again, we are told, "Beloved, let us love one another: for love is of God; and everyone that loveth is born of God, and knoweth God" (1 John 4:7). It is obvious that one who loves the brethren deeply has the Son and thus has life. This brings assurance that he is not still on "death row."

15. Whosoever hateth his brother is a murderer: and ye know that no murderer hath eternal life abiding in him.

John doesn't mince any words about those who harbor hatred in their hearts toward their brothers. They are murderers! In the Sermon on the Mount, Jesus had stated that the real source of sin was internal. The actual test of a person is what takes place in his heart. The external act, whether it be murder or lying, is always preceded by sin in the heart.

Hatred toward another person is a terrible thing. Given enough time, its deadly toxins will poison every aspect of one's life. Further, the energy we spend hating is wasted; it cannot be used for positive good. But worse, the way of hatred is the way of eternal death. Jesus put it this way: "Whosoever is angry with his brother without a cause shall be in danger of the judgment" (Matthew 5:22).

II. Love in Action
(1 John 3:16-18)

A. Christ's Example (v. 16)

16. Hereby perceive we the love of God, because he laid down his life for us: and we ought to lay down our lives for the brethren.

Since John is writing a practical letter rather than a theological treatise, he does not attempt to give a definition of love. Instead he gives us a picture of love in action. The words *of God* are not in the original text and have been supplied by the translators. In this context, the reference is to Jesus, who *laid down his life for us.*

By going to the cross, Jesus laid down His life that we might have the possibility of receiving eternal life. Jesus expressed this idea when He described himself as the good shepherd who was willing to lay down His life for the sheep (John 10:15-18). Jesus' death stands as an example for all who would follow Him. The ultimate test of one's love is whether he is willing to die for the brethren. Not many will be called upon to make this kind of a sacrifice, but the example stands to remind us of just how demanding *agape* love can be.

But in John's situation, this challenge may not have been entirely theoretical. By the time this letter was written, many Christians had already been martyred for their faith, including James, Peter, and Paul. John very well may have been looking toward events soon to happen that would test their love by the cross, the stake, or the sword. So warned, they would have been better prepared to wear the martyr's crown as a demonstration of their love for the brethren.

B. To Love Is to Give (v. 17)

17. But whoso hath this world's good, and seeth his brother have need, and shutteth up his bowels of compassion from him, how dwelleth the love of God in Him?

Most of Christ's followers would not be called upon to show their love by walking the martyr's path. And so John turns to a less heroic, but just as important, way to show love. Poverty was common in the first century, and there were very few institutions to minister to human need. Further, the ordinary citizens were not so insulated from the hungry and the homeless as we are today. Thus they would not have to hunt far to find those who were in need.

Bowels is from a word that refers to the inner parts of the body, the viscera. Many of the ancients believed that the passions, emotions, and affections had their source there. *Shutteth up his bowels* of compassion means simply "Ignores human need and refuses to help." We would say that a person who does this "closes his heart," which also is a metaphorical expression.

John then closes this verse with a penetrating rhetorical question: How can the love of God dwell in such a person? The only effective way of showing our love for God is by showing love for others, love such as God has already shown for us through His Son. In our day there are emotional, mental, spiritual, and material needs. We dare not confine our concerns to only one aspect of men's needs when there are many others.

C. Love Is Not Words Alone (v. 18)

18. My little children, let us not love in word, neither in tongue; but in deed and in truth.

John does not imply that we should not tell others that we love them, but that we should do more than tell them. Words don't cost very much and they won't provide much food for the hungry or shelter for the homeless. By our deeds of helpfulness to those who are in need, we give visible expression to the love of God in our hearts. To love *in truth* is to show that our love is real, not a sham or pretense. John here echoes the words that James had written earlier: "If a brother or sister be naked, and destitute of daily food, and one of you say unto them, Depart in peace, be ye warmed and filled; notwithstanding ye give them not those things which are needful to the body; what doth it profit?"

III. Love Brings Blessings
(1 John 3:19-24)

A. Assurance to the Heart
(vv. 19, 20)

19. And hereby we know that we are of the truth, and shall assure our hearts before him.

Hereby refers to what John has said in the verses immediately preceding (vv. 16-18). By our deeds we show the sincerity of both our faith and our love. If faithfully we put into practice the teaching of Christ and the apostles, we give evidence that *we are of the truth* that we proclaim.

And shall assure our hearts before him. The promises of God are clear in His Word; if we obey his will, we are assured of the promises. We do not rest upon our own personal feelings with no outside check upon them. The assurance we possess depends upon the revelation God has given.

20. For if our heart condemn us, God is greater than our heart, and knoweth all things.

Deep in our hearts we at times realize that we do not measure up to the high standards that Christ has set for us. In those moments, our heart condemns us. But we need not agonize in guilt. Our hearts are not the final judge in such matters. God, because He knows everything, knows the sincerity of our hearts. He also knows that even with the best of intentions we often fall short. In the first chapter, John has already stated that God is faithful and just to forgive sins (v. 9). Here he gives additional assurance that God's love can cover the condemnation our own hearts bring upon us.

B. Confidence Before God (vv. 21, 22)

21. Beloved, if our heart condemn us not, then have we confidence toward God.

While our hearts condemn us, we cannot have confidence before God. But because we know His love, we no longer need live under this condemnation. In 2:28 John spoke of the confidence we may have when the Lord returns. Here he assures us that we can have confidence to approach Him with our requests.

22. And whatsoever we ask, we receive of him, because we keep his commandments, and do those things that are pleasing in his sight.

We must not misunderstand what John is saying here. He is not saying that God will grant us anything that we wish. The requests God honors are those that are in keeping with His will (see 1 John 5:14, 15; John 14:13, 14; 15:7; 16:23).

Because we keep his commandments. This does not mean that God, in answering prayer, is rewarding us for our obedience. John is saying that our obedience indicates that we are living a life that is in harmony with the Father. When we so live, we will not pray for foolish and un-Christian things or with selfish motives. We always add that most vital limitation, "Not my will, but thine, be done" (Luke 22:42).

C. Obedience to God (v. 23)

23. And this is his commandment, That we should believe on the name of his Son Jesus Christ, and love one another, as he gave us commandment.

In the previous verse John speaks of keeping God's commandments—plural. Here he speaks of commandment—singular. But John is not confused. What he means is that all of God's precepts can actually be summed up in one commandment that has two sides. First of all, *we should believe on the name of his Son Jesus Christ.* To believe on the name of Jesus means to accept all that He taught and did and is, and to pledge our lives to the doing of all He commanded. This belief will inevitably cause us to *love one another, as he gave us commandment.* In this text, John has shown us several ways in which to demonstrate this love.

D. Unity With God (v. 24)

24. And he that keepeth his commandments dwelleth in him, and he in him. And hereby we know that he abideth in us, by the Spirit which he hath given us.

John once more speaks of commandments—plural. He is not contradicting what he has just said in the previous verse. There is really only one commandment—that we believe on the name of Jesus and love our fellowmen as He directed. But there are many ways by which we show this love, and each of these becomes a commandment.

At first reading, one might suppose that John is saying that because we keep His commandments we dwell in Him. In the light of other Scriptures, however, we ought to interpret this the other way around. Because we dwell in Him, we keep His commandments (Romans 6:2-7). Indwelling has two sides: we dwell in Him and He dwells in us.

We need not guess about this precious relationship. We can know for a certainty that we

visual 10

WE CAN
GIVE
WITHOUT LOVING,
BUT
WE CANNOT LOVE
WITHOUT
GIVING.

are in Him and He in us because of the Spirit. The comforting gift of the Spirit is bestowed at our baptism (Acts 2:38). He produces fruit in our lives that can be observed by others. One who can freely exhibit love for the brethren without reservation demonstrates that the Spirit is within his heart.

How Do You Know?

How do you know when an elephant's in your bath? It's such an old joke, surely everyone knows the answer by now: "You can smell peanuts on his breath!"

Some instructive corollaries can be drawn from this nonsense. How do we know that God lives in us? We know it "by the Spirit *which he hath given us.*" Interestingly enough, the Greek word translated *Spirit (pneuma)* means breath, wind, or air. Thus we have words in English such as *pneumatic* (air powered), and *pneumonia* (infection that interferes with breathing).

We can be certain God abides in us when we sense His breath (Spirit) in our hearts. God breathes His Spirit into our consciences and into our consciousness, and we are most aware of His presence when we act or speak in a manner that is godly, Christlike, holy.

The reason the elephant joke makes us smile is that it overlooks the obvious. The presence of an elephant in your bath would certainly be detected in more than one way. Sure signs of God's indwelling include peace beyond understanding, joy unspeakable, and hope for things not seen. If you possess contentment, a spirit of obedience, and love for all your brothers, you have evidence that God resides in your soul.

—R. W. B.

Conclusion

A. Living Martyrdom

"I'd be willing to lay down my life for the faith!" the preacher said, and the audience responded with hearty "amens" and affirmative

nods. That seemed quite a bold thing to say— but also quite a safe thing to say. After all, when was the last time anyone in this country actually died for his faith. Of course, there are places in the world today where witnessing for Jesus can earn one the martyr's crown. It was certainly true in the day when John lived and wrote.

In verse 16 John holds up *dying* for our faith or for our brethren as a model of Christian love and courage. But in the following verse, he commands us to make *living* for our faith and for our brothers a model. And after everything has been said and done, this may be more difficult than martyrdom. For one thing, it is a lifelong commitment, because we will never run out of opportunities to serve those about us.

If we have the love of God dwelling in us, we will not hesitate to give of our possessions to one who is in need. But our giving will not be limited to the giving of money, food, or clothing. After all, government agencies can provide these things. Often the most important gift that we can give is ourselves. Even more than the world needs food and clothing, the world needs to know that there is a God who cares. Most people will not discover that fact unless those who seek to serve the Lord seek also to give of their time and loving care to others. We may very well call this kind of loving service *living martyrdom!*

B. As One Thinketh in His Heart

The Scriptures teach us that as one thinketh in his heart, so is he (Proverbs 23:7). If one plans a robbery, he is a robber even if he never carries out his plans. If one seeks to deceive others with falsehoods, he is a liar even if he never utters a word. In the same way, one who hates another person is a murderer even though he never raises his hands against that person. That is the reason that we must guard the issues of our hearts with all diligence. The best way to do that is to fill our hearts with love.

C. Let us Pray

Most gracious Father, let us never forget the message that we have heard, that Your Son loved us enough to die for us. Give us the courage to be willing to die for You. But also give us the strength and wisdom to be willing to live for You under conditions that are not always easy or pleasant. In the name of Him who died for us we pray. Amen.

D. Thought to Remember

Love is the doorway through which the human soul passes from selfishness to service, and from solitude to kinship with all mankind.

Learning by Doing

This page contains an alternate lesson plan emphasizing learning activities. Classes desiring such student involvement will find these suggestions helpful.

Learning Goals

Students should accomplish the following in today's class session:

1. Contrast God's love as described in 1 John 3:11-24 with the world's kind of love.

2. Agree that Christian love is active.

3. Choose one action they will be able to do that will demonstrate love to another Christian.

Into the Lesson

Choose one or several of the following ideas for beginning today's class session:

1. Mix-up. Write each of the following words on a separate piece of poster paper: LOVE IS SOMETHING YOU DO. Give each word to a different class member. Arrange the people in front of the class so that the sentence is mixed up. Ask class members to arrange the people in the right order so that their words make a sentence.

2. Point/counterpoint. Divide the class into pairs. One half of the pairs should think of reasons the following sentences are true: "Love is a feeling. The most important part of love is what it does to your heart." The other half of the class should try to prove this proposition: "Love is a command. The most important part of love is what it does to your actions." After five minutes or so, let the class discuss.

3. Graffiti. Write LOVE IS in big letters on a sheet of butcher paper you have mounted on the wall ahead of time. As students arrive, they complete the sentence with words or even pictures they draw on the paper.

4. Neighbor nudge. Ask half of your students, in pairs, to discuss "The best example of love I've ever seen." The other half should discuss "The worst example of hate I've ever seen." After about three minutes, discuss these examples as a class.

5. Brainstorm. Ask class members to tell you the names of as many love songs as you can write on your chalkboard in sixty or ninety seconds. Challenge the class to rate each love song title from one to five (one is highest or best): How adequately does this title really describe love?

After any of the above introductory activities, tell class members that today's class session will examine a Biblical definition of love to see how God's kind of love is different from what the world often means when it uses the word.

Into the Word

Any of the activities above can become a springboard for today's Bible study. The numbers below correspond to the introductory activities.

1. Ask class members, in groups, to survey today's text and list answers to this question: How do these verses show that love is something you do?

2. In groups, students should seek answers to these questions: "What is the relationship between what is in the heart and what happens in the life? How does this text show how actions grow out of thoughts and feelings?"

3. After completing the graffiti wall, students will see many definitions of love. Now they should survey today's text to list how John finishes the sentence.

4. In pairs or groups, students should list: "What examples of love and hatred does this passage contain? How do you explain the hatred that John predicts? How can the love he describes compensate for it?"

5. Divide the class into an even number of groups. One half of the class writes a song about love based on principles from today's text. They may use a familiar tune and write new words. The other half of the class lists principles from the text and then surveys hymnals to find hymns that express some of these principles.

Allow time for your groups to report back to the whole class, sharing their ideas. During this time, you will be alert to the ideas they share, filling in gaps or tactfully correcting errors. Also be prepared with explanations for difficult-to-understand portions of the text.

Into Life

Ask class members to reflect again on the "Love Is Something You Do" idea. Ask volunteers to share specific actions of other Christians that have communicated love to them. Ask class members to think silently about this question: "When did I last perform some action that shows a fellow Christian that I love him or her?"

Distribute slips of paper and ask class members to privately jot down the names of three or four Christians who need a demonstration of love. Beside at least one of these, students should write how they will show that person love. Close the session with prayer.

Let's Talk It Over

*The questions on this page are designed to encourage review of the lesson
Scriptures and to promote discussion of the lesson by the class. The answers
provided are only discussion starters. Let your class talk it over from there.*

1. In today's text, John reminds us that, as the children of God, we are to "love one another." What are some specific ways in which we may do that?

The Greek word that John uses for love is *agape*. This is an unselfish love that sees the need in others, moves to meet those needs, does not count the cost, does not calculate what it will get in return, and does not evaluate the worth of the person with the need. Consequently, to love one another involves being sensitive to the needs other people have and using whatever resources we have (or organizing resources from others) to meet those needs. It may be a financial need, a fellowship need, a forgiveness need, a transportation need, a teaching need, a corrective need, etc. This kind of love looks out for the other person first. It seeks to make the other person feel important.

2. How does loving our brothers and sisters show that we have passed out of death into life (1 John 3:14)?

To pass from death to life is to change eternal positions. It is to be transferred from the kingdom of Satan into the kingdom of God's Son. Satan hates. Jesus loves. Satan is the agent of death. Jesus is the agent of life. Death signifies a separation. Life signifies a union. To love our brothers and sisters, as defined in question 1 above, is evidence that we have left Satan's kingdom and have moved into Christ's kingdom where *agape* love reigns.

3. In what ways can we "lay down our lives for the brethren" (1 John 3:16)?

To lay down our lives does not necessarily mean that we give up our physical lives. If it meant only that, we could do it but once. There is another thought here: that we do what Jesus did on the cross—voluntarily sacrifice self. We lay down our lives for the brethren continually as we die to selfishness and live unselfish lives of love. Sharing our material goods with our brothers in need, as John makes plain in the very next verse, is one way that we can crucify self. A Christian is to work to provide for himself (2 Thessalonians 3:10); to provide for his family (1 Timothy 5:8); to provide for another in physical need (Ephesians 4:28; 1 Timothy 6:17-19). God

is concerned about our finances, not because He is interested in raising cash, but because He is interested in raising children to become like Christ. We are kidding ourselves if we claim to love the way God loves, while at the same time we remain stingy.

4. What is the difference between loving with tongue and loving in deed and truth?

To love in tongue is to say with words that we love someone. To love in deed is to do some deed to show the love. To love in truth is to be sincere in our acknowledgement that we are disciples of Jesus. The kind of love deed we do shows our sincerity. To our knowledge, Jesus never once said to anyone, "I love you." He may have said it many times, but we do not know about it. But we do know that He demonstrated love. This is not to suggest that we should never use those three powerful words; but it is to suggest that rather than just "word" love, we must also "work" it. That is the challenge—declare it by doing it. Then we know that our lives on the outside are what we claim to be on the inside—we are being truthful to our claim of being God's children.

5. What is the practical, emotional, and psychological value of knowing that although our hearts condemn us, God is greater than our hearts (1 John 3:20)?

Each of us knows himself or herself very well. Our hearts know the wrong we do; they know also our impure thoughts, attitudes, and motives. Because this is so, we may judge that our relationship to God is in jeopardy, that if Jesus came back tonight, we would not go to Heaven. But God is greater than our hearts, for He forgives us when we often do not forgive ourselves. He considers us worthy even though we may consider ourselves unworthy. He looks at us in a more kindly manner than we look at ourselves. It is time for us to accept God's acceptance of us, even when we may not feel acceptable. That is His decision, not ours. And He has made that decision in His Son Jesus on the cross. He is greater than our hearts, and He knows *all* things—He knows that we are His forgiven children, even though sometimes we may not feel like it.

Fear and Love

LESSON SCRIPTURE: 1 John 4:7-21.

PRINTED TEXT: 1 John 4:7-21.

1 John 4:7-21

7 Beloved, let us love one another: for love is of God; and every one that loveth is born of God, and knoweth God.

8 He that loveth not, knoweth not God; for God is love.

9 In this was manifested the love of God toward us, because that God sent his only begotten Son into the world, that we might live through him.

10 Herein is love, not that we loved God, but that he loved us, and sent his Son to be the propitiation for our sins.

11 Beloved, if God so loved us, we ought also to love one another.

12 No man hath seen God at any time. If we love one another, God dwelleth in us, and his love is perfected in us.

13 Hereby know we that we dwell in him, and he in us, because he hath given us of his Spirit.

14 And we have seen and do testify that the Father sent the Son to be the Saviour of the world.

15 Whosoever shall confess that Jesus is the Son of God, God dwelleth in him, and he in God.

16 And we have known and believed the love that God hath to us. God is love; and he that dwelleth in love dwelleth in God, and God in him.

17 Herein is our love made perfect, that we may have boldness in the day of judgment: because as he is, so are we in this world.

18 There is no fear in love; but perfect love casteth out fear: because fear hath torment. He that feareth is not made perfect in love.

19 We love him, because he first loved us.

20 If a man say, I love God, and hateth his brother, he is a liar: for he that loveth not his brother whom he hath seen, how can he love God whom he hath not seen?

21 And this commandment have we from him, That he who loveth God love his brother also.

mistrst anognre

GOLDEN TEXT: There is no fear in love; but perfect love casteth out fear.—1 John 4:18.

John Writes of Life, Light, and Love

Unit 2: Abiding in Love
(1, 2, 3 John, Lessons 8-13)

Lesson Aims

As a result of this lesson, students should:
1. Understand that love can conquer fear.
2. Desire to develop a maturing love toward others.
3. Determine to demonstrate Christian love by a specific action in the coming week.

Lesson Outline

INTRODUCTION
  A. Loving Rats
  B. Lesson Background
  I. GOD IS LOVE (1 John 4:7-12)
  A. Love Comes From God (vv. 7, 8)
  B. God's Love Manifested (vv. 9, 10)
  C. Love Brings Obligations (vv. 11, 12)
 II. LOVE BRINGS ASSURANCE (1 John 4:13-16)
  A. Assurance From the Spirit (v. 13)
  B. Salvation Through Jesus (vv. 14-16)
III. LOVE BANISHES FEAR (1 John 4:17, 18)
  Love Is Never Having to Say You're Afraid
 IV. LOVE CHANGES ACTIONS (1 John 4:19-21)
  A. Motivation of Love (v. 19)
  B. Meaning of Love (vv. 20, 21)
  Lovers and Liars
CONCLUSION
  A. Love's Reward
  B. Let Us Pray
  C. Thought to Remember

Visual 11 in the visuals packet highlights the attributes of love that are mentioned in today's text. The visual is shown on this page.

Introduction

A. Loving Rats

A young woman fell in love with a young man who was a scientist doing medical research. His research involved working with hundreds of laboratory rats. When the young man began to tell her of his work, she almost broke off their relationship, for she had a deep sense of revulsion toward rats. The very mention of the word brought shivers of horror to her.

But the young scientist was patient and persistent, trying to convince her that rats were not all that bad. Finally he persuaded her to visit the laboratory where he worked. It was all that she could do to enter the laboratory, and she stayed only a few minutes. But her affection for the young man was growing, and she eventually visited him in the laboratory again. This time he took a rat from its cage and, after much persuasion, got her to touch it. Before long she visited the laboratory again, and this time he even got her to hold a rat in her hands. Finally, after several visits, she was able to walk over to a cage and pick up a rat and play with it.

Some time later, as her wedding date approached, a friend, knowing of her fear of rats, asked her how she was ever able to overcome this fear. "Love," she replied, "overcomes fear, and if it is great enough, it will even overcome the fear of rats!"

Love for God and for our fellowman commands much of John's attention in his first epistle. In today's lesson, he touches on the power of that love.

B. Lesson Background

John begins the fourth chapter of his first epistle with a warning that believers should test the spirits. False teachers had arisen who were questioning those facts that lie at the very heart of the gospel. Some were denying that Jesus Christ had come in the flesh. The essence of the gospel is the incarnation, and to deny this was to deny the gospel. The test, then, was very simple. Every spirit that acknowledged that Christ had come in the flesh was of God. Any who denied this were not of God.

However, those who denied Jesus Christ were so eloquent that many Christians were being swept into the heresy. John was trying to strengthen them against this threat. His word of assurance was based on the fact that He who was in the faithful Christians was greater than the one who was in the world.

This threat to the gospel was not laid to rest in the first century. In almost every generation since then, it has arisen to plague Christians.

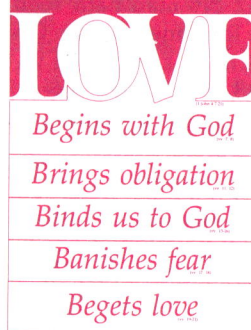

Begins with God
Brings obligation
Binds us to God
Banishes fear
Begets love

visual 11

Today, some who are hailed as leading theologians have taken positions denying that the divine Son of God came in the flesh as Jesus Christ. They may obscure their unbelief with subtle words, but it is still unbelief. The simple test that John proposes in the first verses of this chapter still stands as a valid test.

Another way of knowing if one is of God is by the test of love. John returns to this subject in today's lesson text.

I. God Is Love
(1 John 4:7-12)

A. Love Comes From God (vv. 7, 8)

7. Beloved, let us love one another: for love is of God; and every one that loveth is born of God, and knoweth God.

John addresses his readers as *beloved*, a most appropriate designation, for love is to be the subject of the following verses. *Let us love one another.* The family of God is to be characterized by mutual love. There is no place in this family for selfishness, jealousy, or hatred, which destroy peace and harmony and break its fellowship.

Love is divine in origin. God's love led Him to create man in His own image. His love caused Him to provide for man's needs. And when man fell into sin, God's love made provision for man's redemption. Thus the commandment that Christians love one another is grounded in the very nature of God.

Every one that loveth is born of God. This does not mean that everyone who displays love, no matter the nature of that love, is a child of God. John is writing to Christians, who understand that to be a child of God one must be a believer in Jesus Christ. The point John makes is that one who is a believer will demonstrate love in his life. One cannot be a true believer and not show that faith.

It is possible for a non-Christian to demonstrate a commendable love in his life. Even those who have never acknowledged the lordship of Jesus Christ retain enough of the divine image that they can, under some circumstances, still display genuine love. Certainly, Christians have no monopoly on love. At the same time, one cannot truly be a Christian unless his life bears the fruit of love.

8. He that loveth not, knoweth not God; for God is love.

Children of God should be expected to resemble their Heavenly Father. One way in which this resemblance can be seen is in their love for one another. God has many attributes and qualities, but none of these is so obvious as the attribute of love. It is, in fact, so much a part of His very nature that John equates God with love. When love is lacking in the life of a person, this clearly demonstrates that he does not know God.

B. God's Love Manifested (vv. 9, 10)

9. In this was manifested the love of God toward us, because that God sent his only begotten Son into the world, that we might live through him.

John's language here reminds us of John 3:16, one of the most beloved verses in the Bible. God's love cannot be measured with a yardstick, nor weighed on the scales. How then are we to know that He loves us? We can point to the many wonderful provisions He has made for us in the physical world. But none of these can really show us the full measure of His love. The supreme revelation of God's love for us is seen in the death of His Son on the cross at Calvary. Only when we realize that it was God's only Son who suffered and died there, and that He died so that we who are sinners might live, can we begin to comprehend God's love for us.

10. Herein is love, not that we loved God, but that he loved us, and sent his Son to be the propitiation for our sins. *(atoning sacrifice)*

Not that we loved God. We are selfish by nature. The experience of each of us testifies to the fact that love does not originate from within ourselves. Any explanation of love must begin with God's love for us. In verse 9 John tells us that God revealed His love by sending His Son into the world that we might have life. Thus He showed us what love does—it gives itself away for the good of others. God gave His Son *to be the propitiation for our sins.* Some modern translations render propitiation, "atoning sacrifice." Eternal life is possible only when the price has been paid for our sins. Under the Old Covenant, men sacrificed animals as a means of atoning for their sins. But the New Testament leads us to understand that it is impossible for the blood of bulls and goats to take away sin (Hebrews 10:4). Thus, if our sins are to be removed, we must look to the perfect sacrifice, which is God's own Son.

C. Love Brings Obligations (vv. 11, 12)

11. Beloved, if God so loved us, we ought also to love one another.

Once more John addresses his readers as *beloved.* He wants them to understand that whatever he has to say to them comes because he does indeed love them. The love that God has demonstrated to us is unselfish and serving. In the same way, then, our love ought to express itself in love and concern to others. It may seem that John would have said that, because God loves us, we ought to love *Him*. That would be the natural response to God's love for us. This certainly is implied in all that John says, and, indeed, he makes a direct statement to this effect in verse 19. It is easy to love God who has done so much for us. It is quite another thing to love those about us who at times are anything but lovely. But this is what we must do.

12. No man hath seen God at any time. If we love one another, God dwelleth in us, and his love is perfected in us.

The first part of this verse, *no man hath seen God at any time*, is a truth found in the Old Testament. In John 1:18 it is stated directly in order to emphasize the fact that no one can see God by his own power. Only the Son, who was intimately associated with the Father, could really know Him. God is known to us, not because we see Him, but because He has made himself known. In making this statement, John may have been refuting some of the heretics, who, if they were leaning toward gnosticism, held that in some mystical way they had seen God. The *New International Version* suggests another possibility by inserting the word *but* between the first and second clauses of the verse. The idea is that although no one has seen God at any time, yet if we love one another, God will dwell in us, and His love is made complete in us. Even though God cannot be seen, He dwells in the lives of those who love others. When God dwells in the life of a person, that person is changed. Those changes become so obvious that others can tell the difference and begin to catch a glimpse of what God's love is like.

II. Love Brings Assurance (1 John 4:13-16)

A. Assurance From the Spirit (v. 13)

13. Hereby know we that we dwell in him, and he in us, because he hath given us of his Spirit.

Our relationship with God is a mutual one. We dwell in Him and He in us. It is normal for a person to want some kind of evidence for this mutual relationship. This verse affords two possibilities for this evidence. The word translated *hereby* from the Greek literally means "in this," and can be taken to refer back to the previous verse. One has evidence that God dwells in him, (and he in God) when that person's life shows love to others.

The other possibility is that hereby (in this) refers to what follows. We have evidence of this mutual indwelling because God has given us the

Holy Spirit. Every person who becomes a Christian is promised the gift of the Holy Spirit at his baptism (Acts 2:38). Paul assures us that God's Spirit bears witness with our spirit that we are His children (Romans 8:16). Those who have the Holy Spirit produce the fruit of the Spirit (Galatians 5:22-25), and the first-named fruit is love, the love for one another of which John is speaking in this section of his epistle.

B. Salvation Through Jesus (vv. 14-16)

14. And we have seen and do testify that the Father sent the Son to be the Saviour of the world.

The *we* of this verse is the same as that of 1 John 1:1-4. The apostles who had been with Jesus and had seen Him could testify that He was the Son of God and Savior of the world.

In one brief sentence, John gives us the essence of the gospel. In verses 9 and 10 he pointed out that God had sent His Son to be an atoning sacrifice for our sins. Because Jesus made that sacrifice, He is now our Savior. John's words here remind us of the words of the angel who told Joseph that the child to be born to Mary was to be called Jesus, "For he shall save his people from their sins" (Matthew 1:21). The Samaritans affirmed the same truth after Jesus had preached to them: "This is indeed the Christ, the Saviour of the world" (John 4:42).

15. Whosoever shall confess that Jesus is the Son of God, God dwelleth in him, and he in God.

Jesus came into the world to save the world, but the salvation He offers is available only to those who confess Him as the Son of God. This confession of Christ as the divine Son of God is much more than just an intellectual acknowledgment of that fact. It involves the total surrender of one's life to Him. When and only when one makes this kind of commitment can God dwell in him and he in God. The false teachers who were no longer willing to make this confession were denying themselves this precious relationship with God.

16. And we have known and believed the love that God hath to us. God is love; and he that dwelleth in love dwelleth in God, and God in him.

John here testified to the love of God that he had experienced. His experience had led him to know and believe in this love. God's people come to know His love so well that they trust it with the utmost confidence. *He that dwelleth in love.* He who lives in the atmosphere of love, he whose life is filled with love, can rest assured that he dwells in God and He in him, because by nature, *God is love.*

III. Love Banishes Fear
(1 John 4:17, 18)

17. Herein is our love made perfect, that we may have boldness in the day of judgment: because as he is, so are we in this world.

The word *perfect* means "complete" or "mature." Love matures as we live in fellowship with God daily and as we put into practice His kind of love for our fellowmen. In this kind of love there is no room for petty jealousies or self-glorification. Such love is no longer attracted to the things of this world. A person who has reached this level of love has set his eyes upon things eternal, and for that reason he does not need to fear in the day of judgment. He does not trust in his own righteousness to bring him through that day. Because his love is mature, he has learned to trust in Christ who died for him.

As he is, so are we in this world. This does not mean that we are as perfect as God, but our intention and purpose are that we be godlike even while we remain in this sinful world. Thus living with God and trying to be like Him, "we may have confidence, and not be ashamed before him at his coming" (1 John 2:28).

18. There is no fear in love; but perfect love casteth out fear: because fear hath torment. He that feareth is not made perfect in love.

John is not saying that a Christian will have no fear. Fear is a quite normal and necessary part of our emotional makeup. Without fear, we might take all kinds of risks that would endanger us physically. What John has in mind in this context is the fear of the judgment. If our lives are lived in close fellowship with God and are characterized by the unselfish attitude that expresses itself in willing service, we need not fear the day of God's judgment. This kind of mature love *casteth out fear.* Indeed, this kind of love and fear cannot dwell together. Fear brings dread, torment, and agony in the present. Love brings peace, trust, and confidence for the present and for the future. Obviously the one who lives in dread of judgment gives evidence that he has not reached the level of completed love that John has been writing about.

LOVE IS NEVER HAVING TO SAY YOU'RE AFRAID

When I wrecked my father's new car, I was reluctant to go home. One might even say I was *afraid* to go home. But home I went, confessed my "sin," and was granted forgiveness by a loving father.

Twenty-five years later, *my* son wrecked *my* new car. Police officers, emergency-room personnel, and friends all reported that Sam kept repeating, "Dad's gonna kill me! Dad's gonna kill me!" That was his exaggerated expression of apprehension over what my reaction might be. Almost everyone would say he was *afraid.*

Needless to say, I did not execute my son. I was relieved that he was not hurt more seriously in the accident, and the incident was forgiven. Neither Sam nor I truly feared our fathers' judgment, for both relationships are built on love. Loving sons can face their fathers without terror; loving fathers forgive their sons without restraint.

God's plan includes a day of judgment, when all people will be held accountable for all deeds done in the flesh. But we who are in Christ are not afraid; for God is our loving Father, and through His Son whom He sent to be our Savior, He forgives us of all our sins. —R. W. B.

IV. Love Changes Actions
(1 John 4:19-21)

A. Motivation of Love (v. 19)

19. We love him, because he first loved us.

Fear is a powerful emotion. Fear can prompt us to do many things, things that we don't particularly want to do, things that we would not do if we were not driven to them. But love is an even more powerful motivating force. Love does not drive, it leads. Like fear, love can lead us to do things that we don't especially enjoy, but it can also lead us to enjoy many activities that at first seemed boring or even repulsive.

We are motivated at several different levels. We do some things out of fear, or we avoid doing some things because we fear the consequences if we do them. At another level we do things or avoid doing them out of hope of receiving a reward. At the highest level, we are motivated by love. We love God, not out of fear or of the hope of reward, but because *He first loved us.*

When we first began to learn about God, we learned that He is good, that He gives us the sunshine and the rain and our food. As we grew in our awareness of God, we came to understand that He sent His Son into the world to die for us. As our understanding grew, we learned that He is just, and holy, and merciful. These facts stir within us a positive response. How can we help but love Him, when we consider all that He has done for us?

B. Meaning of Love (vv. 20, 21)

20. If a man say, I love God, and hateth his brother, he is a liar: for he that loveth not his brother whom he hath seen, how can he love God whom he hath not seen?

Love does not exist in a vacuum. If a person loves, there must be an object of that love. It is easy to love God, who has given us so many wonderful blessings. It is a different story when it comes to loving those about us. Yet it follows naturally that if we love God, we must love those whom God has made.

Hateth his brother. The hatred mentioned here is not limited to a bitter animosity that would do violence to a brother. It may be contempt for a person (see Matthew 5:22) or neglect for a brother when he is in need (see James 2:14-16; 1 John 3:17). If one harbors such unloving attitudes toward fellow human beings whom he can see, then his claims to love God whom he cannot see are a lie. These are strong words, but true nevertheless.

21. And this commandment have we from him, That he who loveth God love his brother also.

John concludes this section with a final reminder that it is a commandment of God that we love our brothers. If we love God, we cannot escape the compulsion to love those about us, who are made in God's image.

Lovers and Liars

"Be sure it's true when you say, 'I love you;'
It's a sin to tell a lie.
Millions of hearts have been broken,
Just because these words were spoken:
'I love you, yes, I do; I love you;
If you break my heart I'll die!'
So be sure it's true when you say, 'I love you,'
It's a sin to tell a lie."

That song is so old I can't remember its title or who recorded it. But I do remember hearing it on the radio when I was a teen. It's a cute novelty number, but also gives some good advice.

Home Daily Bible Readings

Monday, May 7—Peter and John: Bold Disciples (Acts 3:1-10)
Tuesday, May 8—Peter and John: Effective Witnesses (Acts 4:5-22)
Wednesday, May 9—The Disciples: Strengthened by Prayer (Acts 4:23-31)
Thursday, May 10—The Disciples: A Community of Love (Acts 4:32-37)
Friday, May 11—The Multitude: Seeking Healing (Acts 5:12-21a)
Saturday, May 12—The Council: Losing Control (Acts 5:21b-32)
Sunday, May 13—The Apostles: Faithful Through Persecution (Acts 5:33-42)

Why is it so easy to lie about love? In romance, people often confuse strong emotions that accompany love, for love itself. Affection, infatuation, excitement, and comradeship—all of these feelings have been wrongly identified as love. But sometimes when you get a feelin', you also get a foolin'! Emotions are tricky that way. They can be misleading, and often are fickle. That is essentially why "millions of hearts have been broken."

Love is strongly linked to emotion, but it also requires commitment and action. This is true also of our love for God. We must demonstrate it by acting in loving ways toward God's children. Otherwise, it is simply a lie.   —R. W. B.

Conclusion

A. Love's Reward

Only those who love can know the meaning of love. Since God is love, we know Him only if we love; but if we love, we most certainly know Him.

Love unites and unifies. Once estranged, men and God are bound together again with the cords of love. He who loves dwells in God, and God abides in him. Love creates the only atmosphere in which fellowship between God and man can begin and continue.

Love calms the fearful heart. "Perfect love casteth out fear." Love and trust go hand in hand. If we love God and are assured of His love for us—and who can doubt this fact?—we will never fear to meet Him, even in the judgment.

Love purifies the heart. True love cannot be debased through envy and jealousy, or vulgarized through carnal passion. It is love that reaches out to grasp the hand of love offered by the Savior. Love transforms and revitalizes the life; for, under the redemption made possible through the love of Christ, the sinful heart is cleansed and the dead heart comes alive.

B. Let Us Pray

Our loving Heavenly Father, we thank You for the love You have shown us. We thank You for life and the things that make life possible and the things that make life enjoyable. We thank You most of all for Your love in sending us Your Son, Jesus Christ, to make salvation available to us. May we learn to follow His loving example that love may grow in our lives. In His name we pray. Amen.

C. Thought to Remember

Genuine love, residing in the heart and shining brightly on all who come within its compass, most makes a person like God.

Learning by Doing

This page contains an alternate lesson plan emphasizing learning activities. Classes desiring such student involvement will find these suggestions helpful.

Learning Goals

Help class members to achieve these goals:

1. Describe, according to today's text, how God's kind of love can eliminate fear.

2. Determine to help eliminate another Christian's fear by demonstrating love to him.

Into the Lesson

Before class, write on a long strip of paper, "Perfect love casts out fear." Tape it on the chalkboard upside down with the words facing the chalkboard.

Ask class members to brainstorm, naming common statements that express how the world feels about love. Examples are, "Love means never having to say you're sorry" or "Love makes the world go 'round.'"

If you have space and time, next brainstorm Scriptural statements regarding love. Did students mention today's theme? Turn up the sheet of paper and tape it so that everyone can read it.

Ask, "Can you think of an example from your childhood when a fear was removed because of the support and help of someone you loved?"

Remind students that last week's lesson contrasted love with hatred. Today's lesson contrasts love with fear.

Into the Word

Before class, duplicate the following Bible-study questions and distribute them to the students now. The four italicized headings over the questions are the points in the outline of the first lesson plan. (These questions are included in the student book, also.)

Divide your class into groups of four to six students to discuss the questions. If time is limited, ask each group to discuss the questions under only one of the points. In the latter case, have a class member read the whole text aloud before the groups begin their study. Appoint one member of each group to be responsible to keep the discussion focused on the assigned questions. Each group should choose a recorder who will share the group's answers with the whole class.

God Is Love (vv. 7-12)

How do we know that God is the source of love? What does His love do for us? How should we respond to His love? What evidence of His love is seen in the world today?

Love Brings Assurance (vv. 13-16)

What assurances or evidences of God's love are mentioned in this section of Scripture? What reason does John give that we should believe what he is saying? How may we be assured that God dwells in us?

Love Banishes Fear (vv. 17, 18)

What major benefit of love does John explain in this Scripture? How is God's love unique among all the kinds of love we know about? Why does our love for God remove our fear of punishment by God?

Love Changes Actions (vv. 19-21)

What does God's love have to do with our love? How do we show our love for God? Why is it so important for us to show love to others?

After about five or six minutes, let the groups report to the whole class. Before each recorder shares results with the class, read aloud the verses of Scripture pertaining to that group's questions. After each report, let the whole class discuss.

If you prefer not to work in groups, you may use the discussion questions to guide your study with the whole class. In this case, write each point of the outline on your chalkboard before you begin that section of discussion.

Into Life

This week we are again discussing the need for Christians to love one another. Ask students to brainstorm words that describe the love that Christians must demonstrate. Point out that love must be active. We can't ignore the needs of our brothers and claim to love them.

Today's Scripture states that love eliminates fear. We have discussed the Scripture's teaching that love eliminates our fear of God. In what sense can love between Christians eliminate other kinds of fears a person may have?

Explore this idea by brainstorming fears prevalent or possible among Christians. Ask students to name as many fears as they can in ninety seconds. Write them on the chalkboard.

For each fear listed, discuss how Christian love demonstrated toward a person with that fear could help eliminate the fear.

Ask class members to survey the list and privately decide whether they know someone with this fear. Can they show love to help eliminate the fear?

Let's Talk It Over

The questions on this page are designed to encourage review of the lesson Scriptures and to promote discussion of the lesson by the class. The answers provided are only discussion starters. Let your class talk it over from there.

1. Why does John repeat so many times that Christians should love one another?

One of the devil's chief tactics is to get Christians to be at odds with one another. The devil knows that the church is strong when it possesses the unity for which our Lord prayed. The cement of that unity is love. Love is the primary characteristic of God, Jesus, and the Holy Spirit. Unless Christians love one another the way God loves, they cannot communicate to the world God's true nature. And if Christians do not love one another, how will they have the maturity or commitment to love non-Christians?

2. What is the relationship between loving and being born of God (1 John 4:7)?

Many people who are not born of God demonstrate love, but their love is restricted. They may love only those who are lovable, or those who agree with them, or those who love them back. But God's love is unrestricted. His love is unconditional. His love doesn't consider a person's physical attractiveness, or intellect, or economic status, or any other attribute. We are to love others as God loves. The only way anyone can live like that is to be born of God. To be born of God means that God's nature lives in us.

3. How is love related to God's commandments?

A Christian who really wants to love as God loves wants to know what God's kind of love does and does not do to another person. Most of the New Testament epistles were written to straighten out false notions people had about what constituted love. Today we have the same problem with the Hollywood hype that communicates false love. To really love is to do what God wants, for God is love; and everything He wants is an expression of love. Every commandment tells us at least one dimension of love. Now read and discuss Romans 13:8-10.

4. Identify different dimensions of love that are implied in verses 9 and 10 and apply them to your life.

Love is openly exhibited (manifested, v. 9). Do we make our love visible? Love is sacrificial (God sent His only begotten Son). Do we sacrifice for others? Love takes risks (God made His Son vulnerable to the world). Do we take risks or do we hold back? Love takes the initiative (v. 10). Do we do that, or do we wait for someone else to make the first move? Love is contagious (v. 11). Is what we are doing being imitated by others? If not, it may not be very significant love.

5. Explain the difference between our love for God and His love for us that provides the basis for John's argument in verse 10.

The essential difference is that God's love for us is free, unmerited, spontaneous. It is not generated by something lovely in us; it overflows from God's heart. Our love for Him is not so, but is a response to His love and goodness and mercy.

6. What application can we make from John's statement that no one has seen God, but if we love one another God abides in us? (1 John 4:12)

Although God cannot be seen by any human being face to face, He can be known through our actions. A person cannot see gravitation, but gravitation can be experienced. A person cannot see electricity, but electricity can be experienced. A person cannot see a virus with the naked eye, but a virus can be experienced. How can God, who cannot be seen with the naked eye, be experienced? He can be experienced by our living out His characteristics. We are to "work out" what God has "worked in." People today who want to know what God is like have the visual aid of observing Christians. God's nature becomes visible as it flows through the lives of Christians who love. That's part of what it means for the church to be called the body of Christ. We are to carry on what Jesus began.

7. How is God's love perfected in us? (1 John 4:12)

This is a staggering thought. God's love is actually made more perfect, that is, more complete, more concretely expressed in our actions. While God can and does express His love directly to individuals, often His love is expressed as Christians minister to others. His love is truly completed when it generates a like love in the hearts of Christians.

Faith and Life

LESSON SCRIPTURE: 1 John 5:1-15.

PRINTED TEXT: 1 John 5:1-13.

1 John 5:1-13

1 Whosoever believeth that Jesus is the Christ is born of God: and every one that loveth him that begat loveth him also that is begotten of him.

2 By this we know that we love the children of God, when we love God, and keep his commandments.

3 For this is the love of God, that we keep his commandments: and his commandments are not grievous.

4 For whatsoever is born of God overcometh the world: and this is the victory that overcometh the world, even our faith.

5 Who is he that overcometh the world, but he that believeth that Jesus is the Son of God?

6 This is he that came by water and blood, even Jesus Christ; not by water only, but by water and blood. And it is the Spirit that beareth witness, because the Spirit is truth.

7 For there are three that bear record in heaven, the Father, the Word, and the Holy Ghost: and these three are one.

8 And there are three that bear witness in earth, the spirit, and the water, and the blood: and these three agree in one.

9 If we receive the witness of men, the witness of God is greater: for this is the witness of God which he hath testified of his Son.

10 He that believeth on the Son of God hath the witness in himself: he that believeth not God hath made him a liar; because he believeth not the record that God gave of his Son.

11 And this is the record, that God hath given to us eternal life, and this life is in his Son.

12 He that hath the Son hath life; and he that hath not the Son of God hath not life.

13 These things have I written unto you that believe on the name of the Son of God; that ye may know that ye have eternal life, and that ye may believe on the name of the Son of God.

GOLDEN TEXT: This is the record, that God hath given to us eternal life, and this life is in his Son.—1 John 5:11.

John Writes of Life, Light, and Love
Unit 2: Abiding in Love
(1, 2, 3 John, Lessons 8-13)

Lesson Aims

As a result of studying this lesson each student should:

1. Understand that eternal life comes as a gift from God through His Son, Jesus Christ.

2. Have a growing desire to please God by obeying His commandments.

3. Determine specific expressions of love and caring to enhance a particular relationship this week.

Lesson Outline

INTRODUCTION
    A. Counterfeit Tickets
    B. Lesson Background
I. THE VICTORY OF FAITH (1 John 5:1-5)
    A. Believers Are Born of God (v. 1)
    B. Evidence of Love for God's Children (vv. 2, 3)
    C. Overcoming the World (vv. 4, 5)
II. THE WITNESSES TO CHRIST (1 John 5:6-13)
    A. Heaven and Earth Bear Witness (vv. 6-8)
    B. God Bears Witness (vv. 9, 10)
        A Credible Witness
    C. Life Eternal Tells of Him (vv. 11, 12)
    D. Blessed Assurance (v. 13)
        Life in the Son
CONCLUSION
    A. On Belief and Behavior
    B. The Only Way
    C. Let Us Pray
    D. Thought to Remember

Visual 12 in the visuals packet highlights the Christian's victory through faith. The visual is shown on page 323.

Introduction

A. Counterfeit Tickets

In the last century, millions of immigrants came to the United States from Europe. Some steamship lines made handsome profits transporting these people to the New World. To promote this business, they advertised extensively and even employed agents to travel in some areas in order to encourage people to buy passage to America.

Many bought their tickets in advance to make certain that they and their families would have a place when the ship sailed. With so much money changing hands, it should not surprise us that charlatans soon appeared on the scene. They falsely represented themselves as agents of the steamship lines and sold counterfeit tickets. Many of the unwary bought these tickets believing that they had assured themselves a trip across the Atlantic. Many who had sold all their possessions to buy their tickets were tragically disappointed when they tried to board the ship with their counterfeit tickets.

In John's day there were false teachers who offered their followers many glorious promises by this false Christ or that. Times have not changed much, for in our day there are false teachers promoting false saviors. Many follow these false teachers, supposing that they have assured themselves passage on that last great voyage that we must all take. Great indeed will be their disappointment. John's words are decisive: "He that hath the Son hath life; and he that hath not the Son of God hath not life."

B. Lesson Background

In last week's lesson, drawn from chapter 4, John discussed God's love for us and the corresonding requirement that we must also love our brothers. John continues this theme in chapter 5. He gives this theme added emphasis by using the example of the family.

In nature we see the strength of family ties. Among many animals may be found examples of care and devotion to the point of self-sacrifice for the benefit of family members. John's point is that we are born into the family of God, which makes us brothers and sisters of all others who are born into this family. Just as in nature there are close ties among family members, close ties ought also to exist in the family of God. Today's lessons begins with this thought.

I. The Victory of Faith (1 John 5:1-5)

A. Believers Are Born of God (v. 1)

1. Whosoever believeth that Jesus is the Christ is born of God: and every one that loveth him that begat loveth him also that is begotten of him.

Because our relationship with God is spiritual in nature, it cannot be defined precisely in physical terms. Yet examples drawn from the physical realm can shed light on the relationship and help us understand it better. For this reason, John uses physical birth to depict the Christian's relationship with God.

Here he returns to a theme that he has stressed before. Belief in Jesus Christ is an absolute essential if one is to be a child of God. First John 4:15 makes it clear that the *believing*, which makes one a child of God, is more than just an intellectual acceptance of the facts about Christ. It includes all that is involved in confession of Him as Lord and Savior and reliance on Him. While faith is a prerequisite of the new birth, John also states that it is evidence of the new birth.

In the latter part of this verse, John lays stress on another theme that he has raised earlier in this letter. In a normal situation, everyone who loves his father will also love his father's children, his brothers and sisters. In the same fashion, those who are children of God should also love their Christian brothers and sisters (see 1 John 4:20).

B. Evidence of Love for God's Children (vv. 2, 3)

2. By this we know that we love the children of God, when we love God, and keep his commandments.

The conclusion that John draws from the previous verse is not exactly what we might have expected. We might have anticipated him to argue that evidence for our love of God is seen in our love for His children. But here John concludes just the reverse—we show our love for God's children by loving God and by keeping His commandments. Actually, John is once more emphasizing his thesis that Christians ought to love their brothers and sisters. As far as John is concerned, it follows logically that if one loves God, he must love God's children. And just to make it clear that no one misunderstands the love of God to be an easy, emotional attachment, he also adds the necessity of keeping His commandments. That stress is certainly needed today, when so many try to get by with sentimentality without any commitment to duty.

3. For this is the love of God, that we keep his commandments: and his commandments are not grievous.

Earlier in this epistle John connected knowing and loving God with obeying His commandments (2:3-6). Jesus had expressed this same thought (John 14:15, 21). John mentions it again here to show that obeying God's commandments is not burdensome. In one of the striking paradoxes that characterized His teachings, Jesus referred to obeying Him as putting on a yoke. It is hard to imagine anything more burdensome or galling than a yoke. Yet Jesus offered it to all those who labored and were heavy laden, giving the assurance that His yoke was easy and His burden light (Matthew 11:28-30). Sweeping aside all the burdensome regulations of the Pharisees, Jesus insisted that there were really just two commandments: Love God with all your heart, soul, and mind, and love your neighbor as yourself.

C. Overcoming the World (vv. 4, 5)

4, 5. For whatsoever is born of God overcometh the world: and this is the victory that overcometh the world, even our faith. Who is he that overcometh the world, but he that believeth that Jesus is the Son of God?

We who love God are to obey the commandments of God (v. 3). But the world makes this obedience seem to be such a grievous burden that we have come to feel that it is a hopeless task. Against this pessimistic background, John gives us reassurance. We who have become the children of God are in the process of overcoming the world. This victory is accomplished through our faith in Jesus Christ. Our belief in Jesus and our reliance on Him gives us the strength to overcome Satan's allurements and to continue in the way of obedience to God. Christ has assured us that He has overcome the world (John 16:33). Having believed and accepted Jesus as the Son of God, we are *born of God*, we are His children. Thus we are joint-heirs with Christ in the family of God, and we shall participate with Him in His ultimate victory (see Romans 8:16, 17).

II. The Witnesses to Christ (1 John 5:6-13)

A. Heaven and Earth Bear Witness (vv. 6-8)

6. This is he that came by water and blood, even Jesus Christ; not by water only, but by water and blood. And it is the Spirit that beareth witness, because the Spirit is truth.

Various interpretations have been given for this verse. Some think that the water and blood refer to the two ordinances of baptism and the Lord's Supper. Others think that the reference is

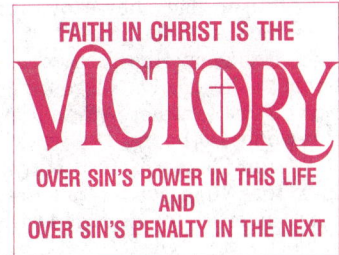

FAITH IN CHRIST IS THE **VICTORY** OVER SIN'S POWER IN THIS LIFE AND OVER SIN'S PENALTY IN THE NEXT

visual 12

to Jesus' death on the cross when the soldier thrust the spear into His side, and blood and water gushed out (John 19:34). It seems best to understand the water and the blood to represent the beginning of Jesus' ministry in His baptism and its conclusion in His death on the cross. Some of the heretics that John was refuting denied the incarnation of the Son of God. By emphasizing Christ's ministry, John was affirming that Christ really did come in the flesh and offered himself as a sacrifice for the sins of the world.

John had been present during Jesus' ministry, and he brought personal testimony about it. But his testimony did not have to stand alone. The Spirit also bore witness to it. Jesus had promised that the Holy Spirit would testify of Him (John 15:26), and the Day of Pentecost saw the beginning of the Spirit's testimony (Acts 2). The Spirit continued to bear witness through the preaching and writing of the apostles.

7, 8. For there are three that bear record in heaven, the Father, the Word, and the Holy Ghost: and these three are one. And there are three that bear witness in earth, the spirit, and the water, and the blood: and these three agree in one.

Much of verses 7 and 8 is omitted in the oldest Greek manuscripts. As a result, several modern translations either omit these parts of the verses or carry them as footnotes. The *New International Version* reads like this: "For there are three that testify: the Spirit, the water, and the blood; and the three are in agreement."

In verse 6 John states that the Spirit has born witness to Christ. Now to this witness he adds the witness of the water (Jesus' baptism) and the blood (His death on the cross). These three agree in affirming the same thing—that the Son of God did appear in the flesh as Jesus Christ. Of course, in the baptism and death of Jesus, testimony concerning Jesus' deity was given by the Father, Son, and Holy Spirit.

B. God Bears Witness (vv. 9, 10)

9. If we receive the witness of men, the witness of God is greater: for this is the witness of God which he hath testified of his Son.

In the normal course of human events, we have learned to accept the testimony brought by men. It is generally trustworthy. Yet men do on occasion lie or give inaccurate testimony concerning matters that pertain to our earthly lives. But God's testimony is always infallible, without error. Thus His testimony is greater. It is great for two reasons: it is more trustworthy because it is divine, and it testifies to a greater subject, God's Son.

A CREDIBLE WITNESS

Perry Mason often tries to discredit witnesses whom the district attorney calls to the stand. In turn, Hamilton Burger uses the same tactic to persuade the jury that little credence should be given to the testimony of witnesses for the defense. If either lawyer can cast a shadow of doubt upon the character or qualifications of any witness, the strength of that person's testimony is diminished.

Not everyone is to be believed. Even under oath, many people perjure themselves, withholding or distorting the truth to protect their personal interests. Judges and jurors have to decide who is most likely telling the truth. Ultimately, testimony on one side or the other is accepted as an accurate reflection of the facts. A decision must finally be made on the basis of *human* judgment of *human* credibility.

John points out that we are willing to "accept man's testimony" *(New International Version)*. On a daily basis, we trust "witnesses" who give us information on which we base both minor and major decisions. Otherwise, our lives would be plagued with suspicion, fear, and doubt. But when it comes to the information on which we base life's most important decision, we don't have to depend upon mere human testimony. *God* is our witness. If He says it, we believe it, and that's the end of it!   —R. W. B.

10. He that believeth on the Son of God hath the witness in himself: he that believeth not God hath made him a liar; because he believeth not the record that God gave of his Son.

One who believes on God's Son has done so because he has accepted the witness that God has given. Faith comes when one accepts the truthfulness of the testimony. He *hath the wit-*

Home Daily Bible Readings

Monday, May 14—A Roman Centurion's Faith (Matthew 8:5-13)
Tuesday, May 15—A Canaanite Woman's Faith (Matthew 15:21-28)
Wednesday, May 16—A Paralytic's Friends' Faith (Mark 2:1-12)
Thursday, May 17—A Hemorrhaging Woman's Faith (Mark 5:24b-34)
Friday, May 18—A Blind Man's Faith (Mark 10:46-52)
Saturday, May 19—A Sinful Woman's Faith (Luke 7:36-50)
Sunday, May 20—A Disciple's Growing Faith (Luke 9:18-26)

ness in himself, that is, he has internalized it, making it a part of his life to the point that it alters his thoughts and actions. There is nothing here to indicate that the believer has received testimony different from that received by the unbeliever. The difference comes in the response that is made to God's testimony concerning His Son. Some readily believed when they heard Him and saw the miracles He performed. The religious leaders, on the other hand, heard the same message and saw the same miracles and yet hardened their hearts in unbelief.

When one refuses to believe the witness that God brings, he, in effect, is saying that God is not truthful. So long as a person persists in this attitude, there is no way that he can respond positively to God.

C. Life Eternal Tells of Him
(vv. 11, 12)

11. And this is the record, that God hath given to us eternal life, and this life is in his Son.

This is the record. Here John refers back to what he said in the first part of verse 10. The witness that the believer has in himself is the fact that he is conscious of God's gift of eternal life, which he has in the Son of God. John speaks of eternal life as a present reality so well established that it becomes evidence in God's testimony to Jesus.

12. He that hath the Son hath life; and he that hath not the Son of God hath not life.

Lest anyone misunderstand the vital truth he has just stated, John repeats it, with emphasis: eternal life, which is a gift from God, is found only in His Son.

If one has the Son, he has life; if one does not have the Son, he does not have life. For John there is no middle ground. That may strike our generation as more than a little harsh, given as we are to compromise and toleration of viewpoints that are mutually exclusive. We have learned to "accentuate the positive" and "eliminate the negative" to the point that we have become intolerant of anything that does not involve compromise. Yet God's messenger has spoken in clear, unmistakable terms that all can easily understand.

D. Blessed Assurance (v. 13)

13. These things have I written unto you that believe on the name of the Son of God; that ye may know that ye have eternal life, and that ye may believe on the name of the Son of God.

John wrote this epistle to show men and women that eternal life comes through faith in the Son of God, and to reassure those who have already taken the first steps along that way, so that they may *know* that they have eternal life.

In the first century, John was addressing himself to a specific problem. Some false teachers had appeared in the flock, proclaiming another way of obtaining eternal life. As a result of their teachings, some Christians were in danger of being led astray. John's purpose was to point them back to the Son of God, who alone could offer eternal life. Even after nearly two thousand years, that message is still a timely one, and we do well to pay it heed.

LIFE IN THE SON

Just as surely as swallows return annually to Capistrano, college students on spring break migrate to Florida. This social phenomenon has been growing in popularity for decades, and now even includes high schoolers who spend Easter vacations on the beaches. Thousands of teens drive hundreds of miles and spend tons of money to leave colder climes and boring classrooms for "fun in the sun." Some go for incessant partying; others go simply to "lay out" on the warm sand, toasting their flesh to just the right shade of tan so when they return to their respective campuses, they will be the envy of all who didn't make the pilgrimage.

Sun worshipers, of course, come in all ages. Scores of senior citizens retire every year to Florida, California, and all the southern states in-between. Like heat-seeking missiles, they fly (or drive motorhomes) to some warm spot for comfort, convenience—and some for convalescing. Life in the sun can be very pleasant and healthful.

Regardless of where you reside, life in Christ is abundant. The quality of eternal life excels any other existence, and it lasts forever! Christians should reflect such warmth and glow from living for Jesus, that all of our neighbors will envy us for our life in the SON.   —R. W. B.

Conclusion

A. On Belief and Behavior

The world is likely to judge a person by his behavior, not his beliefs. After all, what one does is certainly more important than what he thinks, isn't it? One's actions sooner or later affect the lives of others, and so they become matters of public concern. But what one thinks is his own business, and so it need not involve others.

At first this logic seems reasonable enough. At a time when Americans have made a fetish of personal privacy, we are especially vigilant against any intrusions into a person's private world of thoughts and beliefs. Thus we are inclined to let a person think and believe whatever he wants to, if he doesn't hurt anybody.

But there is a serious fallacy in this kind of reasoning. A long time ago Solomon wrote, "As he thinketh in his heart, so is he" (Proverbs 23:7). In other words, what we think determines what we do. When one thinks right thoughts, his actions will be good; and when one thinks wicked thoughts, his actions will be evil. Some may insist that this does not hold true in real life. For example, well-known religious leaders have in recent months been caught in grievous sins. But this does not negate the basic principle that what we think determines what we do. All that these cases prove is that these men's minds were closed to public scrutiny. The evil thoughts that were harbored in the inner recesses of their minds were carefully concealed from others. We can be sure that evil thoughts preceded their sinful deeds.

Let us take another example. Some hold that an unborn fetus is nothing but a bundle of protoplasm developing within a woman. Holding such a view, one could dispose of an unwanted fetus with no more concern than one would have for an infected appendix or a wart. But if a person believes that human life is sacred and that the unborn fetus has all the potential to become fully human, then one will protect that fetus with all the love and care at one's disposal.

All of this may seem somewhat remote from today's lesson. Actually it bears on the very heart of what John wrote about. Into the group to whom John addressed his letter some false teachers had come. They brought new doctrines that challenged the orthodox teachings about who Jesus Christ is and about His relationship to God. Some might dismiss all of this as an unimportant theological discussion about obscure points that don't really matter. But that isn't the way John saw it, and John had the advantage of writing as he was led by the Holy Spirit.

What one believes about a situation will determine the actions he will take in that situation. If one believes that he is a child of God, then he will love God as His Father. A further implication of this belief is that he will love other children of God because they are his brothers and sisters. The very heart of this matter deals with how one becomes a child of God. John insists that one is born of God when he comes to believe that Jesus is the Christ. If he does not believe this, or if he believes that Jesus Christ is someone other than the divine Son of God, he cannot be born of God.

What one believes about God will determine what he believes about God's commandments and how he obeys them. What a person believes about Jesus Christ determines whether he can overcome the world, and, most important, it will determine whether he has eternal life.

Belief versus behavior—clearly this is a choice that we do not have to make; indeed, it is a choice that we dare not make. John makes it quite evident that the two go together. Faith and life are inseparably joined in God's plan for mankind. Let us keep them that way.

B. The Only Way

Christians have insisted that there is but one way to God and that is through Jesus Christ, His divine Son. This teaching is expressed in many ways, but nowhere is it stated more plainly than by Peter as he spoke about Jesus before the Jewish rulers: "There is none other name under heaven given among men, whereby we must be saved" (Acts 4:12).

In an age that prefers to see all views as equally valid, Christianity's doctrinal exclusiveness is not very popular. We must, of course, avoid being judgmental toward other people. After all, salvation comes as a gift of God, and it ill behooves us to usurp God's authority by limiting the number to whom He may give that gift. But as Christians we have a mandate to take the gospel to every creature. The only message that we have a right to proclaim is the message revealed to us in the Scriptures. To change that message or to delete portions that may seem objectionable to non-Christians is to disobey our divine marching orders. John did not hesitate to point out the false teachers and challenge their false doctrine. He did so, not because he hated them, but because he loved them. He knew that "he that hath the Son hath life; and he that hath not the Son of God hath not life" (1 John 5:12). John did not shrink from emphasizing this exclusive doctrine, because he knew that it is man's only way to Heaven.

C. Let Us Pray

Dear Father, we thank You for Your Son, who came into the world to bring us life eternal. Teach us to obey You more fully, to trust Your Son more earnestly, and to love Your children, our brothers and sisters, more dearly. We lift up this prayer in the name of Him through whom we have the promise of eternal life. Amen.

D. Thought to Remember

I need no other argument,
    I need no other plea,
It is enough that Jesus died,
    And that He died for me.
                    —LIDIE H. EDMUNDS

Learning by Doing

This page contains an alternate lesson plan emphasizing learning activities. Classes desiring such student involvement will find these suggestions helpful.

Learning Goals

Challenge students to accomplish at least one of the following goals this week:

1. Decide on the relationship between faith and life, as described in 1 John 5:1-13.

2. Choose one way they can demonstrate more faith and thus experience more life.

3. Speak to one person outside of Christ about the life that only He offers.

Into the Lesson

Use one of the following ideas to begin:

Anonymous sentences. Write the words *Faith* and *Life* on your chalkboard as class members arrive. Distribute note cards and ask each class member to write a sentence or two using both these words. After ninety seconds, collect the note cards and read the sentences to the class. (If you have an overhead projector and enough blank transparencies, distribute transparencies and markers to students and ask them to write their sentences there. Then you can project each of the sentences so everyone in the whole class can read them at the same time.)

Remind students that today's lesson is titled "Faith and Life." Tell them that the verses they will study from 1 John show the relationship between these two.

Informal debate. Ask students, "Do you believe it is difficult or easy to live the Christian life?" Give them thirty seconds to think about the question. Then take a poll of the class, asking students to raise their hands to indicate how they would answer the question. Then ask volunteers to explain the reasons for their choice. Actually, there is something to be said for each position, and students can advance good reasons for choosing either one.

Tell the class that today's text addresses the question and gives some answers that the person outside of Christ may not understand. As today's text is read, the students can decide which option the apostle John would choose.

Into the Word

Regardless of which introductory activity you choose, ask students to decide if living for God is difficult or easy as they listen to a volunteer read aloud 1 John 5:1-5. Discuss: What is it that helps us want to obey God? Why does the non-Christian sometimes fail to see the attraction of following God's commands? How does obeying God prove our love for His children?

Before reading verses 6-8 aloud, remind students that one of John's purposes for writing this epistle was to counter the false teaching that said the Son of God had not actually come to earth in the flesh. As the students listen to these verses read, ask them to decide how John refutes that idea. Ask students what "water" and "blood" may represent. Present the possible interpretations of these verses as explained in the first lesson plan, stressing our commentator's conclusion that John is referring to those acts by which Jesus' earthly ministry was begun and concluded: the water symbolizing His baptism, and the blood symbolizing His death on the cross. About what fact do the Spirit, the water, and blood agree (v. 7)?

Ask students, "Why did the Son of God come?" Tell them that the next verses (10-12) answer this question once again. Read them aloud and ask students to tell you the answer they give. Ask, "Where does eternal life come from?" (Only God.) "Who deserves it?" (No one. It is a gift.) "What one way has God provided for us to have this eternal life?" (Jesus alone is "the way, the truth, and the life.")

Ask, "Is it possible to *know* that we have eternal life?" Read verse 13 aloud. Discuss, "Let's contrast two people. One person *knows* he has eternal life. The other person does not have eternal life. How will their behavior now be different? In what sense will the first person be truly alive while the other person is 'dead?'"

Into Life

If you wrote the "faith" and "life" sentences suggested above, look at them again now. Which ones seem best to describe the relationship between these words that the lesson text teaches? If you did not do that activity earlier, it could be a closing activity. Write some of the sentences on the board; then challenge students:

Are you alive or dead? Where does your faith need to grow?

Do you know someone who is dying because he has no faith in Jesus? Will you pray for an opportunity to introduce him to Christ?

Give students time to privately make one or both of these commitments.

Let's Talk It Over

The questions on this page are designed to encourage review of the lesson Scriptures and to promote discussion of the lesson by the class. The answers provided are only discussion starters. Let your class talk it over from there.

1. Our God is a God of love. He desires our love in return. What does He look for as evidence of our love?

Our text reminds us "every one that loveth him that begat loveth him also that is begotten of him" (5:1). In other words, we show love for our Father by loving our brothers and sisters (see also 1 John 4:11, 12). We also demonstrate our love for God by keeping His commandments (5:2, 3). At the death of Dorcas (Acts 9:36-43), there were many widows who could show the physical evidence of her love. They were deeply grieved at her death because of their personal loss. Are there neighbors or fellow Christians who could testify to the love you have shown them? Could they name times and places when the love of God in you has overflowed for their benefit?

2. Why are God's commandments not a burden for Christians?

A burden is something we carry that is not really a part of us. A donkey is called a beast of burden because it carries so much baggage. The baggage that it carries belongs to someone else. But God's commandments belong to us. His commandments are a part of our new nature, because all of His commandments square with the nature of the Holy Spirit who lives within us. Not obeying His commandments is burdensome. For instance, lying is burdensome, because we always have to remember the lies we told. Unfaithfulness to our mates is burdensome, because we have to design ways to cover it up and hope we are never caught. Carrying a grudge is burdensome, because it affects our internal nervous and vascular systems. To be born again in the image of God is to have seeded in us the character that squares with the principles of conduct contained in the commandments of God.

3. What are some of the ways that Christians overcome the world?

The world is temporary. Christians are eternal. The world will be destroyed, but Christians will be saved. The world's system is a "me-ism" system; the Christian system is a "we-ism" system. The world tempts us to be competitors against each other; God equips us to be compan-

ions for each other. The world has no hope beyond death. Christians look through death to eternal life. The world sees only the visible and the possible. Christians see the invisible and believe the impossible.

4. What is eternal life, and what is its value for us today?

Eternal life involves two dimensions. The first is quality—the quality life of the Son of God that is transplanted in us through the Holy Spirit. Some of the expressions of that quality life are found in Galatians 5:22-25. That quality life begins here and now. Eternal life is not something that begins the moment we die physically. It begins the moment we receive Jesus' life into our lives. *He* is eternal life.

The second dimension of eternal life is quantity—that is, life that will never end. It will last forever. Again, the beginning of that life is not dependent upon one's death. The Christian is in eternal life now. Physical death is simply a means of transporting us from this temporary dwelling place to the continual, everlasting dwelling place. The person who is in Christ will never die. He will just change residences.

5. Why does John say, "He that hath not the Son of God hath not life" (1 John 5:12), since there are so many unbelievers living in the world?

Did you ever lease a piece of property or equipment? You do not own the property; you simply have use of it for a specified period of time. At the end of the lease period you must forfeit the property back to its owner. The unbeliever may continue to breathe and function, but he has no claim upon life. Every day that passes, the unbeliever is closer to death and eternal judgment (2 Thessalonians 1:7-9). To those who believe, however, God gives the gift of eternal life. Life, then, is our possession to enjoy for eternity. Our breath may cease and our body of flesh may decay, but life remains ours; and life will be enhanced with a glorified body at the time of Christ's coming again. Knowing that those who do not have the Son of God do not have life, can we remain unconcerned over their plight and make no effort to make the Son of God known to them?

Loyalty and Discipleship

LESSON SCRIPTURE: 2 John; 3 John.

PRINTED TEXT: 2 John 1-6; 3 John 1-8.

2 John 1-6

1 The elder unto the elect lady and her children, whom I love in the truth; and not I only, but also all they that have known the truth;

2 For the truth's sake, which dwelleth in us, and shall be with us for ever.

3 Grace be with you, mercy, and peace, from God the Father, and from the Lord Jesus Christ, the Son of the Father, in truth and love.

4 I rejoiced greatly that I found of thy children walking in truth, as we have received a commandment from the Father.

5 And now I beseech thee, lady, not as though I wrote a new commandment unto thee, but that which we had from the beginning, that we love one another.

6 And this is love, that we walk after his commandments. This is the commandment, That, as ye have heard from the beginning, ye should walk in it.

3 John 1-8

1 The elder unto the well-beloved Gaius, whom I love in the truth.

2 Beloved, I wish above all things that thou mayest prosper and be in health, even as thy soul prospereth.

3 For I rejoiced greatly, when the brethren came and testified of the truth that is in thee, even as thou walkest in the truth.

4 I have no greater joy than to hear that my children walk in truth.

5 Beloved, thou doest faithfully whatsoever thou doest to the brethren, and to strangers;

6 Which have borne witness of thy charity before the church: whom if thou bring forward on their journey after a godly sort, thou shalt do well:

7 Because that for his name's sake they went forth, taking nothing of the Gentiles.

8 We therefore ought to receive such, that we might be fellow helpers to the truth.

GOLDEN TEXT: Beloved, thou doest faithfully whatsoever thou doest to the brethren, and to strangers.—3 John 5.

John Writes of Life, Light, and Love

Unit 2: Abiding in Love
(1, 2, 3 John, Lessons 8-13)

Lesson Aims

This lesson should enable students to:

1. Better understand the influence they can exert for the cause of Christ.

2. Walk more faithfully in the truth revealed in Christ.

3. Select one way they will render service to those who faithfully proclaim the gospel, especially to those who are strangers.

Lesson Outline

INTRODUCTION
  A. The Power of a Godly Life
  B. Lesson Background
I. FELLOWSHIP IN THE CHURCH (2 John 1-6)
  A. Christian Greetings (vv. 1-3)
  B. Cause for Rejoicing (v. 4)
  C. Exhortation to Mutual Love (vv. 5, 6)
II. A FRIEND IN CHRIST (3 John 1-8)
  A. Greeting (vv. 1, 2)
  B. Commendation (vv. 3, 4)
     Second Generation Christianity
  C. Hospitality Reported (vv. 5, 6)
  D. Helpers in the Truth (vv. 7, 8)
     Strangers/Brothers
CONCLUSION
  A. Walking
  B. In the Truth
  C. Let Us Pray
  D. Thought to Remember

Visual 13 contains a thought-provoking statement that will be helpful as you consider the generosity of Gaius (3 John 5, 6). The visual is shown on page 331.

Introduction

A. The Power of a Godly Life

A minister had served for many years in an inner city mission. Many felt that he was wasting his time there, for he seemed to have little to show for his efforts, and least in terms of large numbers or an attractive building. But across the years, he had built a good rapport with the street people of the area and had gained their respect. As a result, he could safely go places that others feared to enter.

One night during a meeting at the mission, a bedraggled man entered. This man returned night after night and seemed to listen intently to the sermons. Finally, one night during the invitation, the man came forward. "Do you want to give your life to Jesus?" he was asked by one of the workers.

"Well, I don't know," came his reply. "I don't know much about Him."

"Haven't you read in the Bible about Jesus?"

"Nope. I ain't never had a Bible. And besides, I can't read."

"Then, why did you come forward?"

"Well, I'll tell ya. I've been a watchin' that preacher man. He walks like he talks, and so whatever he's got, that's what I want!"

Many people will never read the Bible. The only gospel they will ever know is the one they see written in the lives of Christians. But this kind of message has the power to reach the lives of many people. Gaius, who is mentioned in today's lesson, lived that kind of testimony.

B. Lesson Background

Today's lesson is based on the two shortest letters in the New Testament—2 and 3 John. The apostle John wrote 2 John to "the elect lady and her children" and 3 John to a friend named Gaius. It is believed that John resided in Ephesus when he wrote these letters, and that the recipients were located in the province of Asia.

Second John reflects some of the same themes we have been studying in 1 John. The writer exhorts Christians to love one another and to abide in the truth revealed in Christ. He further warns the "elect lady" against receiving or encouraging false teachers, lest she become an accessory to their evil deeds. In 3 John Gaius is encouraged to receive and help faithful teachers that he might participate in the good they do. The principle is the same in both instances. We become responsible participants in what we help someone else do, whether it is for good or evil.

I. Fellowship in the Church (2 John 1-6)

A. Christian Greetings (vv. 1-3)

1. The elder unto the elect lady and her children, whom I love in the truth; and not I only, but also all they that have known the truth.

In the ancient world, letter writers usually identified themselves at the beginning of the letter rather than at the conclusion as we do. The writer here designated himself as *the elder* rather than by his own name. Never in his writings did the apostle John refer to himself by

visual 13

IF THERE BE ANY TRUER MEASURE OF A MAN THAN BY WHAT HE DOES, IT MUST BE BY WHAT HE

GIVES

name. His advanced age—probably near ninety—made him truly *the elder* statesman among the churches.

The letter is addressed to *the elect lady and her children.* This may have been a mother and her family in one of the first-century churches. At least one commentator holds that the name of the recipient was deliberately omitted to protect her during a time of persecution. However, others believe that the *elect* (chosen) *lady* was a figurative designation for a congregation, whose members were her *children.* John's message is the same in either case.

Even before he extended his greeting, John expressed his love for the *elect lady and her children.* He loved them sincerely because of their fellowship with him *in the truth* of the gospel. They were loved not only by the apostle, but also by all in the Christian community who were committed to that truth.

2. For the truth's sake, which dwelleth in us, and shall be with us for ever.

John loved the elect lady and her children because they loved the truth, the teaching of Christ. Those who are committed to the truth will naturally feel bonds of affection for others who share that truth. This truth is for all times. When standards and values on every hand seem to be in a constant state of change, it is reassuring to know that God's truth is eternal.

3. Grace be with you, mercy, and peace, from God the Father, and from the Lord Jesus Christ, the Son of the Father, in truth and love.

The expressions *grace*, *mercy*, and *peace* were commonly used in salutations. Paul, for example, used this same threefold greeting in 1 Timothy 1:2 and in 2 Timothy 1:2. *Grace* is God's unearned favor, which He has directed to all men. *Mercy* suggests God's willingness to forgive, even when persons have sinned and turned away from Him. He is willing to stay the judgment that we so rightly deserve and give us yet another chance. *Peace* suggests a state in which the cares and threats of the world no

longer prove upsetting. The ultimate source of these blessings is God the Father and His Son. John's use of this expression is more than just a conventional introduction. We saw that in 1 John, the apostle went to some lengths to emphasize the deity of Jesus Christ against the claims of the heretics. He continues that theme in 2 John.

B. Cause for Rejoicing (v. 4)

4. I rejoiced greatly that I found of thy children walking in truth, as we have received a commandment from the Father.

Of thy children. Several modern translations have this "some of your children," suggesting that not all of the children had been walking in the truth. This may have been the case. However, if only some of the children (or members) had been faithful, one would think that John's joy would have been only partial, not great. More likely John was commending the faithful ones that he knew about. This information may have come to him through a letter or a visit from some of these *children.*

Walking in truth. This expression is commonly used to convey the idea of one whose life is committed to serving God in truth. It suggests more than an intellectual holding of truth or a life-style that is only incidentally concerned about truth.

C. Exhortation to Mutual Love
(vv. 5, 6)

5. And now I beseech thee, lady, not as though I wrote a new commandment unto thee, but that which we had from the beginning, that we love one another.

I beseech thee. John's exhortation is both urgent and tender. What he urges upon them is not a new commandment, but one that they had long known. It was new when Jesus first introduced it: "A new commandment I give unto you, That ye love one another; as I have loved you, that ye also love one another" (John 13:34). But now, sixty years or so had passed since Jesus had uttered those words. During that time this commandment had undoubtedly been repeated again and again until it had now become an old commandment.

That we love one another. This was one of the major themes in 1 John. Here it is repeated again, either because the audience is different or because some truths are so basic and essential that they have to be stated again. Some object to love being called a commandment, insisting that an emotion cannot be legislated. This is *agape* love, which is not really an emotion at all but is the showing of good will toward another.

Of course, in the showing of good will toward another, emotions are certain to follow. The emotions do not cause the actions, but are produced by the actions. This kind of love can be commanded.

6. And this is love, that we walk after his commandments. This is the commandment, That, as ye have heard from the beginning, ye should walk in it.

Christian love and obedience are so interwoven that one may scarcely be distinguished from the other. We know that we love when we obey, and we know that we obey when we love. In verse 5 John speaks of "commandment," singular. Here he uses the plural, *commandments*. The commandment tells us to love; the commandments tell us how to show that love. Many centuries ago Augustine said, "Love God, and then do whatever you want." This could be very dangerous, especially among young Christians. Not only do we need general principles to live by, but we need guidance on how to apply those general principles in specific situations. That is why a Christian must use both his head and his heart to walk in truth. His heart motivates him to want to do right, but the head provides the directions necessary to carry the desire to fruition. For this reason, a Christian must continue to study and grow so that he will be better able to apply properly, in real life situations, God's commandment to love.

II. A Friend in Christ (3 John 1-8)

A. Greeting (vv. 1, 2)

1. The elder unto the well-beloved Gaius, whom I love in the truth.

Like 2 John, this epistle begins with John identifying himself as *the elder*. It is reasonable to suppose that this designation was widely understood and accepted among the churches where John had worked. More than one Gaius is mentioned in the New Testament. One was a man of Macedonia, a companion of Paul in Ephesus (Acts 19:29). One Gaius of Derbe accompanied Paul from Greece into Asia (Acts 20:4). A third was a Corinthian whom Paul had baptized (1 Corinthians 1:14). But we cannot tell whether any of these is the Gaius to whom John addressed his third epistle. The fact is, we know nothing more about this Gaius than what is mentioned here. The one thing we can be certain about is that John considered him a beloved and trusted friend *in the truth*.

2. Beloved, I wish above all things that thou mayest prosper and be in health, even as thy soul prospereth.

John extended his greeting by wishing (the word actually means "praying") for Gaius' prosperity and good health. John knew that Gaius was prospering spiritually. John's prayer was that Gaius would enjoy a balance of material and spiritual assets, to be used for the furtherance of Christ's church.

B. Commendation (vv. 3, 4)

3. For I rejoiced greatly, when the brethren came and testified of the truth that is in thee, even as thou walkest in the truth.

We don't know where John was residing when he wrote this letter, but wherever it was, it was possible for brethren from Gaius' church to visit him there. Perhaps these brethren were traveling evangelists who had enjoyed the hospitality of Gaius' home and had come to John with a heartwarming report.

The news that these brethren brought about Gaius was good—he was walking *in the truth*. Perhaps Gaius had been baptized by John, or perhaps John had given him special training. In any event, John took great pleasure in knowing that Gaius was remaining true to the faith.

4. I have no greater joy than to hear that my children walk in truth.

No greater joy. John's life was so invested and bound up in the lives of those he taught that he succeeded or failed, lived or died with them. (Compare 1 Thessalonians 2:19, 20; 3:8.) *To hear.* The real test of the converts' faithfulness came when their teacher was no longer with them. *My children.* An affectionate address to those John taught. (See 1 John 2:1, 12, 18, 28; 4:4; 5:21.)

SECOND GENERATION CHRISTIANITY

My father's middle name is *William*; my middle name is *William*; my son's middle name is *William*. If/when my son and his wife have a male child, his middle name may be *William*, too. It is a tradition that seems worth keeping.

Most people consider it desirable to have male children, who, if the Lord wills, may carry on their family name into the future.

Still more important than carrying on the family name, is passing along our *faith* to future generations. John rejoiced because his spiritual children (those to whom he had taught God's truth) were remaining faithful to Christ. We can understand the satisfaction that the apostle felt.

Those of us who are parents can relate to John's experience and expression in a special way. Is anything more gratifying than seeing your own children follow in your steps of Christian faith? Perpetuating discipleship from generation to generation is at once a challenging

How to Say It

Derbe.   *Der*-be.
Gaius.   *Gay*-us.

responsibility and a thrilling opportunity. Who will carry on your family faith? If you have no natural heirs, those to whom you reach out with the gospel can carry on your "family name": *Christian*.   —R. W. B.

C. Hospitality Reported (vv. 5, 6)

5, 6. Beloved, thou doest faithfully whatsoever thou doest to the brethren, and to strangers; which have borne witness of thy charity before the church: whom if thou bring forward on their journey after a godly sort, thou shalt do well.

We learn in these verses one way in which Gaius was walking in truth. He extended hospitality to Christian *brethren* who were *strangers* to him. These brethren were traveling evangelists. In those days there were no missionary organizations to provide for the needs of those who traveled to spread the gospel, nor were there nationwide chains of motels to provide accommodations. The traveling evangelists were on their own to find accommodations when they came into a town or city. Limited public facilities meant that they were dependent upon local Christians for food and shelter. Of course, in many situations there were no Christian homes available or they were closed to these ministers.

Gaius had apparently made an exceptional effort to care for the traveling evangelists who came through his town. It is clear from these verses that "walking in truth" means more than maintaining our belief in God and in His Son. It necessarily requires that our faith be put into action in our daily lives.

The traveling evangelists who had benefited from Gaius' hospitality had borne witness to his actions *before the church*. This was probably the church where John was serving in Ephesus, and perhaps from which these evangelists had been sent out with the gospel. No doubt John and the entire church rejoiced in this report of Gaius' hospitality extended to these evangelists. *Whom if thou bring forward on their journey.* If these same brethren or others like them came again to the community, they were to be treated with like consideration. The expected encouragement includes not only hospitality for the time of their visit, but supply for their continuing journey. *After a godly sort*, that is, in a manner worthy of God. John was confident that

Gaius' support of these brethren would not be miserly, but would reflect the generosity of God.

D. Helpers in the Truth (vv. 7, 8)

7. Because that for his name's sake they went forth, taking nothing of the Gentiles.

The evangelists mentioned in the preceding verses had left their homes to carry out the commission Jesus had given. Their missionary efforts were carried out by the authority of His name and for the glory of His name. As they traveled about, they took nothing from the Gentiles, that is, the non-Christians, so that they might not in any way hinder the reception of the message. This made the help of brethren the more needful.

8. We therefore ought to receive such, that we might be fellow helpers to the truth.

In 3 John, the apostle gives three reasons why Christians ought to extend hospitality to those engaged in service for the kingdom. First, we ought to be hospitable to everyone who has need, because this is one way that we walk in the truth. Second, Christian workers ought not to depend upon Gentiles (non-Christians) for their support. Verse 8 gives the third reason. In helping those who are furthering the gospel, we become *fellow helpers to the truth*. This was what Paul meant when he wrote to the Philippians, thanking them for the financial help they had provided for him. In so doing they had "fellowship in the gospel" (Philippians 1:5).

What are our attitudes and practices concerning those who travel in the service of the Lord? Do we always make adequate provisions for them? Are we even concerned enough to know how they are being cared for? Let us, like this man Gaius, share generously of our material possessions to support those who have given themselves to the furtherance of the gospel.

Strangers/Brothers

The text of one Sunday's sermon was Hebrews 13:2: "Be not forgetful to entertain strangers: for thereby some have entertained angels unawares." A little boy reported to his parents that the preacher had talked about "angels in their underwear!"

We can understand the child's missing the point. But more unfortunate is the fact that many adults miss the opportunity of which the writer of Hebrew spoke. Gaius, John's friend in the faith, had learned this important lesson: the virtue and value of Christian hospitality.

Christian hospitality is a godlike ministry. But many church folk are reluctant, even unwilling, to entertain strangers. Traveling evangelists and visiting missionaries are typically housed in hotels these days. Though that seems to be the preference of some, the trend developed as fewer people could be found who would open their homes to church guests.

All of us are the losers when hospitality is gone. The sharing of mutual faith and encouragement between Christian hosts and Christian visitors is an irreplaceable quality of fellowship.

—R. W. B.

Conclusion

A. Walking

As we read 1, 2, and 3 John, we might suspect that John enjoyed walking, for he used the words *walk* and *walking* several times. But he was not prescribing a physical exercise. He used the term symbolically to describe one's conduct, how he lived his life.

Walking can be used to describe conduct that is either good or bad. For example, in 1 John 2:11, John states that a person who hates his brother "walketh in darkness." On the other hand "if we walk in the light, as he is in the light, we have fellowship one with another, and the blood of Jesus Christ his Son cleanseth us from all sin" (1 John 1:7).

In 2 and 3 John, the expression *walking in truth* is used. With this expression, John meant to convey the idea that those who walk in truth believe sound doctrine and are applying this sound doctrine to their daily living. There was a special need to emphasize sound doctrine when John wrote, because the church was under attack by false teachers who were denying some of the cardinal points of the Christian faith.

Across the centuries, the church has struggled to maintain a balance between sound faith and pious living. The temptation has been to empha-size one to the exclusion of the other. Those who put their emphasis on an orthodox faith sometimes become so involved in defending the faith that they fail to show the love that God expects. On the other hand, those who minimize sound doctrine and emphasize good deeds may lose sight of the divine motivation for their good works.

John insists that a sound faith and a life of love for others must go together. He especially commends Gaius, who had succeeded in keeping his faith and his life in balance. We would do well to follow the example of Gaius.

B. In the Truth

John rejoiced not only that his children walked, but that they walked "in truth." The Christian religion is not just sentiment or emotion. It is based on historical facts. God sent His Son into the world to die for the sins of the human race. Christ was crucified, was buried, and then came forth from the tomb alive. To deny any of these facts is to deny what is absolutely essential to Christianity. But for now, to walk in the truth means that one must know the truth. God gave man intellectual powers, and He intended these to be used. That means we have an obligation to study His Word at every opportunity. It means also that every church has a duty to stress Bible study.

But to *know* the truth is not enough. We must also *do* the truth. It is important in our teaching that we help students understand how to do the truth. In our complicated society, even mature Christians need help in knowing how to apply their faith to everyday situations. We must also motivate students to do what they believe to be right. All kinds of pressures are at work to keep us from living up to our convictions. But there were pressures in the first century, too, and undoubtedly Gaius felt these; still he "walked in the truth."

C. Let Us Pray

Dear Father, we thank You for the example given us by these first-century Christians. May we learn from them how to stand firm in the faith and yet demonstrate love to our fellowmen. Help us to see that Christ's yoke is not heavy but will bring us joy and peace if we are willing to bear it. In His name we pray. Amen.

D. Thought to Remember

Doctrine is the necessary foundation of duty; if the the theory is not correct, the practice can not be right. Tell me what a man believes, and I will tell you what he will do.

—TRYON EDWARDS

Learning by Doing

This page contains an alternate lesson plan emphasizing learning activities. Classes desiring such student involvement will find these suggestions helpful.

Learning Goals

Lead students to do the following today:

1. Survey 2 and 3 John to compare the qualities of the main characters described there.

2. Compare the loyalty or disloyalty of these Christians with their own faithfulness to Christ.

3. Choose ways to become more loyal to Christ.

Into the Lesson

On your chalkboard or on a poster that you mount before the class, write, "This person walks in the truth." Ask students to brainstorm answers to this question: "What are some characteristics of a person who walks in the truth?" Write the characteristics on the chalkboard as students shout them out. Ask students to find a partner. Then let each have one minute to tell their partner about someone they know (or knew) who walks (walked) in the truth of Christ.

Let several students share briefly. You may want to poll the class and simply list the names of those they described to their partners. Are there a couple of outstanding people from your congregation who were mentioned by more than one class member?

Point out to students that today's Scripture text mentions several Christians, and one of them is characterized as a person who walks in the truth (3 John 3). In today's class session, students will consider several aspects of what John meant when he spoke of walking in the truth.

Into the Word

Before class, ask several people to prepare brief reports on the main characters of 2 and 3 John: The "lady," Gaius, Diotrephes, Demetrius, and the author of the epistles. Their reports can be based on information from the commentary in the first lesson plan, plus material in other commentaries or a Bible dictionary, Bible encyclopedia, or Bible handbook.

To begin today's Bible study, write the five names on your chalkboard. Distribute blank paper and ask students to jot the names there, leaving room under each one. (Or direct them to the student book, where provision is made for this.) As someone reads 2 John and then 3 John aloud, students should jot down what is said there about each of these people.

Divide the class into fifths. Assign one of the five names on the chalkboard to each fifth of the class. Students should group themselves into twos or threes to compare notes on their assigned character and then to study the text more carefully. Give them several minutes to jot down as much information as possible.

If your class is large enough for a sixth or seventh grouping, some students could survey the text to look for the following:

1. What themes from 1 John are repeated in 2 and 3 John?

2. One of John's concerns in 2 and 3 John is of providing hospitality for itinerant religious teachers. Second John looks at this issue from one perspective, and 3 John addresses it from another. What are John's concerns about these teachers and the church? (Second John warns against offering hospitality to those who teach false doctrine concerning Jesus Christ. Third John encourages readers to provide hospitality for true teachers of the Word.)

Let students share what they have written about their assigned characters or in answer to the two questions above. After students share, the students who prepared their reports before class should give them at this time. They should have information available from their sources that could not be found in the text itself.

Into Life

Choose one of the following activities. Or read all three to your students and allow them to choose which one they will do.

1. Write a letter to a Christian whose example and influence have meant much to you. This may be someone in your congregation or someone in a church you used to attend. In the spirit of 2 and 3 John, thank this person for the impact he or she had on your life for Christ.

2. Write a letter about yourself, as though it were written by an observer of your congregation. What would someone like the apostle John say about you, your faithfulness to Christ, and your contribution to His cause through the local church?

3. Write a letter about yourself, but as if it were a year from now. How do you want to grow in faithfulness and service? Reflect this in your letter as you describe yourself living in the future.

Let's Talk It Over

The questions on this page are designed to encourage review of the lesson Scriptures and to promote discussion of the lesson by the class. The answers provided are only discussion starters. Let your class talk it over from there.

1. How may others be persuaded that the Christian gospel is truth?

The gospel must be proclaimed before it can be believed (Romans 10:14), but those proclaiming the gospel must be genuine. We must walk in the truth, that is, we must practice what we preach. We must obey the commandment to love one another. Insincere Christians will not persuade others of the truth of Christ.

2. How would you counsel someone who finds it difficult to love other Christians outside his pet group of friends?

The Bible does not give us much choice in this matter. Since it is a direct command that we love one another, to fail to love all in God's family is sin. Those who limit their love to a certain group within the fellowship may be preoccupied with self. If we ask only, "What will happen to me if I broaden the scope of my love?" we may be disappointed with the answer. We may be hurt. It will cost us something. We may be bored. Our present friends may turn to other associations. These are the risks of loving.

Consider a different question: "What will happen to them if I do not love?" They may be discouraged. They may suffer deep need alone. They may turn away from the church (and from Christ) because they found only coldness there. Love, genuine love, does not calculate what will be received in return. It does not wait for the right feelings. We should love because we care about Christ (Matthew 25:40, 45) and because He commanded it. We should love because we care about our spiritual family in Christ.

3. John, the apostle of Christ, was in his nineties when he wrote his encouraging letter (3 John) to a friend, Gaius. What applications can we learn from that?

None of us should consider ourselves too old or too important to write encouraging letters to others. Growing older is no excuse for uninvolvement in the lives of others. Growing older is not a reason to become grouchy, but to become more gracious. For the older we get, the more time we have spent with the Lord and the more we should permit His Spirit to bring us to spiritual maturity. Is it possible that one of the most important things that could happen to a discouraged Christian would be for some of the senior citizens to write that person an uplifting letter?

4. Can you recall a time when you enjoyed the fellowship of other Christians even though you had just met them for the first time? What is the basis for that fellowship?

It is our great privilege as Christians to consider ourselves part of God's adopted family on earth. Whenever we meet other Christians on vacation, at a convention, at a retreat, etc., we can be sure we have much in common, even though the common bond is the faith we share. Fellowship is sustained not just because we believe in Jesus, but because we mutually hold as truth a body of knowledge about Jesus and about His will for us. If we are trusting in the same Lord and striving to conform our lives to the same moral pattern, then we are "fellows in the same ship"—fellowship.

5. What are some factors that might motivate strangers to come back to our church's services after their first visit?

Visitors may be motivated to return if they are made to feel wanted. After all, the church is for strangers as well as for members. The church is for the searching, the hurting, the bleeding, the wounded, the depressed, the perverted, the sinners. That is why the church is for us and for others. Thus, strangers need to be given a warm greeting. They also may be motivated to come back if they hear lessons and sermons that relate the Bible to life today. They may be motivated to come back if the members repeat their names often when speaking to them, and if they introduce them to others. They may also be motivated to return if they are given a list of ministries (not just meetings) that the church is actively involved in—that lets them know that the church is a caring and sensitive church. They may be motivated to return if they see that the regular members are enthusiastic in Bible study and worship. If the regular members are bored, why should strangers return?

Summer Quarter, 1990

Theme: Wisdom as a Way of Life

Special Features

Lessons

Unit 1: Wisdom in the Psalms

Unit 2: Proverbs of the Wise

Unit 3: The Limits of Human Wisdom

Unit 4: Wisdom in the New Testament

Related Resources

The following publications give additional help for the lessons in the Summer Quarter. They may be purchased from your supplier. Prices are subject to change.

A Loser, A Winner, and a Wise Guy, by David McCord. This book contains some lessons learned from the lives of Saul, David, and Solomon. Order #11-40084, $2.25.

Check Your Morality, by Knofel Staton. In this book, moral issues confronting our society are considered from a Biblical perspective. Order #11-39971, $3.95.

How to Know the Will of God, by Knofel Staton. This book shows how you can find the answers to many important questions. Order #11-39948, $2.95.

Teach With Success, by Guy P. Leavitt; revised by Eleanor Daniel. Explains how to teach successfully and contains an update on terms and trends. Order #18-03232, $7.95

You Can Teach Adults Successfully, by Ronald G. Davis, Mark Plunkett, Daniel Schantz, Rick Shonkwiler, and Mark A. Taylor. Order #18-03208, $2.95.

Jun 3
Jun 10
Jun 17
Jun 24
Jul 1
Jul 8
Jul 15
Jul 22
Jul 29
Aug 5
Aug 12
Aug 19
Aug 26

The Principal Thing

by Orrin Root

WISDOM IS THE PRINCIPAL THING; therefore get wisdom." This is the advice of Solomon (Proverbs 4:7), whose own wisdom qualifies him to speak.

"Get wisdom." At any university, the big and busy student body indicates that the wise king's advice is being followed by many who never read the book of Proverbs. Parents, high-school counselors, lecturers, and writers all unite in urging a young person to go to college and get wisdom. Solomon said, "She shall promote thee: she shall bring thee to honor" (Proverbs 4:8); but modern advisers more often say, "She will help you make money."

The pursuit of wisdom is not always successful. Teaching a course in "Public Education in the United States," a distinguished professor began by tracing a person's training from kindergarten through elementary school, high school, college, and graduate school. At the end of the narrative he announced triumphantly, "At last we make him a PhD!" Then after a dramatic pause he added, *"And he's still a fool."*

Sometimes the search for wisdom is handicapped by a bad start. "The fear of the Lord is the beginning of wisdom" (Psalm 111:10; Proverbs 9:10). If we ignore God and rely on human thinking, the best of wisdom will elude us.

Philosophy is a name we sometimes give to the search for wisdom. Literally it means love of wisdom. Philosophy is not worthy of that name if it shuts out the divine revelations and searches only in the natural world and the human mind. As a thoughtful lecturer put it, "Philosophy is a blind man, in a dark cellar, looking for a black cat, that isn't there."

Philosophy is blind if it relies on human thinking only. The mind of man by itself is not capable of discovering the highest wisdom. Philosophy is in a dark cellar if it searches the natural world without the light of God's revelation. Philosophy is looking for a black cat: ultimate truth and wisdom are not easily seen. Finally, the cat isn't there. Wisdom in its height and depth and breadth and length is not in the natural world and the human mind. It is in the Lord God Almighty. Anyone who denies Him will find only bits and pieces of wisdom.

Do you want to be wise? Do you want to know the truth? Don't stop your own thinking; but excite it, improve it, tune it to the Word of God. Let the light of divine revelation flood the dark cellar of the natural world and human experience. You may never capture the cat of truth and put your collar on it, but it will sit beside you and purr.

In this book, we have thirteen short studies drawn from the "wisdom literature" of the Bible. They will not teach us all we would like to know, but they will point a direction for us. Why not read all of Proverbs, all of Ecclesiastes, all of the Sermon on the Mount, and all of James as we study these lessons for the next three months?

Wisdom in the Psalms

Since these studies are all about wisdom, it may seem strange that the word *wisdom* does not appear in the texts of the first two lessons. Nevertheless they are about wisdom.

Lesson 1. Two ways are described. If I take one of them, I am like a tree by the river: firm and handsome and fruitful. If I take the other way, I am like chaff blown away in the wind. Is it hard to see what that has to do with wisdom?

Lesson 2. Again two ways are seen. One brings riches and then disaster. The other brings not riches, but enough to live on—and forever. Which way is wiser?

Lesson 3. Now comes a clearer picture of those who get rich and don't care how they do it. "Their way is their folly" (Psalm 49:13). They heap up wealth, but they can't take it with them. They come to the end of life and have nothing; but the upright man can say, "God will redeem my soul from the power of the grave" (v. 15).

Proverbs of the Wise

The book of Proverbs is the world's most famous collection of wise sayings. Compiled nearly three thousand years ago, they fit the circumstances of our time with amazing precision. Lessons 4 to 8 bring us some samples.

Lesson 4. Here is the purpose of Proverbs:

> To know wisdom and instruction;
> to perceive the words of understanding;
> to receive the instruction of wisdom,
> justice, and judgment, and equity;
> to give subtilty to the simple,
> to the young man knowledge and discretion.
> —Proverbs 1:2-4

In this book, wisdom is not hiding herself or playing hard to get. She is standing in the street and shouting for attention:

How long, ye simple ones, will ye love simplicity?
and the scorners delight in their scorning,
and fools hate knowledge?

—Proverbs 1:22

Foolishness clings to those who cling to their own way. Wisdom is available to those who will take instruction from the inspired Word.

Lesson 5. "Get wisdom!" That urging is central in lesson 5. One way to get it is to hear the instruction of a father. The father's duty is to have the words of Scripture in his heart and teach them diligently to his children (Deuteronomy 6:6, 7). If a father is negligent in this duty, his children can bypass him and go directly to the source, God's Word, for their wisdom. "She shall bring thee to honor, when thou dost embrace her."

Lesson 6. Wisdom! How glorious she is! When the Almighty created the heavens and the earth, wisdom was His tool and His delight. How could anyone imagine that creation came without a mind and a plan? That error is denied by the intricate interrelationship of the things that are. By wisdom the Lord God made them all. By wisdom He made us. Today and always wisdom calls to us:

Hearken unto me, O ye children:
For blessed are they that keep my ways.

—Proverbs 8:32

Lesson 7. "Experience keeps a costly school, but fools will learn in no other." So says an old proverb that is not written in the Bible. Lesson 7 presents a number of things that can be learned from costly experience, but how much better it is to learn them from the Word of God and avoid the cost and pain of learning them from experience!

Lesson 8. In picturesque language the poet lists four things that are wonderful, four things that are intolerable, four things that are little but wise, and four things that move gracefully. Everything, good or bad, has consequences. So if you feel boastful, or if you have an evil thought, "lay thine hand upon thy mouth" (Proverbs 30:32). Don't let the bad thought get out.

Limits of Human Wisdom

The book of Ecclesiastes brings us the inspired musing of King Solomon in his later years. His accomplishments were tremendous, but he found them strangely unsatisfying. Still he came to a magnificent conclusion. At the end of the book, his advice to a young man is threefold:

Rejoice in thy youth.
Remember thy Creator.
Fear God and keep His commandments.

Two short samples of Ecclesiastes are chosen for our study, and they too present wise conclusions.

Lesson 9. Gifted with wisdom, riches, and power, Solomon had the opportunity and the inclination to try everything. He came to the conclusion that there is nothing better than to work for a living and enjoy the living one earns. How many discontented workers would be happier if they could realize that their lot is the best there is!

Lesson 10. One thing that King Solomon learned was the importance of timing. There is "a time to every purpose under the heaven" (Ecclesiastes 3:1). With his limited wisdom, man cannot know all about the work of God; but he can know enough "to rejoice, and to do good" (3:12), to "enjoy the good of all his labor" (v. 13). This is "the gift of God" (v. 13). Have we all learned to appreciate it?

Wisdom in the New Testament

Job, Proverbs, Ecclesiastes, and some of the Psalms are commonly called "wisdom literature." Of course, there is wisdom also in the law and the prophets and in the books of history. Even more notable is the wisdom of the New Testament, and three samples of it will complete our study.

Lesson 11. Jesus the Son of God is wiser than Solomon the son of David. In different words, Jesus confirms the statement that wisdom begins with the fear of God. He tells us to take the way that leads to life, though the other way is more popular. The narrow way is the way in which He leads.

He leadeth me, O blessed thought!
O words with heavenly comfort fraught!
What-e'er I do, wher-e'er I be,
Still 'tis God's hand that leadeth me.

Jesus says to beware of false prophets, and adds that character is indicated by what one does rather than by what he says. Jesus' teaching is the solid foundation for a good life.

Lesson 12. Solomon said, "Get wisdom," and emphasized the importance of listening to instruction. James indicates that wisdom can be had for the asking, but he does not say by asking alone. "Receive with meekness the engrafted word" (James 1:21). Wisdom is gained by asking and study together, and it is shown in a good way of life.

Lesson 13. James echoes Jesus' teaching about doing. Hear the word of God, but "be ye doers of the word, and not hearers only."

Let us then be diligent both in studying these lessons and in living by them. This is the way of wisdom.

Wisdom and the Good Life

by Charles E. Cook

NEVER BEFORE in the history of mankind has there been so much information available to so many. As a result of recent developments in the fields of communication technology and data processing, we are informed within moments of any major occurrence almost any place on the earth or even in outer space. We have the ability to gather data, store it, retrieve it, assimilate it, analyze it, and communicate it faster and with more accuracy than any other generation. This ability has made it possible for us to predict accurately the outcome of elections before all the votes are counted, as well as to track severe weather developments and to give adequate warnings for evacuation. Not only have we made great strides in the area of information systems; but in almost every other field of learning, we are taking giant steps also. The fields of science and technology are constantly amazing us all with their discoveries.

Having and Being

As a result of these advances, this generation stands head and shoulders above all others in terms of *having*. We are deluged with the "things" of life. One of the most complex challenges of our time is to solve the problem of the safe disposal of the growing piles of refuse we have accumulated—the outmoded, undesirable things that now clutter our lives. We have inundated ourselves with the unnecessary and the unwanted. We are being choked to death by the consequences of our own cleverness.

Yet, we remain a restless, unsatisfied, unfulfilled people. Regarding the subject of *being*, we seem to be no closer to understanding the meaning of our personal existence than some of the most primitive cultures. In many ways we seem to have regressed in our grasp of some of the most basic truths of life. In his book, *The Illusion of Technique*, William Barrett, the distinguished professor of philosophy, reminds us that, "Despite the great triumphs of a technical civilization, humankind still exists in the bosom of nature." Barrett asks the question, "How does technical man exist in relation to Being?" He concludes, "We can draw one prosaic and sensible conclusion, that technological advance in itself is not sufficient to secure the happiness of mankind."

One would think this conclusion might be obvious to us, but this is a truth not easily accepted by modern man. We are consumed with the belief that somehow, given enough time, money, and raw material, our human intellect will enable us to construct a Utopia for ourselves. We are counting on "better living through chemistry." Our problem is that we insist on equating *living* with the *things* of life, and we think that *having* is *being*. We have failed to accept the conclusion of Solomon that this is "a chasing after the wind" (Ecclesiastes 1:17).* Life is more than a problem to be solved. It is more than answers to questions that are raised. It is more than all the knowledge that we may accumulate related to our existence. Living has to do with the quality of *being* in relationship to the One who said, "I have come that they may have life, and have it to the full" (John 10:10), and, "I am the way and the truth and the life" (14:6). It is wise for us, therefore, to pursue with diligence an understanding of those principles and practices taught in His Word that serve to enhance and enrich our lives.

Dark Alleys and Dead-End Streets

The world's wisdom has not been very helpful in this regard. It has lead us down dark alleys and into dead-end streets. It has made promises that it could not fulfill, offered hope where there was no hope, and given answers that have only raised more questions to which it had no answers. The bankruptcy of the world's wisdom is described by Paul in 1 Corinthians 1:19, 20: "For it is written: 'I will destroy the wisdom of the wise; the intelligence of the intelligent I will frustrate.' Where is the wise man? Where is the scholar? Where is the philosopher of this age? Has not God made foolish the wisdom of the world?" The answer to Paul's question should be self-evident, but it seems not to be for many. We continue to be duped into accepting the world's wisdom. We persist in believing that our way is better than God's. Yet, throughout the wisdom literature of the Bible, the contrast between divine wisdom and human wisdom is clear. Solomon said, "With much wisdom comes much sorrow; the more knowledge, the more grief" (Ecclesiastes 1:18). His human wisdom had led him into the pursuit of every pleasure, but the result was not pleasure at all. He said, "I denied myself nothing my eyes desired; I refused my heart no pleasure.... Yet ... everything was meaningless" (2:10, 11).

Contemporary Examples

At the risk of being misunderstood, allow me to use a few examples to show just how the world's wisdom has been shown to be foolish. First, with regard to our contemporary views of the family. The Bible is rather clear about the roles and relationships that are appropriate within the family. It advocates a covenant relationship based upon a common bond of self-giving love and a commitment to Jesus Christ. It identifies the mutual responsibilities of leadership, faithfulness, respect, and obedience as they relate to husbands, wives, and children. And some of these roles and responsibilities are clearly gender-related. (See Ephesians 5:21—6:4.) But the world has chosen "in its wisdom" to advocate a non-gender position in relation to the roles and responsibilities in the family. The result has been identity confusion, inner personal conflict, and interpersonal conflict, resulting in a breakdown in family life.

Again, the wisdom of God's Word teaches that casual, promiscuous sex outside of marriage, including homosexual practices, degrades the human body and results in a tragic penalty both physically and psychologically. Paul clearly identifies these awful consequences in Romans 1:18-32. Yet, the world "in its wisdom" increasingly approves such sexual behavior and insists that those who take a position of opposition are old-fashioned, judgmental, or unsophisticated. So, we are not counseled to change our behavior but to "take precautions" so as to avoid what Paul says is inevitable. We still believe we can sow our wild oats and then expect God to hear and answer our prayer for a crop failure!

Related to this is the growing acceptance, even by professed Christians, of "living together unions." A high percentage of those who marry have lived with their spouses before marrying them. The wisdom of the world suggests that this is a desirable choice, both for economic and social reasons. However, a recent study found that women who had made this choice were eighty percent more likely to separate or divorce than those who had not. Especially liable to divorce or separation were those women who had lived with the future spouse for three years or more before the marriage. The study concluded that couples who cohabited premaritally were not as committed to the values and interests of marriage as those who did not. (*Psychology Today*, July/August 1988, p. 15.)

One of the signs of immaturity is the inability or unwillingness to learn from experience. We seem to have self-imposed blindness that keeps us from seeing the relationship of our troubles to our unwise choices. We are intoxicated with our knowledge and have taken on an air of omnipotence that causes us to feel that we are an exception to all the laws of life. It is not unlike the deep sea diver who becomes a victim of nitrogen narcosis and thus unknowingly puts himself in grave peril.

When will we learn that to ignore the wisdom of God and the principles of His Word is absolute foolishness? When will we learn that intellectual power without moral control leads to man's downfall? The One who made us surely knows what is best for us. His wisdom is of inestimable value (Proverbs 4:7). And, it is available to all who desire it. "For the Lord gives wisdom, and from his mouth come knowledge and understanding" (Proverbs 2:6). Our first task is to seek the truth for living found in His Word so that we may be truly wise. This means that we must not only increase our knowledge of the way God desires us to live, but also *desire* that life which is abundant and fulfilling. The real issue is obedience. In contrasting the two kinds of wisdom, James asks, "Who is wise and understanding among you?" Then he answers his own query: "Let him show it by his good life, by deeds done in the humility that comes from wisdom. But if you harbor bitter envy and selfish ambition in your hearts, do not boast about it or deny the truth. Such 'wisdom' does not come down from heaven but is earthly, unspiritual, of the devil. For where you have envy and selfish ambition, there you find disorder and every evil practice. But the wisdom that comes from heaven is first of all pure; then peace loving, considerate, submissive, full of mercy and good fruit, impartial and sincere" (James 3:13-17). Application of the wisdom of God is essential for this good life.

*Scripture quotations are from the *New International Version*.

Reflections on Wisdom

by R. Edwin Groover

IF YOU WERE to identify the ten wisest people in the world, where would you begin your search? Would you go to the cabin of a reclusive author, to the office of a powerful politician, to the lecture hall of a great university? No doubt, you can think of other people as likely candidates. But you may be thinking that it would be foolish even to begin such a quest, for the people who are the wisest probably would not devote their energies to promoting themselves. They would not bother to respond to inquiries from the *Directory of the World's Wisest People*—if such a volume existed.

A better use of our time would be to cultivate those relationships and traits associated with wisdom that make our lives more productive and then to help others do the same.

But still there is a search. Where do we begin? What are we looking for?

In his epistle, James speaks of two kinds of wisdom. One is earthly; it is associated with the devil, and, when people follow its dictates, every evil work results. The other wisdom, true wisdom, the wisdom James exhorts us to desire and nurture, is from above (James 3:17). It is a gift of God's grace to those who gladly receive it. The wisdom from above does not inspire pride. Gratitude—not arrogance—is the proper response to a gift.

Wisdom Is Active

True wisdom, which comes from God, is not to be confused with theoretical knowledge, with mere possession of information. The wisdom from above is active; it serves others. It provides the basis for harmonious and healing relationships. The wisdom described in James 3:17 promotes the welfare of others; it fosters a sense of community, of belonging to the Creator and to those made in His image.

James informs us that "the wisdom from above is first pure."* Here, purity refers especially to the absence of self-centeredness. Godly wisdom is not contaminated with the world's preoccupation with personal convenience and the acquisition of power. The attitudes and actions produced by godly wisdom are free of all ulterior motives.

The wisdom from above is also "peaceable." This quality of wisdom is not born of indifference. Wisdom is active, forgiving, genuine: it is "gentle, open to reason, full of mercy and good

fruits, without uncertainty or insincerity." Others have nothing to fear from the person who lives under the guidance of this kind of wisdom. This person respects the feelings of others, is open to persuasion, and shows compassion. One who is wise listens attentively and patiently. This person can admit mistakes, and is eager to grow in wisdom. On the other hand, one who is given to pronouncing judgments, who has little time or inclination to be gentle, or approachable, or merciful toward others, and who shows by his or her actions that people do not matter, is not exhibiting the wisdom from above.

It is helpful to note the similarities between the characteristics of the wisdom that is from above and *agape*—the godlike love taught and exemplified by Jesus and described particularly by the apostle Paul in 1 Corinthians 13. The way of wisdom and the way of love are parallel and overlapping paths. Wisdom and love come into focus sharply in the person of Jesus Christ. He unites these virtues in himself and in His teachings.

We may know the characteristics of godly wisdom, as taught in God's Word and exemplified in His Son, but our knowledge is inadequate if it is not translated into life. Our knowledge about the wisdom from above is merely theoretical, if it is something we only recite but do not allow to govern our lives.

The Fruit of False Wisdom

James wrote to first-century Christians, "But if you have bitter jealousy and selfish ambition in your hearts, do not boast and be false to the truth. This wisdom is not such as comes down from above, but is earthly, unspiritual, devilish. For where jealousy and selfish ambition exist, there will be disorder and every vile practice" (James 3:14-16).

We twentieth-century Christians need to hear these words. We need to hear for the sake of ourselves and for the sake of those outside of Christ, who understandably tend to judge the legitimacy of the Christian faith on the basis of their perception of our lives as individuals and as a community.

Ungodly living by Christians damages the reputation of the church in the eyes of the world. The news media provides ample evidence of the general tendency of headlining the faults of the church—and particularly of its leaders. Regardless of how we may react to those television evangelists who have admitted to serious misconduct in highly publicized cases in recent years, many non-Christians have used these scandals to justify a negative view of the church.

The world can also point to the failings of those of us who do not have national or international reputations. As individuals and as a community, we confess that we sometimes exhibit "jealousy and selfish ambition," "disorder and every vile practice" rather than the "good fruits" of the wisdom from above.

The Christian community is hurt when any of us jockeys for power. If we treat a brother or a sister as a rival, if we rejoice at the thought of some misfortune befalling that person, then we are guilty of sinful attitudes and behavior. We most certainly do not act in accordance with godly wisdom. The church suffers when contentiousness is the order of the day among any Christians in any place. And the world hurts—and dies—if the church does not provide a clear alternative to the wisdom of the world.

Scriptural examples of believers who exhibited the wisdom of this world come to mind readily enough. Paul warned the Christians at Corinth, for instance, about the consequences of their continuing to rely upon this false wisdom. The apostle urged his brothers and sisters there to forsake selfishness, party-spirit, and other sinful attitudes. He reminded them of the better way, the way of love.

True wisdom issues in peace, but "earthly, unspiritual, devilish" wisdom generates confusion and conflict of the sort that afflicted the Corinthians Christians—and that has continued to hamper the effectiveness of the church to the present. This false wisdom presents itself cleverly. It seeks to recruit others to its side. And when it gains a foothold in a congregation, a family, or any group, it engages in subtle and relentless attacks against the harmonious relationships nurtured by the wisdom from above. Devilish wisdom drives people apart and delights especially in driving Christians apart. And when the unspiritual masquerades as the spiritual—as false wisdom will do at its diabolical best—the rifts that result are likely to be especially deep and devastating. What a wickedly clever scheme it is to promote the heresy of disunity among Christians under the banner of right thinking and proper procedures!

If you have read all or just a part of C. S. Lewis' *Screwtape Letters*, you have noticed that the views and actions of Satan's minions tend to be quite logical—once you observe that the points on the spiritual compass are reversed. You may also have noticed in *Screwtape* that the most effective work done on behalf of the "Father Below," as the tempter's lackeys call him, is not the frontal assault but the subtle challenge, often delivered in a whisper or a nudge. Devilish wisdom seeks to be recognized as true wisdom. But the identity of this unspiritual wisdom is established by its results.

Wisdom Incarnate

It was the apostle Paul who more forcefully than any other New Testament writer called attention explicitly to Jesus Christ as wisdom incarnate (see 1 Corinthians 1:24, 30, for example). Thus a question even more basic than, "What is wisdom?" is, "Who is Jesus?" Because we believe that He is the Christ, the Son of the living God, we are convinced that He is more than one who taught about wisdom. It is through submission to Him that we have access to the wisdom from above. And through Him, wisdom becomes a way of life rather than a list of abstract principles. Our joy is to live in Jesus Christ, who is the wisdom of God. Our search for wisdom leads us to Him who reveals himself to us, who has always sought us, and who reconciles us to himself and to one another. Our search for wisdom leads us to discipleship.

Our Mission

We who are privileged to teach in the church devote ourselves to informing, equipping, and encouraging people in their walk with Jesus Christ. A Christian who teaches embarks on a vital mission. Rigorous self-evaluation is required, because the teacher is called upon to reflect godly wisdom in motives, words, and actions. Thus, this ministry must not be entered into hastily or rendered carelessly. It is better not to be a teacher at all if the nature of this service is not understood and accepted. James, a teacher himself, warned in James 3:1.

Still, Christian teachers count the cost, accepting responsibilities along with the joys. We are—we should be—disciples growing in the wisdom that is from above. If we are truly wise, we care for the people whom we teach. We encourage them to be growing disciples, to grow as we are growing. We are blessed as we walk with others and lead them toward ever-higher levels of maturity in Christ. Our mission is momentous indeed. Together, in Christ we find insight into what life ought to be, and the courage to live it as our Creator intends. Together, we seek to grow in the wisdom that is from above.

---

*Scripture quotations are from the *Revised Standard Version*.

Quarterly Quiz

The questions on this page may be used in several ways: as a pretest at the beginning of the quarter; as a review at the end of the quarter; or as a review after each lesson. The questions are based on the Scripture text of each lesson (King James Version).
Answers are on page 341.

Lesson 1

1. The man who does not walk in the way of the ungodly has his delight in the _____ of the Lord. *Psalm 1:2*

2. The ungodly are like the (dried leaves, chaff, dust of the earth), which the wind drives away. *Psalm 1:4.*

Lesson 2

1. We are cautioned not to envy the workers of iniquity, for they shall soon be cut down like the grass. (T/F) *Psalm 37:1, 2*

2. The meek shall inherit the earth, and shall delight themselves in the abundance of (prosperity, possessions, peace). *Psalm 37:11*

Lesson 3

1. Though a person may boast of the multitude of his riches, he cannot give to God a _____ for his brother. *Psalm 49:6, 7*

2. The psalmist says that the wise, the foolish, and the brutish person all die and leave their _____ to others. *Psalm 49:10*

Lesson 4

1. "The _____ of the Lord is the beginning of knowledge: but _____ despise wisdom and instruction." *Proverbs 1:7*

2. Proverbs tells us that "wisdom" cries aloud, but that she is found only in the remote places of the earth. (T/F) *Proverbs 1:20, 21*

Lesson 5

1. According to Proverbs, what is the principal thing a person should get? *Proverbs 4:7*

2. The father tells his son to get a good grip on instruction and never let her go, because she is his _____ . *Proverbs 4:13*

Lesson 6

1. Wisdom is spoken of as being with God before the creation. (T/F) *Proverbs 8:22, 23*

2. Wisdom praises the person who watches at her gates daily. (T/F) *Proverbs 8:34*

Lesson 7

1. The writer of Proverbs 22 says that something is rather to be chosen than great riches. What is it? *Proverbs 22:1*

2. "Train up a _____ in the way he should go: and when he is _____ , he will not depart from it." *Proverbs 22:6*

Lesson 8

1. Two of the four things Agur did not know were the way of an _____ in the air, and the way of a _____ upon a rock. *Proverbs 30:19*

2. Agur mentioned four things that are little upon the earth, but he said that they are exceeding _____ . *Proverbs 30:24*

Lesson 9

1. Solomon observed that one generation passes away, and another comes. But what did he say abides for ever? *Ecclesiastes 1:4*

2. Solomon said that he had seen all the works that are done under the sun. What was his conclusion? *Ecclesiastes 1:13, 14*

Lesson 10

1. Solomon said that God has made everything (meaningful, beautiful, helpful) in its time. *Ecclesiastes 3:11*

2. Whatever God does is done so men may fear Him. (T/F) *Ecclesiastes 3:14*

Lesson 11

1. Of whom was Jesus speaking when He warned of ravening wolves who come to God's flock in sheep's clothing? *Matthew 7:15*

2. Jesus spoke of a wise man and a foolish man, each of whom built a house. What did each man build his house on? *Matthew 7:24, 26*

Lesson 12

1. If we lack wisdom, James urges us to ask God for it. But in what manner are we to ask? *James 1:5, 6*

2. The wisdom that creates envy and strife does not come from God, but is (earthly, sensual, devilish, all three). *James 3:14, 15*

Lesson 13

1. James commanded, "Be ye _____ of the word, and not _____ only." *James 1:22*

2. The Scriptural commandment, "Thou shalt love thy neighbor as thyself," is referred to by James as the _____ law. *James 3:8*

The Two Ways

of Living

June 3
Lesson 1

LESSON SCRIPTURE: Psalm 1.

PRINTED TEXT: Psalm 1.

Psalm 1

1 Blessed is the man that walketh not in the counsel of the ungodly, nor standeth in the way of sinners, nor sitteth in the seat of the scornful.

2 But his delight is in the law of the Lord; and in his law doth he meditate day and night.

3 And he shall be like a tree planted by the rivers of water, that bringeth forth his fruit in his season; his leaf also shall not wither; and whatsoever he doeth shall prosper.

4 The ungodly are not so: but are like the chaff which the wind driveth away.

5 Therefore the ungodly shall not stand in the judgment, nor sinners in the congregation of the righteous.

6 For the Lord knoweth the way of the righteous: but the way of the ungodly shall perish.

GOLDEN TEXT: The Lord knoweth the way of the righteous: but the way of the ungodly shall perish.—Psalm 1:6.

Wisdom as a Way of Life
Unit 1: Wisdom in the Psalms
(Lessons 1-3)

Lesson Aims

This lesson will:

1. Show that Psalm 1 points out the two basic and divergent paths a person can take in life.

2. Encourage the students to choose and to continue in God's way in Jesus.

Lesson Outline

Display visual 1 from the visuals packet. It highlights the First Psalm's description of a righteous person. The visual is shown on page 350.

Introduction

A. Which Is the Right Road?

We are used to driving on well-marked highways with route numbers and destinations clearly delineated. But have you ever traveled away from the main roads, in a rural area, seeking a church building or home? Perhaps you stopped and asked directions and were told to go so many miles on a certain highway. No doubt, assurance something like this was given: "You can't miss it. It has a large red barn right near the road." But before you got there, you came to a fork in the road. The two roads seemed equally well "blacktopped," but only one could be leading where you wanted to go. At this point a choice had to be made.

So in life, we are confronted with spiritual and ethical choices. In making these choices, we determine the direction our lives will take. Is our general direction to be self-seeking or self-giving? Will we aim always to be straightforward and honest, or will we tend to be underhanded and tricky in our dealings? Is our quality of life to be positive, joyful, and friendly, or negative, gloomy, and antisocial?

Psalm 1 presents a picture of the two fundamental and diverse ways of living and depicts the qualities and destinies involved in both. It will be seen that God shows man the right way, blesses him in it, and rewards him for continuing on it.

B. Lesson Background

Various types of literature are found in the Bible. There are historical accounts, laws, genealogical records, prophetic pronouncements, and biographical and autobiographical narrations. There also are examples of a type of "wisdom literature," which was prevalent in the ancient Near East and in other areas as well. This consisted of brief sayings that capsulized the experience of the past and "packaged" it for the instruction of the readers or hearers. It is found in its purest form in the Biblical book of Proverbs, but it appears in a modified way in other Scripture material, too.

It is true that Psalms is the "songbook" of the Hebrew people. Many psalms are of a celebratory nature, reflecting God's triumphs through and with His people. Of course, some psalms are prayers of deep penitence, remorse, or thanksgiving. But some have the teaching quality common to "wisdom literature."

The psalms we shall consider in lessons 2 and 3 fall into the latter category. In them, the psalmist points out the way of true wisdom for man and urges the reader to walk in it.

In Psalm 1, the psalmist sets before us several contrasts. It will be our happy privilege in this study to see what these contrasts involve, to explore their ramifications, and to apply to our lives the truths and insights they reveal.

I. The Righteous Road (Psalm 1:1-3)

A. What Is Bypassed (v. 1)

1. Blessed is the man that walketh not in the counsel of the ungodly, nor standeth in the way of sinners, nor sitteth in the seat of the scornful.

The book of Psalms begins with the word *blessed.* This expression of the "blessedness" or the supreme well-being of those who love and serve God is found frequently in the psalms.

The nature of the blessedness known by the righteous is found in what they do *not* do, as well as in what they do. Certainly, there is much to be said for an "affirmative attitude" toward life. There is a great need for a stress on all that is good, pure, wholesome, and uplifting. Yet, there is no evading the reality of wickedness and those attitudes and actions that degrade and destroy. We are blessed not only by the benefits we enjoy, but by the many perils and problems we escape. So this psalm begins by indicating that the happy condition of the righteous can be seen in the evil ways they have avoided.

Walketh. Often in the Biblical writings, the "walk" of a person stands for that individual's manner of life. To walk *in the counsel of the ungodly* is to arrange one's life by following the advice of those who have no faith in God or love for Him. Will ungodly people advise us to engage in any activity that honors God or reflects our obedience to His commands? Rather, the godless person will fail to see God anywhere and will advise against acknowledging or serving Him at any time. He who repudiates God will be very delighted when others heed his advice to forsake God's way and reject God's will.

Those "without God" will never see any use in giving time and money to the work of God. To expend energy or effort to know the Bible, to lead persons to become followers of Jesus, to devote time to prayer and worship—all these activities would be considered worthless by the ungodly. "The man without the Spirit does not accept the things that come from the Spirit of God, for they are foolishness to him, and he cannot understand them, because they are spiritually discerned" (1 Corinthians 2:14, *New International Version*).

Nor standeth in the way of sinners. Three times in this brief psalm the expression, *the way,* is used: "the way of sinners," "the way of the righteous," and "the way of the ungodly." Like the term *walk,* the expression *the way* is often used in Scripture to designate a manner of living. It is the kind of activity that has become a pattern of conduct for an individual or a group. Thus, the characteristic speech, recurrent actions, and usual attitudes of people become their "way" of life.

Just as there is a way of righteousness, faith, and salvation, so there is a way of sin, disbelief, and spiritual disaster. Obviously, those who have committed themselves to God should have no part in the latter. Of course, as Jesus recognized, we cannot be entirely (nor should we be) separated from sinners, but we must not stand up for or stand in favor of their sinful ways (see John 17:15; 1 Corinthians 5:9, 10).

Nor sitteth in the seat of the scornful. It has been noted often that the description of the behavior to be shunned by the person who would be "blessed" shows a pattern of progression. All too often this is also the process of spiritual deterioration. First one *walks* in the counsel of ungodly people, then one *stands* in the way of sinners, and finally one takes a place where he *sits* among the scornful.

The scorner is an individual who feels superior to others. He regards himself as on a height of excellence from which he can demean or ridicule someone else. Of scorners, Henry Howard wrote, "Instead of unmasking badness, they are more concerned with defacing goodness, casting the shade of suspicion across the fairest reputations, chuckling suggestively at every mention of honour, curling a contemptuous lip when fidelity is praised, holding duty in derision and God in defiance, despising authority and flouting law" (*The Threshold,* p. 53).

B. What Is Enjoyed (v. 2)

2. But his delight is in the law of the Lord; and in his law doth he meditate day and night.
The "blessed man" is to be known not only by what he shuns, but also by those attitudes and actions that fill his life. God's revelation of His will points out what the righteous person considers not only his duty, but also *his delight,* to accomplish. To such a person, the rules of the "game of life" and its boundaries are not limiting, constraining burdens. Rather, they are the Creator's wise provisions, through which the activity of living can be enjoyed and fully experienced with verve and vitality.

God's law is like a railway track, on which we may run our lives. As long as we stay on the track, we can go toward our destinations with speed and ease. Further, in underground rail systems, a third, electrified track provides a stream of power to enable the train to run. So as we live by God's Word, we not only refrain from wrecking, but we receive a continuous supply of power for the movement of life in directions laid out by God's revelation of His will.

To *meditate* on God's law means to contemplate it with thoughtful reverence and respectful scrutiny. It is to give attention to the possible reasons for the admonitions or restrictions contained in it. It is to see how these directives apply to various areas of our lives. It is to appreciatively contemplate the love and wisdom that underlie certain commands and to see if we can think of examples by which they have been illustrated and their value enforced.

The cow and some other animals called "ruminants" store grass, hay, or herbs in an extra stomach, and then they bring them up as a cud on which they chew until all the juice and nutrients in them are extracted. So, in meditation, we bring back material previously read, heard, or experienced, and consider it reflectively to obtain guidance in determining future attitudes or actions.

In the Biblical sense, meditation is not a focusing of the mind on a certain word or phrase in an attempt to *stop* thought and induce a "free floating" disconnection with temporal reality. Rather, it is a thoughtful consideration of Biblical truths so our hearts and minds may be filled with an increased awareness of God's presence and purpose for our lives.

C. What Is Imitated (v. 3)

3. And he shall be like a tree planted by the rivers of water, that bringeth forth his fruit in his season; his leaf also shall not wither; and whatsoever he doeth shall prosper.

This comparison of the "blessed" man with *a tree* is concerned only with certain aspects of a living tree. Of course, a tree is nonreasoning, stationary, and vegetative. What the psalmist means is that a person who is aware of God and is obedient to Him is like a tree in terms of *rootage, fruitage,* and *leafage.*

One of the most vital parts of a tree—its root system—is almost totally invisible. It has been said that a tree is like an organism upside down, with its head and mouth in the ground and its body and bushy tail in the air. The tree absorbs or drinks in water and minerals from the soil through its roots. These also serve to anchor the tree.

The person who knows and obeys God's truth, in any age, draws nourishment for the health of his soul and also finds that he is securely grounded when the tempests of life blow over him. Psalm 138:3 speaks of the result of rootage in God: "In the day when I cried thou answeredst me, and strengthenedst me with strength in my soul." The godly person's assurance of a firm anchorage in God is sounded in Psalm 16:8: "I have set the Lord always before me: because he is at my right hand, I shall not be moved." A constant renewal of strength and

the assurance of stability are the results of seeking, understanding, and trusting in God.

Those persons who commit themselves to God and His ways will also have fruitage. All healthy trees, especially the kind the psalmist is contemplating, bear fruit at some time of the year. We know Jesus urged His followers to bear fruit and to expect life experiences that would help them bear "more" fruit. Jesus said also that the one who abides in Him will bring forth "much" fruit and so will glorify the Father in Heaven (see John 15:1,2,4-8). The apostle Paul spoke of "the fruits of righteousness, which are by Jesus Christ" (Philippians 1:11), and the fruit that the Holy Spirit helps to bring forth in our personalities (Galatians 5:22, 23).

It is significant that the *leaf* of that tree, which is symbolic of the godly person, *shall not wither.* The life of a tree is dependent on its roots, but not more so than its reliance on its leaves. In the leaves, the minerals and other elements brought up from the roots are transformed into living matter that is necessary to the tree's health and growth. If the leaf *withers,* the life of the tree is doomed. Its death is sure. So the righteous person's trust in the Lord is the means of the constant renewal of his spiritual life energies.

The leafy section of the tree thrusts up into the sky, and from the sunlight above it draws its sustenance and strength. It lives not just on elements drawn from this world, but from the radiation that comes from above. "Though rooted in this world, yet like the tree he [the godly man] will stretch forth appealing and appropriating hands toward another upon which he will draw for his dynamic to be and to do and to endure" (HOWARD, *The Threshold,* p. 111).

The psalmist closes his description of the righteous person by saying that he will *prosper.* In Old Testament times, prosperity was largely understood to be the enjoyment of the material blessings of health, wealth, progeny, and a good name. The fuller revelation Jesus brought helps us to see that the greatest prosperity is *spiritual.* In Him we have the forgiveness of sins, the fellowship of the church, the knowledge of God as our Father, and the hope of life everlasting.

II. The Wicked Way (Psalm 1:4, 5)

A. Instability (v. 4)

4. The ungodly are not so: but are like the chaff which the wind driveth away.

There is a difference between the righteous and the sinful. The psalmist points out the condition and blessing of the person who is dedicated to God, and then insists that *the ungodly are not so.* While devout people are stable, anchored, flourishing, and vital, the impious are without foundation and driven about by many external forces. The currents of fashion, impulse, and popular opinion all exercise an influence that drives such individuals this way and that. Because of this drifting quality, such persons are apt to become shallow, purposeless, unsettled, and uncertain. This instability is likened to the chaff, which the wind blows away when threshed grain is being winnowed.

B. Insecurity (v. 5)

5. Therefore the ungodly shall not stand in the judgment, nor sinners in the congregation of the righteous.

This verse speaks of the day of judgment, when all persons will come before God, and the final estimates of life will be made (Matthew 25:31-46; Revelation 20:11-15). The house built on the sand of indifference to God's truth will collapse, and "great will be the fall of it." Since the ungodly are like chaff that is blown about and scattered by the wind, lacking stability and sound character, they will receive consideration in the judgment and will find no place among the righteous ones assembled.

JUSTICE PREVAILS

Jack Eckerd is the founder of the drugstore chain that bears his name. Some years ago he accepted Christ, and not long after that, as he walked through one of his stores, he noticed that the magazine racks were filled with copies of pornographic magazines. Though retired from actual leadership, Eckerd called the president of his company and urged him to get rid of the magazines. Management protested, citing the substantial profits they stood to lose; but using his power as the largest stockholder, Eckerd prevailed. The pornographic materials were removed from all 1,700 drugstores in the chain.

When Eckerd was questioned as to what motivated him to take such a stand, he simply replied, "God wouldn't let me off the hook."

As Christians, it is vital for us to realize that we are accountable for our actions. Psalm 1 pronounces a blessing on the follower of God; it also rebukes the wicked and promises that all sinners will be punished. Though we may attempt to blame our faults and mistakes on others, the Bible teaches personal accountability. "What a man sows, that will he also reap," is its teaching.

Though at times it seems that the wicked prosper, we would do well to remember that those who persist in wickedness will eventually experience God's wrath. As the psalmist said, "The ungodly shall not stand in the judgment, nor sinners in the congregation of the righteous" (Psalm 1:5).   —T. T.

III. Where the Roads End (Psalm 1:6)

A. Fulfillment in God (v. 6a)

6a. For the Lord knoweth the way of the righteous.

It is true that God *knows* all things, and He knows the way of the wicked as well as *the way of the righteous.* But these words are not just an indication of God's mastery of information, but an assurance that He knows of the faithfulness of the righteous and that He upholds and blesses their lives. In the Sermon on the Mount, Jesus frequently assured His hearers that God knows our needs and that He takes note of and will remember our deeds of kindness, helpfulness, comfort, or generosity. (See Matthew 6:17, 18, 26, 30; 7:11. See also Matthew 10:29-31, 42.)

B. Frustration in Emptiness (v. 6b)

6b. But the way of the ungodly shall perish.

Only the life that finds its direction, purpose, and goal in the living and eternal God can endure. "What is your life?" James asks. Then, speaking of our mortal existence in human terms, he answers, "It is even a vapor, that appeareth for a little time, and then vanisheth away" (4:14). But, as Jesus says, when our deeds are "wrought in God" (John 3:21), they link us with the One who is "from everlasting to everlasting" (Psalm 90:2). Only God's way is fulfilling. The way of sin is self-destructive and futile. Everything divorced from God's presence and purpose is frustration and folly, and is certain to perish.

Home Daily Bible Readings

Monday, May 28—God Nourishes Us (Jeremiah 17:5-10)

Tuesday, May 29—God Is Our Rock (Psalm 62:1-7)

Wednesday, May 30—God's Love Is Steadfast (Psalm 62:8-12)

Thursday, May 31—True Blessedness (Matthew 5:1-12)

Friday, June 1—Reverence Christ as Lord (1 Peter 3:8-16)

Saturday, June 2—God Knows Our Journey (Psalm 1)

Sunday, June 3—Strive for Peace With All (Hebrews 12:12-17)

THE UNPOPULAR ROAD

I shall be telling this with a sigh
Somewhere ages and ages hence:
Two roads converged in a wood, and I—
I took the one less traveled by,
And that has made all the difference.

These oft-quoted words of the great American poet, Robert Frost, are from his poem entitled, "The Road Not Taken." The author was expressing his thankfulness for having chosen the more difficult, less traveled road of life, since it had led to more fulfillment.

Many years earlier, the psalmist spoke of two roads that stand before all men. The first, the way of the wicked, leads away from God, and those who take it will be condemned. The second, the way of the righteous, leads to blessing and eternal life, which God will bestow on those who travel it.

The key to the psalmist's pointed words lies in the fact that all persons are faced with a choice. We can take the path that is beaten down and made wide, and be accompanied by many travelers; or we can choose "The Road Not Taken." This latter road promises at times to be steep, narrow, and lonely. It may cause its travelers a great deal of difficulty. Yet to those who willingly choose it, and persevere, it will make a great deal of difference; for this is the road that leads to life.

—T. T.

Conclusion

A. No Middle Road

Just two ways of life are pictured in the First Psalm—the way of the godly, which endures, and the way of the ungodly, which dissipates and disappears. There is no semi-righteous path or a way that is only partly wicked. We have only the choice between that which is holy and wholesome, and that which debases and destroys.

Again and again the Biblical revelation points out the necessity of *choice*. Moses said to the Hebrews before his death, "I have set before you life and death, blessing and cursing: therefore choose life" (Deuteronomy 30:19). Joshua confronted the people of his time with the words, "Choose you this day whom ye will serve" (Joshua 24:15). On Mount Carmel, Elijah asked, "How long halt ye between two opinions?" (1 Kings 18:21). He insisted that the people had to make a choice. Jesus affirmed that there are two "gates," which open upon two different roadways—one leading to life, the other to destruction (Matthew 7:13, 14).

No one ever drifted into righteousness or dozed into an increasing awareness of God. To

visual 1

decide not to walk in God's way is to choose to go in the way of failure and frustration in life. The fact that the choice between these two ways of life is pointed out often in Scripture underscores our Heavenly Father's desire that we make right choices as His children. It should not be thought that the divergent ways we face in our choice of life's path is presented to us in a cold, neutral manner. God loves us and He wants us to choose the way that will bless us and save us.

After Moses outlined the alternative "lifestyles" to Israel, he didn't add, "And it's indifferent to me what you choose," or, "You will have to choose, I don't care." Rather, he closed with a note of pleading and entreaty, "Therefore choose life!" So God calls us today to come to life and blessing and salvation by following Jesus along the path of release, radiance and redemption.

B. Prayer

Our Father, we come with a new awareness of the inevitable alternate paths that open before us through life. May we choose to walk with the Son of God in His way of humility, spirituality, simplicity, and helpfulness. Keep us, we pray, from those ways where "sin's allurement is." Save us from pride, selfishness, and greed. Grant us the persistence to practice righteousness with enthusiasm and to turn from the sordid and the crass.

Dear Lord, help us to find joy and peace in believing. May part of that joy be found in assisting others to be joyful, and may our peace make us ever more willing to bring the Prince of Peace to others. It is in His name that we pray. Amen.

C. Thought to Remember

We need to realize that even now we are walking in one of the two ways of life described by the psalmist in today's text. May we make sure it is the right one.

Learning by Doing

This page contains an alternate lesson plan emphasizing learning activities. Classes desiring such student involvement will find these suggestions helpful.

Learning Goals

In this lesson, the students will:

1. Chart the characteristics of the godly and the ungodly, as seen in Psalm 1.

2. Be encouraged to commit themselves to reading and meditating upon Scripture daily.

3. Be challenged to walk more fully in the way of righteousness.

Into the Lesson

Divide your students into groups of four and have them discuss these questions in their groups: "When is the best time for you to read or study the Bible?" and "Why is this the best time for you?" After allowing two or three minutes for sharing, call the class to order and instruct them to discuss the following in their groups: "To what degree is it possible to read the Bible faithfully and yet live a life that is contrary to its teachings?" Give the groups about five minutes for discussion, then ask one group to share its conclusions. Following this initial report, ask if there is any group whose views were different. Encourage them to speak out.

Have a volunteer read Psalm 1:2 aloud. Point out that the psalmist indicates that one of the characteristics of the blessed and godly person is that he meditates upon God's law day and night. Ideally, our life-style should be shaped by what we learn from God's Word, but in reality this does not always occur. Call upon another volunteer to read James 1:22 aloud.

Into the Word

On the chalkboard or an overhead projector transparency, make a chart with two adjacent vertical columns. In one column, list the blessed man's characteristics that are mentioned in Psalm 1. Encourage your class members to find these qualities and share them aloud as you record their findings. (There are three characteristics in verse 1 and three more in verse 3.) Then have the class find the ungodly man's characteristics (see verses 4 and 5), and write these in the other column.

Single out the characteristic, "Whatsoever he doeth shall prosper," and ask the following question: "To what extent, if any, are Christians promised that they will prosper?" After the class has responded, remind them that material prosperity as a result of godliness is basically a concept found in the Old Testament. With the coming of Christ, a fuller understanding unfolded. His was a life of poverty, but He prospered spiritually, and His followers were promised spiritual prosperity as they receive the forgiveness of sins and the gift of eternal life.

Into Life

Encourage class members to determine if they are walking on the right path as outlined in Psalm 1. Reproduce and distribute the following evaluation statements and ask each student to rate himself or herself. Tell them to mark an X under the word that represents their response to each statement. After they have completed their marking, instruct them to connect the X'S with a line. The line will show the kind of spiritual path they are presently walking.

1. I ask the advice of ungodly persons concerning vital decisions in my life.

Never   Occasionally   Frequently   Always

2. I tend to follow the crowd.

Never   Occasionally   Frequently   Always

3. I form close relationships with those who are scornful and contemptuous.

Never   Occasionally   Frequently   Always

4. I have difficulty in making time to read or study the Bible.

Never   Occasionally   Frequently   Always

5. My life seems to bear little or no fruit for Jesus Christ.

Never   Occasionally   Frequently   Always

After your students have had adequate time to rate themselves, comment that the average Christian's rating may show a somewhat crooked way. The ideal rating is a straight line connecting the *nevers*. Close the study of the lesson by asking each person to choose one item on the rating scale that he or she would like to improve. Suggest that work be done on that one item exclusively during the month of June. Dismiss the class with a time of silent prayer, during which class members can dedicate themselves to change and improvement with the Lord's help.

Let's Talk It Over

The questions on this page are designed to encourage review of the lesson Scriptures and to promote discussion of the lesson by the class. The answers provided are only discussion starters. Let your class talk it over from there.

1. Psalm 1:1 seems to describe a kind of progression that some people follow on their way to increasing sinful involvement and rebellion against God. How can we warn people about the danger of becoming caught up in this progression?

Some Bible teachers see an illustration of this danger in the experience of Lot, Abram's nephew. Genesis 13:11, 12 tells us that Lot separated from Abram and "dwelt in the cities of the plain, and pitched his tent toward Sodom." A little later (Genesis 14:12) we find Lot dwelling *in* the wicked city of Sodom, and in 19:1 he is described as sitting in the city gate, indicating he had become a leading citizen of Sodom. While he apparently did not partake of the worst of Sodom's sins, he put himself and his family in tremendous moral and physical peril by his choice to live there. We must stress today that it is possible to walk "in the counsel of the ungodly" by focusing our attention too long on the literature, entertainment, conversation, and goals, etc. that are produced and espoused by ungodly people. That focus can result in our standing up for the principles of sinners, and at last in our practicing such principles.

2. Why is it important to stress the fact that prosperity from the New Testament standpoint looks beyond material success and physical well-being to the far-superior blessings of the spiritual realm?

The New Testament does not exclude material success as an aim for Christians. Jesus in Matthew 6:33 and the apostle Paul in 1 Timothy 6:17 show the legitimacy of acquiring and enjoying material goods. But some New Testament believers appear to place too great an emphasis on material possessions, while neglecting the greater goal of spiritual enrichment. Material prosperity may contribute to our spiritual growth, if we respond to it with continual thanksgiving and with faithful stewardship to God. But the absence of material prosperity may result in even richer spiritual advantages. It may be that the lack of what we regard as necessities will be a benefit to us if such lack strengthens our dependence on God. A period of ill health may prove invaluable in causing us to awaken to the sufferings of others. The loss of some precious material possession may lead us to put greater emphasis on laying up treasures in Heaven (Matthew 6:20).

3. With our jam-packed schedules, how can we find ways to meditate on God's Word day and night?

While "day and night" is an expression that speaks of constant attention to the Scriptures, it suggests for us the use of early morning and late evening as excellent occasions for meditation. We may need to arise thirty minutes or so earlier than normal to allow time for this important spiritual exercise. Perhaps it will be necessary to wash our faces, do some physical exercise, or get a cup of coffee or tea to help stir our minds to alertness. If we will give ourselves time to "soak in" Biblical truth at the outset of the day, we may find it recurring in our thoughts at appropriate moments during the day. A nighttime effort at meditation can be especially valuable, since it may prove effective in generating a sense of peace and relaxation that will contribute to restful sleep. It is certainly better to occupy our thoughts at bedtime with Scriptural truths and promises than to worry about what the coming day might bring.

4. How can we help those who choose to follow Jesus Christ see that their choice involves a lifelong commitment?

Much has been said and written about the "back door of the church." It is a distressing fact that many who receive Jesus Christ as Savior and enter the fellowship of the church soon drift away and resume the life-styles they participated in prior to their decision for Christ. It is true also that many more Christians, who sporadically continue to attend the church's services, demonstrate few of the other characteristics of discipleship. These circumstances suggest that in our evangelistic efforts we must point out more clearly that Jesus Christ calls us to absolute commitment. Perhaps we need to make more frequent usage of passages such as Luke 14:25-33 as we invite people to become followers of Jesus. That might reduce the number responding to the invitation, but those who would choose to follow Jesus would be more likely to develop into genuine disciples.

Justice Will Prevail

LESSON SCRIPTURE: Psalm 37.

PRINTED TEXT: Psalm 37:1-11.

Psalm 37:1-11

1 Fret not thyself because of evildoers, neither be thou envious against the workers of iniquity.

2 For they shall soon be cut down like the grass, and wither as the green herb.

3 Trust in the Lord, and do good; so shalt thou dwell in the land, and verily thou shalt be fed.

4 Delight thyself also in the Lord; and he shall give thee the desires of thine heart.

5 Commit thy way unto the Lord; trust also in him; and he shall bring it to pass.

6 And he shall bring forth thy righteousness as the light, and thy judgment as the noonday.

7 Rest in the Lord, and wait patiently for him: fret not thyself because of him who prospereth in his way, because of the man who bringeth wicked devices to pass.

8 Cease from anger, and forsake wrath: fret not thyself in any wise to do evil.

9 For evildoers shall be cut off: but those that wait upon the Lord, they shall inherit the earth.

10 For yet a little while, and the wicked shall not be: yea, thou shalt diligently consider his place, and it shall not be.

11 But the meek shall inherit the earth; and shall delight themselves in the abundance of peace.

GOLDEN TEXT: The Lord loveth judgment, and forsaketh not his saints.—Psalm 37:28.

Wisdom as a Way of Life
Unit 1: Wisdom in the Psalms
(Lessons 1-3)

Lesson Aims

As a result of this lesson, the students should:

1. Understand why they should not envy the prosperity of the wicked.

2. Have greater trust in God and commitment to Him.

Lesson Outline

INTRODUCTION

    A. Rx for Defeatism

    B. Lesson Background

I. FIRST SYMPTOMS—SUGGESTED REMEDIES (Psalm 37:1-6)

    A. Unrest and Envy (vv. 1, 2)

       Envy's Revenge

    B. Trust in the Lord (vv. 3-5)

    C. Promised Improvement (v. 6)

       Two Views of Life

II. SECONDARY SYMPTOMS AND HELP (Psalm 37:7-11)

    A. Dismay at Sinners' Success (v. 7)

    B. Correctives Commended (vv. 8-10)

    C. Endurance and Enjoyment (v. 11)

CONCLUSION

    A. Long-term Investments

    B. Prayer

    C. Thought to Remember

Visual 2 in the visuals packet is designed to be used with the Conclusion section. The visual is shown on page 357.

Introduction

A. Rx for Defeatism

Who among us has not taken notice of the seemingly good fortune of many evil people? And who has not, at one time or another, envied their good fortune? We see gamblers, drug dealers, crime "bosses," and other unsavory characters displaying every evidence of prosperity. They own luxurious homes in exclusive areas, drive powerful cars, employ skilled financial advisors and attorneys, and dine in sumptuous restaurants. Why should such persons flourish, while many godly people live in harsh and strained circumstances, hampered by high costs and low incomes? Certainly it is not difficult to become "envious against the workers of iniquity" (Psalm 37:1) and to resent the fact that the person "who bringeth wicked devices to pass" still "prospereth in his way" (v. 7).

Psalm 37 is a valuable prescription against this malady. It contains repeated reminders that the apparent success of the wicked is only temporary. Further, it indicates that trust in God, delight in Him, commitment to His way, stillness or rest in Him, and continued hope in Him will bring blessings abundant. The ultimate assurance is that the one who looks to God in obedient faith will know lasting joy and the possession of all that is most worthwhile on earth. These blessings will be crowned and fulfilled by the possession of a profound sense of peace.

B. Lesson Background

Psalm 37 is an alphabetical psalm in form and a "wisdom" psalm in content. In the Hebrew text, several psalms are so arranged that successive stanzas begin with the letters of the Hebrew alphabet in order. Psalms of this type are 9, 25, 34, 37, 111, 112, 119, and 145.

Of course, Psalm 119 is the most unusual and intricate illustration of this literary device. In that psalm there are twenty-two stanzas with eight verses in each stanza. Every verse in the first stanza begins with the first letter of the Hebrew alphabet. Every verse in the second stanza begins with the second letter of the Hebrew alphabet, and so on through all twenty-two stanzas. No explanation is given for the alphabetic structure of these psalms, but it is presumed that they were so arranged as an aid to memorization.

Psalm 37 is also one of the "wisdom" psalms, about which comment was made in the Lesson Background section of last week's lesson. As in the first Psalm, the major stress in this psalm is on God as the *reason* for some of the questions men raise, and as the one who is the *answer* to those same queries.

I. First Symptoms—Suggested Remedies (Psalm 37:1-6)

A. Unrest and Envy (vv. 1, 2)

1. Fret not thyself because of evildoers, neither be thou envious against the workers of iniquity.

To *fret* is to turn things over in the mind repeatedly in such a way that one's inner peace and calm are "rubbed raw" by some irritating thought. If the thought is allowed to go unchecked it will continue to chafe the soul and rob one of tranquility of life.

In this instance, the psalmist cautioned against undue concern regarding persistent, seeming prosperity of evil persons. God has indicated that whatever the righteous man does "shall prosper" (Psalm 1:3). Yet, often those who are not righteous appear to prosper also; in fact, sometimes they seem to prosper more than the godly. Why should a God who is holy and who wants men not to steal, not to bear false witness, and to serve Him above all, allow evil men to flourish, even sometimes to take advantage of those who are sincerely striving to live according to God's commands?

2. For they shall soon be cut down like the grass, and wither as the green herb.

When we understand that the seemingly favorable lot of evil people is only temporary, we can see the folly of being alarmed or envious of them. The grass seems so green, almost pulsating with life; but as soon as it is cut down, it begins to become dry and brown. Green vegetables begin to decay after being picked. So the wicked may appear invulnerable, attractive, and vibrant, but their condition is subject to sudden change. A drop in prices, a change in the public's buying habits, or a plunge of the stock market can quickly alter the circumstances of such persons' lives. Sudden physical illnesses, and natural catastrophes occur frequently. All of these factors and many more may at any time turn blessings into bitterness, and triumphs into tragedies. But even if the wicked live long and prosper all the while, how can even that length of time be compared with eternity?

ENVY'S REVENGE

Admiration and envy are closely related, yet they are never the same. The one, admiration, is a virtue; the other, envy, a vice. While we are taught to admire those who have qualities worth imitating, we are never permitted to envy anyone, the good or the bad.

Envy can have disastrous results. Dr. Seuss, in one of his children's books, has a character named Grinch. Grinch is a jealous sort, one who can't bear the sight of anyone's enjoying himself. When he sees someone doing so, it makes him so angry he bites himself! Admittedly, that is unusual conduct, but it does help us see that envy often turns on itself. Said another way, "Envy shoots at others and wounds itself."

While it is wise to admire the good, it is foolish to envy the evil. Psalm 37 explains why the latter is true. Instead of fretting about evil ones and envying their prosperity, David admonishes us to, "Trust in the Lord and do good" (v. 3); "Delight ... in the Lord" (v. 4); and, "Hope in the Lord" (v. 9, *New International Version*).

Hopefully, such conduct may cause many to admire you and want to imitate you.   —T. T.

B. Trust in the Lord (vv. 3-5)

3. Trust in the Lord, and do good; so shalt thou dwell in the land, and verily thou shalt be fed.

In the Old Testament, *trust* is a word that has much the same meaning as *faith* in the New Testament. That faith is more than intellectual belief; it involves an obedient throwing of oneself on God's love and care. In "the faith that works," James sees the example of that yieldedness and submissive devotion involved in *trust* in the Lord (James 2:17-20, 24, 26). Characteristically of the Old Testament, the reward of trusting the Lord is that one shall *dwell in the land*. God's covenant with Israel involved the conquest and inhabitation of Palestine. He had promised them that they would dwell safely in that land, so long as they honored Him and lived according to His laws.

For the Hebrew people, the promise was also that they would *be fed* from the bountiful harvests they would enjoy in "the land flowing with milk and honey." As Christians, trust in Christ leads to spiritual nourishment. Jesus said, "I am the living bread which came down from heaven: if any man eat of this bread, he shall live for ever: and the bread that I will give is my flesh, which I will give for the life of the world" (John 6:51).

4. Delight thyself also in the Lord; and he shall give thee the desires of thine heart.

The person whose life is surrendered to God will find joy in that submission. To think of God will not be painful, but pleasant. To do God's will will not be something to be endured, but enjoyed. Many who have undertaken tasks for God have found such duties to be wings that have lifted them up rather than weights that have brought them down.

The promise here is that God will give the one who delights in Him *the desires of [his] heart.* The person whose life is focused on the Lord is the only one to whom this assurance could be given. God cannot give the unregenerate person his inner wishes, because they are evil. But to the one who trusts in Him, God can make such a pledge. Yearnings to know God more fully, earnest desires to do His bidding, and efforts to love and help His children more effectively— such wishes God can bless and forward.

5. Commit thy way unto the Lord; trust also in him; and he shall bring it to pass.

Again the psalmist urges that we surrender our wills to God, and trust in His purpose to use and bless our lives. If we do this, the outcome will be clear and unmistakable in its goodness. The *New International Version* translation of this and the following verse makes it clear that the *way* commended in verse 5 is revealed in the blessings described in verse 6.

C. Promised Improvement (v. 6)

6. And he shall bring forth thy righteousness as the light, and thy judgment as the noonday.

The *light* is that which enables everyone to see clearly, and at no time is the light of the sun brighter than at *noonday*. At present, those who are evil may seem to prosper, and the righteous may seem to be overshadowed by clouds and darkness; but in God's own time He will reveal the righteousness of His people. The justice of their cause will shine as brightly as the sun, and all injustice in this life will be remedied.

Two Views of Life

Doubtless the pleasure is as great
of being cheated as to cheat.

These are words of the poet Samuel Butler, written in the seventeenth century. There may be some who would agree with him, but surely not the majority. Frankly, I find no pleasure in the thought of either one. I do not enjoy being cheated, nor do I cheat others.

In that same century, the poet John Dryden portrayed the thoughts of a pessimist with these words:

When I consider life, 'tis all a cheat;
Yet, fool'd with hope, men favor the deceit;
Trust on, and think tomorrow will repay.

I suppose most pessimists feel they are being realistic in describing all of life as a cheat. And, apart from God, perhaps the pessimist can make a case for his dark view of life. Too often in this life, the righteous suffer and the evil prosper. Seeing this happen, or, experiencing it, can cast one into a dark mood and cause him "to suffer seasickness during the rest of his journey of life."

There is, however, a brighter view of life, one that takes God into consideration. The psalmist urges us to believe in God and anchor our hope in Him. If we do, we will not be "fool'd with hope," but rewarded by it.   —T. T.

II. Secondary Symptoms and Help (Psalm 37:7-11)

A. Dismay at Sinners' Success (v. 7)

7. Rest in the Lord, and wait patiently for him: fret not thyself because of him who prospereth in his way, because of the man who bringeth wicked devices to pass.

To *rest* here means "be silent." The idea presented is that one should not whine or complain. The seeming success of evil persons, the apparently favorable outcome of their devious devices, tends to vex the righteous and draw complaints from them (see Job 12:6; 21:7-9; 24:2-12). Many times we find ourselves aghast as some obvious wrongdoing has gone unpunished and has even seemed to have been rewarded. "How can they get away with that?" we object. "Is there absolutely *no* justice?" The psalmist encourages us to be content to wait the Lord's time, when He will set all things right.

B. Correctives Commended (vv. 8-10)

8. Cease from anger, and forsake wrath: fret not thyself in any wise to do evil.

We are cautioned not to react angrily when we see the prosperity of the wicked. If allowed to run its course, such agitation of life can lead to unwise actions. We may even be tempted to say, "If that's the way things are, I might as well cheat or misrepresent some matters myself. Those who are dishonest are getting away with it and are much more successful than people who try to do the right thing." *The New English Bible* translates this last clause, "Strive not to outdo in evildoing." So the psalmist calls us to greater patience and a keener perception of the ultimate outcome of such behavior.

Notice that the expression *fret not* is used again in this verse. This is the third time the psalmist employs it in the first eight verses of this psalm. (Others are in verses 1 and 7.) Regarding our reaction to the apparent successes of evildoers, perhaps one could say, "The more faith, the less fret."

9. For evildoers shall be cut off: but those that wait upon the Lord, they shall inherit the earth.

The psalmist insists that, in spite of every appearance to the contrary, those who do evil shall not go unpunished forever. In our own lifetime, we have seen many people *cut off*, who at one time were perpetrators of injustice and who seemed invulnerable to judgment because of their positions and power. Mussolini seemed entrenched in authority, but was executed and hung by the heels in Milan. Hitler controlled vast armies and ruled as *Der Fuhrer*, but died a suicide amid the ruins of his own capital city. Because of wrongdoing, presidents and vice-presidents of the United States have been driven from office. Congressmen have been imprisoned. Even judges have gone from their high positions to the ignominy of confinement in penitentiaries.

The *New International Version* translates the last part of this verse, "those who hope in the Lord will inherit the land." So we are urged not only to be patient when evil appears to flourish, but to be mindful that our real hope is in God.

visual 2

I.R.A.
FOR THE RIGHTEOUS

INHERITANCE
TO BE RECEIVED (v. 9)

RIGHTEOUSNESS
TO BE REVEALED (v. 10)

ABUNDANCE
OF PEACE TO BE ENJOYED (v. 11)

After all, we can expect God's ultimate blessing to be *ours* if we truly are *His*. Hope is essentially future-oriented. If we become despondent when we observe the prosperity of the wicked, it is because we are looking at the *present only*. The future of the wicked is only one of frustration and failure; their success is only temporary, and their deficient characters will be a curse to them forever. The person who trusts in God and looks to Him will find peace, joy, satisfaction, and serenity. The godly person experiences these now in some measure, and will find their complete fulfillment in the "new heavens and . . . new earth, wherein dwelleth righteousness" (2 Peter 3:13).

10. For yet a little while, and the wicked shall not be: yea, thou shalt diligently consider his place, and it shall not be.

The thought of verse 2 is repeated here. When God renders the final judgment of all human life, the wicked shall be swept away.

C. Endurance and Enjoyment (v. 11)

11. But the meek shall inherit the earth; and shall delight themselves in the abundance of peace.

The Hebrew word here translated *meek* seems to mean poor, lowly, or less favored. The Greek expression appears to carry with it the ideas of submissiveness and capability of being easily controlled. In both testaments, the quality indicated is the opposite of being high, haughty, arrogant, or unbending. Here we see an apparent clash with reality, as many understand it. To say that people who are of lowly demeanor, quiet, patient, and undemanding, will receive inner strength or know a quietude of spirit, is one thing. But to indicate that such persons *shall inherit the earth* seems to be contrary to the facts. Do not the assertive, the demanding, the ones determined to receive their "rights" have their way and "get ahead" in the world?

Of course, it depends on whether one takes a short view or a long one, whether one looks at externals only or is aware of the deeper dimensions of life. Many times, advances won by clamor and self-promotion are given with reluctance and utilized in an atmosphere of animosity or hostile cooperation. But the person who renders quiet service and helpfulness will win a place in the hearts of co-workers and companions that is affectionate and enduring.

Meekness does not mean weakness, but strength that has come under the control of a spirit yielded to God. Moses is said to have been unusually meek: "Now the man Moses was very meek, above all the men which were upon the face of the earth" (Numbers 12:3). Moses was fired with indignation and killed an Egyptian who was beating an Israelite. Yet the proud, violent prince of Egypt learned patience and humility tending sheep for four long decades in the desert. He still could be wrathful, as was illustrated by his reaction to the Israelites' worship of Aaron's golden calf. But he was one who had learned to listen to God and to obey Him.

Jesus illustrated meekness in a beautiful way, too. He was willing to be a servant to men, to touch the diseased, to cleanse the sinful, and to bear suffering and loss for mankind. Yet He blazed with anger at men's "hardness of heart" and also expelled the money changers from the temple, overthrowing their tables and driving out the sheep and cattle. It may be significant that Heavenly victors are pictured as singing "the song of Moses the servant of God, and the song of the Lamb" (Revelation 15:3).

R. H. Fisher wrote, "The conquerors can get the outside trappings of earthly possession; but what do they really gain even of the world they seek? . . . A man may seem to have inherited the earth when he has gained nothing more than some new anxieties and burdens to fill his days with pain. 'Dost thou wish to possess the earth?' asked St. Augustine. 'Beware, lest the earth possess thee.' But the meek enter into a fuller inheritance of the earth, even the treasures of its honour and love."

In his book, *The Beatitudes*, Dr. Elbert Russell pointed out that the classical Greek word for *meek* in Jesus' echoing of this Old Testament verse is an expression relating to the "breaking" of horses. A horse was said to be "meeked" when it was subdued so it could be bridled, saddled, and ridden, or when it could be harnessed for drawing carts or wagons. "The underlying contrast is between the wild 'unbroken' animals and those which have learned to work with and for man" (p. 49). So the student who refuses to submit himself to the disciplines of study will have a poor academic record. The athlete who refuses to conform to the rules of a game will be disqualified. The driver who ignores traffic laws and drives "wildly" will be arrested. Only those willing to be *meek*, in the sense of controlled or cooperative, will *inherit* any earthly blessing or quiet status.

Our text tells us the *meek* also will *delight themselves in the abundance of peace.* Rebellion against the way of the Lord and imitation of the behavior of the unrighteous are certain paths to unrest and disruption in life. Isaiah said, "The wicked are like the troubled sea, when it cannot rest, whose waters cast up mire and dirt. There is no peace, saith my God, to the wicked" (57:20, 21). They may appear prosperous or popular or powerful, but they have little peace. Cheating, lying, deceitfulness, selfishness, pride—all these lead to instability and an underlying sense of insecurity. Only those who are obedient to God—honest, faithful, sharing, humble people—can find the peace that stills the spirit, calms the soul, and brings to us supportive, encouraging, and comforting friends. Truly abundant peace is the *delight* of the *meek.*

Conclusion

A. Long-term Investments

Direct the class's attention to visual 2 in the visuals packet as you present the thoughts in this section.

Many a person has invested money in some sort of "retirement account." The money may be invested in insurance, bonds, a pension plan, or the more recent Individual Retirement Account (IRA). These arrangements do not promise quick financial returns. Instead, the investment programs are designed so that they will "pay off" in years to come. Eventually, perhaps after a person has paid in to the account for many years, the time of retirement arrives, and the income from the years of "paying in" begins to appear. Month after month, a check comes to that person—the result of the planning and preparation made in his or her earlier years of life.

The mode of life recommended in Psalm 37 is quite like that. We are cautioned not to envy those who are squandering their lives pursuing present pleasures and who have no regard for their spiritual future. The psalmist exhorts us to trust in God, to commit ourselves to Him, and to continue quietly and joyfully in well-doing; to make preparations for that time in the future when God will reveal the shallowness of those who placed their trust in this life, and will reward those who, by obeying Him, wisely planned for their eternal future. Eventually the rewards of a disciplined life will bring rich and continued contentment and quiet delight. Paul

Home Daily Bible Readings

Monday, June 4—Delight in the Lord (Psalm 37:1-6)

Tuesday, June 5—Wait Patiently for God (Psalm 37:7-11)

Wednesday, June 6—God Loves Justice (Psalm 37:27-31)

Thursday, June 7—God's Vindication (Luke 18:1-8)

Friday, June 8—"God, Be Merciful" (Luke 18:9-14)

Saturday, June 9—God Cares for Us (1 Peter 5:6-11)

Sunday, June 10—God Sustains Us (Psalm 55:1-8, 16-22)

stated, "Godliness is profitable unto all things, having promise of the life that now is, and of that which is to come" (1 Timothy 4:8).

Of course, many of the qualities commended in Psalm 37 are summed up in the Christian concept of love. It is this love that suffers long and is kind, is not puffed up, does not behave in a rude manner, does not just seek its own benefit, etc. The earnest William Cowper wrote,

Our days are numbered, let us spare
Our anxious hearts a needless care:
'Tis Thine to number out our days;
Ours to give them to Thy praise.

Love is our only business here,
Love, simple, constant, and sincere;
O blessed days Thy servants see,
Spent, O Lord! in pleasing Thee.

B. Prayer

Our Heavenly Father, we are grateful for Your love for us, which is seen in the gift of Jesus as our Savior and Lord. We are also thankful for the unfailing testimony to Your creative wisdom, which the wonders of the natural world constantly present to our inquiring minds. But we ask forgiveness for the mistrust and unrest we feel when we see the prosperity and power of evil men. Enlighten our understanding, Lord, that we may see that all such arrogant and unrighteous prominence and power is temporary. Help us to possess the qualities of trust, commitment, delight, patience, and hope, which will clarify our perspectives and confirm our faith. In Jesus' name, amen.

C. Thought to Remember

The roadway of the irreligious seems paved with gold, but it leads to eternal doom. Only committed trust in God leads to liberty and life.

Learning by Doing

This page contains an alternate lesson plan emphasizing learning activities. Classes desiring such student involvement will find these suggestions helpful.

Learning Goals

As a result of studying this lesson, each student should be able to do the following:

1. Be able to list several reasons for not being troubled by or envious of the prosperity of the wicked.

2. Memorize Bible verses that will strengthen them against the temptation to be envious.

Into the Lesson

Bring a bag of donuts and distribute some of them on napkins to a select few in the class before the session begins. Instruct them to display the donuts prominently, but not to eat them, or share with others, or give any explanation as to why they have the donuts. After a few moments, during which other class members may comment on the scarcity of donuts or ask about their share, go around to those holding donuts and have them return them to the bag. Ask those who did not receive a donut to share how they felt when they saw some get one and yet they themselves had been offered nothing. Explain that this brief exercise underscores how easy it is to envy others. Add that there are enough donuts for everyone and that they will be shared at the end of class time.

Into the Word

Direct the class to read Psalm 37:1-3. Ask, What attitude and action are recommended in place of being upset by and envious of the prosperity of the wicked. (Trust in the Lord and do good.) Elaborate upon why trust is a good substitute for envy.

Comment that not much is said in Psalm 37:1-11 about what will happen to the wicked, but many verses are devoted to what the attitudes and actions of the righteous should be. Distribute index cards, and ask each student to make a list of the key verbs or phrases in verses 4-8 that are instructions given to the righteous. After allowing a few moments for this, ask the students to state them aloud. As they do, write the words on the chalkboard. They are *delight, commit, trust, rest, wait, fret not, cease, forsake.* Have the students reread the verses and note how many of the instructions pertain to the righteous person's attitude or relationship to God. (Five of them do. Only three relate to one's actions or attitudes toward others.) Underline the five directives

and mention that you will say more about them later. Point out that verse 8 implies that fretting about the prosperity of the wicked may result in our doing evil.

Now have a volunteer read verses 1-11 aloud, while the class listens and notes which three verses tell of the punishment of evildoers (vv. 2, 9, 10). Let the class discuss this question: When does the retribution for their wicked ways occur in the lives of evildoers? After some discussion, remind the class that God does not *always* settle His accounts during a person's earthly existence. For some, divine retribution may be delayed until Judgment Day. This delay may cause the righteous to become indignant about the unfairness of life. However, this delayed retribution further underlines the importance of concentrating upon our relationship to God rather than upon how others are prospering. Indicate that the rewards of the righteous are recorded in verses 6, 9, and 11. Ask what they are. (Their righteousness will be seen, they will inherit the earth, and they will live in peace.)

Into Life

Divide the class into five study groups. Assign to each group one of the directives underlined earlier. Have them construct a real life situation that illustrates how one would act if he applied the assigned directive to a troublesome experience in life. Here is an example to guide the groups: A young couple pledged to give $75.00 a month to the support of a missionary in Asia. The husband has since lost his job, and the couple must rely upon the income from the wife's job to support them. If they are following the directive of committing their way unto the Lord, they will continue to give their $75.00 to the missionary and will reduce their other obligations and their personal and recreational expenses. They will rely upon God to see them through.

Let the groups share with the whole class the real life situations they construct.

Lead the class members in finding three Bible verses that can serve as steps to deeper trust and commitment to God. Possible verses are Matthew 6:33, Philippians 4:19, and Hebrews 13:5. Suggest that these verses be memorized during the coming week and put to work in daily life.

Let's Talk It Over

The questions on this page are designed to encourage review of the lesson Scriptures and to promote discussion of the lesson by the class. The answers provided are only discussion starters. Let your class talk it over from there.

1. Why is the verb *fret* an appropriate term to describe the reaction we may have toward evil persons who prosper?

"Do not fret because of evil men" (Psalm 37:1, *New International Version*). We have a nagging, gnawing feeling that life is unfair, when we see outright sinners enjoying more of this world's blessings than ourselves. The communications media have expanded and intensified this feeling. By means of newspapers, magazines, and television we obtain a closer look at prominent people throughout the land who spurn God's laws and outwardly bask in wealth and fame. If we allow it, this constant exposure can chill the fervor of our praise to God and cause us to lose sight of the superior worth of spiritual blessings. We need to be aware of the presence of this irritating feeling and deal with it before it spreads and affects our entire beings.

2. Is it appropriate for us to express satisfaction when the wicked suffer a downfall? How can we make sure our attitudes are proper in regard to this?

In Proverbs 24:17, 18 we have this warning: "Do not gloat when your enemy falls; when he stumbles, do not let your heart rejoice, or the Lord will see and disapprove and turn his wrath away from him" *(New International Version)*. It seems that a distinction may be made between the personal desire to see judgment visited on an enemy and the general wish to see justice fairly administered in our society. We may take a measure of satisfaction when a criminal is apprehended and sentenced for his crimes. Or we may sense the fitness when an immoral person reaps the harvest of wild oats sown. But rather than rejoice over such calamities, we should pray that the wrongdoer's downfall will prove to be the means by which he or she will be led to repentance and surrender to God.

3. How may we delight in the Lord?

One way is to take delight in reading, understanding, and obeying His Word. Psalm 119:16, 24, 35 remind us that this is a proper attitude to take toward our reading of the Bible. Another activity that offers a means of delighting in the Lord is our public worship. Our attitude should be like that of the psalmist, when he confessed, "I was glad when they said unto me, Let us go into the house of the Lord" (Psalm 122:1). If we enter into worship with the attitude "Let's get this over with, because I have other things to do," we will experience little godly delight. We may also delight in the Lord by the way we serve one another. We may apply Paul's exhortation to the Colossians at this point: "Whatsoever ye do, do it heartily, as to the Lord, and not unto men" (Colossians 3:23).

4. The psalmist exhorts us to "rest in the Lord." What does this involve?

The *New International Version* renders the first statement in Psalm 37:7, "Be still before the Lord and wait patiently for him." So the picture is not of a person resting after a day of toil. Instead, we may see this invitation to rest in the Lord as a matter of depending on Him to handle the ultimate issues of justice. There are times when justice is fairly administered here on earth, but on other occasions justice is thwarted. This is frustrating, but we can rest in the assurance that the Judge who sees all will ultimately "judge the secrets of men by Jesus Christ" (Romans 2:16).

5. How can we cultivate the attitude of meekness?

One of the first steps is to recognize that meekness is not equivalent to weakness. It is quite the opposite—a sign of true strength. Solomon expresses that fact in these words: "Better a patient man than a warrior, a man who controls his temper than one who takes a city" (Proverbs 16:32, *New International Version*). Another step is to investigate the example Jesus provided. Of Him, Peter wrote, "When he was reviled, [he] reviled not again; when he suffered, he threatened not" (1 Peter 2:23). Prayer is a major step. We can probably think of circumstances in which we tend to become hostile or argumentative. Or we may be able to identify people whose personalities so affect us as to make us irritable and unduly critical. We need to pray with honesty and humility about our reaction to these.

No Security Without God

LESSON SCRIPTURE: Psalm 49.

PRINTED TEXT: Psalm 49:1-15.

Psalm 49:1-15

1 Hear this, all ye people; give ear, all ye inhabitants of the world:

2 Both low and high, rich and poor, together.

3 My mouth shall speak of wisdom; and the meditation of my heart shall be of understanding.

4 I will incline mine ear to a parable: I will open my dark saying upon the harp.

5 Wherefore should I fear in the days of evil, when the iniquity of my heels shall compass me about?

6 They that trust in their wealth, and boast themselves in the multitude of their riches;

7 None of them can by any means redeem his brother, nor give to God a ransom for him:

8 (For the redemption of their soul is precious, and it ceaseth for ever:)

9 That he should still live for ever, and not see corruption.

10 For he seeth that wise men die, likewise the fool and the brutish person perish, and leave their wealth to others.

11 Their inward thought is, that their houses shall continue for ever, and their dwelling places to all generations; they call their lands after their own names.

12 Nevertheless man being in honor abideth not: he is like the beasts that perish.

13 This their way is their folly: yet their posterity approve their sayings.   Selah.

14 Like sheep they are laid in the grave; death shall feed on them; and the upright shall have dominion over them in the morning; and their beauty shall consume in the grave from their dwelling.

15 But God will redeem my soul from the power of the grave: for he shall receive me.   Selah.

GOLDEN TEXT: God will redeem my soul from the power of the grave: for he shall receive me.—Psalm 49:15.

Wisdom as a Way of Life
Unit 1: Wisdom in the Psalms
(Lessons 1-3)

Lesson Aims

This lesson will:

1. Point out the folly of placing our trust in riches.

2. Help the class see that our security in life and death is found only in God.

Lesson Outline

Display visual 3 from the visuals packet. It illustrates the thought that Christian hope far outweighs any temporal security one can buy. The visual is shown on page 365.

Introduction

A. The Search for Security

Across the ages, mankind has been aware of the uncertainties of existence and has looked for protection from those things that threatened. So, men sought caves as refuges from rain and sleet. They built fires at night to ward off nocturnal wild beasts. Shelters of some sort were constructed to shield against adverse weather. In later times, castles were encircled with moats. In our times, armies, navies, and air forces are considered part of a "national security network."

Meanwhile, special diets, regimens of exercise, and various preventive medical procedures are followed as a key to health and longevity. We have locks on doors, smoke alarms, and pest control inspections—all in the interests of a greater "sense of security." We have life insurance, automobile insurance, fire insurance, and insurance of bank deposits. In the United States we have national public insurance as a "Social Security System." It may well be that the quest for security is one of the main concerns of our age. The psalmist shows us that in his time, too, security was sought, and where it is found.

B. Lesson Background

The Forty-ninth Psalm expressly claims to speak of "wisdom" (vv. 1-3). As is true of most wisdom writings, especially the book of Proverbs, not Israel alone but mankind in general is addressed. In common with all such literature in the Bible, however, the wisdom that is held up and held out to us is centered in the recognition of the reality of God.

The psalmist is concerned that the arrogantly rich and powerful will have too great an influence on the molding of human conduct. One feels that the writer himself has felt the temptation to be unduly impressed with the prominence and seeming permanence of rich and powerful persons. He cautions all against this tendency by strikingly emphasizing the leveling influence and certainty of death.

The psalmist directs our thinking to a desire that is universal in mankind—that of security. Most of what he says has to do with men's foolish efforts to achieve it, before he finally points the reader to the only One in whom lasting security is found.

I. Advice Advertised (Psalm 49:1-4)

1. Hear this, all ye people; give ear, all ye inhabitants of the world.

This is a graphic way of seeking attention for an important message. The town criers of an earlier age rang a bell and cried, "Hear ye! Hear ye!" when some "public interest" announcement was to be made. Because it deals with universal truths, this psalm is addressed to the people of all nations.

2. Both low and high, rich and poor, together.

The advice about to be given is for those of diverse social classes and economic statuses. The normal condition would be for *low and high, rich and poor*, to be separated. That this is something they need to hear *together* is unusual.

3. My mouth shall speak of wisdom; and the meditation of my heart shall be of understanding.

What the psalmist is now to declare will be an expression of *wisdom*. The wisdom is not his own, but that which has been communicated to him and upon which he has meditated. The following verse speaks of the psalmist as listening to this communication.

4. I will incline mine ear to a parable: I will open my dark saying upon the harp.

The *New International Version* translates this, "I will turn my ear to a proverb; with the harp I will expound my riddle." *The New English Bible* has, "I will set my ear to catch the moral of the story and tell on the harp how I read the riddle."

The Hebrew word translated *parable* in this verse includes all types of sayings, proverbs, allegories, or parables. That this is to be declared *upon the harp* indicates that it is to be recited with a harp accompaniment. It is not just a lecture or a dry presentation of alternative views of life, but a serious song or chant.

II. The Impotent Impious (Psalm 49:5-9)

A. Wickedness of the Worldly (vv. 5, 6)

5. Wherefore should I fear in the days of evil, when the iniquity of my heels shall compass me about?

This verse is clearer in the *New International Version*, which has, "Why should I fear when evil days come, when wicked deceivers surround me?" The *Revised Standard Version* translates the last section of this passage, "when the iniquity of my persecutors surrounds me." Here the psalmist states the subject of the "dark saying." Evil persons surround the righteous, lying in wait to trip them up. Do the righteous have reason to fear, or may they trust in God's protection?

6. They that trust in their wealth, and boast themselves in the multitude of their riches.

The sense of this verse continues from the preceding verse. The psalmist is asking, "Why should I fear when evil persons surround me—those who trust in their wealth and boast about how rich they are?" Such persons are worldly and carnal, and give no thought to God. Seeking only to amass "things" to themselves, they have no qualms in persecuting the righteous.

NOTHING TO FEAR

Most Americans are familiar with the words of the late president, Franklin Delano Roosevelt, who said in his first inaugural address, "The only thing we have to fear is fear itself." Interest-

ingly, another American had earlier expressed that truth. In his journal in 1851, Henry David Thoreau said, "Nothing is so much to be feared as fear." And others before him stated the same truth in slightly different words.

It seems to be human nature to fear the future and what it will bring. Even more, most all of us have at least some fear of death, since it takes us into uncharted waters. However, as Christians we do not need to fear either of these. We have placed our faith in God, who has promised to sustain us on earth and to redeem us from the grave. As a result of these promises, our fear is in vain; and worrying only steals our joy and shortens our days.

The beautiful message of God's Word rings out loud and clear. When we give our lives to the Lord, we have nothing to fear. Not Satan. Not evil men. Not death or the grave. Not even fear itself! We have overcome fear through Jesus Christ our Lord.   —T. T.

B. Where Wealth Fails (vv. 7-9)

7. None of them can by any means redeem his brother, nor give to God a ransom for him.

Leviticus 25:47-54 tells how a man who had been sold for a debt could be "redeemed" by a certain payment of money; or, if he could accumulate enough, he could "redeem" himself. This redemption was a release from physical and legal slavery. But that is not the "redemption" that the psalmist is speaking of. The following verses show he is thinking about the impossibility of evading death. Even if a person could be redeemed from servitude by a brother, no one could ever purchase another person's freedom from death. There is no way God's sentence of death for sinful mankind can be reversed.

We who are Christians can see how much we owe to Jesus, our Lord. He brought "life and immortality to light" by His resurrection from the grave, so that we have "everlasting consolation and good hope through grace" (2 Timothy 1:10; 2 Thessalonians 2:16).

8. (For the redemption of their soul is precious, and it ceaseth for ever:)

The redemption of a soul is costly, too costly for the wealthy to effect, no matter how great their riches (compare Job 36:18, 19). *It ceaseth for ever.* Once death comes, the opportunity for redemption ceases.

9. That he should still live for ever, and not see corruption.

This verse should be read with verse 7 (verse 8 is parenthetical). There is no "price" a human can pay to prevent death or deliver him from the grave. But praise God, we have assurance through Jesus' conquest of death that we as His disciples shall live beyond the dissolution of our bodies at death. So we have Paul's words, "O death, where is thy sting? O grave, where is thy victory? . . . But thanks be to God, which giveth us the victory through our Lord Jesus Christ" (1 Corinthians 15:55, 57).

A Worthless Obsession

A number of years ago, a woman in Florida died, alone, at the age of seventy-one. The coroner's report read, "Cause of death—malnutrition." The lady had actually wasted away to fifty pounds! Investigators who found her said that her home was a pigpen, the biggest mess they had ever seen. Amid the rubble, however, they found two keys, which led officials to safe-deposit boxes at separate banks.

What they discovered was incredible. The first box contained over seven hundred AT&T stock certificates and a stack of cash worth nearly $200,000. The second box contained only currency, some $600,000 worth of it! The starved woman was in reality a millionairess!

Such a miserly attitude is rare, but the principle it is founded upon is all too common. Simply stated, our society teaches that money equals success and security. God's Word will have nothing to do with such a view. The psalmist reminds us that wealth and riches are temporary, and do not have the power to purchase one's salvation. Eternal security comes only from God, who has purchased us from sin and eternal death through the blood of Jesus Christ. When we rely on Him and stop looking to self, we have true security; and we will overcome even the power of the grave.   —T. T.

III. The Difference Death Makes (Psalm 49:10-13)

A. Death, an Unheeded Reality (vv. 10, 11)

10. For he seeth that wise men die, likewise the fool and the brutish person perish, and leave their wealth to others.

The rich person must see that his wealth cannot keep him from dying. Indeed, nothing can cancel out the sentence of death under which all humans exist. No one escapes death—not the wise, neither the fool, nor the senseless person. All at last come to death's unchanging silence and impotence and, in so doing, leave all of their earthly possessions to others.

11. Their inward thought is, that their houses shall continue for ever, and their dwelling places to all generations; they call their lands after their own names.

Home Daily Bible Readings

Monday, June 11—Our Lives Are Priceless (Psalm 49:1-9)
Tuesday, June 12—God Ransoms Our Souls (Psalm 49:10-15)
Wednesday, June 13—The Great Commandment (Luke 10:23-28)
Thursday, June 14—The True Neighbor (Luke 10:29-37)
Friday, June 15—Love Fulfills the Law (Romans 13:8-14)
Saturday, June 16—Our Freedom in Christ (Galatians 5:1-12)
Sunday, June 17—Called to Freedom (Galatians 5:13-15, 22-25)

The wealthy know that all men are mortal, but they cherish the *inward thought* that in a certain sense they may escape death. So they establish their families and leave their houses to them to keep up the family reputation. They accumulate large estates and name them after themselves, all with the intent of keeping their memories alive to future generations.

B. The Doom of Death (vv. 12, 13)

12. Nevertheless man being in honor abideth not: he is like the beasts that perish.

This verse stresses the fact that earthly position and prestige last only a short time. One day a person may be president of a large corporation and possess all the attributes of authority and power. He may be one to whom others defer and whose presence is authoritative. Yet a sudden stroke, heart attack, or accident may strike him down. So quickly may he fall from his position of honor among men, only to be helpless in death. Others must take his place and execute directives in his stead. Someone else will delight in all the power and privileges he once enjoyed.

The statement that man *is like the beasts that perish* does not mean there is no difference between them. But there is a similarity between them in that both man and beasts pass from the earth. After death, the physical bodies of both experience dissolution. This reminds one of these words in Ecclesiastes: "I also thought, 'As for men, God tests them so that they may see that they are like the animals. . . . As one dies, so dies the other. . . . All go to the same place; all come from dust, and to dust all return'" (3:18-20, *New International Version*).

The Christian dies, too—physically, as do all who live "in the flesh"—but he dies in hope of the resurrection and the life eternal. Probably few greater poems about death have been written than the one John Donne included in his "Holy Sonnets," issued between 1619 and 1623.

> Death, be not proud, though some have called thee
> Mighty and dreadful, for thou art not so:
> For those whom thou think'st thou dost overthrow
> Die not, poor Death; nor yet canst thou kill me.
> From rest and sleep, which but thy picture be,
> Much pleasure; then from thee much more must flow;
> And soonest our best men with thee do go—
> Rest of their bones and souls' delivery!
> Thou'rt slave to fate, chance, kings, and desperate men,
> And dost with poison, war, and sickness dwell;
> And poppy or charms can make us sleep as well
> And better than thy stroke. Why swell'st thou then?
> One short sleep past, we wake eternally,
> And Death shall be no more: Death, thou shalt die!

13. This their way is their folly: yet their posterity approve their sayings. Selah.

This their way refers to the course of conduct described in verses 6-12. Those who trust in their wealth, boast of their riches, and who live unmindful of the certainty of death are tragically mistaken. Jesus told of the prosperous man who planned to expand his material resources so he could enjoy years of selfish luxuriance. Suddenly he was confronted with death. Because the man was unprepared for it, God called him a fool. While he was laying up things for himself, he was "not rich toward God" (Luke 12:16-21).

The fact that the descendants of such people give attention to their *sayings* shows they have not understood the real tragedy of their ancestors' lives. Having inherited their wealth, they adopt also their principles and live by them.

The *Selah* at the close of this verse appears to be a note for those using this psalm in worship. The word is found seventy-one times in the

Psalms, and it is thought to have been a musical or liturgical sign of some kind. It may have been the direction for an instrumental interlude, or for a doxology to be sung.

IV. The Abiding Righteous (Psalm 49:14, 15)

A. All Die—The Righteous Endure (v. 14)

14. Like sheep they are laid in the grave; death shall feed on them; and the upright shall have dominion over them in the morning; and their beauty shall consume in the grave from their dwelling.

As sheep follow one another, so one after another, men, however rich, eventually pass into the silence of *death*. Death is pictured as a hungry monster who waits to devour all the pomp and pride of those who are prosperous but perverted. Thomas Gray writes in his famous "Elegy Written in a Country Churchyard,"

> The boast of heraldry, the pomp of power,
> And all that beauty, all that wealth e'er gave,
> Await alike the inevitable hour:
> The paths of glory lead but to the grave.

The upright shall have dominion over them in the morning. The time of repression and difficulty brought about by the wicked and powerful is considered a bad, dark night. As even the longest night of loneliness or anxiety, sadness or pain, at last gives way to dawn, so the *morning* will come when the godly will be made alight with blessing and peace. When the resurrection morning comes, everlasting dominion will be assured to God's saints.

Their beauty . . . their dwelling. The *New International Version* translates this, "their forms will decay in the grave, far from their princely mansions."

B. Personal Hope Affirmed (v. 15)

15. But God will redeem my soul from the power of the grave: for he shall receive me. Selah.

Some people claim that no thought of personal immortality is expressed in the Old Testament. It certainly is true that in the Old Testament, there is a major stress on the blessing of prosperity and on the fact that God would bless Israel's faithfulness by allowing them continued possession of the "land of promise." However, there are notes in the Biblical literature that point to a hope for future union with God and to blessings beyond this life. (See Job 19:23-27 and Daniel 12:2, 3.)

This verse is another of those reassuring passages. Indeed *the grave* has *power*; it stretches forth its hand and will take each one of us in its

visual 3

dark grasp. But death cannot *keep* the righteous in its power, for God will redeem them from its grip. There was one, our Savior and Redeemer, who himself broke the bonds of death and promised to do so for others as well. In his great sermon on the Day of Pentecost, Peter said of Jesus, "But God raised him ... from the agony of death, because it was impossible for death to keep its hold on him" (Acts 2:24, *New International Version*). Or, as Paul asserted in his second letter to Timothy, "Our Saviour Jesus Christ ... hath abolished death, and hath brought life and immortality to light" (1:10). This is the solution of the "dark saying," the psalmist delivered (v. 4).

CERTAIN SECURITY

The news of January 5, 1988, was shocking: "Pistol" Peter Maravich, basketball legend, was dead at age forty! Who would have suspected that he would collapse and die suddenly? He had kept his body in top-notch shape through athletics, his diet consisted solely of health food, and he was living a clean, Christian life. Besides, he had become a useful tool in the kingdom, using his fame to gain opportunities to testify for his Lord. Why, then, had Pete Maravich died?

Only God knows the answer to that question, but His Word helps us gain some understanding. For instance, the psalmist proclaims that all men, whether wise or foolish, rich or poor, must someday face death. Indeed, we know that we are destined to die, and that our bodies will decay. But God's Word has a message for us, and it is this: He will redeem our souls from the power of the tomb, and we will live on.

Maybe that's why Pete Maravich was taken at a relatively early age. His death serves as a reminder to us all. No matter who we are, how important we may appear, how healthy we may seem, our earthly life can end in an instant. Yet, we who are in Christ need not fear the grave; it conquers only our fragile body, never our soul. We can rest secure in knowing that we will dwell with our Father eternally.   —T. T.

Conclusion

A. Spiritual Perspectives

We are aware of how a scene may vary in appearance when viewed from different locations. From one viewpoint, an object may seem to have a dimension of depth that it does not have when viewed from another angle. In the city of Jaipur, in the Indian state of Rajasthan, there is a beautiful rose-red building on the main street. When viewed from the front, the building looks like a large palace. But viewed from another

position, it is seen to be just a high, rather wide wall with windows. Behind it, there are places to stand and many "apertures." There the wives of the Rajah could stand and view parades and various street activities without being seen. It looks as if it is a large, beautiful building, but it really is only a facade.

As in the psalmist's day, there are affluent persons who trust in their wealth and boast of their riches. Thoughts of God and/or responsibility to Him are far from them. Their lives appear to be solid and significant; but when they are viewed from a Christian perspective, they are seen to be frivolous and futile.

At first, the psalmist was tempted to become discouraged when he considered the prestige and power of the unrighteous rich. But then he changed his viewpoint, and it revealed to him the temporary nature of their power. Their inevitable fate was to die, never to be released from the grip of death. By contrast, the righteous would be redeemed from death's power to live in God's presence.

If we are tempted to envy the wealthy of this world who live with no regard for God, may we change our perspective, as did the psalmist, and look at this world and all that is in it from the viewpoint of eternity.

B. Prayer

We are thankful, Father, for the many blessings we enjoy every day. We are grateful for shelter from storms, for nights of rest, for occupations that challenge our best efforts, for the many varieties of food we can eat with pleasure. We are mindful of friends and congenial workmates. We remember always our families and the intimate ties of parents, wives, husbands, brothers, sisters, and children. Above all, we have the spiritual blessings of worship, faith, and fellowship.

Dear Lord, help us to concentrate on what we have, rather than on what we do not have. Especially help us never to be tempted to be overawed by riches secured by deceit, or pandering to evil desires. Enable us to foresee the inevitable death and disaster that come to those who give no heed to their Creator and His truth.

As we face our own death, grant us the assurance of hope that Jesus, our risen Lord, brings us by His own words and His own resurrection. In his name we pray. Amen.

C. Thought to Remember

At the grave, all earthly possessions, all titles, honors, academic degrees, and distinctions must be laid down. Only our characters and our standing with God will go with us into eternity.

Learning by Doing

This page contains an alternate lesson plan emphasizing learning activities. Classes desiring such student involvement will find these suggestions helpful.

Learning Goals

This lesson should help students to:

1. Face and accept the reality of their own death.

2. Identify the things in which they may be trusting for their security.

3. Place their trust only in God.

Into the Lesson

Before the class arrives, tape strips of colorful construction paper on the wall or the chalkboard at eye-catching angles. On each strip of paper, print one of the following: smoke alarms, missiles, safe-deposit boxes, diets, Army, life insurance, savings accounts. As the session begins, direct the class's attention to the words and ask, "What do all of these have in common?" (Answer: Each is viewed as a means of providing some kind of security.)

Draw a time line on the chalkboard. Divide it into three segments and label them, Ancient, Medieval, and Modern. Ask the class to name some things people trusted during each of those eras for security. (Ancient: fortresses, fire, armies. Medieval: moats, castles, knights in full armor. Modern: insurance policies, missiles, and smoke alarms.) After answers are listed under each segment, say that wealth has been regarded in all three periods of history as a source of personal security.

Then state that in Psalm 49, a different point of view is given to encourage the righteous poor. Inquire if anyone can state it in one sentence. (Answer: Wealth may seem to provide security and influence in this life, but it cannot keep anyone from dying.)

Into the Word

Use the following questions to guide the students in exploring Psalm 49 together.

1. To whom is this psalm addressed, and how important did the writer believe its truths to be? (vv. 1-3). (It is addressed to all peoples of all estates. The writer calls it wisdom and sets out to instruct people about what he believes is a fundamental issue in life.)

2. What mistake do some wealthy persons make in regard to their wealth? (v. 6). (They trust their wealth to provide *all* of their needs.)

3. What event in life cannot be avoided, regardless of one's financial status? (vv. 7-9).

(Death. Elaborate by saying that wealth may enable a person to receive special medical attention and the latest drugs, and thus postpone death; but death must come to all.)

4. What blessed state of the righteous is referred to in verse 14? (The resurrection from the dead, when the righteous will reign with God.)

5. Why should those who are righteous not fear death? (v. 15). (God will break death's hold on them and take them to himself.)

Summarize this portion of the lesson by saying that Psalm 49 attempts to deal with people's tendency to allow the wealth of others to intimidate and impress them unduly. There are many things that money cannot buy. Escape from death is one of them.

Point out that verse 15 implies the concept of life after death. The Old Testament peoples, however, had limited insight into life beyond the grave. Ask if anyone can recall Old Testament passages referring to life after death. Assign the following verses to be read aloud: Genesis 5:24; 2 Kings 2:11; Job 19:23-27; Psalm 17:15; Isaiah 26:19; Daniel 12:2, 3.

Into Life

Make copies of the following obituary form. Have each student fill one out.

Your Name   Age   Date of Death
At the time of death, his/her principal interest was _____
He/She was a member of _____
                             (clubs, organizations)
He/She will be remembered by _____
because _____.
He/She made a significant contribution in the area of _____.
The funeral service will be at _____.
In lieu of flowers, contributions may be sent to

_____.

After allowing students time to fill out their forms, have students pair off and share answers to the following questions: How did I feel as I filled out this form? What statement was the most painful or most difficult for me to complete? Dismiss the class by saying that wealth may seem to be important now, but facing our own death should make us aware of the greater importance of our eternal future.

Let's Talk It Over

The questions on this page are designed to encourage review of the lesson Scriptures and to promote discussion of the lesson by the class. The answers provided are only discussion starters. Let your class talk it over from there.

1. It seems that the temptation to envy the rich is one that few Christians are able to avoid consistently. Why is this so?

One of the lesser-known psalmists, Asaph, confessed, "For I envied the arrogant when I saw the prosperity of the wicked" (Psalm 73:3, *New International Version*). Then he described his impressions of the lives of these prosperous, wicked persons: "They have no struggles; their bodies are healthy and strong. They are free from the burdens common to man; they are not plagued by human ills" (Psalm 73:4, 5, *New International Version*). We realize that these impressions are exaggerated, and Asaph also realized that, for he later spoke of the calamities awaiting the wicked (vv. 18-20). Like Asaph, we can almost convince ourselves that the acquisition of wealth would solve all of our problems and bring us unbounded contentment.

2. The psalmist addressed all the citizens of earth. We also should pray that people all over the world would be reminded of the inevitability of death. Why is this reminder needed?

Though they experience the passing of relatives and friends, and they read of the deaths of prominent individuals, many persons tend to think death will not come to them. Or perhaps their view is that death will come someday, but it is so far off they can merely ignore it. This psalm can be a starting-point to prayer that human beings will be brought face-to-face with the inevitability of their death and with their need to respond to the only one who holds the key to eternal life—our Lord Jesus Christ.

3. We have probably known occasions when we desperately wished we could save a loved one from death. But we could not make that wish come true. How, as Christians, may we respond to the impossibility of saving others from death?

While we may not be able to prevent another person's physical death, we can enable other people to escape eternal destruction. So, for us, the frustration of death's unavoidable grip on our circle of loved ones may give way to the rejoicing that is made possible through Christ's resurrection triumph. Christ's death accom-

plished something greater than anything we can do. "For scarcely for a righteous man will one die: yet peradventure for a good man some would even dare to die. But God commendeth his love toward us, in that, while we were yet sinners, Christ died for us" (Romans 5:7, 8).

4. Does the accumulation of wealth tend to make people feel immortal? If so, how can we correct this tendency in ourselves and others?

Perhaps we can view our possessions as distractions that so occupy our attention that they leave us little time to ponder our mortality. When one's focus is on objects that are material, especially enduring objects such as houses and their furnishings, it is easy for that person to assume that life will just keep on going in the same comfortable way. This may be one reason for Jesus' exclamation, "How hardly shall they that have riches enter into the kingdom of God!" (Luke 18:24). We who are Christians can also get caught up in the quest for material things, and we may tend to overlook the danger that it poses for us. Jesus' warning concerning riches must be reemphasized in sermons and lessons, so that His people will be shaken out of the complacency that wealth brings and will be led to face their mortality, their responsibility toward God, and their need to cultivate the spiritual life.

5. Eternal life is one of the brightest prospects that the Christian faith offers us. Why do you think the Old Testament was comparatively silent about this prospect?

It may not be so silent as we may believe. We note that when Jesus demonstrated to the Sadducees the reality of the resurrection, He referred to Moses' experience at the burning bush. God had told Moses that He was the God of Abraham, and Isaac, and Jacob. Jesus then declared, "God is not the God of the dead, but of the living" (Matthew 22:32). In other places in the Old Testament, the resurrection of the dead is assumed, though not spelled out. But it is true that the Old Testament has little to say on this subject in comparison with the New Testament. Perhaps this was because it was a major part of Jesus' mission to bring "life and immortality to light through the gospel" (2 Timothy 1:10).

Wisdom Cries Aloud

June 24
Lesson 4

LESSON SCRIPTURE: Proverbs 1

PRINTED TEXT: Proverbs 1:1-9, 20-23.

Proverbs 1:1-9, 20-23

1 The Proverbs of Solomon the son of David, king of Israel:

2 To know wisdom and instruction; to perceive the words of understanding;

3 To receive the instruction of wisdom, justice, and judgment, and equity;

4 To give subtilty to the simple, to the young man knowledge and discretion.

5 A wise man will hear, and will increase learning; and a man of understanding shall attain unto wise counsels:

6 To understand a proverb, and the interpretation; the words of the wise, and their dark sayings.

7 The fear of the Lord is the beginning of knowledge: but fools despise wisdom and instruction.

8 My son, hear the instruction of thy father, and forsake not the law of thy mother:

9 For they shall be an ornament of grace unto thy head, and chains about thy neck.

. . . .

20 Wisdom crieth without; she uttereth her voice in the streets:

21 She crieth in the chief place of concourse, in the openings of the gates: in the city she uttereth her words, saying,

22 How long, ye simple ones, will ye love simplicity? and the scorners delight in their scorning, and fools hate knowledge?

23 Turn you at my reproof: behold, I will pour out my spirit unto you, I will make known my words unto you.

GOLDEN TEXT: The fear of the Lord is the beginning of knowledge: but fools despise wisdom and instruction.—Proverbs 1:7.

Wisdom as a Way of Life
Unit 2: Proverbs of the Wise
(Lessons 4-8)

Lesson Aims

As a result of this lesson, students should:

1. Understand the nature and purpose of the book of Proverbs.

2. Realize that God is the source of all true wisdom.

3. Choose to walk in wisdom's way.

Lesson Outline

INTRODUCTION
  A. A Look at Life's Values
  B. Lesson Background
I. THE PURPOSE OF PROVERBS (Proverbs 1:1-6)
     Brains and Wisdom
II. WISDOM'S WAY (Proverbs 1:7-9)
     Badges of Joy and Glory
III. WISDOM'S CRY (Proverbs 1:20-23)
CONCLUSION
  A. Now Hear This!
  B. Prayer
  C. Thought to Remember

Display visual 4 from the visuals packet and let it remain before the class throughout this session. The visual is shown on page 371.

Introduction

A. A Look at Life's Values

A question we all ask frequently is, "What is it worth?" or, "What is its cost?" The question usually relates to the price of items offered for sale—clothing, houses, appliances, autos, food, etc. The comparison between any merchandise's cost and its worth to us helps us determine whether or not we will buy it. The shrewd shopper is one who makes wise decisions concerning values in relation to prices.

However, some realities are more important than those involving commercial purchases. These are the qualities that go to make up the foundations of character, on which all other activities involving life's choices are based. The great British writer, G. K. Chesterton, said the most important question to ask before renting a room in a lodge or inn does not relate to price, the view from the windows, heating, or lighting. The most vital inquiry is, "What is your view of the universe?" In other words, "Do you believe in God, in His creative work, in His presence in life as Observer and Judge?" If one truly believes in a God of power to whom we will give an account, one may well imagine that prices and arrangements and facilities will be all right.

We recognize that values *are* important, but it is much more essential to determine *what* our values should be. The book of Proverbs is designed to increase our wisdom and understanding, so we can make that determination.

B. Lesson Background

All nations have pithy sayings that are quoted as the wisdom of "the voice of experience" in various areas of human behavior. It has been said that proverbs are "the wisdom of many and the wit of one," or "short sentences drawn from long experience," or "the cream of a nation's thought." "Maxims" or "aphorisms" are other terms applied to such statements.

Biblical proverbs differ from those of a general and popular nature, because they speak constantly of life in the light of God's will and purpose. The stress is on "wisdom," but it is a wisdom illuminated with the awareness of the Lord and of His presence. Of course, there are many sayings in which God is not mentioned, but there is always the insistence that wisdom begins with "the fear of the Lord."

Proverbs is a book that has few chapters on single topics, though there are sections dealing with certain matters at some length. (See 7:6-27; 8:12-36; 31:10-31.) Usually the single sayings are one verse in length and are linked together like pearls on a thread or string. Some of the principal recurring themes of Proverbs are (1) the praise of wisdom, (2) the condemnation of sloth and strong drink, (3) warnings against evil speech and wicked women, (4) the commendation of diligence, righteous speech, and godly women, (5) the futility of being a "fool," and (6) the importance of relying on God and obeying Him. With the exception of the last two chapters, Proverbs is attributed to King Solomon.

I. The Purpose of Proverbs (Proverbs 1:1-6)

1. The Proverbs of Solomon the son of David, king of Israel.

We know Solomon wrote hundreds of proverbs and doubtless collected many others (1 Kings 4:31, 32). It is true that he became unwise in his conduct in his later years. However, that does not mean the truths contained in the proverbs are any less valid. Indeed, it is in the light of many of these sayings that his own failure can be seen very clearly.

2. To know wisdom and instruction; to perceive the words of understanding.

Through the pondering of proverbs one will come to the possession of wisdom. The Hebrew word here translated *wisdom* has particular reference to the moral and religious life of the individual. It involves ordering aright all relations with man and with God. *Instruction* refers to the disciplining of life. The student of Proverbs, then, is to know wisdom and the discipline of life that comes by following it.

To perceive the words of understanding. To be able to understand or comprehend the words of wisdom and instruction; to see the implications of, and the values to be derived from, the application of these "words of insight" in daily living.

3. To receive the instruction of wisdom, justice, and judgment, and equity.

Wisdom. The Hebrew word that is translated *wisdom* in this verse is not the same word as that found in verse 2. The *New American Standard Bible* gives us "wise behavior" in this verse; others suggest "thoughtfulness," or "good sense," as nearer the meaning.

Justice means "doing what is right." Here, indeed, *wisdom* is greatly needed. Proverbs 12:15 states, "The way of a fool is right in his own eyes," and Proverbs 14:12 affirms, "There is a way which seemeth right unto a man; but the end thereof are the ways of death." So we are urged to carefully consider our course and to do what is *really* right, in accordance with the will and ordinances of God, and thus avoid the pitfall that awaits those who are self-willed.

Finally we are to learn to exercise *judgment, and equity.* In the balancing of wrongs and of disputes, probably nothing can be absolutely just and fair. But we can make every effort to act or decide in such a manner that there will be as little injustice and unfairness as possible. Since determining the really *fair* course amid a multitude of choices is so perplexing, the necessity of wisdom—especially divinely enriched wisdom—becomes very obvious.

4. To give subtilty to the simple, to the young man knowledge and discretion.

It is apparent from this verse that the Proverbs were originally designed to constitute a teaching manual for young men, and it is generally believed that these were men being trained to administer the affairs of the empire of Solomon. The word *subtilty* has come to have an adverse connotation, suggesting crafty concealment or deceit, but such was not its meaning originally. Here it means prudence or good judgment. The word *simple* refers to one who is immature, open to receive instruction. In Proverbs, it generally

visual 4

Wisdom cries out to be heard and known.

LISTEN!

indicates a person who is "open" to the enticements of evil. *Discretion* is the ability to make right choices for the conduct of life. The word is equated with *subtilty* or prudence in the first part of the verse.

5. A wise man will hear, and will increase learning; and a man of understanding shall attain unto wise counsels.

Learning is for the young and inexperienced, but not for them only. One who has already learned much and who is naturally perceptive can still continue learning by means of the wisdom that these proverbs offer. The second part of this verse repeats the thought of the first part. *Wise counsels.* This Hebrew word means steering, guiding, or governing. A wise person will diligently seek divine instruction so he will be able to control his life successfully in all of its activities.

6. To understand a proverb, and the interpretation; the words of the wise, and their dark sayings.

Here we see another purpose that is served by the book of Proverbs. The *New American Standard Bible* reading here is, "To understand a proverb and a figure, the words of the wise and their riddles." The *New International Version* has, "for understanding proverbs and parables, the sayings and riddles of the wise." Thorough familiarity with the proverbs set forth here would help the young and unlearned to understand more and deeper teaching.

Some of the proverbs are in the plainest language. Verse 10 of this chapter is an example. Others are figurative, needing interpretation to make their meaning plain. Verse 17 is an example. Many teachers sometimes made use of *dark sayings*, enigmas or parables with hidden meanings. Compelled thus to search for the truth, a student might understand it better, appreciate it more, and remember it longer. On one occasion, Ezekiel was told to reveal truth to Israel in this way (chapter 17), and we are familiar with Jesus' use of this method of teaching.

Of course, understanding these proverbs includes more than comprehending their meaning. To really understand them is to incorporate them in life, to use them as guides in daily living.

BRAINS AND WISDOM

Max Born, who died in 1970, was a brilliant man and co-winner of the 1954 Nobel Prize for Physics. Once, in an interview on television, he said, "I'd be happier if we had scientists with less brains and more wisdom." In so saying, he pointed out that there is a difference between knowledge and wisdom.

Knowledge is "a clear and certain perception of something, an acquaintance with facts." Wisdom, on the other hand, is "the faculty of *making the best use of knowledge*, the power of true and right discernment." Said another way, "Wisdom is that something that enables us to use knowledge correctly."

Notice that Born didn't say he'd be happier if scientists *had no brains* and more wisdom. He knew that both are important.

Solomon knew this, too. In writing Proverbs, he wanted to increase his people's knowledge (1:4) and their ability to understand hard sayings (1:6). But he also wanted to help his people in "attaining wisdom and discipline," in "understanding words of insight," in "acquiring a disciplined and prudent life," in "doing what is right and just and fair" (1:2, 3, *New International Version*).

In introducing this book, Solomon might well have said, "I'd be happier if my people had *more brains and more wisdom*." During this study, we should strive for both.   —T. T.

II. Wisdom's Way
(Proverbs 1:7-9)

7. The fear of the Lord is the beginning of knowledge: but fools despise wisdom and instruction.

The Hebrew word for *beginning* refers to the primary principle, the basic governing factor. The awareness of and reverence toward God is basic to the attainment of proper *knowledge*, as well as ultimate *wisdom*. To recognize God's creative activity is to understand that there is rationality, design, and purpose behind every aspect of the natural world. Genuine *knowledge* of principles, processes, and the mutual relationship of things is attained only by believing there is purpose and intelligence behind the phenomena we observe. We may not know "why" or "how" something is, but if we believe it must have a purposeful "connectedness" with other

things, we may eventually understand it. When a living person's body is cut, blood flows. For centuries men did not know just why. Ultimately, the circulation of the blood and the whole complex intertwined network of blood vessels, capillaries, arteries, heart action, etc. was determined. It was all part of a design and order. If the world were all irrational, there would be no incentive or ability to find out the answer to all the "whys" that confront us everywhere. Thus, a reverent awareness of the infinite, living God is foundational to all *knowledge*.

But the awareness of God leads also to awe and utter humility before Him. This is especially true when not only His creative wisdom but His forgiving love is understood. As William Arnot says in *Laws From Heaven for Life on Earth* (1889), "What God is inspires awe; what God has done for his people commands affection" (p. 17).

In spite of the distinctions that may be made between wisdom and knowledge, Dr. Arnot indicates that in the verse we are considering, "knowledge" and "wisdom" are not distinguished. "But when they are placed in antithesis, wisdom is the nobler of the two.... The two terms, taken together indicate, in this text, the best knowledge wisely used for the highest end" (p. 18).

The contrast to the best use of *knowledge* is the disdainful attitude of foolish people. Those who are lacking in sense not only fail to use the knowledge that reverent inquiry will provide, but ridicule and reject those who seek to instruct them. It is only the foolish person who deems himself so self-sufficient that he can dispense with all instruction, or who feels that his wisdom is so great that he can learn nothing from others, or who considers himself above any obligation to God.

8. My son, hear the instruction of thy father, and forsake not the law of thy mother.

This is similar to the commandment, "Honor thy father and thy mother" (Exodus 20:12). Our first teachers are found in our own homes. To have respect for our parents and to accept their guidance are both extremely important to our well-being and our later learning. The duty of parents is to know and teach truth and godliness to their children; the children's responsibility is to submit to and act in accordance with their parents' directions (see Ephesians 6:1-4).

The breakdown of stable and spiritually attuned families is a great evil and one of the greatest causes of social problems in modern society. It is significant that after the mention of our responsibility relating to God, the very first command that involves relationships between people is the one concerning the life of the family. Jesus indicated the importance of this command in Matthew 15:3-9.

9. For they shall be an ornament of grace unto thy head, and chains about thy neck.

An *ornament* is literally a wreath or garland. The *chains* referred to are not the *chains* of penal confinement or enslavement. Rather, they are decorative *chains* or necklaces of pearls or some other type of precious stones. Just as ornaments and jewels are popularly regarded as setting off the personal form, so obedience to parents' godly instruction beautifies the moral character.

Let us hear Dr. Arnot once again on this verse: "Put on now, O son! daughter! put on these beautiful ornaments; love, obey, cherish, reverence your parents. These are in God's sight of great price ... they are thought becoming by all but fools. These ornaments will not be out of date when time has run its course. They will be worn on the golden streets of the New Jerusalem, when the fashions of this world shall have passed away" (p. 26).

BADGES OF JOY AND GLORY

Years ago in old Southern Rhodesia—indeed, in any number of countries where the British had had influence, it was customary for chiefs to wear emblems about their necks to reveal their status. The emblems, about the size of an automobile plate, were made of good metal, were attractively designed, and were generally worn with a degree of pride.

The wearing of such emblems is not of recent origin. In fact, a similar practice may be found in the Bible. When, for example, Pharaoh put Joseph in charge of the land of Egypt, he "put a gold chain about his neck" (Genesis 41:42). Also, when Belshazzar exalted Daniel to the place of third ruler in his kingdom, he "put a chain of gold about his neck" (Daniel 5:29). For Joseph and Daniel, as well as for Jews in general, such a chain was not only a sign of authority, but was also a badge of joy and glory.

In similar fashion, Solomon says, should the instruction of the father and the law of the mother be considered. For surely, the young person who receives godly instruction from his parents, and lives by it, will be rewarded with both joy and glory. Today would be a good day

---

for each parent to ask himself or herself, "Am I giving my children such marvelous badges to wear?"

—T. T.

III. Wisdom's Cry (Proverbs 1:20-23)

20. Wisdom crieth without; she uttereth her voice in the streets.

This verse is one of many in Proverbs in which wisdom is personified as a woman. (Note, among others, such passages as 3:13-18; 4:5-9; 8:1-3; 9:1-6.) The fact that wisdom, as a lady, *cries* aloud *in the streets* is unusual and arresting. In the Biblical world, most women were quiet in public. Their voices were not heard as priests in the temple or in later years as participants in the synagogue services. That a good and marvelous woman such as *wisdom* should not only speak in public but cry aloud in the streets was almost unthinkable. However, this is how wisdom's anxiety to reach men is depicted.

The wisdom of which Solomon is speaking is essentially divine. Her words, whether they convey the promises of blessings, threat, or vengeance, are the authoritative words of God. Wisdom uses the instrumentality of God's creation, prophets, teachers, and even life's experiences to preach to mankind.

21. She crieth in the chief place of concourse, in the openings of the gates: in the city she uttereth her words, saying.

This is a further explanation of the previous verse, emphasizing both the public nature and the insistency of wisdom's call. This invitation is not a secret solicitation offered quietly to only a few selected individuals. Rather, it is spoken in the places where people gather in the cities. It is widely heard and freely broadcast so that many may hear and that any may come.

22. How long, ye simple ones, will ye love simplicity? and the scorners delight in their scorning, and fools hate knowledge?

Wisdom asks three questions—questions not meant to be answered with any specific reply. These are rhetorical questions designed to cause men to pause and consider their attitude toward wisdom's overtures. Three classes of persons are addressed and described. These are: (1) the *simple* who love *simplicity;* (2) the *scorners* who delight in *scorning;* and (3) the *fools* who *hate knowledge.*

(1) *The simple who love simplicity.* The Hebrew word for simple is the same as that used in verse 4. It refers to those who are immature, those who are easily led into ways that prove to bring them nothing but misery and harm. They

---

+-----------------------------------+
| **How to Say It** |
| |
| BELSHAZZAR. Bel-*shazz*-er. |
| PHARAOH.   *Fair*-o or *Fay*-ro. |
+-----------------------------------+

just go blundering on, oblivious of warnings and heedless of the consequences of their deeds. They don't anticipate consequences, nor do they listen to the words of caution that would "complicate" their lives.

(2) *The scorners who delight in scorning.* These are people who think it "smart" to poke fun at everything. They deride those who are careful to consider the possible circumstances of their actions before undertaking them. They sneer about attitudes of reverence or reticence. They scoff at the prospect of future judgment or the ill consequences of evildoing. As the apostle Paul remarks about sinners in the Roman letter, "They know well enough the just decree of God, that those who behave like this deserve to die, and yet they do it; not only so, they actually applaud such practices" (1:32, *The New English Bible*).

(3) *The fools who hate knowledge.* These people do not desire to know either the God of wisdom or the wisdom of God. They are offered instruction about how life can be benefited and blessed by doing God's will, but they reject it. God, our Creator, offers mankind what is, in essence, a manufacturer's "owner's manual" for the use of the life He has created and given us. But this is derided and thrown away. Such people are indeed "fools."

23. Turn you at my reproof: behold, I will pour out my spirit unto you, I will make known my words unto you.

Turn you. This is wisdom's call to the simple, the scorners, and the fools. It is a call to repentance and conversion. All through Scripture, God called to His people to repent, to change their ways, to return to Him. This was the message of the prophets, who urged Israel to give up idolatry and evil practices and to walk in ways of genuine worship and righteous living. John the Baptist, Jesus, and the apostles all included repentance in their messages. (See Matthew 3:1, 2 ; 4:17; Mark 6:12; Luke 24:47; Acts 2:38; 26:20.) God's blessings and spiritual help are promised to those who turn from sin to Him.

Conclusion

A. Now Hear This!

On ships in the United States Navy, public announcements are prefaced by the words, "Now hear this!" This phrase indicates that directives or news of a general importance will soon follow. We read in Proverbs that wisdom calls aloud in the gates and open areas of the city. Wisdom's counsel is not given secretly or in some covert manner. Everyone can hear, and anyone may heed, the advice and admonitions being uttered. The way of wisdom is made clear by the teachings delivered in Proverbs.

Wisdom "calls aloud" to us today in reference to our own life activities. The general "rules" for health certainly are well known by most adults. Foods that are known to promote good health should be eaten regularly. Other foods that may harm us, should be restricted. Some substances should be avoided. Moderate exercise and proper amounts of rest and sleep are known to be helpful. General counsels such as these are "called aloud," and those persons who desire to have and maintain good physical health listen to them and order their lives accordingly.

Wisdom cries aloud to us in regard to our moral and spiritual health also. That call is vital, to both our earthly and our eternal well-being. This wisdom which is final and fulfilling, is found in Christ Jesus (1 Corinthians 1:24). God has made Him to be for us "wisdom" as well as "righteousness, and sanctification, and redemption" (1 Corinthians 1:30). Let us hear His call, and come to Him, and find *eternal* life.

B. Prayer

Our Father, in our quest for more and more information and knowledge, help us not to forget our great need for wisdom. We realize, Lord, that as humans we have devised many ways by which we can destroy human life. Help us, rather, to seek those truths that will keep people together, promote their spiritual well-being, and save them physically and spiritually. Lead us to the knowledge of Jesus, the Christ. In His name we pray. Amen.

C. Thought to Remember

God is to be reverenced, honored, and obeyed. This is the first step in wisdom.

Home Daily Bible Readings

Monday, June 18—Fear God (Proverbs 1:1-9)

Tuesday, June 19—Forsake Violence (Proverbs 1:10-19)

Wednesday, June 20—Wisdom Cries Aloud (Proverbs 1:20-23, 32, 33)

Thursday, June 21—Don't Stray Into Speculation (1 Timothy 1:3-7)

Friday, June 22—A Holy Calling (1 Timothy 1:8-14)

Saturday, June 23—Mystery Revealed; Christ in You (Colossians 1:9-12, 25-28)

Sunday, June 24—"We Are the Lord's" (Romans 14:5-9)

Learning by Doing

This page contains an alternate lesson plan emphasizing learning activities. Classes desiring such student involvement will find these suggestions helpful.

Learning Goals

This lesson should enable students to:

1. Compare and contrast Biblical proverbs with secular proverbs and adages.

2. Define the meaning of wisdom as used in Proverbs and demonstrate how it is acquired.

3. Illustrate specific ways that wisdom can enhance the quality of life.

Into the Lesson

Prepare handouts of the incomplete proverbs listed below. Distribute them at the beginning of the session, and allow time for class members to complete the assigned task. (This same material is in the student's quarterly.)

Can You Tell the Difference?

Complete the following familiar proverbial expressions:

1. A penny saved is a penny _____.

2. When a job is first begun, never leave it till it's _____.

3. Pretty is as pretty _____.

4. God helps them that help _____.

5. A soft answer turns away _____.

6. Early to bed and early to rise, makes a man healthy, wealthy, and _____.

7. _____ goeth before destruction.

8. God tempers the storm to the _____ _____.

9. A good name is rather to be chosen than _____ _____.

10. He that falls in love with himself will have no _____.

11. Train up a child in the way he should go: and when he is old, he will _____ _____ from it.

12. Beauty is only _____ _____.

13. Spare the rod and spoil the _____.

After the class has filled in the blanks, ask them to mark an x beside the ones found in the Bible. *Answers:* earned, done, does, themselves, wrath (x), wise, Pride (x), shorn lamb, great riches (x), rival, not depart (x), skin deep, child (x).

Mention the fact that all countries have pithy, wise sayings that are often quoted and accepted as directives for human behavior. Explain that Biblical proverbs differ from those of a general and popular nature in that they relate to living in the light of God's revealed will and purpose.

Into the Word

Introduce the book of Proverbs by using the material in the Introduction section of the lesson commentary. Then divide the class into groups of four to six students each. Assign the following questions for them to answer as they study Proverbs 1:1-9, 20-23. Have each group appoint a scribe, who will report the group's findings to the class. Allow ten to fifteen minutes for this activity.

1. What was an often-quoted saying in your family as you were growing up? How did you feel about it?

2. According to Proverbs 1:1-6, what are the aims of the Proverbs? Who may profit from a study of them?

3. What is your understanding of the expression, "the fear of the Lord" (v. 7)? How would one behave who had "the fear of the Lord"?

4. To whom does "wisdom" call out, and what is her message? (vv. 20-23).

Have the scribe from each group share the insights his or her group gathered. (Responses to the first question need not be shared with the entire class. It was intended as a means of helping the class members share something of themselves with others before getting started on the Bible study.) Develop more fully the concept that "the fear of the Lord is the beginning of knowledge" Point out that there is a *false* wisdom, which many persons espouse. It centers in time, in this present world, but ignores eternity. *True* wisdom, the wisdom that Proverbs exhorts us to seek, begins with reverence for God. Emphasize that reverence for God is more than an emotional attitude. It is a recognition of who God is and who we are. True wisdom must be built upon this foundation. Our relationship to the Author of all wisdom and truth is more crucial than any other information we may acquire and apply.

Into Life

Since God desires for us to acquire wisdom, ask the class to suggest some steps they can take to accomplish it. List their suggestions on the chalkboard. Be sure this one is included: Engage in some sort of systematic Bible study. Encourage the students to read the book of Proverbs in conjunction with this five-lesson unit of study based on that book.

Let's Talk It Over

The questions on this page are designed to encourage review of the lesson Scriptures and to promote discussion of the lesson by the class. The answers provided are only discussion starters. Let your class talk it over from there.

1. While it does not appear in the *King James Version* of our text, the word *discipline* seems to describe the kind of life Solomon outlined in Proverbs 1. Why is this a timely word for our society to consider?

The most popular words in our society seem to be *rights*, *freedom*, and *opportunity*. But each of these, apart from discipline, offers very elusive benefits. We may demand our rights, but if we fail to exercise discipline in the use of those rights, we will lose them. Similarly, we cry out for freedom, but freedom without discipline will lead to chaos. It is well that we strive for equal opportunities in education, employment, housing, etc. However, once opportunity comes, it takes discipline to grasp its potential. It would be refreshing to hear a political leader issuing a challenge to our society to enter a new era of personal discipline. Of course, the public would have every right to look for an equal emphasis toward personal discipline on the part of its governmental officials.

2. How does the expression, "the fear of the Lord," affect people in general today?

Unbelievers tend to scoff at those fearful aspects of the Lord, which are presented in the Scriptures. They joke about Hell and poke fun at real or imaginary "hellfire-and-brimstone" preachers. Some unbelievers take a more serious view of this Biblical concept and attack Christianity for fostering guilt and fear. They may suggest that the church has found this a handy doctrine for frightening people (and their money) into its ranks. Among Christians, on the other hand, are those who tend to minimize the fear of God in comparison with the love of God. They find some justification for this in John's reference to the "perfect love [that] casteth out fear" (1 John 4:18). But John was apparently speaking of a gnawing fear, a paralyzing dread, which keeps one from recognizing God's Fatherly love. In contrast, many passages in the New Testament show that a healthy fear of the Lord is a vital aspect of Christian living.

3. There are both favorable and unfavorable ways of being simple regarding God's instruction. How can we cultivate the favorable form of simplicity?

Paul informed the Corinthians of his concern that their minds "should be corrupted from the simplicity that is in Christ" (2 Corinthians 11:3). There are certain fundamental elements in our Christian faith that we dare not lose sight of. They are profound, and we cannot fully understand or explain them. Our faith in God the Father and Christ the Son is one of these. No matter how much we may speculate about the nature of the Almighty and the mystery of the Godhead, we must rest our faith at last on the simple, clear teachings of Scripture on these subjects. Such topics as salvation; the ministry of the Holy Spirit; the nature of prayer; and the mysteries of death, the resurrection, and the final judgment also tend to promote speculation. It is a mark of simplicity to learn diligently and to hold firmly to the Biblical teaching regarding these matters, and to keep opinion and speculation in a separate category.

4. The attitude of scornfulness toward what is sacred or toward traditional values is widespread today. What are some forms this attitude takes?

While the term may be a bit outdated, the tendency to be "cool" or a bit detached and unemotional toward much of life is still popular in our society. Those who value "coolness" are inclined to scorn their neighbors who feel that religion, patriotism, or social concerns are matters worthy of their emotional involvement. This is a particularly difficult problem in the church. Certain members prefer what could be called a "lukewarm" approach to spiritual matters (see Revelation 3:15, 16). They want worship services that are brief and formal, and fellowship that maintains a good measure of aloofness. Any service that they are asked to render must be something they can do without "getting too involved." When they see other members demonstrating enthusiasm and excitement in worship, fellowship, and service, they may react with scorn and criticism over what strikes them as emotionalism. If this is true within the church, it is even more pronounced outside of it. Many unbelievers, proud of their refusal to commit themselves to anything outside of themselves, are quick to scorn Christians who demonstrate such commitment.

Get Wisdom at All Cost

LESSON SCRIPTURE: Proverbs 4.

PRINTED TEXT: Proverbs 4:1-13.

Proverbs 4:1-13

1 Hear, ye children, the instruction of a father, and attend to know understanding.

2 For I give you good doctrine, forsake ye not my law.

3 For I was my father's son, tender and only beloved in the sight of my mother.

4 He taught me also, and said unto me, Let thine heart retain my words: keep my commandments, and live.

5 Get wisdom, get understanding: forget it not; neither decline from the words of my mouth.

6 Forsake her not, and she shall preserve thee: love her, and she shall keep thee.

7 Wisdom is the principal thing; therefore get wisdom: and with all thy getting get understanding.

8 Exalt her, and she shall promote thee: she shall bring thee to honor, when thou dost embrace her.

9 She shall give to thine head an ornament of grace: a crown of glory shall she deliver to thee.

10 Hear, O my son, and receive my sayings; and the years of thy life shall be many.

11 I have taught thee in the way of wisdom; I have led thee in right paths.

12 When thou goest, thy steps shall not be straitened; and when thou runnest, thou shalt not stumble.

13 Take fast hold of instruction; let her not go: keep her; for she is thy life.

GOLDEN TEXT: Wisdom is the principal thing; therefore get wisdom: and with all thy getting get understanding.—Proverbs 4:7.

Wisdom as a Way of Life
Unit 2: Proverbs of the Wise
(Lessons 4-8)

Lesson Aims

As a result of this lesson, the students should:
1. Understand the importance of knowing God's wisdom.
2. Never let go of that wisdom.
3. Communicate God's wisdom by teaching and example.

Lesson Outline

INTRODUCTION
    A. Wooing Wisdom
    B. Lesson Background
I. PARENTAL TEACHING (Proverbs 4:1-4)
    Passing It On
II. WISDOM'S PREEMINENCE (Proverbs 4:5-7)
III. WISDOM'S PRIZES (Proverbs 4:8-10)
    A. Promotion and Honor (v. 8)
    B. Beauty of Character (v. 9)
    C. Longevity (v. 10)
    Wisdom for Life
IV. WISDOM'S PATH (Proverbs 4:11-13)
CONCLUSION
    A. Adult Delinquency
    B. Prayer
    C. Thought to Remember

Display visual 5 from the visuals packet and let it remain before the class throughout this session. The visual is shown on page 379.

Introduction

A. Wooing Wisdom

In the previous lesson, mention was made of the fact that in Proverbs wisdom is sometimes personified as a woman. In this week's lesson, wisdom is likened to a most desirable marriage partner. She is said to be one who will preserve and promote the one who possesses her. She will provide beauty for one's life, and will keep one from stumbling. Longevity, and life itself, are said to be in her hands.

The idea of *courting* wisdom reminds us of the fact that wisdom is more than the accumulation of knowledge. By diligence and perseverance, we can acquire many items of information. The understanding of the *meaning* of this information and its most effective and worthwhile *use* is a different matter. By itself, information does

not teach us *how* it may be used. It can be used to defraud and destroy, to harass and harm, or to liberate and lift human life. Knowledge, ability, and cooperation all help in the production of an automobile. But the automobile may be used to aid in a bank robbery, to bring people to hospitals, to give pleasure and variety to life, or to facilitate work. How the automobile will be used shows the presence or lack of wisdom.

Just as all the blessings of a life-enhancing marriage depend on a man's persuasion of a woman to yield to his entreaties, so wisdom must be wooed. That is, wisdom must be developed and won by effort and desire for it. It will not come by accident.

B. Lesson Background

The advice of a father to his children is a prominent feature of this lesson. This theme is seen in several places in Proverbs, where sections begin with the address, "My son,...." While Solomon did not write all of the book of Proverbs, he did have a hand in the collection of many of the "sayings," and doubtless wrote large numbers of them himself (1 Kings 4:32).

The frequent warnings in Proverbs about "strange women" are graphic and vivid. The sad fact is that Solomon did not take his own advice. His marriage to hundreds of wives, many of whom were foreign women who worshiped false gods, was a major factor contributing to his departure from the devotion to Jehovah that had characterized his youth. In addition to his "regular" wives, he also became involved with hundreds of concubines.

Solomon's example is a potent factor as we evaluate the father's admonitions to his son. No wonder there was conflict, unrest, and, ultimately, revolution in Solomon's kingdom. It sprang from the unrestrained luxuriousness and sensual license of Solomon himself. He praised wisdom, and urged the young to hold tightly to it when they attained it. But Solomon failed to live by the wisdom he taught to others. The fact that one with all the power, riches, intelligence, and ability of Solomon failed when he didn't follow his own instruction shows us how true and valid that insight was.

I. Parental Teaching (Proverbs 4:1-4)

1. Hear, ye children, the instruction of a father, and attend to know understanding.

In this section of Proverbs, the fact is forcefully presented that parents serve an important function as *teachers*. We realize that parents are the ones to whom, from a human standpoint, we owe our very existence. They *preserve* our lives during our infancy and childhood, when we cannot provide our own shelter, clothing, or food. They *protect* us from disease by providing medical attention, and they keep us from harm, which fire, flood, wild animals, or cruel human beings might bring to us. And they *teach* us. They teach us by their examples, by their attitudes, and frequently by their oral instruction. Their instruction progresses from the teaching of elementary things—such as how to wash, brush teeth, comb hair, tie shoestrings, and "tell time"—to matters relating to life's values, choices, and purposes. This latter type of *instruction* is what is considered in this and the following verses.

2. For I give you good doctrine, forsake ye not my law.

For I give you good doctrine. The teacher speaks with authority. He has certain definite convictions, and he believes that his instruction is important in a high degree. In modern English, the word *doctrine* is not used much except in connection with religious teaching, but it means teaching of any kind. Here it is *good* teaching that is offered the children. The teacher has confidence that what he offers is sound and helpful; teaching that leads in the right way, and has as its ultimate source the Spirit of the eternal God.

Forsake ye not my law. This admonition had been given before, and it was to be repeated many times in the future. The Hebrews measured the gravity of a problem by the frequency with which they gave their warning. *Law* here means the same as *doctrine*. As usual, the author repeated the thought of the first clause and thus gave it greater emphasis. Now, as in the days of Solomon, the danger is always present that as young men grow up, they may forsake their parents' teaching that would lead them in the right way.

3. For I was my father's son, tender and only beloved in the sight of my mother.

For I was my father's son. These and the following words correspond well with what we might expect Solomon to say. He was the child of David's old age, the one whom David, passing by several of Solomon's older brothers, selected to be the crown prince of Israel, the successor as king on the throne. This being true, it was natural that he was in David's presence much, and received from him wise words that would guide a young king in administering the affairs of a nation. *Tender and only beloved in the sight of my mother.* These words indicate that the child had been the object of his parents' special care. It is interesting to note the place held by

visual 5

Solomon's mother in his own personal esteem. He had good reason thus to regard her. She, more than any other person, was responsible for his selection as king, when he had several brothers who were older and normally would have been in the line of succession (1 Kings 1). However, the Hebrews as a rule exalted their mothers more than did the children of other nations. In their code of laws the fifth Commandment reads, "Honor thy father and thy mother" (Exodus 20:12). Bathsheba may well have had much to do with Solomon's early education, even as, in later years, the mother Eunice and grandmother Lois carefully taught the child Timothy the way of the Lord. This verse is a picture of the method used in the family education of the child. The father was responsible for the instruction, but certainly in special instances, and increasingly so in later times, the mother shared in this work.

4. He taught me also, and said unto me, Let thine heart retain my words: keep my commandments, and live.

Apparently, Solomon's more advanced training was given him by David. No doubt, Solomon learned much about government, as well as righteous living, from the life of him who was both a wise administrator and a righteous man—one who loved "justice and mercy."

The fact that a father is the author of one's existence on this earth gives him a special place in one's heart. However, David desired more than Solomon's emotional attachment; he wanted his son to remember what he had taught him, and obey that teaching, so Solomon might live a godly life.

It is obvious that moral and spiritual teaching given to children is very significant. As children grow up, some may for a time neglect or reject these truths, but they will still retain them in memory. Those truths have a part in the formation of inner concepts of right and wrong, which frequently surface in later years to serve as healing, restoring, and correcting influences.

PASSING IT ON

A leading authority on the family says, "Your home is the number one influence in the life of your child." To substantiate his claim, he offers the following statistics. He says the average church has a child 1% of his time; the school has him 16% of his time; and the home for the remaining 83%!

Those statistics do not minimize the need for churches and schools, but they do reveal that parents have the greatest *opportunity* to influence the thinking and behavior of their children. Not only so, but the Scriptures indicate that parents have the greatest *obligation* to provide ethical and spiritual guidance for their children.

We live in an age when many parents shirk their responsibility and expect school systems, television, baby-sitters, or the church to provide such training. Yet children are best reared to fear God by the careful efforts of Christian parents. Godly wisdom is acquired from fathers and mothers who daily teach their children the principles of God's Word, and live them out as examples for them.

The responsibility of parents is great, but their reward is greater as they see their children embrace God's truths and walk in His ways.—T. T.

II. Wisdom's Preeminence (Proverbs 4:5-7)

5. Get wisdom, get understanding: forget it not; neither decline from the words of my mouth.

Beyond all factual knowledge, more than learning the techniques by which bricks or tiles are laid, or boards are fashioned into rooms or furniture, lies the *wisdom* that dictates why, where, and when such knowledge and skill are to be used. After one has learned how to accomplish some activity—whether it is planting a field, or constructing a dam—there still remain those questions only wisdom can decide. Is such activity really constructive, or do we *want* to do something destructive? Should this be done, even if we can do it? Is this the time or place to do it? What will such action cause others to do or not to do? All such questions cry out not just for the power to do, but the ability to decide. This is the place where *wisdom* and *understanding* are of vital significance.

6. Forsake her not, and she shall preserve thee: love her, and she shall keep thee.

Here wisdom is presented as a woman. We are told we must not be unfaithful to wisdom, if we want to be *preserved*, that is, kept from destruc-

tion. Solomon, who wrote or collected many of these proverbs, serves as a good example. God granted him wisdom and understanding regarding the physical world and human behavior (see 1 Kings 4:29-34; 3:16-28). However, Solomon was led astray by his inordinate sexual drives and by his desire to placate and make marriage alliances with bordering nations (1 Kings 3:1; 9:16, 24; 11:1-11). The seeds for the dissolution of the nation of Israel were sown during Solomon's reign, because he forsook the ways of God, toward which wisdom led.

7. Wisdom is the principal thing; therefore get wisdom: and with all thy getting get understanding.

Since wisdom is self-evidently more important than mere knowledge, and since the lack of wisdom is so tragic, the conclusion follows— the most important thing is to acquire wisdom. In most cases, we can make up for a lack of knowledge. For example, we know that few of us can fashion chains of gold, cut diamonds, or dive for pearls. Yet these objects can be purchased, so that we can enjoy them. Likewise, many insights into law, medicine, business, or literature can be secured from those who have special knowledge in those fields of learning. But how to utilize such information involves the use of *wisdom*.

With all thy getting get understanding. The *New International Version* translates this, "Though it cost all you have, get understanding." No price is too high to obtain her. This causes us to think of Jesus' parables of the hidden treasure and the pearl of great price (Matthew 13:44-46). In both instances, the man sold all he had to obtain the valued prize.

III. Wisdom's Prizes (Proverbs 4:8-10)

A. Promotion and Honor (v. 8)

8. Exalt her, and she shall promote thee: she shall bring thee to honor, when thou dost embrace her.

Some of the persons who became prominent in Bible history were persons of diligence and dedication, who made wise use of their talents wherever they were. This was true of Joseph—as slave, prisoner, and ruler in Egypt. Young David was wise as he tended and defended his flock. Later, as a leader in Saul's army, "David went out whithersoever Saul sent him, and behaved himself wisely: and Saul set him over the men of war, and he was accepted in the sight of all the people, and also in the sight of Saul's servants" (1 Samuel 18:5).

The same wise conduct may be seen in the life of Nehemiah, who was promoted from the position of servant to the Persian monarch to that of governor and administrator of a city. He was entrusted with the use of the government's resources, all because of his wisdom and the character that this wisdom provided.

When thou dost embrace her. If wisdom is thought of as a woman to be wooed and won, this concept becomes significant. We must have more than a nodding or a speaking acquaintance with wisdom. A commitment must be made to her. She is to be embraced or held fast with affectionate enthusiasm. We must yield to wisdom's way, so that wisdom becomes part of life and a joyful possession.

B. Beauty of Character (v. 9)

9. She shall give to thine head an ornament of grace: a crown of glory shall she deliver to thee.

True wisdom clothes the life of its possessor with a special beauty. By way of contrast, vices such as bigotry, unfairness, greed, and cruelty are ugly and destroy the harmony and loveliness of living.

C. Longevity (v. 10)

10. Hear, O my son, and receive my sayings; and the years of thy life shall be many.

In normal circumstances, the way of God, the path of wisdom, tends to stability of life, serenity of spirit, and security of person. Of course, some have been persecuted and have died "for righteousness' sake." However, the way of moderation, good relations with others, peace of heart—these contribute to the kind of living that prolongs life. On the other hand, excesses of every kind, animosity, fighting—all drive persons to lay waste their existence in "riotous living."

WISDOM FOR LIFE

Sam Poole was my wife's grandfather. He was one of those remarkable people who became a legend in his own time. He is still remembered as a Christian gentleman, a leader of the church, and an example who inspired others to follow the Savior. Among other blessings, he lived to be 104, never entering a hospital as a patient until after he was 100!

A jack-of-all-trades, Sam was a man noted for his wisdom, which leads to the topic for discussion: Did his wisdom come because of his long life, or did his long life come as a result of his wisdom? Surely the former is true. Yet, in Sam Poole's case, as is true of other Christians, wisdom helped produce longevity. Undoubtedly, his lifelong habits of attending church, abstaining from evil practices, and obeying God's ethical commandments contributed to his long life.

Solomon testifies that this is true. He says that by heeding good advice and walking in an upright path, one will live many years. I know this worked in Sam Poole's life, and I have confidence it will work in the lives of others as well.
—T. T.

IV. Wisdom's Path
(Proverbs 4:11-13)

11. I have taught thee in the way of wisdom; I have led thee in right paths.

The one who is instructing here is aware of the importance of both example and oral teaching. We may note that the parent who is rearing a child is teaching that child, whether or not any formal instruction is given. The child sees what the parent does. Does he (or she) pray? Does he show a concern for the worship of God? Does he conduct his affairs at home with kindness and with love? What are his relations with others in the family and with those outside the immediate family circle? What sort of books are found in the home? What music? The child observes all these, and from them he forms his opinions of life's values. So it is the writer says, *I have led thee in right paths.*

12. When thou goest, thy steps shall not be straitened; and when thou runnest, thou shalt not stumble.

When thou goest may refer to the daily walk of life. The word *straitened* means confined, hemmed in, or narrowed. The path of wisdom leads to the greatest possible liberty of life. One of Satan's worst lies is that Jesus' call to righteous living confines a person and robs life of joy. In truth, sin is what enslaves to destructive habits and modes of life, which constrict life more and more. Jesus came that we might have *abundant* life. He said, "If the Son therefore shall make you free, ye shall be free indeed" (John 8:36).

When thou runnest may refer to life's emergencies and extreme crises. At such times, when prompt and decisive action is required, we are less apt to *stumble* if wisdom directs our way.

13. Take fast hold of instruction; let her not go: keep her; for she is thy life.

Instruction here refers specifically to the instruction the father gave his son. In a wider sense, however, "wisdom" is meant, as the use of the feminine pronouns suggests (see verses 7-9). The youth is urged not only to "get" wisdom but also to hold it tightly and to never let it slip from his grasp. So far as wisdom is kept and guarded, to that extent life is secured.

An interesting story is told of the days of whaling with wooden sailing ships. In remote Antarctic seas, such a ship was butted fiercely by a wounded whale. An opening was made in the ship at the waterline, and the ship began to sink. All crewmen got into "long boats," with large amounts of supplies and water, since weeks might pass before a ship would find them. They were pulling away from the ship, when suddenly two sailors jumped out of one boat and swam back to the sinking vessel. They went below, even as the water arose till the ship's deck was nearly level with the sea. They quickly emerged, jumped overboard, and swam frantically back to join their shipmates. The item they had retrieved was the compass! How would they have been likely to find their way without the compass? So the Word of Life is our compass, and the instruction contained in its wisdom should not be let go, for indeed it is "our life."

Conclusion

A. Adult Delinquency

The section of Proverbs we have been considering reminds us of two of the major responsibilities of adults to the younger generation. This includes not only our own children, but the many other younger people with whom we associate. The *example* of an older generation does have a marked effect on those who consider them "older." To a certain extent young people may resist shaping their lives in the same molds that their elders chose. Frequently, such changes are innocent enough, when they simply involve hair and clothing styles or harmless recreational preferences.

There ought, however, to be standards of honesty, integrity, purity, faithfulness, and thoughtfulness, which changing fashions should not affect. Above all, examples of prayer, concern for the salvation of others, and faithfulness to corporate worship should be very evident. The attitudes and actions of older folk, whether parents or not, make a difference in the life of younger people. They indicate the value judgments of the older generation. Thus, however much we may *say* that church attendance and ethical behavior are important, if by our actions we say something else, our oral protestations will avail little.

Direct *teaching* about right conduct and Christian values should also be given in our homes and family circles. This is true when children are young and impressionable, and it should be continued when young people begin to probe, question, and examine matters of faith and life

Home Daily Bible Readings

Monday, June 25—Get Wisdom (Proverbs 4:1-9)
Tuesday, June 26—Hold On to Wisdom (Proverbs 4:10-19)
Wednesday, June 27—Wisdom—Life to Those Who Find Her (Proverbs 4:20-27)
Thursday, June 28—God's People (1 Peter 2:1-5, 9-10)
Friday, June 29—We Are Examples (1 Peter 5:1-5)
Saturday, June 30—Wisdom Is Priceless (Proverbs 3:13-20)
Sunday, July 1—Do Not Envy Evildoers (Proverbs 3:27-35)

on their own. We should encourage the acquisition of meaningful Christian literature for our homes, promote participation in wholesome, Christian-oriented youth activities, and be as understanding, open, and spiritually, socially and intellectually relevant as possible.

Very often, adults are insensitive to these needs. The problem of so-called "juvenile delinquency" is in many instances really "adult delinquency." Too many times young people are not *taught* the way of Christ. People do not automatically "grow up" as Christians apart from being *taught* the ways of Christ. Additionally, a Christian *example* must be set. One Christian thinker said, "The problem today is, when the Prodigal Son begins to think of going home to his father, he finds his father right in the pigpen with him." May we truly be able to say to the younger people of our era, "I have taught thee in the way of wisdom; I have led thee in right paths" (Proverbs 4:11).

B. Prayer

Dear Father, we recognize how desperate is our need, and the world's need, for wisdom. We have accumulated much knowledge. Help us, Lord, to be concerned with how to utilize the knowledge we possess. Grant us wisdom to make proper choices and to be aware of the nature and implications of such decisions.

Help us also, Heavenly Father, to be wise not only for ourselves, but also for the sake of those who look to us for guidance and graciousness in life. In Jesus' name we pray. Amen.

C. Thought to Remember

The greatest folly is to fail to seek, to know, to embody, and to teach the wisdom that is from God.

Learning by Doing

*This page contains an alternate lesson plan emphasizing learning activities. Classes
desiring such student involvement will find these suggestions helpful.*

Learning Goals

The study of this lesson should enable students to:

1. Name the benefits that wisdom provides, according to Proverbs 4.

2. Identify people in the Bible who had practical wisdom and used it for righteous purposes.

3. Enumerate specific ways adult authority figures and parents can best communicate to children the wisdom of Christ's teachings.

Into the Lesson

Bring several common household items of varying prices, and display them prominently on a table at the front of the room. Distribute paper and pencils to the students as they arrive, and ask them to guess the price of each item and to total the prices. Tell them that the person whose estimate comes closest to the total value of the items will receive a prize. (The prize can be one of your choosing, but be sure that it has appeal for your class.) After determining the winner and awarding the prize, introduce the lesson by saying that we are able to discern the relative value of items that we use regularly. Today's Bible text speaks of something that is of the highest value and urges us to seek it above all else, namely, "wisdom." Ask the class, "What is the price of wisdom in today's culture?" (Get them started by asking what it costs to attend college or business school for one year. Also, ask them if there is ever a price to be paid in terms of time spent in gaining experience.) Let the discussion flow according to the interests of the class.

Into the Word

In the book of Proverbs, wisdom is presented as being of the highest value, and its benefits are praised. Give each student a sheet of paper and direct them to draw a line down the middle of it, thus forming two columns. Instruct them to label one column "Benefits" and the other "Prerequisites." Ask the students to study Proverbs 4:5-13 in pairs. Have them list in one column the benefits of wisdom, and in the other column, what a person must do to attain those benefits. Allow about five minutes for this. The lists should contain the following. *Benefits:* preserve and keep you; promote you; honor you; give you an ornament of grace and a crown of glory; keep your steps from being straitened; keep you from stumbling. *Prerequisites:* Acquire wisdom; do not forget it; do not forsake it; love wisdom; exalt wisdom; embrace wisdom; don't let go of wisdom. As the students share their findings, make a master list on the chalkboard. Using the comments of explanation in the commentary section of this manual, clarify any entry the students do not understand.

If, as it seems, Solomon himself wrote this part of Proverbs, he failed to heed his own advice. Have the students turn to 1 Kings 11:1-8, and guide them in compiling a list of the ways in which Solomon failed to use his wisdom well. Call attention to 1 Kings 11:9-11 and ask how God responded to Solomon's failure in this regard.

Put the following Scripture references on the board: Genesis 45:4-8; Ruth 3:1-5; 1 Samuel 18:5; Nehemiah 2:1-8. Ask the class to read these Scriptures and identify the Bible characters who acted wisely to advance the cause of the Lord. (Answers: Joseph, Naomi and Ruth, David, Nehemiah.)

Into Life

Point out to your class that parents need to be the wisest people of all as they share God's wisdom with their children. As Proverbs 4:1 indicates, fathers (and mothers) are to instruct their sons (and daughters) in the ways of wisdom. Divide the class into groups of four and assign one of the following questions to each group for discussion. Allow five or ten minutes for this. (1) What are some possible reasons why many teenagers refuse to listen to the teachings of their parents? (2) What are some practical and interesting ways to teach children to enjoy reading the Bible? (3) What are some common mistakes parents make as they attempt to impart wisdom to their children? (4) If you could teach your children one facet of wisdom and be assured that they would listen and obey, what would it be? When the groups have finished their discussion, let them share their conclusions with the whole class.

Conclude today's class session by urging your students to continue to seek God's wisdom, to live wisely, and to share that wisdom with those who are younger. Pray for God's help to accomplish this.

Let's Talk It Over

The questions on this page are designed to encourage review of the lesson Scriptures and to promote discussion of the lesson by the class. The answers provided are only discussion starters. Let your class talk it over from there.

1. What can the church do to assist the parents within it to become more effective teachers of righteousness to their children?

The church can make parents aware of how important it is that they take on the task of teaching in their homes. One familiar way of doing this is by comparing the relatively small amount of time children spend at church with the many hours they spend in the public school classroom. To follow up on this, perhaps the church can help parents evaluate the kind of public school education their children are receiving. If humanistic values are taught in textbooks, if the Bible and Christian morality are attacked, if evolutionary theory is emphasized, parents will need help in dealing with these. Concerning Bible teaching tools, the church should acquire a good supply of books, filmstrips, video tapes, audio tapes, games, etc., and instruct and encourage parents in the use of them.

2. Why is it encouraging to know that children's hearts may retain the words they are taught, as Proverbs 4:4 indicates?

Both parents and teachers of children become exasperated at times with the apparent fruitlessness of their instruction. The children will either exhibit an indifference to the spiritual truths that are imparted, or they will make clear their rejection of certain Biblical principles. Even the children who appear to be absorbing the lessons will occasionally demonstrate, by their words or behavior, that the truths have not really affected them. But if those lessons are made vivid and memorable, if they are repeated often and stressed, and if they are related to life situations and decisions, the instructor has good reason to hope that in future years they will yet bear a rich harvest in the child's life.

3. Since Proverbs suggests that wisdom is like a woman to be wooed and won, what are some practical applications we can make of this concept?

Recalling the period of their courtship, a husband or wife may think of a number of comparisons between their relationship then and this matter of wooing Biblical wisdom. For example, it is customary to regard a couple in love as thinking of little else than one another. If we are to win wisdom as an intimate part of our lives, we must surely give it significant thought and attention. As the Song of Solomon may remind us, a man and woman in love delight in extolling one another's charms. It is also important that we marvel over the glories of God's Word and exclaim to Him our wonder over His wise and holy ways of dealing with man. Human courtship at its best leads to a lifelong commitment in marriage. Our quest for the true wisdom also involves such commitment.

4. What are some ways in which poor parental examples influence the attitudes children have regarding the church?

One of the most familiar examples is the case of parents who send their children to church while they themselves stay home. The implication taught by their behavior is that church is "kid stuff," and their children may later see it as a mark of their own growing-up process to stop attending. Parents who teach their children to "get along" with their peers may negate this message by slandering fellow Christians while in their children's presence. It may be that parents will display a Bible in the home and perhaps read it occasionally. But if its importance is clearly secondary to the television set or to other literature, children will soon perceive that.

5. What are some ways in which positive parental examples influence the attitudes children have regarding the church?

When parents invest a significant portion of their time in serving within the church, a favorable impression regarding the church will be made upon their children. Of course, parents must not let their involvement in church activities crowd out quality family time, or the good impression may fade. Another positive example comes from using the home itself as a place of ministry. If parents open the home to needy people for a meal, to missionaries or Bible college students for rest and relaxation, or to troubled persons for counseling and encouragement, children will see that "Love thy neighbor as thyself" is not just a nice-sounding bit of church talk, but a principle to be practiced.

Wisdom—the Creator's Delight

LESSON SCRIPTURE: Proverbs 8.

PRINTED TEXT: Proverbs 8:22-36.

Proverbs 8:22-36

22 The Lord possessed me in the beginning of his way, before his works of old.

23 I was set up from everlasting, from the beginning, or ever the earth was.

24 When there were no depths, I was brought forth; when there were no fountains abounding with water.

25 Before the mountains were settled, before the hills was I brought forth:

26 While as yet he had not made the earth, nor the fields, nor the highest part of the dust of the world.

27 When he prepared the heavens, I was there: when he set a compass upon the face of the depth:

28 When he established the clouds above: when he strengthened the fountains of the deep:

29 When he gave to the sea his decree, that the waters should not pass his commandment: when he appointed the foundations of the earth:

30 Then I was by him, as one brought up with him: and I was daily his delight, rejoicing always before him;

31 Rejoicing in the habitable part of his earth; and my delights were with the sons of men.

32 Now therefore hearken unto me, O ye children: for blessed are they that keep my ways.

33 Hear instruction, and be wise, and refuse it not.

34 Blessed is the man that heareth me, watching daily at my gates, waiting at the posts of my doors.

35 For whoso findeth me findeth life, and shall obtain favor of the Lord.

36 But he that sinneth against me wrongeth his own soul: all they that hate me love death.

GOLDEN TEXT: Hear instruction, and be wise, and refuse it not.—Proverbs 8:33.

Wisdom as a Way of Life
Unit 2: Proverbs of the Wise
(Lessons 4-8)

Lesson Aims

As a result of this lesson, your students should:

1. Be more aware of the evidences of God's creative wisdom everywhere in the universe.

2. Understand that Jesus is the embodiment of God's wisdom.

3. Commit themselves more fully to Jesus.

Lesson Outline

INTRODUCTION

Display visual 6 from the visuals packet and let it remain before your class throughout this session. The visual is shown on page 389.

Introduction

From the point of view of style, the "wisdom literature" of the Bible takes its place among much similar proverbial lore. This material, found in writings of Egyptian, Persian, Indian, and Chinese antiquity, is succinct, urges the use of good sense in daily conduct, and is largely this worldly. That is, it is concerned with such matters as the proper conduct toward superiors, the need to be temperate in living habits, the harmfulness of lying, indolence, gossip, lack of thrift, and drunkenness. The Biblical literature, however, stresses the great importance of the fear of the Lord and trust in Him. This emphasis is not found in wisdom writings among non-Jewish peoples.

There is another unique characteristic of Hebrew wisdom literature, namely, the personification of wisdom. In the text for this lesson, for example, wisdom speaks as a kind of independent entity, who was with God at the time of the Creation. Such phrases as "I was brought forth" (v. 24), "I was there" (v. 27), "I was by him" and "I was daily his delight" (v. 30) seem to indicate wisdom's individual existence.

Furthermore, wisdom is presented as giving counsel to men so they can conduct their lives in ways that will be wholesome, constructive, and pleasing to God. Wisdom pleads with mankind to choose good, not evil; wisdom, not folly; the way of life, rather than the way of death.

No matter what our fellowmen *say*, we tend to evaluate their sincerity, their comprehension, their interests, their dispositions by what they *do*. So it is with a sense of wonder that we see the creative wisdom of God in the universe He has made, and further in the way He advises men and yearns to help them live more fully and constructively.

I. Wisdom Before Creation (Proverbs 8:22-26)

22. The Lord possessed me in the beginning of his way, before his works of old.

The Lord possessed me. "Wisdom" has been speaking in the preceding verses of Proverbs 8, and continues to speak here. Wisdom was a quality God possessed before the general creative process began. The wisdom of God is that ability or competence that has always lain within God's personality and that became obvious as the Lord created the physical universe as the external expression of His purposes.

Before his works of old. That is, as has just been said, the latent wisdom of God became evident as the creative processes unfolded.

23. I was set up from everlasting, from the beginning, or ever the earth was.

The infinite wisdom of the Creator was seen in the creation, but it existed long before any creation occurred. Some groups of the ancients believed the earth itself was eternal. On the contrary, the Biblical view is that God always was. We believe He possessed all of what we may call His "attributes," but some of these qualities of His being became exposed only as He acted in creation, revelation, redemption, judgment, and in the expression of compassionate concern for man.

24. When there were no depths, I was brought forth; when there were no fountains abounding with water.

The *New International Version* translates this, "when there were no oceans." While *depths* may be a more literal rendering, *oceans* expresses the general idea more graphically. It is a comforting and a marvelous truth to contemplate that He who will exist in power and wisdom when there shall be no more sea (Revelation 21:1) already lived before ever any sea was. *Fountains* refers to springs in the earth's interior.

25. Before the mountains were settled, before the hills was I brought forth.

With us, wisdom is an ability to use knowledge most effectively. This wisdom must be acquired, and we need to use it as a precious possession more valuable than any diamond, ruby, or emerald. But God did not learn to be wise. He is the living treasure of wisdom, which flows out for the use of all the sons and daughters of men.

The words of this verse, spoken of wisdom, call to our minds the psalmist's affirmation of Jehovah: "Before the mountains were brought forth, or ever thou hadst formed the earth and the world, even from everlasting to everlasting, thou art God" (Psalm 90:2).

26. While as yet he had not made the earth, nor the fields, nor the highest part of the dust of the world.

The earth . . . the fields. The distinction here seems to be between those land areas that are cultivated and occupied and those areas of land that are uninhabited. *The highest part of the dust of the world* may be best understood to mean all the mass of the dust of the earth. Before any of this existed, wisdom was with God.

II. Wisdom During Creation (Proverbs 8:27-31))

27. When he prepared the heavens, I was there: when he set a compass upon the face of the depth.

Surely the *heavens*—all the galaxies, the planetary arrangements of our own solar system, the ordering of elements by which the atmospheric *heaven* permits the formation of clouds, and the jet streams, by which clouds and air are circulated around the earth—are all evidences of unique and unmatched intelligence. The sea with its great depths and extent is remarkable also. It is so broad that one can see that the horizon forms a kind of circle. The *New International Version* has for the last part of this verse, "When he marked out the horizon on the face of the deep," while the *Revised Standard Version* reads, "When he drew a circle on the face of the deep." The next verse expands on this present verse.

28. When he established the clouds above: when he strengthened the fountains of the deep.

Clouds are one of the most remarkable features of the environment of our planet. Water is heavier than air, but water can be absorbed into those formations we call *clouds* and be carried by wind currents for hundreds of miles. When thermal conditions are right, the vapor is condensed and the water then falls out upon the earth in rain, sleet, hail, or snow. Elihu questioned Job about the wonders of this when he asked, "Dost thou know the balancings of the clouds, the wondrous works of him which is perfect in knowledge?" (Job 37:16).

Only in recent years, because of the development of deep-sea diving mechanisms, has man been able to explore the ocean depths. In several places, springs have been found welling up from the ocean floor and creating strange "islands" of life about them. We know now that the phrase *fountains of the deep* is not just poetic.

29. When he gave to the sea his decree, that the waters should not pass his commandment: when he appointed the foundations of the earth.

The earth is two-thirds water, and the depth and immensity of the earth's seas is stupendous. One might wonder why the *waters* do not completely cover the earth. But there is the attraction of the moon, which draws the waters in the oceans one way and another so they go only "so far." The divine arrangement for the *decree* that *the waters should not pass his commandment* is beautifully and poetically indicated by God when He asked Job, 38:8-11: "Who shut up the sea behind doors when it burst forth from the womb, when I made the clouds its garment and wrapped it in thick darkness, when I fixed limits for it and set its doors and bars in place, when I said, 'This far you may come and no farther; here is where your proud waves halt'?" (Job 38:8-11, *New International Version*).

Though the earth is rotating on its axis at a rate of more than one thousand miles per hour at the equator, and though it is hurtling through space at the speed of 66,600 miles per hour on its multimillion mile annual journey around the sun, the earth seems very stable and solid. So one can speak about the earth's *foundations*. The firmness of earth is as great a tribute to the Creator's wisdom as is the leashing of the sea's tides or the formation and use of the clouds.

30. Then I was by him, as one brought up with him: and I was daily his delight, rejoicing always before him.

The personification of wisdom continues. Wisdom is pictured as a familiar and close companion of God. Of course, we know God was never *brought up* in the sense of passing in sequence from infancy, to childhood, to adolescence, and then to maturity. But the closeness of wisdom to the Lord, its intimate association with God's nature and activity, is what is stressed. *The New International Version* renders the first part of this verse, "Then I was the craftsman at his side." This emphasizes the part wisdom played in the fashioning of the many designs and mechanisms so cunningly wrought into the fabric of the universe.

The joy resulting because of the creation is clearly brought out in the last part of this verse. The gladness that accompanied God's creative activity is suggested in other sections of Scripture as well. We think of the creation account in Genesis, where the creative acts were called "good" and "very good," and in Job 38, where the angelic delight in God's creation is vividly described, "When the morning stars sang together, and all the sons of God shouted for joy" (v. 7).

Those who come to understand more and more of the beauty and intricacy of God's creation share that joy. When one understands the mechanisms of the pollination of flowers, or the structure of cells, or any of thousands of complex processes, one is filled with awe and a sense of delight at the order and fitness of what is seen.

A GLORIOUS UNIVERSE

I have just finished reading Jonathan Weiner's intriguing book, *Planet Earth*. It is a fairly large book that deals with scholarly ideas about the universe, but it is written so that a non-scientific person, such as myself, can grasp the concepts. That's why I like it, and why I recommend it to others with similar limitations. If you choose to read it, you will have to stay on your toes. The author is an evolutionist, and much of what he says is contrary to our Christian beliefs.

Weiner pictures the earth as a marvelous planet, still in the process of creating itself, with wonders on every hand, and with built-in qualities of change and adaptability.

He suggests the possibility that just as the human body has the ability to adjust to changing conditions (sweating when it's hot; shivering when it's cold), so the entire planet may have its own mechanisms by which it makes allowance for the abuse it suffers at the hands of man.

How wonderful is the universe; how marvelous is the planet Earth! Indeed, wisdom "was there when he [God] set the heavens in place, . . . and when he marked out the foundations of the earth" (Proverbs 8:27, 29, *New International Version*).   —T. T.

31. Rejoicing in the habitable part of his earth; and my delights were with the sons of men.

The *New American Standard Bible* reads, "Rejoicing in the world, His earth, and having my

---

How to Say It

ELIHU.   Ee-*lye*-hew.
CHUANG-TZU.   Juang-zu.

---

delight in the sons of men." Among all the vastness of the universe, we know this earth best. And we are constantly amazed as modern technology enables us to observe more and more of God's creative wisdom. Study of the other planets, so far as now possible, reveals them as too hot, too cold, or too lacking in oxygen or nutrients to serve as a home for man. Our beautiful world is marvelously fashioned to be suited to our life.

When we study man—man with his complex body, and his capability for feeling and willing, for wonder and worship, for faith, hope, and love—we are truly enthralled. Of course, man has the capability for hatred and horror, terror and torture, perversion and persecution. But this is also the world to which the Son of God came to unite His life and destiny with *the sons of men*, delighting to call himself "the Son of man." Thus, wisdom can rejoice in the sons of men, who are capable of turning to God, of sacrifices for love, of the creation of beauty, of the redeemed life, and of the renewed spirit.

III. Wisdom's Benefits Today (Proverbs 8:32-36)

32. Now therefore hearken unto me, O ye children: for blessed are they that keep my ways.

As is often true in Proverbs, wisdom is pictured as urging men to listen to her instruction. It is not as though wisdom is saying, "Here it is; take it or leave it." Rather, wisdom pleads with men. One is reminded of God's words, quoted by Isaiah, "I have spread out my hands all the day unto a rebellious people" (65:2), and of Jesus' beautiful invitation, "Come unto me, all ye that labor and are heavy laden, and I will give you rest" (Matthew 11:28).

Of course, it is not enough to *hear* wisdom's directions for life; one must keep her ways. In like manner, Jesus pronounced blessings upon those who heard His sayings and *did* them (Matthew 7:24-27). A major stress on being *doers* of God's word is found in the book of James (1:22; 2:17, 18, 24, 26).

33. Hear instruction, and be wise, and refuse it not.

It is impossible to make someone act wisely. We can give *instruction* that is correct, honest, worthwhile, and vital. But we cannot compel a person to really listen to, or accept, that instruction. Directions for living life in a wise manner are available, but each person must decide for himself or herself whether or not to yield to wisdom's entreaties.

34. Blessed is the man that heareth me, watching daily at my gates, waiting at the posts of my doors.

Here wisdom is presented as inhabiting a house, which probably is surrounded by a wall with *gates* to guard admittance to the property. As people seeking favors of the resident would *wait* at the gate or the doors of the house for his appearance, so those desiring wisdom are urged to be present and eager to receive the blessings and benefits that wisdom can provide. The concept of wisdom's house or mansion is taken up in Proverbs 9:1, where we read, "Wisdom hath builded her house, she hath hewn out her seven pillars."

BANISH WISDOM

Chuang-tzu was a Chinese philosopher of the fourth and third centuries B. C., who followed a way of life known as Taoism. He left behind some of his thoughts in a small book whose title is the same as his name. It contains allegories, parables, etc., and is highly mystical, as is almost everything associated with this religion.

"Banish wisdom, discard knowledge, and gangsters will stop," is one of Chuang-tzu's statements. Sound logical? Not at all. I assume he is saying, "If people will stop striving for wisdom and knowledge, if indeed they will cease all striving, then there will be no criminals; for crime is the result of craving for what others possess."

Inasmuch as wisdom came from the Lord, and is His delight, it is impossible for man to banish it. In fact, God's Word makes clear that rather than banish wisdom and discard knowledge, we should strive to attain them and use them to our own benefit, for the benefit of others, and to the glory of God. —T. T.

35. For whoso findeth me findeth life, and shall obtain favor of the Lord.

Wisdom can help man see God's works in all things, and can also bring to man a revelation of God's will for man. While the heavens do declare the glory of God, and the earth also is full of God's glory (Psalm 19:1; Isaiah 6:3), God reveals a way of *life* to man in His Word. This is indeed the way wisdom brings life to man—the life that will know God's blessing and special presence. (Note Deuteronomy 30:11-16.)

Jesus, God's living Word, brought to man spiritual life from God. "In him was life; and the life was the light of men" (John 1:4). Jesus himself said, "I am come that they might have life, and that they might have it more abundantly" (John 10:10). And on the night of His betrayal, Jesus prayed, "This is life eternal, that they might know thee the only true God, and Jesus Christ, whom thou hast sent (John 17:3).

If we hear wisdom's pleadings and walk in her ways, we will *obtain favor of the Lord.* Because wisdom is from God, it follows that we shall be pleasing to Him when we accept wisdom's leading. To seek to please God is surely the highest ideal to which we can aspire.

HORACE'S ADVICE

"To flee vice is the beginning of virtue, and to have got rid of folly is the beginning of wisdom." The statement sounds like something out of the Bible, probably out of the book of Proverbs. But it is not. The statement was made by Horace, Roman poet of the first century B.C., who some claim is the most read of all Roman writers. The expression is not untrue because it is not from the Bible; it just isn't inspired.

Here is another quotation from Horace: "It is not the rich man you should properly call happy, but him who knows how to use with wisdom the blessings of the gods, to endure hard poverty, and who fears dishonor worse than death, and is not afraid to die for cherished friends or fatherland." Of course, I disagree with his reference to the "gods"; but with that exception, I endorse his advice. Horace suggested we "use with wisdom" our blessings. Solomon portrays wisdom as saying, "Whoever finds me finds life and receives favor from the Lord" (Proverbs 8:35, *New International Version*)

All of us receive blessings in life, and those blessings take various forms. Wise is the person who recognizes God as the source of all blessings and who, through the use of them, brings honor to God. —T. T.

36. But he that sinneth against me wrongeth his own soul: all they that hate me love death.

visual 6

In the natural world, harm can come to man in many ways. But wisdom teaches us how to protect ourselves from that which would threaten our physical safety. Thus, we take shelter in the time of a violent storm, we avoid exposure to extreme weather conditions, and we respect the deadly capability of many wild animals and poisonous snakes. But if we disregard what wisdom teaches us concerning these, or any other, sources of harm, we will surely experience difficulty and may even suffer death.

The same is true in the spiritual realm. Wisdom teaches us to avoid the evils of greed, pride, selfishness, hatred, lust, anger, and jealousy. Wisdom leads us to obey God, accept His Word, and conform to His will. To reject wisdom's leading is to turn from life to death.

Conclusion

A. Christ—The Wisdom of God

A study of the book of Proverbs reveals the important place assigned to wisdom in the economy of God. As we noted earlier, wisdom is personified in the book of Proverbs. In certain sections of Proverbs, this personification seems to give way to complete personalization, and wisdom takes on the character of a real being, one "clothed with personal life, in closest fellowship with the Eternal, inseparably one with Him" (Cook). Take, for example, such words as these in today's text: "The Lord possessed me in the beginning of his way, before his works of old. I was set up from everlasting. . . . When he prepared the heavens, I was there. . . . I was by him, as one brought up with him: and I was daily his delight, rejoicing always before him" (Proverbs 8:22-30). Some associate this personalized wisdom with the second person of the Trinity, Christ, and find further identification with the *Logos* (Word) of John's Gospel, which John asserts was "in the beginning with God" and later "was made flesh, and dwelt among us" (John 1:1-14).

Paul described Jesus as "the power of God, and the wisdom of God" (1 Corinthians 1:24), and taught the Colossians that in Him "are hid all the treasures of wisdom and knowledge" (2:3). Who else but Jesus could say, "The words that I speak unto you, they are spirit, and they are life" (John 6:63)?

The wisdom of God is seen in Jesus. He came to do the will of God (Hebrews 10:7). His words are the words of God; His works are the works of God (John 14:10; 9:4). He speaks of himself as "the way, the truth, and the life" (John 14:6). He made known God's way of righteousness by living a fully righteous life. He lived a life completely sanctified, separated, and surrendered to Him, and thus pointed the way for others to do the same. And by His life, death, and resurrection, He provided the way for redemption.

On two occasions during Jesus' ministry, the Father said of Him, "This is my beloved Son, in whom I am well pleased." If we too would please our Heavenly Father, let us accept and follow Jesus, "who of God is made unto us wisdom, and righteousness, and sanctification, and redemption" (1 Corinthians 1:30).

B. Prayer

Our Father, we stand in awe of Your wisdom, which we see displayed everywhere we look in this marvelous universe. The precise movements of planets, the ceaseless rise and fall of the oceans' tides, and the delicate artistry of a butterfly's wings alike are evidences to us of Your creative mastery. Whether we look at the fashioning of our blood cells, or the mechanisms of the senses of sight, hearing, or touch, we pause in admiration.

But beyond all physical marvels are the wonders of Your love and mercy, which brought our Savior, Jesus, into our world. We are grateful for His words of truth, for His acts of compassion, and for His willingness to give His life a ransom for us. We are possessors of undying hope, because He lives as conqueror of sin and death.

Help us to be more and more aware of that wisdom from above, which you have revealed in all these realities of life and especially in Your Son. In Jesus' name, amen.

C. Thought to Remember

God has revealed His wisdom to us. Let us open our eyes and hearts to *perceive* it and *embrace* it.

Home Daily Bible Readings

Monday, July 2—Wisdom Calls Us (Proverbs 8:1-11)

Tuesday, July 3—Wisdom's Way Is True (Proverbs 8:12-21)

Wednesday, July 4—God Created Wisdom First (Proverbs 8:22-31).

Thursday, July 5—Wisdom Is Life (Proverbs 8:32-36)

Friday, July 6—The Wise Grow in Wisdom (Proverbs 9:7-12)

Saturday, July 7—The Wise and Foolish Contrasted (Proverbs 15:1-11)

Sunday, July 8—God's Knowledge (Romans 11:33-36)

Learning by Doing

*This page contains an alternate lesson plan emphasizing learning activities. Classes
desiring such student involvement will find these suggestions helpful.*

Learning Goals

After studying this lesson, your adult students should:

1. Experience a sense of wonder and awe at God's wisdom that is seen in the creation of the universe and man.

2. Demonstrate wisdom in caring for the earth, our bodies, and our minds.

3. Know that Jesus Christ is the ultimate personification of wisdom.

Into the Lesson

Bring a variety of old magazines to the classroom. Include travel magazines in the collection. Provide scissors, newsprint, and paste. Divide the class into groups of four to six and ask each group to choose a different verse from Proverbs 8:22-31 to illustrate. Have each group cut out pictures and make a montage on the newsprint, illustrating the feature of the physical world mentioned in their verse. This will provide visual reminders of the magnificent wisdom God demonstrated in creating the universe. When the montages have been completed, tape them to the chalkboard for all to see.

If your classroom is not conducive to such an activity, assign selected verses from Proverbs 8:22-31 to three or four students the week before this lesson. Ask them to prepare at home montages of pictures of various features of the physical world, label them with the assigned verse, and bring them to class to be displayed. Briefly discuss the marvels of our world that are shown on these montages.

Into the Word

Point out that the montages that have been constructed illustrate the results of God's great creative wisdom. Explain that the entire eighth chapter of Proverbs is dedicated to the praise of wisdom. It is presented as an independent entity that speaks about itself and all it has witnessed. Wisdom seems to be God's companion, instead of one of His characteristics.

Ask the class to find the answer to the following questions by reading the assigned verses. Encourage participation by as many as possible. (1) In Proverbs 8:22-26, what basic concept regarding wisdom is presented? (Wisdom was with God from eternity, before anything was created.) (2) According to verses 27-31, what was

wisdom doing as God created the heavens, the seas, and mankind? (Wisdom is described as being beside God, working with Him, and rejoicing in what was created.) (3) What do verses 32-36 indicate that mankind's response should be to all that wisdom has done and has said about itself? (People should listen, heed instruction, not neglect wisdom, wait and watch for wisdom.)

Put the following letters on an overhead transparency or on the chalkboard and ask the class to unscramble them: CYLOGOE. The word is *ecology*, and it reminds us that we need to have the wisdom to exercise good stewardship in the care of the world in which we live. Distribute paper and pencils and ask the students to list as many ways as they can think of in which people can show stewardship over natural resources. Instruct them to be specific. For example: Avoid being careless with matches and camp fires. Conserve electricity by keeping thermostats set at moderate instead of extreme temperatures. (Allow five minutes for this activity before asking everyone to share their conclusions.)

Call attention to Proverbs 8:35, and explain that although wisdom claims that it enables people to find life, the fuller truth is that he who is wise looks to Jesus Christ as the one by whom we may find eternal life. Have someone read John 1:4 and John 5:40 aloud. Ask the class if they can remember some other Scriptures that indicate that life comes through Jesus Christ. Encourage students to use their Bibles and to share their findings. As they do so, record the Scripture references on the chalkboard or an overhead transparency and have the Scriptures read aloud. (Some possible answers are Mark 8:34, 35; John 3:16, 36; 5:24; 6:47-51; 14:6; Colossians 3:4; 1 John 5:12; Revelation 2:10.)

Into Life

The Scripture text for this lesson has reminded us of the wonders that surround us in the physical universe. Further, we have seen that God delighted in all those things that His creative wisdom brought forth. Earlier, the students suggested a list of ways in which we can exercise good stewardship over God's earth. Have each student select one item from that list and make a sincere effort to put it into practice in the coming week.

Let's Talk It Over

The questions on this page are designed to encourage review of the lesson Scriptures and to promote discussion of the lesson by the class. The answers provided are only discussion starters. Let your class talk it over from there.

1. One of the mysteries surrounding our Creator is how He could have always existed. Is this a barrier to faith, or may it contribute to a person's developing faith in God?

The Bible nowhere explains this divine attribute. It opens with the words, "In the beginning God" (Genesis 1:1), and only occasionally gives us glimpses of what happened before creation. We are clearly shown that everything material owes its existence to God. The person who rejects the idea of God must assume that matter is eternal or that it originated on its own. Surely that viewpoint requires a greater stretching of one's imagination than faith in an eternal Creator. To ponder these matters is to recognize the severe limits of the human mind. We may not be able to lay hold on tangible, scientific proof that God is and always was. But then, neither can non-believers prove their viewpoint. So faith in God is a sensible option to the person who thinks seriously about these mysteries.

2. Why may it be advantageous for Christians to be well informed as to the stars and other heavenly bodies?

Such knowledge could be a means of strengthening our faith in God. When we gaze into the heavens at night, we are impressed anew with our relative smallness and the immensity of the creation. That leads in turn to a sense of awe and humility, which is conducive to faith. Also, when we become acquainted with the precise movement of the heavenly bodies, we experience what the psalmist stated: "The heavens declare the glory of God; and the firmament showeth his handiwork" (Psalm 19:1). Since the universe is a kind of "book" that reveals the Creator, we would do well to "study" it, even as we do the Bible. A knowledge of the heavens may give us opportunity to testify of our faith in God on occasions when our listeners may not be open to direct Biblical truths.

3. Some readers of the Bible are disturbed by its failure in places to use scientifically accurate terminology. What can we say to this?

In our lesson text we have reference to "the foundations of the earth." In Psalm 19:4-6, the sun is pictured as traveling across the heavens in its daily journey. We know that the earth does not have literal foundations, and we are also aware that the earth travels around the sun, rather than the opposite. We can respond to this by pointing out that if God had given Biblical writers scientifically-precise terms, their writings would have made little sense to the readers of their time. It was obviously God's intention that scientific knowledge be progressively discovered by man. Also, we must take into account the Biblical use of poetic description. In both of our examples, the expressions used are in poetic, not scientific, contexts.

4. Why may it be advantageous for Christians to be well informed as to the beauties and intricacies of nature?

In connection with Solomon's wisdom, we read that "he spake of trees, from the cedar tree that is in Lebanon even unto the hyssop that springeth out of the wall: he spake also of beasts, and of fowl, and of creeping things, and of fishes" (1 Kings 4:33). Jesus, the one "greater than Solomon," also spoke frequently of nature. Obviously, spiritual lessons may be gained through the observation and study of nature. Also, a knowledge of nature may be a means of sharing our faith in God with people who also delight in the creation, but have not yet become personally acquainted with the Creator.

5. Those who reject wisdom harm themselves; those who hate it demonstrate their love of death. This principle found in Proverbs 8:36 is expressed in various ways throughout the Bible. What are some of these other ways?

This is similar to Moses' challenge to Israel, "I have set before you life and death ... therefore choose life, that both thou and thy seed may live" (Deuteronomy 30:19). It is the same kind of choice Jesus set before His hearers when He spoke of the broad way that leads to destruction and the narrow way that leads to life (Matthew 7:13, 14). Paul set forth the principle in terms of sowing and reaping (Galatians 6:7, 8). In each case, human beings are addressed as free moral agents. They may choose to follow God's way, which results in blessing. Or they may reject God's message and live as they please, but they must accept the disastrous consequences of that decision.

Clue FOR we do Living

Lessons From Life

LESSON SCRIPTURE: Proverbs 22:1-16.

PRINTED TEXT: Proverbs 22:1-16.

Proverbs 22:1-16

1 A good name is rather to be chosen than great riches, and loving favor rather than silver and gold.

2 The rich and poor meet together: the Lord is the maker of them all.

3 A prudent man foreseeth the evil, and hideth himself: but the simple pass on, and are punished.

4 By humility and the fear of the Lord are riches, and honor, and life.

5 Thorns and snares are in the way of the froward: he that doth keep his soul shall be far from them.

6 Train up a child in the way he should go: and when he is old, he will not depart from it.

7 The rich ruleth over the poor, and the borrower is servant to the lender.

8 He that soweth iniquity shall reap vanity: and the rod of his anger shall fail.

9 He that hath a bountiful eye shall be blessed; for he giveth of his bread to the poor.

10 Cast out the scorner, and contention shall go out; yea, strife and reproach shall cease.

11 He that loveth pureness of heart, for the grace of his lips the king shall be his friend.

12 The eyes of the Lord preserve knowledge; and he overthroweth the words of the transgressor.

13 The slothful man saith, There is a lion without, I shall be slain in the streets.

14 The mouth of strange women is a deep pit: he that is abhorred of the Lord shall fall therein.

15 Foolishness is bound in the heart of a child; but the rod of correction shall drive it far from him.

16 He that oppresseth the poor to increase his riches, and he that giveth to the rich, shall surely come to want.

GOLDEN TEXT: A good name is rather to be chosen than great riches, and loving favor rather than silver and gold.—Proverbs 22:1.

Wisdom as a Way of Life
Unit 2: Proverbs of the Wise
(Lessons 4-8)

Lesson Aims

As a result of this lesson, a student should:

1. Appreciate the relevance of these ancient proverbs to life in the twentieth century.

2. Desire the eternal riches God offers more than the material wealth of this world.

3. Select one proverb from the Scripture text and put it in practice this week to enrich his spiritual life.

Lesson Outline

INTRODUCTION

I. PATHS TO AND PERILS OF PROSPERITY (Proverbs 22:1-5)
   A Good Name

II. ACTIONS—WISE AND OTHERWISE (Proverbs 22:6-12)

III. FOUR FATAL CHARACTER FLAWS (Proverbs 22:13-16)
   A. Laziness (v. 13)
      Any Excuse Will Do
   B. Lustfulness (v. 14)
   C. Permissiveness (v. 15)
   D. Greediness (v. 16)

CONCLUSION
   A. Ancient Advice for Living Today
   B. Prayer
   C. Thought to Remember

Visual 7 in the visuals packet is designed to be used with your study of verses 13-16 (point III in the lesson outline above). The visual is shown on page 397.

Introduction

The book of Proverbs contains many separate "sayings" or maxims that appear to be independent. Some of them do stand alone. Others of them, however, are phases of a larger topic that is treated again and again in different ways. Thus certain subjects are encountered often in the book. Some of these subjects are the contrast between the rich and the poor, the wise and the foolish, the pure and the impure, the thoughtless and the considerate.

One is reminded of a symphony in which two or three thematic musical "phrases" are discernible. Amid the various major "movements" will be heard these haunting melodic phrases. Sometimes they will be touched upon by the woodwinds, sometimes sounded by the brass, sometimes echoed by the stringed instruments. Even so, various emphases can be picked out of the seemingly disorganized material in many chapters of Proverbs. Themes such as those mentioned above are found in the Scripture text for this lesson.

I. Paths to and Perils of Prosperity (Proverbs 22:1-5)

1. A good name is rather to be chosen than great riches, and loving favor rather than silver and gold.

In the Old Testament, Israel's reward for obedience to God's will is often expressed in terms of material blessings. That concept is found also in the wisdom literature of the Old Testament. In Psalm 1:1-3 we read that the man who does not walk "in the counsel of the ungodly" but instead delights "in the law of the Lord," shall be blessed: "whatsoever he doeth shall prosper." But here we are told that there is something better than *great riches*, and that is *a good name*. It is possible to have riches and a fine reputation; but if a choice must be made between the two, a good reputation is better.

This thought is reflected in Shakespeare's *Othello*, a play in which a great deal is made of reputation. In Act III, Scene III, we read,

> Good name in man and woman, dear my lord,
> Is the immediate jewel of their souls:
> Who steals my purse steals trash; 'tis something, nothing;
> 'Twas mine, 'tis his, and has been slave to thousands;
> But he that filches from me my good name
> Robs me of that which not enriches him
> And makes me poor indeed.

Allied with *a good name* is the enjoyment of *loving favor*. The *New International Version* translates this, "to be esteemed is better than silver or gold." Notoriety itself is not that which is considered significant. One can be well known and yet be regarded with contempt, or be feared because of one's power. But much better than this, of course, is to be widely known and looked to with deep affection.

A GOOD NAME

Few would quarrel with Shakespeare's logic, which is expressed in the quotation above from *Othello*. A stolen purse is but a minor loss compared to a filched name.

How can a person's name be stolen? Through gossip and slander. Some unknown poet expressed this well in a poem entitled, "Gossip Town." Three stanzas are especially appropriate:

> The principal street is called They-say,
> And I've Heard is the public well;
> The breezes that blow from Falsehood Bay
> Are laden with Don't-You-Tell.
>
> In the midst of the town is Tell-tale Park,
> You're never quite safe while there,
> Its owner is Madame Suspicious Remark,
> Who lives on the street Don't Care.
>
> Just back of the park is Slander Row—
> 'Twas there that Good Name died,
> Pierced by a dart from Jealousy's bow,
> In the hands of Envious Pride.

Of course, good names are not always stolen; sometimes they're lost through the carelessness of their owners. But whether lost or stolen, the damage is almost irreparable. —T. T.

2. The rich and poor meet together: the Lord is the maker of them all.

Many situations arise where the *rich* and the *poor* do not *meet together*. Some more wealthy people send their children to private schools, have first-class seats on airplanes, and patronize restaurants poorer folks ordinarily cannot afford. But while rich and poor diverge in many ways, they do *meet together* at several points. Rich and poor are born the same way, in a mother's pain and in nakedness. While the food and clothing and shelter of the rich and poor may differ widely in quality and quantity, the *need* for these is a reality to both.

All face illnesses, too. While the more affluent may be able to secure more competent medical help, still the flesh of all men share susceptibility to bruises, abrasions, and all sorts of infections. The appendix of a well-to-do person can be inflamed in the same manner as that of a pauper.

Of course, in our society all read the same newspapers, listen to the same radio stations, attend the same baseball, football, hockey, and other games. Above all, in the church, all worship God in the same pews. In one church of my acquaintance, millionaires sat in the same sort of pews, on the same level, as mill workers, or office workers, or nurses. The coming of Jesus, born in a stable, yet the royal Son of David and Son of God, forever makes it possible for the *rich and poor* to *meet together*. All alike seek the redemption of His cross and share the radiant hope of His resurrection.

That God is our Maker means that all mankind shares the commonality of creation by a Heavenly Father. All who share this human kinship can come into the finer kinship of Christian brethren, if they will accept God's Son and the salvation He offers.

3. A prudent man foreseeth the evil, and hideth himself: but the simple pass on, and are punished.

Dr. Arnot, in *Laws From Heaven for Life on Earth*, points out that evils, which one may see and from which a *prudent man* will hide, may be classified as (a) practical and financial, (b) moral and ethical, and (c) spiritual.

Often, with some forethought, it is possible to see that certain feverish economic activities are doomed to collapse. Purveyors of schemes and "investments" may arrive on the scene and promise fabulous profits from their business ventures. One should be insightful enough to keep away from all "get-rich-quick" endeavors. This should not be difficult for Christians, who of all people, should realize that to "lay . . . up . . . treasures upon earth" is not to be a major concern in life (Matthew 6:19, 20).

With forethought, it is possible to see that certain associations and practices, situations and choices, are apt to lead one to a wrong and harmful way of life. The *prudent* person will shun such companions and occasions. For instance, a certain bowling "league" may introduce one to a place where there is much drinking, swearing, and abandoned behavior. It would behoove one to consider changing bowling activities to a more congenial, less morally threatening, environment. Certainly we need to maintain contact with sinful persons, if we are to win them to Christ. However, it would be well to *hide* ourselves from some situations that have proven themselves to be morally and spiritually threatening. An individual must determine what the proper course of action is in such matters by the circumstances in each case and by his own strength or weakness in the spiritual areas involved.

4. By humility and the fear of the Lord are riches, and honor, and life.

Great promises are held out here to the person who is *humble* and lives in reliance upon God, who is reverent toward Him, and who constantly reorders his life in relation to God's will. Great wealth or blessings, as the world considers these to be, may not come to the person who lives in simplicity before men and in surrender to God. But that person will find favor with God and will receive the true riches that are uncorrupted by moth and rust, honor from God and men, and the life that now is and that which is to come—the life eternal in Heaven. He may have little now in the way of material wealth, but the one who trusts God is content and grateful. He feels extremely blessed, for he knows that, in reality, he possesses "all things" (2 Corinthians 6:10).

The person who is greedy for gain and who lives only for things never gets enough. He will always find other people whom he considers *rich* compared with himself. He himself may possess, say, $3,000,000 worth of assets, but someone else has $300,000,000. His own relative "poverty" will breed only discontent in his heart.

What peace of mind or true poise of life can such a person hope to have if he is arrogant and proud and has no trust in the Heavenly Father? Such a person can have no riches that are meaningful or satisfying. "The wicked are like the troubled sea, when it cannot rest, whose waters cast up mire and dirt. There is no peace, saith my God, to the wicked" (Isaiah 57:20, 21).

5. Thorns and snares are in the way of the froward: he that doth keep his soul shall be far from them.

Froward is a word that has dropped out of regular English usage. It is a term that is the opposite of *toward*. Thus it means "away from," turning aside or being somehow diverted from a path that leads somewhere. The *froward* person is one who doesn't move toward a definite goal; he thus falls into trouble and runs into traps, by which he is entangled or unwillingly restrained. One who steadfastly keeps on the road of conformity to God's purposes will be saved from the disasters of spirit that await the one who turns from the narrow way that leads to life (Matthew 7:14).

II. Actions—Wise and Otherwise (Proverbs 22:6-12)

6. Train up a child in the way he should go: and when he is old, he will not depart from it.

The Hebrew word translated *train up* can be translated "initiate," "dedicate," or "discipline." Its proper meaning is said to be "to narrow" or "constrict." The picture is that of a growing bush or plant, which is tied up or secured so it grows in a certain direction rather than spreading out in uncontrolled profusion. Similarly, this proverb urges that a *child* be controlled so the focus of his life is fixed or "zeroed in" on certain behavioral patterns and ideals. This is done by encouraging development in what is considered the most desirable and profitable way of life.

Even when constraining a plant to grow in a certain manner, one must carefully apply cloths or strings or wires so the branches are not harmed or the circulation of nutriment from roots to tendrils impeded or cut off. How much more wisdom and delicacy of touch is required in guiding and molding the developing person-

ality of a child! But the promise is given that proper discipline and control will result in benefits in future years.

7. The rich ruleth over the poor, and the borrower is servant to the lender.

One who owns property or is investing what we today call "capital" in an enterprise can dictate the work to be done, the place it will be done, and what the product will be. Therefore, the person who seeks employment must adjust his time, place, conditions, and type of endeavor to suit the demands or needs of the one whose resources make the work possible.

It also is true that if one is to *borrow* money or any commodity, the *lender* can indicate when he expects to be repaid and how, as well as what interest must be paid, or what services are to be rendered in the repayment of the loan.

8. He that soweth iniquity shall reap vanity: and the rod of his anger shall fail.

Shall reap vanity. The person who sows iniquity shall ultimately have nothing substantial to show for his life. But the word translated *vanity* also means "calamity," "trouble." So the truth expressed is that those who do evil shall meet with punishment in their very sins. Job 4:8 says, "They that plow iniquity, and sow wickedness, reap the same." By contrast, "To him that soweth righteousness shall be a sure reward" (Proverbs 11:18). We are reminded of the apostle Paul's statement, "Whatsoever a man soweth, that shall he also reap. For he that soweth to his flesh shall of the flesh reap corruption; but he that soweth to the Spirit shall of the Spirit reap life everlasting" (Galatians 6:7, 8).

The rod of his anger shall fail. The writer is thinking of the violence and cruelty that the evil person intends against his neighbor. It has no permanence. Eventually, it will vanish away.

9. He that hath a bountiful eye shall be blessed; for he giveth of his bread to the poor.

Again and again in Scripture, the importance of consideration for the *poor* is stressed. It is said of the Lord, "He raiseth up the poor out of the dust" (Psalm 113:7). In speaking of his manner of life, Job said, "I delivered the poor that cried, and the fatherless, and him that had none to help him" (29:12) We are told in Psalm 41:1, "Blessed is he that considereth the poor: the Lord will deliver him in time of trouble." A call to live in the light of God's reign is sounded strongly in Psalm 82. Two duties facing mankind are to "defend the poor and fatherless" and to "deliver the poor and needy" (3, 4).

The prophetic writings are aflame with indignation that the poor are exploited and oppressed. "What mean ye that ye beat my people to pieces, and grind the faces of the poor? saith the Lord God of hosts" (Isaiah 3:15). He says again in 32:7, "The instruments also of the churl are evil: he deviseth wicked devices to destroy the poor with lying words."

In voicing God's condemnation of the inhabitants of Jerusalem, Ezekiel charges, "The people of the land have used oppression, and exercised robbery, and have vexed the poor and needy" (22:29). Amos is especially vigorous in his denunciation of those who take advantage of the poor. He warns of punishment for those selling "the poor for a pair of shoes" (2:6), of those who "oppress the poor" and "crush the needy" (4:1), whose "treading is upon the poor," and who "turn aside the poor in the gate from their right" (5:11, 12).

Jesus indicated that one of the evidences of His messiahship was that "the poor have the gospel preached to them" (Matthew 11:5). James 2:5, 6 tells us God has chosen the poor of this world to receive blessing, if rich in faith. Further, he speaks severely of those who have "despised the poor."

10. Cast out the scorner, and contention shall go out; yea, strife and reproach shall cease.

This is an incisive analysis of why troubles and disturbances arise in many social situations. The reason is that some people are scornful, or derisive. That is, they look down on others and feel "superior"; thus they deride others and refuse to work with them. The solution is to get rid of the one whose antagonistic attitudes cause problems.

11. He that loveth pureness of heart, for the grace of his lips the king shall be his friend.

In contrast with the "scorner," the person described in this verse acts from sincere and uncontaminated motives. His attitude promotes social harmony and creates good instead of ill feeling. No wonder *the king*, or anyone in a leadership position, is a *friend* to such a helpful, earnest, constructive individual. No wonder Jesus had high praise for those who are "pure in heart" (Matthew 5:8).

12. The eyes of the Lord preserve knowledge; and he overthroweth the words of the transgressor.

The *New International Version* renders the first part of this verse, "The eyes of the Lord keep watch over knowledge." God is interested in man's *knowledge*. This may well be because every bit of true understanding is a comprehension of something more God has done in the intricate and interconnected wonder of His creative work. While all genuine knowledge is pleasing to God, those who boast about violating His ways will find such rebellion to be useless.

III. Four Fatal Character Flaws (Proverbs 22:13-16)

A. Laziness (v. 13)

13. The slothful man saith, There is a lion without, I shall be slain in the streets.

The lazy person always seems to have an excuse for postponing his work or for his failure in meeting his obligations. The most improbable peril or obstacle is sufficient to justify his inactivity. He cannot go here or there, because it may snow, sleet, hail, or rain. The date is such that there will be too much traffic on the road, or possibly someone in the family to be visited has a contagious disease! Let us reject such slothful inclinations. Instead, let us resolve to do the duties we know we should perform and to deal with difficulties as they arise.

ANY EXCUSE WILL DO

The Hebrew text reveals that there is satire in verse 13, but it's easy to miss in our English versions. A surface reading makes it appear that the man spoken of has a legitimate reason for not wanting to go outside. I, for one, would prefer to stay inside and enjoy the protection of my home, if I knew there was a lion prowling the streets of my city. But that's not the case. This lazy fellow says, "There's a lion *without*," that is, "out in the open country." And, "because there is, I am not going to venture out into the streets of my city."

This is a classic example of the maxim, "Any excuse will serve when one has not a mind to do a thing"; or, simply stated, "Any excuse is better than none."

How true that is! For example, if one doesn't want to attend church, he can always find some excuse for not doing so. I recall the story of the two men out golfing on the Lord's Day. One looked down at his watch, and, noticing that it was 10:30 A.M., commented to his partner, "If I were home, I'd just now be getting in the car to go to church." To which his companion replied, "Not me. If I were home, I wouldn't be going to church today; my wife is sick."

Enough said.   —T. T.

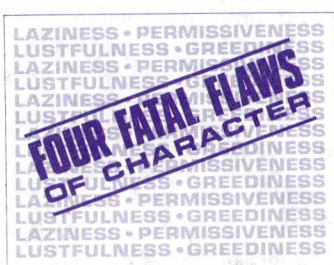

visual 7

B. Lustfulness (v. 14)

14. The mouth of strange women is a deep pit: he that is abhorred of the Lord shall fall therein.

Proverbs frequently warns us against the wiles of prostitutes and adulteresses. The tragic events in the lives of Samson, Judah, David, Solomon, and others teach us that such warnings are important and relevant. Many careers of political, economic, and religious leaders have been ruined because such warnings as are in this verse were unheeded. *He that is abhorred of the Lord* is the person who has incurred God's wrath by previous unfaithfulness and sin. Having abandoned God, that man is left to himself to fall prey to the seductive words of wicked women.

C. Permissiveness (v. 15)

15. Foolishness is bound in the heart of a child; but the rod of correction shall drive it far from him.

A *child* is *bound* by his or her very nature to do *foolish* things. In many areas, life's experiences bring the needed correction. For example, a child learns by experience that it is uncomfortable to get wet feet and legs in snow and slush. If he is burned once by playing with matches, he understands the pain that fire can inflict. But traits such as inconsideration, selfishness, and waywardness are not abandoned by the child so quickly. To rid a child of these requires effort by the parents. Instruction, correction, and discipline—lovingly, patiently, and consistently given—can overcome these tendencies and assist in the child's proper character development. A parent's permissiveness in these areas will eventually lead to heartbreak for parent and child alike.

D. Greediness (v. 16)

16. He that oppresseth the poor to increase his riches, and he that giveth to the rich, shall surely come to want.

The person so greedy for gain that he exploits *the poor* is not likely to profit much in the long run. Even if the poor are "taken advantage of," they have so little from which they can be parted. Further, to sell to the poor on "easy credit" is to be in danger of losing much when they are unable to pay. The effort to gain riches by "cultivating" wealthy people is apt to cause frustration, for the wealthy generally possess a greater alertness to exploitation. All who strive to get rich in any way, at any cost, are in danger of losing friends, financial status, and stability of life.

Conclusion

A. Ancient Advice for Living Today

The book of Proverbs comes to us across a great span of time. One may be inclined to think that such ancient writings can have little to say to man in such a "high-tech" age as ours. Yet the same evils, about which Proverbs speaks, are with us yet today. Men are still led astray by "strange women," greed, and sloth. Conversely, a good reputation is just as important as it was thousands of years ago. Humility, prudence, and foresight are still admirable qualities. And how shall godliness and the knowledge of the Creator continue on earth, if we do not teach and discipline our children regarding His ways?

Surely Jeremiah 9:23, 24 could be used as a summary statement of the teaching of Proverbs: "This is what the Lord says: 'Let not the wise man boast of his wisdom or the strong man boast of his strength or the rich man boast of his riches, but let him who boasts boast about this: that he understands and knows me, that I am the Lord, who exercises kindness, justice and righteousness on earth, for in these I delight,' declares the Lord" *(New International Version)*.

B. Prayer

Our Heavenly Father, we offer our prayer in the flow of our life in this busy, beautiful, and mysterious world. We are grateful for what we have been able to learn *about* the world, but we are also thankful for the directions given us in Your Word for living *in* the world. May we learn to live wisely and serve faithfully. Amen.

C. Thought to Remember

The root and flowers of wisdom depend on the same thing—the fear of the Lord.

Learning by Doing

*This page contains an alternate lesson plan emphasizing learning activities. Classes
desiring such student involvement will find these suggestions helpful.*

Learning Goals

In studying this lesson, students will:

1. Analyze and chart Proverbs 22:1-16 according to its major topics.

2. Compare the teachings of Jesus in the Sermon on the Mount with the wise sayings in Proverbs 22.

3. Come to a greater awareness of the spiritual danger that lies in the desire for riches.

Into the Lesson

Begin by commenting that the book of Proverbs abounds with a wide variety of wise sayings and statements offering sound advice regarding life and conduct. To point up the importance of such advice, ask each class member to find a person who is not their relative and discuss the following question: If you were asked to help and advise a foreign student or tourist who is visiting in our country for one year, what three pieces of advice would you offer? Allow about five minutes for the pairs to discuss this. Then let the whole class share and discuss their suggestions for a few minutes. Then say, "Let's see what important lessons for life we can gain from today's lesson text."

Into the Word

Lead into a study of today's Scripture passage by saying that Proverbs 22:1-16 deals with three major areas of concern. They are not developed consecutively, but the discerning reader can find them. Give each student a sheet of paper and pencil, and ask them to make three vertical columns and label them as follows: "Riches," "Undesirable Spiritual Qualities," "Desirable Spiritual Qualities." Then instruct them to read Proverbs 22:1-16 and find the verses that relate in any way to these topics. Have them list the verses in the appropriate columns. (Their charts should resemble the following: Riches—vv. 1, 2, 4, 7, 16; Undesirable Spiritual Qualities—vv. 5, 8, 10, 13, 14, 16; Desirable Spiritual Qualities—vv. 1, 3, 4, 9, 11.)

In the Sermon on the Mount, Jesus spoke of riches. He also mentioned desirable spiritual qualities that we should incorporate in our lives, as well as undesirable spiritual qualities that we should avoid. Divide your class into three groups and have them survey this Sermon, which is found in chapters 5-7 of the Gospel of Matthew. Assign one chapter to each group. Let the students work in pairs to study their assigned chapter. Instruct them to use the reverse side of the sheet you gave them earlier and to make a chart like the one they made for their survey of Proverbs 22. The three columns should be given the same headings. As they read their chapter, have them fill in the chart by listing the verse references under the appropriate headings. When the groups have completed their surveys, have them share their findings with the class. Each group can add to their chart the information given by the others.

Elaborate upon the topic of riches. Tell the class that a study of the four Gospels shows that Jesus talked much more about man's use of money than about any other topic. Ask them why they think He talked so much about this subject. Summarize the answers by reading Matthew 6:21. Jesus wanted people to give their hearts to God. He knew that the attraction of wealth was so strong that it could keep them from making that commitment, if they let it.

Into Life

Point out that the issues mentioned in Proverbs 22 are as current as today's newspaper. The advice given in Proverbs for successful living is as pertinent and helpful today as it was when it was first written. People today are faced with the same temptations, although some of the sins have been given more respectable names. Adultery, for example, may now be referred to as "an affair" or an "extra-marital relationship" or "open marriage." It may well be asked, "Whatever became of sin?" Summarize the lesson by saying that whether the sin be that of adultery, greed, or oppression of the poor, each individual is responsible before God for the choices that he or she makes. The advice contained in Proverbs for a happy and successful life before God is offered to all. We must choose to follow it.

Conclude the lesson by asking the class to mention some everyday examples of ways in which adults are tempted to compromise their integrity for personal gain. Some examples are shady business deals, cheating on income tax returns, or neglecting to give to the needy. Close with prayer seeking God's help as we strive to live according to the high standards of conduct that are presented in His Word.

Let's Talk It Over

The questions on this page are designed to encourage review of the lesson Scriptures and to promote discussion of the lesson by the class. The answers provided are only discussion starters. Let your class talk it over from there.

1. Why is it beneficial for wealthier Christians and poorer ones to have frequent contact with one another?

Such contacts may arise when a church in an affluent area plants a new congregation in a poorer section of their community. Or, in some large congregations that draw worshipers from a widespread area, rich and poor may well sit side by side in the same pew. However the contact arises, it should be cultivated so that the stereotyped views, which rich and poor frequently hold regarding one another, may not be reproduced in the church. The poor may assume that wealthy people are callous and contemptuous toward those who are below them on the economic scale. The rich may have the impression that poorer people are envious of them. By having fellowship with one another, each can see that they share in struggling with problems and fears and that they have a similar love for the Lord and desire to do His will.

2. What are some ways in which we can "hide" from evil that might tempt us or ensnare us?

It is well for us to take time to work out our own code of restrictions—points at which we will "draw the line" when influenced toward a certain form of behavior. For example, though we recognize that movies with something other than a general rating could have some redeeming value, we will determine to refrain from viewing them. Another way of "hiding" is simply avoiding certain persons who tend to have a strong negative influence on us (see 1 Corinthians 5:9-11; 15:33). It may make us feel guilty to shun someone who wants to associate with us. But if their ungodly influence on us seems stronger than our godly influence on them, avoidance may be the safer course.

3. Some parents feel that it is not right for them to exercise too strong an influence on their children. They insist that the children should be free to choose their own religion, moral standards, vocation, etc. How do you feel about this?

Our lesson text contains a command that plainly calls for parents to influence their children: "Train up a child in the way he should go: and when he is old, he will not depart from it" (Proverbs 22:6). The fact is that our children are subject to many influences in our society. The school, television programs, coaches of athletic teams, schoolmates, and playmates are among these. Certainly it is unwise for parents to attempt to *dictate* all their values and goals to their children, but they do the young people no favor if they fail to influence them for what is right and good.

4. Applying Proverbs 22:13 to the church, what are some of the imagined perils that keep members from completing the church's work?

One that comes readily to mind pertains to the task of making evangelistic calls. Members tend to shy away from this task, because they imagine themselves being embarrassed or insulted or having a door slammed in their faces. Of course, these happen occasionally, but not nearly so often as we may fear. Another fear is that regarding teaching or speaking before the congregation. We may fear that our minds will go blank in the middle of our presentation or that we will accidentally say something that is doctrinally wrong. But if we have prepared well beforehand, neither is likely to occur.

5. Because the physical abuse of children receives so much media attention, some readers may be disturbed by our text's reference to "the rod of correction" (v. 15). What can we say about this?

Perhaps we have all read or heard of an instance in which a parent has administered cruel and abusive punishment to his children and has claimed simply to be following Biblical guidelines. We may even feel that our text and the later statements found in Proverbs 23:13, 14 contribute to such misunderstandings of the nature of parental discipline. It is well to point out that in the Christian era we have passages such as Ephesians 6:4 and Colossians 3:21 to guide us in our application of the instructions in Proverbs. If we believe in the appropriateness of physical punishment, we must make sure that it is administered in such a way that children are not unduly provoked to wrath or exasperated.

Proverbs in Pictures

LESSON SCRIPTURE: Proverbs 30.

PRINTED TEXT: Proverbs 30:18-33.

Proverbs 30:18-33

18 There be three things which are too wonderful for me, yea, four which I know not:

19 The way of an eagle in the air; the way of a serpent upon a rock; the way of a ship in the midst of the sea; and the way of a man with a maid.

20 Such is the way of an adulterous woman; she eateth, and wipeth her mouth, and saith, I have done no wickedness.

21 For three things the earth is disquieted, and for four which it cannot bear:

22 For a servant when he reigneth; and a fool when he is filled with meat;

23 For an odious woman when she is married; and a handmaid that is heir to her mistress.

24 There be four things which are little upon the earth, but they are exceeding wise:

25 The ants are a people not strong, yet they prepare their meat in the summer;

26 The conies are but a feeble folk, yet make they their houses in the rocks;

27 The locusts have no king, yet go they forth all of them by bands;

28 The spider taketh hold with her hands, and is in kings' palaces.

29 There be three things which go well, yea, four are comely in going:

30 A lion, which is strongest among beasts, and turneth not away for any;

31 A greyhound; a he goat also; and a king, against whom there is no rising up.

32 If thou hast done foolishly in lifting up thyself, or if thou hast thought evil, lay thine hand upon thy mouth.

33 Surely the churning of milk bringeth forth butter, and the wringing of the nose bringeth forth blood: so the forcing of wrath bringeth forth strife.

GOLDEN TEXT: If thou hast done foolishly in lifting up thyself, or if thou hast thought evil, lay thine hand upon thy mouth.—Proverbs 30:32.

Wisdom as a Way of Life
Unit 2: Proverbs of the Wise
(Lessons 4-8)

Lesson Aims

As a result of this lesson, a student will:
1. Have a greater appreciation of the wisdom of God, as seen in nature.
2. Learn to look for lessons in events and things that seem small and insignificant.
3. Help resolve conflict among people.

Lesson Outline

INTRODUCTION
    A. Marvelous Matters
    B. Lesson Background
I. THINGS WONDERFUL AND WOEFUL (Proverbs 30:18-23)
II. THINGS MINUTE AND MASTERFUL (Proverbs 30:24-31)
    Lessons From Ants
    A Strutting Rooster
III. CAUTIONARY COUNSELS (Proverbs 30:32, 33)
CONCLUSION
    A. Poetic Pictures
    B. Prayer
    C. Thought to Remember

Display visual 8 from the visuals packet and let it remain before the class throughout the session. The visual is shown on page 405.

Introduction

A. Marvelous Matters

In the Biblical literature, we see a mixture of appreciation and caution regarding nature. There is a constant awareness of the power and wisdom of God, which are seen everywhere in the physical universe He created. God called "good" all the material things He had formed (Genesis 1:4, 10, 12, 18, 21, 25, 31). The psalmist declared that the heavens reveal "the glory of God" and the "firmament" His "handiwork" (Psalm 19:1). Psalm 104 has a long list of natural phenomena such as clouds, springs, birds, grass, trees, and various animals. At one point the psalmist exclaims, "How many are your works, O Lord! In wisdom you made them all; the earth is full of your creatures" (v. 24, *New International Version*).

Yet we also find a reticence in the references to nature. There was a good reason for this. In

Biblical times, the nations surrounding Israel were for the most part worshipers of nature. Many worshiped the sun. Others trusted in the influence and "favorable" positions of the planets and the stars. Some regarded trees or animals as sacred, and did obeisance to them.

The false gods of many Canaanite religions were worshiped in groves on high hills. But the hills were not to be exalted—only God, who had created them. So it is we find the psalmist declaring, "If I lift up my eyes to the hills, where shall I find help? Help comes only from the Lord, maker of heaven and earth" (Psalm 121:1, 2, *The New English Bible*). Hence it came about that care had to be exercised in comments concerning such natural features as hills, trees, stars, etc. This makes all the more impressive the inclusion of the perceptive and appreciative notes about the ways of nature described in Proverbs 30.

B. Lesson Background

The *King James Version* ascribes Proverbs 30 to one named "Agur" (v. 1). The Hebrew text here is declared by all Hebrew scholars to be very difficult to translate. This is because several words in this verse occur nowhere else in the Old Testament. Agur was a seer, about which nothing else is known for certain. The *Revised Standard Version* says Agur is a "son of Jakeh of Massa." "Massa" was the name of a son of Ishmael (Genesis 25:13, 14), so some believe Agur may have been an Arabian.

This chapter apparently is one of two appendices added to Proverbs to complete the collection of wise sayings that had been assembled. Among the notable features of chapter 30 is not only the stress on the mysterious character of the natural world, but the form in which the writing is cast. We have a series of what have been called "numerical proverbs." These begin with the formula, "There are three things ... yea, four ..." and are found in verses 15, 18, 21, 24, and 29. Some have suggested these may have had their origin as riddles, which later were fashioned into "wise sayings."

I. Things Wonderful and Woeful (Proverbs 30:18-23)

18. There be three things which are too wonderful for me, yea, four which I know not.

This is the formula that introduces a numerical proverbial saying, as noted above.

19. The way of an eagle in the air; the way of a serpent upon a rock; the way of a ship in the midst of the sea; and the way of a man with a maid.

The four marvels enumerated here may be briefly considered as follows:

A. *The Eagle's Flight.*—Now that men can soar with gliders and hang gliders, as well as more conventional aircraft, we are aware of thermal updrafts and the effects of air currents. The ancients must have wondered at the way eagles and other birds lifted effortlessly up and up without flapping their wings or seeming to make any effort. We now know that before cliffs fronting on the sea and in other places there are many thermal air disturbances. Some of them move upwards with significant force. By spreading its wings and adjusting to the upward flow of air, birds can soar to a considerable height. This ability was considered quite inexplicable by numerous ancient observers.

B. *The Serpent's Movements.*—Snakes have no legs, and yet they move with surprising speed. This becomes especially puzzling when they cross smooth, flat surfaces, such as a rock formation. Of course, their locomotion is through muscular contraction as they move slightly from side to side. However, this mobility is still noteworthy.

C. *The Ship's Buoyancy.*—When a ship is passing through rough seas, it seems to disappear in the trough of waves, but emerges upon the top. Then it descends again in a kind of downslope, uphill maneuver. This seeming sinking and heroic rising again, time after time, was viewed with pleasurable awe by Agur.

D. *The Man's Wooing.*—Because of the intensity of their mating urges, men are naturally attracted to women. The mystery is how men, generally much less comely, are yet able to attract and win the adherence and devotion of women. Many birds have especially colorful plumage, and some stage elaborate and spectacular "courtship" movements of one kind or another. The courtship of men is much less obvious and overt, but nevertheless is a reality. The writer regarded this whole process with wonderment.

20. Such is the way of an adulterous woman; she eateth, and wipeth her mouth, and saith, I have done no wickedness.

Placed in contrast with the modesty of a virtuous maiden is the moral insensitivity of a woman who is brazen in her infidelity. She convinces herself that her unfaithfulness to her husband really does him no harm. To her, her act of adultery is just another physical experience, such as the consumption of a meal. In her view, the disobedience of God's command is of little moment.

21. For three things the earth is disquieted, and for four which it cannot bear.

How to Say It
AGUR. *A*-gur.
ISHMAEL. *Ish*-may-el.
JAKEH. *Jay*-keh.
MASSA. *Mass*-ah.

For three things. The formula that began verse 18 is seen again here. In this case the four *things* are matters that are jarring and so unlovely that they seem to cause everything to be "out of joint."

22. For a servant when he reigneth; and a fool when he is filled with meat.

A. *A Servant Made Sovereign.*—The man who goes from a position of serving others to a position of authority and control tends to become arrogant and obnoxious in his use of power. We speak of someone who misuses the power of his position as one who is "throwing his weight around." Or, as Shakespeare expressed it in *Measure for Measure,*

> Man, proud man!
> Dress'd in a little brief authority,—
> . . . .
> Plays such fantastic tricks before high heaven
> As make the angels weep.

B. *A Food-filled Fool.*—The word for *fool* denotes a low, profligate fellow, who is rich and has no concern for others or society's conventions. If such a person rises to a position of prominence and power, he becomes obnoxious and unbearable in his manner and in his treatment of others.

23. For an odious woman when she is married; and a handmaid that is heir to her mistress.

C. *The Scornful Spouse.*—An *odious woman* is one in whom there is nothing lovable. The writer pictures a woman who has passed much of her life without love, and who, as a result, has become sour of disposition. If such a woman finally wins a husband, she uses her new position to make others as miserable as she can.

D. *The Dominant Domestic.*—The sudden elevation of a maidservant to the position of mistress of the house would create an equally intolerable situation. Such a person, Agur observes, would in all likelihood become conceited, arrogant, and repugnant to all around her. We see something of this in the behavior of the Egyptian maid Hagar, who bore a son to Abraham when Sarah seemingly could not do so (see Genesis 16:4, 5). Doubtless, she assumed airs of superiority and scorn toward Sarah.

II. Things Minute and Masterful
(Proverbs 30:24-31)

24. There be four things which are little upon the earth, but they are exceeding wise.

The observation here is very astute. Not everything that is significant is large and bulky. We have become increasingly aware of the importance of the tiny. The awesome force of nuclear explosions is unleashed by the rupturing of atoms—elements of matter so small they are almost invisible. The inheritance factors that relate to color of hair and eyes, the texture of hair and skin, and many other qualities, are determined by "genes," or little cells almost infinitesimal in size.

In his poem "Fable," Emerson portrays an argument between a mountain and a squirrel concerning their comparative value. The poem concludes with the squirrel saying,

> I'll not deny you make
> A very pretty squirrel track;
> Talents differ; all is well and wisely put;
> If I cannot carry forests on my back,
> Neither can you crack a nut.

25. The ants are a people not strong, yet they prepare their meat in the summer.

A. *The Anticipation of the Ants.*—Surely the *ants* are one of the tiniest of observable insects. One marvels at the organization of their "ant hills" and the division of labor that scholars have discovered they exhibit. As the writer of this proverb indicates, they *prepare* for the winter season with provisions stored in advance. Their industrious work is commended in Proverbs 6:6-8. Here again we are reminded that the natural world provides many "lessons" man would do well to learn.

LESSONS FROM ANTS

Ants, I suppose, may be found almost everywhere on this earth. From my own experience, I can testify that they inhabit North and South America, Europe, the Mideast, and Africa. I know also that they come in various shapes, sizes, and colors. Most of them are harmless, going about their work without any intention of being offensive.

The writer of this text cites one of their traits, which man would do well to emulate—their preparation for the future. Other qualities also come to mind.

They are industrious. Sometimes as many as thirty thousand of them inhabit one colony. Without any "guide, overseer, or ruler" (Proverbs 6:7), they work together and get the job done.

They are also purposeful. Few things deter them. They have been known to tunnel under rivers to get to their destination. They well exemplify Paul's philosophy, "This one thing I do" (Philippians 3:13).

Ants are very small insects, but the lessons they teach can have great significance for us if we will receive them. Solomon is correct. We should "go to the ant . . . consider her ways, and be wise" (Proverbs 6:6).   —T. T.

26. The conies are but a feeble folk, yet make they their houses in the rocks.

B. *The Conies Among the Crags.*—Conies are animals now known as "hyraxes" or "rock badgers." Approximately the size of a rabbit, these creatures make their homes in areas on the faces of cliffs where rocks have fallen down. In Biblical times, the majority of houses were constructed of mud bricks that were made in kilns. To dwell in substantial stone houses was the prerogative of those who were wealthy. Yet the *conies* made their houses of rock, even though, as compared with the strength of animals like the wild ox or the deer, they indeed were *feeble*. The writer of Hebrews spoke of heroes and heroines of faith who "out of weakness were made strong" (11:34). Paul bore testimony that even in the midst of physical disability, he had strength because of the power of Christ that rested upon him. He said, "When I am weak, then am I strong" (2 Corinthians 12:10). When we take our shelter in the rock that is higher than we are, like the *feeble conies* we find ourselves girded about and protected as by walls and supports of stone (Psalms 61:2; 62:1, 2; 71:3).

27. The locusts have no king, yet go they forth all of them by bands.

C. *The Logistics of Locusts.*—The *locusts* were voracious insects that devoured all vegetation in their path. Coming in swarms, they would suddenly zoom down, as if on command, to attack certain areas. They would sweep over the land with the apparent order and discipline of an invading army. A vivid picture of a locust "invasion" is given us in Joel 2:3-11.

28. The spider taketh hold with her hands, and is in kings' palaces.

D. *The Lore of the Lizard.*—This is one place where a better understanding of the Hebrew text has resulted in a translation quite different from that of the *King James Version.* Many of the more recent versions of the Bible translate the creature named here as "lizard" rather than *spider.* In general, these versions all agree with the *New International Version*, which renders this verse, "a lizard can be caught with the hand, yet it is found in kings' palaces."

Few places are more guarded than *kings' palaces*, few places where unauthorized entrance is more difficult to secure. Yet lizards have penetrated these privileged domains. So small and vulnerable that it can be caught with the hand and crushed, yet so swift and quiet it can be found amid the most regal surroundings! The mighty lion, the fierce wolf, the savage bear have been so hunted that now they are found only in the wildest, most inaccessible places. But the tiny, inoffensive lizard still is to be found in the habitations of men—even of monarchs. This reminds us of Jesus' words that the meek shall inherit the earth.

29. There be three things which go well, yea, four are comely in going.

The *New International Version* translates this, "There are three things that are stately in their stride, four that move with stately bearing." Here again the numerical formula is utilized—this time to depict the regal demeanor of some living creatures.

30. A lion, which is strongest among beasts, and turneth not away for any.

A. *The Lordly Lion.*—In Old Testament days, *lions* were still found in Palestine. The lion long has been recognized as "the king of beasts." Sometimes in Scripture the lion is a symbol of royal authority—indeed, of Jesus as king (Revelation 5:5). Also, the savage power of Satan is likened to that of a lion (1 Peter 5:8).

31. A greyhound; a he goat also; and a king, against whom there is no rising up.

B. *The Regal Rooster.*—The Hebrew expression translated *greyhound* here is vague and is not used of an animal anywhere else in the Old Testament. Some suggest that a zebra is meant; others, a war-horse, or a leopard. Several ancient translations call it the cock. Following these readings, the *New American Standard Bible*, the *Revised Standard Version*, and *The New English Bible* have "the strutting cock," and the *New International Version* has "a strutting rooster."

SEEING GOD THROUGH GLASS

visual 8

C. *The Graceful Goat.*—The *he goat* is singled out for attention, too, as a creature that moves with a stately manner as he heads the flock. John Geikie, nineteenth-century English churchman and writer, observed, "Flocks of goats are very numerous in Palestine at this day, as they were in former ages. We see them everywhere on the mountains, in smaller or larger numbers; at times also along with sheep, as one flock, in which case it is usually a he-goat that is the special leader of the whole, walking before it as gravely as a sexton before the white flock of a church choir."

D. *The Masterful Monarch.*—A *king, against whom there is no rising up* is translated in *The New English Bible* as "a king going forth to lead his army." One thinks of an army drawn up in battle array, with its crowded ranks of grim warriors at attention, its cavalry unit mounted. One can see the horses pawing the ground and tossing their heads with flowing manes. Banners flutter, armor glistens, trumpets sound, and the king rides forth on a powerful steed, with great shouts of acclamation and cries for victory sounding in his ears.

This is a scene similar to ones that Shakespeare's Othello remembers as he says good-bye to his career as a commanding general:

Farewell the plumed troop and the big wars,
That make ambition virtue! O, farewell!
Farewell the neighing steed, and the shrill
    trump,
The spirit-stirring drum, the ear-piercing fife,
The royal banner, and all quality,
Pride, pomp, and circumstance of glorious war!

A Strutting Rooster

Whenever I see, or hear, the phrase, "a strutting rooster," I am reminded of a true story that a friend shared with me.

Sometime ago he raised a rooster that grew meaner and meaner, as it grew older and larger. In fact, it became so mean that even he disliked going near it. On more than one occasion, it attacked or threatened to attack him. Naturally, it dominated the chicken lot, pecking the pullets and hens, and wounding all would-be male challengers.

One young rooster, however, had thoughts of owning its own harem! After months of avoiding conflict with the old barnyard king (months during which the aspirant grew stronger), it one day threw down the gauntlet. Instead of running away, it stood its ground and fought. The fight was rather bloody; and when it had ended, the chicken lot had a new ruler. Thereafter, if the usurper even looked in the direction of the past ruler, the old rooster took off running. His bluff had been called. He had lost control of his barn-yard kingdom.

Bullies, whether neighborhood ones or international ones, are often like that. Someone always comes along to challenge their right to rule.

Agur's advice is good: "If you have played the fool and exalted yourself, or if you have planned evil, clap your hand over your mouth!" (Proverbs 30:32, *New International Version*).   —T. T.

III. Cautionary Counsels
(Proverbs 30:32, 33)

32. If thou hast done foolishly in lifting up thyself, or if thou hast thought evil, lay thine hand upon thy mouth.

There are two circumstances in which one should put one's hand over one's mouth; that is, in which one would be wise to keep silence.

(1) If one has somehow acted in a very unwise manner, it is best not to speak about such behavior. While the foolish action may have been seen by a few, it does not pay to give any publicity to it. If one keeps quiet about it, it may soon be forgotten. At least as an old couplet by George Wither (1588-1667) states, it is well to remember,

> And I oft have heard defended,—
> Little said is soonest mended.

(2) Silence is truly "golden" when one has *thought evil*, that is, planned evil. Most persons, at some time, allow a harsh or devious idea to come into the mind. We may be resentful, suspicious, proud, have evil desire, or harshly criticize some act others have done or that we might do. If we never *speak* of these concepts, no one else will be discouraged, offended, or tempted by us.

Home Daily Bible Readings

Monday, July 16—God's Word Proves True (Proverbs 30:1-9)
Tuesday, July 17—Dishonorable Living (Proverbs 30:10-17)
Wednesday, July 18—Wonderful and Terrible (Proverbs 30:18-23)
Thursday, July 19—Say No Evil . . . (Proverbs 30:24-33)
Friday, July 20—Salt and Light (Matthew 5:13-20)
Saturday, July 21—"Imitators of God" (Ephesians 5:1-14)
Sunday, July 22—Respecting One Another (Ephesians 5:15-21)

33. Surely the churning of milk bringeth forth butter, and the wringing of the nose bringeth forth blood: so the forcing of wrath bringeth forth strife.

The same Hebrew word is translated *churning*, *wringing*, and *forcing* in this verse. The word means "pressure" in all cases, though with a different application. What the proverb says is that as pressure applied to milk produces butter (or cheese), and as pressure applied to the nose produces blood, so the pressure of wrath (that is, the brooding over anger) will result in quarrels and strife. Taunting, insulting, and demeaning words create anger in others. The wise and thoughtful person will heed the suggestion to avoid such provocative speech.

Conclusion

A. Poetic Pictures

Through the eye of the poet, we have observed the manner of creatures and human beings in this world God has created. We too stand in wonder as we consider the marvelous works of God's hands.

There are lessons to be learned from the animal kingdom and from the world of insects. May we not only marvel at God's majesty displayed therein, but also meditate on the lessons these creatures would teach us.

The sage has also shown us pictures of human behavior not so wise and not so pleasant. The examples given should help us develop self-restraint in our speech and conduct, and thereby avoid the turmoil and strife that plague self-willed and foolish persons.

B. Prayer

Our Creator God, we approach You in reverence, awed by the thought of Your great power and wisdom that confront us everywhere in the world of nature. We are also aware of the same wisdom in the ordering of our own bodies, minds, and emotional makeup. Grant that we may be observant so we do not take all these wonders as commonplace. Make us to be appreciative, thankful, and humble.

Help us, Father, to trust the One without whom "was not any thing made that was made." May we know and love this One who came among us, illumined our darkness, and died for our sins. May we live in His life, rejoice in His grace, and know His peace. Amen.

C. Thought to Remember

God never wrought a miracle to convince [refute] atheism, because His ordinary works convince it.   —Francis Bacon.

Learning by Doing

This page contains an alternate lesson plan emphasizing learning activities. Classes desiring such student involvement will find these suggestions helpful.

Learning Goals

After this lesson, a student should be able to:

1. Recognize and understand the nature of numerical proverbs.

2. Give more attention to the small things in creation, especially the animal world, in order to learn the lessons that they provide for life.

3. Discern when it is wise to keep silent and exercise self-restraint.

Into the Lesson

Display these words on the chalkboard or on an overhead transparency: *Talk to the Animals.* Distribute pencils and blank sheets of paper and tell the class members that they have two minutes to write the names of as many different animals as they can (this includes insects, too). At the end of that time, recognize the person who has listed the most animals. Next, ask the students to examine their lists and put an x beside the name of each animal that is known for possessing a positive trait, which we as humans should develop in our lives. Have them write one word that describes the trait for which the animal is known. (For example, the dog is *faithful* and a beaver is *industrious.)* Take a few moments and share some of your students' responses.

Point out that people have observed the animal world for centuries and from it have derived valuable insights about life. *Aesop's Fables* is one of the most famous collections of insights from animals. The writer of Proverbs 30:18-33 also observed the animal world and derived insights from the creatures therein.

Into the Word

Have the class open their Bibles to Proverbs 30:18-33. Instruct them to read the verses and then refer to their list of animals. Ask them to circle each animal on their list that is mentioned in verses 18-33. On the chalkboard or on the overhead transparency, under the title *Talk to the Animals*, print the names of the animals that are mentioned in today's Scripture text: eagle, serpent, ants, conies, locusts, spider ("lizard" in some translations), lion, greyhound ("rooster" in some translations), and goat.

Call everyone's attention to verses 18 and 19. Ask, "Why is each of these four things both wonderful and mysterious? Begin with the eagle and the serpent, since you have been talking about animals. (See the explanation given these verses in the lesson commentary.)

At this juncture, explain what numerical proverbs are and how they can be recognized. (Use the material in Lesson Background.) Show that Proverbs 30:18 has the markings of a numerical proverb. Have the students glance through the rest of the chapter and see how many others they can identify. (They are verses 21-23; verses 24-28; and verses 29-31.) Save verses 21-23 for later development.

Ask, "Why are ants, conies, locusts, and spiders (or lizards) pointed out?" (They are little but very wise—v. 24.) Likewise, why are the lion, the greyhound (or rooster), and the goat singled out for attention? (For their stately bearing—v. 29.) Note that the writer draws attention to an admirable quality or qualities in the animals.

When the writer moves from the animal world to human beings, he no longer points out virtues, but shows their faults and shortcomings. Ask what the ruling servant, the food-filled fool, the odious woman, and a maid who succeeds her mistress illustrate. (They are all so unappealing and repulsive that they disquiet the earth.) If time allows, explain what each one does that is so unlovely.

Into Life

Proverbs 30 warns us against carelessness in our speech. Direct the class's attention to verse 32. Ask, "According to the writer of today's Scripture text, what are two occasions when a person should be quiet?" (When one has behaved unwisely, and when one has thought evil.)

Mention the fact that we all need confidants, those with whom we can share our deepest thoughts and feelings; but we need to be discriminating in our choice of those persons. Have someone read James 5:16 aloud. Explain that talking about our sins is helpful only in the context of praying for one another. We need not dwell on our sins or give word to our evil thoughts. We do need to confess them to God and ask for His cleansing and forgiveness. We must ever be aware of the fact that our speech can be damaging to others and to our personal witness for Christ.

Let's Talk It Over

The questions on this page are designed to encourage review of the lesson Scriptures and to promote discussion of the lesson by the class. The answers provided are only discussion starters. Let your class talk it over from there.

1. Although we now understand the physical principles that enable birds to fly, we still often feel a sense of awe in watching a bird in flight. Why is this?

Perhaps we still feel something similar to David's longing when facing troubles: "And I said, Oh that I had wings like a dove! for then would I fly away, and be at rest" (Psalm 55:6). It is tempting to think that the gift of flight could enable us to escape all our troubles. Of course we do have access to flight, and no doubt many who travel by airplane to distant places for vacations enjoy that sensation of "getting away from it all." But a bird's flight is so effortless, so expressive of a sense of freedom, that it continues to generate a longing within all of us. This may be the reason why some people find it very appealing to picture themselves as possessing wings in Heaven.

2. How would a fresh emphasis on wonder at "the way of a man with a maid" be a welcome change today?

In today's movies and television shows, there is little wonder shown over the God-given attraction between the sexes. Instead, viewers are led to believe that mere physical gratification is the key to this attraction. Over and over the same crude and unimaginative portrayal is set forth: man meets woman; man goes to bed with woman; man and woman then go their separate ways. The idea of a meeting and blending of personalities, the concept of loving, lifelong commitment, and the Biblical ideal of a total union as "one flesh" are generally absent. The fact that so many marriages end in divorce today has surely resulted in part from our over emphasis on the physical pleasure and emotional satisfaction couples are led to expect. A restoration of this sense of awe at the attraction between man and woman could lead to a healthier view of marriage as the joining of two complementary personalities, and not just two bodies.

3. What are some of the feelings that we commonly hold toward small creatures such as ants? What feelings should we have?

Ants, flies, bees, spiders, and the like are often easy to ignore. As long as they stay out of our way, we may not think about them at all. But in our home or on our picnic table, they become a nuisance; and in the case of a stinging bee or a biting spider, they may cause us to fear. As the book of Proverbs demonstrates, we miss some very practical lessons if we fail to give the small creatures more attention than this. Their organization, their industriousness, the fact that they plan for the future by storing up food, and the way in which they protect themselves are all worthwhile matters for study.

4. What characteristics of the lion remind us of our Lord Jesus Christ (Revelation 5:5), and what characteristics remind us of Satan? (1 Peter 5:8).

We have seen lions in films or in zoos and circuses, and we can surely testify to the aptness of their title as "king of beasts." Even at rest, a lion is a very commanding creature. This symbolizes vividly the authority and majesty of Jesus Christ. He once offered himself meekly to be the atoning Lamb of God, but now He is a mighty ruler to whom we must willingly yield. Satan, on the other hand, is well-represented by the swiftness and strength by which the lion attacks its prey. We dare not underestimate the danger he poses to us, although through Jesus Christ we can see him as "a roaring lion" whom we are capable of resisting (1 Peter 5:8, 9).

5. We may all remember occasions when we wish we had "laid our hands upon our mouths," that is, not spoken. What are some examples of such occasions?

Hasty words spoken in anger may come to mind. If only we had not spoken in the heat of anger, we would not have damaged a friendship or intensified the conflict between ourselves and an enemy. We may also recall a time when we spoke words in jest, which the hearer interpreted in a negative way. In line with Proverbs 30:32 in our text, we may now regret that we did not stifle a boastful or arrogant statement, which has come back to haunt us. Or perhaps we made an unwise promise or a foolish vow. The advice to clap our hand over our mouth may be the writer's figurative way of urging us to verbal discretion; but there may be occasions when it is profitable to follow his advice literally to halt our unadvised words.

All Is Vanity

July 29
Lesson 9

LESSON SCRIPTURE: Ecclesiastes 1, 2.

PRINTED TEXT: Ecclesiastes 1:2-8, 12-17; 2: 24, 25.

Ecclesiastes 1:2-8, 12-17

2 Vanity of vanities, saith the Preacher, vanity of vanities; all is vanity.

3 What profit hath a man of all his labor which he taketh under the sun?

4 One generation passeth away, and another generation cometh: but the earth abideth for ever.

5 The sun also ariseth, and the sun goeth down, and hasteth to his place where he arose.

6 The wind goeth toward the south, and turneth about unto the north; it whirleth about continually, and the wind returneth again according to his circuits.

7 All the rivers run into the sea; yet the sea is not full: unto the place from whence the rivers come, thither they return again.

8 All things are full of labor; man cannot utter it: the eye is not satisfied with seeing, nor the ear filled with hearing.

. . . .

12 I the Preacher was king over Israel in Jerusalem.

13 And I gave my heart to seek and search out by wisdom concerning all things that are done under heaven: this sore travail hath God given to the sons of man to be exercised therewith.

14 I have seen all the works that are done under the sun; and, behold, all is vanity and vexation of spirit.

15 That which is crooked cannot be made straight: and that which is wanting cannot be numbered.

16 I communed with mine own heart, saying, Lo, I am come to great estate, and have gotten more wisdom than all they that have been before me in Jerusalem: yea, my heart had great experience of wisdom and knowledge.

17 And I gave my heart to know wisdom, and to know madness and folly: I perceived that this also is vexation of spirit.

Ecclesiastes 2:24, 25

24 There is nothing better for a man, than that he should eat and drink, and that he should make his soul enjoy good in his labor. This also I saw, that it was from the hand of God.

25 For who can eat, or who else can hasten hereunto, more than I?

Jul
29

GOLDEN TEXT: I have seen all the works that are done under the sun; and, behold, all is vanity and vexation of spirit.—Ecclesiastes 1:14.

Wisdom as a Way of Life
Unit 3: The Limits of Human Wisdom
(Lessons 9, 10)

Lesson Aims

As a result of studying this lesson based on Ecclesiastes 1:2-8, 12-17; 2:24, 25, students should be able to:

1. Acknowledge that the outlook of Ecclesiastes is of value to the believer.

2. Identify the weaknesses of a worldly philosophy of life.

3. Live one day at a time, understanding life's simple pleasures as gifts from God.

Lesson Outline

INTRODUCTION

  A. The Meaning of Life

  B. Lesson Background

  C. Authorship of Ecclesiastes

 I. THE VANITY OF LIFE (Ecclesiastes 1:2)

II. LIFE'S ENDLESS CYCLE (Ecclesiastes 1:3-8)

  A. What Profit? (v. 3)

  B. Motion Without Change (vv. 4-8)

III. A SEARCH FOR MEANING IN WISDOM (Ecclesiastes 1:12-17)

  A. Vain Works (vv. 12-15)

  B. Vain Wisdom (vv. 16, 17)

    The Vanity of Wisdom

IV. SIMPLE PLEASURES AND GOD'S BLESSING (Ecclesiastes 2:24, 25)

  A. Enjoying Good (v. 24)

  B. Verification (v. 25)

    A Reason to Live

CONCLUSION

  A. Faith in God and Life's Meaning

  B. Prayer

  C. Thought to Remember

Display visual 9 from the visuals packet and let it remain before the class throughout this session. It highlights the thoughts presented in the "Conclusion" of this lesson. The visual is shown on page 412.

Introduction

A. The Meaning of Life

"What's it all about . . . ?," asked the lyrics of a popular song a few years ago. This song was simply one point in a long line of religious, philosophical, artistic, and musical quests for meaning. Children wonder what they will be

when they grow up. Young people wonder about how they will spend their lives and with whom they will go through life. Mature adults give thought to their lives' accomplishments and the questions of retirement. But throughout one's lifetime, one wonders about the meaning of it all. What *is* it all about? Without an answer to this crucial question, life's activities cannot fall into their proper places. Some people have concluded that their lives have no meaning; countless souls around the world come to life's end in despair, finding no coherence, no rhyme nor reason in their time on earth.

A young minister was shocked when he saw a motto embroidered on a handmade purse carried by one of the church's most faithful ladies. "Eat, drink, and be merry, for tomorrow we die," he thought it said. Before he could reprimand this Christian sister for such a view of life, a second look revealed the full text of her humorous slogan: "Eat, drink, and be merry, for tomorrow we diet."

This young minister (who happens to be the writer of this lesson) was not very familiar with the so-called wisdom literature of the Old Testament. Proverbs, Job, and Ecclesiastes talk about the meaning of life, and, just as important, they tell us how we ought to conduct our lives and how we ought to view ourselves in the face of life's meaning.

Because of his relative ignorance of these wisdom writings, the young minister mentioned above did not stop to think that the book of Ecclesiastes does indeed say, "A man hath no better thing under the sun, than to eat, and to drink, and to be merry" (8:15). But the Biblical book does not stop there. The writer's awareness of God tempered his thinking. His final conclusion was, "Fear God, and keep his commandments" (12:13).

We too must learn that the presence of God in our lives makes the difference between a meaningless quest and a meaning-filled lifetime.

B. Lesson Background

What we find in the book of Ecclesiastes is a man of faith seeking to reconcile his disappointing search for meaning with his awareness of God. His pessimism was shared by many who

How to Say It

QOHELETH (Hebrew). Koh-*hel*-eth.

QAHAL (Hebrew). Kah-*hal*.

HEBEL (Hebrew). *heb*-el.

YITHRON (Hebrew). yith-*rone*.

were searching for meaning, but his awareness of God makes the book of Ecclesiastes stand apart from other ancient and modern quests for the meaning of life. In today's lesson, we shall see how this book speaks to our generation's continuing search for meaning in a world filled with despair.

C. Authorship of Ecclesiastes

The opening verse of this Old Testament book provides us with both the book's title and the title of its writer. Ecclesiastes contains "the words of the Preacher." The English term *Preacher* is a translation of the Hebrew word *qoheleth*, whose Greek and Latin equivalent has given us the more familiar name of the book, *Ecclesiastes*. Qoheleth was a teacher or preacher whose words of wisdom were respected. In fact, the word *qoheleth* is related to the term *qahal*, which means "to assemble" (as a verb) and "assembly" (as a noun). This indicates that the author was a preacher to Israel, the congregation of God.

The Preacher is further identified in verse 1 as "the son of David, king in Jerusalem." This almost certainly means Solomon, and other verses also point to Solomonic authorship (2:8; 12:9).

I. The Vanity of Life (Ecclesiastes 1:2)

2. Vanity of vanities, saith the Preacher, vanity of vanities; all is vanity.

The first verse tells us about the book's author and provides the title; verse 2 states the theme of Ecclesiastes. It's concise and blunt statement is difficult for some readers to reconcile with the rest of the Bible. *Vanity of vanities . . . all is vanity*, sounds skeptical and pessimistic when compared with other Old Testament books. Even more obviously it contrasts with the more optimistic perspective of the New Testament. Solomon's philosophical inquiry is not given to easy answers or pat conclusions, but the book of Ecclesiastes does contain a valuable discussion of life and its meaning. It gives us a realistic understanding of what life is all about, if measured with a strictly materialistic world view. The value of Ecclesiastes to modern readers is found in the thorough search that its author made. The great lessons that the Preacher found can be ours, if we are willing to appropriate their truth. Ecclesiastes offers us a marvelous opportunity to discover life's meaning the easy way, by learning from the mature, sound experience of one of history's wisest individuals.

What is it that Solomon said in 1:2 and 12:8? Quite simply, he discovered that all human ex-

perience is, in the long run, futile: *Vanity of vanities, saith the Preacher. . . .* The *King James Version* uses the word *vanity* to translate the Hebrew noun *hebel*. This word is capable of being translated in a variety of ways, but all of the possibilities, literal and figurative, convey a similar meaning.

Literally, *hebel* means wind, breath, or vapor, all of which represent realities with little substance or permanence.

Figuratively, *hebel* carries the meaning of futility, emptiness, transitoriness, or meaninglessness. So *hebel* refers to something that is real and recognizable, but without much substance or permanence. In other words, Solomon observes that everything in the human experience is fleeting and perishable. His blanket statement is couched in the superlative. Just as *holy of holies* means most holy of all, *vanity of vanities* means most vain of all. It means total vanity, utter worthlessness. Thus Solomon gave his evaluation of life's activities: all human effort ends in frustration.

This pessimistic outlook may appear to be extremely negative, perhaps even blasphemous. Is this what Solomon believes down in his heart, now that life has been tasted and found to be bitter? Or is he saying that this is how some people view life at the end of their journey, especially if they have no personal faith in the Lord? In other words, is the writer stating his own personal philosophy, or is he attacking the secularists and materialists of ancient times? Either interpretation is possible, since either one can be harmonized with the rest of the book.

The present writer believes that the conclusion *all is vanity* is Solomon's own view, a perspective he has reached on the basis of experiences described in Ecclesiastes. However, his use of the negative word *vanity* is not extreme, sacrilegious, or blasphemous. Instead, he has chosen his key word very carefully. Does this mean that he had an extremely low level of expectation because life had dealt him an unusual number of severe blows? Not necessarily. His use of the word *vanity* can be understood as the proper terminology for a realistic appraisal of life, if life is attempted with no relationship with God. Many of us have tried to get along without God at some point in our lives. Now that we have come back to God, however, we can see how empty and meaningless those times in which we were alienated from God actually were.

Remember that the writer of Ecclesiastes was not an atheist. Indeed, an uncompromising belief in God is found at the base of his thought (5:2; 7:13; 12:1). To understand the message of

Ecclesiastes, one must accept God as a presupposition, as did the Preacher, and come to see that the pronouncement *all is vanity* is God's ordinance. God has made everything futile under the sun, that men may look to Heavenly realities beyond the sun. As one astute writer has suggested, the Preacher demolishes in order to build. *Vanity of vanities* is not his judgment of life's total meaning, but frustration and emptiness will be the result for one who endeavors to find all meaning in the created world. God himself says this attempt will be utterly futile, like chasing after the wind. Since all pursuits of man are vain and useless, man is ultimately forced to think about spiritual matters. When seen in this light, the Preacher is not blasphemous but evangelistic.

II. Life's Endless Cycle (Ecclesiastes 1:3-8)

In this passage, Solomon supports his theme with several observations from life. He documents the monotony that is part of the human experience and is built into nature itself.

A. What Profit? (v. 3)

3. What profit hath a man of all his labor which he taketh under the sun?

Solomon began by asking a logical question derived from his thesis. He asked how one could find *yithron* through *labor*, that is, what gain, profit, or advantage results from human effort? Labor was one of the experiments that Solomon tried in his quest for meaning, all of which failed (1:8).

B. Motion Without Change (vv. 4-8)

4-8. One generation passeth away, and another generation cometh: but the earth abideth for ever. The sun also ariseth, and the sun goeth down, and hasteth to his place where he arose. The wind goeth toward the south, and turneth about unto the north; it whirleth about continually, and the wind returneth again according to his circuits. All the rivers run into the sea; yet the sea is not full: unto the place from whence the rivers come, thither they return again. All things are full of labor; man cannot utter it: the eye is not satisfied with seeing, nor the ear filled with hearing.

One point is made by this series of verses. Mankind is surrounded by numerous signs of change, but in reality human beings are caught up in an endless, monotonous cycle in nature in which no real change occurs. This relentless cycle is evident in the passing of generation after generation, none of which seem to make

any real impact on the scheme of things. Mankind's efforts are measured against the endless cycle of nature, as witnessed in the movement of the sun, the wind, and rivers. More durable symbols could not be mentioned.

III. A Search for Meaning in Wisdom (Ecclesiastes 1:12-17)

Verses 4-8 illustrate the futility of seeking permanent meaning in labor. Solomon's second attempt to find meaning in life was through wisdom.

A. Vain Works (vv. 12-15)

12, 13. I the Preacher was king over Israel in Jerusalem. And I gave my heart to seek and search out by wisdom concerning all things that are done under heaven: this sore travail hath God given to the sons of man to be exercised therewith.

As the Preacher describes this experiment, he identifies himself once more. This is especially appropriate here, since Solomon was internationally famous for his wisdom. Verse 13 says he wanted to exercise his wisdom in the examination of all human activities.

14. I have seen all the works that are done under the sun; and, behold, all is vanity and vexation of spirit.

Once again Solomon draws attention to the futility of human labor. The effort to lose oneself in work will not satisfy, as many men and women have discovered the hard way. Nor do the results of labor—salary and material advantages—provide lasting meaning. The temporary nature of the satisfaction found in work is described as *vanity and vexation of spirit*. The same Hebrew word means either *spirit* or *wind*, and the *New International Version* reads *a chasing after the wind* instead of *vexation of spirit*.

15. That which is crooked cannot be made straight: and that which is wanting cannot be numbered.

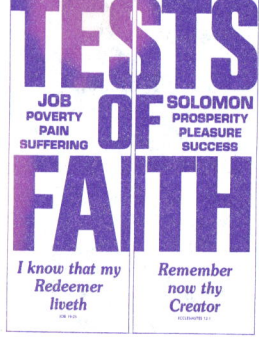

visual 9

Here Solomon quotes two proverbs that must have been known to his ancient readers. He was using something they already knew to reinforce the lesson that he wanted to teach. Since the crooked cannot be straightened and that which is lacking cannot be counted, we are to understand that there are definite limits to what man can do. According to Ecclesiastes 7:13, God is responsible for the way things are. The scheme of things cannot be altered by man's feeble attempts.

B. Vain Wisdom (vv. 16, 17)

16. I communed with mine own heart, saying, Lo, I am come to great estate, and have gotten more wisdom than all they that have been before me in Jerusalem: yea, my heart had great experience of wisdom and knowledge.

Solomon's self-examination led him to an awareness that his intellectual achievements were great, surpassing those of his predecessors and contemporaries. The opportunities for learning in Jerusalem had been great, and the writer had taken advantage of them to increase his store of wisdom.

17. And I gave my heart to know wisdom, and to know madness and folly: I perceived that this also is vexation of spirit.

Solomon looked at both sides of any issue. He considered *madness and folly* as well as *wisdom*. Still all his thinking was nothing but *vexation of spirit* or *a chasing after the wind*. The theme of Ecclesiastes ("vanity of vanities") applied to this endeavor as well.

It is surprising that Solomon was disappointed with wisdom. This is one thing in which we would expect him to find meaning. His honest analysis of this pursuit ended with the same indictment: even wisdom brought no lasting results. Probably all of us have come to the realization that knowledge itself cannot bring satisfaction. The more we know, the more we realize how ignorant we really are. This conforms with our earlier suggestion that "vanity of vanities" is God's way to drive humanity back to a proper relation with the divine.

THE VANITY OF WISDOM

In Switzerland stands a small stone church building. On a marble slab above its door is carved this statement: "Built by Voltaire." Tourists often ask, "Why would one who did not believe in religion build a church?"

Voltaire came to this area in order to write, and some of his writing was against Jesus Christ. But when he saw the simple village people going faithfully each Lord's Day to an old frame church, and genuinely living for the Lord during the week, he was deeply impressed. Out of his respect for these people, he built the small stone building.

Like all of us, Voltaire sought for the meaning of life. Believing he could find it through wisdom and higher learning, he pursued these things. Perhaps the humble life and simple faith of the villagers with whom he lived made him wonder if they had found something he had missed.

Long before Voltaire, Solomon perused human knowledge as a possible source of life's meaning, and concluded it was not to be found there. He said, "I set my mind to know wisdom and to know madness and folly; I realized that this also is striving after wind" (Ecclesiastes 1:17, *New American Standard Version*).

We can look in many directions for meaning and joy in life. Yet, like Solomon, in the end we will discover that true worth and meaning come from but one source, God. —T. T.

IV. Simple Pleasures and God's Blessing (Ecclesiastes 2:24, 25)

After passing judgment on the fruitless effort to find meaning in pleasure, wisdom, and labor, Solomon finds meaning in life's simple pleasures. Such acknowledgements come often in the rest of the book (2:24-26; 3:12, 13, 22; 5:18-20; 8:15; 9:7-10).

A. Enjoying Good (v. 24)

24. There is nothing better for a man, than that he should eat and drink, and that he should make his soul enjoy good in his labor. This also I saw, that it was from the hand of God.

Food and drink are to be enjoyed as the fruit of one's labor. This does not mean that the writer has suddenly adopted a hedonistic life-style. He is still pointing to the limitations placed on human endeavor. The search for meaning comes up short until one sees that life's simple pleasures are, in fact, blessings from the Lord. Pleasure must not be regarded as the goal of life; it is a by-product of recognizing that real meaning is found in one's relation with God on a day-to-day basis. *The hand of God* produces positive results when this level of spiritual maturity has been reached, but a materialistic perspective eventually leads one to conclude that "all is vanity."

B. Verification (v. 25)

25. For who can eat, or who else can hasten hereunto, more than I?

Solomon with his wealth and wisdom was able to compare all the activities of mankind, and so he was qualified to testify that there is nothing better than the simple pleasures that all can enjoy. Such is the meaning of the *King James Version*. Some other versions follow the ancient Greek Old Testament here. It verifies the last part of verse 24, saying that no one can eat and drink without God. All of us must depend on God to supply what we need.

A Reason to Live

It is called the "Suicide Belt"—ten wealthy towns strung together along the shore of Lake Michigan north of Chicago.

The teens who live there are not poor, deprived youth. Most of them live in huge houses with swimming pools and servants' quarters. They vacation in Europe, on the Caribbean, or wherever their affluent parents wish to take or send them. Yet many of these youth are miserable. Suicide attempts are common and often successful.

Of course, suicides are not confined to a few towns on Lake Michigan. Unfortunately they are occurring frequently all over the land. In a recent year over thirty thousand successful suicides were reported. The reason behind these self-inflicted murders is simple—many people have failed to find anything in this world worth living for.

A casual glance at the first few verses of Ecclesiastes would lead one to believe that is how Solomon felt. "All is vanity," he said. In fact, after considering everything the world had to offer, Solomon surmised that there was little in life but eating, drinking, and working. Eventually this great Jewish king learned that life is worthwhile—under one condition. He gave everything a try, and found that serving God and trusting Him are all that really matter.

How much happier we would be if we too would accept that conclusion!   —T. T.

Conclusion

A. Faith in God and Life's Meaning

Two of history's greatest thinkers, Job and Solomon, were also two of history's greatest men of faith. Both of these Biblical figures overcame serious doubts because of their profound trust in the sovereignty of God. Job weathered a storm of skepticism brought on by his suffering. Following his dialogues with friends and his encounter with God, Job's faith emerged stronger than ever. For Job, life had meaning and coherence because his personal relationship with God was reaffirmed.

Solomon's faith was tested by a lifetime of prosperity, and the uncertainty he experienced

about life's meaning resulted from living in the lap of luxury. He had experience with everything that is supposed to provide a sense of meaning and accomplishment—ambition, materialistic prosperity, pleasure, and intellectual achievement. Yet after a lifetime of experiments, all he could say about the meaning of his life was, "Vanity of vanities ... all is vanity." Though this key phrase appears throughout the book of Ecclesiastes, it must be seen for what it actually is, not for what modern skeptics want to make out of it. "Vanity of vanities" is not Solomon's negative assessment of life in general; it is his critique of a life that seeks its greatest fulfillment in materialism, without leaving room for faith in the Lord. Solomon observed that his own life was blessed with meaning only when he recognized the reality of God's activity in his day-to-day activities. For him, the highest good was not measured in terms of the accumulation of wealth, prestige, or honors. Life's highest good, the summum bonum, he says, is discovered in a daily recognition of God's presence and an awareness of life's simple pleasures as divine blessings. The Bible allows us to learn from the finding of Solomon, thereby saving us from a lifetime of frustration in our own search for meaning.

B. Prayer

Lord, we ask for wisdom in understanding the meaning of our lives. Give us strength and courage to face life's challenges. We thank You for the eternal hope that we find in Christ. In His name we pray. Amen.

C. Thought to Remember

Let's recognize God's blessings in our lives day by day.

Learning by Doing

This page contains an alternate lesson plan emphasizing learning activities. Classes desiring such student involvement will find these suggestions helpful.

Learning Goals

As a result of studying this lesson, each student should be able to do the following:

1. Understand and be able to state the central theme of the book of Ecclesiastes, and tell in what the writer found meaning and satisfaction.

2. Compare the ways through which the Preacher learned about the meaning of life with the ways in which we learn about it.

3. Select and cultivate one specific attitude or activity that will give a deeper meaning to his life.

Into the Lesson

During the week before this lesson, collect magazine pictures that depict the pleasures, the possessions, and the activities that the secular world values. (Be sure to include pictures of books.) Before the class arrives, tape the pictures to the chalkboard and intersperse these scrambled words in their midst: disowm (wisdom), bralo (labor), replesua (pleasure), nosep-sissos (possessions). Tell the class that the pictures are clues to the scrambled words. Direct people to work together in twos. Distribute paper and pencils for the pairs to use in unscrambling the words. Share the unscrambled words and point out that they are things that many people seek in hopes of finding meaning for life.

Into the Word

Make a transition into the Scripture by saying that the writer of Ecclesiastes tried all of the above-mentioned ways to find meaning in life. Ask the students to turn to Ecclesiastes 1 and 2. Tell them to find the verses that refer to the Preacher's involvement in each of the unscrambled words on the board. Remove the pictures and write each reference beside the word on the chalkboard as class members skim the text and find the verses. (Pleasure, 2:1-3; Labor, 1:3; 2:4-6; Wisdom, 2:12-16; 1:16, 17; Possessions, 2:8.)

Direct the class members' attention to 1:2 of Ecclesiastes. Explain that this verse expresses the Preacher's evaluation of all his pursuits. Be sure to explain that *vanity* means emptiness and futility. Suggest that the class skim chapter 1 again and search for passages that describe a sense of futility. (Vexation of spirit or striving after the wind, 1:14; nothing new under the sun, 1:9; no remembrance, 1:11; endless cycle of life, 1:4-7.)

Indicate that Ecclesiastes 2:24, 25 reflects Solomon's one positive evaluation of the activities of life. He found it futile to depend upon pleasure, wisdom, labor, or possessions to give meaning to life, but in the simple pleasures of daily life, he saw blessings from God. Have a volunteer read these verses aloud. Show that the well-reasoned conclusion of the writer is that the only real meaning for life is found in one's relationship with God on a day-to-day basis. Ask that the following verses be found and read aloud because they support the same insight: 3:12, 13, 22; 9:7; 12:13, 14.

Summarize the study of chapters 1 and 2 by reminding the class that labor, wisdom, possessions, and pleasure are not intended to be ends in and of themselves. They are all transitory and offer little in terms of ultimate meaning for life. Explain that "under the sun" living is described as being empty and futile, but the child of God relates all the things he does and possesses to God. "Under the sun" living is transitory, but "under the Son" living has eternal value.

Into Life

Lead the class in a discussion of this question: What are some negative things that people tend to do when they decide that life is empty and meaningless? (Some possible answers are: commit suicide, live self-indulgently, spend vast sums of money to protect themselves from harm, etc.) Then ask the class to contrast these negative responses with some positive responses that might be made. (Help others explore the spiritual aspects of life, truly search for some eternal significance in life.) Point out that a feeling of futility may be the turning point in one's life. Suggest that class members keep in touch with the non-Christians around them so they can share the good news of the eternal significance that belief in Jesus Christ gives.

Pass out slips of paper and ask each class member to write one activity that he should include in his daily schedule because of the added dimension of life he has because he knows the Lord. Collect the papers and share a few of them with the class. Close with a prayer of thanksgiving for being able to live "life under the Son" and not merely "life under the sun."

Let's Talk It Over

The questions on this page are designed to encourage review of the lesson Scriptures and to promote discussion of the lesson by the class. The answers provided are only discussion starters. Let your class talk it over from there.

1. There is little doubt that people's lack of any sense of meaning or purpose in life is responsible for much of the turmoil of our time. Can you think of examples of this?

Various forms of violence against human beings testify to a pervading viewpoint that life is cheap. We hear of acts of international terrorism, gang wars among young people, rapes and murders and other violent crimes throughout our society. Also, the continued abuse of drugs and alcohol points to a widespread "don't care" attitude. If a person sees himself as little better than a machine or an animal or a purposeless speck of matter in a meaningless universe, he is not likely to be very concerned about ruining his body and mind. We can say something similar about the practice of abortion. When people can refer to the unborn infant as a mere mass of tissue, does it not reflect the more general idea that perhaps we are all little more than masses of tissue, and it matters not how we live?

2. What comparisons can we draw between Solomon's life and the lives of materialistic-minded people today?

In Ecclesiastes 2:4-11 we learn of Solomon's effort to find satisfaction in his wealth. It sounds very much like the "good life" to which many aspire today. That involves lavish homes, sleek automobiles, fine furniture, etc. Solomon's conclusion is striking: "Then I looked on all the works that my hands had wrought, and on the labor that I had labored to do: and, behold, all was vanity and vexation of spirit, and there was no profit under the sun" (Ecclesiastes 2:11). We often hear similar conclusions today from people who have "climbed the ladder of success" and reached their material goals.

3. Some people we know actually seem at times to worship their work. What can we say to them?

Aside from the material gain, these individuals seem to find satisfaction in applying their minds and hands and feet to a constant round of labor. The term *workaholics* has been coined to describe them. They need to see the temporal nature of what they are doing. It is a sobering fact to contemplate that our human creations will soon crumble away, that the products of our labor are quick to perish. But it is necessary to realize this fact so that we may come to terms with eternal realities. Once we put our trust in God and commit ourselves to serving Him, our daily labor takes on a different character. Paul urges us, "Whatsoever ye do, do all to the glory of God" (1 Corinthians 10:31). Rather than worship our work, we worship the One who has given us strength to work, and we aim to do all of our work in such a way as to glorify Him.

4. Some people we know actually seem at times to worship knowledge and wisdom. What can we say to them?

These people appear to have an almost insatiable thirst for learning. They read books on a wide variety of subjects, attend lectures and seminars, and perhaps take classes offered by a local college. There is nothing wrong with learning, but for some it becomes the focal point in their lives. Like those whom Paul described, they are "ever learning, and never able to come to the knowledge of the truth" (2 Timothy 3:7). Perhaps we can demonstrate to such individuals that their thirst is one that can never be satisfied. Worldly knowledge is ever-changing and always incomplete. But Jesus Christ came to provide satisfaction for man's deepest thirsts (John 4:13, 14). If we center our quest for knowledge and wisdom around Him, then we have access to a fountain that will not fail to supply us.

5. The lesson writer points out, "Pleasure must not be regarded as the goal of life; it is a by-product of recognizing that real meaning is found in one's relation with God on a day-to-day basis." Can you think of specific examples of this principle?

One of our most pleasurable experiences is eating. Those who "live to eat" have only a brief time each day when they delight their palates with a variety of tastes. But Christians thank God for the gift of food and use the strength it supplies for God's glory. Thus they enjoy a kind of continual feast in all that they do. Sexual pleasure provides a similar contrast. The world seeks it as an end in itself, and never is fully satisfied. But Christians find fulfillment in utilizing it as God's gift within the context of marriage to express self-giving love.

Times and Seasons

LESSON SCRIPTURE: Ecclesiastes 3.

PRINTED TEXT: Ecclesiastes 3:1-15.

Ecclesiastes 3:1-15

1 To every thing there is a season, and a time to every purpose under the heaven:

2 A time to be born, and a time to die; a time to plant, and a time to pluck up that which is planted;

3 A time to kill, and a time to heal; a time to break down, and a time to build up;

4 A time to weep, and a time to laugh; a time to mourn, and a time to dance;

5 A time to cast away stones, and a time to gather stones together; a time to embrace, and a time to refrain from embracing;

6 A time to get, and a time to lose; a time to keep, and a time to cast away;

7 A time to rend, and a time to sew; a time to keep silence, and a time to speak;

8 A time to love, and a time to hate; a time of war, and a time of peace.

9 What profit hath he that worketh in that wherein he laboreth?

10 I have seen the travail, which God hath given to the sons of men to be exercised in it.

11 He hath made every thing beautiful in his time: also he hath set the world in their heart, so that no man can find out the work that God maketh from the beginning to the end.

12 I know that there is no good in them, but for a man to rejoice, and to do good in his life.

13 And also that every man should eat and drink, and enjoy the good of all his labor, it is the gift of God.

14 I know that, whatsoever God doeth, it shall be for ever: nothing can be put to it, nor any thing taken from it: and God doeth it, that men should fear before him.

15 That which hath been is now; and that which is to be hath already been; and God requireth that which is past.

GOLDEN TEXT: I know that, whatsoever God doeth, it shall be for ever: nothing can be put to it, nor any thing taken from it: and God doeth it, that men should fear before him.—Ecclesiastes 3:14.

Wisdom as a Way of Life
Unit 3: The Limits of Human Wisdom
(Lessons 9, 10)

Lesson Aims

After studying this lesson students should be able to:

1. Know some ways to live with the unexpected.

2. Have some guidelines for making choices.

3. Be persuaded that God is completely trustworthy.

Lesson Outline

INTRODUCTION
  A. The Facts of Life
  B. Lesson Background
I. A TIME FOR EVERYTHING (Ecclesiastes 3:1-8)
  A. Importance of Timing (v. 1)
  B. Examples (vv. 2-8)
     A Time for Joy
II. GOD'S GOOD ANSWER (Ecclesiastes 3:9-15)
  A. Man's Puzzle (vv. 9-11)
  B. Man's Good (vv. 12, 13)
     Worry-free Living
  C. God's Permanent Work (vv. 14, 15)
     A Sure and Steady Way
CONCLUSION
  A. The Appropriateness of Things
  B. The Value of Things
  C. The Choice Is Ours
  D. Prayer
  E. Thought to Remember

Display visual 10 from the visuals packet and let it remain before the class. The visual is shown on page 421.

Introduction

Some things in our life are not just as we want them to be, but we have to accept the facts, as a starting place for the decisions we make, the feelings we have, and the action we take. Sometimes the hardest part of solving a problem is to know and accept the facts. We need to think clearly until we know what the facts are. Then we can honestly appraise how we feel about these facts. From these two starting points we are ready to move forward toward meaningful solutions.

We are indebted to the writer of Ecclesiastes for reminding us of some pertinent facts.

A. The Facts of Life

So long as the universe continues as we know it, we accept the idea that some things are fixed. All science depends upon this concept. The sages of all generations have charted the rhythms, and in the process have formed all sorts of "ologies" such as astrology, biology, zoology, and meteorology.

Through the years many people have believed that the cosmic, physical, and moral orders are definitely related. Moral law is as rigid and changeless as natural law.

Faced with the many contrasts that people of all generations have observed, and faced with the sadness that many of life's realities bring to us, it is most important that we gain as much wisdom as we can for living victorious lives in spite of difficulties.

B. Lesson Background

In our search for wisdom, who can help us better than Solomon, the most famous wise man of the ages? Some scholars doubt that Ecclesiastes is his work, but most conservative commentators agree that he is "the Preacher, the son of David, king in Jerusalem" (Ecclesiastes 1:1). What we read in Ecclesiastes 1:12—2:12 fits what is recorded of Solomon in 1 Kings 4:29-34. The book seems to reflect many years of his experience as well as the inspiration of God.

I. A Time for Everything (Ecclesiastes 3:1-8)

A. Importance of Timing (v. 1)

1. To every thing there is a season, and a time to every purpose under the heaven.

One part of wisdom is knowing that time is important. Many actions are not inherently bad or good, but problems arise sometimes because our timing is wrong. More than one sandlot ball player has gotten into trouble because his timing was off. His swing was slow, and he hit a foul through a neighbor's window—but that does not mean sandlot baseball is bad.

B. Examples (vv. 2-8)

2. A time to be born, and a time to die; a time to plant, and a time to pluck up that which is planted.

An untimely birth is sad, and so is an untimely death. In our gardening we do not all follow the "signs of the moon," but we know that planting when the ground is too cold is a waste of time, energy, and seeds.

3. A time to kill, and a time to heal; a time to break down, and a time to build up.

If we are cornered by a poisonous snake, with no escape route, that is a good time to kill. When a building is no longer safe for occupancy, it is time to break it down.

4. A time to weep, and a time to laugh; a time to mourn, and a time to dance.

Jesus shed tears over Jerusalem, the beloved but wicked city (Luke 19:41). He joined in the sorrow at the death of Lazarus (John 11:35). Thus He indicated that tears are a part of life. He set the example for us in perceiving the right kind of response for a given situation.

5. A time to cast away stones, and a time to gather stones together; a time to embrace, and a time to refrain from embracing.

From gathered stones the mason selects those he can use, and he throws the rest away. Even married couples, if they are wise, know how to limit their love life.

6. A time to get, and a time to lose; a time to keep, and a time to cast away.

Buying groceries or harvesting them from the garden, and throwing away garbage—these actions apply Solomon's principles in every home.

7. A time to rend, and a time to sew; a time to keep silence, and a time to speak.

There is nothing unusual about this. The filled rag bag is clear indication that we consider some things good only to rend. All mature people know that "silence is golden" at times.

8. A time to love, and a time to hate; a time of war, and a time of peace.

The perfect love of God reaches out to all the world (John 3:16), and our modern emphasis on love is good; but there is a place for hate as well (Proverbs 6:16-19).

The preceding verses urge us to use wisdom in timing our enterprises, to know when to seize the opportunity, to feel for the open door. This is true in attempting a good deed or in moving to stop one that is definitely detrimental. Since the good and the bad of life have been handled well by others, there is good reason to hope that we too can live victoriously.

We may see in these verses also a warning to cultivate patience in waiting for the right time before entering on an activity.

A TIME FOR JOY

Mark Twain is a familiar name. We know him as the professional humorist whose lectures and writings made people around the world laugh and, for a short time at least, forget their troubles. Yet Mark Twain was in private a man whose life was broken by sorrow. When his beloved daughter Jean died suddenly of an epileptic seizure, Twain, too ill to go to the funeral, said to a friend, "I have never greatly envied anyone but the dead. I always envy the dead."

What a shame that one who gave so much joy to others found so little for himself!

The author of Ecclesiastes mentions that there is "a time to weep, and a time to laugh," but he also lets us know that God intends for man to live joyously, doing good works, and thus finding happiness in living.

One of the beautiful things about this passage (Ecclesiastes 3:1-8) and, all of God's Word is that it never seeks to conceal the truth. Solomon knew that life included death as well as birth, mourning as well as dancing, war along with peace. Not everything in life is enjoyable, not everything makes us laugh, as Mark Twain discovered. Yet God promises continual joy to the believer, a joy that cannot be taken away by the world. Circumstances, people, material things may all attempt to bring us down, but the joy that comes from Jesus can never be snatched from us. It is steadfast and unshakable. —T. T.

II. God's Good Answer (Ecclesiastes 3:9-15)

A. Man's Puzzle (vv. 9-11)

9. What profit hath he that worketh in that wherein he laboreth?

This perpetual question seems to be common to the human race. We want to know about purpose in life. Can any satisfaction accrue to a person toiling in a world that is marked by this continuous cycle of events, a world where what is has already been, and what is to be has already been?

10. I have seen the travail, which God hath given to the sons of men to be exercised in it.

It would seem from this verse, and the almost identical thought in chapter 1, verse 13, that God wants us to give serious thought to what is going on in life and how we should deal with it. It is not enough for us to say that we are going to live our lives with no real concern for the reasons for things.

11. He hath made every thing beautiful in his time: also he hath set the world in their heart, so that no man can find out the work that God maketh from the beginning to the end.

In a way, this verse states the human problem. In some translations it is "eternity" instead of *the world* that God has set in the heart of men. This word with a disputed meaning may refer to the desire for eternal life, or to the hidden meaning of life, or to our love of the world. Whatever else may be involved, the verse indicates that we are frustrated in our attempt to know how everything fits together. Regardless of how strong our desire may be, we can't get all the answers. We are forced to live with a fragmented view, but God's revelation can aid in our understanding.

B. Man's Good (vv. 12, 13)

12. I know that there is no good in them, but for a man to rejoice, and to do good in his life.

After describing the futility of some human striving, the writer turns to what is often overlooked in times of feverish activity. The statement in Ecclesiastes 2:24-26 helps us to see one permanent truth: God is always within reach and is the key.

The story of Dr. William Larrimer Mellon, Jr. is a thrilling one. Larry, as he was known to his friends, was thirty-seven years old. He had everything that one could want. He had family, money, prestige, a life of leisure and pleasure. But one night he read a magazine article about Dr. Albert Schweitzer, who years before, at the age of thirty, had put aside successful careers in music, in writing, and in teaching to go to Africa as a medical missionary. This magazine article planted a seed in Larry Mellon's mind. He read all he could find about Dr. Schweitzer, eventually corresponding with him. Then Larry Mellon made a decision.

He enrolled in Tulane University School of Medicine and was awarded his Doctor of Medicine degree. After serving as an intern, he decided to work in the disease-ridden tropics of Haiti. His work is well known in the hospital that he built with his own money.

Larry's decision was not easy or automatic. It came because he had made a serious evaluation of his life and of the world. Because he had been entrusted with much, he felt a responsibility to do much. Like Solomon, he felt that there is nothing better than to rejoice in doing good.

13. And also that every man should eat and drink, and enjoy the good of all his labor, it is the gift of God.

Here is a key reminder for our own sense of victory in life. Happiness can be enjoyed in the very act of living. Even the common things must be received as gifts of God. He gives us the strength of body and mind to work for a living. If we are willing to receive it, He gives us the ability to be content with what we earn by our own efforts.

WORRY-FREE LIVING

A recently published book, *A Sense of History*, opens with a section entitled, "I Wish I'd Been There." Numerous historians, scholars, authors, and editors were asked to choose one event in American history they would like to have witnessed. Some chose the moment Columbus first discovered America, others looked to the issuing of the Emancipation Proclamation, while still others mentioned Pearl Harbor on December 7, 1941. Almost all who were polled mentioned different events, and everyone seemed to have a slightly different angle. For that reason the book proved to be fascinating reading.

Obviously there is no time machine, so we cannot go back and view historical events any more than we can move forward and view the future. Yet many of us live every day with either the past or the future on our mind. For that reason we fail to live each day to its fullest, and thus never achieve Jesus' promise of abundant living.

We can do nothing to alter what has happened in the past, and it may seem that we can do but little to affect the future. But, as Solomon mentions, we can find satisfaction in our labor and the tasks God gives us. It is useless to struggle through life filled with anxiety and burdened down with stress. God has control of the universe and only asks that we do our best each day to live and labor for Him. In so doing we may change the future more than we think.   —T. T.

C. God's Permanent Work (vv. 14, 15)

14. I know that, whatsoever God doeth, it shall be for ever: nothing can be put to it, nor any thing taken from it: and God doeth it, that men should fear before him.

We are to fear God. This is a pivotal truth that we must learn if we are to sort things out in life. Aware of our ultimate ignorance and dependence, we can appreciate our state as creatures and appreciate our God who is beyond our comprehension. In many instances modern man would rather resolve things in his own way, ignoring the eternal truth in God. The Preacher would have us know that the Creator is supreme and that the basic nature of creation will not be altered. It may well be that we are kept from knowing all to keep us from thinking that God can be replaced as the sovereign of our lives. We should learn that lesson from the record of Adam and Eve in the garden; but if we do not, it is repeated daily in our lives.

15. That which hath been is now; and that which is to be hath already been; and God requireth that which is past.

Nothing is really new. From the beginning, God has ordained the seasons. Deep thinkers who study the past are united in the conclusion that "history repeats itself." What we do, no matter how great, is neither new nor final. Similar things have been done before; and if the world stands they will be done again. Consider the way we look at the ancient pyramids. Will

visual 10

The PAST cannot be changed.
The FUTURE may not come.
Only the PRESENT is in our control.
Rejoice, and do good.
NOW

not future ages look at our elaborate mausoleums in the same way, while devising their own ways of honoring their dead?

How shall we look at human life on earth? Is it an endless cycle, governed by a rigid framework of repeated events, and ending in futility? Or is it a series of events repeated many times, but at all times moving toward a future settlement?

The apostle Paul seems to choose the latter view. He sees God revealing the eternal, Christians seeking the qualities and values that endure forever. See Colossians 3:1 and Philippians 4:7, 8.

People who lose the sense of eternity lose something vital and sink to new lows. "What's in it for me now?" is a question that often leads to destructive behavior. Try to count the conceptions outside of marriage that have resulted from the desire for a brief moment of pleasure. Then think how long the consequences remain. Think about the "high" that a person receives from the use of certain drugs. Then remember how long the user is dead after the overdose. To keep us from self-destruction we need to believe in an eternal God who knows and cares.

A SURE AND STEADY WAY

The World Almanac 1988 provides vital statistics for a twelve-month period ending with March, 1987. The statistics paint an interesting portrait of life in America. During that period there were in the United States 3,770,000 births, 2,085,000 deaths, 2,425,000 marriages, and 1,184,000 divorces. More people left the rural areas of America to move to our cities, and more mothers of infants joined the working force.

What does all of this tell us? It says that you and I are living in a fast-changing world that does not even allow us to catch our breath. Every day we move forward technologically, and wave good-bye to the past. Many of us find that all of this change makes us uncomfortable. We feel powerless concerning our own destiny.

It is as if the world controls us, dragging us along as it moves ahead.

However, it does not have to be that way. The writer of Ecclesiastes affirms what is said throughout God's Word—the Lord is unchangeable, and his truth endures forever. He has provided guidelines for living that will never change and that provide for abundant life in every age. We do not have to be unsure of ourselves in the midst of a hectic, unsteady world. God provides us with solidity and strength that can never be taken away. —T. T.

Conclusion

A. The Appropriateness of Things

One who reads this chapter of Ecclesiastes will come to the conclusion that *we are to be concerned about the appropriateness of things in our lives.* In a matter so simple as changing clothes, we think about the appropriate place to do it. But we must go beyond the obvious matters, many of which are covered by laws. In all facets of life we are to be concerned about the impact that our actions, words, attitudes, and even thoughts will have on other people.

Appropriateness of a deed or thought must be judged in large part by the total circumstances that are involved. These include attitudes of others, foreseeable results, the effect that it will have on the one who does it, and the rather nebulous but still important way in which it bears upon the entire picture of one's life.

The example we set with our choices is one place at which we can apply the test of appropriateness. If others do as we do, will they be uplifted or debased? If we are seeking first the kingdom of God, every word or act will be judged by whether the kingdom is advanced. We must ask ourselves just how appropriate is our action in light of God's eternal purpose for us.

B. The Value of Things

Also, from this text we see that it is important for us to be involved with the relative value of all things. Without really thinking about it, we make choices of this nature. It is good to sleep. It is good to be awake. Each morning we decide which is of greater value at the appointed waking-up hour. Life is filled with choices. Often the choice is not between good and evil, but between two good things. Which, then, is most valuable in the eternal judgment of God?

One of life's most frequent evaluations is that made in the spending of our money. For some, of course, if there is money in the pocket the purchase can be made. To be Christian, we must ask: Will it be spent purely for pleasure? Will it be for things that appear to be attractive at the moment? Will you be spending your money just because you have been hooked by an advertising campaign? How will the valuation be made? There is no choice but to make a choice. The money is going somewhere, even if it is only into the mattress at home. All elements involved in a Scripturally good and proper evaluation are to be considered.

Two truths run throughout the Bible to give us guidance as we determine the relative value of things. One such truth is that of stewardship. All that we are, all that we have, and all that we can be is a sacred trust, given to us by almighty God to be used for His glory.

The second is that all things are to be seen in light of the commands that we are to love God with all that is within us, and to love our neighbors as ourselves.

The degree to which these two truths operate in our lives will have much to do with the relative values we attach to things.

C. The Choice Is Ours

We also learn from the Preacher that we are called upon to make decisions. Many people allow themselves to be pushed, influenced, or led in many of their choices. Personal responsibility is thus evaded. Peer pressure, the desire for popularity, the tendency to take the path of least resistance, or the wish to escape personal blame takes the place of sound judgment in the light of eternity.

Jesus approached four people who had followed Him and asked them to leave their nets and become fishers of men. We don't know all about what was done with their fishing business, but we know that they personally made a decision that was based on their faith in Jesus.

The fishermen-followers of Jesus grew up by the Sea of Galilee. They knew what it was to toil on the lake through the hours of darkness. They knew the work and frustrations involved in fishing by net. They knew the difficulties involved in trying to meet the needs of the day with the catch of the day. Theirs was a routine of much sameness, much frustration, much work, and some reward. Peter, Andrew, James, and John appear to have known little more than this pattern of life. Yet after they had been with Jesus for a while, and had seen what He could do, they responded affirmatively and apparently without hesitation when Jesus said, "Follow me." They left their nets and followed Him.

How many people today would make the same decision under the same circumstances? What a tremendously and potentially traumatic experience it was to turn their backs on the occupation they had always known! And yet, because of what they had seen in Jesus and because of what they believed to be true in Him and through Him, they determined to leave their nets in order to be followers of Jesus.

Our text calls upon us to make a fundamental decision—not for a particular act, but for a basic premise of life. That is, that God is in ultimate control, and that to be found under His control is the greatest expression of wisdom.

At no time in one's life can he expect to enjoy the greatest blessings and the most benefit unless he is giving active consideration to the prior claim that God has upon his life. The gift of life and the fact that God will some day judge the affairs of life should give us pause. When we try to take things into our own hands, we are in trouble!

D. Prayer

Our Father, we pray that we may not lose the sense of the eternal in our rush to find an answer to "what's in it for me now?" At the same time, we pray that we may not think we need to know all about eternity. We pray that we may be kept humble and be driven to know You so that we may be on the right course when something happens in our lives. Please, then, lift us above the dust, put true significance into every earthly activity, keep us from surrendering to the unworthy, and help us know that even the dark corners of our lives can be illuminated by what You have to offer us. We are glad that we have a reason for our faith, and we pray that You will increase that faith. In Jesus' name, amen.

E. Thought to Remember

Let's put our confidence in that one who is not affected by time or circumstances—even God.

Home Daily Bible Readings

Monday, July 30—A Season for Everything (Ecclesiastes 3:1-8)
Tuesday, July 31—All Is Beautiful and Eternal (Ecclesiastes 3:9-15)
Wednesday, Aug. 1—Be Joyful and Consider (Ecclesiastes 7:1-14)
Thursday, Aug. 2—True Piety (Matthew 6:1-15)
Friday, Aug. 3—True Treasure (Matthew 6:16-24)
Saturday, Aug. 4—"Do Not Be Anxious" (Matthew 6:25-34)
Sunday, Aug. 5—"My Hope Is in Thee" (Psalm 39)

Learning by Doing

This page contains an alternate lesson plan emphasizing learning activities. Classes desiring such student involvement will find these suggestions helpful.

Learning Goals

As a result of studying this lesson, each student should be able to do the following:

1. Demonstrate the importance of discovering and following God's timetable.

2. List some specific ways to deal with the bad times in life.

3. Identify some creative choices that can be made in response to some of the predictable and inevitable events in life.

Into the Lesson

Before the class arrives, draw a horizontal line on the chalkboard. On one end of it write "birth" and on the opposite end write "death." Put five dots on the line. Then draw a short vertical line under each dot. As the students arrive, pass out a blank sheet of paper and a pencil to each. Ask each person to draw lines on the blank paper like the ones on the board. Then tell each class member to write five significant events that have occurred in his life, and on the vertical line below each event write the date of that event. Demonstrate by sharing two or three from your own life, such as high-school graduation, new job, baptism, new career, etc.

Arrange the class in groups of four to share answers to the following:

1. When you were in grade school, what was your favorite pastime? (Ask the question and give your own answer to the whole class. Then say that the person whose birthday is closest to Christmas gets to go first in each group.)

2. Now that you are an adult, how would you spend the time if you were given an extra twenty-four hours each week to use exactly as you please? (Teacher, you need to answer this first before turning it over to the small groups.)

3. Tell the members to share their time lines with one another.

If you have a large class and no room to separate in small groups, each person may share these activities with one seated beside him. Allow about fifteen or twenty minutes for small groups to share this exercise. If you do it one on one, allow about seven or eight minutes.

Into the Word

Choose two class members in advance and ask them to be prepared to read Ecclesiastes 3:1-8 antiphonally to the class. At this point in the lesson, have the antiphonal reading done. For example, reader 1 reads, "To every thing there is a season," and reader 2 responds, "And a time to every purpose under the heaven." Each verse can be separated in this fashion. At the conclusion of the reading, comment that we are indebted to the writer of Ecclesiastes for reminding us of some pertinent facts of life. Ask the class to read Ecclesiastes 3:9-15 and see what verse seems to indicate that life is full of predetermined events over which man has little or no control. (Verse 15.) Point out that we need not be mere victims of our circumstances. We can choose the timing of many events. What do we consider in choosing a time to take a vacation, a time to be married, a time to buy a home, etc.?

Direct the class members to use the reverse side of the paper on which they drew their personal time lines. Have them draw a line down the center of the page and thus create two columns. Ask them to select all of the negative occurrences in Ecclesiastes 3:2-8 and write them in the first column. In the second column have them give an example of each occurrence. Use the chalkboard to demonstrate: "a time to weep" the loss of a wonderful job opportunity. Reserve time to share the work of the class and to discuss some of the controversial events. For example: "When, if ever, is the time to kill?" (This activity is also in the student quarterly.)

Call attention to Ecclesiastes 3:14. Ask the class what truth found in this verse can help us know how to respond to the bad times in life. (Men should fear before God.) Indicate that regardless of how bad some events are, we can be comforted and strengthened by our reverence for and faith in God. Select three people to read the following verses aloud: Job 13:15; Isaiah 26:3; Philippians 4:6, 7.

Into Life

To show that it is important to discover God's timetable, have the class look up the following verses in the Old Testament and the New Testament. Direct one half of the class to study these verses in the Old Testament and determine what significance timing had in them: 1 Samuel 13:8-14; Genesis 16:1-4. The other half of the class should use these verses: John 7:7; Galatians 4:4, 5; Luke 9:51. Close by urging the class to spend time seeking God's timing in their own lives.

Let's Talk It Over

The questions on this page are designed to encourage review of the lesson Scriptures and to promote discussion of the lesson by the class. The answers provided are only discussion starters. Let your class talk it over from there.

1. Some Bible readers interpret the phrases "a time to be born, and a time to die" as indicating that the day of each person's death is predetermined. What shall we say to this?

While we cannot control the day of our birth, we can influence the timing of our deaths. Many individuals shorten their life-spans through health-destroying habits, through careless operation of their automobiles, and through other high-risk activities. When someone we know has died suddenly, we may say, "It was his time to die" or, "His number was up"; but he may have hastened that day by the life-style he chose. This leads us to think of stewardship of our life. Though "our citizenship is in heaven," and though we presently dwell in "lowly bodies" (Philippians 3:20, 21, *New International Version*), we still need to treat our bodies well and preserve them to be used in the Lord's service.

2. Ecclesiastes 3:1-8 is sometimes read or referred to in connection with a wedding ceremony. How may this be appropriate?

It does not speak of "a time to marry, and a time to delay marriage," but that contrast is a fitting application. The timing of marriage can have far-reaching consequences. A couple may rush into marriage before they have prepared themselves for the radical change it will make in their lives. On the other hand, a couple may put off their wedding unnecessarily because of family pressures or economic considerations. Christian couples will want to pray for God's leading. If the reading of this passage at a wedding reflects the couple's wish for God's guidance, then it is quite appropriate.

3. Some translations of Ecclesiastes 3:11 say God has set "eternity" in the hearts of men. What does this suggest in regard to our evangelistic efforts?

Here is a characteristic that sets human beings apart from animals. We are capable of looking beyond our day-to-day existence and pondering our ultimate destiny. Along with a concept of eternity we have a longing for eternal life, but we are confronted by the awful reality of death. Many prefer not to think about death and eternity as they lose themselves in an endless round of projects and activities. In evangelism we may try to awaken their inclination toward eternity. This is in line with Jesus' dealing with Nicodemus (John 3). Because of Jesus' death and resurrection, we have a convincing response to the universal longing for eternal life. "He that raised up Christ from the dead shall also quicken your mortal bodies" (Romans 8:11).

4. The book of Ecclesiastes reminds us that nothing is really new, that human behavior and human events follow the same pattern in every era. What are some examples of this?

Human goals remain much the same. Now as in Solomon's time, people are seeking wealth, pleasure, and security. And the temptation is as strong as ever to use devious means to obtain these goals. Stealing, cheating, and extortion have continued as popular methods. That leads us to say that the human tendency to make mistakes is as prevalent as ever. An oft-quoted observation notes, "Those who fail to learn from the mistakes of the past are doomed to repeat them." That describes our era well. It is also pathetically true that human beings remain convinced that they can save themselves. This humanistic viewpoint has often been proved to be inaccurate, but many individuals still believe that man has the capacity in himself to build the perfect society.

5. God wants us to be people of decision, and not merely to drift along with the tide of popular opinion. What are some opinions from which we need to separate ourselves decisively?

There is a popular idea that we ought to be responsible for no one but ourselves, but the Bible asserts that we are responsible for others— for winning them to Christ, for ministering to their needs. In thinking of morals it has become commonplace for people to abandon the Bible's absolute standards of right and wrong. Popular opinion allows almost any kind of sexual behavior, "as long as it is done in love." Lying, cheating, stealing, etc. are regarded as legitimate under certain conditions. The moral chaos this has generated is one line of evidence that shows how much we need to return to God's eternal standards.

A New Teacher of Wisdom

August 12
Lesson 11

LESSON SCRIPTURE: Matthew 7.

PRINTED TEXT: Matthew 7:13-29.

Matthew 7:13-29

13 Enter ye in at the strait gate: for wide is the gate, and broad is the way, that leadeth to destruction, and many there be which go in thereat:

14 Because strait is the gate, and narrow is the way, which leadeth unto life, and few there be that find it.

15 Beware of false prophets, which come to you in sheep's clothing, but inwardly they are ravening wolves.

16 Ye shall know them by their fruits. Do men gather grapes of thorns, or figs of thistles?

17 Even so every good tree bringeth forth good fruit; but a corrupt tree bringeth forth evil fruit.

18 A good tree cannot bring forth evil fruit, neither can a corrupt tree bring forth good fruit.

19 Every tree that bringeth not forth good fruit is hewn down, and cast into the fire.

20 Wherefore by their fruits ye shall know them.

21 Not every one that saith unto me, Lord, Lord, shall enter into the kingdom of heaven; but he that doeth the will of my Father which is in heaven.

22 Many will say to me in that day, Lord, Lord, have we not prophesied in thy name? and in thy name have cast out devils? and in thy name done many wonderful works?

23 And then will I profess unto them, I never knew you: depart from me, ye that work iniquity.

24 Therefore whosoever heareth these sayings of mine, and doeth them, I will liken him unto a wise man, which built his house upon a rock:

25 And the rain descended, and the floods came, and the winds blew, and beat upon that house; and it fell not: for it was founded upon a rock.

26 And every one that heareth these sayings of mine, and doeth them not, shall be likened unto a foolish man, which built his house upon the sand:

27 And the rain descended, and the floods came, and the winds blew, and beat upon that house; and it fell: and great was the fall of it.

28 And it came to pass, when Jesus had ended these sayings, the people were astonished at his doctrine:

29 For he taught them as one having authority, and not as the scribes.

Aug 12

GOLDEN TEXT: The people were astonished at his doctrine: for he taught them as one having authority, and not as the scribes.—Matthew 7:28, 29.

Wisdom as a Way of Life
Unit 4: Wisdom in the New Testament
(Lessons 11-13)

Lesson Aims

This lesson is designed to help the students to answer the question, Am I an authentic disciple of Jesus?

Lesson Outline

INTRODUCTION
    A. Making Choices
    B. Lesson Background
  I. THE TWO WAYS (Matthew 7:13, 14)
    A. The Easy Way (v. 13)
    B. The Hard Way (v. 14)
       Free Will Versus Determinism
 II. THE TWO TREES (Matthew 7:15-20)
    A. The Camouflage (v. 15)
       False Prophets
    B. The Exposure (v. 16)
    C. The Consistency (vv. 17, 18)
    D. The Destiny (v. 19)
    E. The Conclusion (v. 20)
III. THE TWO CLAIMS (Matthew 7:21-23)
    A. The Authentic Claim (v. 21)
    B. The Unauthentic Claim (v. 22)
    C. The Denial From Jesus (v. 23)
IV. THE TWO BUILDERS (Matthew 7:24-27)
    A. The Wise Builder (v. 24)
    B. The Stable Building (v. 25)
    C. The Foolish Builder (v. 26)
    D. The Unstable Building (v. 27)
 V. THE REACTION (Matthew 7:28, 29)
    A. The Reaction (v. 28)
    B. The Reason (v. 29)
       Crazy Gods?
CONCLUSION
    A. Hearers and Doers
    B. Prayer
    C. Thought to Remember

Visual 11 from the visuals packet highlights the main points of the lesson outline. The visual is shown on this page.

Introduction

A. Making Choices

It happened close to Carmel, California. An eleven-year-old boy was surfing with a friend when an unusually large wave caught him off guard and took him under. It soon became ap-

parent that the wave was stronger than the lad; he was not going to make it to shore.

A man walking along the beach saw the danger, dove into the water, grabbed the boy, and took him to shallower water. The boy lived, but the man drowned.

For a few days he was dubbed the mystery man by the newspapers because he did not have identification on him. When his body was identified, some interesting things were learned about him. He loved children dearly. He also very much feared the water.

He had to make a decision between love for a drowning child whom he did not know and fear of water which he did know.

And love overcame the fear. John wrote about it when he said, "Perfect love casteth out fear" (1 John 4:18).

We have many choices to make as disciples of Jesus. Will we choose the easy way or the hard way?

Some choices may be met with fear—fear of rejection, fear of being misunderstood, fear of change itself. But our decision will measure our love—our love for Jesus. And perfect love will drive away fear.

B. Lesson Background

Jesus was concluding what has been called His Sermon on the Mount. He talked about the inner characteristics that produce either good fruit or bad fruit (7:15-20). He made it clear that He wants more than desires; He wants deeds. He wants more than promises; He wants productivity. He wants more than attendance; He wants obedience. He wants more than lives comfortable and satisfying to us; He wants lives continually changing into Christlikeness.

The two ways illustrate our start in the Christian life. The two trees illustrate growth toward maturity. The two claims illustrate godly action that comes out of growing into maturity. The two houses illustrate the destiny of our lives.

Will we react the way the people in Jesus' day reacted when they heard these words? They were astonished at His teaching, for they knew He had authority.

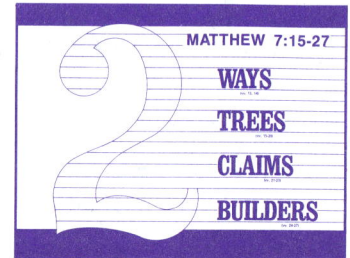

visual 11

I. The Two Ways
(Matthew 7:13, 14)

A. The Easy Way (v. 13)

13. Enter ye in at the strait gate: for wide is the gate, and broad is the way, that leadeth to destruction, and many there be which go in thereat.

This verse and the next describe two different entrances—one is narrow, the other is wide; one is popular, the other is not; one leads to life; the other leads to destruction.

The original word for *strait* suggests a confining and compressing situation, like the narrow end of a funnel. Have you ever seen a "fat man's squeeze"? Not everybody can get through it, and not everybody can get through this strait gate. We can't carry all of our former baggage—life-style, habit patterns, perspectives, character, etc. We come through this gate after repentance. Repentance is the change necessary to become "thin enough." But repentance on our part meets forgiveness on God's part. Forgiveness eliminates the sin-baggage in our lives. That's why Jesus told His apostles that "repentance and remission of sins should be preached in his name among all nations" (Luke 24:47).

Look at yourself now. Are you any different on the way than you were before you went through the gate? Did coming through the gate of Jesus Christ cost you anything in attitudes, in actions, in your love life, in your tongue life, in your priorities? If not, then you may have gone through the wrong gate—the wide one. The easy way is the popular way, because the gate is wide enough for us to "go with the flow" and follow the crowds.

B. The Hard Way (v. 14)

14. Because strait is the gate, and narrow is the way, which leadeth unto life, and few there be that find it.

What is this strait gate? It is Jesus himself. He says He is the door, and people must enter by Him (John 10:9). He also says, "I am the way . . . no man cometh unto the Father, but by me" (John 14:6).

When the crowd is teaching us that casual sex is okay, Jesus teaches us not to look lustfully at another person. When the crowd says it is okay to engage in premarital sex in order to check out compatibility, Jesus says not to commit adultery. When the crowd says that homosexuality is an acceptable alternate life-style, Jesus affirms the destruction of Sodom and Gomorrah, two cities that were filled with homosexuality. When the crowds say it is all right to cheat on taxes, Jesus says to give to the government what belongs to it. When the crowds say that we should look out for number one, Jesus says we should give up selfishness. When the crowds say to be macho by retaliating, getting even, and holding grudges, Jesus says to forgive.

These verses cause us to ask, "Where am I?" Am I on the way to Heaven and eternal life, or am I on the way to Hell and eternal death?

FREE WILL VERSUS DETERMINISM

Years ago I used a college textbook entitled, *The Psychology of Adjustment.* I have long since forgotten the author and much about the text. I do recall, however, that the premise of the book is that all living matter continues to make adjustments. When an organism can no longer make adjustments, it has ceased to live.

There are different theories as to how adjustments are made. Some give a mechanistic interpretation to man, thinking all his acts are as automatic as that of Pavlov's dog that was conditioned to salivate in anticipation of food. They say we are so conditioned that we must inevitably respond in a certain way to any situation we face. In other words, they say we cannot choose what we shall do.

Jesus teaches rather that man is an intelligent being who is able to make choices for himself. In this light He speaks of two ways and advises us to choose the narrow one. Unless man is indeed free to make choices, he is neither guilty nor innocent, good nor bad. Judgments of right or wrong go out the window, and so should rewards and punishments.

I am urging you, as Jesus did, to decide for the way that leads to life. If you can make a decision, then the mechanist is wrong and Jesus is right.

—T. T.

II. The Two Trees
(Matthew 7:15-20)

There is a close connection between the two ways and a warning against false prophets. False prophets stand at the wide gate and use all sorts of gimmicks, motivations, nice-sounding teachings, and emotional appeals to usher crowds in. Masses of people may follow a certain teacher, but that does not mean the teacher is right (or wrong).

A. The Camouflage (v. 15)

15. Beware of false prophets, which come to you in sheep's clothing, but inwardly they are ravening wolves.

The Christian life is a life of vigilance, not a life of slumber in early retirement. We must *beware* before entering the gate to be sure we are entering the right gate, and we must continually remain aware while we are on the right way.

Prophets are not concerned about events in the future only, but also about people in the present. In fact, most of the preaching and teaching of prophets in the Bible deals with the character of God's people—how they treated God and how they treated one another. The prophets called people to repentance.

Prophets were to bring God's revelation to people's lives. Without that revelation, people would cast off moral restraint and adopt any popular life-style (Proverbs 29:18; the word *vision* refers to God's revelation). Speakers can be camouflaged to look good on the outside without being good on the inside. In fact, they may be *ravening wolves*. Wolves damage, destroy, and scatter sheep. Wolves bring disunity to the unifying fellowship of a flock.

A teacher may sound good and look good, but what are the results (fruit) of his ministry? Are people hooked on a method rather than the Master? Do people follow the teacher in an emotional way and think others are insincere Christians if they do not? Do the fruits include commitment to unity in God's family, or is God's family becoming divided? A true prophet will help bring God's people together.

While Jesus is the entrance gate (vv. 13, 14), He is also the true prophet. We have the responsibility to evaluate the work of anyone or any system that is seeking to direct us through a gate or on a way, and the standard of judgment is to be found in Jesus' words and actions.

There are many kinds of false prophets besides those claiming to be spokesmen of God: the horoscope, the Ouija board, fortune tellers, witchcraft, a persons' own conscience, non-Christian counseling, humanistic education.

False Prophets

Years ago I received a letter from a woman who was trying to set me straight concerning the second coming of Christ. She agreed with Jesus that no man knew the day nor the hour of His coming (Mark 13:32), but she claimed to know the year. The year she predicted has gone, and the lady is proved to be a false prophet.

Such people do not intend to be wolves, but their mistaken predictions do tend to destroy faith rather than to build it. When they lead people to abandon their work and wait idly for Jesus to come, that is not good fruit (2 Thessalonians 3:11, 12). When anyone appears with "inside information" that no one else knows, we need to be cautious. Wait and see what the result is.

—T. T.

B. The Exposure (v. 16)

16. Ye shall know them by their fruits. Do men gather grapes of thorns, or figs of thistles?

The teacher is measured by the results. Fruit grows slowly, so it is not always easy to tell the fruit immediately. But after a time, a person's teachings can be evaluated by what happens. A person's public reputation may not correspond with his private character. Be wary of those whom you know only by their public exposure. If a person is getting richer and richer with funds from people who are getting poorer and poorer, he is a false prophet. What he says may be good, but the results are not.

C. The Consistency (vv. 17, 18)

17, 18. Even so every good tree bringeth forth good fruit; but a corrupt tree bringeth forth evil fruit. A good tree cannot bring forth evil fruit, neither can a corrupt tree bring forth good fruit.

A tree can be known by its fruit. A Christian teacher helps people become more like Christ. One who is not growing in Christlikeness has entered the wrong gate or is going the wrong way. Even if we enter the right gate, it is possible to switch roads afterward.

D. The Destiny (v. 19)

19. Every tree that bringeth not forth good fruit is hewn down, and cast into the fire.

Roads go somewhere. The road we travel in this life will take us either to Heaven or to Hell. The primary test is this: are we in Christ? John made it clear that the one who has the Son has eternal life (1 John 5:11, 12).

E. The Conclusion (v. 20)

20. Wherefore by their fruits ye shall know them.

Christians have the responsibility to make evaluations. But don't just look at what a person says. Look also at the results. If a leader asks his followers to send money to help feed the poor, while he himself refuses to live simply so that others can simply live, that leader has not strapped on the sandals of Jesus nor carried the towel and basin in his hands.

III. The Two Claims
(Matthew 7:21-23)

A. The Authentic Claim (v. 21)

21. Not every one that saith unto me, Lord, Lord, shall enter into the kingdom of heaven; but he that doeth the will of my Father which is in heaven.

Verses 13 and 14 ask the question, "Where am I?" Verses 15-20 ask the question, "How am I?" Verses 21-23 ask the question, "Whose am I?" That question is not answered just by what we say, but also by what we do. The test here is the test of obedience.

We are to follow Jesus' example here. He claimed to be God's Son, but at the same time made it clear that He lived to do the Father's will (John 5:30). "I do always those things that please him" (John 8:29).

B. The Unauthentic Claim (v. 22)

22. Many will say to me in that day, Lord, Lord, have we not prophesied in thy name? and in thy name have cast out devils? and in thy name done many wonderful works?

Doing sensational things and attaching the name of Christ to them is not the test of being a genuine Christian. Other questions need to be asked: (1) For whom is a person really doing those sensational things—for God or for self? (2) Who is getting the most credit and benefit—God or the person? (3) Has the person doing these things entered by the correct gate—Jesus Christ—through faith, repentance, and baptism?

Before we get harsh with others, though, we need to look at ourselves. Do we live during the week by the words of the songs we sing on Sunday? "Take it to the Lord in prayer"—do we? "O worship the King"—do we really? "I surrender all"—do we? "Rescue the perishing"—how many have we rescued lately?

C. The Denial From Jesus (v. 23)

23. And then will I profess unto them, I never knew you: depart from me, ye that work iniquity.

The issue is not just what are we saying about God and His Son, but what is God saying about us. How could prophesying, casting out demons, and doing many mighty works be considered by Jesus to be evil? Perhaps it is because those who were doing those things lacked Christlikeness and were not producing Christlikeness in others. That would mean they were doing these sensational works upon the wrong foundation, which squares with what Jesus says next.

IV. The Two Builders (Matthew 7:24-27)

A. The Wise Builder (v. 24)

24. Therefore whosoever heareth these sayings of mine, and doeth them, I will liken him unto a wise man, which built his house upon a rock.

Christianity is not just hearing; it also involves doing. It is not just memorizing, but also mimicking. It is not just believing, but also behaving. Christianity is not something we just enter into; it enters into us and changes us.

The rock upon which we are to build our lives is Jesus himself (1 Corinthians 3:11; 1 Peter 2:4-8). The taller the building is, the deeper the foundation must be. We are to stand tall for Christ.

The false prophet builds for himself; the true prophet builds for others. The evildoers build for show (the sensational activities in verse 22). The righteous doers build for eternity. The wise person who builds upon the foundation is the person who not only reads or hears Jesus' teachings in the Sermon on the Mount, but also makes the life-style changes to apply them.

B. The Stable Building (v. 25)

25. And the rain descended, and the floods came, and the winds blew, and beat upon that house; and it fell not: for it was founded upon a rock.

A person's character is like a house. Every internal attitude is like a beam, a joint, a window seal. A solid character built on the solid Christ will stand through the storms of life. To say that the house did not fall is another way of saying the positive things in the Beatitudes—"theirs is the kingdom of heaven" (Matthew 5:3); "they shall be comforted" (v. 4); "they shall inherit the earth" (v. 5); "they shall be filled" (v. 6). Read the rest in verses 7-12.

To build on the foundation is to build a character upon the solid model of Jesus—His words, His works, His commands. It is to allow our spirits to lessen and the Spirit of Christ to grow until we become like Him.

C. The Foolish Builder (v. 26)

26. And every one that heareth these sayings of mine, and doeth them not, shall be likened unto a foolish man, which built his house upon the sand.

On what am I building? To hear God's will but not do it is to build on quicksand, and the house built there will come tumbling down. To build on the sand is to call Jesus Lord, but to construct our lives according to our own guidelines, desires, and feelings.

Christ is not teaching salvation by works. We are not saved by works but by grace. Salvation is from the rock, who is Jesus. Building is applying His teachings to our lives. We are not saved by good works, but we are saved *to* good works (Ephesians 2:10).

D. The Unstable Building (v. 27)

27. And the rain descended, and the floods came, and the winds blew, and beat upon that house; and it fell: and great was the fall of it.

Many houses in southern California are marvels to view—fantastically lovely, sitting on a hillside overlooking the ocean. Many people drool over those houses as they drive by—until the major rains come and the houses go sliding down the hillside. What looked so extravagant and so attractive became mere piles of mortar and lumber.

V. The Reaction
(Matthew 7:28, 29)

A. The Reaction (v. 28)

28. And it came to pass, when Jesus had ended these sayings, the people were astonished at his doctrine.

It was not unusual for people to be astonished at Jesus' teachings (Matthew 13:54; 22:33; Mark 1:22; 6:2; 10:26; 11:18). To be astonished was to be overwhelmed, dumbfounded, amazed, and awed.

B. The Reason (v. 29)

29. For he taught them as one having authority, and not as the scribes.

Jesus did not get His teaching from commentaries nor quote other scholars. The authority rested in himself. He spoke the truth, while many scribes were evasive. He spoke about matters of great importance rather than majoring in minors. He used many illustrations from common life rather than being stifled and impersonal with principles only.

However, it is not enough just to be astonished. Men could be astonished and still build upon the sand. We must move from astonishment to obedience.

Crazy Gods?

"The Gods Must Be Crazy" is a movie set in the Kalahari Desert of Africa. The story is simple. A pilot flying over the Kalahari throws out a Coca Cola bottle. The bottle lands near a Bushman village. These simple people conclude that since the bottle came from the sky, it must have come from the gods.

They are greatly intrigued with the bottle, finding numerous uses for it. Soon, however, contentions arise among them. Everyone wants to use the bottle for his or her own purposes. Arguments start and turn into fights. The leader of the group determines that the gods must be crazy to send only one such bottle. He determines to take it to the end of the world and throw it off.

If indeed there are many gods, and if they are but "humans writ large," and make mistakes as we do, then it is a valid conclusion that on some occasions the gods may do something crazy. But there are not many gods, and we Christians know it. There is but one God, and Jesus is His Son. What He has said on any subject is the final word. Because it is, He could say, "Therefore whosoever heareth these sayings of mine, and doeth them, I will liken him unto a wise man, which built his house upon a rock."

Make no mistake—God makes no mistake!

—T. T.

Conclusion

A. Hearers and Doers

Jesus wanted people to hear His sermons; but when He finished, He was not interested in their shaking His hand and saying, "That was a great sermon." He would much rather see them living the life-style He talked about. Now you must make some decisions—to enter the narrow gate, Jesus; to walk the narrow path, living out Jesus' life-style; to close your eyes and ears to the deceivers who try to get you to believe that other ways of life are just as pleasing to God.

You must be aware that you can deceive yourself if you do not remember that God wants the inside of a person to be as pure as his outer actions appear to be.

B. Prayer

Father, may I not only seek to master Your words, but seek to let Your words master me.

C. Thought to Remember

Not all roads lead to the same place.

Learning by Doing

This page contains an alternate lesson plan emphasizing learning activities. Classes desiring such student involvement will find these suggestions helpful.

Learning Goals

After this lesson, students will be able to do the following:

1. Tell some differences between false prophets and true prophets.

2. List some signs that indicate that a person is on the way to spending eternity with God.

3. Contrast the wisdom of the world with the wise teachings of Jesus.

Into the Lesson

Read the following multiple-choice statements and have students jot down their answers:

1. False prophets are (a) easily recognizable; (b) difficult to distinguish from true prophets; (c) non-existent in our time.

2. Some signs that indicate one is on the way that leads to eternal life are (a) bringing forth good fruit; (b) believing and trusting in Jesus Christ as the Son of God; (c) both of the preceding; (d) uncertain and hard to read.

3. The teachings of Jesus are different from what the crowd says because (a) the crowd usually opts for the easy way; (b) the teachings of Jesus are impossible to obey.

4. The teachings of Jesus were different from what the scribes said because (a) He was not as well educated; (b) His ideas were radical; (c) He did not get his teaching from other scholars, but spoke with personal authority.

Tell the students that these sentences reflect the main themes of today's study.

Into the Word

Direct the class to read Matthew 7:15-20 silently and look for the answer to this question: Why does Jesus talk about false prophets and trees in the same message? (Because both are known by the fruit they bear.) Ask the class to cite examples of fruits that a false prophet often bears. (Some possible answers: accumulation of great wealth under false pretenses, great personal glory and recognition, ostentatious luxury.) Follow this discussion by asking what the possible fruits of a true prophet are. Write students' suggestions on the chalkboard. (Some desired answers: honor and glory to God, people learning without being exploited, converts to Jesus Christ, repentance among those who are taught.) Put the following matching game on the chalkboard or make a copy for each student. Explain that we are constantly being bombarded with so-called wisdom, but that we must be on the alert not to accept it without comparing it with the teachings of Jesus. Ask each one to use his/her Bible and refute these statements by the worldly-wise with the appropriate teaching by Jesus. (This exercise is in the student quarterly.)

_____ 1. All roads lead to Heaven.
_____ 2. Look out for Number 1.
_____ 3. Don't get mad. Get even.
_____ 4. You can never be asked to forgive that!
_____ 5. Religion is the opiate of the people.

Possible answers:
  a. Matthew 6:14, 15
  b. John 8:32
  c. Matthew 16:24, 25
  d. Matthew 5:43, 44
  e. John 14:6
(Answers 1. e. 2. c. 3. d. 4. a. 5. b.)

Call attention to Matthew 7:21-23. Help the class members form pairs to discuss whether they agree or disagree with the following statement and why. "We cannot be sure that we will spend eternity in Heaven with God." After about three minutes of discussion, have these verses read aloud by volunteers: 1 John 5:13, John 3:36, Romans 8:1. Summarize the discussion by saying that we can be sure of our eternal destination because we trust Jesus Christ. Our entrance into Heaven is a gift from God that we can confidently rely upon.

Into Life

Remark that the words of Jesus in Matthew 7:23 strike fear into the hearts of some believers. They wonder if those words may be spoken to them on Judgment Day. To allay such fears, some pertinent verses of Scripture may be memorized. Put these verses on the chalkboard, leaving out the *underlined* words. Assist the class in filling in the blanks. "For the wages of sin is *death*; but the *gift* of God is *eternal life* through *Jesus Christ* our Lord" (Romans 6:23). "There is therefore now no *condemnation* to them which are *in Christ Jesus*" (Romans 8:1). Close the session by suggesting that Romans 8:35-39 also should be memorized to sustain us and prompt us to bear good fruit.

Let's Talk It Over

The questions on this page are designed to encourage review of the lesson Scriptures and to promote discussion of the lesson by the class. The answers provided are only discussion starters. Let your class talk it over from there.

1. Instead of emphasizing the "strait and narrow" we often seem to be looking for ways to make Christianity more comfortable. What are some aspects of comfortable Christianity?

We love air-conditioned auditoriums and padded pews. True, there is no added virtue in discomfort, but our stress on physical comfort in worship may indicate an overall softness in our discipleship. Comfortable Christianity is the kind that does not give up anything in the pursuit of holiness. Many Christians watch the same television programs, tell the same coarse jokes, and practice the same body-destroying habits that non-Christians do. Comfortable Christianity is the kind that makes no sacrifices in order to stand up for Biblical morality. Church members may lament among themselves over the woes of pornography, abortion, humanistic influence in public schools, etc.; but how many do anything to oppose these evils?

2. What are some examples of the "sheep's clothing" in which false prophets may appear?

False prophets are capable of quoting Scripture. We remember that Satan himself used Scripture (Matthew 4:5, 6) in his efforts to tempt Jesus. So the fact that a speaker or writer cites various passages from the Bible is no guarantee of his soundness. Also, Jesus' name and great Christian terms like "faith," "love," "salvation," and "eternal life" can be misused by the false teacher. Acts 19:13-16 describes how some men endeavored to use the name of Jesus without a genuine faith in Jesus. We should note that false prophets are also capable of a great show of emotion. They can exhibit much joy over Jesus, much sadness over sin. However, even when such emotion is genuine, it does not necessarily indicate soundness in the truth.

3. It is often noted that there is a significant difference between "talking a good religion" and living out our faith. How is this true?

Those who engage in evangelistic calling frequently encounter people who love to talk about the Bible and the church, but are not interested in making a commitment to the Lord. These people seem to pride themselves on being able to discuss the Christian faith intelligently, and they delight in bringing up tough questions about the Bible, but they sidestep any reference to a personal relationship with Christ. Similarly, in the church we often "talk to death" such matters as missions, local evangelism, our convictions concerning the Bible, our hopes regarding prayer, etc. But we do not consistently take actions in accord with our talk. Even leaders in the church are sometimes guilty of substituting high-sounding talk for decisive action.

4. How can we engage in Christian character-building within the church?

Perhaps we can use our teaching programs more effectively for this purpose. We put a great deal of emphasis on the learning of Bible facts or the developing of skills for Christian service. Sometimes we use our teaching time to acquaint people with church history, inform them as to the teachings of various cults, or stimulate their thinking about the Bible's influence on modern social issues. All of this has value, but nothing is more important than building a Christlike character. This is the goal Paul enunciated in Ephesians 4:15: that we "may grow up into him in all things, which is the head, even Christ." It is well to concentrate much teaching on developing Christlike qualities such as love, compassion, kindness, faithfulness, patience, and others. See Galatians 5:22, 23 and 2 Peter 1:5-7.

5. Why would it be a good thing if even church members were to be freshly astonished at Jesus' teachings?

Many of Jesus' teachings are so familiar to us that we have lost our sense of wonder concerning them. For example, several of the features of the Sermon on the Mount (Matthew 5—7) have appeared so often in sermons and lessons that we may no longer be excited by them. But the Beatitudes (Matthew 5:1-12) offer remarkable challenges to us, and we should feel a constant amazement in regard to them. The model prayer (Matthew 6:9-13) is a masterpiece of brevity and yet so comprehensive that we should be ever attracted to it and influenced by it in our own prayers. We may view the Golden Rule (Matthew 7:12) as something particularly appropriate for children to ponder. It should strike us also as a simple but stupendous standard of behavior, not only to ponder, but also to live by.

Who Is Wise?

LESSON SCRIPTURE: James 1:1-8; 3:1—4:12.

PRINTED TEXT: James 1:1-8; 3:13-18.

James 1:1-8

1 James, a servant of God and of the Lord Jesus Christ, To the twelve tribes which are scattered abroad, Greeting.

2 My brethren, count it all joy when ye fall into divers temptations;

3 Knowing this, that the trying of your faith worketh patience.

4 But let patience have her perfect work, that ye may be perfect and entire, wanting nothing.

5 If any of you lack wisdom, let him ask of God, that giveth to all men liberally, and upbraideth not; and it shall be given him.

6 But let him ask in faith, nothing wavering: for he that wavereth is like a wave of the sea driven with the wind and tossed.

7 For let not that man think that he shall receive any thing of the Lord.

8 A double-minded man is unstable in all his ways.

James 3:13-18

13 Who is a wise man and endued with knowledge among you? let him show out of a good conversation his works with meekness of wisdom.

14 But if ye have bitter envying and strife in your hearts, glory not, and lie not against the truth.

15 This wisdom descendeth not from above, but is earthly, sensual, devilish.

16 For where envying and strife is, there is confusion and every evil work.

17 But the wisdom that is from above is first pure, then peaceable, gentle, and easy to be entreated, full of mercy and good fruits, without partiality, and without hypocrisy.

18 And the fruit of righteousness is sown in peace of them that make peace. ▪

Aug
19

GOLDEN TEXT: Who is a wise man and endued with knowledge among you? let him show out of a good conversation his works with meekness of wisdom.—James 3:13.

Wisdom as a Way of Life
Unit 4: Wisdom in the New Testament
(Lessons 11-13)

Lesson Aims

After this lesson students should be able to:
1. Explain the difference between wisdom and knowledge.
2. Develop a positive attitude when facing difficult situations.

Lesson Outline

INTRODUCTION
  A. Joy Is Not the Absence of Problems
  B. Lesson Background
I. THE GREETING (James 1:1)
  A. The Writer (v. 1a)
  B. The Readers (v. 1b)
II. GROWING TOWARD MATURITY (James 1:2-4)
  A. The Attitude Needed (v. 2)
  B. The Test Provided (v. 3)
  C. The Goal Desired (v. 4)
III. RECEIVING WISDOM (James 1:5-8)
  A. The Prominence of Prayer (v. 5)
    Tokyo, France?
  B. The Potency of Faith (v. 6)
  C. The Poverty of Doubting (vv. 7, 8)
IV. TWO KINDS OF WISDOM (James 3:13-18)
  A. Wisdom That Produces Good Deeds (v. 13)
    The Arrogance of Wisdom
  B. Wisdom That Produces Bad Deeds (v. 14)
  C. Source of Bad Wisdom (v. 15)
  D. Results of Bad Wisdom (v. 16)
  E. Source and Nature of Good Wisdom (v. 17)
  F. Results of Good Wisdom (v. 18)
CONCLUSION
  A. Developing a Christlike Environment
  B. Prayer
  C. Thought to Remember

Visual 12 in the visuals packet contrasts good and bad wisdom as seen in James 3:13-18. The visual is shown on page 437.

Introduction

A. Joy Is Not the Absence of Problems

There is a hospital for the treatment of leprosy in Carville, Louisiana. One day the chaplain was giving a visitor a tour of that hospital. They stopped to talk to a lady who had lost a leg and whose face was terribly marred by leprosy. The chaplain remarked that the lady sang in the hospital choir. The visitor then said to her, "Would you sing me a verse of your favorite hymn?"

The lady smiled. Then out of her blemished, disfigured face came the beautiful melody and words of a familiar song: "I sing because I'm happy, I sing because I'm free, for His eye is on the sparrow, and I know He watches me."

That is an example of joy in the midst of trials. And that is wisdom—real wisdom—wisdom that looks at the facts and responds to those facts with the character of a Christian.

B. Lesson Background

Jesus made it clear that Christianity could not be reduced to a set of rituals and external trappings such as those that had captivated the religion of His day. He talked about ethical decisions, caring for the poor, providing for widows, guarding our tongues, being generous, caring for strangers.

The early church followed Jesus' example. It was not a cold institution but a caring family (Acts 2:44, 45).

At the time our text was written, nearly thirty years had passed. The church then was in danger of keeping up the externals—the meetings, the ordinances, the hymns, the prayers—but not being full of grace, compassion, gentleness, and mercy. The personal was becoming the impersonal. Compassion was turning into coldness.

In that setting James wrote this powerful epistle. It balances doctrines with deeds, faith with works, prayer with activity, scholarship with self-discipline. Thus it confronts the members of the church with the responsibility of the Christian life-style.

I. The Greeting
(James 1:1)

A. The Writer (v. 1a)

1a. James, a servant of God and of the Lord Jesus Christ.

This simple description of *James* causes us to believe that he was well known and respected among the churches. Most students believe this was the Lord's brother, who became a very influential person in the early church (Galatians 1:19; Acts 15:13; 21:18).

The word *servant* comes from the Greek word for slave, but slavery did not always mean menial or unimportant work. Many slaves held high positions in civil service and in business. Some slaves were doctors, nurses, and teachers. Sometimes a slave was adopted into the family and became heir of the family property. Most owners treated their slaves better than employers treated their employees.

Still, to call oneself a servant-slave was to admit a humble submission to an owner. It is interesting that the only title this well-known Christian leader gave to himself was that of a servant-slave of God and Jesus Christ. He wanted to be seen as one who lived to please his Master.

Wouldn't it be great if we could forget about emphasizing title and status, and emphasize service and responsibility instead? Many problems in the church might be solved if we weren't trying to jockey for position.

The Master of James was not a council of men, an institution, or a committee. His Master was *God and . . . the Lord Jesus Christ.* The word *Lord* means the Master (Owner) of the servant. The word *Jesus* means Savior, and the word *Christ* means anointed one. Jesus has been anointed by God to be our Savior and our Owner/Master. Whom God has anointed, none of us have the right to displace.

B. The Readers (v. 1b)

1b. To the twelve tribes which are scattered abroad, Greeting.

The twelve tribes which are scattered abroad are Christians everywhere. There were twelve tribes in Israel, but this letter seems to be meant for Christians, God's New Israel (Romans 2:28, 29; Philippians 3:3; Galatians 3:29; 1 Peter 2:9, 10).

II. Growing Toward Maturity (James 1:2-4)

A. The Attitude Needed (v. 2)

2. My brethren, count it all joy when ye fall into divers temptations.

Christians are *brethren.* They are all members of the family of which God is the Father. We are to treat each other the way God wants His children to be treated.

We usually connect the word *joy* with delight, not *temptations,* or trials, as some versions have it. We are tempted and tried by circumstances that disappoint us, displace us, disadvantage us, or discourage us. *Divers* means all kinds of— all the various sorts of troubles that come our way.

How can we have joy in the face of trials? One way is for us to look beyond the trials and see what is on the other side. People went through various trials when they came to North America on the *Mayflower,* but the hope of freedom gave them joy. Pioneers traveled from the east to the west in covered wagons, amid all kinds of hardships. But there was joy because there was the hope of having a homestead in Oklahoma or a gold mine in California. People looked for the positive beyond the negative.

Circumstances or events by themselves cannot put us into the pits. That's why one person can be paralyzed from the neck down and be cheerful, while another can run out of hair spray and be miserable all day long. The difference lies not in the events themselves, but in the thoughts that go through our minds as we look at those events.

Proverbs 23:7 says, "As he thinketh in his heart, so is he." When trials hit us we often begin to think negatively: "I am no good; I am rejected; I am worthless; I am a failure; I am ugly." We talk to ourselves at the rate of thirteen hundred words per minute. When we talk to ourselves in such a negative way, we are headed to "the pits."

When trials hit us, we need to look beyond the negative for the positive. That's what Paul was getting at in Philippians 4:8-10. We also need to remember that all things work together for good to those who love the Lord. One good they work toward is that we be conformed to the image of Jesus (Romans 8:28, 29).

B. The Test Provided (v. 3)

3. Knowing this, that the trying of your faith worketh patience.

One thing trials can do is to bring out qualities of character that would not be acquired without those tough times. Testing often burns off excess baggage and inappropriate priorities. It often helps us to see where real value lies.

The Greek word for *patience* literally means remaining under. Patience is the ability to stick with it during difficult times. It is fortitude, staying power, persistence. Trials can help develop our determination.

A few years ago the news media were filled with stories about a little girl who fell into a narrow well. Do you remember what happened then? It was a good example of patience. There was determination, persistence, and hard work till the child was rescued. The toughness of the situation called for toughness of character, and people responded. As the saying goes, "When the going gets tough, the tough get going."

C. The Goal Desired (v. 4)

4. But let patience have her perfect work, that ye may be perfect and entire, wanting nothing.

The word *perfect* may be translated *mature.* In Christianity it describes one who has grown up into Christlikeness. That is God's goal for us (Luke 6:40; Ephesians 4:11-16; Romans 8:29). *Wanting* here means *lacking*. When we are mature Christians, we do not lack any of Christ's characteristics. We act and react the way He would. There is no unfinished part of our Christianity.

When we were children physically, we wanted to grow up. When we are children spiritually, some of us are satisfied to stay that way. The trials that come to us may force us to grow up.

III. Receiving Wisdom
(James 1:5-8)

A. The Prominence of Prayer (v. 5)

5. If any of you lack wisdom, let him ask of God, that giveth to all men liberally, and upbraideth not; and it shall be given him.

In the Bible, *wisdom* does not mean knowing facts or data. It does not mean knowing what house we should buy or which stocks will do the best. That's knowledge. Biblical wisdom is the moral disposition to use whatever knowledge we have in a way that will please God and fulfill His will.

To ask for wisdom is to ask for the sensitivity to make the choice that will lead to the Christian good of all concerned. Isn't it interesting that we are not told to read the Bible, or go to college, or study, but to ask God for this kind of wisdom? Such moral discernment is a gift from God, and He desires to give it to all of those who want it. To ask God for it is to draw near to Him. If we draw near to God, He will draw near to us (James 4:8).

To ask for wisdom is to ask God for an understanding mind that we may discern between good and evil in various decisions. We should not ask for wisdom just when we need to make tremendous decisions; we should ask for it daily, so that God's character will form all of our decisions as we become more and more like Christ each day.

We are to ask *God* for wisdom. That does not mean we should never seek counsel from other people. But we need to ask God, because He gives us the inner characteristic to make moral decisions in all kinds of trials.

God gives generously without putting us down. Asking means that we are open and ready to receive. Too often we decide without God; we are hardhearted; we are stiff-necked; we are not about to give in to Him. If we hurt someone, so what? We've done it before. But to make decisions that are harmful to others is to be foolish, the opposite of wise.

TOKYO, FRANCE?

A high-school student seemed to be in a daze. When a friend asked what was wrong, he explained that he was praying. He said he had just taken a test in geography, and that he was praying for Tokyo to be the capital of France!

Some things are worthy topics of prayer, but some aren't. You can't expect God to change historical or geographical facts to make your answer right.

It is easy to learn that Tokyo is the capital of Japan, and Paris the capital of France. We ought to work for such knowledge rather than pray for it. It doesn't come with a sudden burst of light from God. Wisdom, the ability to use knowledge properly, can and should be sought from God. James says, "It shall be given him." But that does not mean we make no effort of our own. We need to learn the teaching of the Bible and the facts of the world around us, and consider them carefully as we pray for wisdom to make our decisions in the light of God's Word.   —T. T.

B. The Potency of Faith (v. 6)

6. But let him ask in faith, nothing wavering: for he that wavereth is like a wave of the sea driven with the wind and tossed.

"Faith is being sure of what we hope for" (Hebrews 11:1, *New International Version*). We are to ask confidently, with the assurance that we will receive what we ask for. We are to ask for God's moral character to enable us to make decisions that will be pleasing to Him and beneficial to others.

The person who asks for this moral wisdom with doubts is the person who has not yet decided whether or not he wants to make unselfish decisions. Consequently he is tossed around like waves on the sea, tossed by circumstances and not the will of God.

C. The Poverty of Doubting (vv. 7, 8)

7, 8. For let not that man think that he shall receive any thing of the Lord. A double-minded man is unstable in all his ways.

A double-minded person has difficulty making decisions. Something other than the will of God influences him—he is *unstable in all his ways*. He decides to "go with the flow" rather than to go with God. He may want something badly, but his double-mindedness reminds him of something else he wants—something that is incompatible with his first desire but may be more pleasing to his selfishness.

Christians must develop a sensitivity to make ethical decisions in ways that will please God and benefit others. That is a mark of maturity.

IV. Two Kinds of Wisdom
(James 3:13-18)

A. Wisdom That Produces Good Deeds
(v. 13)

13. Who is a wise man and endued with knowledge among you? let him show out of a good conversation his works with meekness of wisdom.

Note again that Biblical wisdom is not academic knowledge, but moral insight and skill in advising on practical issues of conduct. Some people are more interested in being right than in being righteous. They would rather have a head filled than a heart that reaches out. Sometimes the longest distance of space yet unconquered is that distance between the head and the heart.

When James asked, *Who is a wise man and endued with knowledge?"* he probably was not asking about two different characteristics. This is a literary parallelism such as the Jews used often. One word is followed by another that means the same thing. The person who is *wise* is also the person who is *endued with knowledge.* This phrase is one word in the Greek. It means understanding, not just knowing facts. The understanding man thinks about how his decision will look to God and what it will do to others. Such a person shows his wisdom and understanding by *a good conversation*, which means a good way of life. He does not boast, but does his *works with meekness of wisdom.* He does not call attention to his good conduct, but his good conduct calls attention to his wisdom.

Meekness is the opposite of arrogance and stubbornness. A meek person is disciplined, useful. The word *meek* was used to describe a horse that had been tamed. Such a horse is under control. He doesn't buck and fight to get his way, but makes his strength useful. Meekness is not weakness, but strength controlled and used properly. Jesus described himself as meek and lowly (Matthew 11:29). He was not weak, but

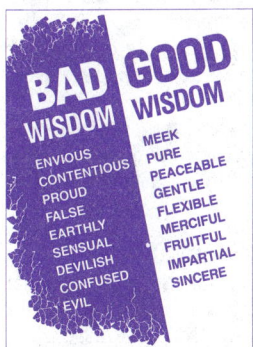

visual 12

His unlimited power was used to do God's will and to benefit others rather than himself.

The meek person wants to benefit others, even if it means giving up his own way. For example, he may not like loud music in the worship service, but he tolerates it because many others like it. The meek person is humbly flexible, but not a doormat. His flexibility is for the benefit of others, not because he is afraid to take a stand. No wonder a meek person produces good deeds.

THE ARROGANCE OF WISDOM

James speaks of "meekness of wisdom." That is seen in the teaching of Jesus. He impressed the hearers with His authority (Matthew 7:28, 29) rather than with scholarly erudition. He often spoke in a simple language about simple things—sheep and goats, grapes and thorns, figs and thistles. His aim was to give a message rather than to make an impression.

Unlike Jesus, some specialize in the arrogance of wisdom. I once read the following statement: "The either/or of the existential situation presents a plethora of alternatives both specific and non-specific when one grasps the eschatological aspect of incarnational Christology." I wonder if its author was trying to explain or to impress, to give counsel or to darken it.

James is right. The truly wise and understanding in this world show by their good life their works in the meekness of wisdom, not in the arrogance of it!
—T. T.

B. Wisdom That Produces Bad Deeds
(v. 14)

14. But if ye have bitter envying and strife in your hearts, glory not, and lie not against the truth.

Now we see some things that oppose meekness: bitter envying, strife, glorying (boasting), and lying.

Instead of *envying* the *American Standard Version* has "jealousy." Our words *jealousy* and *zeal* are both derived from the Greek word that is used here. It is good to be zealous and even jealous for God's will and for the benefit of our fellowmen. But James is thinking here of a selfish jealousy that he calls *bitter*. Such jealousy involves a fierce devotion to one's own way, one's own wishes, one's own opinion, one's own advantage, one's own position. Such a selfish devotion is coupled with hostility toward others when they have their way, when they make a profit, when they receive honor.

Strife is translated "selfish ambition" in the *New International Version*. Ambition is not necessarily wrong, but selfish ambition tries to advance self at the expense of others. This is evident in the age in which we live. It is reflected in the popular adage, "Look out for number one!"

When a person is filled with selfish ambition and selfish jealousy, he will use any means to support his own cause, program, priority, or principles. He has no regard for truth, and so James warns, *Lie not.* He is proud and wants to be recognized, and so James says, *Glory not.*

C. Source of Bad Wisdom (v. 15)

15. This wisdom descendeth not from above, but is earthly, sensual, devilish.

The selfish wisdom of jealousy and strife (v. 14) is not from above. It is *earthly*, belonging to this world. It is *sensual*, opposed to the fruit of the Spirit (Galatians 5:22, 23). It is *devilish*, not godly. A person with that selfish wisdom is not necessarily a non-Christian; he may be an immature Christian, a spiritual infant, regardless of how many years he has been in Christ (1 Corinthians 3:1-3).

D. Results of Bad Wisdom (v. 16)

16. For where envying and strife is, there is confusion and every evil work.

Selfish decisions bring disorder to the body of Christ. *Evil work* is not always things like murder, adultery, and theft. Sometimes it is looking down on others, not maintaining the unity of the Spirit in the bond of peace, being divisive, being quarrelsome, or keeping strife alive.

Another evil work is done when people use all their energies for themselves, ignoring the problems that others have with hunger and poverty. Selfish wisdom among Christians may have called for James' writing about taking care of widows and orphans and expressing faith in acts of benevolence (James 1:27; 2:14-17).

E. Source and Nature of Good Wisdom (v. 17)

17. But the wisdom that is from above is first pure, then peaceable, gentle, and easy to be entreated, full of mercy and good fruits, without partiality, and without hypocrisy.

This verse presents a checklist to help you know whether your decisions are from above or from below. Are your decisions free of selfish motives *(pure)*? Do they avoid hostility and alienation *(peaceable)*? Are your decisions considerate and kind *(gentle)*? Are you quick to agree when you can *(easy to be entreated)*? Are you sensitive to the needs of others *(full of mercy)*? Are your decisions beneficial to others *(full of good fruits)*? Are you free from prejudice *(without partiality)*? Are your decisions sincere *(without hypocrisy)*?

F. Results of Good Wisdom (v. 18)

18. And the fruit of righteousness is sown in peace of them that make peace.

God's wisdom, His moral discernment for the benefit of others, produces a harvest of *righteousness*. Righteousness involves a right relationship with God and others. Such a harvest does not happen by accident, but by intention. It is a result of seed that is *sown in peace.* The sowers are those who make peace, and their aim is to produce righteousness.

Are you a peacemaker or a peace breaker? Are you known as a person who helps put people in right relationships with each other?

There is a correspondence between the wisdom that comes from below and the works of flesh (Galatians 5:19-21). And there is a relationship between the wisdom that comes from above and the fruit of the Spirit (Galatians 5:22, 23).

Conclusion

A. Developing a Christlike Environment

It is difficult for anything good to develop in an environment where people are at odds with each other; but where the environment is filled with Christlike wisdom, people relate to others with fairness, humility, graciousness, and love.

B. Prayer

O Lord, give us this day the moral disposition of Jesus to make decisions to please You and to benefit our fellowmen.

C. Thought to Remember

People do not care how much you know until they know how much you care. Knowing has to do with facts; caring has to do with wisdom.

Learning by Doing

This page contains an alternate lesson plan emphasizing learning activities. Classes desiring such student involvement will find these suggestions helpful.

Learning Goals

As a result of studying this lesson, each student will:

1. Describe the best kind of wisdom.

2. Discover that prayer plays a vital part in the acquiring of wisdom.

3. Learn how to distinguish between "wisdom from above" and "wisdom from below."

Into the Lesson

Begin the class session with the story of the lady with leprosy from the Introduction of the lesson. Ask class members to think about this question: What enabled that woman to be wise enough to find joy in spite of her illness? (Some possible answers: her relationship with Jesus Christ, the ability to see beyond her own limitations, her interest in helpful activities such as singing in the choir.) Point out that true wisdom equips us to respond to bad times with joy and patience.

Provide paper and pencil to each student. Ask the students to complete each of the following sentences as you read it aloud:

1. The worst thing that could happen to me would be _____ .

2. One of the wisest choices I have made in my life was _____ .

3. When I feel the need for wisdom in making a decision I _____ .

After completion of the questions, direct each student to share his sentence with one person not related to him. Allow about six minutes for this sharing.

Make the transition into the Bible study by saying that the book of James shows the practical nature of wisdom.

Into the Word

Put four W's on the chalkboard vertically. Tell the class you have four questions about the book of James. Have the class respond orally to the first three questions. Write their answers beside the W's. *W*ho wrote the book of James? (James, the half-brother of Jesus.) *W*hen was it written? (The specific date is uncertain, but it was about thirty years after the church began.) To *W*hom was it addressed? (The twelve tribes scattered abroad, Jewish Christians; and so to all Christians, God's New Israel.) Use thoughts from the Lesson Background to expand these answers.

When you get to the fourth W, ask people whose last names begin with letters between A and M to read James 1:1-8. Ask the rest to read James 3:13-18. Tell both groups to find and list verses that speak of wisdom or being wise, and also to write one or two thoughts about wisdom that they get from this casual reading. Encourage people to work in pairs, with one person of each pair recording the findings. (This exercise is in the student quarterly.)

After five to ten minutes, have students share their findings as you list them under the fourth W on the board.

Put an X beside James 1:5 on the board. Emphasize that God is the giver of wisdom and that we need to go to Him in prayer when we feel a lack of wisdom. Ask for a show of hands of people who used *pray* to complete sentence number 3 at the beginning of the class session. Say that two things should characterize the praying we do for wisdom. Refer the students to James 1:6-8 and ask them to find those two things. (Faith and single-mindedness.) Discuss what it means to be single-minded.

Put X's beside James 3:15 and 17. Draw two columns on the board and label them "Wisdom From Below" and "Wisdom From Above." Ask for volunteers to give you words that describe each kind of wisdom in verses 14-18 of chapter 3. Write their responses in the appropriate columns. The lesson writer's comments on verses 14-18 will help with the discussion.

Into Life

Lead the class in thinking of real-life situations that exhibit the use of both kinds of wisdom. (For example, wisdom from below, which is earthly and sensual, might lead you to buy pornographic literature; but wisdom from above would find better literature to read.)

Pose this situation and ask the class to discuss how each kind of wisdom would answer: You are a college professor. One of your students has done research under your direction which you hope to use in writing a new book. Should you use the material and give him credit for it, or should you use his work without crediting him because he prepared it for you and will never use it himself? Close by saying that we need to be in constant prayer to have wisdom in dealing with the so-called gray areas of life.

Let's Talk It Over

The questions on this page are designed to encourage review of the lesson Scriptures and to promote discussion of the lesson by the class. The answers provided are only discussion starters. Let your class talk it over from there.

1. James and other New Testament teachers exhort us to rejoice in the face of trials. How do we learn to do that?

In Acts 5 the apostles were imprisoned, beaten, and threatened with death because they were preaching about Jesus; but "they departed from the presence of the council, rejoicing that they were counted worthy to suffer shame for his name" (Acts 5:41). The apostles must have meditated often on the example of their Master. They also must have prayed that they would not be fearful, complaining, or bitter. We have access to these same two means of developing a joyful response to our trials.

2. Patience is one of the most difficult virtues to learn. How can we gain it?

The Old Testament has many exhortations to wait on the Lord. For example, David writes, "Wait on the Lord: be of good courage, and he shall strengthen thine heart" (Psalm 27:14). But we want what we want now, and waiting for victories and blessings is at times almost unbearable. We need to remember that the Lord knows what is best for us, and that His timing is always perfect. Also, we must remember that patience is a spiritual virtue without which we would be stunted in our growth as Christians.

3. Is the prayer for wisdom one that we offer regularly? Why is it important?

It is easy for us to fall into the habit of asking only for the most obvious needs that we and our loved ones have. Someone needs a job; some other is lacking money for college; still others require help in facing an emergency. It is well that we pray about these matters, but we must not pray for material things only. Wisdom is obviously a gift we should eagerly desire. It affects our day-to-day moral decisions, regulates our relationships with other people, and generally aids us in putting Biblical truths into action in our lives. Along with praying, "Give us this day our daily bread" (Matthew 6:11), we do well to pray, "Give us this day our daily wisdom."

4. The lesson writer describes the meek person as "humbly flexible, but not a doormat." How does this flexible meekness make the church a more harmonious place?

We claim to allow liberty in matters of opinion, but many conflicts arise in the church over them. These sometimes pertain to the building itself (what color a room should be painted, how the house should be decorated, etc.), to the kind of worship (new hymns versus old hymns, the length and style of sermons, etc.), or to the habits and personalities of fellow members (this one talks too much, that one is too bossy, etc.). We may feel that our opinions are neglected, and so we complain. We may notice that another member gets most of his opinions accepted, and so we resent it. But opinions are still opinions. As long as they do not oppose Scriptural teaching, we should be flexible enough to tolerate them and promote Christian harmony.

5. How can we deal with a person who dominates any group he is in and insists that his opinions be accepted?

This is the individual who tends to dominate a committee, men's group, women's group, or any other group of which he or she is a part. Sometimes the other members "humor him" and let him have his way for the sake of peace, even though most of them prefer another way. If one person is always overbearing, can we find the courage to talk to him about it? A private one-to-one discussion is better than a public confrontation. Humble prayer together, a mutual searching of the Scriptures, and a frank discussion of the problem may produce beneficial results.

6. If we try seriously to be peacemakers in our family, at our place of work, or in our church, we run the risk of being labeled meddlers. How can we minimize this risk?

A meddler is motivated by pride in his knowledge, while a peacemaker is motivated by love. A meddler is disturbed by the inconvenience that conflict causes him, while a peacemaker is distressed at seeing human beings at odds with one another. The meddler relies on his supposed persuasiveness, while the peacemaker relies on prayer to resolve the conflict. If we are earnest and careful and loving in our efforts, we find Jesus' promise fulfilled: "Blessed are the peacemakers: for they shall be called the children of God" (Matthew 5:9).

Hearing and Doing

LESSON SCRIPTURE: James 1:22—2:26.

PRINTED TEXT: James 1:22—2:8.

James 1:22-27

22 But be ye doers of the word, and not hearers only, deceiving your own selves.

23 For if any be a hearer of the word, and not a doer, he is like unto a man beholding his natural face in a glass:

24 For he beholdeth himself, and goeth his way, and straightway forgetteth what manner of man he was.

25 But whoso looketh into the perfect law of liberty, and continueth therein, he being not a forgetful hearer, but a doer of the work, this man shall be blessed in his deed.

26 If any man among you seem to be religious, and bridleth not his tongue, but deceiveth his own heart, this man's religion is vain.

27 Pure religion and undefiled before God and the Father is this, To visit the fatherless and widows in their affliction, and to keep himself unspotted from the world.

James 2:1-8

1 My brethren, have not the faith of our Lord Jesus Christ, the Lord of glory, with respect of persons.

2 For if there come unto your assembly a man with a gold ring, in goodly apparel, and there come in also a poor man in vile raiment;

3 And ye have respect to him that weareth the gay clothing, and say unto him, Sit thou here in a good place; and say to the poor, Stand thou there, or sit here under my footstool:

4 Are ye not then partial in yourselves, and are become judges of evil thoughts?

5 Hearken, my beloved brethren, Hath not God chosen the poor of this world rich in faith, and heirs of the kingdom which he hath promised to them that love him?

6 But ye have despised the poor. Do not rich men oppress you, and draw you before the judgment seats?

7 Do not they blaspheme that worthy name by the which ye are called?

8 If ye fulfil the royal law according to the Scripture, Thou shalt love thy neighbor as thyself, ye do well.

GOLDEN TEXT: Be ye doers of the word, and not hearers only, deceiving your own selves.—James 1:22.

Wisdom as a Way of Life
Unit 4: Wisdom in the New Testament
(Lessons 11-13)

Lesson Aims

This lesson study is designed to help the student to:

1. Become sensitive to the needs of others.

2. Design practical ways to help people in need.

3. Understand and apply the connection between what we know and what we do.

Lesson Outline

INTRODUCTION
    A. He Is Our Wisdom
    B. Lesson Background
I. BE A HEARER AND A DOER (James 1:22-25)
    A. Don't Be Deceived (v. 22)
    B. Don't Be Forgetful (vv. 23, 24)
    C. Live Out What You Hear (v. 25)
II. BE A HELPER TO THE HELPLESS (James 1:26, 27)
    A. By Checking the Tongue (v. 26)
    B. By Caring for the Hurting (v. 27)
      Pure Irreligion
III. BE A HELPER TO THE POOR (James 2:1-4)
    A. What Not to Do (v. 1)
    B. A Test (v. 2)
    C. A Failure (v. 3)
    D. An Exposure (v. 4)
      Preferential Treatment
IV. BE A DOER OF THE ROYAL LAW (James 2:5-8)
    A. A Reversal (v. 5)
    B. A Rejection by Some Christians (v. 6)
    C. A Rejection by Some Pagans (v. 7)
    D. The Royal Law (v. 8)
CONCLUSION
    A. Proverbs Says It Too
    B. Prayer
    C. Thought to Remember

Visual 13 in the visuals packet emphasizes the main instructions of the lesson text. The visual is shown on this page.

Introduction

A. He Is Our Wisdom

He never had a degree—not even an honorary one. He quit His profession at the age of thirty and became an unemployed itinerant. From then on, He did not settle down in one place for very long. When He slept at night, it was either under the stars or in a borrowed bed.

When He went from place to place, He walked. He invested in no stocks and had no savings account. He never traveled more than two hundred miles from His place of birth.

He was born in borrowed quarters, rode a borrowed colt, was buried in a borrowed tomb.

But when He was twelve years old, He amazed the theological giants of His day. When He taught, people left the shops, the fields, the classrooms, and the homes to hear Him. In the midst of confusion, He modeled clarity. In the midst of hatreds, He demonstrated love. In the midst of an X-rated society, He lived a life of moral purity. In the midst of antagonism, He was a peacemaker.

His name—Jesus of Nazareth. And He is our wisdom (1 Corinthians 1:30).

B. Lesson Background

God has always called His people to both privilege and purpose—status and service, forgiveness and function, gift and demand.

God's people in the Old Testament (Israel) began to stress their privilege and neglect their purpose. The prophets preached that they should repent so that purpose would be connected to their privilege.

Finally one person came who put privilege and purpose in perfect balance. That person was Jesus. He called a new people, the church.

We are called to both privilege and purpose. "By grace are ye saved through faith"—that's privilege (Ephesians 2:8). "Unto good works . . . that we should walk in them"—that's purpose (Ephesians 2:10).

By the time James wrote, some Christians evidently were beginning to stress privilege and neglect purpose. It is easy to stress privilege when we become regular sermon hearers and Bible-study attenders. It's easy to rejoice because we are rich in doctrine, even while we forget that many people are poor in the basic

visual 13

necessities of life. It's easy to think we are special people because we are children of God, even though we neglect others who are different from us in education, in social status, in economics, or in racial identity.

What James says in our text was not only relevant for his audience in the first century, but is contemporary stuff for us today.

I. Be a Hearer and a Doer
(James 1:22-25)

A. Don't Be Deceived (v. 22)

22. But be ye doers of the word, and not hearers only, deceiving your own selves.

Be ye doers of the word, and not hearers only. This is a command. One translation puts it this way: *Be sure that you act on the message.* As new creatures, we are to think differently, act differently, and react differently. Obeying the Word makes a difference between a Christian and a non-Christian.

James is not putting down hearing. It too is essential. Our faith comes by hearing (Romans 10:17), but it is more than hearing.

Not the hearers but the doers will be justified before God (Romans 2:13). Prayer, Bible reading, attendance at meetings for worship and teaching—all these are important, but they are not final goals. They are means for equipping us for service. They are not the whole of our service. The person who is faithful in attendance is not necessarily a good Christian. Knowing about the good and thinking about the good are not the same as being good. We must not substitute hearing for action, but let hearing equip and motivate us for action.

Those who equate hearing with action are those who are deceiving themselves. One of the ways we deceive ourselves is by rationalization. We rationalize that we do not have time for serving God because we are spending so much time attending meetings, studying, hearing. That's like saying we have no time to live because we are spending so much time eating and sleeping.

B. Don't Be Forgetful (vv. 23, 24)

23, 24. For if any be a hearer of the word, and not a doer, he is like unto a man beholding his natural face in a glass: for he beholdeth himself, and goeth his way, and straightway forgetteth what manner of man he was.

The person who is a hearer only is like a person who looks into a mirror and walks away and forgets what he sees. The idea is that we look into a mirror and see that changes need to be made—a dirty face needs to be clean, hair needs to be combed, a dress or shirt needs to be straightened. In fact, we look into the mirror so that we can step out into the street properly groomed.

We hear God's Word so that we can step into service properly prepared. We do not look into the mirror and then refuse to do anything about what we see. But do we hear the Word of God on Sunday and refuse to make any changes in our living? When we hear or read God's Word, how often do we actually commit ourselves to make some practical, specific, and measurable change? In the Word of God we can see the person God meant us to be, the person we can be. We can see that in Jesus himself.

His natural face is literally *the face of his birth.* In a mirror one sees the face he was born with. In the Bible also we see the face of our birth, the kind of person we have been born again to be. God puts Christ's nature in us. When we see that Christ helped the poor, we know that that nature is now in us. When we see that Christ was patient, we know that that nature is now in us. When we see that Christ forgave, we know that we can forgive. Now we need to grow up and allow Christ's nature to shine out of us. We need to make a conscientious commitment to change whatever is not in accordance with the new face of our new birth.

C. Live Out What You Hear (v. 25)

25. But whoso looketh into the perfect law of liberty, and continueth therein, he being not a forgetful hearer, but a doer of the work, this man shall be blessed in his deed.

The forgetful person in the two preceding verses is contrasted now with the person who *looketh into . . . and continueth therein.* The Greek word for *looketh* means literally to stoop down, and so it means to have a very close look. Our study of the Word is not to be a touch-and-go, in-and-out, superficial reading so we can put another star on the chart. We need to do some close scrutiny, some serious studying. The person who *continueth therein* is the person who lives in its company. He does not just read it; he also puts it into practice. One reason he does not forget is that he is *a doer of the work.* Memorize something and you may soon forget it. Do something and you will not soon forget it, nor will others.

What is *the perfect law of liberty?* It is the New Covenant that liberates us from living as we have in the past. We are set free from being hooked on status to become volunteers for service. We are loosed from hoarding that we may help. We are emancipated from protecting self and learn to defend others. We are indeed free to love (Galatians 5:13).

II. Be a Helper to the Helpless
(James 1:26, 27)

A. By Checking the Tongue (v. 26)

26. If any man among you seem to be religious, and bridleth not his tongue, but deceiveth his own heart, this man's religion is vain.

We can fake being religious *(seem to be religious)* and deceive even ourselves, but we cannot deceive God. One thing that exposes fake religion is an unbridled tongue. We need to ask thoughtful questions about the things we say: (1) Would we want someone to say that about us, even if it were true? (2) Is it kind? (3) Will it impart grace to people who hear? (4) Is it necessary?

We do not need to say everything that is true. We are stewards of the truth as we are of our wealth. The fact that we have money does not mean we must spend it today.

An old Jewish proverb says, "A person's tongue is long enough to cut his own throat." A person's tongue is also long enough to cut another person's throat. Children may say, "Sticks and stones may break my bones, but words will never hurt me"; but it is false. Words do hurt. And sometimes the wounds never heal.

Fortunately, the tongue can help as well as hurt. It can bring healing (Proverbs 15:4). Pleasant words are sweet to the soul and are like medicine to many (Proverbs 16:24).

B. By Caring for the Hurting (v. 27)

27. Pure religion and undefiled before God and the Father is this, To visit the fatherless and widows in their affliction, and to keep himself unspotted from the world.

To visit does not mean just to drop by and leave a calling card. It means to care for the needy and supply what they need. *The fatherless and widows* are most likely to be in need, but there may be others who also need our care.

If God the Father sees that caring for needy people is a part of *pure religion*, then shouldn't we do more about it? Perhaps Christianity is not measured in Heaven by how large a congregation is, but rather by how well that congregation meets the needs of the needy—and there are emotional and social needs as well as physical needs.

James' use of the word *Father* reminds us that we are His children. He has put His divine nature in us so that we can carry out His desires. Jesus spoke plainly about what will happen to us in the Day of Judgment if we do or do not care for the needy (Matthew 25:31-46).

But our Christianity is more than personal generosity. It is also personal integrity—*to keep himself unspotted from the world*. The word *world* is used in different ways. Here it means the worldliness that stands against the teachings of God. It is almost synonymous with *evil*. Is it possible that Christians are too close to the world? We don't want to be identified with the pagan world, but do we stay so close that its fun becomes our fun? The stains of the world will splatter on us if we are close. We live in the world, but we are isolationists from its immoral practices.

PURE IRRELIGION

James cites two parts of pure religion: "to visit the fatherless and widows in their affliction, and to keep himself unspotted from the world" (1:27). If these are pure religion, does it follow that their opposite constitutes pure irreligion? If so, I have a candidate for the category. His name is Daniel Quilp. You may remember him as the villain in Dickens' classic story, *The Old Curiosity Shop.*

Quilp never visited orphans and widows except to produce or increase their hardship. The story is focused in the mischief he tried to work on Little Nell, and graphically relates the pain for Kit's mother, a widow with several children.

Far from trying to keep himself unspotted from the world, Quilp did everything in his power to corrupt himself and others. He was a drunk and a gambler. He tortured his wife, abused his help, tormented his mother-in-law. He was always on the lookout for some way to cheat any unsuspecting person.

Daniel Quilp's actions made him a man without a friend. When he died a tragic death, there was none to mourn his passing. In contrast, those who practice James' standard of pure religion may never amass a fortune as old Quilp did; but, oh, the happiness that is theirs!—T. T.

III. Be a Helper to the Poor
(James 2:1-4)

A. What Not to Do (v. 1)

1. My brethren, have not the faith of our Lord Jesus Christ, the Lord of glory, with respect of persons.

Favoritism and faith do not belong in the same person. When James says we should not have *respect of persons*, he does not mean that we should not respect people. He is talking about lifting some people up while putting others down. Rich people in the early church sold their possessions in order to help the poor. But today, we hear, "Why don't they get a job?"

God shows no partiality (Romans 2:11), and neither should we. Our attitude toward our fellowmen, regardless of their status in life, should reflect the attitude of God.

During the first World War a group of Christian men behind the fighting lines opened rest houses for Christian fellowship in which all soldiers were welcome. Over the entrance were printed words that became famous: "Abandon all rank, ye who enter here." When any person walked through that door, it made no difference whether he was a four-star general or a private first class. It is the same when one enters the church. His position or his title or his wealth makes no difference.

B. A Test (v. 2)

2. For if there come unto your assembly a man with a gold ring, in goodly apparel, and there come in also a poor man in vile raiment.

How do we greet people at the door of the church? Here comes somebody of significant status and wealth. Is his welcome any different from the one we give to somebody who is unkempt, obviously poor, wearing a torn shirt? Is it possible that we think that one can give (the rich person), while the other will take (the poor person)? Is it possible that we think one will become a helpful friend (the rich), while the other will become a leech (the poor)? Do poor people serve in public ways, such as ushering, greeting, serving the Lord's Supper? Do we have an unspoken rule that a person has to dress in a certain way before he becomes a full-fledged member?

C. A Failure (v. 3)

3. And ye have respect to him that weareth the gay clothing, and say unto him, Sit thou here in a good place; and say to the poor, Stand thou there, or sit here under my footstool.

Would you give your favorite place to a migrant worker? Would you stand so a vagrant might be seated? Would you even sit in the middle of a pew so a late-comer could find a seat more easily?

D. An Exposure (v. 4)

4. Are ye not then partial in yourselves, and are become judges of evil thoughts?

Making class distinctions is wrong because in Christ there is neither slave nor free (Galatians 3:28). By the same principle there is neither poor nor rich, neither lower nor upper class. Christ's people are united in Him. Each one is entitled to the same courtesies, the same gentleness, the same welcome, the same grace, the same consideration.

PREFERENTIAL TREATMENT

Years ago when I was a missionary in Southern Rhodesia, some stores gave preferential treatment to anyone whose skin was white. Should you enter a store while the clerk was serving a Black customer, the clerk would say to the Black person, "Wait till I serve this White customer."

I must confess this is a heady experience. It makes a person feel he is more important than the one who has been put on hold. But imagine what it does for the ego of the other. It says to such a person, "You are inferior; you are not worth much; you are dispensable. I'll deal with you when I have nothing better to do."

God knows the harm that comes from preferential treatment. Through His spokesman, James, He warns us against giving preference to rich people. Such preference harms the poor man by demeaning him. It also harms the rich man by giving him an exalted view of his own importance. Perhaps the rich man is harmed more severely. The poor, neglected man will survive the experience, and perhaps become stronger because of it. He may serve God and be rewarded with eternal life. The rich man, on the other hand, may come to depend upon himself rather than God. Since his pocketbook buys everything else, he may feel that it can purchase Heaven as well.

Let's be careful not to abuse the poor or the rich.

—T. T.

IV. Be a Doer of the Royal Law (James 2:5-8)

A. A Reversal (v. 5)

5. Hearken, my beloved brethren, Hath not God chosen the poor of this world rich in faith, and heirs of the kingdom which he hath promised to them that love him?

God calls the poor to be rich in faith, to trust Him and not their materials, depend on Him and not their savings accounts. Knowing of His resources, His abilities, His grace, they are content. They do not get nervous every time the President of the United States sneezes or the stock market goes down. They have "true riches" (Luke 16:11).

B. A Rejection by Some Christians (v. 6)

6. But ye have despised the poor. Do not rich men oppress you, and draw you before the judgment seats?

Whom God has cared for, some Christians have despised. Paul likewise noted that some Christians in Corinth humiliated those who had nothing (1 Corinthians 11:22). It is ungodly to despise anyone just because he is poor, and it is unreasonable to honor anyone just because he is rich. Some of the hardships of the early church came from people of status, wealth, and position, especially when they thought their sources of income were threatened. For example, think of the makers of idols in Ephesus (Acts 19:27).

But the rich are not always oppressive. We should never think that people of wealth do not have the capacity to love the Lord. Some of the most dynamic, generous, caring, humble people in God's family are people of wealth. Some of God's greatest leaders were wealthy—Solomon, David, Abraham, and probably Nicodemus, Joseph of Arimathea, Philemon, Lydia. God does not hate riches; no one is richer than He. God accepts both rich and poor if they give themselves to Him, and so should we.

C. A Rejection by Some Pagans (v. 7)

7. Do not they blaspheme that worthy name by the which ye are called?

James continued to point out that some of the opposition to the church came from the rich. Wealthy emperors blasphemed the name of Jesus by claiming such titles as "god," "savior," "lord," and "redeemer." Many affluent unbelievers made light of God's name, and they still do.

D. The Royal Law (v. 8)

8. If ye fulfill the royal law according to the Scripture, Thou shalt love thy neighbor as thyself, ye do well.

Instead of having favorites, we are to apply *the royal law*. That means the law of God the King. His law is the law of love. When we love God with our total being and love our neighbors as ourselves, we have fulfilled the intention of God's law and prophets (Matthew 22:37-40; Romans 13:8-10).

We are to love others as we love ourselves. We are to care for others as we care for ourselves. Some people fail at this point because they do not even love themselves. They wallow in their discouragements because they don't esteem themselves as they should. But God expects us to have a healthy love of ourselves without self-ishness. Then we can love others.

To *fulfill the royal law* is not just to hear about it. It is to apply it in our relationships with others. It is to put into practice God's kind of law and God's kind of love.

Love is the most important principle for the Christian to apply. It is first among the characteristics mentioned as fruit of the Spirit (Galatians 5:22). After listing many elements of Christian character and life, Paul wrote, "Above all these things put on charity [love], which is the bond of perfectness" (Colossians 3:14).

It is possible to serve without love (1 Corinthians 13:1-3), but it is not possible to love without serving. Our love ought to be as wide as God's love. While some people draw small circles to keep us out, we need to draw bigger circles to include them.

Conclusion

A. Proverbs Says It Too

Many Proverbs deal with our relationship to the poor:

"He that hath pity upon the poor lendeth unto the Lord; and that which he hath given will he pay him again" (19:17).

"Whoso stoppeth his ears at the cry of the poor, he also shall cry himself, but shall not be heard" (21:13).

"The rich and poor meet together: the Lord is the maker of them all" (22:2).

"He that oppresseth the poor to increase his riches, and he that giveth to the rich, shall surely come to want" (22:16).

B. Prayer

Our Father, we recognize that from Heaven's viewpoint all of us are extremely poor, but we thank You for touching our poverty with the riches of Your grace. Now help us to become more generous with what we have, that others through us can have a taste and a touch of your unselfishness. We ask it in Christ, who gave up that we might grow up.

C. Thought to Remember

He who gives to the poor makes a loan to the Lord. The Lord will repay.

Home Daily Bible Readings

Monday, Aug. 20—"Doers of the Word" (James 1:22-27)
Tuesday, Aug. 21—Impartial Christians (James 2:1-7)
Wednesday, Aug. 22—Fulfilling Royal Law (James 2:8-13)
Thursday, Aug. 23—Faith *and* Works (James 2:14-26)
Friday, Aug. 24—God's Word Is a Lamp (Psalm 119:105-112)
Saturday, Aug. 25—Apple of God's Eye (Psalm 17:1-9)
Sunday, Aug. 26—Vain Builders (Psalm 127:1-5)

Learning by Doing

This page contains an alternate lesson plan emphasizing learning activities. Classes desiring such student involvement will find these suggestions helpful.

Learning Goals

This lesson should enable students to:

1. Cite specific examples from the book of James that demonstrate wisdom in action.

2. Examine themselves to determine whether they are only hearers of the word or if they are also doers of the word.

3. Be wise enough to be sensitive to unfair or preferential treatment of others, and make a personal commitment to relate impartially to all.

Into the Lesson

Pair off your students. Let each person make ten responses to the question, "What do you see when you look in the mirror?" Give some examples to help them get started: "I see a teacher, a wife, a musician, a happy face," etc. After all have shared, ask them to rank the ten responses in order of importance.

While students remain paired off, ask them to share answers to an additional question: "Why do I look into a mirror?" After a minute or so, record some of the answers on the board. Make the transition into Bible study by saying that one of the most common reasons we look into a mirror is to see if we need to make any changes in our appearance. So it is that we need to look into God's Word and see if we need to make any changes in our way of living. The book of James is that mirror for us today as we learn how wisdom is revealed through our actions and our relationships with others.

Into the Word

Use the chalkboard to make a chart with four columns headed To This; What to Do; What Not to Do; Scripture. List the following items in the column under To This: The Word; Orphans and Widows; The World; The Rich; The Poor; Your Tongue. Class members are to read James 1:22—2:8 and fill in columns two, three, and four, as they relate to the things and people listed in column one. See the student quarterly for a drawing of the chart. You may prefer to make copies for the students instead of putting it on the board.

When the class has finished this study, use it as a springboard for discussion of the following questions:

1. What guidelines can we follow that will help us to bridle our tongues? (The lesson writer gives some helpful thoughts in part II of the lesson. Have a volunteer read Ephesians 4:29.)

2. What are some ways that the contemporary church sometimes caters to the wealthy?

3. What does the church hope to accomplish through preferential treatment?"

4. According to James 2:5, the poor of this world are rich in faith. What does that mean?

Into Life

Put this statement on the chalkboard and have each class member silently choose one ending:

Care of the deprived and disadvantaged ("fatherless and widows") is the duty of:

_____ the public sector (government, federal and local).

_____ the private sector (business, private enterprise).

_____ charitable organizations (fraternal and ethnic groups).

_____ the church (religious agencies).

_____ all of the above.

Have those who chose each ending form a group and write out statements to support their choice. Let each group share its statements with the class. Conclude by commenting that James 1:27 seems to indicate that each Christian does have a responsibility. We may help the needy through any of the groups listed, but we cannot ignore our duty. Let someone read Matthew 25:31-46.

Distribute the Wisdom Inventory below. Have each student draw a face beside each of the criteria listed to indicate how wisely he is acting in his personal life. For example:

 I'm doing great!

 Oops! I neglect this.

 Hmmmm. I need to think about this.

1. I read or study the Bible daily.
2. I visit shut-ins, widows, the ill.
3. I don't cater to the wealthy.
4. I give regularly to the poor and hungry.
5. I give generously to the church.
6. I speak encouraging words to others.
7. I do volunteer service in the community.
8. I recognize and confess my sins.

Let's Talk It Over

The questions on this page are designed to encourage review of the lesson Scriptures and to promote discussion of the lesson by the class. The answers provided are only discussion starters. Let your class talk it over from there.

1. Sometimes it seems that even the best sermons are soon forgotten. What can be done to help the hearers to put into action the Biblical principles they hear?

Some churches use a section of their Sunday bulletins for an outline of the sermon, space for notes, and suggestions for putting the preacher's points into practice. This at least reminds the preacher that he must issue a clear call for action, and it encourages the hearers in making a definite, personal application. A further step in joining hearing and doing may be to arrange for a discussion period soon after the sermon so that hearers may exchange their thoughts about it. The idea is not just to dissect or criticize the sermon, but to find ways of putting its teaching into action.

2. What are some guidelines involved in using the Bible as a mirror?

When we look into a literal mirror, we must be prepared to see things as they are. If we have blackened an eye or cut our chin, or if we have neglected washing or shaving, we are going to see an unpleasant sight. So in Bible study we must be willing to see that some of our goals, attitudes, and habits are not what they ought to be. We do not break a mirror when it shows us an unwelcome sight; neither should we abandon the Bible because it judges our thoughts and behavior. We use the mirror as an aid in making our face look better, and we should use the Bible as a means of making our actions better.

3. What help can be found in the idea of bridling the tongue?

James mentions this in 1:26 and returns to it in the third chapter: "If any man offend not in word, the same is a perfect man, and able also to bridle the whole body" (James 3:2). This suggests that the tongue is comparable to a wild horse. It certainly can run wild, leaving destruction behind it. If we do not control it, it can wreak its damage as rapidly as a mustang can gallop across the plain. This warning helps us to recognize the tremendous potential for harm in that innocent-looking organ. It also warns that we must make an effort to tame the tongue and direct its energies into constructive purposes. We cannot do this without trying.

4. While "the fatherless and widows" are not the only needy people, they are two important groups we should not neglect. What are some ways in which we can minister to them?

An obvious answer is the visiting of children's homes and retirement or nursing homes. But if this is obvious, it is not universally practiced. These facilities can be depressing places to visit, and some Christians are a bit squeamish about them. Widows, whether in retirement homes or in their own homes, should not be forgotten. They may need transportation or help with repairs on an automobile, assistance with lawn care or home repairs, legal advice, or visitors to bring brightness into a routine existence.

5. Do we make distinctions in our church on the basis of wealth, education, social standing, or marital status? If so, how?

We may pride ourselves on being a church in which wealth and social standing are matters of no consequence. And yet we may in subtle ways favor certain members. In remodeling or decorating, we may cater to the whims of those who can give most. In choosing leaders, we may prefer people who are prominent in the community. In selecting teachers, we may value formal schooling more than demonstrated character and ability. We may be so family-oriented that single persons feel neglected and lonely. We may neglect quiet people because it is more fun to be with vivacious ones.

6. What are some practical ways in which we can fulfill in the church the royal law to love our neighbor as ourselves?

Our neighbor may need transportation to and from worship. Are we willing to go out of our way to provide it? It may even be that our neighbor needs some better clothing in order to feel comfortable attending church. Can we make the extra effort to obtain that clothing for him or her? Loving our neighbor in the next pew can involve simply taking the time to ask about his welfare, or to see if he needs our prayers or to answer any questions he may have. Loving our neighbor in Christ may take the form of telephoning him if he is absent from worship, or sending him a card of encouragement. Do we really care about our neighbors?